John Leigh......	....LY
Diana Gayelorde-Sutton	.....JENNY SEAGROVE
Young John	.........STEPHEN J. DEAN
Young Diana	...............PATSY KENSIT
Mark	......JACK WATSON
Luke	......FRED BRYANT
Reuben	......IAIN ANDERS
Thirza	......JUNE MARLOW
Drip	......GILLIAN RAINE
Mr. Gayelorde-Sutton	...HAROLD INNOCENT
Mrs. Gayelorde-Sutton	...ELIZABETH BENNETT
Miss Westcott	......MARY MORRIS
Yves de Royden	......YVES AUBERT
Mr. Priddis	......PRESTON LOCKWOOD
Mr. Blackler	......FULTON MACKAY
Twining	......JONATHAN LYNN
Mary	......CHRISTINA BARRYK
Alison	......LYNNE MILLER
Starkey	......ADAM NORTON
Adjutant	......CHRISTOPHER GOOD
Col. Ackerley	......JEFFRY WICKHAM
Raoul de Royden	......YVES BENEYTON
Rance	......JEAN BOISSERY

Dramatised by	......ANDREW DAVIES
Script Editor	......DEVORA POPE
Directed by	......DAVID TUCKER
	RICHARD STROUD
Produced by	......KEN RIDDINGTON

*Front cover photograph
shows Kevin McNally and Jenny Seagrove*

Diana

R. F. Delderfield

CORONET BOOKS
Hodder and Stoughton

For John Steinbeck, who knows Sennacharib—*in acknowledgment of all the happy reading hours his work has given me over a quarter-century.*

Part One

Chapter One

TWO MIRACLES occurred that October, the October of my fifteenth birthday. This story begins with those miracles, so I must record them in the order in which they took place; first the miracle of landscape, which was purely personal, secondly the encounter in the larch wood, involving Diana and myself.

I had been living with Uncle Luke and Aunt Thirza for a fortnight or so, and the change of scene, from a second-floor apartment in the Brixton Road to a quayside cottage in a small Devon holiday resort, had done little to cure the wretchedness caused by watching my mother die, or seeing her buried in the hideously crowded cemetery where they laid her.

People were kind. Uncle Luke came up from Devon the day she died and I had no uncertainty about the future, for he assured me of a home the moment he arrived. My mother and I, however, had been very close, for my father, a second cousin of my mother's who shared the same name, had died years before and I barely remembered him. We had shared the genteel squalor of the Brixton boardinghouse and when she wasn't at work and I wasn't at school, we were seldom apart.

On Saturday afternoons, and on fine Sundays, we explored London together. We went to all the usual places—the Tower, Westminster Abbey, Hampton Court. We also went to the Tate Gallery and it was here, only a short time

1

before her death, that she revealed to me the fact that she carried in her mind the remembered scents of West Country gorse and purple heather. This puzzled me at the time, for I knew that she had left Devon as a small child and had never once returned. I knew also that since that time she had lived all her life in cities.

We had been looking at a big landscape by an artist whose name I have forgotten, and the background of the picture was a rich blaze of golden gorse and purple heath, the kind of heath that most people mistake for heather. My mother said, "There John, that's how it is! That's how it looks and that's how it smells!"

The predominant smell at that moment was London fog, seeping through the dome of the gallery, and I made a feeble joke about this but she didn't laugh, just shook her head and said, very quietly, "Ah, but *I* can smell it! It's a kind of frosty freshness. You've got to see it first, though, then when you see it, a picture like that can easily conjure it up."

I forgot this conversation almost at once and I didn't remember it again until that Saturday afternoon, the first Saturday of October, when Uncle Luke, who was paying forfeit of his weekend ramble because he had watched herring gulls all morning instead of delivering furniture, handed me twopence for the bus ride to Heronslea Cross and advised me to explore the country behind Shepherdshey and see if I could identify the holding that we Leighs were said to have farmed for eight generations.

I went off eagerly enough, glad of an opportunity to be alone with my grief and put myself out of reach of Aunt Thirza's well-meant but irritating endeavors to distract me. Uncle Luke had given me directions and I left the bus at the fork, walking down the unsurfaced road to Shepherdshey.

It was a fine, keen afternoon and the road that I later came to know so well was firm underfoot. In summer the Shepherdshey road was thick with dust, so thick that it whirled up when disturbed and settled on the stalks of cow parsley, bending them forward until they were almost horizontal to the road. In winter the track was a slough, without a dry spot anywhere. Only after fine autumn weather was the surface firm as far as the village.

In those days Shepherdshey was a hamlet that had strayed out of an eighteenth-century sporting print. Each side of the single street was lined with humpbacked cob cottages and the only two breaks in the frontages were the general shop on the left and the half-timbered pub on the right. I looked at the pub with interest. It was called The Jolly Rifleman, and I knew it, for it was the place where Grandfather Leigh had drunk himself to death.

Heronslea House, the only sizable home in the area, lay on my left, on slightly rising ground. I couldn't see much of it because it was approached by a winding, beech-lined drive, and further concealed by a clump of tall elms that grew beside the Teasel Brook. At Shepherdshey the brook ran out of its gully, or "goyle" as they called it in these parts, and the path up to the common followed the stream as far as its sharpest curve, a mile north of the village. On the left of this path were the huge rhododendron clumps of Heronslea House and on the right a broad slope that climbed to Teasel Wood, a vast tangle of fir, spruce, beech, chestnut and dwarf oak.

I was not especially interested in the landscape, not at least until I had left the village behind and climbed the first ridge behind the big house. Then, as I approached the plank bridge that crossed the rushing brook, something stirred under my heart and I began to run without knowing why.

When I reached the first trees of Teasel Wood I stopped and turned around, looking down over the half-moon of timber screening the rear of the big house and beyond it across five miles of pasture to the sea. It was on this spot that the personal miracle occurred. It was here that I first looked upon the area that Diana and I, but no one else on earth, were to know as "Sennacharib."

The sensation was as much physical as spiritual. It was as though something had struck me a sudden blow in the pit of the stomach, a fierce, winding blow that made me reel and reach out to steady myself against the smooth bole of the nearest beech. I saw on the instant the whole sweep of

3

the country, the woods, dove-gray and russet, the white ribbon of road, the smoky, purple woods beyond, the patchwork green of the pasture, the red brown of the plowed land and finally, as a frame to the picture, the pale blue of the Channel on the skyline.

I saw all this but it was the flaming gorse and purple heath that made me cry out, for it lay along each side of the valley like a hoard of guineas flung slantwise across a shallow bowl and at each point where the gold was thinly scattered the purple of the heath showed through, like an imperial mantle spread to catch the money.

It was then that the tag of verse came into my head, the first two lines of "Sennacharib" that I had chanted in the tiled prison house of Brixton Road School:

> The Assyrian came down like a wolf on the fold
> And his cohorts were gleaming with purple and gold . . .

The entire valley—gorse, heath, beechwood, larch-wood, elms, brook and all that lay between sea and the moor became mine and because it was mine I named it Sennacharib. Even the white mansion, glimpsed through the wood far below, was included and on entering into possession I experienced a moment of pure joy that has never been mine since. Grief, and a boy's luxury in grief, fell away from me at the memory of my mother's odd remark in the Tate Gallery and I sniffed a long, long, satisfying sniff that brought with it not only a calm acceptance of death but also a consciousness of ancestral heritage, the realization of the presence here, on this very spot, of all the long-dead Leighs who had stood and looked down on Sennacharib in the past. Dead they were and yet they were not, not while I lived; and I was gloriously, exultantly alive.

This was the measure of my discovery on that October afternoon; this was the first of the two October miracles.

I went over into Sennacharib the following Saturday and the Saturday after that. I wanted to know every bridle path, every bush, every fold in the valley between Shepherdshey and the frontier of the London Road, where it bordered the common seven miles inland.

It was very quiet down here in the autumn. During those early expeditions I did not meet a soul and when I stood quite still on the edge of Teasel Wood the only sounds that I could hear were the gossip of the larches in Heronslea Wood, or the sudden crackle of bursting gorse pods shooting seeds into the thickets. The oaks and beeches of Teasel Wood never talked unless there was a stiffish breeze, and the air was very still that October, so still that sometimes it seemed to me that everything had stopped growing in Sennacharib and that I was its sole inhabitant.

I came to understand this curious isolation of the area. Geography, and the pace of Edwardian development, had conspired to isolate the area. Our part of the West was a broad triangle, jutting into the Bristol Channel, and the estuary of the Whin and the town of Whinmouth on its left bank had been bypassed when the main railway line drove due west to the county town, fifteen miles inland. Whinmouth had a modest holiday industry and an even smaller fishing and coastal trade, but for the most part Whinmouth folk lived by taking in one another's washing. Such visitors as found their way to the town came down the river road, or via the branch line that ran beside the river. Few of them turned east into the scrub, common and pasture of the Shepherdshey district. This fact delighted me; the fewer people who challenged my right the better I was pleased. But here I ought to speak briefly of my family, the Leighs, although none of them play more than a casual part in my story.

I soon found Foxhayes Farm, where my mother had been born, and shortly afterward I crossed Teasel Wood and introduced myself to my Uncle Mark at his ramshackle riding stable on the edge of my domain. Uncle Mark was the second of my three Devon uncles, Uncle Reuben being the eldest, and Uncle Luke the youngest. Between them, during that first month in the West, I began to make sense out of our family history and learned how, although all were the sons and grandsons of farmers, not one of them had held a scythe or turned a sod since they were small boys.

They were an odd, contrasting trio, with nothing in common but the big, loose-limbed bones and the drifting gait of the Leighs. My mother had spoken to me about this gait when she recognized it in myself. "You can always tell a Leigh by his walk," she said. "A Leigh never puts one foot in front of the other, he drifts like a leaf on a pavement."

As I said, Grandfather Leigh had drunk himself to death, and he accomplished this before he was forty. Up to the moment that his wife died during her fourth childbirth he had been a strict Methodist and was looked upon as being an exceptionally pious man. Like many religious men, however, he challenged the wisdom of his God to interfere with the continuity of a well-ordered life, and when his wife died he was not so much despondent as furiously angry. He marched straight into The Jolly Rifleman on the day after the funeral and ordered rum. Having once tasted it he decided that he liked the flavor and continued to drink it in prodigious quantities until the day came when the landlord refused to serve him.

After that he took to riding his cob farther afield, down into Whinmouth, or over to the Pilot, at Nun's Bay. He was often drunk for days at a stretch but no matter how much liquor he swallowed he never reached the stage where he was unable to sit his saddle and ride off in search of more.

When I got to know the Shepherdshey folk I met people who could talk of his antics during the last two years of his life. They were in the best traditions of the Victorian drunkard and included scenes of the wildest improbability. He must have behaved something like Masefield's hero in "The Everlasting Mercy," smashing up bar parlors and whirling his fists at rash friends who tried to remonstrate with him. One night he stripped himself stark naked and carried a torch up the main drive to Heronslea House. On another he set fire to some of his own ricks and then drove a blue farm wagon at a breakneck speed down the Teasel track and through Shepherdshey as far as the crossroads.

He went to jail several times but the moment he came out he started all over again, and was soon regarded as an intolerable nuisance in the district. Everybody was relieved when they found his cob crushed to death under Nun's Head one morning. His battered body turned up on the estuary cockle sands a week or so later and it was assumed that he had missed the cliff path after leaving the Pilot at closing time.

At the time of his death his eldest son, Reuben, was eight, and the two younger boys, Mark and Luke, were respectively a year and three years younger. My mother was not much more than a baby, and former Methodist friends came forward to give the children homes after the tenancy of the farm had gone to a nominee of the Gilroy Estate, for at that time a cousin of Lord Gilroy was occupying Heronslea House.

Uncle Reuben was adopted by the Methodist minister, who subsequently apprenticed him to Mr. Handford, the founder-proprietor of the little weekly newspaper in Whinmouth. The boy showed an aptitude for printing and was soon a steady journeyman and later the foreman printer in Handford's works behind the newspaper office, in High Street.

Reuben was a solemn, humorless man, a very kind and thoughtful soul, animated by an almost fanatical sense of duty toward his neighbors and employer. In due côurse he became a town councilor and was much respected, though never very popular in the Whinmouth area. He was a local preacher and a confirmed radical, so that he could deliver an impressive address on salvation or free trade, whichever his audience demanded. I was glad I had been taken in by Uncle Luke and Aunt Thirza. Life with Uncle Reuben would have been more comfortable but very dull.

It wasn't at all dull at Uncle Luke's. Luke had been given a home by a general dealer, who occupied ramshackle premises near the dock. He had never learned a trade but when he grew up he inherited the business, such as it was, and earned his living buying and selling second-hand household goods.

He was not very interested in this means of livelihood

and had no business acumen whatever. He was a country-man pure and simple, with eyes and ears for nothing but things that grew in the hedges and fields, or the wild life of the cliffs and the banks of the estuary. His knowledge of birds in particular, and of wild life generally, was prodigious. Everywhere he went he carried a pair of binoculars and everything he saw that interested him he wrote down in fat exercise books that he stuffed into his roll-top desk at the Mart and never referred to once they were full.

He could tell you the smallest details about the habits of unusual birds—what they lived on, when they appeared in Britain, where they nested, how many eggs they laid and anything else about them. He would sit in a hedge for hours with his binoculars glued to his eyes watching lapwings patrol their nests against the descent of hawks. He loved wild flowers, all wild flowers, and could tell you just where to find yellow rattle or round-headed rampion. With colored chalks he could sketch the hue and structure of every significant plant that grew in hedge, field or copse.

He was a spare, shambling man, with iron-gray hair and mild, myopic eyes, but despite his gentle nature he could be madly exasperating if one was obliged to work with him. It was often difficult to get through to Uncle Luke, for his brain was hedged around with trefoil, butterbur and bristly ox-tongue, or patrolled by protective flights of screaming jays and wailing herring gulls. His wife, Aunt Thirza, treated him like an idiot child. She was a shrewish, bustling, efficient little body, with restless eyes that gleamed from behind gold-rimmed spectacles. She took a fancy to me, however, and almost from the moment I arrived she seemed to expect me to make up for her husband's deficiencies as a provider.

I was expected to work hard but as a reward I was given plenty of pocket money. At sixteen I was virtual master of the house.

Uncle Luke showed a lively interest in my rambles about Sennacharib during the weekends.

"There's a pair of buzzards up there," he said, ignoring the disgusted grunt of his wife. "Buzzards disappeared from these parts when I was a boy and these are the first

8

I've seen in twenty years. Birds are slaves to fashion just like us, and they tire of districts every now and again. I don't know what brought 'em back here but I know what made 'em go. Lord Gilroy's kin had a keeper who was deadly with a rook rifle. He must have shot a dozen and draped 'em on his vermin pole before they up and left. That keeper shot himself in the end, climbing through a hedge into Teasel Wood, and it was about the best thing that ever happened on that estate!"

Uncle Luke never killed anything, not even a fly or a cockroach, and the only thing that could summon him from his endless contemplation of nature was the witnessing, or even a description, of a wanton act of killing. The mere memory of the marksman with the rook rifle, dead more than twenty years, was sufficient to spoil his midday meal.

Uncle Mark, the middle son, was the one reputed to be most like his father. He was over six feet in height and broad as a barrel. His skin was as rough as a last year's apple and his eyes, when they weren't challenging, gleamed with sardonic humor. He was the only member of the family who used the broad Devon bur of his forefathers and his speech was so thick, and so full of archaic idiom, that it was months before I was able to understand more than half the words he uttered.

He had a terrible reputation with women and was reputed to be paying several affiliation orders in the district. Notwithstanding this he always had a roll of filthy bank notes in his breeches pockets and I never did discover how they got there. His livery stable, situated on the far side of Teasel Wood, was a hopeless, ramshackle affair, a motley assembly of clapboard stables and tin sheds, housing a few unclipped ponies, three rawboned hacks, and one well-cared-for gelding that he maintained for his own use.

In his younger days he had been huntsman to the Gilroy pack and was still seen on the fringe of the hunting field, though he never actually attended a meet in case someone should demand his subscription. He was a mean, gruff, picturesque old rascal, and did not go far out of his way to welcome me when I called on him. He was still on nodding terms with Uncle Luke but he and Uncle Reuben detested one another. Uncle Reuben regarded him as a reincarnation of Grandfather during the days of his decline, whereas Uncle Mark dismissed his elder brother as "a bliddy ole humbug, wi' no more go in 'im nor a zick cow!" On the few occasions they met in Whinmouth Bay their greeting was limited to a mutual growl.

It was on the afternoon when I had met and been repelled by Uncle Mark that I first saw the buzzards.

I had hoped to spend the entire afternoon at the stables, but Uncle Mark was in a foul temper over something or other and after looking me up and down with obvious disfavor he simply said:

"Huh! So you'm Miriam's boy, be'ee? Can you zit a horse?"

When I told him that I had never bestridden a horse in my life he was so disgusted that he swore aloud. I backed away and dodged behind the stables, awaiting a chance to slip back to the woods. He waddled off mumbling to himself and I remember thinking how neatly he fitted my conception of Billy Bones, in *Treasure Island,* and wondering if he too was drinking himself to death on Jamaica rum, like Bones and Grandfather Leigh.

I misjudged Uncle Mark at that time. He was good company once you had learned to take his gruffness for granted, and he never touched rum or any other spirit, confining himself to rough cider which, he declared, "stayed in the legs, didn't maze the ade, an' left a man all his faculties to take full use of such hoppertoonities as come his way!"

By "hoppertunities" Uncle Mark simply meant a chance encounter with any obliging women who crossed his path, and his expectations were frequently gratified. At fifty he was a very lusty man and certain types of women were attracted by his heavy masculinity.

I escaped to the tangle of Teasel Wood and across the goyle into the larch and chestnut woods, behind Heronslea House. It was here, on a rail that marked the limit of the park, that I first saw the two buzzards and instantly mistook them for eagles.

10

They were magnificent birds, the female noticeably larger than the male, with plumage of deep, rich brown and conspicuously lighter patches on the underparts. Their tails were beautifully barred and they sat hunched on the crossbar, their bright yellow feet gripping the decaying bark, their arrogant eyes regarding me with mild disapproval, as though daring me to cross the fence and enter the grounds of the enclosure.

I had a good long look at them before they rose on blunt, mothlike wings and wheeled over the sparsely timbered paddock, uttering a duet of long, mewing cries, a note unlike that of any bird I had ever heard.

Fascinated I watched them soar and drift at about a hundred feet and then, entirely discounting me, they dropped again with wonderful deliberation and perched on the second fence that enclosed the inner plantation.

I don't think I saw the notice board but if I had, the warning would not have deterred me. I climbed the rail and crossed the paddock but the buzzards rose again before I could dodge behind the tree close to them. I ran and leaped over the second paling and through the trees into the wood, but it was impossible to see them here although I could still hear their *Mee-oo! Mee-oo!* from above the feathery heads of the larches.

The wood was new ground for me and I went on down the gentle slope until I broke through to a narrow ride, a glorious, green aisle, as cool and still as a cathedral. It was the kind of wood one reads about and sometimes sees on a calendar cover but rarely discovers, not even in unspoiled country. Rides intersected it and every now and again two rides merged and huge bracken fronds crowded into the slender triangle formed by the junction.

Nearly all the flowers had gone but there were still tall fox-glove stems and one or two late campion and lady's slipper. The trees were so closely set that a kind of green mist hung over the wood. There had seemed to be no breeze outside, but in here the faintest breath of wind set the larches tissing and they seemed to me to be whispering the same word over and over again: "Assyria—Assyria—Assyria."

11

I was standing on a curve of the main ride when I heard a sudden crackle in the undergrowth behind me. Swinging around I came face to face with a keeper, carrying a double-barreled shotgun in the crook of his arm.

I took an instant dislike to the man. He was dressed in rough, patched tweeds, corduroy breeches, gleaming leggings and a drooping weather-stained trilby, but somehow he did not look like a countryman. His face was too pale and too narrow and his eyes were red and angry, like a ferret's. It was clear too that he was going to be as truculent as most of his kind, for he neighed at me in a strong Cockney accent, as alien as my own.

"Wotcher think *you're* up to, eh?"

Uncle Luke had given me casual advice about trespassing.

"If anyone challenges you offer 'em a farthing damage and walk off without arguing the toss!" he had told me. I had also read about this somewhere and the dignified compromise intrigued me. I happened to have a farthing in my pocket, change from a loaf I had bought for Aunt Thirza earlier in the day, so I plunged my hand into my trouser pocket and produced it as the keeper strode clear of the bracken and faced me in the ride.

"This is for any damage I've done," I said, trying to keep a steady voice, for despite the grand gesture a townsman's fears caused my heart to hammer wildly and I hated the man's red eyes.

With a downsweep of his hand he struck the coin from my hand and thrust his narrow face to within an inch of mine.

"Saucy young bastard! Been after rabbits, you 'ave! Seen the notice, 'aven't you? *Read,* doncher?"

I mumbled that I had not seen a notice and that if I had I would not have entered the wood, but he cut my excuses short and pushed me so vigorously that I staggered back and struck my elbow a sharp blow on a tree. Either the pain, the man's manner, or both enraged me and the spurt of anger gave me a little courage.

"You can't do that to me!" I shouted at him. "I wasn't doing any harm!"

12

"Shut yer mouth an' open yer jacket!" he roared, shifting his grip on the gun and advancing so close to me that I recoiled from the stench of his bad breath.

"I won't and you can go to hell!" I screamed, my back to the tree and my fists clenched.

Townsman or countryman, he knew his business. In a trice he had dropped his gun and grabbed me above the elbows, whirling me around and throwing me violently against his extended leg so that I fell flat on my back in the bracken. In another second he was on top of me, had lifted me sideways and seized my arm in a half nelson. I cried out with pain and fright but he only jerked the wrist higher and higher, until I almost fainted and began to thresh out with both legs.

"Assaultin' a keeper! We'll see abaht this, cock!" he said, and was in the act of dragging me to my feet when I saw, through a film of tears, a horse and rider walk into view around the broad curve of the ride and heard a girl's voice say:

"Let him go, Croker! Don't be such a damned fool! *Let him go I tell you!*"

He released me at once, jumping back so quickly that I fell forward on my hands and knees. When I regained my feet I saw pony and rider advancing into the main ride and Croker, now harassed and confused, retreating to the spot where his gun lay in the long grass.

The girl came on slowly, her feet free of the stirrups, her body loose in the saddle that creaked as though very new. Apart from this rhythmic creak, and the almost noiseless impact of the pony's hoofs on the beaten earth of the ride, it was curiously silent in the glade.

There was something stately about her advance, as though she was a young queen riding to acknowledge the obeisance of a respectful multitude, and she sat her pony as though she had never used any other means of progression. This regality, and the utter confusion of the keeper, suddenly communicated itself to me, so that I dropped my glance and pretended to look about for my cap, lost in the struggle.

"You know perfectly well that you're not supposed to

13

do that, Croker!" she said, and her voice, pitched pleasantly low, had a ring of authority. Her presence was so commanding that I began to feel almost sorry for the wretched keeper, now so ill at ease that he had forgotten to retrieve his gun.

He flushed and blurted out:

"He showed fight, Miss Em'rood, proper young d—"

He was going to say "devil" but the girl cut him short, lifting her gloved hand from the pommel of the saddle.

"Bring me your gun—*quickly!* Bring the gun here!"

The man bent, picked up the gun and almost ran across the ride. She took it from him and glanced at the hammers.

"It's cocked, you fool!"

The man began to squirm under her merciless contempt.

"I know it is, Miss Em'rood, but I didn't 'ave it in mind to shoot! Cor Jesus, I wouldn't do that, miss, I was just—"

"You're a liar, Croker! You cocked it to scare him and it might easily have gone off while you were rolling about near it! Then you'd have been charged with murder and strung up and I should have been a witness against you! I would have been, I can tell you! I'd have even turned up to read the notice on the prison gate!"

I suppose this was meant as a joke but Croker did not take it as such. He began stammering more excuses: He was trespassing . . . there's the notice up on top . . . he must have seen it . . . he started the fight . . .

"That's not true," I said, speaking for the first time. "I offered him a farthing damages and said I'd go. Look, there's the farthing on the ground."

While we were talking the pale sun had passed the open part of the ride and I could see the new coin gleaming in one of Croker's heel clips.

The girl glanced at the coin and then at Croker. Severity and the touch of haughtiness left her expression and she smiled. It was a swift, boyish kind of smile and when she spoke again the rasp had vanished from her voice.

14

"You certainly *will* hang one of these days, Croker! Imagine leaving a clue like that farthing!"

Croker recognized the change in her voice and was pitifully grateful for it. He began to weave more excuses, repeating over and over again that he had strict instructions to eject all trespassers and referring once more to the notice board on the edge of the wood, but again she cut him short with the regal lift of the hand.

"Oh, *stop* it, Croker! Don't *whine* so! I hate people who whine and snivel. And I hate people who hide behind other people's orders. Do you know what you are? You're the sort of person who encourages the Bolshies. People like you would have us all guillotined in no time!"

I am sure that Croker failed to follow her odd line of reasoning and equally sure that it was employed for my benefit rather than his. She returned his gun but he seemed reluctant to go without some assurance on her part that the incident would not be reported.

"After all, I did 'ave me instructions," he mumbled, "and if yer Pa gets to hear about it—"

"You had no instructions to commit assault and battery on my friends!" she told him, and saw his jaw drop with renewed dismay.

"Gawd, Miss Em'rood, 'ow was I ter know he was a friend o' yours? *Ow* was *I* to know. . . ? He never said nothing!" He turned to me for corroboration. "You didn't, did you?"

"I don't imagine you gave him much of a chance," replied the girl crisply, and then, as though conversation with Croker bored her, she pulled off her riding hat and dismounted.

I had never seen anyone dismount from a horse the way Diana dismounted. She threw her right leg over the pommel and pointed both feet before floating rather than leaping from the horse and then landing with half her weight against the mount's shoulder. It was such an effortless, graceful movement that you wanted to see it performed over and over again. It set you wondering whether it had been acquired after months of practice, or was merely one of a whole repertoire of lithe, graceful movements, like the

15

casual lift of her hand, or the way she moved with the horse when it had walked toward us across the glade. Everything about her had this smooth practiced fluency, even her voice and the movements of her wrist as she gently danced the hat on its elastic chin strap.

To watch her, to be with her, was like listening to a famous actor declaiming well-remembered lines, or hearing a brilliant concert pianist play a familiar passage from one of the classics. There was something exciting and accomplished about everything she did, yet it was the kind of accomplishment that contained no element of surprise or shock, so smoothly and effortlessly was it achieved.

"Hold the pony," she ordered me, "I won't be a moment," and she handed me the reins and crossed to where Croker stood, taking him firmly by the arm and leading him away from me and down the ride in the direction of the house. They walked together as far as the curve and then stopped for a moment out of earshot. I saw her talking to him earnestly, and Croker listening with every mark of attention. Then, with a vigorous nod, he shouldered his gun and marched off between the trees and she came slowly up the ride toward me. It was then that I really saw her for the first time and the second of the October miracles occurred.

She was about my own age and not nearly so tall or mature as I had imagined her to be when she was mounted. Up to that moment, with her hair bundled under the hard little hat, I had judged her to be at least sixteen, but with her lovely hair loose on her shoulders she did not look as old as I and I wondered again at the deference shown to her by such a truculent man as Croker.

From a distance it was the quality of her hair that impressed me, that and the strange transparency of her skin, the paleness of which was so vividly emphasized by her dark chestnut hair. She had a short, straight nose and a small, slightly jutting chin with a single dimple, the largest dimple I had ever seen, a finger's breadth below her mouth. This much I saw as she advanced up the glade, but it was not until she took the reins from me that I noticed her eyes. They were huge and the shadows around them

16

made them seem even larger and more expressive. When she had first approached us, and put a period to the agony of my twisted arm, I had noticed that her eyes were blue, but not until this moment had I realized just how blue they were. They were like the patch of sky between cotton-wool clouds on the calmest April day, or the strip of Channel beyond the first line of sandbanks in Nun's Bay, where the sea floor shelves away from the lip of sandstone and the sudden depth of the water is apparent from the clifftop. They were the blue of Teasel Wood periwinkles, the blue of the irises growing alongside Shepherdshey reservoir; they were Sennacharib blue, a christening gift from the fairy godmother of the woods, moors and cliffs of the lands I claimed.

I looked into their depth for perhaps three seconds while she took the reins from me and swung herself into the saddle with the same effortless hoist as she had left it. I think she must have known that, at this moment, I passed from boyhood to manhood and was hers for life, that everything awaiting me in the future, every ambition that stirred in me, every emotion I was to experience, would be prompted by her dimple, her dark tumbling hair and her eyes. She knew too, as I did, that from then on everything that happened to me that had no bearing on her would be smaller change than the farthing at our feet.

The conquest pleased her, that much was evident by her manner during that first afternoon, but it made no lasting impression on her, so that our relationship was destined to be lopsided from the very beginning.

At the time, however, I did not quarrel with this. Her ascendancy had been established from the moment she lifted her gloved hand to terminate the pain of Croker's half nelson. It was more than that, for she was who she was, the daughter of Eric Gayelorde-Sutton, Squire of Sennacharib and stockbroking overlord of everything in it, a girl in beautifully cut riding clothes, mounted on a sleek, well-mannered pony, a girl who, at the lift of a hand, could make a bully like Croker wriggle with fear and embarrassment.

Against this I had nothing but my secret claim, and that seemed ridiculous in the presence of Diana Gayelorde-Sutton.

2.

The strange thing about that first hour in Diana's company was that I felt no shyness in her presence. We exchanged information about one another as readily as two people who find themselves embarking on a long railway journey in one another's company.

The first thing I wanted explained to me was her name. The keeper had addressed her as "Miss Em'rood" and it seemed an unlikely name, even though I had imagined it to be a surname and not, as it turned out, his interpretation of her Christian name.

"It's *Emerald*," she told me, laughing, "not 'Em'rood' —'Em'rood' is just his way of saying it. He comes from Kent and you ought to understand, for you talk rather like him. Do you come from Kent?"

I said I did but I did not tell her it was unlikely to be the part of Kent from which a gamekeeper had been recruited. Somehow it was terribly important to me to impress her with the fact that Devon was my real home and that my childhood among the terrace houses and tramway clang of the Brixton Road had been incidental. I told her my name and she savored it.

"John Leigh . . . that's a country name . . . *John*, yes, you do *look* a John but it's still not quite right somehow . . ."

Suddenly her eyes sparkled and she dropped the reins, leaning back and putting both hands on her narrow hips.

"I know who you remind me of! It's not John, it's *Jan* . . . *Jan Ridd!*"

The fancy excited her so much that she rocked in the saddle. "Jan Ridd, the big solemn boy in *Lorna Doone!* You're tall and lanky and . . . and serious-looking. Haven't you read *Lorna Doone?*"

Mercifully I had. Only a few days previously I had found a copy in a box of books that had been trundled

18

into the Mart on Uncle Luke's handcart and had read as far as Jan's escape with Lorna in the snow. I was not sure that I relished her description, "lanky and serious-looking," but on the whole I found the comparison flattering. Jan Ridd was big, strong and fearless and Lorna was dark, winsome and strong-willed, so that at once my mind began to weave a rich pattern of rustic romance in which Keeper Croker was Carver Doone and this girl had been snatched from him after a merciless contest between us. Then my imagination ran against a bulwark of fact, for in this instance the roles of rescuer and rescued had been reversed, running contrary to all accepted courses. It was the girl who had released me from the clutches of Carver, and sent Carver about his business with his tail between his legs.

I returned to the subject of her name, Emerald.

"It's a funny name," I said, "I've never heard it before."

"I don't use it, only Mother insists on using it! It was her idea . . . she named me after Lady Cunard because she's such a terrible snob. As if a name can do anything for a person—I mean, to make them like anybody else! I always used my second name, Diana. Don't ever call me anything but Diana and don't ever tell anyone about Emerald. You won't, will you?"

"Of course I won't! I like Diana much better. It suits you and I like it. Diana what?"

She laughed again. It was wonderful to watch the play of the dimple and the heavy stir of her hair when she threw back her head. Every moment I spent with her added volume to the tide of worship that rose in me. As we walked along I began to feel lifted on it, just as the earlier miracle in the valley had lifted me, but this time my exhilaration yearned for some form of expression. I wanted to shout and dance and sing. I was no longer John Leigh, odd-job boy at Leigh's Furniture Mart, a clumsy overgrown lout fresh from Brixton Road Council School and wearing a gray serge suit utterly unsuited for a ramble through a larch wood in the company of an angel. I was Jan Ridd, vanquisher of Doones, striding along beside his adored Lorna and conveying her to a place of safety and repose.

"Diana Gayelorde-Sutton," she said, this time with a trace of contempt. "Gayelord is more snobbery, because daddy's real name is Sutton and mother dug up the Gayelorde soon after we took Heronslea. I don't know where she found it, she's very touchy about it when I ask her, but it was all done properly, you know, deed poll and all that!"

I was not at all sure what "deed poll" was but I was beginning to glimpse a formidable picture of her mother, a person for whom it was clear that Diana had no respect whatever. I wanted to know more of her and more of the family, how they came to be here, how rich they were, why it was necessary to name Diana after someone whose name I associated with ocean-going liners and why the family's surname had to be dressed up with the aristocratic-sounding Gayelorde.

She told me a good deal about herself that afternoon and demanded little in return. I told her proudly that my family had once farmed Foxhayes and that I now lived with an uncle in Whinmouth Bay but she showed no real interest in my family or, indeed, how I came to be on the estate. I didn't find out everything about the Gayelorde-Suttons that afternoon but as I walked beside her along the ride she talked very freely and gaily about her life and background, and I listened to everything she said with respect, awed at being the confidant of such a wonderful creature.

It seemed that the Gayelorde-Suttons, father, mother and daughter, had leased Heronslea from the Gilroy Estate less than a year ago, when Diana's father had made a great deal of money in some kind of business that Diana appeared to understand but was utterly unintelligible to me. It was, she said, something to do with shares, holdings, or mines, either in Africa or South America, she wasn't sure which.

He had been rich before this but was not fabulously wealthy, with another house in London, a horde of retainers and a Rolls-Royce sedan, in addition to the coun-

20

try estate, rustic retainers and two more cars, a Bentley for Mrs. Gayelorde-Sutton and an Austin station wagon for use at Heronslea.

All this was impressive enough but there was more to come. The family went abroad a good deal and when they traveled during the holidays they sometimes took Diana with them. She had been to France several times and to Spain and Italy on two other occasions. When they were in London her father spent most of his time "sitting on boards," which struck me as a strange occupation for a man who owned a Rolls-Royce and two large houses. I was foolish enough to probe her statement and Diana, after shouting with laughter, explained that a board was a group of people in charge of a business, and that her father, aside from his African or South American activities, administered dozens of smaller businesses in the City.

She herself, she said, hardly ever stayed at the London house because she was a boarder at a snob school in Surrey. She would have been at school now but there had been a "lovely, lovely, outbreak of measles," and everyone who didn't show spots had been sent home for "a fortnight's mooch, smack in the middle of term!"

She told me a good deal about her school and I was on more familiar ground here, for I was an avid reader of the *Magnet* and *Gem* and I recognized her school as a girls' equivalent of Greyfriars and St. Jims, where every pupil's father was fabulously rich and famous people arrived in limousines on speech days.

She hated school more than most children, finding all the mistresses "stuffy," and all the lessons "grisly." From her description of the place I knew that I should have liked it. It was certainly a very different kind of school from the one that I had attended in the Brixton Road. All the girls had little rooms of their own and the meals, which she described as so-so, sounded to me like a series of modest banquets.

They even had little parties in the evenings, "to learn how to drink sherry without giggling," and after prep, on winter evenings, one of the mistresses read aloud from *David Copperfield,* or *The Mill on the Floss.* There were plenty of outdoor activities too, hockey, tennis, lacrosse and a game of which I had never heard called "squash," but Diana, although very much an outdoor girl, disliked games as much as lessons. "I kick against anything organized," she told me. "That's why I like riding and that's why I love it down here, with no one but dear old Drip."

"Who's Drip?" I asked her, imagining it to be either the pony she was riding, or a favorite dog.

"Drip is a kind of governess that Mummy got for me," she said, "after Passy-Glassy told Daddy that I wasn't doing any work and must cram during the hols. She's a terrible dreary old thing to look at but she worships me and I can do absolutely anything with her. I should be having conversational French right now but I easily talked her out of it. I said I had a bad headache, and needed fresh air. You'd like Drip, she's a pet really!"

"Then who on earth is Passy-Glassy?" I wanted to know.

"Oh, she's Head at Mount Waring and she's a fearful droop! She's called Passy-Glassy because she's always checking up on accents and one day she threw us into fits by telling us about a girl from the north, who said 'Passs me a glasss' with a strong Lancashire accent. She said it ought to have been 'Parse me a glawse, I want to hev a barthe,' and the whole Middle School went up in smoke at the idea of Miss Endicott-Brookes taking a bath in a glass! She's as fat as a barrel, you see."

It was a silly story I suppose, but it made me laugh, partly because Diana was clever at imitating accents but more, I think, from relief that she was so gloriously free of snobbery, and this made an association between us possible.

I don't think I had ever met anyone quite so free of class prejudice. I knew that I possessed a strong Cockney accent, for already the Devonians in Whinmouth Bay had made me conscious of it, but Diana minded it as little as my trespass of her father's property and from the first moment we were alone she always treated me as a social equal.

At the time I mistook this for a natural broad-mindedness on her part; it was only later that I discovered that it was

22

a deliberate act on her part, part of her ceaseless counter-offensive against her mother.

While we had been talking we had followed the ride that led to the eastern edge of the wood and suddenly we emerged from the trees and looked down over the valley. I forgot Diana for a few moments as I studied the view, for I had never seen it from this angle, and the impact of all that color was so powerful that it made me run ahead of her until I came to the extreme edge of the escarpment. Then I looked back and saw her framed against the green backcloth of the larches and I knew that she was the jewel of Sennacharib and as rightly mine as any part of it.

I made a vow then that somehow, at some time, no matter how many difficulties interposed, or how long the conquest took me to achieve, I would marry Diana Gayelord-Sutton and we would live together in that big white house, the roof of which I could glimpse from where I stood.

3.

She kicked her pony alongside and looked down at me curiously but even at that stage of our friendship it wasn't necessary to explain to her how I felt about Sennacharib.

She said, "You love it, don't you, Jan? You feel about it just as I do! You *do*, don't you?"

I don't think I was surprised that she had guessed my secret so quickly. Somehow it had never really been a secret from her.

"It's Sennacharib," I told her, and recited the opening lines of the poem.

She didn't laugh, or look blank, or quarrel with them in any way but sat perfectly still on her pony, looking over my shoulder and down the golden hillside to where the Teasel crept between folds to Shepherdshey, then up the further slope into the blue-black vastness of Teasel Wood.

It was one of those magic moments that come perhaps twice in a lifetime, the moment before a single word, or a sigh of wind, breaks a crystal of pure happiness. We stood together for perhaps a minute and then the buzzards came drifting over the wood, mewing their soft, plaintive call.

The moment passed as we saw them dip across the elm clump in search of fresh wind currents.

"How would you like to come home for tea?" she said, when the birds had disappeared. "There's no one there but Drip and me, and Drip won't mind, she's always saying I spend too much time alone."

I tried not to show elation, mumbling something about muddy boots and the Whinmouth bus, but she ignored excuses and kicked the left-hand stirrup iron.

"Jump up behind," she said. "Nellie can easily take two of us."

"I've never been on a horse," I protested, for the second time that afternoon.

"This isn't a horse," she said, "so do as I say, and hold me around the middle!"

It was as much an order as any she had given Croker. I put my foot in the free stirrup and climbed on the pony's broad back, clasping my hands around her narrow waist and letting my legs swing free.

"Tighter!" she commanded. "Or we'll part company on the bends. Giddup, Nellie! Stir your stumps!" and we were off at a brisk trot, heading back into the wood and down the broad path toward the house.

It wasn't a very comfortable ride but what it lacked in comfort it made up for in exhilaration. Soon I was clinging to her as a drowning man clings to a breakwater and even the fragrance of her hair could not obliterate the fear of being hurled from my seat and flung against the trunks of the close-set firs that replaced the larches farther down the slope. At the same spanking pace we left the wood and entered the level paddock leading to the kitchen garden and stables. Then a madness entered her and she urged Nellie forward, shouting and kicking furiously with her heels.

The pony did not seem to mind its double load and broke from rolling canter into a stretched gallop, streaking across the grass and clattering onto the cobbles of the yard at top speed.

I did not know then that a horse needs no urging when its head is turned for home, but neither did I know that it always stops outside its own stable door. It did so now

24

with an abruptness that sent me flying over Diana's shoulders and onto the cobbles under its feet. The impact drove all the breath from my body and stripped the skin from my knees and knuckles.

Diana did not even leave the saddle. When I struggled to my feet she was helpless with laughter.

"You should have braced!" she gasped. "Braced back, directly we passed through the arch. I say, you haven't really hurt yourself, have you?"

I had but I wasn't going to admit it to a girl. My knees and knuckles were smarting horribly but I thrust my hands in my pockets as Diana slid down and a bowed old groom clumped out of the house and led Nellie into a lighted stable.

"I'm all right," I said. "It was fun, but I did tell you I'd never been on a horse before!"

A middle-aged woman, with graying hair scraped back into a tight bun and a permanently worried expression creasing her bespectacled face, appeared on the stone platform that projected from the rear of the house.

"What's happened? Who's that? I was worried about you," she called to Diana. "It's long after teatime!"

"Oh you're always worried about something, Drip," Diana called back. "I've brought someone to tea and we're both ravenous! We'll have it in the kitchen."

"You can't entertain guests in the kitchen," Drip said. "You know very well that your mother would be furious."

"She won't know unless you tell her, so don't fuss, Drip. Just call through and tell Cook we'll have crumpets. Do you like crumpets?" she said, turning to me, and when I said I did she took me by the hand and ran up the steps to the kitchen door where Drip was waiting to usher us into the house.

We went along a dim passage and into the large, cheerful room in which there was a great deal of heavy oak furniture and a large fire burning in an open grate. There was a wonderful smell in here, a smell made up of baking bread, lamp oil and smoldering wood. Diana peeled off her string gloves.

"Good Lord, you're bleeding like a stuck pig!" she suddenly exclaimed, staring at the blood on her glove. "Take him down Hangman's Drop and let him wash off, Drip. Let me see!" and she seized both hands and stared at the gravel rash. "That's nothing at all," she went on. "Put some powdered alum on them. I know there's some in there, I used it this morning."

Drip cluck-clucked almost continuously but she did everything Diana ordered her to do, taking me down three steep steps into a washhouse where there was a big, lead sink and enamel bowl. The room was at least three feet below the level of the kitchen and Diana, who had a nickname for everyone and everything, always referred to it as Hangman's Drop.

Drip, whose real name was Miss Emily Rodgers, superintended the washing and cleaning of my cuts and bandaged a long graze on my knee. She was a simple, sympathetic little body and I didn't envy her chaperonage of a high-spirited fourteen-year-old like Diana.

"She hasn't even introduced us," grumbled Miss Rodgers, when Diana's voice came to us from the kitchen, where she was now beguiling the fat, freckled cook. "Are you one of the boys she met at the Conservative gymkhana in the summer?"

"No," I admitted, "I got lost in the woods higher up. I live in Whinmouth Bay and my name's Leigh, Jan Leigh."

"Well, Jan," she said lightly, "don't let her lead you into any mischief. She'll try, mark my words. I'm not firm enough with her, I know, but she's got such a way with her, and she always does exactly what she chooses to do the moment her mamma's back is turned. There now, that doesn't hurt any more, does it? Come and have tea and then I'll get someone to take you home."

We found Diana lifting the cover from a silver muffin dish stacked high with dripping crumpets. I was ravenously hungry and so, it seemed, was she, for between us we ate a dozen, finishing off with huge slices of rich plum cake.

I don't remember enjoying a meal more than I did that evening. It wasn't simply the food, which was plentiful and beautifully prepared, or the presence of Diana, bubbling

26

on the edge of laughter as she maintained a running fire of teasing aimed at poor Drip and the cook. I think my delight stemmed from a sense of pride arising from where I was and from the coziness of the warm kitchen overlooking the stable yard, where the autumn dusk was creeping in from the woods and isolating the yellow glow of the stable lamps. There was a kind of timeless comfort and security in here, a sense of being wanted that soothed the ache of my mother's death and stilled the upheaval that had followed it, and when Drip, in response to Diana's urgent pleas, brought in her musical boxes, a final drop of delight was added to my cup and I remember thinking how wonderful it would be to live like this always, here, with Diana, in the very heart of Sennacharib.

Drip, or Miss Rodgers as I always preferred to think of her, was a collector of musical boxes, some of them very old and intricately constructed. Her favorite was one made of mother-of-pearl and crowned by a willowy woman in a high-waisted frock and a Quality Street bonnet. It played "Allan Water" and the pure, tinkling notes brought a lump to my throat.

I was surprised and pleased to discover that Diana was affected by the tune, for when I looked at her halfway through the second playing I noticed that her huge eyes were brimming with tears and that she did not seem in any way ashamed of them but let them brim over and roll slowly down her cheeks. I had already noticed how beautiful she looked when she was angry but there in the lamplight, sitting quite still as the music box tinkled out "Allan Water," she looked like a girl out of one of the eighteenth-century portraits I had seen in the Tate Gallery. Her presence filled the room and the whole universe became a place of enchantment.

"I think Mr. Leigh had better get ready to go now," said Miss Rodgers when the tune tinkled to a close. "His people will be getting worried about him and he's missed the last bus from the crossroads."

I was so surprised and flattered at being referred to as Mr. Leigh that I did not hear Diana tell the cook to order the car. It was not until Diana grabbed me by the hand,

27

pulled me into the passage and through a white door into the hall that I realized it was now half-past six and that Aunt Thirza would have been nagging Uncle Luke about my absence since the half-past-five bus had arrived in Chapel Square.

I had a fleeting glimpse at the front part of the house, a large oval hall studded with dark oil paintings and spread with Persian rugs. There were several closed doors leading out of it and I had time to notice the lovely proportions of the staircase that swept in a wide scimitar curve to a three-sided gallery, a gallery lit by a huge crystal chandelier.

"We've got electric in this part of the house. We put in a plant to make our own," Diana told me, "but the current isn't strong enough to supply the back regions yet and Daddy says it'll need another dynamo. I don't care if we never have it, I like the lamplight in the kitchen. Where shall I tell Redman to go?"

Redman was the chauffeur who was waiting, capped and booted, just inside the porch. He said "Good evening, sir" when I came up with Diana but he shot me a shrewd sidelong glance nevertheless.

I told Diana I had better be put off at the bus center in the square, but that it was not necessary to have a car to convey me home, for I could easily walk.

"Don't be so feeble," she snorted, "it's four miles and dark as a bag! Drop him at the bus center, Redman."

"Yes, Miss Emerald," he said and managed to convey the impression that he by no means relished the assignment but would perform it as a personal favor to her.

She followed me out on the half-moon of the graveled approach and the chauffeur opened the rear door and held it while I climbed in. The car was Mrs. Gayelorde-Sutton's Bentley, and far larger and more luxurious than any car I had traveled in up to that time.

Redman walked around and got into the driver's seat, but before he could let in the clutch Diana opened my door again.

"Oh, there's one thing I'd forgotten," she said, a little breathlessly. "You can go anywhere in Sennacharib when I'm back at school, and I'll see that Croker and the others are told about it. Good-by, Jan. See you again sometime —next hols perhaps."

"Yes," I said, "and thank you for everything . . . it's been wonderful . . . I . . ."

The chauffeur moved off then, just at the moment when a huge dog, either a Great Dane or a St. Bernard, ran barking from the house and thrust his great muzzle into Diana's hand. Greeting the dog she seemed to forget about me and as the car sped down the drive I twisted around and looked back at the house, only to see that the front door was now closed and that a single spotlight shone out over the portico, picking out the tall Doric columns that graced the front of Heronslea.

I was the tiniest bit put out by the speed with which she had withdrawn, but soon I forgot this in rich contemplation of all the wonderful things that had happened since Croker had jumped at me out of the wood. I found this contemplation so rewarding that I forgot I was traveling in a chauffeur-driven Bentley, owned by the wife of the overlord of Sennacharib, and only awoke from my daydream when the car stopped and Redman's voice rasped from the speaking tube. "This is it, I think!"

He didn't say "sir" and he didn't jump out to open my door.

Chapter Two

THE FIRST week in November brought a series of violent southwesterly gales. One after the other they beat upon the coast, drenching the town with fine, sticky spray, knocking holes in the promenade and reducing to debris such of the beach huts as had not been dismantled and carted away for the winter.

I had never seen seas like this and I enjoyed the spectacle very much. I liked to stagger along the esplanade, with the wind in my back, and scramble over the landship rocks to Nun's Bay Head, where a little coast guard hut had been built on the highest promontory.

From here you could see the coastline from the estuary in the west to Nun's Bay in the east, an entire seascape of heaving brown mantled in misty rain. The roar of the breakers provided a continuous undertone to the shriek of the wind, as it made its first landfall after a three-thousand-mile-haul across the Atlantic.

When the tide was out and the sandbanks were exposed it was sometimes possible to see the stark remnants of the *Bonadventure,* the wreck that had given a name to this part of the coast. Uncle Luke told me that the great ship had gone aground there in the early nineteenth century and that almost everyone aboard it, including a company of nuns on their way to the West Indies, had been drowned. Most of those that the sea returned were buried in Whinmouth but two were interred on the little island, now known as Nun's Island, that stood about a mile out to sea. When the clouds lifted I could see the mouse-shaped rock with its thin covering of trees and scrub and farther east the abandoned lighthouse, put there by Winstanley years before his more famous lighthouse was built off Plymouth.

I did not go out to Sennacharib until late in the month and when I did I discovered that the gales had played havoc with my valley.

Two of the giant elms on the edge of the Heronslea rhododendron plantation were down, and one of the avenue beeches had fallen across the drive and was being cleared by estate timbermen. The Teasel Brook, which Diana and I had last seen as an insignificant stream some two yards wide, was now a brown torrent carrying a flotsam of twigs and leaves out of Teasel Wood. At Shepherdshey Bridge the water was almost up to the arch and the village street was ankle deep in frayed thatch, broken tiles and sodden twigs from the Heronslea timber.

I went on up the Teasel for a mile and found that the October colors had faded. The gorse guineas had turned to a dull copper and the purple sheen of the heath was rust red. It was still an exciting spectacle but its full glory had gone. There was loneliness in place of the mellow welcome of a month before.

I entered the estate boundary, partly to test the strength of the license Diana had promised me, but also in the vague hope of seeing her or getting some news of her. I met no one, not even Croker, who I suppose was busy clearing the rides behind the house, where the gales had done considerable damage among the larches and firs.

In the following month, as Christmas approached, my uncle's business took me to Shepherdshey Village several times in one week and I came to know some of the folk who lived there.

They were a picturesque community, almost untouched by the twentieth century and in some ways as archaic as the tumble-down buildings they occupied.

There was Half-a-Crown Sam, the village cretin, so bowed and hunched that when seen from a distance he looked almost round. Sam was a professional idiot, with a smooth shining skin and great tufts of yellow hair peaked up like the hair of a circus clown. His eyes were the lightest blue but could narrow to the merest slits when someone invited him to demonstrate the trick that earned him his name—a choice between a half crown and a halfpenny. He invariably chose the halfpenny, muttering that it was less trouble to carry away. Shepherdshey people told me that he had been amassing money by this means for close on thirty years, so perhaps he wasn't really an idiot at all.

There was Ada Macey, the shrill-voiced proprietress of The Jolly Rifleman. Ada said she could remember my Grandfather Leigh taking his first noggin of rum the night he buried his wife. She had a high color and hard eyes and her reputation had penetrated as far as Whinmouth Bay, where she was said to have two husbands, the landlord, Jack Macey, and his man-of-all-work, Harry Venn. Jack, so the story went, had been reported missing early in the war, and Ada had married Harry soon after Armistice Day. She was not in the least put out when Jack turned up in 1919, and since then all three had continued to live

31

lively but by no means quarrelsome lives in the ancient hostlery, west of the Teasel bridge.

It was difficult to imagine Ada as a source of solace to one man, much less two. She was sharp-featured, short-tempered, and not averse to boxing the ears of any male customer who crossed her. I delivered some furniture there on one occasion and happened to scratch the paint off the banisters on my way upstairs. Her protests followed me down the street as far as the crossroads and some of her expressions were such as the Whinmouth fishermen used when trippers walked over their nets spread to dry on the quay.

Across the street from Ada's pub was the village general shop, maintained by a swart, foxy little man called Pat Bristow. Pat was a bachelor and his bosom friend was the sexton, Nathaniel Baker, who seemed to spend all his time seated on Pat's counter.

Nat was a huge, slow-speaking man and the main occupation of these two consisted of issuing a running commentary on every customer who passed the window.

They were ruthless character slayers and in any less tolerant community would have soon been summoned to answer a slander writ. Pat would lay the accusations and wait for Nat's thoughtful corroboration. Having secured it he would then cast about for new charges in respect of the next person to pass the window. Both male and female sinners were referred to as "'er."

"There 'er goes, ol' Nell Josling, looking as though butter wouldn't melt in 'er mouth!" Pat would say, jerking his pipe stem at an elderly woman on her way to the bus stop. "Wouldn't think to look at 'er she owed me four-pun-ten, would 'ee? Owes everyone over Whinmouth, so I hear. Ought to county court 'er, I ought, but I'm zoft. That's my trouble, zoft as a feather bade I be!"

Nat would ponder the customer's shortcomings for a few moments before adding, "They zay 'er insured old Trev Josling bevore 'er passed on. Dree-hundred-pun I 'eard it was. Tidy sum for a man in 'is condition, dornee think, Pat? And him a-bade two year or more, bevore us got round to burying 'un!"

Then Ada Macey would appear in the porch opposite to shake a mat and Pat would abandon the Joslings in order to comment on Ada's experiment in polygamy.

"Going on long bevore 1914 it was! I used to stand here an' zee 'em bob upstairs the minute old Jack Macey went out to his allotment. Time it to the split second they would. First you'd zee Jack, spade in hand, then Harry carrying out the empties, then Ada taking off her apron on the way upstairs. Always in a hurry *she* was, but Harry, he took his time like. He'd watch Jack out o' zight around the church bevore he went up, then draw isself a pint on the way up, never mind 'er shouting for him from the best room! Makes 'ee laugh, dorn it, blamin' it on the war?"

Then Nat would add his corroborative evidence regarding Ada's character in earlier life: "Never no different she wasn't! Smut Stover was the first there when she was fifteen. Zore 'em once I did, in the corner o' the churchyard when I was a choirboy. Fine place to start eh, top of a grave, but it's true. Smut gimme a penny to forget what I zee!"

Smut Stover, the man they referred to, was still about the village. He was a notable poacher, always at odds with the keepers on the Heronslea estate and on Lord Gilroy's coverts farther east. He was a cheerful ruffian and a crony of my Uncle Mark, who was said to have nameless business with him. Perhaps this accounted for Uncle Mark's roll of notes, for Smut was half a gypsy and was regarded as a thief as well as a poacher.

There were respectable folk of the community, of course, but I had no occasion to meet them at that time, for they never patronized Uncle Luke's Mart. They consisted of several farming families scattered around the area and one or two retired folk living in remote houses on the east side of the brook.

The farmers were as backward as everyone else in Shepherdshey. One never saw a tractor at work in the fields, only big, lumbering carts, painted sky blue and drawn by huge, patient shire horses. The vicar, Mr. Shelton, was as out of date as his parishioners.

He looked like a character in a *Punch* cartoon, trotting

33

to and from the vicarage in shirt sleeves, a black bib and rusty clerical hat. He spent most of his time with his bees and usually had to be fetched from his hives on the edge of Teasel Wood when he was wanted to visit the sick, or perform a ceremony. He was said to be deep in the pocket of the Gayelorde-Suttons and dined with them whenever they were in residence. Another regular visitor to Heronslea was Colonel Best, V.C., a Zulu War veteran, who had taken part in the defense of Rorke's Drift and received an assagai wound that left him with a withered arm. The village as a whole, however, thought very little of the new occupants of Heronslea, dismissing them as foreigners, or "foggy-do-men." Everyone whose father had not been born in Shepherdshey was a foggy-do-man and the Gayelorde-Suttons, particularly Mrs. Gayelorde-Sutton, were objects of derision, welcome enough for the gifts they distributed at Christmas and at various fetes held in their grounds but far short of what the villagers called "real gentry," like the Gilroys.

The steady milking of the Gayelorde-Suttons was the principal hobby of the villagers. Mrs. Gayelorde-Sutton was invited to become president of every social group and a fairy godmother to every activity sponsored in the area. Her delight in these forms of patronage ensured a steady flow of funds, jumble, produce and free labor, and in return for these bounties the villagers were ready to eat as much feudal pie as she set before them, mumbling their thanks, tugging their forelocks and laughing heartily at the provider the moment she drove away in her Bentley or Rolls-Royce.

During that first winter I wondered how much Diana knew of this rustic charade or whether she cared two straws what the village folks thought of her parents, but soon I had an opportunity of assessing Mrs. Gayelorde-Sutton myself and guessing at the reasons for Diana's hostility toward her mother.

I heard heels clicking on the slate slab outside the main door and looked up to see Diana standing there. She was standing sideways to me, talking to someone out of my line of vision.

34

I slammed the book shut and jumped up to greet her, but at that moment she shrugged and moved away as a well-dressed woman came through the doorway. I guessed at once that this was her mother, the celebrated Mrs. Gayelorde-Sutton, so I swallowed my welcome and remained quiet in order to get a good look at her.

She was a great deal younger than I had imagined, not more than thirty-three or thirty-four, and so stylishly dressed that anybody in a town like Whinmouth Bay would be sure to turn around and stare at her when she passed by. Skirts were at their very shortest just then and this made her look almost girlish, for her tailor-made costume finished well above her knees. She had very shapely legs and smart shoes, with heels that looked almost as long as her feet.

She was not particularly good-looking and possessed few of Diana's striking features but the general impression she gave was one of sensational smartness, like a model on the cover of an expensive periodical, the kind of magazine you see people reading in first-class railway carriages. She had dark, close-cropped hair and greenish slightly prominent eyes. She was medium height, with a neat figure somewhat too thin. The only thing about her that reminded me of Diana was her chin, well rounded but very firm, too firm for a woman as willowy and elegant as she.

I studied her and was a little disturbed by what I found. There was something arrogantly aggressive about the way she sauntered around our pathetic display of goods, as though she were doing us a favor by just being there and was afraid of touching things as she tip-tapped among kitchen chairs, tables, mangles, washstands and battered commodes.

Then I heard her voice and realized instantly why the people in Shepherdshey made unpleasant jokes about her. It wasn't a woman's voice at all but a voice that belonged to an extravagant puppet. Its accent was so strained and strangled that it made you feel ashamed to listen and it struck me at once that her voice was in key to her personality, a whole jigsaw of effort and contrivance in striking

35

contrast to her daughter's effortless way of moving, talking and smiling.

When Diana moved and smiled everyone about her relaxed. The person at whom she smiled wanted to acknowledge the rhythm and orderliness of the universe, for contact with her made you feel tolerant and generous *inside*. When her eyes sparkled you knew that it was good to be alive and that everything was going to turn out all right in the end.

Mrs. Gayelorde-Sutton's presence had an exactly opposite effect. It made you feel tense and apprehensive, as though you were walking over rough ground in the dark and not sure what you would bump into, or how much you would be hurt in the process. It armed all your defenses against indignities and humiliations and even when she wasn't addressing you the sound of her voice talking to somebody else made you feel edgy and small.

I've thought a good deal about Mrs. Gayelorde-Sutton's accent in the last twenty years. I've even gone to considerable pains to get it down on paper, but to do so with any accuracy is almost impossible, for it was the kind of accent that didn't use any rules regarding the articulation of vowels or the emphasis of syllables. It was meant, of course, to be a high-hat accent, the kind the best people have used since accents became stock-in-trade in this country, but hers overreached itself so ludicrously that it plunged down into farce and was lost in a whirl of despair, laughter or downright incredulity, according to how important she was to you.

I knew that she was important to me because I was already hopelessly in love with her daughter, and the first dry crackle of her voice made me shy away in alarm and want to hide myself behind Uncle Luke's junk.

I was still standing there, book in hand, when she swung round and tip-tapped into the Mart, her prominent eyes roving here and there for someone to hector. That was the very worst thing about her; you were always absolutely certain she *would* hector, it was so clear from the way she walked and held herself. Diana trailed along behind, almost submerged, I noticed, under this tide of arrogance.

Then Mrs. Gayelorde-Sutton spied me, rooted to the spot in our pigsty of an office.

"Boy!" she pronounced. "Come over heah, boy!"

I edged forward like a pupil of Dotheboys Hall anticipating a sound thrashing.

"How mache is *thet!*" she said, flicking her hand from the wrist and indicating a marble-topped washstand marked ten shillings in Uncle Luke's chalked scrawl.

I made a bad mistake straightaway. Licking my lips, and trying hard not to look at Diana who was now standing immediately behind her mother, I said that the article was marked and could be sold for ten shillings, plus delivery charges.

She screwed up her mouth, already very small, into a pink ball about the size of a florin.

"Ai ken see it's marked, boy! Ai've got eyes in mai head! Is there no adult on the premises?"

I quavered that I was in charge during the temporary absence of Mr. Leigh, but that I had his authority to sell anything that was priced.

She thought about this for a moment and then Diana suddenly spoke up. She did not look at me, and gave no sign at all of recognizing me as the boy to whom she had once extended the freedom of Heronslea and entertained in the kitchen less than three months ago.

"You'd better tell him we're buying a lot of things for the cottages," she said, quietly. "Then he'll probably let you have everything a lot cheaper."

I welcomed the compromise. Up to that moment I had been wondering what on earth a person like Mrs. Gayelorde-Sutton could want with our stock. I had seen some of the furniture inside her home, and the very least of it would have been unlikely to find its way on to Uncle Luke's handbarrow. I realized now that she was furnishing some of the Heronslea estate cottages and that made her presence clear. I managed to master my awe and embarrassment in the prospects of doing a profitable piece of business in Uncle Luke's absence and enjoying the handing over of money when he came in, cold and tired after six hours at the auction.

"We could certainly come to some arrangement like that," I said briskly.

She laughed at that and her laughter was like a gleam of sunshine, but sunshine on a February afternoon, without a particle of warmth in it. It was a laugh that made you wince and stammer, and what made it so much worse for me was Diana's silent presence.

I was rescued by Uncle Luke's entry. He came in trundling his handbarrow and even the presence of three chamber pots, roped to the barrow rails by loops of cord, did nothing to reduce the relief his entry afforded me.

"This is Mrs. Gayelorde-Sutton, from Heronslea," I muttered. "She wants some pieces for her cottages, Uncle Luke!"

She whipped around on me like a striking cobra.

"How do you know who I am?" she snapped, and it seemed to me that Diana disembodied herself into the windowless part of the store. I had realized my mistake as soon as it was uttered, however, and this time I was ready for her.

"Everybody knows you in Whinmouth, ma'am!" I said, and it was almost pathetic to see her bridle at such a hoary way of complimenting a customer.

"We hev been renovating on a considerable skeale," she told Uncle Luke, who was not particularly impressed by her. "Mai husband and I hev rebuilt all the cottages on the spinney side of the avenue and we shall be buying somewhat extensively, providing, of course, that we don't quarrel over praices!"

Uncle Luke, who treated every customer alike, assured her that this was unlikely and switched on a naked electric light in the angle of the store made by the office partition. As she followed him across the Mart I saw Diana jerk her head toward the main door and I gladly took the hint, slipping outside and across the road to the edge of the quay, where she joined me.

"Didn't she know about me?" I asked, breathlessly, for the encounter had shaken me badly.

"Good Lord, of course not," said Diana. "I don't tell her anything important."

The words warmed me through, thawing me out and uncoiling the knots in my inside.

"I've been up to Sennacharib several times since," I said, "but I've never even seen Croker. You've had a lot of damage up there, haven't you?"

"Don't let's waste precious time on small talk," said Diana, shortly. "She'll be out in a minute and she wouldn't even trade here if she saw me talking to you! Have you seen our buzzards again?"

I told her no and she smiled a secret kind of smile.

"I have," she said. "I saw them yesterday. I've got a thing about those buzzards, Jan. They only show up when we meet, so I knew I'd see you today. I saw them from my bedroom window but you won't ever see them unless I'm there."

It made all buzzards lovelier than birds of paradise and I accepted her prophecy on the spot.

"Will you be at Boxing Day meet?" she wanted to know. "We're having it at Heronslea . . . it was always at Teasel Wood, but Mummy's decided to give a lawn meet and the Master has fallen in with it because there'll be plenty of everything—you know, stirrup cup and all that!"

"Muffins?" I said. My knowledge of hunting ritual was lamentable but this query made her laugh so much that I had time to feast my eyes on her and notice that she wore a rakishly tilted Cossack cap and that her soft brown curls cascaded from beneath it and lay thickly upon her shoulders. She looked more grown up than when I had last seen her, but perhaps this was because of her London clothes and elegant Russian boots, which were tight-fitting and as high-heeled as her mother's.

"You don't eat muffins on horseback, Jan," she said, but the touch of mockery was compensated by her easy use of the name she had given me. "You've grown even taller and broader, yet you aren't sixteen. When *are* you sixteen?"

"Next October," I said, trembling a little, "October the 6th."

"I'll remember," she said and then, looking across at

39

the ramshackle shed: "What exactly do you do in a dump like this?"

"I help my uncle, we buy furniture at sales and sell it again at a small profit."

"Is that all?"

"Well, yes, I suppose so. We deal in secondhand books, of course, and sometimes sell bits of china and other antiques."

"It's not much of a job, is it? Why don't you get a real job?"

Up to that moment I had been rather proud of the position of right-hand man to the proprietor of the Quay Furniture Mart. It had seemed to me a much more important job than those occupied by most of the Whinmouth Bay boys who had passed school-leaving age. Most of them were grocer's errand boys, or newspaper and milk deliverers. Her obvious contempt, however, wrought an instant change in my heart. Suddenly the job of wheeling used-up furniture about on a barrow seemed mean and degrading and I knew that I would have to seek an occupation that found more favor in her sight. The prospect elated rather than depressed me. I said, rather recklessly:

"Oh, this is only temporary. I've got my eye on something much more exciting!"

"What?" she demanded.

"You'll find out when the time comes," I promised, and my stomach contracted as I reflected that the prospect of finding an exciting job in Whinmouth Bay was remote indeed.

She didn't press the point but simply looked me up and down, a half-smile playing hide-and-seek around the corners of her wide mouth. Finally she nodded, as though she had made up her mind about something.

"You're sweet, Jan. I like you because you're different!"

I could have fallen at her feet on the quayside. I could have told her that I was worth ten of Jan Ridd when it came to adoring and protecting the girl I loved, but I had no words at my command, and even if I acquired them I was aware that I had nothing to buttress a declaration, not even a job that she considered superior to that of a glorified errand boy in the seedy old store of an unfashionable seaside town. I realized that my declaration must wait and all I said, in a desperate endeavor to prolong this delicious conversation, was "How do you mean, different?"

"Oh, just different," she said, and then: "Most boys of your age are show-offs!"

She turned and walked back into the store and I followed her at a safe distance. Uncle Luke called to me from the shadows and asked me to help him move a washstand into the center floor space and after that I was fully occupied, dragging furniture to one side and calling out the prices to Uncle Luke, while Mrs. Gayelorde-Sutton probed and peered and squeaked among the dusty stock. She finally settled for a small vanload and Uncle Luke reduced the total price by more than 20 per cent. I decided that for one so fabulously rich she was careful with halfpennies.

She bought one thing for herself, a pretty porcelain vase that she singled out in order to demonstrate her knowledge of china. From time to time Uncle Luke bought pictures and ornaments at the sales, but he could never afford to compete with the dealers for articles of any value, and this vase was Victorian and of little account.

"I'll take the little Rockingham vawse," she said, when they had agreed on a figure for the furniture, and when Uncle Luke, who was a lamentably honest dealer, explained that the vase was not Rockingham but of a much later date, her mouth again contracted into a pink ball and she called upon Diana for corroboration.

"Aim'rald," she said, pronouncing the name with a sigh-like emphasis on the first syllable and then almost ignoring the "rald," "wouldn't you say that this was Rockingham? Laike the figures in the small kebinet in the morning room?"

Diana drifted over but nothing could induce Uncle Luke to sell an article under false pretenses. He said, very firmly, "It's not Rockingham, ma'am. If it was it certainly wouldn't be priced at fifteen shillings!"

"It's slightly chipped," said Diana, woodenly, "and inside it's full of hair cracks."

"I'll hev it anyway," said Mrs. Gayelorde-Sutton, and put fifteen shillings on the table. "Rep it carefully and put it in the car, boy."

Diana shrugged and moved away again, while I wrapped the vase in tissue paper, placed it in a cardboard box and carried it out to the Rolls which was parked some distance down the quay.

I hoped that Diana would follow me out but she didn't. When I opened the door I found the rear compartment was full of dogs. They were handsome, amiable dogs, not disposed to resent a stranger. One was the huge beast that I had seen Diana fondle when I was driving away from Heronslea, and I saw now that it was a Great Dane. Half obscured by its vast bulk was a sleepy, golden Labrador, with a spiked red collar, and behind the Labrador a silky cocker spaniel who sat up and whimpered. I put the box in the glove compartment and petted the dogs, noticing that they all had their names and addresses engraved on their collars. The Great Dane was Beau, the Labrador was Sheila, and the spaniel was Flop. I wondered which of them was Diana's and whether it was she who had named them. Then Diana and her mother came out and I heard Uncle Luke promise to deliver the furniture by carrier's van and Diana and her mother got into the car, both without another glance in my direction.

As they drove off I hoped that Uncle Luke would close the store and go in to tea, because I yearned to slip away to my bedroom, light the gas fire and savor everything Diana had said during our brief conversation. I had plenty to think about—the fact that she considered me important enough to keep my visit a secret and not attempt to pass it off as a chance encounter with a village boy bribed by muffins and plum cake to keep his mouth shut about a bullying keeper. There was also her frank use of the name Jan and the admission that she considered me sweet, though I was not sure that I liked the adjective. Then there was the more flattering statement that she found me different. In fact the whole atmosphere of our second meeting had been distinctly encouraging, so much so that I made up my mind to go to any lengths in order to deliver the goods to Heronslea. I also decided to attend the Boxing Day meet despite Uncle Luke's strong disapproval of fox hunting. I went to bed happier than I had been since the evening of the second October miracle.

2.

As it happened, the furniture was not delivered until after Christmas.

Ned Gilchrist, the carrier who undertook our deliveries, was booked all that week and although I begged him to accommodate us, and told him that the good will of people like the Gayelorde-Suttons was important to us, he was unable to fix a delivery date earlier than Old Year's Eve, so I had to wait until Boxing morning before I could hope to see Diana again, and then I knew that I would have no chance of talking to her alone, for a local meet, especially a lawn meet on a bank holiday, was certain to attract half the population of Whinmouth Bay.

It was just as I thought. The exodus from the town after breakfast on Boxing morning required the attention of the entire local police force, a sergeant and two constables, and apart from the buses and a few private cars conveying people to the Shepherdshey crossroads, the road was thronged with cyclists, pony carts and groups of pedestrians in their Sunday best.

I resented this invasion into Sennacharib and set off rather sullenly on Uncle Luke's ancient cycle. On the way I passed half a dozen horsemen and three or four pigtailed girls riding plump ponies. I reflected bitterly that these people would have the privilege of spending an entire day in Diana's company, whereas my own contact with her would be limited to a respectful gaze from the edge of the lawn and perhaps a wave of recognition if I was lucky enough to be noticed in such a crowd.

I was unduly pessimistic. In the first place, I soon forgot the stir and chatter around me in the glory of Sennacharib, now looking its winter best in strong December sunshine. The beeches that lined the approach to the house were splashed to their summits in red gold and every rusty leaf glittered with tiny beads of moisture, so that the trees looked like a long row of golden candlesticks sprinkled with silver dust. The sky between them was a cloudless blue and the air was so clear and frosty that it made your eyes and nostrils smart. The turf of the outer paddock was rimed and springy underfoot, and behind the house, which stood against the long slope of rhododendrons and Scotch firs like a squat wedding cake, was the high, feathery crest of the larch wood, the dearest spot in Sennacharib, for it was here I had met Diana.

The graveled forecourt, immediately in front of the portico, presented an animated scene by eleven o'clock. About a hundred people were sitting their horses there and sipping stirrup cup from glasses carried round on silver trays by members of the staff wearing spotless aprons and long Edwardian streamers. I recognized the fat cook dispensing pastries from the terrace, and at the first stroke of eleven the huntsman released the pack from a station wagon and they poured onto the gravel, trotting with nose down and tails up around and about the horses until they were chivied into a dejected group by the cries of the hunt servants and the pistol cracks of their long whips.

The Master himself, bull-necked Doctor Kingslake, stood on the terrace chatting to a tall, squarish man with a head that looked far too big for his thin neck. Somebody close by said that this man was Mr. Gayelorde-Sutton, so I paid the group on the terrace special attention. Presently a groom led two horses around from the stable yard and I watched him hand the reins of the smaller horse to a younger man and then move over to assist Diana's father to mount.

Gayelorde-Sutton climbed up very awkwardly and when he was there he sat slightly forward, with his legs stuck out at wide, ungainly angles. When the groom moved away he wobbled slightly, then steadied himself by gathering reins and crop into a tangled ball. Then I forgot him, for Diana came out through the tall French window and it seemed to me that the chatter all around us subsided as she drifted across the terrace, took the reins of the smaller horse and floated up into the saddle, settling herself like a bird on a nest and making some last-minute adjustments to the girths.

She looked as enchanting as ever in a dark blue habit, fawn jodhpurs and a blue hunting hat crammed down over her curls. I was still gazing at her when somebody nudged me and I turned to find that it was Nat, sexton of Shepherdshey, whom I had last seen sitting on the counter of the Shepherdshey shop.

Nat was commenting on the uncertainty of Mr. Gayelorde-Sutton's seat and doing so in the tone of tolerant contempt that all the Shepherdshey folk reserved for foggy-do-men and foreigners.

"Look at 'un," he muttered, "zittin' there like he was hatching out a pan o' live coals. Gordamme, the bliddy vool'll break 'is bliddy neck if they 'as any kind of a run! They won't though, never do Boxing Day, not with 'alf the bliddy county standing around and sp'iling the scent wi' they ol' charrybangs and whatnots! Be a laugh though, wouldn't 'er? Praper job if the pervider of all this 'ere toddy valled flat on 'is face afore they so much as got goin'!"

I deduced from Nat's speculation that Mr. Gayelorde-Sutton was a beginner, and now that he was mounted I edged closer to get a better look at him.

He was far less impressive than Mrs. Gayelorde-Sutton and on horseback he looked almost pitiful, for you felt that you wanted to stand around and catch him when, as must soon happen, he fell down on one side or the other.

His head was so round, and his body so square that the contrast was almost grotesque, and while I could see some slight physical resemblance between Diana and her mother I could see nothing at all to connect this nervous, awkward man with the girl who sat beside him, looking as if she had grown out of the glossy creature she was riding.

Then the Master mounted and called gruffly to the hounds, who shook off their dejected look and trotted up to him adoringly as he addressed them by a string of John Peelish names. When they had gathered, and he had tossed back his final flagon of stirrup cup, the crowd surged in and the huntsman blew a long, tuneless blast on his horn.

The thought of not being seen by Diana made me bold enough to push through the ranks of followers and cross the drive to where she was sitting her horse. The riders were beginning to close up behind the Master and she touched her mount with her heels and passed within a few feet of me, frowning slightly, as though irritated by the impeding presence of so many pedestrians.

"Hullo!" I faltered, touching her foot rather desperately, and she turned in the saddle and glanced down at me. Her frown disappeared and she smiled rather absently.

"Hullo, Jan! Glad you could get here. Are you going to follow on foot?"

"Are we allowed?"

"Of course. We'll be drawing Big Cover behind the house to begin with, and after that we'll probably move over to Teasel Wood. I should go there first and get away from this awful mob."

The horn sounded again and the followers fell back, forming up behind the last of the horsemen and moving around the western clump of rhododendrons toward the paddock over which I had galloped on Nellie. I grabbed my bicycle and pedaled madly down the drive and along to the village, where I left my bike in the yard of The Rifleman and continued on foot along the path beside the brook as far as the long sloping hill that crowned Teasel Wood.

Nobody followed me, they were all pounding after the field in the broad rides behind the house. I could look down on it here and, although field and followers were invisible under the close-set trees, I could hear the horn and presently a chorus of faint halloos.

I waited up there until after one o'clock, and my patience was rewarded. Just as I was thinking of surrendering to the pangs of hunger (I had been so excited that I had been unable to eat more than a spoonful or two of porridge for breakfast) there was a wild outcry from

46

the far side of the brook and I saw the huntsman and one or two other riders burst through the gorse, jump the brook and pound up the slope directly toward me, led by about a dozen hounds in full cry.

Then I saw the fox, a brown, unhurried streak, daintily picking its way among the half-exposed roots of the gorse and heading, no doubt, for the shelter of Teasel Wood on the crest of the slope. He was invisible to his pursuers but I had him in view for several minutes and saw him turn right-handed to approach the trees at an oblique angle.

I marveled at his coolness and the deliberation he showed in threading his way through the obstacles that lay in his path. For a moment or two I forgot Diana and the hunt in a prayer that he would find sanctuary before hounds overtook him.

He made it with three hundred yards in hand and even tricked them into thinking he had headed directly up the slope, for they kept on until they had overrun his scent and reached the edge of the wood where I was standing. There they paused and ran aimlessly to and fro while the huntsman pounded up, his horse snorting with the effort of breasting the slope and glad enough to check while his rider glanced left and right, screwing up his nut-brown face in an effort to guess the likeliest line.

His sharp eye caught sight of me where I was standing against a tall pine.

"Did you see our fox, sonny?"

"Yes, sir," I said, "he ran along under the hedge and went in there!" and I pointed in the opposite direction to that taken by the fugitive, indicating a stony track that wound along the edge of the wood toward the common proper.

He did not thank me, for which I was grateful, but simply shouted, "Left-handed, Charlie!" to a farmer on a huge gray, who had breasted the slope behind him. Then he bellowed some jargon to the hounds and cracked his whip, driving them around the left-hand curve of the wood and riding out of my line of vision.

Seeing him from below, a stream of riders who had negotiated the brook now bore off at a sharp angle, spurring to overtake him on the gentler slope of the hill.

I was so frightened by the effects of my lie that I did not dare to watch any longer but retreated into the wood and took up a position in some hazel bushes beside the broad cart track that cuts Teasel Wood into two equal halves.

Dismally I wondered what Diana would think of such unsporting behavior and I was almost sick with shame and fear when I heard them pounding back along the cart track, slowly at first, then more resolutely as a stray hound picked up fresh scent outside the wood and drew them on at a brisker pace.

I stayed hidden in my cover when the huntsman, cursing like a madman, thundered by, followed by the farmer on the gray and after him three or four more riders, including the Master, who was so tall that he had to lie flat on his horse's mane to avoid low-hanging branches.

There was a fallen fir a few yards up the path and the huntsman jumped it, but all the others thought twice of setting their horses at the jagged cluster of broken branches and picked their way around near the small crater dug by the roots.

At last, after a dozen or so had gone by, along came Diana crouched low in the saddle and calling softly and persistently to her mount.

She was moving in long, easy strides and made straight for the fallen tree, adjusting her bunched reins as she went and shouting "Up, Glory, *hup!*" as the horse rose and cleared the highest branch by a good six inches. They made a perfect landing on the far side of the obstacle and I remained hidden in the hazel bush until the last of the field had cantered by, still shamed but for all that secretly pleased with myself, for my stratagem had at least enabled me to see Diana in action and Diana riding a fence that had scared all but the professional in the field.

The hunt went whooping away over the arable land in the direction of the sea and I stayed in the wood long enough to watch the stragglers toil across the gorse hill in twos and threes, their horses finding the plowland heavy going after the beaten rides of the estate thickets.

Last of all came **Mr.** **Gayelorde-Sutton**, his hat swinging on its guard, his reins, crop and string gloves tangled into a skein and held against his stomach by his wrists, while his fingers groped and groped for the lifeline of his mount's breastplate. He was only moving at a shambling trot, and as his forlorn figure crossed the skyline I could not help wondering whether active participation in the hunt had been his idea or his wife's. In spite of his money and cars, in spite of his undisputed sovereignty of Sennacharib, I felt sorry for him. I was always to feel sorry for him, for then and later he always had the air of an ungainly, unpopular child, bullied by a vain parent into entering a contest that could bring him nothing but bruises and humiliation.

Halfway along the brook path I came face to face with Drip and she recognized me at once.

"I thought you'd be riding, Jan!" she said and the warmth her greeting showed told me that she was predisposed in my favor and might prove a valuable ally. I pulled off my cap and admitted that I was not yet a good enough horseman to hunt but hoped to join the Pony Club and become proficient in the near future.

"That's a very sensible outlook, Jan," she said. "Emerald thinks everybody has got as much confidence as she has, and because she's a girl all the boys she knows try to outdo her and get into trouble of one sort and another. Are you walking back to Whinmouth or did you come over by car?"

I said I had cycled and wished I could think of some way to rid her of the impression that I was a member of the same social set as the rest of Diana's contemporaries. I hated the thought of her finding out who I really was, where I lived, what I did for a living, and how impossible Mrs. Gayelorde-Sutton would consider me as a squire for her daughter, but I lacked the courage to make the necessary confession and see dismay creep into Drip's lined face. Then she gave me something else to think about.

"I'm on my way to Miss Westcott's, at Hawthorn Cottage by the crossroads," she said. "She's collected a parcel for me from the midday bus. I went into Whinmouth for it on Christmas Eve but it wasn't ready. It's Emerald's Christmas present and I think it's going to be a big surprise for her!" Drip smiled. "She's a very difficult girl to buy for, you see, because she's got everything a child could possibly need or want. If I tell you what it is you won't repeat it to her and spoil it, will you?"

"Of course not!" I promised, and added that it was unlikely I should see Diana again before she went back to school for the Lent term.

"Then I'll show you when we get to Hawthorn Cottage," said Drip. "I think I'd like to know what someone her own age feels about it."

We turned into the village street and walked up the gentle rise to the crossroads. On the way Drip talked ceaselessly about Diana and, although she told me little that I did not already know, she made it clear that she was as much Diana's slave as I was, and a far more unselfish one to boot, for her livelihood depended on Diana's progress and good behavior, and from what I had seen of the relationship of governess and pupil it was obvious that Diana dictated her own terms to this gentle, friendly soul.

I also gathered that Drip was terrified of Mrs. Gayelorde-Sutton.

"Her mamma is very keen to bring her on," she explained plaintively, "but Mrs. Gayelorde-Sutton is away such a lot and nobody else has any kind of authority over her. I'm sure *I* haven't and I know that her father hasn't. She can coax him into promising anything, even when it runs contrary to her mamma's wishes, and that sometimes makes trouble for all of us! It's not that she's naughty, mind you, she's the most lovable gel in the world when she wants to be, but she's not afraid of anything or anyone, except perhaps her mamma, and when she's down here she likes to run wild, you know, the way she did when she put you up on that pony and raced across the paddock into the yard. She needs somebody much stricter than me, I'm afraid, but I think I'd break my heart if I couldn't watch her finish growing up, now that I've had her so long. You see, Jan, I'm a kind of auntie about six times removed, and I was her nanny before I was made governess."

Drip had been talking half to herself as we went along but now, as we reached the gate of Hawthorn Cottage, she suddenly recollected herself and smiled.

"There now, I am a goose. As if you'd be interested in all this chatter! Just wait there and I'll pop in and see if the present has come, I won't be a moment." She tripped up the path and disappeared into the cottage without knocking.

In less than a minute she was out again, carrying a large oblong carton that appeared to be heavier than she could comfortably manage. She set it down on a stone garden ornament and whipped off the lid in a flurry of pride and excitement.

"There!" she said. "What do you think of *that?*"

I gazed at the contents in wonder. The box was full of exquisitely bound books that fitted into a neat, backless bookshelf, the kind of shelf made to stand on a large bedside table. The edges of the pages and the lettering of the authors' names and titles were picked out in gold and the bindings were of tooled Moroccan leather, with a silken bookmark hanging from each spine. I went down on my knees and examined the titles, a fanfare of all the titles I had already gathered into my own private box at the Mart, *Robinson Crusoe, Treasure Island, Kidnapped, Tom Brown's Schooldays, Huckleberry Finn, Silas Marner, The Mill on the Floss, Pilgrim's Progress, Water Babies, Westward Ho!, Don Quixote,* and half a dozen more; but these were more than just books, each was a work of art, exciting to look at and thrilling to handle.

"It's an absolutely wonderful present, Miss Rodgers!" I exclaimed and saw that my unconcealed delight brought her intense pleasure, for she flushed and bit her lip, as though about to burst into tears.

"I . . . I'm so very glad you think so, Jan . . . I thought and thought and then, about a week or so ago, Diana happened to make a joke about how she used to plague me into reading one more chapter before I turned out the

51

light. I picked all her favorites, you see, and strictly between ourselves, they're *my* favorites too. I thought she'd have them for always and maybe remember me when she dipped into them, perhaps when she has children of her own and begins reading aloud to them."

"*Lorna Doone* isn't there," I said suddenly. "She likes *Lorna Doone,* doesn't she?"

"The case only held fourteen," said Drip, so apologetically that I instantly regretted my comment, "besides, I . . . I just *had* to draw the line somewhere. They were rather expensive."

I wondered how much the Gayelorde-Suttons paid her and how many weeks' salary had been paid over the counter for this wonderful demonstration of affection. The thought, together with Drip's eager expression, formed a lump in my throat, so that I could only blurt out once more that it was a marvelous birthday present and that Diana would be certain to value it above all her more spectacular possessions.

Drip was so delighted with this halting speech that she gave me an impulsive hug and said that I was a nice boy and must come to tea again during the holidays and hear another of her musical boxes, one that played "Lass of Richmond Hill." Then, as she was replacing the lid of the box, she had an inspiration.

"Why don't you buy her *Lorna Doone?*" she suggested. "You're quite right, *Lorna* was always a great favorite with her, but of course, you must know that, mustn't you? After all, you're Jan, aren't you?"

"It was Diana who christened me Jan," I told her. "My proper name is John. I like Jan much better, though," I hastened to add.

"Well, if you haven't already got her a present it might be a good idea, don't you think? I know they've got a copy in Beatty's because I saw one. It won't be exactly like these, of course, because these had to be specially ordered from Agnews', in London, but it's a very nice edition, in dark blue, for seven-and-six."

I said it was a very good idea and thanked her for show-

ing me the books. Then I said good-by and began to push
my bike up the long hill. As always, whenever I had seen
Diana, I had plenty to think about on the way home.

3.

Uncle Luke paid me ten shillings a week and I was expected to save half this sum for my clothes. There was
nothing in my money box because Christmas had emptied
it and New Year's Day fell before another payday. I
couldn't ask Uncle Luke for an advance, for my money
was always doled out by Aunt Thirza and I knew that she
would ask me why I needed it so urgently. I hadn't told either of them about Diana, sensing that they would raise a
whole string of objections to my associating with a family
like the Gayelorde-Suttons. Drip's idea was a nuisance in
some ways, because the raising of seven-and-sixpence occupied my thoughts all next day, and I wanted to devote
my attention to the much more important problem of finding a job that Diana would consider a worthier occupation
for a Jan Ridd than that of carting kitchen furniture and
chamber pots around town on a handbarrow.

I had already given long and careful thought to this
problem but as yet had not produced a solution, not even
a temporary one. I even went so far as to borrow one of
Uncle Luke's nature notebooks and jot down a list of my
possible qualifications. They were not impressive. I discovered that I was an inch and a half above average
height, nearly a stone above average weight, could swim
two lengths of the Brixton Baths breaststroke and one
length backstroke, had written a composition on "A Day
at Hampton Court" that had been included in the school
magazine during my final term at school, and had since
shown a mild aptitude for getting bargains in the slow bid-
ding that opened the local auction sales.

There was, so far as I could see, nothing here to indicate that I would one day develop into the kind of man
whom Diana Gayelorde-Sutton would admire and respect.
Physically she seemed to find me pleasing but I was aware
that men who earned their living by physical accomplish-

53

ments—lifeguards, gymnasts, athletes, and even police-men and professional boxers—seldom became the masters of large country estates, with a string of hunters and several expensive cars.

I finally decided to put the problem on one side until I had settled the more immediate one of finding seven and sixpence for the blue *Lorna Doone* and until I had had an opportunity of questioning Diana as to the type of occupation she would consider fitting for a future husband. It was necessary, I felt, to explore the ground very carefully before making a decision that might lead me into another blind alley.

I set these thoughts down now across an interval of more than twenty years and it may seem an exaggeration on my part to claim that, at the age of fifteen and two months, I was already planning my life along lines that led directly toward marriage and the overlordship of Senna-charib, with Diana as vice-regent, but I know that it was so. I realize now that the normal pursuits and dreams of a boy played but a small part in my development after the October miracles; I was now the victim of a twin obsession, the ownership of a country estate, and the sharing of that estate with Diana Gayelorde-Sutton. Everything I dreamed, and everything that I pursued, had to do with one or other of these ambitions. I was not as yet physically in love, for Diana was too remote and far too elevated in my imagination to encourage me to ponder the act of touching her hand, or breathing one word to her of my devotion, but I know now that her mere presence uplifted me and inspired me in a way that all the heroes of romantic fiction had been uplifted and inspired by their sweethearts and wives.

Perhaps my insatiable appetite for books had something to do with it, or perhaps my spirit, badly bruised by the recent death of my mother, responded to the spontaneous friendliness she had shown a gawky boy who had settled among strangers. It may have been either or both of these things that drew me to her, or it may have been the fact that she represented, in a single attractive human being, all the good things of life, and all the comforts and security that spring from wealth and the manifestations of wealth.

I solved the present problem by an act of sheer desperation.

On the following day, when the last post had gone and I had abandoned hope of being able to take her a surprise parcel, I remembered that there were one or two articles of furniture in the Mart that had been put on one side to await the collection by the Council refuse van. They had been brought away from the last sale, where the auctioneer had included them in a final lot as too battered and broken to be itemized, and Uncle Luke loaded them onto his barrow in one of his absent-minded moods. When he saw their condition he flung them aside as items unlikely to coax coppers from the lowliest customer.

I went out and took a good look at them. There was a three-legged chair, a cabin trunk with its lid hanging on a single hinge, and a badly frayed wickerwork plant stand. All the pieces were there and I set to work on them by candlelight, for there was no electric point in the repair shop. We often restored furniture, so I had all the right tools and a gluepot.

In less than two hours I had completely repaired the chair, rehinged the lid of the trunk and replaited the frayed patches in the plant stand.

I estimated that we could now ask fifteen shillings for the three items and I carried them up to Aunt Thirza in the flat we occupied behind the Mart and told her that I had spent the evening working on them.

Aunt Thirza was a parsimonious soul and I knew that I could count on her commendation. She did not disappoint me. When I told her I was going to ask Uncle Luke to price the items at five shillings apiece she at once opened her purse and extracted three half crowns. "This'n to encourage 'ee in the belief that someone'll buy everything, providing 'er's furbished up to look praper," she told me.

I slipped out at nine o'clock the next morning and ran along to Beatty's, in Chapel Street, to buy *Lorna Doone*, telling them to leave it unwrapped because I wanted to write in it and wrap it myself.

I should have liked to buy a card to go with it, but the purchase of the book consumed my entire capital. During the lunch interval I took the gift to my room and sucked a penholder throughout the greater part of the dinner hour while composing the inscription.

Finally, I wrote: *To Diana, a New Year gift, from Jan, with all my Love.* I hesitated a long time before I added the final words but finally decided that they could pass as a formality and could not be taken to mean anything forward on the part of the donor.

I now had to wait three days until the carrier called for the goods that Mrs. Gayelorde-Sutton had bought before Christmas, for I had made up my mind to give Diana the present rather than risk a maternal interrogation that might follow the arrival of an unexpected parcel.

On the last day of the year the van arrived about eleven o'clock in the morning and Aunt Thirza packed me some sandwiches to take for lunch, as I was expected to stay and help with the unloading. My one fear was that Diana might not be sufficiently interested to come over to the cottages when we arrived or, worse still, that her mother would superintend the whole operation and keep us in view all the time.

I was lucky again, for not only was Diana awaiting us at the entrance to the drive but at once hopped on the tailboard and gave the driver his directions. She was dressed for work too, in blue jeans, a green sweater and a scarlet beret. She told me that her mother and father had returned to London the previous day and that Drip was expecting me to tea when the job had been completed.

"It won't take us all the afternoon," I protested, though secretly overjoyed at the invitation. "We shall be finished about three and the van will be going back."

"Oh, I've fixed all that," she said, airily. "I telephoned your uncle and said we wanted some help clearing out one of the cottages and that you were to stay and sort out anything he might want to buy."

"Good Lord!" I said, aghast at her nerve. "Whatever did he say to that?"

"He said it would be all right and you could come home

on the bus at six. Why should he object? You're not scared of him, are you?"

"No," I said, "not of him, but I'm scared of your mother."

"Well, most people are," she said tolerantly, "but she's well over two hundred miles away, thank heavens! Praise Him from Whom all blessings flow for Boards!"

The van branched off the main drive and lurched along a narrow track that led through rhododendrons to the cottages, built on the Teasel side of the big paddock. Somehow it was much easier to be myself with Diana when she was dressed in hand-me-downs, a dirty sweater and the beret. On all three of the previous occasions that we had met her expensive-looking clothes had intimidated me, but today she looked just like one of the fishermen's daughters who played and flirted on the quay outside the Mart. I asked her about her Christmas gifts (being careful to drop no hint about my present) and she said that she had been given a silver toilet set by her mother and that the horse I had seen her riding on Boxing Day was a combined Christmas and birthday present from her father. She made no mention of Drip's wonderful gift.

This led us on to discuss the Boxing Day hunt and she told me that they had run the fox to ground at Nun's Bay, where it had entered a cliff earth too deep to be opened with the crowbars. They had hung around there most of the afternoon, and apart from the initial gallop that I had witnessed it had been a blank day.

I had half a mind to tell her then that it was I who had saved the fox by misdirecting the huntsman but I checked myself, fearing that such a confession would endanger our relationship and spoil what promised to be a wonderful day. I had made up my mind that I would tell her but in my own time, when our friendship had thrown out stronger roots.

We got through the unloading in double-quick time and the van left soon after two o'clock.

"Now," I said, finishing my sandwiches, "where's all this other stuff I'm supposed to look at?"

She laughed and shook her curls. "Why, Jan, you great

booby, there isn't any! I made that up. I guessed you'd have to go back and I wanted you to stay, but it's perfectly all right, you can say none of it was worth buying."

I wasted no time pondering her ethics. I was far too flattered by the discovery that she wanted my company enough to invent lies to get it. The sky was overcast and rain was threatening, so I imagined that we should now return to the house. Instead, however, she suggested that we go up through the larch wood and across the common to another wood that I had not yet explored but had seen from a distance on the day of my encounter with the keeper.

"It's the most exciting place in Sennacharib," she said, "because it's got the Folly in it."

"What's the Folly?" I asked and she told me that it was a kind of tower, built by one of the mad Gilroys nearly a hundred years ago, and was not ruinous and abandoned but quite habitable and just like a corner tower of a French chateau on the Loire.

It sounded well worth exploring so we set off at once, Diana having called to a woodsman and told him to tell Drip that she had had lunch with the furniture men and would be back at dusk for tea. I was on the point of giving her my present then but I decided it would be better to wait until we got to the Folly. The book was carefully packed in my knapsack, along with Aunt Thirza's thermos flask and sandwich tin.

We climbed the main ride of the larch wood and crossed the fenced paddock to Foxhayes Common. The Folly was in a large, straggling copse that occupied the highest piece of land on the estate, apart from Overhang Head, above Nun's Bay on the coast. This wood was not a plantation but a wild and lonely jumble of dwarf oaks, chestnuts and silver birches, and as we drew near it I could see the top of a leaded conical tower peeping from the seaward edge of the timber. I thought it very odd that I hadn't noticed such an incongruity before It was, as Diana had described, just like a corner of a castle in an illustrated fairy-tale book, the kind of tower where giants and ogres lived and old women spun magic charms. It was exciting enough, but the excitement it generated was tinged with fear and I was at a loss to understand why anyone had chosen to build a tower in such a lonely spot, or what possible purpose it could have served when first erected.

Diana said she had wondered the same things and had sought information from the oldest estate worker, a man whose father had been a keeper at Heronslea when the house was still occupied by the Gilroys.

"The man who had it built was a bit of a loony," she told me. "He used to come out here and sit by himself for days on end, or so old Venner told me. At one time it had little cannons on the top floor and Lord Gilroy's cousin, or whoever it was who built it, used to play his violin up there. Poachers wouldn't go near the place, Venner said, because they all thought it was haunted after he died. There was even a story that people heard a violin playing there long after he was dead and gone, but I don't believe in ghosts, do you?"

I said I didn't, but the Folly, when we came to it, was the kind of place that encouraged you to believe in them wholeheartedly, particularly on a gray December day, with a cold wind blowing from the northeast and the surrounding common looking pinched and defeated, as though it awaited a spring that would never come.

There was an overgrown path leading to the doorless porch and a flight of church-tower steps to the upper rooms, of which there were two. The triangular steps were hewn out of solid stone and were still in good condition, so we climbed up, passed through the middle chamber and reached the top room without any difficulty.

It was lighter and more cheerful up here, for we were now above the level of the nearest trees and could look down over the whole stretch of country between the tower and the sea.

Sennacharib was laid out like a map, with the blur of Teasel Wood to the east, the blue spirals of smoke marking Shepherdshey in the center, and the vast green clump of the Heronslea grounds to the west. Beyond the road you could see the red and gray huddle of Whinmouth and the estuary, and if the day had been clear the far side of the Whin would have been visible, as would have been Nun's Island in the bay to the north.

Up here the sense of gloom that the first sight of the Folly had provoked was exorcised by the magnitude of the prospect and Diana, noticing my exhilaration, said, "You like it, don't you, Jan?"

"Yes," I said, "it's a marvelous place! Does anyone come here now, anybody but you?"

"No," she said, "not even the keepers. I know that because they were surprised to hear it was still safe to climb and you can see by the briers at the entrance that nobody ever uses the path. I'll tell you what, Jan, it can be *our* place. I won't ever bring anyone here but you and if we ever want to meet, and it isn't possible to make proper arrangements, we can have the Folly as a *thought code*—you know, a prearranged rendezvous that doesn't need any message—we'll just *know* we can always meet here! Later on I'll sneak some chairs and a table, and perhaps a bit of carpet and some tinned stuff and an oil stove for cocoa. It'll be like the cave in *Tom Sawyer* or that place on the cliffs where Stalky and Co. used to hide."

I was overwhelmed by a plan that plainly indicated that I was progressing at a prodigious rate, but the mention of Stalky and Co. suddenly reminded me of the gift and I took it out, my throat dry and my hands shaking a little.

"It's for you, my New Year present," I said, blushing. "I met Drip at the hunt and she said she'd forgotten to include this in that wonderful set she gave you."

The presentation took Diana completely by surprise. She stared at me with parted lips for a moment and then she swallowed twice, very deliberately, and began to tear at the wrappings. I watched, enjoying every second of her suspense, and when she saw what it was, and had cooed her delight over the inscription, I was ready to burst with pride and satisfaction.

"*Why, Jan!*" she cried, holding it close against her chest. "This is the nicest present anyone ever gave me . . . no, no, I *mean* it . . because—well—you haven't got

60

much money and this is like . . . like Daddy giving me a thousand pounds, if you see what I mean!"

I don't know how much Mr. Gayelorde-Sutton was earning in 1927 but the book represented three quarters of my weekly income. If he was drawing fifty thousand a year from his investments, as he did into the middle part of the thirties, then her extravagant comparison probably wasn't far short of the mark.

It was easy to see that she had been reared against a background of dividends and shares values. The first thought that came into her head was the cost of the book and what the outlay had imposed upon the investor, but a more generous reaction followed as soon as she had reread the inscription and flicked through the pages.

"It's the *thought* that's exciting, Jan! You're like old Drip that way. The presents I got from Mummy and Daddy don't really mean anything, you see? They forget until I come home just before Christmas and then they suddenly remember that something is expected of them and rush out and splosh money on the first thing that comes into their heads. It was that way with the pony and the dressing set."

I didn't feel that I could take undue credit for the gift. Although an accomplished liar herself, Diana always made you feel that way, you shied away from pretense and wanted to tell her the whole truth, whatever the consequences.

"As a matter of fact it was an afterthought on my part," I admitted. "I got the idea from Drip, when she showed me the marvelous present she had for you."

"I don't care, I still think it was wonderfully sweet of you, Jan . . . there, that's *how* sweet!" and she placed the book on the broad window ledge, took my face in her hands, and kissed me on the mouth.

Sensations are difficult to recall over a gulf of twenty years. You always promise yourself that you will remember the best of them but you seldom do, not really, not in the active sense. There have been half a dozen moments in my life of which I could have said I was ecstatically happy, and each of those moments was a spon-

61

taneous gift from Diana. This, I believe, was the first of them, not only because it was the first time that I had been kissed by a girl and because that girl was Diana, but because her impulsive affection somehow transformed me from a boy to a man, marking that transition as nothing else could have done.

Adolescence, at least for the male, is a slow, tedious business and not so exclusively physical as is generally believed. I think that its progress involves so many workaday things, things like wages, the lack of privacy in tiny households, the attitude one is obliged to maintain toward parents and employers and even the attitude of bus conductors and civil servants. I had been doing a man's work ever since I came to the West and I had always been treated like a man by Aunt Thirza and Uncle Luke's customers, but I had never considered myself anything more than an overgrown boy until Diana's lips touched mine and I caught the fleeting scent of her hair and my senses registered the pressure of her fingers on my cheeks.

I don't recall whether I returned her kiss but I do know that I must have communicated something of my emotional turmoil to her, for her hands instantly left my face and she had to combat a flurry of embarrassment, rare for her but powerful enough to make her turn back to the window and change the subject.

"Do you ever go to dances in Whinmouth, Jan?"

Her abrupt change of manner shocked me. Somehow it depreciated the value of the kiss.

"No," I said, with a touch of sulkiness, "I can't dance."

"Of course you can," she said impatiently, "anybody can nowadays, there's simply nothing to it but walking around to a rhythm! We have a dance every Saturday at school but it's a bore dancing with girls. I have to be gentleman because most of the girls are smaller."

Talk of her school always interested me, possibly because it was so unlike any school I had attended or visited. From the odd scraps of information she imparted I had conjured up a picture of a kind of social university, where the emphasis was on deportment rather than on dates, sums and irregular verbs.

"What are you going to do when you leave that place?" I asked her, not because I was anxious to know, but because I wanted her to do the talking, leaving my faculties free to imprint the memory of the kiss upon my mind.

"Oh *that's* all mapped out," she said, scornfully. "It's all rather dull and I'm not at all sure I mean to go through with it! I shan't leave till I'm seventeen and then Mummy's determined to send me to Switzerland to be finished. She plans to keep me there about a year, rubbing up on languages and then I'm to go *en famille* to Paris before coming back to be presented."

I had a vague notion what "being presented" and "finished" meant but not the slightest inkling of the meaning of *"en famille."* I never minded displaying ignorance of this kind to Diana, so I asked for more detailed information.

She said that nearly all girls who were finished in Switzerland remained on the Continent for another year or so, living with a French family in order to become fluent in at least one other language. I said that this would probably be fun, but she shook her head and pointed out that her mother would be certain to select a family where boarders were heavily chaperoned and never allowed to leave the house alone. She went on to say that the sister of one of her friends was already domiciled in such a household and had written home to say that it was worse than being in prison.

I asked her to explain to me exactly what being presented entailed.

"Well, it's a kind of here-I-am ritual," she said, laughing. "It happens when a girl is about eighteen and she is prepared for it, the way you get prepared for confirmation. When it happens you have what is called 'a season.' A season means you stay in London and go to parties and naturally you have a big party of your own. The idea of the parties isn't for fun but an opportunity to meet suitable boys."

"Boys to go about with?"

Diana threw back her head. "Oh Jan," she protested, "you're so sweet—*no,* boys who'll propose to you!"

I at once turned my face against seasons and muttered darkly that I had always supposed that this sort of thing was terribly old-fashioned nowadays and that even wealthy people married for love, the way they always did in books.

"Oh that's so," she said lightly, "but the man you happen to fall in love with doesn't have to be poor, does he? Some of them who come to the debs' parties are, of course, as poor as church mice if you did but know it, and all those are on the lookout for a girl with money, but money wouldn't influence me one way or the other, so long as the man I accepted *was* somebody!"

"You mean a . . . a knight, or something?" I asked, guardedly.

"Goodness no!" said Diana, laughing again. "Titles don't mean a thing nowadays. You can buy them if you want to—in a roundabout way, that is. Mummy's been after one for Daddy for years now, but it takes time and it's got to be done tactfully. She'll pull it off, though, mark my words! No, what I mean by *being* somebody is somebody who had done something out of the ordinary, somebody like, well, Jike Scott of the Antarctic, or Evans of the Broke, somebody I could look up to and who didn't give a hoot whether Daddy was well off or not, but wanted *me* as a person. The point is, people like that usually haven't got money, not real money, that is."

Then and later I was fascinated by Diana's phrase— "real money." Our views of money were poles apart. Any money was real money to me but it wasn't to her; "real" implied something over the five-figure mark, the kind of money I associated with film stars, and people like her father.

Her declaration gave me hope, however, for at least I was getting the kind of information I needed. I made up my mind to get more.

"What would you like to do when you leave school apart from what your mother has mapped out for you? I mean, if it was left to you, would you go around the world or something?"

"Not me," said Diana, promptly, "you can have globe-trotting for all I care! Travel isn't anything like as exciting as it's cracked up to be. There's nowhere like this, for instance, at least not where I've been so far. France is flat and bare, and Switzerland is sickeningly picture-postcardy. Italy's all right in some ways but it's ever so smelly and I'm glad Mummy and Daddy are going to Africa on their own in the summer, because then I shall have you and Sennacharib all to myself for seven glorious weeks!"

Suddenly she stopped talking and looked at me speculatively for a long moment, sucking her finger and "freezing" her enormous dimple. "Do you know, Jan," she went on at length, "I think that's what I like about you—apart from your nice wide shoulders and your long eyelashes, I mean—you *feel* about this place as if it was something alive, like an animal. That's exactly how I feel but I don't think I'd have known that if I hadn't met you that day in the wood. What would I do if I wasn't packed off to Switzerland to be finished, and then hauled home for all that presentation flimflam? *I know* what I'd do"—she stood clear of the window ledge and interlocked her long fingers —"I'd run a riding school, hunt all the winter and swim all the summer. I'd teach *you* to ride, so that we could go long hacks together and in the evenings I'd give parties— not the kind of parties that Mother gives, where dreary people stand around nibbling those soppy little sausages on sticks but *real* parties, where we all danced on the terrace and had midnight swims and talked and talked, you know, about interesting things, like books and plays and being in love."

The mention of books was the one chord I recognized in this rhapsody and I pounced on it, recalling my pitiful little success with the essay on "A Day at Hampton Court."

"Would you . . . you *marry* a writer, Diana? A famous one, of course!" I added, seeing a puzzled expression cross her face.

She put her head on one side so that her dark curls swung freely in what I thought an enchanting manner.

"A writer? Ye-es! I think I would, providing he wrote the right sort of books, of course. I wouldn't care to be the wife of a writer like Edgar Wallace, for instance, but it might have been fun to have been, say Mrs. Kingsley, or Mrs. Robert Louis Stevenson! A writer would never be dull, would he? He'd always be surrounded by other interesting people, you know, painters and sculptors and famous people of one sort or another. Yes . . . " she finally made up her mind. "I *would* like to marry an author, Jan!"

There was so much that I wanted to say to her but I needed time and leisure to think it out. I had a conviction now that our relationship was entering a new phase and that it might be fatal to make rash promises I had no power to keep. A vague plan was already forming in my mind but it needed time.

"Can we meet on Saturday, Diana?" I asked her. "I might have something important to tell you."

She pouted. "Oh dear," she said, "I won't be here on Saturday. I should have gone back with Mother and Daddy but I wriggled out of it because I knew you were coming. I tell you what, why not write to me about it? I'll give you my school address too, at least I'll give you a day girl's address to write to, because old Passy-Glassy has a nose a yard long and if she recognizes letters in male handwriting she redirects them to parents! Here"—she whipped a tiny diary and a stub of pencil from the pocket of her jeans and scribbled an address on it—"write to me as much as you like and then I'll be one up on Sheila Bryanstone. She's always showing off about the sloppy letters she gets from the boys she meets in the hols."

I took the address and as I did so I saw through the open casement that dusk was creeping across to the edge of the wood and lights were showing down in Shepherdshey hollow.

"We'd better be going, Diana," I told her. "It'll be dark before we get back."

She looked out of the casement and then picked up her book, opening it at the flyleaf and rereading the inscription. "All my love . . ." she repeated and then, shutting it abruptly: "Do you mean that, Jan, really mean it?"

66

"Why yes," I said, grateful for the fading light, for I knew that I was blushing, "yes, of course I meant it."

The half-smile that was so peculiarly Diana's flickered at the corners of her mouth.

"You mean you haven't got a girl already?"

"No," I said, using the Whinmouth term for an adolescent courtship, "I'm not 'going' with anyone, if that's what you mean."

"That's funny," she said, half to herself, "I always imagined that a boy as big as you and going to work . . ."

She trailed off, as though turning something over in her mind, and then quickly looked at me, with serious eyes.

"You won't see me again until next hols. Wouldn't you like to kiss me, Jan?"

If she had said that before we entered the Folly, before I gave her the book and she had responded with the impulsive kiss given in acknowledgment, I should have been far too shy and gawky to have responded, but I had grown very appreciably during the last half hour, and when she stepped closer and tilted her face I felt no embarrassment, only a great surge of warmth and ecstasy, that lifted me higher than this—the highest point in Sennacharib. I kissed her very softly on the mouth and I think she must have known then that it was the first time I had ever kissed a girl. Then, as gently as I kissed her, she took me by the hand and led me down the staircase and into the wood. As we came out on the path to the paddock there was a flutter of wings in the oak on the very edge of the copse as our buzzards rose and wheeled above the larches below.

Neither of us remarked on them but Diana's fingers tightened on mine before she released my hand to climb the rail and jump down into the field.

Chapter Three

EARLY THE next morning I put on my best suit and went around to the building behind the High Street office of what my Aunt Thirza described as "The Gospel According to Saint Reuben"—that is, the headquarters of Uncle Reuben's *Whinmouth & District Observer*.

I had been there before, of course, but my visits had been impersonal. Then the machines that were engaged in grinding out handbills and posters, and the lumbering great flatbed on which the *Observer* was printed each Friday had been no more than a source of clatter. Now I looked at them with respect, for I knew that they underpinned the bridge I so desperately needed to approach even the most tentative claim to Diana, or Sennacharib.

It was the usual small-town printing office, employing half a dozen men and boys, all wearing indescribably filthy aprons. The machines appeared to me to be but a slight improvement on the apparatus of William Caxton, seen in the famous picture depicting the patronage of Edward IV. Each machine was surrounded by bulkheads of type cases at which men stood, plucking at type and slamming their gleanings into what to me looked like metal pencil boxes. Over all hung a rancid smell of machine oil and printer's ink, together with an air of quiet absorption.

Uncle Reuben greeted me with the professional heartiness of a habitual public speaker.

"Well, young feller-me-lad, and what can we do for you today?"

I had learned to ignore his forced breeziness and look-smart-about-it manner, for I knew that he possessed qualities of kindness and patience. I spoke up without fear or embarrassment.

"I want to be a reporter, Uncle," I told him, adding a conciliatory "I'm quite prepared to start at the bottom."

He stared hard at me for a moment or two and then laughed. A laugh was a luxury in which he rarely indulged.

"God bless my soul!" he exclaimed, laying down his "pencil box" and thrusting both hands into his apron pocket. "Whatever gave you that idea, John? Was it Uncle Luke or Aunt Thirza? Have they decided you're not cut out for a junk merchant?"

"No," I told him, "I think they like me working for them, but there's no future in it."

Suddenly he looked pleased and studied me for a long minute; then he said:

"I daresay you're right at that! It isn't a real trade, like printing. What you really mean, I imagine, is that you want to learn to be a compositor?"

"No," I said pompously, for one glance had assured me that Diana would regard printing as only slightly less degrading than junk dealing, "it's writing I want to do, writing for the paper. You see, I think I'm going to be a writer someday and words and phrases are the tools of my trade."

This impressed him more than it should have done. How was he to know that the statement had been lifted from a book on writing for the radio, borrowed from the local library?

"Come with me," he said briefly, and led the way between type cases into a poky little office behind the flatbed.

It was lit by a single, begrimed skylight and its sole items of furniture consisted of a roll-top desk, a cane-bottomed chair and a vast array of paper, all kinds of paper, from galley proofs and posters to dog-eared ledgers and offcuts. The hardboard walls were plastered with old posters and trade calendars and there was one impressively bold notice that said: FOLLOW YOUR COPY, EVEN IF IT GOES OUT THE WINDOW. The desk likewise was a litter of proofs—"pulls" I later learned to call them—and in here the smell of ink and oil was subordinate to that of my uncle's vile tobacco. He swept papers from the chair and sat down, groping for his pipe.

"A reporter," he began, "has to be observant. Are you

observant? Take a quick look around this office and then close your eyes. Ready? Now then, what's in this pigsty?"

I reeled off a list of nearly two dozen items that had remained in my memory and he was obviously struck by my powers of observation.

"That's very promising," he conceded, "but supposing I sent you to report a funeral, what would you find out?"

"Who was there and who read the burial service."

"Good! And a wedding?"

This was more ponderable so I took my time.

"What the bride had on and what all the people had given them for presents," I suggested.

His eyes smiled. "That's not a bad guess," he admitted, "except that we don't print the presents unless they pay three pence a line for them! Well, you seem to have the right instincts but can you write shorthand?"

I told him that I was willing to learn, adding that I had taught myself to type on Uncle Luke's ramshackle Oliver. When he rose I saw that I had pleased him.

"I don't know why this never occurred to me when your mother died," he said, absently. "It was very remiss of me, for you shouldn't have wasted time in that wretched furniture shed. That's no kind of job at all for a bright boy like you! I shall have to see Mr. Priddis, of course, but I think I can talk him into it."

This was disappointing. I had forgotten for a moment that Uncle Reuben did not own the paper and printing office.

"But everybody says you run the paper, Uncle Reuben," I protested.

"Everybody says wrong," he replied gravely, "I only do as much as I do because Mr. Priddis hasn't been very well lately. Now run along and don't say anything to anyone until you hear from me."

I gave him my promise and went out the back way into the yard. Twenty-four hours later I was junior reporter on the *Whinmouth & District Observer*. Not content with riding two horses, I had cheerfully committed myself to riding three.

In 1927 the *Observer* had a circulation of about three

thousand. This doesn't sound much but it was impressive for all that, as the local population did not exceed twelve thousand and we reckoned to sell an *Observer* to four out of every five houses in Whinmouth Bay.

It was owned and nominally edited by Nick Priddis, a man in his mid-sixties and a chronic sufferer from asthma. People were not much mistaken in supposing Uncle Reuben to be the real editor, for Priddis' ill-health had prevented him from active participation for some years and he spent most of his time in his cottage up the coast.

Uncle Reuben did most of the original writing and I stress the word "original" because at that time less than a third of our copy was written by any member of the staff. About half of it was shamelessly snipped from the columns of the *County Press,* a much larger and more important journal, published biweekly in Whinford, the county town. Much of the remainder was sent in by local contributors who viewed the act of publication as adequate reward for their efforts.

The economics of the paper baffled the uninitiated. Advertisement space was sold at two shillings an inch, and even less if the advertiser was a regular. The *Observer* sold at one penny but local news agents were charged eightpence a dozen, ninepence if we had to deliver. The ready money that did flow into the office came in via small ads, at threepence a line. Lists of wreaths in funeral reports and lists of wedding gifts in wedding reports were the main sources and petty cash was also supplied by the lucrative set pieces—births, deaths and marriage announcements and the "return thanks" panel that invariably followed a funeral. For the rest, the paper existed on quarterly payments for larger advertisements and on the steadier proceeds of its printing office.

The *Observer* had a curiously old-fashioned format. Its front page was devoted exclusively to standard advertisements, built around a huge, blurred block depicting the Whinmouth esplanade as it had looked in the eighteen-seventies. This picture set the tone of the publication. One only had to glance at the bathing machines, the little girls in pantaloons and the lowering clouds in the background,

71

to know that the inside pages would be solid wedges of close print, difficult to concentrate upon and impossible to skim. It gave the paper a dull, self-righteous aspect. It said, in effect: *You may look in vain for sensation in here. Whatever is written down happened just so, whether you like it or not!*

Uncle Reuben was perfectly capable of going out and about town to collect information for the inside columns, but the printing office was the only one for miles around and his presence was needed there as supervisor. He therefore welcomed the idea of having a boy to send here and there for raw material that he could shape into news at his desk under the dirty skylight.

Usually he only had to snip the reports from *The Whinford Times,* rewrite the introductions, change the headings and send the copy down to the keyboard operator to be used in our paper. This meant that most of the paper had to be printed in a single day and a night, and it was becoming clear to Uncle Reuben and his employer that the business would not stand the overtime rates entailed by this makeshift process. The mainstay of the firm was the printing office and my uncle was needed in there to set type and operate the keyboard for the Monotype.

I had a brief interview with Mr. Priddis, the owner, on the day I started work and, although I was to see little of him during the years I worked on the paper, he impressed me as a man with original views on journalism. I never afterwards forgot his handling of my initiation.

He looked like a Victorian actor, tall, spare, and all knees, knuckles and black eyebrows. He had a strong, resonant voice and punctuated his lecture with deft applications of a nasal spray, the use of which might have brought him physical relief but seemed to irritate him to a point of frenzy.

"So you're Reub's boy? What's your name? Well, I don't imagine we shall see much of one another—curse this bloody contrivance—I've got a cottage up at Hartland and have to spend most of my time there. The air's less oppressive, or so they tell me. Reub says you've got a nose for news. What do you say, hey? Drat this pestilential invention, don't know why I use the damn thing—listen, sonny, since you've volunteered for the treadmill your uncle will expect you to put your back into it. *People!* That's your job from now on, people around here—nowhere else, just around here—what they do, what they think, what they eat, what they wear, how they get on with their wives, how they don't—devil take this blasted thing —nothing outside matters, see? Governments fall, war breaks out in South America, records are smashed—earthquakes, plagues, revolutions—none of it matters as much as who runs the woolly stall at the Missionary Sale of Work. There's a coronation in Westminster Abbey—not your business! You've got your eye on the choice of a Carnival Queen right here, d'you follow? Curse this bloody squirt—that's all, boy, that's all!"

It was, too, for Uncle Reuben had entered in with some proofs and jerked his head toward the door, indicating that the explosive interview was over. I made a bewildered exit and a few minutes later I was on my way to get an account of the Whinmouth Club's away match, from the strongly partisan source of the man who won it by kicking a last-minute goal.

Mine was no slow, painful apprenticeship wherein I was led, step by step, from the petty sessional court to a coroner's inquest, from the interschool athletics contest in Harbor Meadow, to the autumn production of the Whinmouth Thespians. I was picked up and flung headlong into the torrent of local politics and social activities, hearing something fresh almost every hour and marveling at the complexity of what I witnessed and learned.

To the impersonal spectator, Whinmouth Bay was a deceptively tranquil community—"dead-and-alive," visitors called it—but to an inquiring boy, engaged in recording its day-by-day history, it seethed like a hot spring. I was so frantically busy during those first weeks, and so tired after my scurryings about the district and my two-hour stint at shorthand after supper, that I barely had time to think of Diana or Sennacharib. At first I was nervous of making mistakes and sometimes I was homesick for the humdrum peace of Uncle Luke's Mart, but on the whole I enjoyed my new importance and a front-row seat at every event that took place in the triangle between the estuary of the Whin and the eastern edge of Teasel Common, the boundaries that marked the extremities of our territory.

I was the impersonal witness at family tragedy and family celebration. I attended concerts, council meetings, lectures, sports meetings, dances and every kind of social function. I got to know every face in town and I saw the inside of every kind of dwelling, from the three-roomed cottages on the quay to the detached houses that stood in their own two-acre plots in the area west of the Shepherdshey road. I was absorbed in the business of becoming if not a writer, then at least a professionally observant chronicler of British provincial life and, as I say, I had almost forgotten how and why this transformation in my life had taken place until the morning that I received Diana's letter.

I went up to my room with wildly beating heart, turning the blue envelope over in my hands and noting the elegant flourishes on the J in John and the L in Leigh, for Diana's handwriting was new to me and as exotic as everything else about her.

It was a chatty, affectionate, schoolgirlish letter and succeeded in putting the *Whinmouth & District Observer* right out of my mind for the next forty-eight hours.

MY JAN [it began]—

As you don't seem disposed to write to me, as you promised, I'm breaking all the rules (social as well as Passy-Glassy's) by writing to you first.

School is as dreary as ever and I'm counting the days until we break up for Easter. Before that, however, we've got Lent exams and I'm sure to flop at practically everything, for I've slacked all term and its partly your fault, because I've been waiting and waiting to hear from you about our lovely Sennacharib and whether you've been to the Folly again and if you think of me as much as I do of you! (This is awful, I'm absolutely throwing myself at you!)

Seriously though, I have been awfully disappointed by your silence, and have made an absolute nuisance of myself with Marion. (She's the day girl whose address I gave you to write to.) I must have asked her about fifty times whether there was a letter for me and now the hateful thing says no before I can ask! I had another and special reason for writing. Is it possible for you to come to London on Saturday? This may sound absolutely mad to you but there is a good chance of us being able to meet, in fact you could take me out somewhere if you wanted to and it would be a terrific adventure and a marvelous score over the school rules! I'm not going into details in this letter, *a* because you mightn't be able to make it, and *b* for the more likely reason that you've cooled off and are going about with someone in Whinmouth Bay, in which case tear this up and forget all about it and me. If you *can* come to town, however, write and say so at once and I'll write again by return and give you all the instructions for what our Lorna would have called "a tryst."

> All my love dear Jan,
> DIANA

There was a single cross, artfully contrived out of the final flourish of her signature, and when I saw it, after rereading the letter for the third time, my hands shook with excitement.

I would have liked to have written a long letter in reply, telling her all about my new job and making it sound much more glamorous and exciting than it really was, but I had a busy day ahead of me and conditions were not conducive to composing my first love letter. Ordinarily I should have waited until I did have a chance to write, but the prospect of actually seeing her was more urgent than the desire to pour out my feelings on paper, and if she was to have time to write back and explain how and where I could meet her it was essential that I reply by return.

I worked out a plan to get to and from London. There was a semifinal Cup excursion from Whinford and I knew that I could borrow Uncle Luke's bicycle and ride it to Whinford Junction on Friday, in time to catch the train at 10 P.M. I could leave the bike in the station yard against my early morning return on Sunday, and the prospect of such an exhausting journey involving the loss of two nights' sleep made the occasion additionally romantic. I wrote a hasty letter explaining my plan and said that I would follow any instructions she sent. Wednesday and Thursday passed in an agony of anticipation. Then, on Friday, her second letter arrived. It said briefly that I was to meet her outside Swan & Edgar's, in Piccadilly Circus, at three o'clock on Saturday afternoon and that I need not reply as she would be passing the rendezvous at that time in any case. The letter contained no endearments. It was blunt, very much to the point and, as I was to discover with the years, entirely characteristic of Diana when she had business to conduct.

I told Uncle Reuben that I wanted to take advantage of the cheap excursion and would like his permission to skip the tedious folding routine of publication day.

He was a good deal surprised at my request, so much so that I did not dare to pretend to a sudden interest in professional football but told him a lie that troubled my conscience. I said that my object in wanting to visit London was to put flowers on the grave of my parents.

He was very touched by this and instantly granted me leave, doubling the burden of my conscience by giving me ten shillings to buy flowers from himself, Uncle Luke and Aunt Thirza. I had no option but to take his money and it burned in my hand. I told myself that I would have to go to the cemetery now whether I had the time or not.

At the last minute I adjusted my plan and went to the junction at Whinford by train, taking Uncle Luke's bike in the luggage van and catching the main-line train in good time. I was far too excited to sleep and sat hunched under the feeble compartment light reading *Lorna Doone*. The romance had become a kind of litany for the worship of Diana.

It was drizzling when I arrived at Waterloo and still wanted an hour or so to daybreak.

I left the station and walked along York Road and over Westminster Bridge toward the Houses of Parliament. It was a dank and dismal morning, and the Thames looked still and sinister in the glow of the Embankment lights. An early tram whined past as Big Ben struck five, telling me that I still had ten hours to fill before meeting Diana. The dreariness of the scene deflated me and I thought how strange it was that, although I was a Cockney born and bred, I should feel so lonely and desolate in the heart of my home town, so much so that I was already beginning to feel homesick for the rusty bracken of Teasel Slope and the dark smudge of Folly Wood against the skyline of Foxhayes Common. The tug of homesickness set me thinking deeply. Why was it, I wondered, that such a remote and rustic corner of England exercised such undisputed sovereignty over my heart, and that after a few short months of the least impressionable period of childhood? Was it the drag of an ancestral memory, or had it nothing to do with long-dead Leighs but everything with a fourteen-year-old schoolgirl, whom I had met but half a dozen times?

When the first gray streaks of dawn began to show over the river I stirred myself and decided that what I needed to cheer myself up was a wash, a brush-up and a hot meal.

I found all three in the Covent Garden area and after some bacon and eggs, and three cups of drayman's tea, I shed my pensive mood and was not even depressed by the prospect of traveling all the way to Brixton to visit the double grave. Somehow it seemed to me that this dismal obligation would be an act of finality, a final breaking of ties that held me to my drab London boyhood. I told myself that my mother, who could conjure up the smell of Devon gorse and heath after a separation of forty years, would surely have approved my new allegiance to Sennacharib and understood my almost physical repugnance for the huddle of slate, asphalt and yellow brick of which some Cockneys are so proud.

I spent Uncle Reuben's ten shillings and seven-and-six of my own on a large armful of daffodils and narcissi and caught a southbound bus to the cemetery. By midday I was back in the Strand and after a modest lunch in a snack bar I walked up Whitehall to spend an hour in my favorite museum, gazing once more on the bloodstained shirt Charles I had worn at his execution and the pathetic skeleton of Napoleon's horse, Marengo. I wondered whether Diana would share my enthusiasm for museums, or whether she would demand more sophisticated entertainment.

When the clock said two-twenty-five I decided that it was time to find out.

I walked up to Piccadilly Circus, arriving far too early. The usual group of anxious-eyed pedestrians were drifting up and down the block, each endeavoring to give an impression that the appointment they had anticipated was of small importance, yet each betraying the same kind of nervous apprehension that I experienced. If ever we met in London again, I decided, it would have to be at a more original rendezvous.

I had no idea from which direction she would come, or what means of transport she would use, so that when, on the stroke of three, a taxi pulled up beside me I did not glance at it until the door slammed and a voice on the brink of laughter said, "Don't scowl so, Jan! People will think we're married and I'm an hour or so late!"

She looked more grown up than ever. I had been half-expecting a girl in a school uniform and one of those dreadful floppy hats, but here she was in the smart little suit that she had worn at the Mart—"mufti" she called it, and added that it was only permissible when you were taken out by one's parents. She had an outdoor coat over her arm and a little yellow straw hat, close-fitting and trimmed with tiny wings, like the hat worn by Gretchens in traditional Dutch pictures. I felt painfully shy in my ready-made suit of gray serge and a soft collar held in place by a narrow tiepin, but from the first moment she seemed to sense my awkwardness and set to work to overcome it, taking my arm and in full charge of the expedition.

"First, somewhere to sit and gossip," she said. "How about Lyons, in Coventry Street? I've got until eight o'clock and it'll take us forty minutes to get back to school. There's a train at seven-thirty-five and you can travel with me as far as the suburban station."

I was impressed by her efficiency and air of dispatch. It was as though she had been planning every moment of our meeting, anticipating each contingency before it revealed itself.

Fresh from Devon, I was bewildered by the swirl of

traffic, but she guided me across to Eros and then over the wide stretch of Coventry Street as though I were one of her big, obedient dogs.

Even in that press of buses and taxis, however, I was conscious of the firm pressure on my forearm and the rhythmic bob of her brown curls that now seemed suspended from the rim of her little yellow hat. Delight in her company swelled inside me and with it came a kind of delicious dependence on her judgment and gently exercised authority.

When we reached the Corner House I made a big effort to assume my responsibilities as a squire. I piloted her to a corner table, far enough away from the orchestra to enable us to converse without raising our voices. It was the post-lunch lull and they were not busy. The waitress brought us tea and cakes almost at once and the orchestra tuned up and began to play excerpts from *The Merry Widow*.

"Jan, you're looking wonderful!" she said, with enthusiasm. "I'm so thrilled you could make it, because I went to so much trouble and it would have been absolutely awful if you hadn't been there after all. Just think, I might have run the risk of being expelled, all for nothing!"

"Expelled? Good Lord!" I exclaimed. "You don't mean . . ."

"Why, naturally!" She laughed and squeezed my hand. "If I was caught here with a boy Passy-Glassy would have a seizure! When she finally came around she'd phone Mummy and I'd be out on my ear in twenty-four hours. This is positively the worst thing you can do short of bringing a man into your cubicle and I don't think that's ever been done, at least not in my time, though May Didcott is supposed to have done it the week before she stowed away for Switzerland."

I would have liked to have heard more of May Didcott, but first I wanted to learn how Diana had arranged our meeting in the first place.

"Oh, it was all very simple really," she said, gaily. "You see, we get one day each term out with our parents and everyone usually takes half-term, which was nearly a month ago. Mummy and Daddy were away in Nice at half-term, so I had a day due to me and they came for me after breakfast this morning. I've just left them at home."

"But you couldn't have," I protested, remembering my five-hour train journey from the West.

"Silly! I mean home up here, in Palmerston Crescent. It's only me who thinks of Heronslea as real home. I don't think they'd go there much if it wasn't for me, or if it wasn't the thing to do—you know—to have a place in the country and play at being a squire weekends."

"But if you're supposed to be with them, and they think you're supposed to be back at school, how on earth can you stay out until eight?" I asked.

"Oh, that's where the brains come in," she replied, lifting the teapot that the waitress had set before her and beginning to pour. "I know that you take sugar, but I forget whether you have milk in first."

"It doesn't matter," I said, impatiently, "tell me what you did."

"Well, I simply told Mummy that I had to be back by three for an important hockey match but I didn't tell her until it was too late to get hold of the chauffeur, so then I had to go by taxi and the taxi brought me here instead of taking me back to school. I was lucky in one respect though. Mummy would have told the driver where to take me and he might have followed his instructions in spite of the big tip that I had ready, but just as he arrived the phone rang and Mummy answered it, so *I* gave him his instructions instead and just kissed Mummy good-by at the door! Now then, that's enough about me, tell me everything about your new job. I'm terribly proud of you, Jan, perhaps because I had a sort of feeling you were just bragging up at the Folly and that when I came home at Easter you'd still be mucking about that awful furniture store. Do you go to fires and wrecks and attend murder trials?"

"I would if there were any," I said, guardedly, "but so far there haven't been. I did go out after the fire engine once but it was only a chimney fire in a semidetached on the Shepherdshey road. I like it, though, and it's going to be exciting when things start happening in the summer.

Uncle Reuben says that the spring is always the quietest time because it's only the visitors who get themselves into trouble and give us the more sensational stories—you know, boating tragedies and beach rescues."

She made me describe everything I did and even asked me to write something in shorthand on the paper napkin. I wrote: *You look very beautiful today!* and she teased me into translating. Then, when I could think of nothing more to tell her, she said:

"You don't know how lucky you are, Jan, to be more or less grown up and earning your own living. Look at me, marking time and likely to be, for years yet!"

It was characteristic of Diana, then and later, to subscribe to the popular fiction that money and a cushioned background were obstacles that stood in the way of full enjoyment of life. She would always pretend that the circumstances surrounding her stifled self-expression and encouraged a general flabbiness of outlook. I don't think that she really believed this, even then, but she found it useful as a banner of rebellion against externally applied discipline. It was also a challenge to her mother, the kind of challenge that she was making now, by sitting in Lyons Corner House instead of returning to school.

I remember that all the charm she exercised over me did not prevent me from debating this claim and that we had an amicable argument about it on the spot. I must have sounded very pompous when I pointed out the obvious advantages of a good education and of the opportunity to travel while still at school, and of all the glittering by-products of wealth, such as ponies and a legal claim to every square yard of Sennacharib.

"Well, all I can say is I'm jolly glad *you* haven't got it anyway, Jan," she said, when I had run out of the advantages of being Emerald Diana Gayelorde-Sutton, of Heronslea, Devon, and Palmerston Crescent, W.9., "because what I admire about you is the fact that you stand on your own feet! That's what makes you different from all the other stuffed dummies Mummy introduces into the house. They're all at public schools, of course, and they take the kind of background that I have for granted, but there isn't one of them who could learn to be a reporter as you have, and on top of that I don't think any of them would take this much trouble just to see me, so there!"

I could have sat there all the afternoon and evening hearing her talk like that, but the restaurant was filling up now and if we wanted to make the best use of our few hours together it was time to move.

"Have you anywhere special you'd like to go?" I asked. "I suppose you've been to the Tower and Madame Tussaud's, and all that. If it had been better weather we could have gone on the Serpentine for a row. I used to go there with my mother sometimes."

"I thought we might go to the pictures," she suggested. "There's a double feature at Marble Arch, a film about Nurse Cavell and a new comedy called *Just Imagine*. How would you like that?"

I said I should like it very much and called the waitress, who had been hovering around our table rather impatiently. It was nearly half past four and all we had ordered was tea, cakes and a second jug of hot water.

I paid the bill and we caught a bus to Marble Arch. A Pathé Gazette feature was showing when we went in and we had time to settle ourselves before the comedy started. I didn't often get the opportunity to go to the cinema because we didn't have one in Whinmouth Bay, so I was determined to enjoy myself, apart from the nearness of Diana. She asked me to help her off with her coat and when it was folded across the empty seat in front she let her shoulder touch mine and presently she took hold of my hand in the most natural way possible. I wouldn't have changed places with a prince of the Indies.

The comedy was an original one to a cinema-goer fed on Harold Lloyd and Buster Keaton. The hero was transplanted into the world of the future, where laughs depended upon his reactions to the new habits of society. I remember how I laughed when, having visions of a large, satisfying meal, he was given a small vitamin pill and exclaimed, "Give me the good old days!" I remember, too, how Diana laughed, and how secretly shocked I was, when a couple put money in a slot and a baby slid down a chute, giving the hero an opportunity to make the same remark, this time in tones of the strongest disapproval.

The Nurse Cavell film impressed us both tremendously and stoked up a tremendous hate for the suave German generals.

Looking back it seems strange that a cinema audience could wax so indignant over the execution of a single British nurse, but in those days Belsen and Lidice were nearly twenty years away and not even Germans used phrases like "total war" or "liquidation."

When we emerged into the foyer we were still in a patriotic fever and I was touched to notice that Diana had been weeping in the darkness and did not appear to be in any way ashamed of the fact.

"I think she was wonderful, just wonderful!" she said, dabbing her eyes. "Daddy showed me the place in Brussels where they shot her but it didn't seem very important then. Gosh! *I'd like to do something like that, you know, stand up to all those bullies because you believe in something!*"

"I'd jolly well come and rescue you long before you got shot!" I told her, identifying myself with Jan Ridd once again, and she squeezed my arm and said that she knew very well I would but that it was high time we caught the bus for Victoria, for we dared not risk missing the train.

It was at that moment that Yves de Royden stepped up and whipped off his cap with a courtly flourish. I looked at him with interest because I thought he was very oddly dressed. He looked very well-to-do but somehow frumpish as well, in his pepper-and-mustard tweed suit and a kind of cravat, instead of a conventional collar and tie. His trousers were unfashionably tight at the ankle, for it was the era of wide Oxford trousers, and I noticed that he carried an ebony-handled cane which he tucked smartly under his arm as he bowed.

"Why, Yves," exclaimed Diana, delightedly, "what a place to run into you! Whatever are you doing over here? Buying more horses?"

The young Frenchman looked at me as I stood slightly behind Diana. I was feeling, and doubtless looking, miserably embarrassed but Diana at once introduced us. "This is a journalist friend of mine, Yves, a Mr. Leigh, from Devon. Jan, this is Yves de Royden. You must have heard of his father, Hervé de Royden. He won the Ascot Gold Cup with Dantonist a year or so ago, and he's quite famous, isn't he, Yves?"

The French boy smiled and extended his hand, his fingers barely touching mine. He was about seventeen, tall and thin, with narrow hips and shoulders, like those of a girl. After the apology for a handshake he turned his attention to Diana and asked three rapid questions in perfect but slightly pedantic English.

"You have been to the films? You like the picture? You are on holiday from school?"

The faint impression of effeminacy was charmed away by his excessively good manners and adult bearing, but notwithstanding this I hated him, then and there, for he seemed to me to be typical of the kind of rival I should have to face in the future. I recognized that he was so much more a part of her world than I could ever be and my nervousness made me rather rude. I said, gruffly:

"We've got to catch that train, Diana!"

He turned his charm on me, repaying good for evil and making me feel more inferior than ever.

"You have a train to catch? But I will take you there! I have a car outside. It would be a great pleasure."

"Oh, you're an absolute darling, Yves!" exclaimed Diana. "Just wait till you see his car, Jan, he wrote me about it. Why, this is wonderful luck, we might have missed that train getting a taxi. Come on, Jan, and you'd better step on it, Yves, it's Victoria!"

She hustled us out of the foyer and he led the way to a side street off Cumberland Place, where a low-slung and exotic-looking cream sports car was parked. It was a Lagonda, the kind of car I had only seen in magazine advertisements. There were no rear seats, so Diana squeezed in between us and we zoomed off down Park Lane, passing every vehicle that showed ahead.

He drove superlatively well, maintaining a consistently high speed but taking no chances. Speech was impossible owing to the rush of air and roar of the engine, but I heard Diana shout "Lovely! Lovely!" as we skimmed past the sentry boxes outside Buckingham Palace. In a very few minutes we were at Victoria and Diana was telling me to buy two tickets for a place called Sanderstead, one single ticket and one return.

When I rejoined them in the yard they were still talking beside the car, but as I approached, Yves drew himself up to attention and extended his hand to its fullest extent, the way all Frenchmen shake hands. Then he gave a little bob toward Diana and to my intense astonishment took her gloved hand and raised it lightly to his lips.

"Until Ascot then," he said, and Diana replied:

"If I can manage it. It's in termtime, you know, but I'll talk Daddy around. Good-by, Yves, dear, and thanks so much for the lift. I adore the car, it's an absolute scorcher!"

He nodded once more to me, wriggled into the car and roared off into the traffic. To my great relief Diana seemed to dismiss him at once. "Come on," she said, seizing my hand, "we'll get a carriage to ourselves if we look spoony enough!"

We went to the far end of the waiting train and although one middle-aged man did ignore Diana's look of savage disapproval as he stepped over our feet, he got out at the third station from the terminus and we made the remainder of the journey alone.

The advent of Yves de Royden and his splendid car had blunted the fine edge of my pleasure and she was quick to notice the fact.

"Why, Jan," she said, smiling and propelling herself toward me, "I do believe you're jealous! You needn't be, silly. I wouldn't *dream* of falling for a foreigner. Yves is a nice foreigner, of course, and fabulously rich but I never think of him as a real man, not like you. Why, if he had to take part in a fight he'd probably kick and scratch! They all do, you know, like Brigadier Gerard in the box fight."

She knew exactly how to banish my gloomy thoughts and by the time we had passed another station I had almost forgotten Yves and his outlandish courtliness.

"I've had a wonderful day, Diana," I told her. "It's one

85

of the best days I remember, like that one back in October, when we met for the first time."

"It's funny, Jan," she mused, tilting her head, throwing out her legs and turning in her toes, "but I can't imagine we've only known each other about six months. It seems as if you've always been part of Heronslea and the Devon half of me, if you see what I mean. Sometimes I feel I'm two quite separate people, the London Emerald and the Devon Diana. I like Diana best, of course, and when I'm with you I grow right away from the other person, so that she seems a stranger. At first I thought it depended on where I was in the flesh but now it doesn't somehow, it's got to do with you, the way you look and talk and even walk. Just now, for instance, in the car I mean, the fact of you being there kept Emerald at a safe distance. Does this sound crazy to you? I'm sure it must because you're so . . . so very much *one* person all the time!"

Before I could think of an answer her practical streak reasserted itself, summoned by the hoarse shout of the station porter calling the name of a station.

"It's the next stop," she warned, "but don't get out until the moment the train is moving and then go right across the bridge and wait for the next up train. It's just possible that there might be someone from school on the platform. Now there's one thing we've got to settle. How much have you spent, I mean altogether, including your fare?"

"Good Lord," I protested, "that's nothing to do with you!"

"Oh yes it is," she said briskly. "I asked you up here and you can't afford to splosh money around. There was the fare and the cafe and the pictures and then these railway tickets. Would two-pounds-ten cover it, or is it more?"

In view of the fact that the return ticket to Devon had only been ten-and-sixpence, two-pounds-ten was getting on for double the amount I had spent but I was horrified at the thought of her financing the excursion, or paying one penny toward the costs of our entertainment.

"I wouldn't dream of taking your money," I said, flushing. "It's . . . it's been wonderful meeting you like this and the man always pays, you know that, Diana."

She looked at me gravely for a moment. "All right, Jan," she said. "I knew you'd make a fuss, so I'll have to make it up to you some other way. We shall be in in less than a minute, so you'd better kiss me, that is if you want to."

In the early stages of our long courtship it was always Diana who took the initiative, not only about when we should meet and how we should occupy our time but when we should embrace or even hold hands. She was so much more adult than I was, and we both knew it, but that occasion was the first that I was more than a passive partner in the act of kissing.

I put my arms around her and kissed her in what I hoped was a fair imitation of the couples on the films and her response was frightening. As our lips touched she tightened her grip on my neck and shoulders, pressing her cheek to mine and murmuring, "Jan, Jan, you belong to me! You're my Jan, aren't you? You *are*, aren't you?" Then I forgot to be frightened and began to drown in a sea of sweetness, so engulfing that I did not even hear the porter shout "Sanderstead" or sense that the train was drawing to a halt.

She pushed me away, jumped up, and pulled her coat from the rack. I noticed then that her eyes were wet and that they had the same look of intensity that I had seen in them when she had gathered up her reins and ridden straight at the fallen tree on Boxing Day.

"Good-by, Jan," she whispered. "I'll write! I promise—good-by, darling Jan, *my* Jan!"

Then she was gone and I heard her footsteps pattering along the platform. The train jerked and I remembered just in time that I too had to alight.

I flung myself out of the carriage and came down on one knee, jarring it painfully, but I was up again at once and waited in the shadows between the station lights until the train was out of sight. Then I crossed the bridge to the up platform, feeling nothing of the smart of my knee but walking in a blissful state of suspension between the greasy planks of the steps and the sky. In this ecstatic trance I somehow found my way back to Waterloo.

I slept most of the way home and when the train ran into Whinford, about half-past four, the night had cleared and the sky was bright with stars.

My road home to Whinmouth Bay ran alongside the river and it was here, in the silence broken only by the steady crank of Uncle Luke's ancient machine, that I emerged from the trance and was able to set about marshaling my thoughts and enjoying the sense of achievement they brought to me.

A little over thirty hours ago, I reflected, I had traveled over this same route toward an uncertain destiny, for despite my new-found confidence in myself, and in Diana's encouraging behavior in the Folly on Old Year's Day, there had remained deep down in me a nag of doubt that she would ever grow to regard me seriously. I had difficulty in ridding myself of the thought that my devotion was simply a scalp to hang on the belt of a spoiled child. Now I no longer had any doubts. Not only was I cheered in retrospect by the encounter with the French boy and by the lightness with which she had dismissed him, but as positive proof of her love I had the image of her tear-stained face when we parted and her whispered claim on me as we had kissed one another and she scurried out of the compartment.

I repeated her words over and over again to myself and each repetition brought more comfort and reassurance. I no longer pondered the outcome of her presentation parties, or feared her mother's opposition to our preposterous courtship. Whatever the future held in store for us, wherever she was sent, however long we were separated, I knew now that Diana and I belonged to each other for all time and that nothing else was of the smallest importance.

By the time I rode into Whinmouth Bay the sky was paling over Nun's Head and the shadows on Whinmouth Flats, on the western side of the estuary, were deeper in contrast. I no longer felt tired and jaded, for the fifteen-mile ride had seemed like five. Instead of going home to bed I propped the cycle outside the Mart and walked along the old jetty at the Point.

This was my favorite part of Whinmouth and I had a secret perch here, under the barnacled timbers near the lock gates. It was still barely light and being Sunday morning there was no one astir. I climbed down the piles and sat looking out over the wide estuary, waiting for sunrise to succeed the false dawn.

It was quiet and pleasant down here. Out on the bar gulls were wheeling over the shallows, wailing greedy protests at one another. The soft tide lapped the timbers of the jetty and across the river one or two early lights were showing under the hills. I always used to think of this scene as the Mississippi and it did indeed correspond in many ways to Mark Twain's vivid descriptions of the big river, for if you took a slantwise view it was heavily timbered on each side and it never occurred to you that open sea lay on the immediate left.

I sat here a long time, my legs swinging from the crosspile, thinking and thinking about love. I thought about it in relation to all the people I knew, Uncle Luke and his querulous Thirza in their poky little bedroom over the Mart, Uncle Reuben in the loneliness of a bed-sitting room behind the High Street, the landlady of The Rifleman and her two husbands over at Shepherdshey and, from thence, to the graceful, porticoed Heronslea, home of Diana and her ill-assorted parents.

I wondered about the relationship of Mr. and Mrs. Gayelorde-Sutton, he with the big, wobbling head and square, clumsy body, she so elegant, groomed and stilted, and it puzzled me that these two people could have created a vital and adorable creature like Diana. People always said that if you want to see what you are getting when you lead a bride to the altar you should look closely at her mother, but how could this apply in my case? What link could exist between the eager, sparkling girl I had left on a suburban platform and the silly, prancing woman who mangled her vowels and performed such monstrous antics in order to impress dour old countrymen like Big Nat, the Shepherdshey sexton? Why had a financial wizard like Mr.

Gayelorde-Sutton chosen such a creature for a mate? How could he suffer her to act such a charade, day in and day out, when his friends and business acquaintances must surely snigger behind their hands every time she opened her mouth? Was she like that when they were alone together?

Did she continue to twist every "i" into a strangled "aiee" when they went to bed together? Would she be more inclined to regard me as a social equal if I did the same thing, or if I learned to ape the courtliness of a boy like Yves de Royden and kiss her hand when I was introduced to her? Or was all this flummery due to money and nothing else? Did the mere possession of property and a big bank balance regulate her attitude toward everyone she met?

I was unable to answer any one of these questions but they were idle and irrelevant in my present uplifted mood. What anyone else thought about pledges exchanged between Diana and myself was unimportant. What mattered, *all* that mattered from now on, was that we belonged to each other, as surely as Heloise belonged to Abelard, Romeo to Juliet, Jan to Lorna.

When the shadows had lifted from the western bank I got up, stiffly. My bruised knee was paining me but I paid no attention to it. I scrambled up the timbers of the jetty and regained a quay now crowded with screaming herring gulls and lesser black-backed gulls quarreling among the lobster pots over gobbets of gutted fish.

I let myself into the apartment above the Mart and crept along to my room. No one was about so I did not wait to make tea but turned in and slept the clock around.

Chapter Four

DIANA'S EASTER holidays commenced on April 1st but she did not come down to Devon for the first week. She wrote to me from London a day or so after breakup to say that she would meet me at the Folly "very early in the morning" on the day after her return. I set the alarm for five A.M. and it was still dark when I cycled up the chalk road to Foxhayes Common and entered the Heronslea estate from the rear. I left the bicycle on the track leading to Heronslea Woods and climbed the spiral staircase of the Folly just as the sun was breasting Teasel Wood and every bird in Sennacharib was awake to greet it.

I had never seen Sennacharib in springtime and its beauty, viewed from the open casement of the Folly, made my heart ache. Every bracken frond of the common was laced with dew and beyond it, across the green downslope of the larch wood, I could just make out the white smudge of Heronslea House. Where the sun touched the southern slopes the primroses were growing in great, trailing clusters along the edge of the plantation, so thickly as to form a yellow hedge.

Our two buzzards were astir, drifting lazily over their favorite hunting ground of the paddock. Every now and again one of them would pretend to swoop, dropping a hundred feet or so, but never pushing home an attack. I remembered then that Uncle Luke had said buzzards were cowardly birds, always waiting for easy prey and never attacking anything that might fight back, but this morning it seemed to me that they were enjoying the wind currents and their mastery of flight rather than searching out a meal.

I was still watching them when I saw something twinkle on the fringe of the larches and after a moment or two

Diana rode into the paddock. She was mounted on her big piebald, Sioux, and was leading a saddled pony.

I could see her more than a mile off, moving toward the Folly at a slow trot, and the sun made the stirrup irons flash like naked swords. I watched her with quiet pride, sitting her splendid Sioux as nonchalantly as her celestial namesake, and when I waved from the window she urged the horses into a slow canter that sent the pheasants karking from the bracken and a pair of pigeons whirring out of the oaks beside the Folly.

When I was sure that she had seen me I ran down the staircase and out into the clearing. The sparkle of the morning glowed in her cheeks as she threw a leg over the pommel and slid to the ground with one of her breathless, good-to-be-alive laughs.

"Isn't this wonderful, Jan? I thought it was the kind of morning you should learn to ride! Slip Nellie's irons down and let's see how you look. How did you get here so early? I made sure I'd be first. Come on, get up, for Sioux is raring to go!"

I obeyed without much enthusiasm, remembering the last occasion that she had bullied me into climbing up on Nellie, the dun pony she was leading.

I did not fear a fall so much as I dreaded to look ridiculous in her eyes, but Nellie seemed quiet enough on the leading rein and when I was awkwardly astride, Diana proceeded to give me my first lesson in horsemanship. I would have preferred a quiet walk along the primrose banks and the chance of starting a hare or fox from the dew-beaded gorse, but Diana was adamant. Once embarked upon the subject of horses she pursued it to the exclusion of all else.

"Hands down—elbows in—*no*, don't turn your toes out! Press in and up, with the strain on the balls of your feet. That's the way you learn to grip with your knees and you won't even stay on old Nellie until you learn to do that. Don't sit *forward*, Jan, not unless you want her to gallop! Loop your reins—look—like this, you're holding them bunched, just like Daddy."

"I feel like Daddy!" I told her, but she stuck to the lesson with the single-mindedness of a professional.

"Relax, Jan—don't *hunch*—you aren't going to fall off so long as you listen to me. Relax, and let all your muscles except your thighs go slack. *That's* better! Now, I can't have you on the leading rein at your age, so tie it up and let's go!"

We jogged out of the wood and across the common to the moor. She rode alongside and kept looking doubtfully at my feet, occasionally tapping them with her crop. After a mile or so I began to feel more confident and presently she shouted something to Nellie, who rolled into a slow, easy canter, pushing ahead of the collected Sioux and widening the gap between us.

I was astonished then to discover how easy it is to sit a cantering pony. I did not know that Nellie was all of twenty years old and that countless children had learned to ride on her broad back. Then Diana flashed past me and blocked the narrow path, forcing Nellie to drop back into an uneven trot, and I had all my work cut out to maintain balance, especially after one foot had slipped from the stirrup and I pitched forward, clutching frantically at Nellie's mane and rolling first to one side and then the other.

"Well, I've seen a lot worse," said Diana, smiling, when at last she wheeled and grabbed Nellie's drooping reins. "You've got long legs and you'll be all right when your muscles build but you'll have to practice for hours and hours until you can hardly limp around."

"If we're going to ride every morning," I protested, "I'll have to get the proper togs. These trousers ruck up and I've rubbed all the skin off the inside of my knee."

"I'll have a square foot of skin off your bottom before I've finished with you!" she promised. "When you come out tomorrow bring corduroys. They'll do to begin with but never mind about riding now, let's walk back to where your bike is, I've got to explain the scheme I've worked out for the rest of the holidays. Now listen carefully and do everything I say, then we can be together all the time until I go back."

The plan had the hallmark of Diana's shrewdness and

reckless gaiety but she explained it in the matter-of-fact tone she invariably used when advancing a harebrained scheme aimed at getting her own way.

"You see, Mummy would squash it flat if she thought we had even a mild crush on one another," she said, frankly, "so I had to think out a foolproof wheeze to explain your presence in Sennacharib for the rest of the hols."

"You can't mean to keep on buying loads of Uncle Luke's furniture," I protested.

"Good Lord, no," she said, impatiently. "You work for a newspaper now, don't you? Well, this has to do with a newspaper, and Mummy'll fall for it hook, line and sinker, because she's an absolute glutton for publicity, even publicity in a little local rag like yours."

It was the first time Diana had spoken slightingly of *The Whinmouth & District Observer*, and I should have challenged her had I been less enthralled with the prospect of spending days in her company. She was right in claiming her plan to be foolproof, however, for it was based on Mrs. Gayelorde-Sutton's snobbery. Providing my employers proved co-operative I didn't see how it could fail.

The idea was that my paper should set about collecting information for a series of weekly articles on Heronslea House and the history of the estate as a whole. I was to be introduced into the house as the gleaner of these facts and then either Uncle Reuben, or someone else, was to collate the information I had gathered into a series of features. The scheme was to be sparked off by a telephone call from me to Mrs. Gayelorde-Sutton, after which I was to sell the idea to Uncle Reuben as having originated from her.

It worked surprisingly well. Uncle Reuben liked local features, though I had a hard job to prevent him from undertaking the fact-finding tour himself. When I pleaded that I needed experience, however, he gave way, and so it was that I donned my best suit and dutifully presented myself at the front door of Heronslea House, equipped with a notebook, three well-sharpened pencils and such confidence as Diana had been able to instill into me during that morning's riding lesson on the common.

I had expected Diana to fly to the door the moment I arrived but when a traditionally disdainful butler led me into the circular hall and across it to a sunny room overlooking the small terrace, she was nowhere to be seen. I was shown a chair and told to wait until it pleased Mrs. Gayelorde-Sutton to attend to me. I don't know whether Masters, the butler, had been informed of the reason for my presence, but I gathered from his manner that I was not the type of guest he was accustomed to admit to his mistress's writing room.

It was an interesting room, especially if you knew Mrs. Gayelorde-Sutton. The walls and bureau photographs screamed her pretensions toward life membership in the Upper Ten. There were several oval oil portraits of bewigged gentlemen and brocaded ladies, a signed photograph of a recently deposed king, more photographs of groups of fashionably dressed people, including herself and husband taken on a racecourse somewhere, and a cabinet crammed with china, part of her Rockingham and Bow collection.

The furniture was mostly French. There was a large writing table, with slender legs and a mass of gilded ornamentation, a lovely rosewood escritoire, decorated with a pastoral motif on its bow front and a set of ribbon-backed chairs, with seats that matched the yellow curtains of the room. Although in many ways a ludicrously counterfeit squireen, it was clear that Mrs. Gayelorde-Sutton possessed genuine taste. There was absolutely nothing wrong with her ideas of furnishing a large country house. Life with Uncle Luke, and attendance at scores of auction sales, had taught me a smattering of these matters and I sensed that everything in the room was what the dealers would call "right," just as she herself always looked "right," until the moment she opened her screwbag mouth and spoiled a good impression by strangled vowels and overstressed consonants.

Suddenly she swept in and subjected me to a long, disapprovingly intense scrutiny.

"The reportah from the peepah? But you're only a boy! I expected someone oldah, *mech* oldah!"

Luckily I had anticipated this and made haste to explain that I was a mere fact assembler and that the proprietor of the paper would write the actual articles.

I must have been learning fast about Mrs. Gayelorde-Sutton, for I scored a direct hit by a deferential tailpiece to the effect that this assignment was considered the most important one our paper had ever undertaken and therefore demanded the maximum preparation.

"Oh, I see, I see!" she murmuerd and then, after a moment's reflection: "Ai'im far too busy to spend mai taime explaining everything to a boy, but there's something in what you say. We don't want to rush the business, do we? Ai think perhaps the best idea is to get mai daughter to show you around; then you ken read me what you've written, before submitting it to your editah."

She opened the door and called, "*Air*-m'ald . . . *Air*-m'ald . . .!" There was the painful sigh in her pronunciation of the name as I had noticed on the occasion when she visited the Mart. "Come in here, Air-merald, Ai want you to meet someone!"

The strong element of farce in the situation made me want to giggle but I forced myself to maintain a mute, respectful expression while Diana was summoned and solemnly introduced to me. Her play-acting was far better than mine. She even managed to look petulant when her mother instructed her to escort me around the house and grounds and tell me what she knew of its history.

"How long is all this likely to take, Mother?" she demanded, implying that she regarded the entire business as a terrible bore.

"As long as Ai think fit, deah!" said Mrs. Gayelorde-Sutton tartly, and I noticed the deep-rooted antipathy that existed between them, even allowing for the fact that Diana was only playing a part and that her mother was addressing her in front of a stranger.

"All right, all right, I only asked," grumbled Diana, "but I don't want to spend the entire holidays cooped up in the house!"

It seemed to me that Diana was overdoing her show of reluctance but I later concluded that she was merely strengthening the knot that was to hold us together for the next three weeks. Her apparent truculence irritated her mother and made her determined to exert her parental authority. She gave Diana a little lecture on the importance of her escort duties and stressed that everything she said was liable to appear in print. Diana played her like a fish, pretending to warm to her duties as soon as Mrs. Gayelorde-Sutton pointed out that the tour was to include a careful inspection of the entire estate and that this would mean rambles about the grounds.

"Does he ride?" she inquired demurely and winked over her mother's shoulder.

"Oh yes, ma'am," I told her, "I learned over at the Tally-Ho Stables, a year or so ago."

"There then," said Mrs. Gayelorde-Sutton, with a certain amount of relief, "you can ride over the estate but Ai shall want the interiah covered first, you understand? All the chinah and pictures and particularly the Dutch and Italian gardens and McCarthy's hothouse displays. When we've sorted it out," she added, turning to me again, "your employer will hev to send a kemerah up heah, so now I'll leave you to my daughter and you can show me what you've done when it's time to go. Start in the library, Airm'ald, and ask Mrs. Beddowes when she's ready to let you go upstairs."

"Yes, Mother," said Diana, dutifully. "Come this way, will you, Mr. . . . Mr. . . . ?"

"Leigh," I said, promptly, and followed her out into the hall, closing the door behind me.

2.

Thus began the charade that lasted the greater part of the Easter holidays, and from everyone's viewpoint it proved a remarkable success. The articles were compiled to Mrs. Gayelorde's satisfaction, the *Observer* filled its center page without the aid of scissors and pastepot, and Diana and I had license to associate whenever we wished. Although it all began as an elaborate joke it soon developed into something more for me. To anyone at all receptive to beauty and good craftsmanship, an inspection of Heronslea House and estate was a rewarding way of spending an April day. Diana was at first incredulous, then mildly amused by my enthusiasm.

"You're taking it all so seriously, Jan," she complained, when I begged her to allow me more time in the library. "Nobody ever *reads* the books in here, they went with the house and they simply aren't readable, none of them."

"They smell exciting anyway," I said and Diana laughed and gave me an affectionate little hug.

"Oh, you're a funny boy, Jan!" she exclaimed. "Funny but nice! You know"—she stood back and regarded me as though making up her mind about a purchase at a counter —"I really think you *are* going to be someone after all. I'll tell you what. For the house tour I'll hand you over to Drip. She's got quite a pash on you and I'll get all my chores done before we start outside and combine this nonsense with some real work on the horses. I've got heaps of letters to write and an awful French holiday task and by the time I've done you'll be through in here."

Without waiting for my agreement she pulled me up the broad staircase, composed of stairs so shallow that one had little sensation of climbing, and along one of the curved corridors to a little suite beyond the schoolroom. This was Drip's quarters and as we went in she said:

"Drip's in our secret, of course, so you might have to grapple with her conscience! She won't give us away, however, so you don't have to put on an act with her."

It was soon clear that poor Miss Rodgers was having a great deal of trouble with her conscience, and because I was genuinely fond of her I was unable to share Diana's detachment. It did not take me long to discover that Drip was very well aware that my world revolved around Diana, and also that I was no more than a glorified errand boy with whom her charge was consorting in brazen defiance of her mother.

Miss Rodgers (I find it difficult to write of her as "Drip") was torn between her adoration for Diana, her genuine kindheartedness, her liking for me personally, and her obvious duty to her employers, but Diana was correct in her assumption that our secret was safe, for Drip's awareness of responsibilities as governess was outweighed by more personal considerations. After a good deal of preliminary tongue clicking and half-hearted protests she consented to take over Diana's duties as guide.

"I don't like all this hole-in-the-corner business, Jan," she admitted, as soon as Diana had left us alone. "After all, I am supposed to be responsible for her whenever her mother isn't here, and although I don't see why you and she shouldn't be friends, I don't like being a party to a shameless deceit."

"It isn't really a deceit, Miss Rodgers," I pleaded, "because we really are going to print the articles. Besides, I like the job and I think Diana's mother will like what we do, so in the end everyone'll be happy, won't they?"

"Yes," said Drip, doubtfully, "but I think you'd better tell me a little more about yourself, just in case anyone finds out later on. I mean . . . well . . . Diana's mother is rather fussy about whom she associates with in the holidays, and I can't help feeling that she might be furious if she found out that Diana had tricked her like this, if you see what I mean."

I saw what she meant far more clearly than the amiable little governess imagined. Diana's mother would be less inclined to explode over being so outrageously hoodwinked than over the discovery that her expensively educated daughter was gaily associating with a boy who had recently graduated from a secondhand furniture store to the post of junior reporter on an insignificant country newspaper, and a boy, moreover, who had left a council school at the age of fourteen and used a reedy, Cockney accent that placed him on a footing with the village boy who cleaned the silver.

My tour of the house in the wake of Drip served to emphasize the existence of the vast social gulf between us. Before I had inspected half of the sixty-odd rooms of the mansion it was plain that the Gayelorde-Suttons were far wealthier than I had supposed. I followed Drip from room to room with mounting dismay. It was like being taken on a conducted tour around Blenheim Palace, or Compton

Wynyates. Drip let me browse in the library and jot down notes about some of the pictures on the staircase. There was a Cotman landscape and several small Fragonards. Down in the vast drawing room was a group of Isabey miniatures and two portraits by Raeburn. I knew very little about pictures and was content to make notes on the insurance figures quoted by Miss Rodgers, but my association with antique dealers had taught me something of the value of the French furniture in the ground-floor apartments.

The furniture alone would have merited a four-day sale and attracted every reputable dealer in London. There were samples of almost every well-known English craftsman of the eighteenth century, as well as a number of exquisite French pieces, of the kind I had already noted in the writing room.

There were Aubusson screens, Chinese carpets, Burgundian tapestries and Sheraton sideboards, loaded with Georgian silver. There was Mrs. Gayelorde-Sutton's personal collection of china ranging from early Chelsea and Plymouth, to exotic groups and centerpieces of Rockingham, Worcester, and Bow. There was a small armory containing chased Spanish morions, exquisitely wrought Italian armor, and a dozen cases of handsome dueling pistols, collected, I was told, by Mr. Gayelorde-Sutton during his various Continental trips. There was a little conservatory, full of oddities left by the Gilroys and containing, among other interesting exhibits, the charred stump of a stake at which the last witch of the district was said to have suffered. Dotted here and there among all these splendors were scores of framed photographs, each of them featuring the Gayelorde-Suttons during their swift rise to power during the opening years of the decade.

It was an early photograph of Mr. Gayelorde-Sutton wearing knickerbockers and deerstalker hat and taken alongside an early model of an open touring car that prompted me to ask Miss Rodgers if the family had always been rich, or whether, as was freely rumored in Shepherdshey, they had acquired their vast wealth during the 1914-18 war.

I saw by the instinctive tightening of the governess's lips that the question challenged her honesty.

"Well er . . ." she temporized, "Diana's father has always been very clever, of course, and he was doing quite well *before* the war, importing something or other from South America, but money makes money, doesn't it? It was really *during* the war that he came to be really well-known, not in the newspaper sense, you understand, not like Rudolph Valentino or that man Lind something or other, who flew the Atlantic last summer, but among the city people who seem to make money without doing anything in particular."

"But what does he really *do?*" I asked, for it seemed important to me that I should know this once and for all.

Drip wrinkled her pudgy little nose and looked very uncomfortable.

"I . . . I don't really know," she admitted. "I don't think anyone here really knows, except that it's something to do with . . . with high finance, and . . . and *selling* something to the government. Perhaps it's something like he was doing before the war—that was nitrates, I believe, Chilean nitrates. I do remember that because I saw some illustrated charts hanging in his office when I had to call there the day war broke out."

That was as much information as I got at that time about the source of the Gayelorde-Suttons' wealth, but before Diana came to claim me and continue our tour of the gardens, Miss Rodgers asked me into her little sitting room adjoining the nursery and talked to me seriously over a cup of tea and some of her favorite muffins. I could see that she was still very worried over our association and at length she forced herself, much as she hated to pry, to explore the future of a friendship between Diana and myself.

"I . . . I know you're very young, Jan," she began, her pendulous cheeks flushing, "but I've got a dreadful conviction that you're . . . well . . . beginning to feel the same way about Diana as I do, and I can't see how you'll be able to stop getting *hurt* later on. You see, I've known Diana from the minute she was born and she's always

101

been this way—thoughtless and terribly impulsive, always rushing into things that she thinks of as ... well ... as *adventures,* I suppose. I don't mean that she's silly enough to imagine she's in love, or anything of that nature, and I suppose I shouldn't even say that to a boy of your age anyway, because I'm sure you won't let your mind dwell on that kind of thing for years yet, but I do think a young person can be hurt as much by a broken friendship as grown-up people are hurt by love affairs, and I don't like a nice boy like you being picked up and ... and well ... *led* to believe things and then dropped and laughed at, do you know?"

Despite her obvious good intentions I found myself resenting her estimate of Diana. I suppose I failed to make sufficient allowance for the fact that Miss Rodgers had been reared in a Victorian atmosphere and accepted rigid class distinctions without in the least resenting them. It seemed to me at that time that she was being stuffy and old-fashioned, as well as slightly disloyal to someone who had never hinted at the social barrier between us, except as a fence to be crossed and recrossed in defiance of her mother's edicts.

I fell back on a rather surly justification of myself as a not altogether-impossible squire for the daughter of wealthy and distinguished parents. Drip's halting references to impending disaster had touched my pride in a way that Diana's frank acceptance of parental opposition had never touched it, and I said, without looking at her:

"I'm not going to stay a small-town reporter, Miss Rodgers. I'm going to get on a bigger paper and be famous, so that in the end we won't have to pretend any more and then Diana and I can be married without any fuss!"

Poor Miss Rodgers was so startled by the mention of the word "marriage" that she dropped her pince-nez spectacles on the carpet.

"Jan, you ... you mustn't *think* about things like that," she protested, her plump hands fluttering as she groped for her glasses. "You must see that just saying them puts me

102

in a dreadful position. I don't know what to say, I simply don't know *what* to say!"

She trailed off miserably and I was sorry then that I had confided in her. At the same time, I felt the necessity of convincing her that it was quite possible for a boy of fifteen and a half to be hopelessly in love, and that I would not accept her disqualification on grounds of age quite apart from those of class and education.

"People grow up quicker than they did when you were young," I declared, quoting from a newspaper feature I had read a day or so before, and feeling a hot flush creep into my cheeks. "I'm nearly sixteen now and all the boys about my age in Whinmouth have a girl they like better than any other girl. I've never met anyone who could compare with Diana, not just to look at, I mean, but as a person, as someone who's wonderful to *be* with. All the girls in the town seem so . . . so feeble compared with her, and she seems to like me, otherwise why should she go to all this trouble so that we can be together?"

Miss Rodgers seemed to consider and for a moment the concern left her expression. When she spoke again she sounded wonderfully gentle and understanding, so much so that instantly I changed my mind about her and was glad that I had forced the matter out in the open.

"You haven't got a mother or father, have you, Jan?" she asked and when I told her they were both dead she folded her hands on her lap and smiled, her faded blue eyes radiating so much kindness and comfort that I swallowed quickly and had to look away.

She went on: "I'm afraid I'm a romantic, Jan, just like you, and what you've just said makes it clear to me that I was quite wrong to pooh-pooh the idea of being in love at your age. You *are* in love, the right kind of love, and I don't suppose anything I can say will stop you being, not for a year or so at all events. All I want to say now is that you must realize Diana isn't in love in the same way, perhaps because she hasn't grown up as fast as you, or perhaps because she's had so much of everything. That means that she hasn't developed in the way that you've had to develop, partly, I think, because you lost your mother and

103

father at a time when you most needed them but more so because you've been pushed out in the world to earn your own living. All the other young people Diana knows have still got two or three years more of schooling ahead of them and this friendship with you is a kind of game to Diana. Although I'm sure she likes you very much, most of the fun to her is just having you around and scoring over her mother; that is, doing something that she knows very well is strictly forbidden."

She paused a moment and then added, "I don't suppose this makes much sense to you now, but I think you'll see the wisdom of it later on. I'm going to have a little talk with Miss Diana and it's going to be tonight!"

She got up and smoothed her dress, looking so resolute that my heart sank at the prospect of our association being severed there and then.

"If you say anything like that to her I won't be able to see her, Miss Rodgers," I pleaded. "You needn't be frightened I'll do anything you wouldn't like. I'll just go on being friends, the way we are."

I thought, fleetingly, of our secret meeting in London, and of the despairing kiss that Diana had given me as the train drew into the station. I wondered what Drip would say and do if she knew the whole truth of our association to date, and whether such knowledge would cause her to regard the matter less sympathetically from my point of view.

"All the same, I'm going to talk to Diana," said Drip, "but don't think for a moment I'll say anything at all to her mother, or that I'll make it any more difficult than it already is for you to see one another. To begin with, that would only make Diana more determined than ever, and the truth is I'm thinking of you more than her because you're the one who is going to be hurt most and I won't have that, ever, do you understand? I won't *have* that!"

I left Heronslea that day without seeing Diana again and my thoughts were so wretched and confused that I made no attempt to sort out the notes I had made, but retired to my room after supper on the pretense of doing this and sat for a long time watching the moon rise over the estuary beyond the empty quay.

Whichever way I looked at the situation, I could see no hope in the immediate future and I slowly came to hate Drip for what seemed to be a monstrously unjust interference in our lives.

I set the alarm for five o'clock again and cycled up to Foxhayes to watch the dawn, but although I hung about the Folly for almost two hours Diana did not appear and I freewheeled back to town in black despondency.

Diana's failure to keep the tryst seemed to me clear evidence that all was now known to her mother, and quite apart from the misery of losing her I began to feel very apprehensive of my reception at the office.

I did Drip a grave injustice. There was no showdown. Uncle Reuben was just as interested in the articles as ever, and was obviously expecting me to bus over to Heronslea for the next day's note taking. He even complimented me on the material I had already gathered and said that if I wished to knock it into a draft article, without first submitting it to him in detail, I was welcome to try as soon as I returned.

His attitude was puzzling but not nearly so puzzling as Diana's. She greeted me the moment I entered the drive, and talked gaily of a book that she had unearthed dealing with the history of the house and estate under the Gilroy who had built the Folly.

We inspected the Dutch garden as she chattered on about this and that until I had almost persuaded myself that Drip's nerve must have failed her at the last moment and that she had never, in fact, had her talk with Diana. Then, as we passed the box hedges and entered the Italian garden, I thought I detected a nervous brittleness about Diana's chatter, as though she were only talking in the hope of preventing me from voicing the subject uppermost in my mind. This conviction grew until at last I was unable to keep silent any longer and blurted out: "Well, did Drip say anything to you las* night, Diana? Anything about us?"

She stopped in the middle of a sentence and looked at

me sharply, her head on one side, her thumb pulling her lower lip.

"What does it matter what Drip said? Who cares about Drip's opinion one way or the other? I told you she wouldn't give us away and that's all that counts, isn't it?"

"No," I said, glumly, "it isn't, and what's more you must know that it isn't!"

She looked at me then with an expression I had never seen in her face. It was hard and challenging, as though at any moment her eyes would blaze with anger. When she spoke her voice was equally harsh and strange.

"Why should you say a thing like that? Just exactly what did Drip say to you about me? What made you afraid of coming here?"

"I'm not afraid, Diana," I protested, "it's just that . . ."

"You *are* afraid, Jan! All the sparkle's gone out of you. Yesterday it was fun and today you're as jumpy as a cat. You'd better tell me everything Drip said and be done with it."

I told her, withholding nothing, and she heard me in silence, keeping her gaze on me in a way that made me feel wretched and ashamed.

"Is that all?" she said, when I had finished.

"All I can remember," I said, sulkily.

She stayed quite still for a moment, reflecting.

"You know what she was getting at," she said at length. "I mean, what she was *really* driving at when you peel away all the cotton wool that she wrapped it in and all that gaff about me encouraging you just to spite Mother, and so on?"

"She didn't seem to me to beat about the bush very much," I growled.

Diana threw back her head and laughed. It was not her pleasant abandoned laugh, the one I loved to hear, but an expression of unspeakable contempt, contempt for Drip, for me, for Heronslea House and everything in it.

"People like Drip always go all around the mulberry bush to soften the blow," she said. "They think they're doing it out of consideration for people but they aren't, you know, it's just lack of guts on their part. Drip's a dear

106

old thing in many ways but she hasn't the spunk of a rabbit. She ought to have said exactly what she meant while she was about it."

"What did she mean, Di?"

"Simply that nothing could ever make you into the sort of person that I should care to be seen with——outside Sennacharib, of course. Just that you weren't 'our class' and never could be, and that everything about you was wrong, clothes, accent, outlook, everything! Well, do you believe that? Because it's what you think that really matters, Jan. Do you believe it, deep down, inside you?"

Did I? I think I did on the rare occasions when I could escape from the web of romantic dreams I had been spinning since the day Diana had ridden out of the larch wood and rescued me from the keeper. I had changed my job because of her. I had obeyed her every command, as a dog runs to a whistle. I had lied to myself, to Uncle Reuben, to Aunt Thirza, to her mother and even to Drip, simply in order to continue dreaming, but if I was once seriously challenged could I continue to fool myself? Would I ever convince myself that Diana and I could ever really belong together, or would I wake up and face the fact that no efforts on my part would ever establish a relationship between us that was capable of outgrowing the friendship of two adolescents, a pair of kids who had absolutely nothing in common but a love of the woods, fields and hedgerows?

I was searching for words to convey this to her when suddenly she took pity on me and her expression softened. She took hold of my wrist and ran her fingers up the sleeve until they were pressing my forearm. Her touch was like a salve, soothing the raw wound of my pride and injecting vigor into my dreams. Confidence and self-esteem seemed to radiate from her finger tips and flow through into me, the glow warming every nerve in my body.

"What you need is a tonic, Jan, a real, live tonic! Meet me at Whinmouth Station after lunch and we'll go out after it, but don't ask me about it now, just be there. We're going on a little trip somewhere."

"How far?" I asked, astonished at both proposal and change of mood.

107

"Oh, not so far," she replied, gaily, "ten or twelve miles. We'll be back before dark and by that time you'll have things straighter, a whole lot straighter, I promise you."

That was all she would say at that time and we devoted the rest of the morning to an inspection of McCarthy's spectacular hothouses and banks of blooms. I made various notes, but my mind was not on my work, it was probing and probing into the mystery behind Diana's knowing smile and her brisk, business-like manner.

I left Heronslea shortly before lunch and gobbled a meal in time to be at our little railway terminus by two o'clock. About ten past Diana came into the booking hall and without glancing in my direction went straight to the window and bought tickets. I heard the clerk say, "Two returns, Castle Ferry, two-and-four, miss," as he gave change.

"Why on earth are we going to Castle Ferry?" I wanted to know, as we passed the barrier.

"You'll find out as soon as we get there!" was all she would tell me. "Now don't keep pestering me with questions and let me enjoy my surprise. I know what I'm doing, I *always* know what I'm doing, Jan!"

I knew her well enough by then to keep my curiosity to myself and find other topics to talk about. Fortunately an obvious one was at hand, for Castle Ferry was a fishing village a dozen miles along the coast and to get to it by rail one had to travel inland to the county junction and then, by branch line, southeast through the pine and bracken country beyond Teasel Wood and the boundaries of Sennacharib.

I had been there once before and knew it for a picturesque little place, just beginning to enjoy popularity as an artist's colony. It was too picture-postcardy for my taste, the kind of seaside one sees in scores of amateur water colors, all pebbles, white cottages and heeled-over boats draped around with nets and lobster pots. It had, I suppose, plenty of conventional charm but lacked the solitude of Sennacharib, or even the strident vitality of the rural slum that is often the hard core of towns like Whinmouth.

108

We had our heads out of the window all the way and vied with one another in spotting landmarks, but before we reached the junction the fact that we were alone in a railway compartment reminded me of the short railway journey we had made together in London, and I began to hope that Diana would say something to stage a repetition of the moment of parting. She was not, however, in a romantic mood, for when I let my arm rest on her shoulder and lightly brushed her hair with my lips, she ignored the gesture and said, rather pointedly, "Look, Jan! You can just see the top of the Folly above the wood."

We left the train at a point a mile or so from the coast and walked down the steep lane between high, flowering hedgerows to the foot of the village, where a shallow stream emptied itself into the bay that divided Castle Ferry into two unequal halves.

The castle, a rounded ruin, was on the far side and under it was an old tavern, The Sloop Inn. There was no bridge and people who wanted to cross from one part of the village to the other used a rowing boat that was hauled along a taut cable by hand. There was no regular service. Ferry customers crossed the shingle to where the boat touched shore, and if the ferry was on the far side the ferryman, who spent almost all his time in the pub, was summoned by a hail.

Easter was gone, the summer season had not yet begun, and there was hardly anyone about. The boat was moored on the far side, so we put our hands to our mouths and shouted in chorus. Nothing happened for a few moments, then the ferryman emerged from the Sloop, a fat, shambling man in a fisherman's jersey and a battered yachting cap. He waved his arm, very irritably I thought, and began to haul the boat toward us.

"Take a good long look at this Johnny, Jan," said Diana as the ferry neared us, "because he's the reason we're here."

The ferryman was worth noting. He was the most picturesque old ruffian I had ever seen, a cross between a W. W. Jacob's illustration and a buccaneer run to seed. He was aged, I should say, between sixty and seventy, and his face was a flabby ham, framed in tumbling iron-gray locks that were almost as long as a girl's. His complexion was a light mahogany but not pleasing, for grime filled the crevasses of his huge ears. His eyes were as soft and blue as Diana's, but the cunning squint in them changed to a surly contempt when he saw that his passengers were only a couple of youngsters and therefore unlikely to pay more than the requisite halfpenny. Seen at close range his bulk, and particularly his belly, was immense; when he seated himself in the bows preparatory to hauling on the cable, the stern was out of the water until we had stepped in and sat down. He smelled very strongly of beer and when he opened his mouth to jam a clay pipe between his discolored teeth I saw that his tongue was horribly furred. One way and another, he struck me as being an extremely unsavory old man, the kind of pseudo-fisherman who hangs about quays cadging from visitors, who usually tell one another: "Here is a real old salt, the kind that are getting rare these days." We had our own contingent of longshoremen at Whinmouth, but none of them were quite so repellent or professional-looking as this one. His hands were as big and rough as everything else about him, and the tar from the cable had ingrained itself as high as the wrist. He looked to me as though he had never washed since he was a boy and apart from the reek of beer it was an unpleasant experience to travel with him, for he also exuded an odor of stale sweat.

He said nothing to us during the five-minute crossing and only grunted when I handed him sixpence, twelve times the fare. We got out and took the path up the knoll to the castle and I saw him stumble into the pub the moment he had moored the boat.

"Well?" said Diana, throwing herself down on a level stretch of grass beside the tower. "What do you think of Dan'l?"

"I think he's a complete phony," I said, "and a pretty smelly one at that!"

"Not a character? Not a tarry chip of Old England?"

"No," I said, "not on your life! Chaps like him are ten-a-penny in Whinmouth, but most of them wash once in a while and all of them say thank you when they get a tip."

She curled her legs under her and leaned back on her hands, the familiar smile playing hide-and-seek round the corners of her mouth, while her eyes regarded me with affectionate mockery.

"Look, what is all this?" I demanded. "What's he got to do with us being here?"

"He's the tonic I told you about," said Diana, "he's your private pick-me-up."

I was always ready to stand a great deal of chaff from Diana but that day I was too nervous about the immediate future to put up with her teasing indefinitely. I said, shortly, "For goodness' sake say what's in your mind and let's begin at the beginning!"

"All right," she said, softly, inserting a grass stem into her mouth with the casual grace she displayed when she slipped from the back of one of her ponies. "Dan'l is Mummy's father and my grandfather!"

I jumped as if I had found myself sitting on a wasps' nest, utter incredulity depriving me of speech for nearly a minute. At last I found my tongue.

"That . . . that ferryman! . . . *Your grandfather!*"

"Uh-huh!" she said, enjoying every moment of my outraged astonishment. "His name is Daniel Best and Mummy is his youngest daughter. She doesn't know that I know, of course; in fact, nobody knows that I know except you, but it's true, all right, and if you look really hard you can see it, at least I can, because I've seen Mummy without make-up."

"I don't understand," I said, weakly, "I just don't understand how the chap and your mother . . ."

I trailed off, for it was impossible to contemplate the relationship, much less put it into words. I thought back to the first glimpse I had ever had of Mrs. Gayelorde-Sutton, tip-tapping on her high heels into Uncle Luke's store, splendidly arrogant in her elegant clothes and addressing me as though I was something left behind by the tide. I remembered how she had screwed her small, red mouth into a tight ball of distaste and called in strangled vowels to

111

Diana, "*Air*-m'alde! *Air*-m'alde! Come heah, Air-m'alde, Ai want you!"

I compared her mincing charade with the sour, uncompromising heaviness of the ferryman Dan'l, searching my memory for some characteristic or suggestion of a characteristic, that might link them as father and daughter, but my mind shied away from the possibility, not only on account of its staggering improbability but because, deep in my heart, I was feeling the first stirrings of pity for Mrs. Gayelorde-Sutton and wanting to absolve her from a relationship with a sullen drunkard who smelled vilely of sweat and stale liquor.

"How did you find out? Why are you so sure?" I asked, holding on to a tendril of hope that this was just one of Diana's elaborate jokes.

"I'd always wondered about Mummy's people," she said. "I think I began to suspect something years and years ago, when I first realized how terribly phony *she* was and why she tried so terribly hard to convince even me that she came out of the top drawer. Then I got a clue from a book of check stubs she left lying around and did some detective work among her papers before coming over here to make sure. It wasn't all that difficult, it only needed common sense and luck. She pays him to stay away, you see, and as long as he gets regular beer money and his cottage rent paid, he never gives any trouble. He isn't anything like as truculent as he looks, just rather pitiful, I always think."

"Do you mean you actually rooted about among your mother's things for clues?" I demanded.

"Certainly, and don't expect me to apologize for it," she said sharply. "I've a right to know who my own grandfather is, haven't I?"

I conceded her this but remained doubtful of the ethics of her action.

"Does he know . . . about you?"

"Well, he knows I exist, but he certainly doesn't recognize me. That was obvious, wasn't it?"

I thought for a moment and then began to ponder her tortuous motive in bringing me here, introducing me, so to

112

speak, to the family skeleton. I remembered the word she had used—"tonic." What exactly did that mean? How was knowing about Dan'l a tonic to me? Then, quite suddenly, I saw her object and she realized that I had understood.

"Well, Jan, do you catch on? Does it make sense now—why I brought you here, I mean?"

I said, "I imagine it was to prove to me that your family wasn't really any better class than mine, Diana."

"I should say you had the edge on us if anything," said Diana, laughing. "I've seen all your uncles and none of them measure up to our Dan'l, do they?"

Suddenly she whisked out of her bantering mood and her eyes became serious. "Don't you *see*, Jan, it isn't what you are, it's what you become that matters! If Mother had just broken away from a family like that and struck out on her own, I think I should have admired her, but as it is, what possible right can she have to choose my companions and lay down rules and regulations for me? She doesn't just laugh at Dan'l, or give him enough money to lie low. She doesn't even send him out of the country—she's too scared to do that and wants him fairly handy where she can keep an eye on him. It's almost as though he was a criminal, and in a way he's worse than a criminal to her, certainly worse than a criminal with a public school background. It makes me absolutely sick when people like her and Drip look down on somebody like you, someone who earns his own living, and tries to keep himself decent on a few shillings a week! I brought you to see Dan'l in the hope that it would help you to see straight, the way I've seen since I was old enough to sit up and take notice. If a person like you wants to change enough, he can always do it. Thousands of people have had worse starts and become all sorts of things without being ashamed of what they were born, as Mummy is. I suppose I've got a thing about this snob business because I've been hedged in with it all my life, and when Drip came up with her pi-jaw last night I wanted to hit her. Then I was angry with you, for letting her persuade you to eat humble pie and pull a forelock at squire's house. Don't *ever* eat humble pie, Jan, and don't ever pull forelocks! If you do I'll hate you, and I don't want

113

to hate you because you being in love with me is the nicest thing that's ever happened to me!"

Her logic wasn't very original but I still think hers was a remarkable outlook for a fifteen-year-old girl who had been brought up to regard almost everyone about her as a social inferior. I know that at the time I admired her for it tremendously, and that my heart, already hers, swelled with pride because she had faith in me and was prepared to go to such lengths to prove it. I loved her honesty and courage. I loved her high spirits and irrepressible sense of fun. I loved her grasp of realism and utter lack of pretension and I was beginning to respond to her physically in a way that was new to me, despite our occasional kisses and childish protestations. This would doubtless have happened before, but until her latest declaration my awareness of her eager, elfin prettiness had been held in check by her unattainability. I had been ready to serve her, to perform any and every feat she demanded of me. I had been eager to worship but, if necessary, to do my worshiping from a respectful distance. Now, within a few months of my sixteenth birthday, I wanted to possess as well as worship, I wanted to begin training as the man who would ultimately soar to the ecstatic position of mastery over her, and as I watched the afternoon sun light up her hair and breeze stir the uneven fringe that seemed always to be reaching for the arch of her left eyebrow, I made up my mind that I would commence that training without confiding in her and then lay my accomplishments, one by one, at her feet as the forfeits of rapture.

We sat there a long time watching the empty bay, talking of other things, apart from beery old Dan'l and what kind of childhood her mother must have had in the crowded cottage that he continued to occupy behind the boat sheds. Then we climbed down from the castle and ordered a Devonshire tea in a tiny gift-shop-cum-café under the red cliff, afterwards re-crossing the ferry piloted by her grandfather, who became embarrassingly servile when presented with Diana's half crown at the point of disembarkation.

We had to share the compartment back to Whinmouth,

114

which distressed me, for I had made up my mind to kiss
her without awaiting her usual invitation. As it happened,
with three other people in the carriage, I was obliged to
remain content with letting my hand rest on hers as we sat
close together on the dusty cushions. I saw her to the bus
stop shortly before dusk and then, with singing heart, went
home to sort my Heronslea notes and file my latest
memories.

Chapter Five

DIANA RETURNED to school the last week in April. By the
first week of May I had made my plans and put the two of
them into operation.

I had learned a good deal in the holidays. It was plain
that Diana was not prepared to share her life with a man
whose achievements were limited to chronicling small-
town events, and while my present job was good enough
to be regarded as a training ground for wider fields, I realized that I must look ahead for something more spectacular and certainly more rewarding. In the meantime I decided to employ the interval by overhauling my social
equipment, leaving my career in abeyance until I was experienced enough to apply for a post in Fleet Street.

It was still nearly three years before the great industrial
slump of the early thirties and the word "unemployment"
did not, as yet, loom very large in Whinmouth. I went so
far as to discuss my future with Uncle Reuben and although he shook his head when I told him, with the brash-
ness of youth, that I was determined to see the world and
start by getting myself a job on a national newspaper, he
commended my ambition and promised that when the
time came he would do everything in his power to help
me.

"You'll find that every middle-aged reporter in Fleet
Street dreams of running a little provincial weekly like

ours, John," he warned me. "Taken all round, there's a lot to be said for being a big fish in a small pond. Up there they earn good money, of course, but it's a rackety life and most of them end up by drinking too much or go to the bad in one way or another. However, I'm not so old as to realize that you won't want to spend the whole of your life in a place like this, and I think you're bright and willing enough to merit something more than a job on a small paper you aren't ever likely to own. Let's shelve the whole business until you're eighteen; then we'll get Mr. Priddis to give us some introductions and try our luck in somewhere a bit bigger than Whinmouth Bay. In the meantime we'll give you a raise to thirty shillings a week."

I thanked him and was ready to leave it at that but privately made up my mind to do something about improving my position before another two years had elapsed. In the meantime, as I say, I reached out in other directions. I learned how to ride properly and began to acquire a working knowledge of French.

The riding lessons were easily arranged. I went over to Uncle Mark's stables, determined to improve my acquaintance with the old rascal. Having studied his battered signboard, which proclaimed lessons were given and liveries received, I demanded to be taught to ride and offered a fee of five shillings per lesson. Uncle Mark was pleased, I think, by my forthrightness, and by my sly admission that I was presenting myself in defiance to staid Brother Reuben's advice.

"You'll get nothing but dirty stories from that scoundrel," he had warned me, when I told him of my intention. "He'll take all your money and give you nothing better than a filthy taste in your mouth!"

I didn't repeat this comment to Mark but I told him that Uncle Reuben had dismissed horsemanship as a giddy pursuit for the idle rich, and that was enough to put Mark on his mettle.

"Damme, I'll teach 'ee for nowt if you've a mind to learn praper!" he growled, and when I told him I had already had a few lessons on one of the Gayelorde-Sutton
116

ponies he looked me up and down much as Diana had done after persuading me to ride Nellie at the Folly.

"Do you think I'll ever make a really good rider?" I asked him.

"I dunno!" he grunted. "Us'll zee when us gets 'ee up!"

He brought out an old cob called Justice and taught me to mount and dismount, and having expressed grudging satisfaction that I "zeemed to get the 'ang of it better'n most o' the young bleeders," he saddled his own horse and took me over the common, thumping out the rhythm of the trot on my left thigh until it was sore to touch.

After that we made remarkably good headway. I slipped out to Uncle Mark's three or four times a week, and by midsummer we had exchanged Justice for a lively mare called Polly, whom I took over some of the smaller jumps in Mark's grid, behind the stables.

I worked very hard, for I was absolutely determined to surprise Diana when she came home for the long holiday, and Uncle Mark became almost amiable as he watched my progress. The day we galloped round Teasel Wood and finished a neck-and-neck race by clearing a fallen spruce in the ride approaching his premises, he rolled from his sweating mount and waddled over to wring my hand in both of his.

"Giddon, us'll 'ave 'ee 'untin' in no time!" he exclaimed. "Damned if you ab'n got a natural zeat, me boy, aye, an' bliddy gude 'ands too, or my name ain't Leigh! I'll tell 'ee what, you come yer an' zaddle up Polly any time you've a mind to, and you tell that bliddy preacher of yours down in the town that Mark's done more to making a man of 'ee than ever 'im an' 'is penny backscratcher 'as!"

Uncle Mark disapproved of my association with the *Observer*, which he always referred to as a penny backscratcher, an implied criticism of the lavish praise it doled out to its regular advertisers in reports of their various social and political functions. I said very little about my riding to Uncle Reuben, however; indeed, I kept it a close secret from everyone, for I was now itching to demonstrate my prowess to the only pair of eyes that mattered.

In the meantime I was making steady if less spectacular

117

progress with elocution and French, under the tutelage of Miss Beddowes, the daughter of a former king's messenger, who lived in one of the big, detached houses on Foxhayes Hill. Miss Beddowes taught elocution free of charge at the local evening Institute. She was a prim, rather leathery little spinster with a passion for dispensing education among the deserving poor. She ran the local Book Club that did duty for a county library in Whinmouth, and we became friends after I was able to help her in an appeal for unwanted books to stock the club shelves. It was through me that she was given a case of classics from Uncle Luke's store and she was so grateful that she invited me to tea in her big, old-fashioned house on the hill.

She was an energetic little woman whose undoubted talents as a teacher had been wasted while caring for invalid parents. Now that both were dead, and she was comfortably provided for, she was trying to make up for lost time by throwing herself heart and soul into all kinds of social work. Apart from running the Book Club and teaching at the Institute, she was a leader of the Girl Guides and the only female member of the Urban District Council. She was not, at first acquaintance, a very likable person, being entirely without a sense of humor and very much inclined to take herself too seriously, but I grew very fond of her later on and exploited her shamefully when she suggested that I should try to shed a Cockney accent that was beginning to crossbreed with West Country brogue.

From these lessons it was an easy step to elementary French, and I was gratified to discover that I had a mild flair for languages. Perhaps the work seemed easy because I was young and eager, or perhaps the real spur was the prospect of astonishing Diana in yet another field of accomplishment. At all events, Miss Beddowes was pleased with my progress and spared no pains to bring me to a point where my own interest in the subject supplied the main impetus.

I was totally ignorant of French when I came to her but this, I gathered, was an advantage.

"You've nothing to unlearn," she said crisply, when I apologized for my utter ignorance of the subject, adding:

"It's quite dreadful when one reflects that of all the thousands of children who are taught French at school not one—not *one*, mind you—can make himself or herself understood when they set foot at Calais. The trouble is, of course, that the method of teaching is ridiculous, quite ridiculous! A child is bored with unintelligible grammar before its ear is attuned to the language. Now you have a dozen of my oral lessons and listen to my set of records on the phonograph, and I'll have you speaking French as well and better than you can speak English before the next Christmas!"

She did not quite justify this boast but she went an appreciable way toward doing so. She spoke perfect French herself, having lived in France during the greater part of her youth, and all that summer, when I had completed any *Observer* assignments, I cycled up to the big, red brick house on Tuesdays and Fridays and sat in Miss Beddowes' study, listening to her carefully articulated conversational French and the excellent supplementary lessons on the horned phonograph. I can see her now, across the years of slumps, booms and wars, sitting bolt upright in a high-backed chair and making a series of careful mouths as she struggled to perfect my accent, both in French and my mother tongue. Sharp at nine o'clock the elderly maid would enter with cocoa and biscuits, and there was a fifteen-minute break while we talked town politics over refreshments. Then on would go the phonograph and lesson until the chiming clock on her mantelpiece struck ten, when she would rise, dust her plain dress with her hands, and say, "Well, John Leigh, that's all for tonight! Remember, you must *think* in French, beginning as soon as you wake, pull back the curtains, and say, 'Does it rain? Is the sun shining? Is my breakfast ready? Did I dream something pleasant?' "

These questions became for me a litany of the French tongue and throughout that summer I was always dreaming something pleasant, although the majority of my dreams came by day as I walked and cycled about Whinmouth Bay, filling my notebooks with lists of mourners, the names of stall holders, and ratepayers' complaints about the smell of decaying fish on the jetties.

Most of the daydreams were inspired by Diana's letters, a spate of which flowed steadily through the letter box all that summer. Their tone differed somewhat from the letters I had received during the previous term. It was at once more serious and affectionate, sometimes almost frighteningly so, for I think that Diana's stage of adolescence coincided with an upsurge of competitive romance among her friends at school. It was, as she confided later, the Thing to maintain a passionate correspondence with a boy friend, and as time went on, her letters became more liberally sprinkled with dears, dearests and darlings, each of which lifted me to a slightly higher plane of ecstatic contemplation.

There were photographs too, all kinds of photographs, snaps of Diana sitting on a log and displaying plenty of shapely leg, snaps of Diana in a hitched-up gym costume, snaps of Diana in a one-piece bathing costume, looking archly aware of her swiftly maturing figure, and each letter and photograph was read and studied a dozen times before being placed in a special box that I had acquired to receive them, a box shaped like a small treasure chest, with a lock and clasp wrought in the likeness of a heart pierced by an arrow.

It is easy to look back on the joy these letters brought me, and dismiss the romantic impulse as the emotional outlet of a half-grown youth, but what letters reach us in later life that compare with those exchanged by adolescents believing themselves to be deeply in love? I don't know whether the delight of receiving them was more or less than a grown man might feel on getting a letter from his fiancée, but I do know that I looked for the postman as impatiently as a shipwrecked sailor watches for a smudge of smoke on the horizon, and when Bill Clipper, the postman, hesitated outside the Mart before pushing one of Diana's blue and gilt envelopes through the letter box, I had to stifle a shout of triumph and then force myself to walk slowly downstairs, retrieve the letter and scamper off to my room to enjoy it in solitude.

120

One day, toward the end of June, she wrote saying that she had spent a day at Ascot and that Yves, the French boy we had met at the cinema, had been there with his father, the famous race horse owner. I was sick with jealousy all that week and some pictures that appeared in one of the smarter periodicals, showing a group composed of Yves, Diana, and their respective parents at the races, depressed me still further. Yves looked the complete man about town, with an expression of polite boredom on his thin, aristocratic face, but Diana, who was wearing a cloche hat and a flowered frock, looked utterly unattainable and almost as grown up as her mother, who was flirting a parasol and in the act, it appeared, of aiming a salvo of tortured vowels at the bland-looking Count de Royden. That was one picture of Diana that did not go into the chest. It was torn to fragments and dropped over the edge of the wharf.

A week later much better news arrived. Her parents, she informed me, had now departed for Capetown, and would be absent from England until the end of September. This meant that she would be virtually unchaperoned throughout the whole of her summer holidays. I began marking off the days to July 27th, the last day of term.

During the final week's vigil I busied myself with certain preparations. I bought a wicker chaise longue, a light, aged armchair, a pair of rugs, an occasional table, and a wall bookshelf, and transported them, piece by piece, up to the Folly.

It was no easy task, for I dared not hire a carrier, not even as far as the point where the path led onto the common, and the transfer of the chaise longue through acres of brambles from the Foxhayes road to Folly Wood occupied me the whole of one Saturday afternoon. The couch was too long for the spiral staircase, so the evening was spent in hauling it up to the top room of the tower by means of an improvised pulley.

The armchair was easier to carry since I was able to upend it on my head, but its passage from the ground to the tower casement proved hazardous, for it slipped its cradle halfway up and crashed down, almost pulling me after it.

By Sunday of the last weekend before Diana was due, however, I had furnished the tower room to my satisfaction, even adding an oil stove in case we should want to cook and a couple of framed reproductions, one of Botticelli's "Venus Rising from the Sea," and one of Fragonard's "The Swing," both stolen from Uncle Luke's store.

I should have liked to have lit a fire in the broken grate but I was afraid that the chimney would catch fire and someone would see the smoke. The crumbling old room looked cozy enough when I had finished, with a westering sun shafting through the unglazed windows and patterning the plaster walls, and I surveyed it all with quiet pride, reflecting that here was yet another surprise for Diana and one calculated to bring her special delight, for it was she who had suggested furnishing the Folly but had forgotten about it in the turmoil of the Easter holidays.

Once or twice during my comings and goings I caught a glimpse of one or other of Mr. Gayelorde-Sutton's keepers in the paddock behind the larch wood, but never once did I see the buzzards who lived there. It was strange how faithfully they fulfilled Diana's early prophecy concerning their appearance. They never showed up unless we were together.

On the morning of the day she was due to arrive I thought up another surprise, arranging with Uncle Mark's hired man to have the old cob, Justice, brought into the stables for the night and left to await my collection. Diana had written to say that she would arrive late at night and that I was to meet her as usual at the Folly, about seven A.M. the following morning. By six-thirty I was over at Uncle Mark's, had saddled Justice and ridden him over to the meeting place, tethering him under the trees and mounting the stairs in order to watch Diana ride from the wood on Sioux. I knew that Nellie, the pony, was out to grass and that she was very difficult to catch, so I banked on Diana leaving her free until she could bridle Nellie herself. Any horse or pony would come for Diana; she only

122

had to lean on a gate and coo, holding the bridle behind her back.

A few minutes after seven I saw stirrups flash on the edge of the wood and Diana came cantering out of the trees and across the paddock, taking a section of broken rail at a bound and calling softly to the big horse as it loped across the heather to Folly Wood.

She was bareheaded and the sun gleamed in her hair, turning it momentarily from dark chestnut to ash blond. When she was within fifty yards of the tower, Sioux scented Justice and whickered, and from my high vantage point I could detect Diana's surprise as she turned in the saddle and saw the cob tethered to the oak. Then I could wait no longer and pelted down the staircase, risking my neck in a frenzy of joy attributable not only to the pleasure of our reunion but to being abroad in Sennacharib on a warm summer's morning and living in the same world as Emerald Diana Gayelorde-Sutton.

I had some doubts that the endearments in her letters were conventional expressions and that, after the exchange of so many extravagantly romantic phrases, we should both feel shy at the actual moment of meeting. I think I was slightly apprehensive about this despite my excitement, but I need not have been, for the moment I emerged from the tower Diana dropped Sioux's bridle and ran to meet me, her face alight with the same joyful expression as I had noted when we kept our first tryst in Piccadilly.

She was as free of inhibitions as a child at a Christmas treat, throwing her arms around me and kissing me half a dozen times, squeezing my shoulders and laughing as she kissed.

"Jan, Jan, this is wonderful, wonderful!" she exclaimed, when she had paused for breath. "There was I, cursing everybody for not catching Nellie and spoiling our first morning's ride, and you've thought to bring your own horse after all."

"I've got lots of surprises," I told her, "come and see the first of them," and I pulled her up the staircase and proudly displayed the tower room, watching her prance from item to item with more delight than I had dared to hope when toiling through the brambles with that unmanageable chaise longue.

"It's wonderful!" she announced. "We can come here whenever we like, especially when it rains. You've got pictures, books and a stove . . . we can make tea and fry sausages . . . oh, it's lovely, Jan, and I love you for it!"

Then she kissed me again, more expertly this time, and the world stood still while I let my hand run along the back of her head. The scent of Sennacharib was in her hair and its freshness and sparkle in her eyes. I thought I had never seen anything so enchanting as the sweep of her long eyelashes, or the bloom on her cheeks.

"I'm so terribly in love with you, Diana," I told her breathlessly and she put her lips to my ear and whispered, "Me too, Jan! Darling, darling Jan! Me too!"

It was strange how swiftly and cruelly the magic of that morning was shattered and how the second of my surprises, the one that I had judged would please her most, was the cause of our first quarrel, a quarrel that, notwithstanding its triviality, was to leave a small scar in my heart that never wholly disappeared.

We returned to the wood and cantered knee to knee over the common as far as the Teasel bridge. As we went along, Diana glanced at me approvingly and I knew that she was noting my vastly improved seat and general management of a horse. Then my vanity urged me to make a false move, how false and ill-advised I could never have guessed, for it was to strike at three things that were fundamental in Diana's nature—her almost hysterical demand for independence, her pride in what she considered the most important of her achievements, and her love of horses.

At the corner of Teasel Wood, where the timber track skirted the northern boundary and ended by cutting across a corner of the covert and out to Uncle Mark's stables, I suggested we should change horses and race the last half mile. I was quite confident of being able to hold Sioux and secretly mortified by Diana's frank expression of doubt on the subject.

"She's very fresh, Jan," she said doubtfully, "and I honestly don't think you'd better."

I told her nothing of my lessons under Uncle Mark or the fact that I was regularly riding Polly, a mare of sixteen hands and often as much of a handful as the piebald Sioux. I wanted her to discover these things for herself and that was the real reason why I had brought the old cob to the first meeting, for I had planned to appear on Polly the following day.

"Oh come on, let me show you how much I've improved," I argued. "After all, you made me learn to ride, and if you're afraid of your own handiwork . . . !"

"Oh I admire you for wanting to, Jan," she said earnestly, "but I don't want her to run away with you and spoil your confidence and she will, you know, she's got a funny temperament with beginners and after all you *are* still a beginner."

This made me more determined than ever. I slid from Justice and threw her the reins.

"You climb down and I'll show you how much of a beginner I am!" I boasted. "I'll give you a head start and be at Uncle Mark's gate by the time you and that old screw have come into the straight."

"All right, Jan," she said quietly, "but take it easy. Don't touch her with your heels and keep her on a tight rein every inch of the way."

She dismounted and swung up on Justice. I got one foot in the stirrup and then shouted, "Away you go!"

The cob moved off in a collected canter and Sioux, savage at seeing her mistress disappear, bounded after her, so quickly that it was several yards before I could settle myself in the saddle and sort out the double bridle. When I did, and had Sioux well in hand, Diana was about thirty yards ahead, flying down the path and throwing up a screen of dust and chippings in her wake.

Sioux was certainly a flier. I gave her her head and she tore over the ground, overtaking and jostling Justice before we reached the wide curve. I was drunk with pride and as Diana swerved to give Sioux more room I shouted, "Take the brakes off!" and swept past her without con-

125

sciously noting her unsmiling expression as she crouched to avoid low-hanging foliage on the inside of the path.

I think I managed the horse well enough and rode straight at the fallen spruce that marked the end of the gallop. I cleared it, or nearly so, for there was the slightest jar as I forced Sioux to slacken her pace. We slowed down reluctantly and as we pounded up to Uncle Mark's gate there he was, leaning on folded arms, his big red face a study of delighted astonishment as he saw me bring the big mare to a standstill and leap from the saddle.

"Gor damme!" he exclaimed. "What you got there, Jan? 'Er's a praper job."

At that moment Diana came in view and I could see that she was driving the cob as fast and faster than he could go. When she came to the spruce tree she crashed through it rather than over it and Justice, landing badly, pecked and dug in his forefeet, throwing Diana over his head and into the blackberry bushes alongside the path.

Then I knew terror and ran toward her, shouting, as she rose unsteadily to her feet and picked up her crop. I reached her at a run as she was dusting dried leaves from her jacket, but she did not look at me when I stopped just short of her.

"Good Lord, Diana!" I gasped. "Are you hurt? You came a fearful cropper! I ought to have warned you about the jump but I forgot."

"Yes," she said almost inaudibly, "you ought."

She looked straight at me then and I saw a very different person from the eager, sparkling-eyed girl who had thrown her arms around me less than an hour before. Her eyes were now smoldering with rage and her wide mouth, the mouth that had covered my face with kisses so recently, was clamped into a crooked line, as though it was holding back a howl of vexation and injured pride.

She looked at me like that for a few seconds and I squirmed under the glance, for it had in it not only rage and hurt pride, but the kind of contempt she had used to humble Keeper Croker. Then she brushed past me to the gate and snatched Sioux's bridle from Mark's hand.

On the edge of tears I ran after her and caught her by

126

the arm just as she was passing in front of Sioux preparatory to mounting.

"Diana!" I quavered. "I'm terribly sorry about the jump. I thought I'd—"

I was going to blurt out my excuses, to confess on the spot to the part Uncle Mark had played in my tuition and how much I had wanted to surprise her, but she gave me no opportunity to submit this abject apology. Suddenly she pointed to the small fleck of blood on Sioux's shin. It was nothing much, just a scratch caused by one of the twigs of the spruce.

"You big show-off!" she screamed. "You cruel, stupid, clumsy lout! I never want to set eyes on you again, *never*, do you understand!"

Then, as though to make her meaning doubly clear, she stood back and swung her open palm at my face, landing a box on the ear that sent me staggering. Before I had recovered my balance she was in the saddle, had jerked Sioux's head around and was thundering down the ride toward the common. She cleared the spruce with a foot to spare and I gaped after her, my hand still clamped to my crimson cheek.

Uncle Mark spoke from the gate on which he had continued to lean throughout the entire incident.

"Ah," he murmured, "there's sperrit there. More real sperrit'n I ever zeed in a maid!"

I said nothing. Turning my back on him I went around behind the stables for my bicycle.

Diana was not the only one to show spirit that morning. For nearly a year now I had been completely under her spell and ready, if necessary, to lie down and die for her, but that did not mean I was ready to concede superiority to a fifteen-year-old schoolgirl, even such a girl as Emerald Diana Gayelorde-Sutton. This was my first experience of feminine unpredictability and I had no philosophy to match it. I had been lifted to the heights and cast to the depths in a period of less than an hour, and as I thought back over her behavior it seemed to me to display grossly bad manners and a lunatic's illogicality.

For a time my loyalty to Diana sought excuses for her. I told myself that she had been shaken and scared by the fall, that she had been upset by the graze Sioux had received at the jump, that she had lost the race after a good head start and was mortified by a defeat at the hands of a beginner. None of these reasons, however, justified the humiliation she had imposed on me in the presence of a witness, and my resentment was increased by the memory that my stock with Uncle Mark, a veteran admirer of pretty girls, had been reduced to nil at the very moment when it should have soared, for I had planned to introduce him to Diana with a great show of nonchalance. I pedaled myself into a fury during the ride home, arriving hot, bad-tempered and ready to quarrel with anyone.

As it happened the means for working myself into a tornado of self-pity were to hand at the office, for when I reached there someone was complaining to Uncle Reuben that I had done some careless reporting on a funeral the previous week and inserted the family mourners in the wrong order of precedence, thereby sparking off a family row. This kind of thing was often happening—the Whinmouthians set great store upon precedence in lists of mourners, and we usually had a good laugh about it the moment the indignant customer was halfway down the High Street. Today, however, it seemed to me that the entire world was conspiring to make what had promised to be a wonderful day into a hell of trivial irritation, and instead of apologizing I argued and then told Uncle Reuben, in the hearing of the complainant, that I was fed up with the pettiness of Whinmouth Bay and everybody in it. This was heresy to Reuben and he lost his temper, not only with me but with an unlucky printer's devil who had just upset a frame of type and wasted two hours' setting time. I was glad to escape from the strained atmosphere of the *Observer* and brood on my miseries in private during a walk over to the sports pavilion to get the latest scores of the tennis tournament.

Here, on the well-kept courts adjoining the squat pier, I found fresh fuel for my resentment against humanity. Whinmouth Sports Club organized a very popular open tennis tournament and first-class amateurs came from all parts of the West to take part in it. They were the kind of young people who spent the entire summer traveling from tournament to tournament in sports cars, and today they were a bitter reminder of Diana's class, the pampered children of the rich, who were never expected to earn money but were experts at spending it. I hated the sleek good looks of the girls and the studied heartiness of the men. I envied them their gay blazers and cars, their easy confidence and haughty bearing toward the ball boys and oafs like myself who were obliged to treat them with respect. They drifted about between sets calling one another "old bean" and "old thing." The men drank small whiskies and soda and flirted with the girls, while discussing games in incomprehensible slang.

Somehow the day passed with an interschool sports meeting, a couple of weddings, and a fruitless quest in search of details regarding a street accident. When I came off duty about eight o'clock I was slightly cheered to see that the sky was overcast and hear a rumble of thunder over the bay. That meant the stuffiness of the day would dissolve in one of our heavy local thunderstorms and all the visitors, particularly the tennis amateurs, might get wet! By nine o'clock the storm had burst and rain was slashing across the estuary, while thunder crashed and lightning flickered in a way that exactly suited my mood. I went to bed early, resolved to think out the phrases of a long farewell letter to Diana composed in terms of dignified sorrow. This, I thought, would be more calculated to wound her than would an explosive renunciation of my homage. Before I had made up my mind how to open the letter I was sound asleep.

Something awakened me with a start and I saw that it was almost one A.M. The downpour had ceased and the thunder was rumbling away on the other side of the river but steady rain was coming down and the guide light on the edge of the wharf, opposite my window, was the only relief in the inky blackness of the bay. I lay still listening for a moment and then the sound that must have awakened me came again, a loose rattle on the windowpane, as of sand or fine gravel flung from below.

I was out of bed in a second and had my head out of the window, peering down on the wharf. For a moment I could see nothing, then I detected the vague outline of a solitary figure standing on the edge of the narrow pavement and looking up.

"Jan!" it called, piteously. "Jan, it's me! Diana! Come down and let me in, Jan, I'm soaked!"

It was some seconds before I was able to persuade myself that I was not dreaming. Then, without stopping to put on the old mackintosh that I used for a dressing gown, I grabbed a flashlight and slipped downstairs and along the passage to the front door.

Aunt Thirza was a fanatical bolter and barrer. There was never anything worth stealing inside the house, and Uncle Luke cheerfully relied on a sixpenny padlock to keep thieves out of his store, but his wife went through an elaborate ritual of locking up each night and I knew that I could never open the front door without disturbing the household. I put my mouth to the letter box and directed Diana to go down the passageway to the kitchen door and opened the door leading to the yard. Diana came in dripping and I was still too astonished to utter a word of greeting.

Luckily for her, Aunt Thirza had another idiosyncrasy. She kept the kitchen stove going winter and summer. I turned on the light and stoked the fire, as Diana kicked off her sopping shoes and crouched close to it, extending her hands to the blaze and looking at me with one of her sly, sidelong grins.

"Well," she said, "aren't you going to gloat?"

"What on earth's happened?" I wanted to know. "What made you come down here at this time of night and in all this rain?"

She settled herself in Aunt Thirza's favorite wooden chair. "Conscience, I suppose," she said. "I was going to leave a letter if I hadn't been able to wake you. Look, I've got it ready, but there's no point in your reading it now. This is a much cozier way of confessing, Jan."

"It won't be very cozy if my aunt wakes up," I said. "If she finds me entertaining a girl at one in the morning, there'll be a fearful to-do."

"Where do they sleep, at the front?"

"Yes, in the room immediately over the store."

"I guessed they would, that's why I took the risk of throwing shingle. The awful thing was I wasn't absolutely certain of your bedroom. I was going to slip the letter through the door and bolt if anyone else popped their head out of the window!"

"How the blazes did you get down here at this time of night?"

"I borrowed the head gardener's cycle, it's always propped up against his cottage. I didn't mind that bit, it was fun riding through that deluge, and the lightning over the woods looked ever so pretty. I oughtn't to have liked it really, because coming here and getting so wet was a sort of penance, and you aren't supposed to enjoy penances, are you?"

There was nothing penitential about her. She was as gay and sparkling as the day we had first met and I had a strong conviction that, however abject her mood had been when she started out, the excitement of riding three miles through a thunderstorm, in the middle of the night, had offered more than adequate compensation for the discomfort suffered.

"Let me read the letter you were going to leave," I demanded.

She hesitated and the fleeting smile at the corners of her mouth worked wonders on my bruised spirit.

"Nnno," she said at length, "it's far to abject! I'd sooner tell you what's in it and keep what's left of my pride."

She ripped the sodden envelope in two halves and stuffed it into the coals. Then she turned toward me, put her arms around my neck and laid her wet cheek alongside mine.

"I'm terribly sorry I was so beastly, Jan darling, as sorry as it's possible to be! There, say I'm forgiven!" and she kissed me twice, once on the mouth and once on the forehead.

Her lips were the only warm part of her. When I put my arms on her shoulders I realized that she was soaked through and shivering. Then I suddenly realized I was in pajamas and quickly released her, stepping away so nervously that she threw back her head and laughed aloud.

"Why, Jan, you're blushing! I believe you're still a bit scared of me but I really can't blame you, can I, you surely haven't ever entertained a girl in your pajamas before! If you'd like to slip something on, I won't stop you and maybe you could find something dry for me. I don't want to catch cold and spoil the first week of the holidays."

It was in my mind to say that the holidays were already spoiled for us but then I realized that this was no longer true and that whatever had happened up at Uncle Mark's that morning was more than atoned for by her presence here and her affectionate apology. Then I had another shock, for she returned to the fire, pulled her sweater over her head and swiftly unzipped and stepped out of her short gray skirt. She shed her clothes as easily and naturally as if she were undressing in the privacy of her bedroom. With a start I pulled myself together and told her I would try to find some things she could wear, but I warned her to be as quiet as possible, for Uncle Luke was a light sleeper and would certainly rouse Aunt Thirza if he heard movements about the house.

I crept back to my room and foraged for a pair of corduroy slacks that I had outgrown and a roll-necked pullover that I used when I went swimming before breakfast. I also put on my mackintosh and slippers and on the way downstairs I pulled the chain of the toilet, hoping thus to account for any movement that had already been overheard.

When I re-entered the kitchen she was sitting before the fire wearing only a silk heliotrope slip. Her sweater, skirt, stockings, shoes and beribboned panties were spread on my aunt's clotheshorse.

She enjoyed my obvious embarrassment and smiled when I offered her the slacks and pullover.

"In a minute, Jan, let me get warm first. You wouldn't

happen to have a comb handy, I suppose? My hair's in a dreadful state, look at it!"

Her hair was certainly very wet and clung to her cheeks but it looked as pretty as ever, slightly darker than usual but retaining all its luster and vitality. I found her a comb in Aunt Thirza's workbox but when I offered it she said, "You comb it, Jan, I'd like that!"

"You ought to have something hot to drink," I said, looking her over with a tenderness that almost choked me. "I could make some cocoa, provided we got rid of all the evidence afterwards. Would you like cocoa?"

"Yes," she said, "but while it's brewing do my hair."

I put the kettle on the hob and got out the cups, milk, sugar and cocoa can. Then I took the comb and stood behind her chair, letting the damp tresses run lovingly through my fingers. I think it was by far the pleasantest task I was ever engaged upon.

"Now tell me why you came," I said.

"Now I'll tell you why I got in such a tizzy," she replied, leaning back and lifting her long legs onto the fender. "It wasn't really because of the jump, or the graze you gave Sioux, and it wasn't because you beat me and made nonsense of what I said about your being a beginner. All those things had a little to do with it, I suppose, and I was a bit rattled by the fall, but when I had time to think about it I knew what it was that had really upset me. It was your going to someone else to learn and taking away the only real advantage I had over you. Does that sound stupid to a man?"

It did really, for any one of the reasons she had dismissed would have made more sense to me at the time. It was hard to understand why she should have resented Uncle Mark's tuition, or what perverse line of reasoning made her regard her familiarity with horses as a hold over someone whose experiences in that field were so limited.

"You see, Jan," she went on, "the main thing I admire about you is the fact that you stand on your own feet and earn your own living, and the only accomplishment I had to compete with that was my riding, and being able to patronize you when we were together. I had a feeling that it was my handling of horses that impressed you more than anything else, and apart from that it was nice to be able to teach you something that you weren't likely to learn from anyone else. It was a kind of present but better than money, if you like."

The kettle began to steam but I was reluctant to stop combing. I let it simmer for a moment and said:

"Riding is only one of the things I like about you, Diana, and it isn't the most important by a long chalk. I like the way you accept me and take awful risks to be with me and I don't see how anyone in my position could keep from being terribly proud that someone as rich and lovely as you bothers to want me around. That was why I spent so much time at Uncle Mark's, learning to ride properly, and that was why I've been going up to Miss Beddowes' twice a week to learn French and how to speak properly. I don't want you to have to apologize for me wherever we go, and I've never forgotten what you told me over at Castle Ferry, about a person being anything they wanted to be, providing they wanted it hard enough."

"What's this about your learning French?" she demanded. "You never said anything about it this morning."

"It was to be another surprise, like furnishing the Folly and the riding," I said ruefully.

"Tell me about it."

I told her and she listened with the closest attention. When I had finished she reached up and took my hand in both of hers, pressing it down to her small breasts and holding it there. There was absolutely nothing provocative about the gesture. Like all Diana's gestures it was simple, natural and spontaneous. I could feel her heart hammering through the damp slip and the exquisite contact made the stuffy little room swim before me.

"That's the loveliest thing anyone's ever done for me, Jan, and it makes me love you more than ever! I did notice too, about the way you spoke, I mean. I'm not a snob about anything, especially accents, but it is the kind of thing I meant when we talked at Castle Ferry last hols. If speaking without an accent gives you more confidence, then it's right, and I think you were brave and clever to think of it. Say something in French, Jan!"

I said, "To learn French correctly one must think in the language. One must wake up in the morning, go to the window and say, 'Will the sun shine today? Am I hungry? Do I want my breakfast?'"

She squealed with delight, so loudly that I had to shush her.

"Jan, that's marvelous!" she exclaimed. "You've got a better accent than old Flossie, our Mam'selle. Say something else!"

I was so elated by her praise that I forgot all about Aunt Thirza and sang a verse or two I had learned from the phonograph, the opening lines of the inevitable *"Au Claire de Lune."* She looked at me with shining eyes.

"Well, who would have thought it! And you did it for me! Would you do *anything* for me, Jan? Would you?"

There was a kind of teasing ecstasy in the question, as though the contemplation of her power was intoxicating and she wanted to proclaim it.

"I'll make you a nice cup of cocoa and then you'd better put on my things, bundle up your wet clothes and get on home before someone finds us and sends a cable for your people," I told her. I said it casually but I felt very far from casual. The delight of being alone with her in the middle of the night was only slightly held in check by the fear of bringing Aunt Thirza down and having to go into a wealth of humiliating explanatory detail.

We sipped our drink and talked on. She seemed quite unconscious of her state of undress and I don't think that the fact that she was sitting in front of me, clad only in a semitransparent underslip, had any other effect upon me than that of increasing my wonder at her loveliness. Zest for life, and uninhibited enjoyment of the occasion seemed to me to be radiating from her smooth white shoulders and pink toes, and I thought I must have been mad to have felt so bitter and resentful about her a few hours before. Now it was enough to live in the same world; anything additional was a bonus.

About two-thirty we washed up the cups and then crept

back into the kitchen to see if her clothes were dry. The stockings and panties were so she slipped them on, laughing when I turned away and saying, gaily, "Poor Jan, I'm always embarrassing you! I wonder if the real Jan blushed the first time he saw Lorna dressing."

"The only thing you and Lorna Doone have in common is the habit of getting swains into awkward situations," I said, partly in jest but also to mask my shyness.

"And love for our particular Jan!" she said, and suddenly caught up my hand again and pressed it to her cheek, like a child demonstrating affection toward its parent. Then, as suddenly, she let my hand drop and stood away.

"Now, how do I look? Good enough for the road?"

She looked as lithe and supple and feminine as when she was dressed in her own expensive clothes. Even my ill-fitting slacks and grubby jersey could not deprive her of natural grace. We crept across the yard and retrieved the gardener's bicycle from the passageway. I walked with her as far as the end of the quay. The rain had ceased and the cobbled paving stones gleamed under the yellow glow of the guard light.

"Am I quite forgiven, Jan?" she said, as we went along.

"Nothing you could do would ever make me stop loving you," I told her, soberly. "If I never saw you again it wouldn't make any difference to how I've always thought about you!"

She stopped and looked at me across the bicycle. The lamplight shone in her hair, as she put her head on one side and said, "Dear Jan, I think you honestly believe that."

"I do believe it," I said.

"Kiss me good night, then."

We kissed lightly across the machine and then she swung herself onto the saddle with the same easy grace as she displayed mounting a horse. I watched her pedal away toward the High Street, remaining still under the light and listening to the rattle of the mudguard long after she had disappeared. Then, on feet that seemed not to touch the ground, I went home and upstairs to bed.

Chapter Six

I HAVE described this quarrel at length because it marked the very beginning of a subtle change in our relationship.

Up to that time the initiative had always been Diana's. She was the democratic little ladyship, I the adoring swain. Never, during our various meetings, had she gone out of her way to emphasize the social gulf between us, but whenever I reflected upon our friendship I did so with a kind of reverence, as though I were acting in a play in which she was the star and I an insignificant, walking-on character.

After our first quarrel and the midnight scene in our kitchen, the relationship between us altered. I lost none of my admiration for her but my pleasure in her company was no longer qualified by awe. I don't think she was conscious of this change, or of the more important fact that all future adventures and expeditions we shared taught me something new and vital about her.

I have a few special memories of the weeks that followed. My work enabled us to meet almost every day and Diana would occasionally appear at some of the local functions I attended on behalf of the paper.

I would see her waving at me from behind the ropes at an athletic meeting and would hasten over between events to ply her with ice cream and a free program. She would drift into a Methodist Sale of Work, or even the annual general meeting of the National British Women's Total Abstinence Union, taking a seat at the back and waiting for me to finish my work before plying me with questions about the activity I was reporting. She even appeared in the spectator's gallery of the petty sessional court and sat through several tedious hearings, listening with the closest attention to the charges, evidence and decisions.

I was sufficiently vain to imagine that she attended these

local events in order to see me as much as possible, but I had to admit, as time went on, that this was not the case Small-town life was totally unfamiliar to her and she was the kind of girl who welcomed the unfamiliar and applied to it an eager, questioning mind. After the first court session, for instance, she plagued me to explain everything I knew of the rules of evidence and the difference between indictable offenses and offenses that could be disposed of summarily. She also wanted to learn something of local politics and this led us to the council chamber, where she was fascinated by the apparent acrimony that existed between our local diehards and the group of business people styling themselves progressives.

Whinmouth Bay was expanding very quickly in those days and in the vanguard of its advance was a former jobbing builder, now a hotelier, called Singleton. Already a comparative newcomer like myself could notice changes about the town, evidence of Singleton's reiterated boast to put Whinmouth on the map.

Through the early part of the twenties his had been a lone voice but now, as the first postwar decade drew to a close, he won over a group of adherents, small businessmen who felt that they stood to gain by equipping the town to cater for a bigger influx of holiday makers.

Thus, almost imperceptibly, Whinmouth began to lose its Peggotty qualities. The promenade was extended, neat flower beds and parking areas began to replace the sand hills, a council estate was built where the Foxhayes road entered the town, and a rough-hewn swimming bath took shape in a rocky natural basin east of the jetty.

I witnessed these changes without either resenting or welcoming them. Uncle Reuben was a progressive and lent the *Observer's* weight to the business interests. Looking at Whinmouth Bay now, and remembering what it once was, I have the strongest sympathies with the old-fashioned councilors, men who fought a rear-guard action to keep the rates low and retain what was left of the town's salty charm. I remember that Diana was more farsighted than I and argued strongly against the Singleton group at the time, pointing out that no amount of money or enterprise

138

could convert our isolated community into a serious competitor with the big, established resorts and that we might as well nurse the benefits of that isolation as long as we could.

In this way we managed to see a good deal of one another but there is a curious blank in dating my memories from the first day and night of that summer holiday. I can recall a number of incidents but I can never assemble them in chronological order. Reckoning back, I know that when we met that first morning on the common I was fifteen and a half and Diana had just passed her fifteenth birthday, but from then until prior to her departure for Switzerland, a period of nearly two years, the development of a boy and girl friendship into that of young man and woman is confused and episodic. I am only sure that each highlight in our friendship taught me something new about her, filling a blank space in the picture of Diana that I carried about with me every waking hour. It was like coloring a printed outline in a child's painting book, and the portrait was never wholly completed.

There was the day she asked me to row her over to Nun's Island, the inviting conical rock that broke the surface of Nun's Bay and lay about a mile from the mainland of Sennacharib's coastal border.

I had asked Uncle Reuben to tell me about this islet and about the wreck that had given it its local name. He, in his grave way, had referred me to the files of the *County Press,* where I read all I could learn of the tragedy in which the vessel foundered during the southwesterly gale and all hands save one had been lost.

The grim story intrigued Diana and as we rowed along the coast from Whinmouth and struck out across the bay toward the island, she made me recount every detail. Was it a paddle steamer, like the one Grace Darling went after? How many nuns were drowned? How many crew? Did they find all the bodies? Was there any salvage? Who was the survivor, and what explanation did he give of the calamity?

I told her all I knew, and she was particularly interested in the recovery of the bodies, all but two of the crew having been found during the next few days and buried in a common grave at Whinmouth Churchyard. I had to promise to take her to see this grave and then she wanted to know if the two missing bodies were ever found. I had been saving this as a dramatic climax and told her that they had come to light years later, a pair of clean skeletons, found by Crusoe Jack, the lobsterman who once lived on the islet as a recluse and remained there until comparatively recent times. These two sailors were Negroes, firemen or greasers who had been trapped below when the vessel wedged itself on the rocks, and their skeletons were found after a particularly heavy gale had smashed the remaining timbers of the wreck and uncovered a deep drift of sand between the ridges.

"What happened to them then?" she demanded, her eyes shining with interest.

"Crusoe Jack buried them up near the trees," I told her, nodding to the tiny copse of pine and dwarf oak that crowned the highest part of the island.

"You mean they were actually buried in unconsecrated ground?"

"Well yes, I suppose so. Uncle Reuben told me that Crusoe Jack—he was as crazy as a coot—didn't say anything about finding them for months and then nobody bothered to have them dug up again and examined. I read the adjourned inquest report in the *County Press* and after Jack had described how and where he found them, the coroner said he saw no point in exhuming them and carting them over to the mainland churchyard; it had all happened so long ago."

"Well, I think that's terrible!" exclaimed Diana, to my great surprise. "I think we ought to *do* something about it."

"What on earth can we do?" I protested.

She thought for a moment, biting her lip, and then, as our skiff grounded on the tiny beach about a hundred yards west of the wreck, she jumped into the shallows and ran ashore shouting, "Come and show me the graves, Jan!"

We went up a gully and climbed the knoll to the trees.

Apart from a magnificent view there wasn't much to see. The island was about two hundred yards long by a hundred yards wide, and the slopes below the knoll, which boasted some twenty trees, was covered with couch grass and a low, fungus type of scrub. On the southern slope, facing the open sea, was the ruin I recognized as Crusoe Jack's shanty, now nothing but a roofless structure of pine boughs and driftwood, with a stone chimney and a pebbled floor. We poked about for a spell and eventually found the graves or rather grave, for there was a single mound with a cross fashioned from driftwood, now leaning at an angle of forty-five degrees. She stood and stared down at it for so long that my own interest began to wane; I was more eager to inspect what remained of the actual wreck.

"He didn't even carve the names," she said at last. "Good Lord, Jan, they bury dogs with more dignity and I'll tell you the heart of the matter, it's because they were only black men!"

This aspect of the resumed inquest had not occurred to me and I readily agreed that the lack of ceremony was probably due to the fact that the two men had belonged to some other religion—that, and the lapse of years between the sensation of the wreck and their discovery as a pile of bones. Suddenly she caught me by the arm and I recognized the expression that always heralded some extraordinary and involved plan.

"Can you get off tomorrow evening and bring the boat along as far as the landslip below Nun's Head, Jan? I could meet you there and we could do it. . . . I'll have all the things we shall need and I can ride over on Sioux. I'll hobble her in the meadow, behind the Pilot Inn, and pick her up on the way back."

"Well yes," I told her, quite bewildered, "I could row along and pick you up easily enough but—"

"Don't ask any more questions now, Jan," she said imperatively. "I'm not sure whether I can manage it without help, but I'd like to try and I'd like to do this on my own —all on my own, do you understand?"

She would not explain any further and seemed then to

dismiss the fate of the two Negro firemen, dragging me down the gully to the humps that were all that remained of the wreck and pointing out the barnacle-covered frame that had once been the paddle wheel of the vessel. She seemed preoccupied during the pull back to Whinmouth and when we said good-by and she rode off on the gardener's ill-used bicycle, she seemed hardly to be aware of me until I called after her and reminded her of our appointment the following day.

"That's right," she said, "about five o'clock! I'll be here on the beach."

She was, too, a lonely little figure, squatting on a lobster pot, with the great red wall of Nun's Head rising behind her like a backcloth in a pantomime. As I pulled around the rocks and hailed her she jumped up, flourishing what looked like a cross, of the kind Peter the Hermit held in my illustrated volume of *The Crusades*.

"What on earth have you got there?" I asked, noting that she was in a high state of excitement, so much so that she could not wait for me to beach the skiff but dashed into the water and flung herself down in the stern, nearly upsetting us.

"We're going to have a proper burial service," she said. "It's high time it was read, and you're going to officiate! I'd like to do it myself, of course, but as I'm a woman it wouldn't be right; it would seem too much like a joke and this isn't a joke, it's terribly in earnest."

I gaped at her for a moment and then looked more closely at the cross. It was neatly jointed, freshly varnished, and finished off with plain black lettering that read: *Two Unknown Seamen. R.I.P.*

She watched me nervously as I examined it and then, when I looked at her, she began to blush, looking so adorably pretty and confused that my throat went dry and I wanted to fall on my knees before her, kiss her hands and tell her what a lovely, exciting girl she was and how proud I was to act as her partner in such an enterprise.

"Then you . . . you don't think it's silly, do you, Jan?"

"No," I said, truthfully, "I think you're very wonderful to think of it, Diana."

142

She was pleased with that and we rowed out to the islet in silence, a silence we enjoyed. When we had beached the boat and thrown out the anchor she took my hand and led me along the high-water mark to gather anemones, and then, as the sun touched the rim of the bay and sent a flood of red-hot brass across the water, we climbed the knoll and replaced Crusoe Jack's rotting pole with our cross. I remembered then that I knew barely a word of the burial service and mentioned as much, almost in a whisper. The hush, the solemnity of the act, and Diana's nervous excitement had combined to extinguish the last sparks of frolic from the occasion.

"I've thought of that," she said and from a satchel worn as a shoulder bag she produced a handsomely bound Book of Common Prayer, with the silk marker inserted in Service for the Burial of the Dead.

She placed the anemones at the foot of the cross and then took her place at the foot of the grave, first covering her head with a white scarf and tying the ends under her chin.

"Go on, Jan," she prompted, very gently, "don't be afraid." And when I still hesitated, fumbling with the prayer book: "You needn't think God doesn't approve, I'm sure He does. I'm quite sure He put the whole thing into my head!"

I was grateful for this assurance and at once began to read, clumsily at first but with mounting confidence. I remember shuddering a little when I came to the passage about worms destroying the body, but I cheerfully raised my voice on the cadences of the Ninetieth Psalm. When I had worked through to the piece preceding the final prayer Diana spoke the responses and our voices rose together in that quiet, lonely place, with only a curious herring gull as an audience. When at length I closed the book and coughed with returning embarrassment, I noticed that her eyes were brimming with tears but I was too near shedding them myself to remark upon the fact. She said, after an awkward pause, "Thank you, Jan dear, you read it quite beautifully," and she took my hand, squeezing it as we walked through the soft sand to the boat.

I lay awake a long time that night pondering what we had done. It seemed to me that the incident had revealed an entirely different Diana from the girl whose exploits included thwarting her mother, tearing about on horses and poking fun at the conventions piled up around her.

It seemed that I had stumbled across a Diana in whom a religious training was something more than a convention, someone who took her recent confirmation seriously, who had an adult sympathy for the friendless and underprivileged, and I wondered if this helped to explain her championship of me when I was in the grip of Keeper Croker's half nelson, or her deep humility after the quarrel we had at the stable. I fell asleep at last, luxuriating in the memory of Diana standing with downcast head, her back to the sea, her white scarf fluttering in the evening breeze, and somehow, in trough of sleep, this endearing memory transformed itself into a picture of Diana standing in her bridal veil before the altar at Oare Church. She was undoubtedly Lorna but I was not conscious of standing beside her as a devoted Jan.

2.

Not all my recollections of Diana's exploits at this period in our lives were as solemn or serene as the latter-day burial service. One particularly is in direct contrast, an uproarious occasion about which I can never think without a chuckle.

This was the intrusion of Alice, the prize sow, into the Conservative Fete held in the grounds of Heronslea, and it revealed to me yet another aspect of Diana, the reckless practical joker, forerunner of the Bright Young Thing who intrigued British newspaper readers a year or so later.

It must have been during the early summer of 1931, when the country was approaching the financial crisis that unseated MacDonald's short-lived government. The Whinmouth constituency was predominantly Conservative and had never returned anyone but a Conservative Member. Our Member at this time was Major Fayne, a terse, soldierly man and, as might be expected, high in favor at Heronslea House where he was a frequent visitor.

Mrs. Gayelorde-Sutton was a very active Conservative. She was president of the Constituency's Women's Association, and organizer of a seasonal succession of Conservative functions, one of which was the annual May Fayre, an ambitious project organized for the dual purpose of raising funds and propagating the gospel according to Stanley Baldwin and Mabel Gayelorde-Sutton.

I attended all these functions as a matter of course and had already acquired the journalist's blasé indifference to politics, regarding them more as a source of copy than the means of advertising a social system under a party banner. It was shortly before the advent of aggressive fascism and fascism's chief exponent at that time, the lamented Benito Mussolini, was regarded as a huge joke by Conservatives, Liberals, and Socialists alike.

As the date for the May Fayre approached, marquees and sideshows sprouted on the broad lawns of Heronslea House, and Diana, together with some of the more socially elevated young locals, were enlisted as usherettes, all the girls being attired in the Quaker uniform of high bodice, gray ankle-length skirt and starched headdress.

Diana did not take kindly to this form of regimentation and the fuss, the uniform, and the inroads these events made into her freedom had already colored her political outlook.

"It's absolutely daft!" she complained to me, the evening before the Fayre, when I had slipped over to Heronslea on the pretext of getting advance data. "Quakers and Puritans weren't Conservatives, were they? They lopped poor old Charles' head off, didn't they? And a good job too, if he was anything like Major Fayne and all the old hens who cackle around him up here. Talk, talk, talk, all about what's happening to their filthy money! As if that was the only thing that mattered to the country! You aren't a Conservative, are you, Jan? I shall loathe you if you say you are!"

I said I supposed that I was a Liberal, like my Uncle Reuben, but she declared that she was going to vote Red when she was twenty-one and that what was needed anyway in Parliament were lots more women who would not be so beastly careful of their dignity. By this I inferred that Diana inclined to the Left because her mother was so staunchly Right.

"If they must put us in fancy dress," she went on, "we ought to look like orange girls, at the time of Nell Gwyn, you know—something off the shoulder, to get the men to buy more programs and draw tickets and suchlike!" She looked despairingly at the array of tents and stalls that had transformed the broad sweep between the terrace and the Shepherdshey road into a genteel fairground. "Well," she added, "I'm praying for rain. That'll put the kibosh on everything!"

"It rained last year," I told her, "but they all crowded into the marquee to hear the Member's address. You couldn't breathe in there and Uncle Reuben said they didn't give him elbow room to write notes."

At the thought of a damp and dripping fiasco she cheered a little. "Come and say hello to Alice," she invited, and when I inquired into the identity of Alice, she told me that Alice was the Heronslea prize sow who, together with a lusty litter, was being offered by Mrs. Gaylorde-Sutton for the fete skittle prize.

Alice was the kind of prize that only Mrs. Gaylorde-Sutton would offer. She was undoubtedly the largest pig in the West. Penned in a temporary sty under the avenue beeches, she lumbered to and fro like a malevolent dinosaur, herding her squealing litter out of range of Diana's bamboo cane and grunting maledictions on those who had transferred her from a comfortable paddock sty to a few square yards of unfamiliar enclosure.

"I love pigs," said Diana, dreamily, "they're so gloriously antisocial. She's very unhappy in there. Do you think we could let her out and give her a bit of a root around under the trees?"

"No jolly fear," I told her. "You leave her where she is! She looks a killer to me and if she got loose there would be hell to pay and I'd be sure to get mixed up in it somehow."

"Well," said Diana, "I'll tell you what, the minute old Pumpjaw"—this was Diana's pet name for the Honorable and Gallant Gentleman representing Whinmouth— "pauses for breath, and all the other old pumpkins on the platform start billing and cooing, you nip out to the old coach house. I'll meet you there with some choice refreshments and wine. The only thing good about this show-off is the grub, it's going to be scrumptious!"

I promised to keep the appointment and went about my business. The following morning a glance at the sky told me that Diana's prayers were about to be answered. By midday the rain had begun to fall, lightly at first but very heavily by midafternoon, the time fixed for the Member's address. Provision had been made for this contingency and everyone crowded into the vast marquee. By the time Major Fayne had got under way the heat inside the tent was suffocating, the sour smell of wet canvas and crushed grass combining with that emanating from the clothes of three hundred damp constituents, packed on benches each side of a narrow gangway.

I was wedged under the platform and not unhappily situated, for there was an exit flap within a few yards of me and a current of air kept the people on the platform awake throughout the long-winded address. The people farther back, however, began to get restive as Major Fayne swam through a sea of Socialist disasters toward the global trouble spot in Manchuria, and thence to the value of the pound. He was about to inveigh against Snowden's monetary policy when there was a ripple of laughter at the back of the tent, followed by a volley of startled exclamations and then two individual screams, as loud and piercing as those of a radio heroine.

Major Fayne stopped speaking but remained standing, his overworked jaws agape, his slightly poppy eyes fixed on the scene of mounting confusion at the extreme end of the long marquee. Then Mrs. Gayelorde-Sutton jumped up and shouted something and after that there was a sudden scramble on the part of the platform party to climb down and head for the exit.

As they all tried to do this in unison, and because the

trestle platform was high and there was only a single pair of steps, the result was a confused struggle just above my head. A row of potted hydrangeas broke away from their fastenings and fell onto the press table, scattering mold over myself and the *County Press* reporter and adding to the general tumult. Mrs. Gayelorde-Sutton rushed past me as I was picking myself up and I saw that her face was white with rage.

I hurried after her toward the flap but the platform contingent had now reached level ground and was trying to charge the exit in a body.

Major Fayne fell headlong over the taut guy rope and somebody, with more loyalty than sense, stooped to pick him up, so that others fell and I was turned back into the rapidly emptying body of the marquee and the heart of a scene of wildest confusion. It was like an illustration from an improbable book of Irish country life. Alice's litter was advancing rapidly up the narrow aisle between the close-packed seats; a yard or so behind, grunting and snorting like a mad elephant, came Alice herself. Behind Alice dodged two of the Heronslea estate workers, armed with goads, both screaming directions at one another and obviously out of touch with a deteriorating situation.

The constituents, mad with fear, were scrambling out of the marquee in every direction, the majority diving under side curtains, others battling their way to the open flap behind Alice's cautious pursuers. As I watched, aghast at the shambles, the marquee emptied like a tube and Alice followed her squealing litter out through the platform exit.

I was too shocked to see the funny side of the incident and after gathering up my notebook I went into the open and pushed through the chattering, gesticulating Mayfayrers to the coach house. Inside, weeping with laughter, was Diana, and I knew at once that she had been responsible for the appearance of Alice at the meeting.

It was some minutes before she could speak.

"Oh Lord! Oh Heaven! Did you see it? Were you there? Did you see the laughter turn to terror the minute Alice showed up in pursuit of the babies?"

I had to laugh too, but the reflection of what might have

148

resulted from such a reckless practical joke sobered me almost at once.

"It was a crazy thing to do, Diana," I protested. "Supposing she'd savaged someone? Supposing there had been a real panic and people had got trampled?" Then my journalistic curiosity prompted me. "How on earth did you manage it, anyway, and how do you know you won't get found out? Your mother would half kill you for this, it'll make her a laughingstock all over the county!"

"If I tell will you swear to keep mum—for ever and ever?"

"Yes, of course."

"Even though you're a reporter?"

"You don't imagine I'd sneak on you, do you?"

She stopped laughing then and looked at me with her teasing, half-mocking expression, eyes half-closed, head inclined to one side.

"Dear Jan," she murmured, "it's very flattering to have a newshawk like you put love before duty." Then, seeing my face cloud, as it usually did when she made fun of me, she put both hands on my shoulders, kissed me on the cheek and told me how she had waited until everyone except the Heronslea staff was inside the tent and then let her horse Sioux out of the paddock to graze among the stalls.

"I knew anyone who was around would try to catch Sioux before she bumped into anything, and you know how difficult she is to halter if I'm not about. Well, it worked just as I knew it would. They all went after Sioux, who cantered around behind the house, and when they were out of the way I drove Alice's litter toward some meal I had scattered outside the marquee. When they were nicely clustered there I let Alice out, knowing that she'd make straight for them and that some of them would trot into the tent. I didn't bargain for such a complete uproar, though! The people at the back were ever so glad to see the piglets, because they were so bored, but they all lost their heads when Alice appeared. Don't worry, Jan," she added, seeing that I still looked harassed, "I let her loose

149

for a bit last night and the estate hands think the pen was insecure. I won't get into trouble over it."

"*They* might!" I grumbled, remembering Mrs. Gayelorde-Sutton's savage expression during the scramble for the exit.

"Oh no," she said calmly, opening a basket and offering me savory pies and sandwiches, "I thought of that! I warned Mummy last night that Johnson, the pigman, thought that Alice ought to go back to her sty on the day but she pooh-poohed the idea and told me to tell Johnson to leave Alice where she was. She always knows all the answers, you see, and this might help her to learn to listen to someone else for a change! Here, have some pâté, it's good, and open this bottle of hock I pinched for us. I brought a corkscrew."

I took the bottle and drew the cork, my misgivings less than half resolved by her assurances.

"All the same, I bet there'll be repercussions," I said gloomily, and, as always where Diana's family was concerned, my pessimism was justified. Mrs. Gayelorde-Sutton's counteroffensive opened the following Saturday, and I narrowly missed becoming its first victim.

Uncle Reuben always stayed in the office on Saturday morning, mainly for the purpose of hearing complaints. We could always rely on a steady stream of irate readers each Saturday, people whose names had been omitted or misspelled in a sale-of-work notice, or the principal mourners I have already mentioned, whose claims to precedence had been jumped by mere in-laws in a funeral report. Uncle Reuben never lost his temper with these idiots and nearly all of them were soothed by his bland explanations. I was engaged in plotting next week's tide table when the door flew open and in stormed Mrs. Gayelorde-Sutton, with her big-headed husband in silent tow and everything about them promising a brisk engagement. She flourished a copy of our paper under my nose but I wasn't unduly worried by that, because we had carried a straight report of the incident and there was nothing in it that had not appeared in the *County Press* on the previous day. Uncle Reuben offered her a chair but she refused it, demanding to know the identity of the reporter who claimed to have witnessed the appearance of Alice into the marquee. When Uncle Reuben gravely indicated me she whipped a small newspaper cutting from her handbag and pushed this under my nose.

"Then Ai suppose Ai have yew to thank for this!" she shrilled.

Before I could protest, Uncle Reuben relieved her of the cutting and glanced at it briefly. It was a piece written by the columnist of a London Socialist weekly, in which the writer had made use of the advantages to be derived from the preoccupation of ex-Premier Baldwin with pig breeding. It was a heavy little gibe, beginning:

We are interested to hear that Stanley Baldwin's interest in pigs has spread to his backbenchers and that one of them, the Honourable and Gallant Member for a West Country Constituency, is now more Catholic than the Pope, inasmuch as he actually invites pigs to his public meetings. . . .

There was a crude cartoon clipped to the extract, the drawing portraying the Whinmouth Member and a hawk-visaged supporter (who might or might not have been a caricature of Mrs. Gayelorde-Sutton herself) standing on a platform and addressing a row of attentive pigs. It was entitled "Pigs in Clover."

I was wondering how Mrs. Gayelorde-Sutton came to connect our little paper with the report and cartoon but her next declaration solved the mystery.

"There were only two pressmen actually present in the marquee," she wailed, "and one of them was *thet* boy! Now Ai've been assured by the *County Press*—a respectable Conservative organ, I might add—thet they had no contact with the London papers as a whole, or this scurrilous publication in particulah!"

"And what makes you think it originated from us?" asked Uncle Reuben, innocently.

For a moment Mrs. Gayelorde-Sutton seemed disconcerted, then she rallied and did her best to intimidate him with her hard blue eyes.

"You *must* hev!" she said. "How else would they have heard of it?"

Uncle Reuben regarded her sadly. I have never admired him so much as I did on that occasion, for somehow he made a reality of the vaunted majesty of the British press, standing, as it were, foursquare as the champion of free speech from Paine and Cobden onwards.

"Mrs. Gayelorde-Sutton," he said, consciously inserting a heavy sigh into his voice, "this incident actually occurred and was faithfully and fairly reported in two West Country papers. Copies of those papers have since been mailed all over the world and their contents, I don't doubt, have since been read and digested by journalists of every political creed and shade of opinion. There is nothing, so far as I am aware, to prevent any such journalist using this factual base as the skeleton of a partisan gibe at you and your party. We can hardly be held responsible for the use made of our straight reporting in any corner of the globe!"

It was a dignified rebuke, magnificently delivered, for somehow it conjured up the picture of the arrival of a bundle of *Whinmouth & District Observers* on the busy quays of Hong Kong or the railway sidings of Chicago, where hordes of white, black and yellow journalists were queueing to seize and comment upon the intrusion of a fat sow into a marquee full of Whinmouth Conservatives. It absolved us from all consequences of their several interpretations, at the same time elevating us to Olympian isolation, alongside the shades of W. T. Stead and the late Lord Northcliffe. Its effect upon Mrs. Gayelorde-Sutton, however, was less salutory than upon her hitherto silent husband, who rose, a little stiffly, and laid a restraining hand upon his wife's glove, addressing her in a thin, nasal voice that I now heard for the first time.

"Come, come, my dear," he said, quietly but not meekly, "you've had your say and you've got your answer! Go back to the car while I have a private word with the editor."

To my intense surprise she obeyed him. Without a word of protest she swung round on her stiletto heels and clacked out of the office, leaving behind her a pleasing aroma of perfume to join hopeless battle with the reek of dust, printer's ink, moldering newspapers and Uncle Reuben's semilethal tobacco.

"Well, sir?" demanded Uncle Reuben, his tone hardening now that he found himself addressing a member of his own sex. "I trust you are satisfied with my explanation? Not that I am under any obligation at all to offer you one, even supposing it was I myself who had telephoned Fleet Street. This is fair comment, you understand? Nothing libelous *there,* so don't waste time and money on lawyers!"

It occurred to me that this little speech was a bit high-handed, but Mr. Gayelorde-Sutton did not resent the advice. He just stood blinking heavy-lidded eyes, his head looking more and more like a pink egg balanced on the extreme end of a collared cabbage stalk.

"My wife is naturally upset," he said very civilly. "She feels that this unfortunate incident has been magnified into something calculated to make her a laughingstock among her friends. I did point out before she called, however, that the local press could not be held responsible and I feel your explanation is a fair and an honest one, sir. I would, in passing, like to proffer my apologies to this young gentleman, who might have made a good deal more capital of the occasion than in fact he did, yet still acted within his rights as a er . . . gentleman of the press! Good day, sir, and thank you for your courtesy."

He left us then and Uncle Reuben looked after him sympathetically. I felt a little dizzy, partly with relief but also with elation, for up until then I had never taken Gayelorde-Sutton into consideration as a man or the father of Diana. He had been a mere symbol of wealth, and a caricature of one at that. I had never forgotten his pitiful appearance at the Heronslea meet on Boxing Day. Diana hardly mentioned him and I suppose I had already written him off in my mind as a hen-pecked nonentity. I saw that he was more than that and I was now able to regard him if not as an ally, at least as neutral in the conquest of Diana. A man like that, I reasoned, would at least be fair-minded about his daughter's choice of a husband.

I could hardly wait to recount the scene to Diana and

when I saw her at the Folly that same evening I was deflated by the discovery that she not only knew all the essentials of the interview but had, in a sense, engineered her father's attitude by taking him on one side and pointing out that Mrs. Gayelorde-Sutton's attack upon a local paper would only injure the cause of the Conservatives in the district. I was warmed, however, by her comment upon an aspect of the matter that had not even entered my head—my honoring of the promise I had given her to keep her part in the matter a close secret.

"I wouldn't have blamed you if you'd blurted out the truth, Jan," she said. "After all, I don't see why you should get a rap over the knuckles for something I did and I don't mind saying I had the wind up a bit when I heard that Mother intended storming into your place about it. You see, for all I knew, it was you who had sent the piece to London!"

It saddened me to reflect that she could even contemplate a betrayal of confidence on my part, to say nothing of presumed willingness on my part to see her family ridiculed. When I told her this she laughed and gave me one of her side-tilted looks.

"You're a real old-fashioned one, Jan! I believe you're a masochist and would enjoy dying for me. I believe it would give you no end of a kick. What is it, Jan? I'm not beautiful and sometimes I'm not very nice to you. I'm not going to pretend that I don't *like* having a true-and-gentle-knight, and I'll always come back to you in the end, you can be quite sure of *that,* but—"

She broke off, as though suddenly deciding she had said enough on the subject. I was far from satisfied, however, and pressed her to say whatever she had begun to say. This brought an obstinate expression to her face.

"It doesn't matter," she said, pettishly. "I'm not in the mood to say it right now and I won't!"

Earlier in our association I should have pressed for an explanation but I was learning very quickly about Diana, and took the hint. It was never the slightest good goading her into explaining anything. Her mother had followed that course throughout her childhood and all she had

154

earned by it was resentment that came close to hatred. We let the subject drop there and then, and whenever we touched on it in the future we did so in a mood of hilarity.

3.

The next glimpse I had of a hidden facet in Diana's character was afforded by a trivial incident that took place at the Whinmouth Fancy Dress Parade.

One of the annual events on my calendar was the Whinmouth Winter Carnival, a week of local entertainment sponsored by a veteran committee and aimed at popularizing the town and raising money for the Cottage Hospital and St. John Ambulance Association.

Few British annuals are as profitless as the seaside carnival, and our local affair was no better and no worse than the average small-town carnival. The Englishman is fundamentally devoid of carnival spirit and even if a sense of civic duty, and frequent draughts of alcohol, induce him to don a paper hat and prance about his familiar streets, the weather is usually at odds with the forlorn strings of bunting and determined good cheer.

Our event was organized by tradesmen who were prevented from staging a summer carnival by the demands of their businesses during the period, May to September. Thus the carnival was always held in the third week of October and had to compete with autumn gales, as well as the national distaste for public enjoyment.

The torchlight procession of tableaux was usually a spectacular affair, providing the rain held off, but somehow the carnival, as a carnival, could never divest itself of its overcoat. The only weatherproof event of any size was the Baby Show and Children's Fancy Dress Parade, both held in the Church Hall, in Fish Street.

I was very busy throughout this event, collecting the names of countless Bo-Peeps and Jack Horners. I had, indeed, been busy throughout the week, so much so that I had overlooked the fact that Mrs. Gayelorde-Sutton, in her role of local patroness, had agreed to preside over the panel of judges for the children's parade. I did not remember this interesting fact until I arrived at the hall for the final selection of prize winners.

The children had been divided into various age groups and there were prizes for the first boy and first girl in each class. The organizers, however, had overlooked the dire need for consolation prizes, and as some of the mothers had gone to very considerable trouble to dress the competitors the stewards were faced with the problem of coping with a dozen or so bitterly disappointed finalists in each group.

We were accustomed to trouble with the Baby Show mothers, and the acrimony among the parents grouped at the far end of the hall after the judges had made their final selections was always regarded as something of a joke among Whinmouth tradesmen. Invariably there were threats that children who had failed to win a prize would not be called upon to face humiliation the following year, but nobody took these threats seriously. Each year the number of competitors increased and the two events were enormously popular, over a hundred children entering the parade in costumes that made judging a difficult task.

Not that its demands worried Mrs. Gayelorde-Sutton. She sat on the dais like an Ice Queen, flanked by a self-effacing Chairman of Council and his even more self-effacing wife. Neither of these worthies had the slightest say in the selections. Deftly and mercilessly Mrs. Gayelorde-Sutton sifted the grain from the chaff. When she had made up her mind she beckoned the winner and extended the palm of her hand to the rejects. The latter gesture was exactly like the Phoenicians' rejection of Celtic furs, in the famous picture dealing with early British trade.

It may have been her regal manner, or it may have been the fact that this year's competitors included a larger sprinkling of intractable children that caused this year's six-to-eight class for girls to develop into a scene of lamentation. Rejects were required to move away from the dais as soon as they had been judged and pass behind the stage and through to the dressing rooms. The hall was packed and spectators were sitting in the aisles, so that there was no way in which the spurned Maid Marians and Columbines could fly to their mothers for comfort. They had either to move around behind the stage or stand blubbering under the eyes of the judges.

There were, as I remember, nine rejects in this class, two others having been warned to stand by for the grand parade while the judges passed on to the nine-to-eleven class.

The trouble began when one little girl, dressed in sacking meant to represent the tatters of a scarecrow, burst into tears the moment she realized that she was not a prize winner and then made an unsuccessful dash for the phalanx of spectators.

She was headed off by a grinning steward and the event caused a titter, but the laughter died under the volume of howls touched off among the other rejects. In a few seconds eight children were screaming their heads off and Mrs. Gayelorde-Sutton, more than equal to the occasion, began to strike a compeer's gong and shout, "Cleah the areah! Ai can't continue while *thet's* going on!"

Mrs. Gayelorde-Sutton intimidated most people. Two of the stewards leaped forward to shoo the wailing children into the dressing room, but none would willingly be removed, so the most active steward tucked one child under each arm and tried to shepherd the others with his knees.

At this juncture several indignant mothers jumped up from the body of the hall and began to contribute to the outcry. Mrs. Gayelorde-Sutton sullenly continued to beat her gong, and the laden steward shouted for help.

It arrived from an unexpected quarter. At the height of the uproar Diana swept from the dressing-room arch, lifted the squealing scarecrow, placed a fairy doll almost as large as the child in her arms, pointed to the arch through which she had moved, and then held up seven fingers!

The action was so expertly timed and so deftly executed that all the children, including the two held by the perspiring steward, ceased their squalls and gazed ecstatically from Diana to the doll and then back to Diana again.

Mrs. Gayelorde-Sutton stopped beating the drum and stared bleakly down on her daughter but the audience cheered, as well they might. I remained staring at Diana as she gathered the children in a bunch and swept them into the rooms behind the stage.

It all happened with the speed of a dream sequence. When I had recovered from my surprise I sidled away from the stewards' table and went into the dressing rooms, but inside I stopped short near the door, looking in upon another extraordinary sight. There was Diana, surrounded by children, each of them squealing with delight as she placed a large package in each pair of upraised arms. Scarecrow was seated at her feet, crowing over the fairy doll.

Another child, wearing a ballerina's frock from which most of the tinsel was missing, was nursing a huge Dutch doll. A third child had just torn the wrappings from a cardboard box and found an exquisite doll's set, in blue and gold china. Each of the others had an expensive-looking gift of one sort or another and Diana was exercising complete control over the brood. There were no bickerings, no displays of greed, just a rhapsodic harmony that recalled the visit of Mrs. Do-As-You-Would-Be-Done-By to Kingsley's water babies. It was as though some other and infinitely mature being had taken possession of Diana and appeared miraculously to arbitrate among us lesser mortals, as though she had suddenly burst from the chrysalis of adolescence and become a patient, tender woman, with a vast experience in the art of handling small children. They looked up at her as though she were a goddess sent to extricate them from an intolerable situation and when I drifted into the room not one of them noticed me, or lifted their eyes from Diana.

I don't think I have ever been as moved, or as genuinely surprised, as I was at that moment, but when Diana greeted me she did not appear to regard her situation as anything other than commonplace. She said, very offhandedly, "Oh, hello, Jan! I rather hoped you'd pop in; go out to the car and help Redman to bring in the rest of the boxes. I think there will be enough to go around."

Mutely I did as she asked. Outside in the forecourt the Bentley was parked and Redman, the aloof chauffeur who had driven me home that first autumn evening, was unloading crates of toys from the back of the car. Together we carried the boxes through the stage door, and as we unpacked them I noticed that here and there was a toy from which paint had been chipped.

"Are these all yours?" I asked Diana. "I mean, you didn't buy them specially, did you? They aren't carnival consolation prizes, are they?"

"Good Lord, no," she said, impatiently, "as if those clots would ever dream up a consolation prize for the poor little toads! I came here with Mother and when she was judging the toddlers before the tea interval I saw what happened, so I nipped out and made Redman take me home for a good old rummage in the playroom. I was never very hard on my toys, Jan. To tell you the honest truth, I didn't go for them very much. I always preferred ponies!"

She began distributing gifts to the next lot of rejects, who came hurrying in from the main hall. Apparently word had got around among the losers that they were in for a far better deal than the prize winners; soon every dressing room was crammed with delighted children. I had a quick look at some of the gifts. The least of them must have cost someone a pound note and some were absurdly expensive-looking—tortoise-shell dressing-table sets, dancing shoes, party frocks, a mother-of-pearl Alice band, set in imitation pearls, books still in their cellophane wrappings, teddy bears, golliwogs, and every other kind of toy and trinket. The bounty represented the Christmas and birthday yield of Diana's entire childhood and it was just as she said, she had not been hard on her presents. Most of them appeared hardly to have been unwrapped.

I waited around until the judging was over. I ought to have gone back into the hall and collected the rest of the winners but I had lost interest in the contests. The music began to play and the children were rounded up by stewards for the grand parade. Only the little girl with the Dutch doll remained behind, tugging Diana's pleated skirt. She had an alien accent, placing her somewhere around Hoxton. Diana told me she was Keeper Croker's daughter.

"Please, miss, 'is eye's aht!" she stated, not unhappily but as one who states a simple fact.

Diana stooped and cocked her head at the one-eyed Dutchman.

"Ah, but it's *meant* to be out, Susan! You see, he lost it in the war, fighting the wicked Germans, didn't you, Hans?" And she lifted the doll close to her ear, paused and nodded thoughtfully, before restoring the doll to the child.

"He says he's glad you've got him, Susan, because nobody else wanted him with only one eye! You'll take care of him now that I'm grown up, won't you?"

The child looked very closely at Hans and nodded, emphatically. It crossed my mind, idiotically perhaps, whether she would still possess the doll when she was old enough to learn that Holland had passed the World War as a neutral. Then the thought was lost in wonder at the assurance and maturity of a girl whom I had always thought of as a high-spirited tomboy, with a penchant for getting in and out of scrapes.

"You're absolutely marvelous with them, Di," I said, as Susan Croker trotted after the others.

"Oh, I like kids," said Diana, yawning. "They don't pretend like all those jackasses in there. Do you have to go back? Couldn't we go and see your printing works? I've never seen them, you know, and you promised me years ago!"

"All right, Di," I said quietly, At that moment I would have taken her to Samarkand or Delhi if she had asked me.

We went along Fish Street and into our squalid little office, empty at this time, for Uncle Reuben was on the committee and the printing staff was working on the tableaux we had entered in the Trades Section. As we stood beside the old flatbed I suddenly put my arm around her shoulder, pulled her toward me and kissed her hair. It was only the second of our embraces in which I had taken the initiative and I think it startled her, so that she had to turn it aside with a little joke.

"Say it with printer's ink!" she said, but she found and

160

squeezed my hand hard. I went out into the street feeling like a man who has stumbled upon the lost treasure of the Incas.

4.

Up to this time—that is, until the summer preceding my eighteenth birthday—I was untroubled by active jealousy. Diana was at school for eight months of the year and during the holidays she was mine almost exclusively, for her parents spent a great deal of their time abroad or in London and only used Heronslea for holidays or special occasions, such as the Conservative May Fayre, when they came down for the week-end.

I was still vaguely suspicious of the French boy, Yves, but he and his family came to Heronslea only very occasionally and Diana had few contacts with local families. She wrote to me regularly when she was at school and the moment she came home we picked up the threads of our association without any trouble. I was always conscious of a threat to our friendship in the person of her mother and I never quite lost the dread of an open challenge from this quarter, but she had conditioned the staff of Heronslea to her erratic and unpredictable programs during the holidays and we were thus often able to spend whole days together in Sennacharib without anyone except dear old Drip being aware of our association.

It seemed to me then that this happy state of affairs might continue indefinitely. It never once occurred to me that sooner or later some other young man, with far greater social advantages than I possessed, would notice that, in addition to being the most eligible girl in the district, Diana was also one of the prettiest.

If I had thought about this at all I should have been alarmed at the prospect of some matchmaking mother entering the field on behalf of her son. At this time, when she was sixteen, she retained all the elfin prettiness of adolescence. Her blue eyes usually held in them a glint of mischief, her heavy chestnut hair was always untidy but its texture was smooth and fine and when the sunlight struck it, or she tossed it back to laugh or exclaim, a shower of stardust seemed to explode in your face. Her skin was smooth and pale, and no amount of sunshine would give her face an outdoor tan. Her ears were unusually small, white and flat, almost as if they had been overlooked and planted there as the afterthought of an affectionate creator. Her mouth was ripe and usually smiling, its broad curve matching the fun-sparkle in her eyes, and it was a mouth that always appeared to be on the point of uttering a gay observation, something of no consequence perhaps but expressing the simple pleasure of being alive.

If you looked only at her face she did not impress you as being more than a pretty and intelligent child, but it was otherwise with her figure, which excessive horseback exercise had prematurely developed. Her shoulders were braced and trim and her bust already that of a grown woman. Her narrow waist accentuated muscular hips and long, perfectly shaped legs, but she was vain only regarding her beautiful hands. They were certainly very shapely hands, with long, slender fingers and perfectly shaped nails. I never saw her ride or row without gloves.

"They're like Queen Elizabeth's," she once told me, with a laugh, and when I challenged this (after carefully studying a Holbein print, in one of Uncle Luke's illustrated *World Masterpieces* she added, "Oh, I mean the hands on Elizabeth's tomb, in Westminster Abbey! They're supposed to be the most perfect pair of hands ever carved in stone."

I was suddenly made aware of opposition in the field toward the end of the summer holidays about a month after the fiasco at the Heronslea fete. All the wealthy local families had attended the fete and among them were the Brett-Hawkins clan, a flock of gentlemen farmers, all interrelated, who held large farms and a communal shoot over in the Brackenhayes country, some five miles beyond Teasel Wood.

The acknowledged chieftain of this yeoman family was Colonel Brett-Hawkins, V.C., a hearty, professional soldier, with an active interest in dairy farming and cattle breeding. He owned a large herd of Guernseys and was al-

162

ways winning prizes at the county shows. He also had a trio of tall, broad-shouldered sons, all at Repton or University, and I first noticed the youngest of these, Gerald, when he had distinguished himself at a local gymkhana. As a matter of fact it was Diana who pointed him out to me and told me that he was leaving school to attend an agricultural college and train to take over his father's farms. I didn't pay much attention to him until I attended a point-to-point meeting in the area, and noticed that he was riding Diana's bay mare, Sioux. I had looked forward to the meeting and discussed it with Diana, so that it struck me as odd and disquieting that she had not mentioned to me that she was entering Sioux in the local hunter class. When I challenged her after the race (I was delighted to witness Gerald Brett-Hawkins fall on his hat at the last fence but one!) she was irritatingly casual about it.

"Didn't I tell you? I'm sorry, I must have forgotten. It was a last-minute arrangement anyhow, as Lance Fayne was down to ride her but funked at the last moment."

Lance Fayne was the only son of Major Fayne, the M.P., and I knew him as a frequent visitor to Heronslea. He had squired Diana on the occasion of his sister's twenty-first birthday party but I had never regarded him as a serious competitor because his physical disadvantages canceled out his social qualifications. He was small, thin and undistinguished, a tough and determined rider to hounds, but so narrow-faced and foxy that it was ridiculous to imagine Diana would ever want to be kissed by him.

Gerald Brett-Hawkins, however, was a much more serious challenger. He was an inch or so taller than I and possessed florid good looks, of the type Diana would classify "dago." He had, in addition, an air of aggressive self-confidence, as I soon discovered when Diana introduced me to him in the car park, where she was drinking claret and nibbling chicken in aspic with her jockey's boisterous family. I had seen her go there and was hanging about impatiently, hoping that she would leave them and rejoin me, when she called me over.

"I say, Jan! This is Gerald . . . did you see him come

163

a frightful cropper down there by the brook? Gerald, this is an old friend of mine, Jan Leigh. He's a journalist and he'll describe the lovely figure you cut, somersaulting over the bank!"

We shook hands and he gave me a single, bleak look. I could see that he deprecated Diana's readiness to introduce us, for his quick glance took in my cheap lounge suite and the fact that I was not wearing riding clothes or sporting tweeds. The word "journalist," however, made him pause.

"Really? What paper?"

"The *Winmouth Observer*," I muttered, flushing.

He dropped my hand as though it had been a soiled dish-cloth and resumed his talk with Diana about her mare's propensity to sweat as soon as she came in contact with other horses.

I stood about awkwardly for a moment or two and then left, mumbling something about having to collect the results of the last race for the paper.

Nobody heard my excuse and nobody looked after me when I moved away. I mooched down to the paddock sick with rage, for it seemed to me utterly unfair that I should have to compete with someone like Gerald Brett-Hawkins, a boy with the terrifying advantages of a public school education, good looks, a powerful physique, well-cut clothes, money and, what was more valuable than all these things put together, a background that gave him complete poise in the company of his equals and an ability to dismiss people like me with a limp handshake. I was glad that he had fallen so heavily and wished heartily that he had fractured his arrogant skull. The feelings of dismay he stirred in me that afternoon, however, were insignificant compared with the alarm I experienced when Diana told me that he was taking her to the Point-to-Point dance, at Swanley Lock Hotel on the following Tuesday.

"With him? With that lout?" I exclaimed. "Why, he can't even manage Sioux! What can you see in a chap like that?"

She looked at me levelly. She had a way of making you feel very small when you lost your temper. I never saw

Diana lose her temper over a trivial issue; she reserved all her fire for targets that she could hardly miss.

"I don't 'see' anything in him, Jan," she replied, quietly. "He's a good dancer and he's good-looking but he's not my type. He's the kind of man who would always try to keep-the-little-woman-in-her-place, and you ought to know by this time that I'm not the kind of a girl who wants to be mastered."

This was a subtle dig at my challenge to her freedom of choice but it brought with it a crumb of comfort. I only had to think about it for a moment to realize that Diana and Gerald Brett-Hawkins would quarrel bitterly after an hour or so in one another's company, so long as they weren't distracted by noise and movement.

"All the same that isn't true about his riding," Diana went on. "Sioux is too excitable for a Point-to-Pointer and neither you nor I would have got her as far around the course as Gerald did!"

This was true, of course, but I continued to sulk and Gerald's invitation to go dancing spoiled what might have been a pleasant evening's ride in Sennacharib. We were on the point of parting at the lane that led to Whinmouth Hill when I roused myself, for I always hated to part from Diana in a sour temper.

"Suppose I was able to get a motorbike?" I proposed. "Would you come to the regatta dance at Highchurch with me on Saturday?"

She was delighted with the prospect. The sheer lawlessness of a night out on a pillion made an instant appeal to her.

"Jan!" she said. "You don't mean you're buying a motorbike?"

"No," I admitted, "but old Coleman, our keyboard operator, owns a secondhand Douglas and he's taught me to ride it in our yard during the lunch breaks. He'll lend it to me, I know, and without some kind of transport we'd never get over and back, for it's a good thirty miles each way. The point is, could you get out of the house and back in again without anyone knowing?"

"Why of course!" she said. "I've done it before. Drip

165

will be away for the weekend because Mother's coming down . . . no, don't look so hopeless, it makes it easier, because Drip always comes in and says good night but Mother never does, for she goes to bed much later. I'll tell you what"—she hopped about, her eyes shining with the prospect of an adventure—"come around to my window at dusk and whistle 'Dolly Gray' and I'll be dressed ready and come down over the conservatory roof. I'll leave a little ladder in the laurels and when you see my light you can get it and put it up for me. It'll be just like that Rowlandson print I've got—you know, 'The Road to Gretna'!"

We said good-by, our humor miraculously restored, and I at once set about making my preparations. First I had to buy a dinner jacket, for I had seen in the advertisement we printed that flannels and lounge suits would be frowned upon by the regatta committee. The town of Highchurch was a kind of rich relation to Whinmouth, a much larger and more popular resort, on the western side of the river. It had a nationally famous yacht club and the dance that concluded its annual regatta was a notable West Country event. Highchurch was too far away, and too awkward to reach by bus or train, for the dance to attract people from our part of the country, so I felt fairly sure we should not be recognized or, even if we were, that word of our presence would be unlikely to reach Heronslea.

I ordered a suit the following morning and it was promised for Saturday midday. It cost me six guineas and was made by a little tailor in Church Street. I wore it for years. Today it would probably cost about thirty pounds.

Coleman, the keyboard operator, was doubtful about encouraging me to risk my neck on his machine and insisted on my having several more lessons and taking out a license. It was before the days of driving tests and L plates, and I soon considered myself sufficiently expert to carry a pillion passenger.

I went in for my suit fitting on Thursday and afterwards met Diana in Shepherdshey in order to perfect final details. She said that everything was going according to plan. Drip was leaving that night and her mother and father were coming on Friday and dining at home on Saturday,

166

which meant that there would be no danger of them coming in late when we arrived back at Heronslea about two A.M. She had earmarked the ladder but would not remove it from the tool shed until Friday afternoon. She had also surveyed the escape route from her bedroom window to the edge of the conservatory roof and located a strip of lead guttering that would serve as a path between the roof panes.

It was dusk about eight thirty that night and I wobbled over to Heronslea at twilight, wearing leggings and an old mackintosh to protect my new suit. It wasn't the most suitable outfit for a long ride on a motorcycle but I had been very pleased with my appearance when I had inspected it in the wardrobe mirror. The suit was a good fit and I now felt capable of doing battle with the Gerald Brett-Hawkinses and Lance Faynes of the world on more equal terms.

Diana had explained to me why she had chosen "Dolly Gray" as a signal. The Gayelorde-Suttons employed a man-of-all-work called Gaff, who sometimes pottered about the premises half the night, attending to horses, boilers and electrical plant. He was a persistent whistler but the only tunes he liked were Boer War music-hall melodies. Diana's devious mind reasoned that a snatch or two of "Dolly Gray" would not be commented upon if overheard by her parents or anyone else on the staff.

Luckily the dining room and main hall of Heronslea were on the side of the house farthest from her wing and as far removed from the glassed-in terrace where the Gayelorde-Suttons and their guests took their coffee. I hid the motorbike in some bushes halfway down Shepherdshey Hill and cut across the paddock from the west, using the cover of the oaks and beeches and remaining at a safe distance from the house until it was quite dark.

It was a warm, dry night, with the promise of a bright moon later on, and I thanked my lucky stars that we were not faced with the choice of abandoning the expedition or driving to Highchurch through West Country drizzle.

Shortly before nine I saw Diana's light flash off, on and off again. I moved into the open, crawled through the laurels outside the conservatory and found the ladder im-

167

mediately. It was a light, ten-runged affair and I was able to drag it noiselessly out on to the gravel and set it up against the glass. Then I whistled "Dolly Gray" and it was answered from above. A moment later Diana's window squeaked and I stood back, waiting for her to appear on the guttering.

The minute or two that elapsed before I saw her seemed at least an hour. In the woods behind me owls hooted and once a rabbit screamed. The rest of the house seemed silent and deserted.

At last I heard Diana call softly from the edge of the roof and I steadied the ladder as she descended. She came down with a prolonged rustle of skirts and a whiff of heady perfume. When she reached the ground she turned and kissed me gently on the mouth.

"Thanks, Jan," she said, with a chuckle, "that was beautifully managed."

"You'll get terribly blown about in that outfit," I warned her, but I should have known better, for out of her beaded handbag she at once produced a compressed oilskin, complete with clipped-on hood.

"I'll put it on when we start," she said. "It will crackle too much if I unroll it out here."

We hid the ladder, stole across the paddock and climbed the low fence into the road. Diana donned her oilskin, and after a few terrifying failures on the part of the kick start we set off, her arms around my waist, her hair tickling the back of my neck. The journey was uneventful and we arrived about ten-thirty, when the dance had got into its stride.

I can recall every detail of that wonderful evening. I can remember what she said, what the band played, how the hall was decorated in club colors, with the stage a blaze of sweet peas, dahlias and early chrysanthemums, how many ices we had and the one dance that we sat out to eat them while Ted Bristow's Rhythm Eight wailed "Mean to Me" before beckoning us for the next fox trot, a peppery little tune called "The Wedding of the Painted Doll."

Diana said I looked "lovely and sveldt," whatever that

meant, and I had no need to tell her how exciting she looked in her dance frock of yellow organdie, with a white rosebud pinned under her breast. We might have been dancing as partners since we were children and as the evening wore on, and we swung to and fro among the hilarious couples, reality faded altogether and we conversed with little pressures and glances.

When they had played "God Save the King" and we went out into the harbor car park to find our Douglas, the moon was full and the moored sailing boats, anchored in little groups under the jetties, bobbed up and down on a silver plate so bright that it hurt your eyes to look at it.

"Jan, it's been wonderful, wonderful!" she said, as she slipped into her oilskin. "I wish tonight could go on for ever and ever, because I'm sure it's the happiest night we'll ever have together."

Happiness buzzed in my head. Gone were vague doubts about her mother, her background, her money, or haughty competitors, like Gerald Brett-Hawkins and Lance Fayne.

"We'll have thousands of nights like tonight!" I promised, with the blind faith of a seventeen-year-old. "Besides, it isn't over yet, we've still got to get home. Hold on, here she goes!" and I jabbed joyously at the kick start and started the engine first time.

I had thought that it might be cold on the way back, particularly as we had only missed a single dance and were both very warm when we came out, but the air was as soft and balmy as Mediterranean spring and we cooled down gradually and comfortably as we chugged along the deserted moonlit roads to the Whin swivel bridge that crosses the river four miles up the estuary.

I had no trouble with the bike and from time to time Diana shouted complimentary remarks about my driving.

When we were coasting down Shepherdshey Hill she thumped my back and shouted something that I failed to catch, so at the junction of the village approach road I stopped on the grass verge.

"We'd better park it here while I see you up the ladder again," I suggested.

"Oh, *no,* Jan," she said, pressing my ribs with both

169

hands, "don't let's go in just yet—in for a penny in for a pound! Let's drive on down to Nun's Bay and have a dip. It's a glorious night for a moonlight bath and I've never had one, have you?"

This seemed to me to be tempting Providence. It was already after two o'clock and if we went down to the coast and bathed it would be getting on for dawn before she was back in her room.

"It's a good idea," I temporized, "except that you daren't risk going in for towels and suit and anyway, even if you get yours, I haven't got mine."

"Oh stuff and nonsense," she said, impatiently, "don't be so prudish, Jan! We'll bathe in the nude and if you're too shy you can keep your briefs on. Come on, this is a night to make history! If we don't go we'll be sorry when we're old and tottery—start her up!"

I drove on down to the sea with a flutter of nervousness in my stomach. I was not much afraid that we should be seen—you could wander about in Sennacharib any time of year after dark and rarely see a soul until you met an early plowman plodding up Teasel Lane—I think my uncertainties stemmed from the exciting prospect of sharing a moonlit bay with a nude Diana and the sense of doom that attended the possibility of her mother learning of such a profligate act.

When I saw the water, however, and the dark huddle of cottages that marked the eastern half of the bay, I could hardly wait to pull my clothes off. I had a good deal of trouble with dress studs and cuff links, but Diana had slipped out of her diaphanous dress in a matter of seconds and was running down the beach long before I was ready. The ripple of her laughter reached me together with her splash, as she dived from the edge of the fishermen's miniature jetty. A few moments later we were swimming out into deeper water, Diana using her unstylish but adequate breaststroke, me overhauling her rapidly with the crawl taught me by the Council School instructor in Brixton Baths, long before I ever dreamed of moonlight swims in Devon.

The water was colder than it looked and after fifty yards

or so Diana, gasping, made for a moored dinghy and gripped the anchor chain. After a moment's rest, however, she let go and rolled over and over like a porpoise, her lovely white body shining like a lily petal, her thick chestnut hair trailing behind her like weed. I was too shy to swim close to her but I kept her in view and presently called from the other side of the dinghy:

"You look like a mermaid, Di!"

"I feel exactly like one!" she called back. Then: "Oh Jan, Jan, why do we ever bother with silly clothes? I feel more a part of the sea than I've ever felt in a tight bathing suit and one of those headachy caps."

Then she dived clumsily under the boat and bobbed up alongside me. "Cheat!" she laughed. "You've left your pants on. How deep is it here? Could we reach bottom?"

I threw up my heels and kicked my way under water. It was not more than twelve feet deep and I easily touched bottom. I was in the act of reaching for a pebble when she touched me, her arms encircling my neck, her lips brushing mine. Effortlessly we drifted, without the will to disengage.

It was the oddest sensation, an embrace down there on the floor of Nun's Bay, as though we were sailing gently through limitless space, our limbs freed of all substance and solidity. There was nothing shameless or even sportive about it; it was as though we were partners in some kind of ritual that belonged to a cult as removed from everyday life as a nymph's dance to the music of Pan. The kiss was symbolic, quite unlike any previous kiss she had given me, and when at last we rose together to the surface and struck out for the jetty, neither of us remarked on it, for to do so would have been to break the spell and convert symbolism into ridicule.

The spell held through the time we were drying ourselves on the lining of my old mackintosh and struggling into our clothes. The clothes themselves seemed incongruous, as though, by the mere act of donning them, we were deliberately removing ourselves from a world of enchantment and returning, glumly and resignedly, to an existence that was drab and futile.

171

I felt this so strongly that I remarked upon it. She didn't answer immediately but sat tugging at her hair with a comb taken from her bag. Presently she said:

"Come and sit beside me, Jan. Don't say anything, just sit here and put your head on my lap!"

"You must be cold," I argued, in spite of myself. "I'd better get you home now, Di."

"No, I'm not a bit cold," she replied, and then, with deliberation: "As a matter of fact I'm glowing. You see, Jan, I think I've discovered something, I think I'm in love with you, really and deeply in love! I don't think I could ever love anyone else after tonight and I don't think anything else will ever matter very much to me, not deep down I mean, except to know that you're in love with me and that we'll always be together. Do you think we've sort of hypnotized ourselves into believing this? You know, the music, the dancing, the moonlight and just being here, with everyone else in Sennacharib fast asleep? Or do you think it's simply that suddenly—just now—we both grew up?"

I thought about this a moment. It was like pondering a symphony of great, stirring chords. Then I said, "I've felt like that about you a long time now, Di. I don't think it's much to do with growing up. I felt it ever since that day you rode out of the larch wood and rescued me from Croker!"

Her admission, sweet as it was, did not electrify me, as I should have imagined only a few hours ago that it might. It seemed a natural and inevitable sequel to the embrace under the water, it only confirmed a subconscious conviction that I had had for almost two years now—that Diana Gayelorde-Sutton and I were predestined to grow up together and inherit, in the spiritual sense, all the slopes, coverts and copses of Sennacharib, and that our coming together then and now was simply a small swirl in the rhythm of the universe, like the unhurried patrol of the buzzards who sailed over Teasel Wood, like the flow of the brook under Shepherdshey Bridge, like the mating and flowering of everything that lived and grew in the few square miles we always thought of as our own.

172

I turned the damp mackintosh inside out and laid it across her shoulders. Then I crouched beside the little rock on which she was sitting and covered her hands with kisses while she lowered her head and laid her cheek against my head.

We sat there a long time, hardly moving, saying nothing, listening to the steady suck-lap of the wavelets on the shingle. And then, when I felt her shudder, I stood up and held her closely in my arms, kissing her damp hair, her eyes, her ears and mouth. I had never kissed her in this way before. Such kisses as we had exchanged in the past had nothing to do with the yearning we experienced for one another at this moment. We had forgotten where we were or how we came to be there. We had no shared past and no future, only this sweet, solemn hour that had coaxed us from childhood into anxious maturity, and changed us from a couple of children out on a moonlight spree, into a man and woman who wanted and needed one another so urgently that at this moment we could not imagine an existence apart.

A faint glow of headlights, moving rapidly along the distant London road seen through the cleft of the cliffs, restored to me but not to her a vague sense of time and place. I led her up to the quay where we had left the bike and slowly we rode back to Shepherdshey, stopping once again on the grass verge of the crossroads.

"Don't come across the paddock with me, Jan," she said, suddenly. "Let's say good night here. I'd much rather do that and I'll get back on my own, I promise you."

"What about the ladder? How will you be able to put it away again after using it? If anyone found it there—"

"Dear Jan," she said, slowly running a finger down my cheek, "do you imagine that I shall sleep when I get in? *Tonight?* After all the wonderful things that have happened? I'll change and wait until I hear the maids stirring. Then I'll slip out as though I'm going for Sioux, take the ladder away and put it back in the shed before old Gaff shows up. It's his day to gravel the drive and he won't come around to my side of the house until after breakfast."

I let myself be convinced by these arguments. It was almost dawn anyway. Already there was a faint glimmer in the sky over Shepherdshey Church and I reasoned that one pair of footsteps outside the conservatory would make less noise than two; besides, in the unlikely event of Diana's being caught, my presence would make matters ten times worse. Alone she might be able to talk herself out of being on the conservatory roof in a yellow dance frock at four A.M. on a September morning.

"What about tomorrow?" I demanded. "You'll be going back to school at the end of the week and I want to make the most of every minute. I won't see you again until just before Christmas!"

As I said this I could have wept but she bobbed forward, pecked my cheek and said, with a rueful laugh, "It isn't 'tomorrow,' it's 'today,' silly! I'll phone you between one and two and fix something for the evening. It depends so much on what Mummy and Daddy are doing. They might be going somewhere and expect me to go with them."

We had used this kind of arrangement in the past. When she was unsure of how and when we could meet I stayed behind at the office throughout the lunch hour, waiting for her to phone while I had the premises to myself. I agreed to leave it at that and kissed her once more while helping her over the fence into the copse bordering the paddock. I listened until I could no longer hear her footsteps cracking the twigs and then pushed the bike up the hill, starting it well out of hearing of the house.

When I got up to my room it was almost daylight and although I too intended to remain wide awake and recapitulate every moment of the past few hours, I confess that I failed to keep the tryst, falling asleep half-undressed and remaining so until I heard Aunt Thirza bustling about in the kitchen, with her usual accompaniment of rattling crockery as she assaulted the night's dust on the dresser. I pulled off my clothes, held my head under a running tap, threw on a pair of flannels and went down for a cup of tea, but Aunt Thirza was not fooled for an instant.

"Been out gallivanting half the night. I 'eard 'ee!" she grumbled, in her rich brogue.

I never had to apologize to Aunt Thirza. I was a grown man in her eyes and took shameless advantage of the knowledge that she had one set of rules for me and another for everyone else.

"Well, youm on'y young once, John!" she relented. "Yer, 'ave zum tay, boy, and dorn 'ee hurry to work, zeein' tiz Zat'day!"

I had forgotten what day it was. I had so much else to think of that it was fortunate for the readers of the *Observer* that Saturday was the day I collected no facts and typed no copy.

Uncle Reuben noticed my preoccupation but put it down to a late night. He didn't hold with dancing and motorcycling, and began to counsel a more serious approach to life, pointing out that I was now nearly eighteen and ought to be thinking of implementing my decision to widen my professional experience on a more important paper.

This gave me an opening and I think I rather surprised him with the sudden enthusiasm I showed for bettering myself. I did not tell him that my reason for wanting more money and greater responsibilities had to do with supporting a girl whose father was reputed to be the wealthiest man in the district. He was always so deeply immersed in his own affairs—the paper, his lay preaching, the treasureship of the local Liberal Party, and many other activities—that he had no knowledge whatever of my friendship with Diana. He had, however, carried out his promise about finding me a better job and had been awaiting a favorable opportunity to discuss it, together with another and more sensational proposal that had been maturing for some time.

"It will probably work out very well all around, John," he told me, "because after you've had a year or two on a bigger paper you can come back here on an entirely different basis. You see, since we're now embarked on the subject, I think I can tell you a good deal more than I was inclined to admit when we had our last discussion about your future. Mr. Priddis is leaving the *Observer* and works to me in his will, and who should I have to pass it on to but you?"

His information, so casually imparted, overwhelmed me. Coming so quickly upon Diana's declaration, it converted my entire future into something reasonably foreseeable. I had never thought of myself as the owner-editor of the paper but simply as a junior employee of the present proprietor, whose health was deteriorating very rapidly and giving all employed on the paper and printing works a certain amount of anxiety about our livelihood. Only the previous day Coleman, the motorcycle owner, had drawn my attention to the possibilities.

"If Priddis kicks the bucket what's to happen to us?" he had speculated. "I'll lay you six-to-four the paper will be bought by one of the big chains and they'll put their own chaps in, you can bet your life on that!"

Unemployment was rife at the time and there was some justification for Coleman's gloom. Our local population in Whinmouth was about twelve thousand but our unemployment figure already stood at over four hundred and would go higher when the season ended.

If the business passed to Uncle Reuben we were likely to remain undisturbed and if, in the course of time, it then passed to me, I had an assured if limited future for as long as I cared to remain in the district.

"How does it appeal to you, taking on here after I've gone?" asked Uncle Reuben, eying me doubtfully.

"It couldn't be better!" I told him and smiled when I saw his face light up with pleasure. "I've been very happy here, Uncle Reuben, and things being what they are, where could I expect to do any better?"

He jumped up and thumped me on the shoulder. "God bless my soul, it does me good to hear you talk like that, John! You know, I expected you to be lukewarm about it and mumble a lot of nonsense about Whinmouth being a dead-and-alive hole and no place for a chap of your age! I still think you ought to have a bit of daily paper experience, mind you, but if you've got something established like this to come back to it makes all the difference in the world, it gives you roots, and a purpose in life. Now I'm off to see Mr. Priddis this weekend and perhaps we'll get something on paper. In the meantime I'll jog him for that introduction to a daily. It would mean leaving here, you understand, and I daresay you'd be away three or four years. How do you feel about that?"

"It depends where it is," I told him, with secret visions of frequent meetings with Diana in London and all the advantages of a press card with which to entertain her. "If it was London I think I should like it very much!"

He looked a little puzzled at this. "But I thought you were a converted countryman, John. Luke tells me you spend all your spare time up on the moor, or pottering about in the bay."

I was tempted to tell him then about Diana and ask his advice, which was always objective. In the light of what happened I rather wish I had, but something prompted me to continue to keep my unlikely courtship to myself and I replied, "I wouldn't care to leave the West Country for good, Uncle Reuben, but it's like you said, the more experience I get at my age the better journalist I'll make in the end."

It sounded rather pious but he was a pious man and took the explanation at face value. He beamed on me, paternally.

"By George, I wish you'd been my boy, John! I think I must have misjudged your father when he took young Miriam away from us all those years ago. He must have had some good stuff in him somewhere."

I felt guilty at deceiving him so outrageously but not nearly as abject as I was to feel a few days later, when his opinion of me was to dip to zero.

He went off to North Devon to see Priddis and I forgot him the moment I had the office to myself. I wasn't able to concentrate on anything but sat drumming my fingers beside the phone, waiting and waiting for Diana's call, and hoping with all my heart that she would be able to meet me at the tower that night. I had so much to say to her, so much to promise, and my yearning for her nearness, for the touch of her hand and the sound of her voice, was so intense that I ached.

One o'clock came, then two, but no call; I was ravenously hungry but afraid to leave the office. I phoned Uncle Luke, using the phone with demoniac speed lest it should block Diana's call, and asked him to tell Aunt Thirza that I was busy and couldn't get home. Then I tried to read, hanging about until late afternoon and pacing the deserted printing works like a man awaiting a reprieve. Over and over again I told myself that there was a perfectly simple explanation for her silence and that her parents had whisked her off on a social visit to a place where she was unable to use a telephone.

By five o'clock I was driven by hunger to call it a day and hurry home to my warmed-up dinner. I decided that I could not hope to get news if I stayed in the town, that my best plan was to go up to Heronslea and hang about on the fringe of the paddocks, hoping to catch a glimpse of her and perhaps get a signal.

By this time I was becoming alarmed, but not seriously so, for I reasoned that even if she had been missed during the night it was unlikely that I would be connected with her escapade. I was equally convinced that her mother knew her well enough by now to regard a descent from the bedroom as something entirely characteristic of Diana and punish it as a mere prank.

There was the dance frock, of course, and then, to complicate matters, her dripping hair, but Diana was a very accomplished liar where her mother was concerned and I had every confidence that she would be able to talk her way out of the situation and persuade her mother to accept it as just one more childish whim on the part of a tiresome daughter.

I went to the tower first but it was silent and deserted. I looked about for a note or message but there was nothing, so I crossed the patch of common and went on down through the larch wood into the paddock behind the house. Sioux was there and Nellie, but the rear of Heronslea was empty of humans. I skirted along the edge of the copse, taking good care to keep out of sight of the windows, and then sat down to wait for darkness, when I could approach the house in comparative safety.

It was a long time getting dark. The wood was full of scuttling life and as the sun went down behind the larches blackbirds sang and once or twice a rabbit frisked across the lawn beneath the beeches. It was a lovely, pastoral scene, with the old, beautifully proportioned house in the near distance, bedded down in a wide circle of deep green timber and tussocky lawns, with the deeper green of the laurels and rhododendrons half-screening the pink walls of the kitchen quarters and stable yard. As I waited, the last rays of the sun struck the sloping panes of the conservatory and they flashed a dull ruby. The air was so still that the swift, rending sound of Sioux's rhythmic grass cropping carried right across the enclosure to where I sat, waist-high in bracken. I was not very receptive to the peace and beauty of Sennacharib that evening, however, for Diana's declaration had changed the direction of my thoughts and feelings about our relative status. I was no longer content to hang about awaiting the fall of Heronslea crumbs, keeping out of sight, and taking advantage of the Gayelorde-Suttons' absences in order to woo their lovely daughter. All this time I had accepted the barrier between us as something in the natural order of things, like a desert to be crossed, or a mountain range to be climbed, but now I wanted to blast my way through the barrier and tell the whole world that Emerald Diana Gayelorde-Sutton was in love with me, that we had swum naked by moonlight in Nun's Bay, that we had pledged ourselves to one another and that, come what may, Gayelorde-Sutton millions notwithstanding, I was going to marry her, care for her and share my life with her, somewhere in this vast green silence with which we, and no others, were in true accord.

It did not occur to me, then or later, that I might with some justice be regarded as a youthful fortune hunter or that I was doing Diana a wrong by encouraging her to imagine that she was in love, at seventeen, with a boy unlikely to earn more than one of her father's head clerks. I never thought of Diana as an heiress, only as the daughter of wealthy, snobbish people, and my daydreams did not embrace Heronslea House but laid claim to Sennacharib as a whole, to its woods, commons and beaches. Somewhere inside this realm I dreamed of building a home of our own, a haven that would be in sharp contrast to the elegant pile that dominated the estate.

This was admittedly illogical but I make no excuses. I was seventeen, and deeply in love with a pretty girl. There was pride and wonder in the knowledge that Diana loved me but it was not the kind of pride that Mrs. Mabel Gayelorde-Sutton would have understood.

When it was dark, and before the moon rose, I slipped out of the wood and went around to the front of the house. Moving very cautiously I approached the glassed-in terrace. It was uncurtained and I peeped into the dining room, the main room upon which the terrace opened.

There was a dim light inside and the door was half open. Presently I saw the butler's figure across the aperture and then, by crawling crabwise along the outside wall of the terrace, I positioned myself to look right into the dining room.

What I saw brought no relief to my anxiety. The Gayelorde-Suttons, father, mother and daughter, were at their meal, waited upon by Masters, the soft-footed butler. The radio was playing "Sleeping Beauty Waltz" and the family did not appear to be conversing. Mr. Gayelorde-Sutton sat at the table end nearest to me, his wife was at the other end, and Diana, wearing a dark evening dress, was sitting midway in between, half facing me. They all looked rather solemn and helped themselves to dishes absentmindedly, as though they were eating not because they were hungry but because someone had struck a gong and told them that it was time to eat.

They had reached the dessert stage before I had an idea. Then, catching my breath with nervousness, I whistled a line or two of "Dolly Gray" and was instantly rewarded by the sight of Diana's head coming up. Her father and mother took no notice of the start but continued to peel fruit. After a pause I tried another note or two, and this time Diana did not look up but Mrs. Gayelorde-Sutton said something to the butler, who crossed over and closed the door, cutting off my view.

Baffled and irritated, I crept back to the main drive and stood indecisively beside one of the largest beeches, ready to bob out of sight if anyone appeared in the front of the house. About a quarter of an hour passed and then I saw a chink of light and heard a dog bark. Almost at once there was a scamper of paws on gravel and a moment later Sheila, Diana's golden Labrador, lolloped up to me, snuffling a welcome and panting with pleasure at being released for a few minutes' probe among the rabbit runs of the paddock.

Sheila and I were old friends. She had accompanied us on dozens of rides and not a few dips in the bay. She was small for a Labrador but very active and almost stupidly affectionate.

"Here, Sheila, here!" I whispered, as she located me and jumped up for a pat. "Where's Diana? Is she with you? Is she coming out?"

Then I noticed that a fold of paper had been tucked into her collar and wound around two or three times to make it fast. I grabbed the dog and unwound the spill, resisting Sheila's attempts to snatch it back and take it in her soft mouth.

It was too dark to read any message that might be written on the paper and anyway at that moment Mr. Gayelorde-Sutton, his cigar end glowing, moved out onto the terrace. I slipped behind the beeches and made off back to the copse, Sheila following until a distant whistle recalled her to the house.

Deep in the wood I sat down and struck a match. The message was only a few words of scrawl and had obviously been written in a desperate hurry. It said: *Don't write or phone. Awful row. You not involved yet. Come to church. Sophia Grangerford's trick. All my love, Di.*

My feelings on reading this extraordinary note were very mixed. I was thoroughly alarmed about the row and apprehensive at the obvious reference to last night's affair implied in the word "yet," but at the same time I was comforted by Diana's ingenuity in warning me, by her alertness at responding to the "Dolly Gray" signal so quickly and, above all, by the invitation to attend church and learn more of what had taken place since we had parted. I had no difficulty at all in ciphering the "Sophia Grangerford" piece. Among the books that Diana and I were fond of discussing was *Huckleberry Finn,* and Diana's favorite chapter in that delightful story was the one in which Huck spends a period with the feuding Grangerfords on the river plantation. We had often talked about Sophia, the girl who caused massacre by running off with Harney Shepherdson, and Diana had remarked that Sophia's trick of exchanging plans with her lover through the medium of a note left in her prayer book was a "marvelous wheeze." It was now obvious that she intended to use the same medium and this, I decided, was very clever of her, because there was nothing to prevent me from attending morning service at Shepherdshey Church tomorrow morning and retrieving a letter from Diana's prayer book when the congregation had filed out. The Gayelorde-Suttons were conventional churchgoers when they were in the country and they occupied a pew near the front. Here they sat, surrounded by their estate employees, like a feudal family at church in Plantagenet times. It was a gesture that must have given Mrs. Gayelorde-Sutton a good deal of satisfaction. This was one occasion when I appreciated her game of squiress.

Sharp at ten fifty the following morning I was in position a few pews away from Diana, in the pretty little church of Shepherdshey. Worshipers were sparse and I knew them nearly all. Nat Baker, the big sexton, was doling out hymnbooks, Half-a-Crown Sam, the cretin, sat moonfaced under the lectern, Ada Macey, flanked by her official and unofficial husbands, sat close to the door, and most of the other villagers I knew were in attendance, including about half a dozen keepers, gardeners and their families from the Heronslea estate.

I was very glad of their company, for I had entertained a horrible suspicion that, apart from the Heronslea contingent, I might prove to be the sole parishioner and this would make the inspection of Diana's prayer book a risky undertaking.

The rector droned through the service and the last

182

hymn, I recall, was Whinmouth's most popular wedding hymn, "The Voice That Breath'd O'er Eden," which I took to be a very good omen. Diana was taking no chances at all. If she saw me she didn't advertise the fact but kept her eyes straight before her as she stood, a small, trim figure in a blue two-piece and white straw hat, between her mother and father in the second pew from the front.

When the service was over I waited until the family had moved past my pew and down the center aisle, burying my head in my hands but keeping a wary eye on Diana as she went by, in order to note any signal she might want to give. She did give one, a slow, solemn nod, and as soon as the church was cleared I hurried to the Gayelorde-Sutton pew and rummaged frantically among the hymnbooks in the rack.

I was unable to find a prayer book but then I noticed that one of the hymnals had an envelope in it. I quickly gathered it up and thrust it into my pocket, allowing a little time for the churchyard to clear, and hurried out into Teasel Lane. From here I made my way up toward the gorse slopes, to the spot where I had watched the hunt move in pursuit of the fox I lied about.

The envelope contained two pages covered with Diana's neat, stylish handwriting; it took my breath away.

John dear, it began (latterly Diana had not been so lavish with written endearments; when she used the word "darling" it meant something).

Thank goodness you had the sense to get in touch! As you will have gathered, I was collared on the way in last night and I'll tell you all about that when we meet. Right now there are much more important things to discuss, so here goes! To begin with Mummy doesn't know the truth, or any part of it. She *thinks* I was at a village hop, with Lance Fayne, the M.P.'s son, and I let her go on thinking so (without actually admitting it) because it spikes her guns. The one person she doesn't want to quarrel with right now is the M.P., not just because he is who he is but because of the coming election! She has, however, made an awful decision. I am not to go back to school at all but to go straight off to the Finishing School, the one in

Switzerland that I was booked for next year. It is a country place, stuck away in a place called Thun, in the Bernese Oberland, and I haven't the faintest intention of going! At first I planned to do a bunk en route and get a job in London, where we could still see each other as you said we might later on, but I see now that my disappearance in that way would start a national hue and cry, and get into all the papers, whereas if it happened down here Mummy would sweat blood to keep it dark until I was located. So I'm going to run away *now*, and stay hidden for about a week, or until they find me. You might think that won't help much but it will, because Daddy will be in such a state by the time I'm found that he won't let me go to Switzerland and all that will happen is I'll leave school and stay on at Heronslea most of the year. Now my plan—hold your breath—is to go and hide on Nun's Island, where no one will ever think of looking for me. I have to get there, of course, and this is where you come in. Get the dinghy and bring it along to the place where we bathed after dark last night. Bring anything you think would be useful to a castaway. I'm bringing food but there is a limit to what I can carry. Can you find a waterproof sheet and perhaps some rugs or blankets? I am absolutely determined on this, Jan, because I think it is the only way to make her see sense and I'm dreadfully afraid that,if she finds out about us I'll be sent even farther away, and probably never see you again, and that I just couldn't bear, Jan, because you are the only person in the world I really care about, darling, and I know now that I'm really in love with you, as I said.

Your own,
DIANA

My head began to spin. There were so many fantastic statements in the letter that I had to read it over and over again before I could absorb the gist of it. My first reaction to the island plan was that it could not possibly succeed, and was no more than the semihysterical ravings of a spoiled, sulky child. I began to think about Diana as the person I had known over the past two years, and then, somehow, it did not seem irresponsible but vaguely Machiavellian, particularly when one reviewed the balance of power at Heronslea. If I had not had an opportunity of studying the real Mr. Gayelorde-Sutton, during his visit to the *Observer* office about the pig, I might have rejected Diana's claim that her father would ultimately step in and take her part about going to Switzerland. After that glimpse of him it did not seem so unlikely. He was a man who would stand so much nonsense from his wife and then, when the limit was reached, quietly intervene and issue all the orders. Also, Diana obviously knew him much better than I did, and could better assess the likelihood of his championship. Then again, she was quite accurate in her estimate of the press reaction to a sudden disappearance. If she left a note, as I imagined she would, it was unlikely that local police would take her flight very seriously, whereas if she jumped the train or boat en route for Switzerland, there was sure to be no end of a fuss. Fleet Street would probably hint at White Slavers and invent other dramatic angles and the prominent social position of the family would lay them wide open to national coverage.

Her introduction of Lance Fayne into Friday night's escapade was a stroke of genius, although, incongruously, I found myself resenting his blameless role. I imagined this part of it could be cleared up by a phone call on the part of her mother but as long as Diana would not actually admit to having danced the night away with Lance, Mrs. Gayelorde-Sutton could hardly complain about it without risking a snub, which was something she would not care to receive from a Conservative M.P. Her object in sending Diana away almost immediately was obviously designed to safeguard her as well as prevent a quarrel between the families. What action she would take if she stumbled on the truth I hardly dared to contemplate.

As to the practical aspect, the plan to hole up on Nun's Island, that was not as silly as it seemed, either. Scarcely anybody went there now that the holiday season was ending, and if the recent good weather continued, the old cabin of Crusoe Jack, the recluse lobsterman, would prove adequate shelter once the roof was repaired. Getting there unseen might be difficult but it was by no means impossible, providing we chose our time and the sea remained calm.

I then moved on to examine my own role in the escape

185

and was surprised to discover that, once the first shock of her letter had been absorbed, I began to feel pleasurably excited about it. It was an essay into the realm of pure romance, a flight of desperate lovers to a desert island, with the object of preventing prolonged separation. From the standpoint of maturity I suppose it all sounds harebrained and even cruel, for whatever happened, the Gayelorde-Suttons were certain to suffer a good deal, but from the standpoint of a lad of seventeen, fast in the web of first love, it was a great and glorious adventure, a chance to prove my devotion to the person I admired more than anyone else on earth.

Thinking along these lines, it was a short step from the role of accessory to that of a full partner in the enterprise. The more I thought about it the more certain I became that I could not possibly take her to the island and then return home, but would be obliged to share her period of voluntary exile.

The prospect uplifted me and I thought less and less of the rights and wrongs of the matter and more and more of the bliss of being marooned with Diana in a place remote from human contacts. After considering this for a spell I worked myself into a mood of reckless abandon and set about making plans with the dispatch and resolution of Willie Douglas, whose rescue of Mary Queen of Scots from Loch Leven castle had always occupied a cozy corner of my imagination. Having made up my mind, I deliberately turned my back on common sense. Diana and I were in love. Diana was about to be spirited away. If she had the courage to fight back then so had I, enough to challenge half a dozen Mrs. Gayelorde-Suttons.

I cycled back to town and gobbled my way through lunch in order to have the rest of the day clear. By two o'clock I was down at the quay, inspecting the dinghy and loading it with things we might need. I took a tarpaulin sheet from the Furniture Mart, and half a dozen tattered rugs used for conveying fragile goods to and from the auction rooms. They were very soiled and smelled strongly of linseed oil but castaways could hardly be bothered by a thing like that. I then raided Aunt Thirza's spotless pantry, filching some flour, sugar, biscuits, cans of fruit, a can opener, a whole Dutch cheese and a packet of salt. As an afterthought I took a bottle of Camp coffee, two cups, two plates, a saucepan, a mended kettle and a bull's-eye lantern.

By the time I had it all stowed away under the tarpaulin it was evening, and while Uncle Luke and Aunt Thirza were at chapel I wrote two letters, one to Uncle Reuben and another to Aunt Thirza. I told Uncle Reuben that I had had a sudden notion of a job and had gone after it, and that he would hear from me shortly. I told Aunt Thirza much the same, but added that I intended combining a job hunt with a week's camping holiday and that I had therefore helped myself to a few stores from her pantry. I knew that both Reuben and Thirza would be astonished by my precipitate departure but it was the best story I could think of at the moment, and if there was any publicity about Diana's flight I wanted to do all I could to avoid our absences being linked.

About dusk I pushed off along the edge of the bay, timing my arrival under Nun's Head with the fall of darkness.

It was not until I had tied up under the deserted jetty that I began to wonder how Diana would escape the house and, having managed this, walk the three miles from Shepherdshey to Nun's Steps carrying such kit as she had decided to bring. I was not overconcerned with these problems, for it was clear that a girl who was sufficiently determined to run away from home and isolate herself on a rock a mile out to sea would certainly contrive the preliminaries, notwithstanding the fact that a close watch was being kept upon her movements.

Fishermen were loafing about on the higher quay until after nine o'clock, so I did not dare to leave the boat for fear of being seen and recognized. I lay in the bottom, looking up at the stars and watching the moon play hide and seek with tatters of blue-black cloud. Out beyond Nun's Island I could hear the bell buoy toll and this meant a swell, but the water inshore was flat calm and the tiny wavelets poured over the shingle with barely a sound. I

187

was anchored in two feet of water and soon the gentle rocking motion sent me to sleep, for I was very tired after two nights' broken rest. I was awakened by the sound of something clanking down beside me and I jumped up to see Diana, duffel-coated and hooded, climbing into the boat with an attaché case in one hand and a large canvas bag in the other.

"Lord, I was scared!" she said. "I was quite worn out when I got here and at first there didn't seem to be any sign of you. I kept wondering if you had got my letter—push off, that's everything!"

It was as casual as that! No explanations, no excited tale of her flight, or nervous speculations on the future; just "push off, that's everything!" and she was gathering up the anchor and fending the boat from the jetty.

The extraordinary thing about that long pull to the island was that I was almost speechless with embarrassment. I don't know why this should be so; I had never been embarrassed in her company before but I now found it almost impossible to begin a discussion on the situation. When we were three parts of the way across, and had entered the choppy water beyond the long finger of Nun's Head, I at last forced myself to say, "I'm staying with you, Di, I'm not going to let you stay there alone, no matter what you say about it! If you don't agree or think this will only make matters worse, then we'll turn around now and go home."

She looked surprised for a moment and then laughed. "I knew you would, Jan, but I wanted that part of it to come from you. Quite honestly, I'd be scared stiff out here on my own but I could have faced it, so long as you promised to row out every night, or very early each morning." Then, "Won't you be missed? And won't it mean they'll be hunting for two of us?"

I told her about the false trail I had left and she said I was clever and that she had left a note on her dressing table in true eloping style. In her letter she said that she was running away because she hated the idea of leaving England but had money and would be quite safe. She promised to write within a week. "That should give them time to have a jolly good bust-up about it all," she said, cheerfully, "and the bit about leaving England will get Daddy right under the ribs! I think he dislikes the idea of my going anyway, but Mummy says she won't be answerable for what happens if I don't, I'm so terribly out of hand."

I pondered this as we swung east and rowed inshore.

"What would be your father's attitude if he knew the real reason—about us?" I asked.

"I don't know and I don't care," she said gaily. "He's so weak that I've lost all patience with him. I hate the way they've brought me up, all this snob stuff, and trying to keep me a child as long as they can. Something like this had to happen soon, Jan, and it was making up my mind about you that sparked it off. If I don't strike a blow for myself now I'll be chivvied along by mother all my life, first this finishing-off nonsense, then being presented, then a 'suitable marriage,' and finally complete boredom with some awful droop like Lance, or a starched shirt, like Gerald Brett-Hawkins! I'll just be pitchforked into leading the kind of life *she* leads!"

"What kind of life does she lead, Di?" I asked, realizing that I had never really known despite all the oblique references Diana had made to it in our talks.

"Oh, playing at Big Business with Daddy and falling over herself to be noticed by the right people in all the right places," said Diana, savagely. Then. very seriously: "It might seem to you that what I'm doing is a desperate thing, and I suppose it is. but then I *am* desperate, Jan, desperate of having my life mapped out the way she maps hers out, in a kind of fantastic calendar—Ascot, Wimbledon, Hurlingham, Henley, the 'Season'—you know, and not because she enjoys the actual events but simply because somebody's told her these are the right places to go and the right time to go there. d'you see?"

I saw a good deal more clearly than she realized. We had had these kinds of discussions before but she had not always been so explicit. I understood, for the first time I think, what caused Diana to go to such extraordinary lengths to resist her parents. It was as though she was being forced to serve an endless apprenticeship to a trade she loathed, and in which she could see no personal future beyond the ennui of aping the gentlewoman. It was her essential honesty that caused her to despise her mother's incessant charade, but, in addition to this, her resistance had to do with the inherited outlook of the seedy old ferryman whom she claimed as a grandfather. Inside her, calling loud for release, was a peasant determined to do battle with the shams prescribed by her mother and buttressed by her father's wealth. I learned a great deal from that conversation in the boat. It became very clear to me (though I would not, at first, admit it to myself) that it was not on my account that she was making this gesture of independence. Her flight was instinctive because, as she emerged from adolescence, she felt her resistance weakening with her threatened removal from the familiar, from Sennacharib that had been a kind of sanctuary all these years, and possibly from me also, for I was the talisman of her freedom.

I do not mean that she did not sincerely believe that she was in love with me but simply that I was of secondary importance in a struggle to develop her own personality. I did not resent this knowledge, then or later. For the moment it was enough for me that she found solace in my company and was drawn to me physically and spiritually. I was confident, as are most males at seventeen, that I could soon convert this warmth into a blaze as bright as my own and here I was, with a wonderful chance to prove it! As the boat grounded and we jumped ashore I set about doing just that.

It was fortunate that I had brought the bull's-eye lantern. In its beam we made a careful examination of the shanty and I was soon able to patch the roof with the tarpaulin, weighing it down with heavy pebbles. We then recovered our kit and climbed the gully to the copse, gathering armfuls of bracken for beds. We were too busy for the next two hours to appreciate the beauty of the night, but when the shanty had been made habitable we stood together on the little rock shelf outside the shattered door and looked out on the huge expanse of moonlit Channel.

The shanty faced south, which was a lucky chance, for it meant that our fire would be screened from any observer on the coast and we could also move about fairly freely without the chance of being observed by the pilot boat or trawlermen, who passed inside the island on their way to the open sea.

To the west we could see the necklace of tiny lights that marked Whinmouth quay and the steep streets of the town: to the east there was only the blurr of Nun's Head. The hamlet from which we had set out was obscured by the knoll and its copse. It was very quiet here, the only sound apart from the steady swish of the water being the irregular clang of the bell buoy three or more miles to the southeast.

"What are we going to do about drink?" she wanted to know.

I told her there was a spring somewhere, for Crusoe Jack had used it for years, but because I knew we should have some difficulty in locating it I had brought along a can of water and we could now make our first pot of tea.

"We can have some toast, too," she said, "because I brought a loaf and we'd better eat it before it gets stale. Oh Jan, this is quite heavenly! It's a kind of secret honeymoon! How long do you think it will last?"

"Don't let's worry about that," I said grimly, for in spite of the *sang-froid* with which I had entered the adventure, I had a far more active conscience than Diana and could not quite banish thoughts of the hurrying and scurrying there would be when the hunt was up.

We had a hard task to find firewood by flashlight but we finally gathered a pile and I lit a small fire behind a carefully screened fireplace. The kettle took a long time to boil but when it did, and we had access to the red-hot ashes, Diana made some toast and I got out the plates and sliced the Dutch cheese. Rummaging about among the stuff we had brought with us, I discovered that the case she had carried wasn't an attaché case at all but a portable phonograph.

"Why on earth did you bring a phonograph?" I demanded, for it seemed to me a ridiculous thing to have on a desert island and must have proved a dragging weight to lug over to Nun's Head.

"Well, you see, I wasn't at all sure you'd stay, Jan," she said, laughing, "and I thought I might get very lonely. I only brought two records, a Gilbert and Sullivan medley and 'Student Songs.' They're both rather pets of mine."

We set it going and listened as we munched our toast and drank our smoked tea. The recordings were good and it added zest to the adventure to sit there listening to "The Lord High Executioner" and "The Duke of Plaza Toro." Somehow it made the shack more like home and banished the eerie loneliness of the rock we shared with sea gulls and the bones of long-dead seamen. I was thinking of these men when Diana, who was uncannily accurate at reading my thoughts, brought the subject into the open.

"I'm jolly glad now that we had that service and put up that cross," she said. "If their ghosts are still not laid then they're absolutely certain to be benevolent."

After supper we had the students' songs and then I was very glad that she had thought of the phonograph, for the strong choruses reintroduced a devil-may-care atmosphere into the cabin. We joined in the ones we knew, *"Gaudeamus,"* "The Eton Boating Song," and the Harrow school song, humming an accompaniment to the German songs on the other side of the record. When we had played them over twice I said it was time we went to bed and she lay down on her bracken couch fully dressed. I tucked her up with the least noisome of the rugs and she looked very like a child when she pronounced herself warm and cozy.

"Dear Jan," she said, sleepily. "Good husband! Kiss me good night!"

I did so very willingly, my love for her sweeping over me like a strong, warm flood.

"Everything is going to be all right about us in the end, Di!" I told her and believed it, deep in my heart.

Her arms wound around me and she kissed me a dozen times.

"Darling, darling Jan!" she whispered. "You're quite the nicest thing that's ever happened to me!"

I made up my own bed on the side farthest from the fireplace but although I was tired out with all the excitement and exertion it was a long time before I dropped off to sleep. I lay awake listening to the mournful notes of the bell buoy, and to Diana's slow, regular breathing, wondering what would be the end of it all and feeling humble and helpless, as well as immeasurably grateful for the opportunity to share the same world as Emerald Diana Gayelorde-Sutton, of Heronslea, Devon and Palmerston Crescent, W.2.

It was a bright day when I awoke and Diana's place was empty. I jumped up and looked wildly around, terrified that she had been spirited away during the night, but almost at once I noticed that the fire had been made up and the kettle was on. A moment later she came clattering into the cabin in slacks and sweater, carrying a large armful of driftwood.

"You were so efficient and come-come-little-womany last night that I thought it was my turn to show off," she said, kissing me lightly. "I've found the spring. It's over on the Whinmouth beach, so I think you had better refill the can before people are about. It's nearly seven already!"

We used the can for washing and I prowled cautiously around the spur of sand to refill at the spring. The distance from this side of the island to Whinmouth was too great for us to be spotted with the naked eye but there were always people on the quays and jetty with telescopes and binoculars, so I decided to take no chances.

We tried to make some salty little cakes with the flour I had brought but they were very unappetizing, so we agreed to ration ourselves with the bread. Diana opened a can of corned beef and we fried slices, exchanging many jokes about one another's cooking abilities. After breakfast we had a swim, then we made more tea and set the phonograph going.

"I wish you'd brought more records," I chaffed her. "We're going to get frightfully sick of 'Three Little Maids'

193

and 'There Lived a King' by the time we're rescued. My favorite isn't here, anyway. It's *The Pirates of Penzance,* the one the amateurs did in the spring."

This led to an amiable discussion on Gilbert and Sullivan, and thence to musical comedies, films and books. During the time we were alone on the island we explored one another's literary and dramatic tastes very thoroughly, for we spent a great deal of our time inside the shanty, being nervous of daylight movement on the western or northern sides of the island.

I remember that first morning we talked a great deal about desert island books and I was rather surprised to discover that her acquaintance with them was slight. I told her the story of *Coral Island* and we discussed *Robinson Crusoe* at length, for she was vaguely familiar with this one. She knew nothing, however, about *Treasure Island* or *The Blue Lagoon,* and was very intrigued by Emmeline's production of a baby without the benefit of Marie Stopes, who was one of Diana's heroines.

I had not been all that impressed by *Blue Lagoon* but I know long passages of Stevenson's classic by heart and recited them with relish. We speculated a good deal on how the vast treasure came to be buried on the island and then moved on easily to poetry, in which field she was far more advanced that I. My acquaintance with verse at that time was limited to ballads like "The Armada" and Kipling's jingles, but she was very scornful about my taste.

"That isn't poetry at all!" she exclaimed. "Those are just rhymes, like longer Jack Horners and Little Miss Muffets! Real poetry is quite different. Miss Thorpe says it's 'emotion remembered in tranquillity'—you know, lovely, lovely groups of words, like Tennyson's *Princess.*"

My knowledge of Tennyson was confined to "The Brook," *Morte d'Arthur* and *The Lady of Shalott* so I asked her if she could quote me some of her favorite pieces.

"My favorite piece of Tennyson is the first and last verse of the song from *The Princess,*" she said, and quoted:

"Tears, idle tears, I know not what they mean,
  Tears from the depth of some divine despair
  Rise in the heart, and gather to the eyes,
  In looking on the happy autumn-fields,
  And thinking of the days that are no more.

"Dear as remember'd kisses after death,
  And sweet as those by hopeless fancy feign'd
  On lips that are for others; deep as love,
  Deep as first love, and wild with all regret;
  O Death in Life, the days that are no more!"

Only a few days ago, after an interval of more than twenty years, I came across these verses and they still retained enough tired magic to restore to me a detailed memory of Diana, sitting with her long legs coiled under her, her small, earnest face frowning with the strain of recollection as she recited them against the background of the rough-hewn logs that formed the fireplace wall of Crusoe Jack's cabin. Then, without effort on my part, the sounds and scents and talks of our idyl came back to me as fresh and gay as growing daffodils, and I remembered how she had run on about poetry, and opened up a new field of cadences that have since brought joy and color into my heaviest hours.

"Miss Thorpe, our English Litt. teacher at school," she told me, "is the only mistress who really understands people our age. Some teachers have a calling, like parsons," she added, "and Thorpey is one of them. She's introduced us to a lot of modern poets, nearly all killed in the war, poor dears, and her favorite, and mine too, is Alan Seager, the American boy. I like everything he wrote because . . . well, because nothing that happened to him could take the sparkle away!"

"What did happen to him?" I asked, curiously.

She told me about Alan Seager, how he came to France a few years before the war, and how, when Paris was threatened by the Germans, decided that he was under an obligation to defend the city that had been his inspiration; how he served through three years of trench warfare and died, obscurely, at the barricade he had visualized in the best known of his verses. When she was discussing something that had captured her imagination she acted quite shamelessly, and as she quoted "Rendezvous with Death" I could see Alan Seager penning the lines among the debris of a shattered Champagne village.

"Do you know any more of that kind of stuff?" I demanded, eagerly. She was flattered by my enthusiasm and went on to quote her favorite verse from Seager, a little poem inspired by the memory of a prewar love. Later on, much later on, I found and learned the verses myself:

"Out of the past's remote, delirious abysses
Shine forth as once you shone—beloved head,
Laid back in ecstasy between our blinding kisses,
Transfigured with the bliss of being so coveted.

"And my sick arms will part, and though hot fever sear it,
My mouth will curve again with the old, tender flame,
And darkness will come down, still finding in my spirit
The dream of your brief love, and on my lips your name."

There was magic in the way she recited those lines, the kind of magic, I think, that Seager himself would have understood so readily, and as she said them it was not the ghosts of the Negro seaman who hovered over Crusoe Jack's shabby cabin, but the benign ghost of someone to whom the ecstasy of first love was still a strong, bright flame, strong enough and bright enough to light a candle in the hearts of two romantic young idiots and persuade them that it was enough to light them down the years.

Toward evening, when there was not much chance of being observed on the south side of the island, we roamed the beach and knoll and caught some flatfish in a pool left by the tide. We took them home and fried them, telling each other that they were delicious, and after our evening record recital we talked again until it was late, neither of us caring to admit that, as the hours passed, we were progressively conscious of the enormity of our situation and terrified of its outcome.

196

So passed three idyllic days, days spent in cautious sun-bathing, talking, preparing picnic meals, gathering drift-wood for the fire and a good deal of innocent love-making of the kind that makes sweaty nonsense of the love-making to which film audiences have been conditioned since the advent of Metro-Goldwyn-Mayer and Para-mount.

Such kisses as we exchanged, and they were not as many as we might have exchanged in that solitude, were spontaneously given and received, and all our caresses were gentle and playful. I don't know why this should be so; we were young, eager, and very well pleased with one another. There was nobody to surprise us or embarrass us, as young lovers are so tiresomely surprised, and so easily embarrassed. We had outgrown the shyness of displaying a mutual desire for affectionate exchanges; we acknowl-edged, with delight, that we belonged one to the other, and therefore had access to all but the innermost chamber of one another's thoughts and feelings. Yet we were not lov-ers in the real sense of the word, not then, not when we could have been and with such complete innocence.

I think we held back for different reasons. On her part she treasured the magic web we had spun, month by month and day by day, since our first meeting in the larch wood. She treasured it, yet was aware of its extreme deli-cacy. She wanted leisure to enjoy its beauty before moving on to explore its intricacies, for there was a kind of time-lessness about this period in our lives and although both of us were acutely aware that the immediate future was peril-ously uncertain, we were yet able to look beyond into the years when we would have outgrown the prohibitions of the present and could contemplate them with laughter and nostalgia.

I, for my part, had another, darker reason for holding back when her lips touched mine and she murmured my name over and over again like an incantation. I wanted to emerge from this strange, sweet interlude free of guilt. I wanted to be ready to challenge her parents and her gilded background without having to explain my deepest feelings for Diana to people who could never measure them in terms of human emotion. I wanted to stand upright and meet their scorn, not to kneel and have it poured over me like scoldings leveled at a willful child. I wanted, even if I had to wait for years and years, to claim Diana as a right, not to beg for her, as one beseeching an impossible favor. This much her trust and declaration had done for me and they brought with them a current of steady triumph, as if the sap of manhood had been pumped into me by my unlooked-for responsibilities. I was no longer afraid of the Gayelorde-Suttons and their money. To a degree Diana's underwater kiss had banished that fear, come what may, threaten who would.

On the fourth night I was awakened by a frightful clamor through which I could hear my name being called, plaintively and urgently.

It was pitch dark and during the night a southwesterly gale had whipped up and was howling across the island like an army of dervishes, piling the sea on the beach in a long thunder of sound.

As I fought the tug of sleep there came a particularly vicious gust that ripped the tarpaulin from the rear of the hut, exposing us to a downpour of slanting rain, cold and mercilessly direct, as though the storm-tossed clouds had singled out our particular corner of the coast for a thorough drenching.

I scrambled up and called back to Diana, torn between the desire to reassure her and the need to save the tarpaulin before it billowed across the island and was lost.

Diana won; we collided in the blustering darkness and instantly her arms went around me.

"Jan, oh Jan, you're there! What's happened? It's so dark and awful . . . !"

I made a great effort and pulled myself together.

"It's all right, Di," I soothed, stroking her streaming hair, "it's just a storm and the wind has ripped the tarpaulin off. Wait, I'll take the light and get it!"

"Don't leave me alone," she wailed. "I can't stay here alone, Jan!"

"All right, then you come too . . . where's the damned light . . . we've got to find the light!"

198

We groped around the hut, stumbling over items of kit and finally locating the bull's-eye near the fireplace. Its weak beam revealed a sorry state of affairs. When we had turned in, the cabin was a warm, cozy haven; now it was a half-flooded ruin, with seventy-mile-an-hour gusts sucking at what remained of its roof and torrents of rain streaming down the ramshackle timber walls.

I took her by the hand and together we staggered out and around behind the hut, flashing the beam from side to side in the hope of spotting the tarpaulin.

The wind was so strong out here that it hammered us like a rain of punches and we had difficulty in remaining on our feet. The loose sand of the hillocks came at us like a volley of darts and the roar of the breakers, fifty yards below us at highwater mark, was deafening. We groped our way, drenched and half-blinded, across the sandhills. On the far side of the island, where the rocks sloped away, the force of the wind abated somewhat, enabling us to reach the inshore tide mark, and here we at last stumbled upon the tarpaulin, soaked and tattered, held in a crevice between two rocks. Somehow we dragged it back to the rear of the shack, where we crouched under the lee of the chimney breast, doing what we could to shelter ourselves under the miserable remnant of tarpaulin. Soon Diana's teeth began to chatter and I thought about trying to light the fire and trying somehow to make a hot drink. Then I remembered that all the driftwood would be wet anyway, in this kind of chaos how could I find kindling and strike matches?

There was nothing to do but wait for dawn, and it was a long time coming.

We lay there, pressed together, sharing what warmth remained in our bodies, until the wind began to drop, the gusts grew more widely spaced and, at last, a gray, reluctant light showed in the sky over Nun's Head.

Then, with infinite difficulty, we stood and spread the tarpaulin over one corner of the cabin, weighting it down with the largest stones we could find. It wasn't much of a shelter and the downpour had given place to a heavy, persistent drizzle, but it was a good deal better than remaining in the open. When it was quite light I scouted around for some paper and sticks, I found a small pile of driftwood that might be coaxed into a fire, but there was nothing to get it going with. By this time, however, Diana had rallied somewhat.

"Use the phonograph records," she suggested. "They're waxy and they've been under cover in the lid."

I found the records and broke them into jagged pieces. After one or two failures we soon had a frail fire going, Diana collecting likely pieces of damp wood, while I slopped along the desolate beach to refill the water can, upset in our groping during the night.

In the half hour the kettle took to boil we surveyed the ruins. Our rugs were soaked and there was no promise of sunshine to dry them. Our food stores, such as they were, were reduced to a soggy paste and the only things left to eat were Diana's two remaining cans of fruit. Neither of us much fancied a breakfast of cold peaches or pineapple, but the tea warmed us and gave us sufficient heart to discuss the situation.

"We'll have to pack it in, Di," I told her. "We can't stay here in this weather without food and shelter. I daresay we could dry out the rugs somehow and maybe patch up the cabin, but suppose we do? By tomorrow we'll be famished."

She said nothing for a moment or two, her small face pinched and strained with the ordeal of the night, her wet hair still plastered in glorious disorder across her cheeks. She sat quite still, hugging her knees and staring into the slow, smoky fire. At last she said:

"Right! Then I'll go back and give myself up, providing we do it separately and providing you aren't involved, Jan."

"How can we do that?" I asked. "It's broad daylight now and we're sure to be spotted going across, or landing."

"Then we shall have to put up with it until dark," she said, firmly. "Then we'll pack up and row across to Nun's Bay. You can drop me there and go on home yourself. I'll get in touch somehow. We'll think up a plan before we actually part."

200

I turned this over in my mind and it seemed about the best course open to us. We dried wood, built up the fire, and decided to take the risk of the smoke being seen, for we could not face the prospect of staying there, wet through and shivering, without the cheering glow and frequent draughts of hot tea.

The weather settled in drear and hopeless, so much so that at midday I was doubtful about making a dinghy trip across open water, but later on, although the rain persisted, the wind dropped altogether and the sea was no more than choppy.

Bad weather has a devastating effect on romance. All the sparkle had died from our island adventure and the rock itself had been changed by dripping skies and chilling southwesterly winds from a remote Eden to a dismal place of exile. We were depressed, too, by the inevitability of a prolonged separation. Perhaps, I thought, we had been away just long enough to persuade Diana's father to cancel her Swiss plans, but whether this was so or not, it was quite certain that the escapade would lead to a much stricter watch being kept upon her and from now on every meeting would necessitate complicated planning and considerable risks of discovery.

We worked out a kind of letter post, inspired, I seem to remember, by an old print Diana possessed, depicting a girl in frills and flounces making her way through a tangled wood to a letter box in a hollow tree. I agreed to call at the "box" every night and pick up any messages, leaving my replies. Even a night and a day under seeping skies could not extinguish Diana's enthusiasm for exploring the secret passages of romance.

Toward dusk the rain ceased, although the sky remained overcast and whitecaps flecked the surface of the bay. Diana said we ought to take the things down to the boat and bale it out before we pulled her down the beach.

"After that downpour last night she'll probably be half full!" she said, gloomily.

I had overlooked this, and we picked up our belongings and went out across the sand pit to the head of the gully, where we had landed and dragged the boat clear of the tide line. When we climbed the dune that looked down on the shallow cleft we stopped and gazed at one another with horror. The gully was empty and the dinghy was gone!

We ran shouting to one another along the entire beach as far as the old wreck. There was no sign of the boat until we reached the extreme southeastern corner of the island and there, left behind by the tide, was one of the floor boards. Apart from that there was nothing but driftwood, cork floats and ragged whiskers of ruined lobster pots. We made a complete tour of the coast in the deepening twilight but there was no sign of the boat. She must have been washed out of the gully by rain and carried away by the ebb tide.

I knew what I must do and I set to work at once. In the last glimmer of light we rooted among the overhang of the dunes for dry or semidry kindling and driftwood. When we had gathered several armfuls we dragged it to the westerly point of the island, directly facing Whinmouth. Then, with dismal solemnity, we carried out the remains of our fire in the saucepan and set the pile alight, heaping the brushwood up until we had a good, strong blaze. I knew that old Tom Yelland, the pilot, would want to know who was tending a fire on Nun's Island the evening following a heavy storm, and it was not long before we saw the light of the pilot boat swing out into the estuary and head out to sea to catch the easterly swell and bear down toward us.

About half an hour passed before the lights bobbed inshore and during that interval we said very little. Finally Diana stood up and tossed back her hair.

"Let me do the talking, Jan," she said. "I'm better at it than you."

"He'll take us back to Whinmouth first," I told her, "and he'll put two and two together at once, so it's no good pitching him an unlikely yarn."

"Listen, Jan," she said, "we've only got a few more minutes and after that it might be months—years even, before we even see one another again."

Her warning bored into me like a drill and involuntarily I began to protest.

"It's true," she went on, relentlessly, "so listen, Jan, and don't interrupt! Promise?"

"I promise, Di."

"Well, then," she said, speaking very levelly, "first I want to say thank you for everything, for coming here and for looking after me so wonderfully. Nobody could have done it so well, not even the real Jan, who was much heavier and stupider than you and really a bit of a bore when he wasn't in action!"

I managed a wry grin at this. It had crossed my mind more than once in the past that Diana would have found Jan Ridd infuriating, notwithstanding his masterful masculinity and heroic mold.

"Secondly, I want you to know that I'm more in love with you than ever and always will be, no matter what happens from now on. Anyone else would seem terribly feeble after you, Jan, and even if they had your kind of hemanship they wouldn't understand me nearly so well as you do, or be anything like so patient with *my* impatience, if you see what I mean. As soon as all this blows over I'll be packed off somewhere, if not Switzerland then somewhere else a long way away, but it can't be forever, because when I'm twenty-one I can do as I jolly well like and I will, don't you fret! I'll come back to you and find you wherever you are and we'll be together, for always. We'll find another Sennacharib maybe and we'll pick up where we left off, doing all the things we like doing and being the sort of people we want to be, d'you understand?"

"Yes, Di, I understand and I feel the same way about everything!"

"I'm glad," Diana went on, "because there's one other thing and that is, we've both got to stop struggling for a bit. Things are too strong for us at the moment and we've got to save our strength and drift with the tide like our poor old boat, waiting until we're in a position to go our own way in spite of all the opposition. That means that you mustn't make a scene when we get back, Jan, and you must just sit quiet and let them say anything, do anything, and treat the whole thing as if it was just a silly sort of a prank and hadn't any real meaning behind it. That's very

203

important, because if they go on thinking that, they'll let up on us sooner or later, and forget about it and that'll be our chance, d'you see?"

It was very sound reasoning for a girl her age and temperament and I compared it, to its advantage, with the sour resentment and defiance that had been smoldering inside me for a long time now. Any kind of honest declaration on our part would be received with anger and contempt, not only on the part of her parents but on the part of people like Uncle Reuben and Aunt Thirza, who would be sure to share Mrs. Gayelorde-Sutton's scorn for a love affair between people as young and as socially remote as Diana and myself. Before I could comment on this, however, Tom Yelland hailed us from the shallows. I picked up our sopping bundles and turned toward the beach.

"Just a minute," said Diana. "I want to kiss you, Jan!"

I dropped my bundles and put my arms around her. My lips tasted the salt on her cheek and she shivered as I murmured her name.

Tom hailed again and Diana whispered, "Darling Jan, darling, darling Jan!" as I stood back and called to Tom. Then, without another word, we crossed the hillock to the mouth of the gully and waded out to the boat.

Chapter Seven

UNCLE REUBEN was the hero of that dismal week. I had always known that beneath his outward crust of holier-than-thou respectability was the core of a social rebel, but until now I had been inclined to share his brother Mark's opinion that, in many ways, Reuben was a hypocrite, that he thundered against others' shortcomings from pulpit and political platform because he had always lacked the courage to expose himself to a man's ordinary temptations. I was wrong and Mark was wrong. Uncle Reuben was a man who drew his inner strength of character from the Old Testament, who really did worship at the altar of self-denial and personal integrity, who believed not only in a fair day's work for a fair day's pay but in a handshake instead of the contract, and in the preservation, at almost any cost, of human dignity in terms of work, truth and resistance to the Devil. He was gruff, intolerant, and sometimes harsh in his judgments but he was no hypocrite; he had more moral courage than anyone I ever met.

In the days that followed our surrender I came to know and respect Reuben in a way that the lobster-helmeted troopers of Cromwell must have revered their Bible-thumping leader in the field. By some standards, I suppose, he was a narrow-minded old stick-in-the-mud but he was also a man, and a good deal more of one than anyone else involved in the repercussions of our flight.

There had been more fuss about our disappearance than I had anticipated. Diana's note about getting a job in a city had fooled nobody and the police were informed of her absence that same night. Extensive inquiries were made and these soon resulted in a report that we had been seen together at the regatta dance on the previous Friday. This at once involved me, and when it was known that I too had left town at short notice, it did not need a trained detective to unravel the basic facts of our long association. Even Keeper Croker was called in to describe how we first met and poor old Drip, the governess, faced recriminations that came near to giving her a nervous breakdown.

There were one or two stormy interviews between Uncle Reuben and Aunt Thirza on the one hand, and Mrs. Gayelorde-Sutton and her solicitors on the other, but the upshot of these was that the hunt veered off on a false scent, for it was assumed that we had run away to try to get married at Gretna Green, in imitation of another teenage couple about whom the papers had had plenty to say a month or so before.

As Diana had prophesied, no one thought of looking nearer at hand, and by the third day, when some of the details had leaked out to the press, Heronslea was picketed by local linage men and so-called special correspondents. These were given a very cavalier reception by Mrs.

Gayelorde-Sutton, who always considered that a free press was the principal drawback of democracy. The result was inevitable. The more she clamped down on news, the wilder and more improbable were the stories printed, and when Diana had been found and packed off home in a taxi by Tom Yelland and the local police, the Heronslea keepers had a full-time task keeping reporters at bay.

We had our share of the press siege but Uncle Reuben was an old hand at dealing with newspapermen and they did not bother us nearly as much; partly, I suppose, because the Heronslea background and Mr. Gayelorde-Sutton's notoriety in the City made Diana a more tempting target.

It all died down after a few days. The story was killed by an earthquake in Japan, then by Germany's abrupt exit from the League of Nations, and later by Diana's heavy cold, which kept her in bed and helped her mother to prevent the press from interviewing her until the story was stone cold.

I stayed indoors most of the time and Uncle Reuben did my work. I was glad of Aunt Thirza that week, for she reserved all her natural belligerence for callers but behaved toward me with extraordinary tenderness—far more, I felt, than I had deserved of her.

Talking to her over our meals (Uncle Luke was already insulated by silent contemplation of the migratory habits of martins and swifts), I realized how wise Diana had been to urge me to encourage the adult world to look upon the whole episode as a teen-age prank.

"Giddon, did 'ee ever zee such a fuss over a couple o' chits takin' it into their ades to go'n live on a desert island?" Thirza snorted, heaping my plate as though I had a dinosaur's capacity for vegetables. "They papermen want something to do, I reckon, writin' all that ole nonsense about something as happens yer every time kids go near the zea!"

The romantic or "sex" angle of the situation entirely escaped her. Diana and I might have been a pair of city toddlers who had succumbed to the magic of blue water and golden sands and sailed away from the harbor to play pirates.

"T'iz all on account o' they Zuttons"—Aunt Thirza would never concede Mrs. Gayelorde-Sutton her double-barreled name—"havin' too much money!" she declared. "If they 'ad to turn to, an' work vor it, zame as most of us, they'd smack her bottom an' think no more of it, so there! Yer, 'ave zum more tatties, boy," she added. "You couldn't have had much to feed 'ee up on that ole rock out there—bliddy silly plaace to go this sort of weather!"

Uncle Reuben, of course, took a much more serious view of the matter The sheer extravagance of our gesture outraged his common sense and I think my willing participation in such a wild adventure permanently lowered his opinion of me as a future editor of the *Whinmouth & District Observer*. What worried him even more, however, was the vague implication, in one of the Sunday newspapers, that we had enjoyed a bizarre honeymoon on the island, and it was this aspect of it that led him to call around and demand to talk to me in private, closing the door on a muttering Thirza and a completely bewildered Brother Luke.

It was the first time we had been alone since I returned, and his brooding presence embarrassed me. When he tried to speak of what was in his mind, however, he became the more embarrassed of the two and finally I had to help him out, for he could never quite bring himself to admit that a child made its appearance via its mother's vagina, or still less that this rather shameful fact was preceded by an even more undignified one in which men played a degrading part.

"If you're wondering what really happened while we were alone out there, you can stop worrying, Uncle," I told him, and was glad to see that my words brought instant comfort to him. "It wasn't that kind of love at all, although I daresay lots of folk around here will always think it was. The whole thing would never have happened if Mrs. Gayelorde-Sutton hadn't decided to send Diana away to a finishing school in Switzerland."

This inclined him more to our side. Despite his ceaseless League of Nations work and Free Trade theories, he was a fanatical isolationist. Deep down he hated and distrusted all foreigners, even the blameless Swiss.

"Why on earth do people like her want to send their daughters to foreign schools?" he growled. "Aren't there good enough schools over here, where she can learn to behave herself properly?"

"It's all part of the setup," I told him, and explained a little of Mrs. Gayelorde-Sutton's plans for Diana's future. He shook his head, despairingly.

"Arrant snobbery! That's all it is!" he muttered. "Too many of those people about nowadays and it's where the Tories get their money from, I imagine. How can you want to go about with a girl like that, John? They aren't our sort at all!"

"Diana is," I said, stoutly. "She hates it as much as you do, and hated it enough to run away from it all."

"But why did you have to get involved? You aren't being sent to a finishing school in Switzerland."

I was tempted to try to explain to him how I felt about Diana, and how she felt about me. It occurred to me that he might be able to understand a little of our love for Sennacharib and the glorious avenues of freedom it offered us, but in the end I thought better of it and simply mumbled:

"We get on, Uncle Reuben We've grown very fond of one another after all this time and it seemed such a shame to spoil it all!"

He sighed and stood up, awkwardly patting my shoulder. There was a good deal more genuine affection in the gesture than he was able to convey.

"Very well, John," he said, "let's forget it all and start afresh. Come back to work tomorrow, and I daresay it'll all blow over in a day or so. Most of these things do, even in places like Whinmouth."

He was wrong in one sense. Whinmouth would have forgotten it almost at once, but the townsfolk were by no means as deeply involved as was Mrs. Gayelorde-Sutton. The day I went back to work we had a visit from her, and it was then that I had an opportunity of estimating Uncle Reuben's full stature.

2.

I thought I knew Mrs. Gayelorde-Sutton as well as anyone by this time, but I was nevertheless amazed by the viciousness of her attack. The moment she saw me she jabbed a trembling finger at me and squealed: *"Thet's* him! *Thet's* the boy! What's he doing here? He ought to be in a reformatory, thet's where *he* ought to be!"

I was badly shaken but stood my ground, reminding myself of Diana's final injunctions about this interview and how it should be handled.

Uncle Reuben, however, was disinclined to be hectored in his own office. He not only disliked Mrs. Gayelorde-Sutton personally but detested everything that she stood for, socially and politically.

"If you've come here for an apology for John's part in this silly business you'll get one, Mrs. Gayelorde-Sutton!" he said, stolidly removing the pipe from his mouth and laying it down on his cluttered desk. "On the other hand, if you've simply called to make trouble, and scream idiotic accusations at everybody, I'll have you removed, if necessary by the police!"

Mrs. Gayelorde-Sutton opened and closed her mouth twice. Her color mounted so rapidly, and her hands fluttered so violently, that I thought for a moment she was going to have a seizure. When at last she did manage to speak, her voice shot into a high, unnatural key and she had to try again, after a few rapid intakes of tobacco-laden air. This made her cough and we waited, with studied politeness, until she had quite recovered. Then Uncle Reuben nodded gravely at me and I took my cue.

"I'm very sorry Diana caused you so much worry," I mumbled, flushing. "I don't think she meant to and I'm sure I didn't!"

As an apology it left a good deal to be desired and Mrs. Gayelorde-Sutton gobbled it up like an insignificant crumb, glaring hard at me, her slightly poppy, green eyes almost starting from their sockets. I had always thought of her as a handsome woman but she did not look handsome now; she looked almost pathetic, like a badly spoiled child who had been goaded into a hysterical temper. Even she realized this, I think, for in the next few moments she made a great effort to calm herself.

"I could hev put you in prison for this," she said. "And I would, too, if Aim'ald hadn't been so . . so utterly *wicked* about it!"

I wondered what this meant and made a guess at it; on Diana's return, no doubt, and after studying the newspapers, Mrs. Gayelorde-Sutton had probably told Diana that she intended prosecuting me on some obscure charge, possibly abduction, or something of that nature. Diana must have countered this by saying that if her mother did anything so stupid she herself would come into court on my behalf. Uncle Reuben, however, cut short my speculations by once more reducing the wretched woman to the point of self-strangulation.

"You couldn't do any such thing, Mrs. Sutton," he said —and I noted that he had taken a leaf from Aunt Thirza's book and dropped the "Gayelorde" in order to reduce his opponent to size. "John certainly did wrong in helping your daughter to run away, and also in not telling you about it when she did, but as the whole thing was your daughter's idea and not his, you could only charge him with being an accessory, and they'd laugh you out of court on that! Believe me, madam, I've a long experience in these matters. If you really want to bring a charge go right ahead and do it!"

Mrs. Gayelorde-Sutton then changed her tactics. Suddenly she began to snivel and her sniffs did nothing to restore her dignity. Uncle Reuben continued to contemplate her gravely until finally she blew her nose into a very expensive-looking handkerchief and wailed:

"It was a *terrible* thing to do! *Terrible!* No *nice* boy would do such a thing, I'm sure." When she said this her vowel-torturing accent disappeared. It was the first time I had ever heard her speak like anybody else and it somehow made her a little more human. Uncle Reuben, however, was unmoved by her tears.

"I'm not sure about that," he said heavily, "but if it is so, then no nice girl would do it either."

This rocketed Mrs. Gayelorde-Sutton out of the doldrums and she began to scream again.

"Ai'll tell you something, Mr. Waht-ever-your-name-is!" she began, her accent returning as all trace of tears disappeared. "The moment Ai hed Aim'ald back Ai called in mai doctor, in order to make a certain examination and set mai mind at rest, once and for all. If his report had been other than it was, then you can be quaite certain that this would be a matter for the police, notwithstanding what yew hev to say about it!"

Her statement so horrified me that I felt physically sick. I saw, as one might regard a series of pictures resulting from a thumb-flick of a book, the sequence of events implied by her admission—the solemn arrival of moonfaced Doctor Barnes, their family physician, his brief interview with Mrs. Gayelorde-Sutton, his heavy tread up the staircase and along the white passage to Diana's room, his routine pulse-feeling of the patient pending the real examination that was to follow, and so on, up to the moment when Diana was face to face with a humiliation that converted our love into an obscene joke. Yet, even while my imagination shied away from this scene, I was ashamed for Uncle Reuben and I think I might have flung myself at Mrs. Gayelorde-Sutton and bundled her out of the room had I failed to notice the curious expression on my uncle's face.

He was not miserably embarrassed, as I had fully expected him to be, and he did not seem to be as irritated as he had been earlier in the interview. He was looking straight at Mrs. Gayelorde-Sutton with a mixture of pity and disdain, as though he had just heard somebody say something that was certain to bring ridicule and disgust upon them, and had said it out of sheer ignorance and lack of ordinary consideration.

He stood up, reaching for the comfort of his pipe and hammering the bowl on his open palm at regularly spaced intervals. When he began to speak he continued this emphatic gesture, punctuating each phrase with a distinct rap, as though hammering nails into the coffin of Mrs. Gayelorde-Sutton's taste and breeding.

"Madam," he said, without raising his voice, yet somehow contriving to enlarge its volume enough to be heard above the clack of the presses in the works, "I feel bound to tell you that I find you a contemptible creature! Thoroughly contemptible, do you understand? If you were a man I should have the greatest pleasure, *the very greatest pleasure,* in picking you up by the scruff of the neck and dropping you into the nearest dustbin!"

I forgot to be horrified when I heard this. I just gaped at them, staring at one another as they stood barely a foot apart. Uncle- Reuben was still rapping away with his pipe, and Mrs. Gayelorde-Sutton, colorless now, was staring at him like a rabbit facing a huge, hungry stoat.

"That you should find it necessary to take such steps with your hapless daughter is one thing," he went on, in the same level tone, "and although I most sincerely pity her it is really none of my business. That you should find it necessary to come here and scream such disgusting admissions to me, in my own office, *is* my business, and I find it insupportable, d'you hear me? *Insupportable,* madam! I am not myself a father but if I was, and it came to my knowledge that you had sought to betray your trust in a girl of mine in that . . . that . . . unspeakable fashion, then I should turn you upside down and deal with you as I fear you neglected to deal with your daughter when she might have benefited from that form of correction! And now, Mrs. Sutton, go back to your big house and endeavor to regulate your family without wasting my time and making me despair utterly of the entire human race!"

With that he strode across to the door and flung it open, waiting beside it while she remained motionless midway between me and the cluttered desk.

I looked away from her then. It hurt me to see a woman in the grip of such a frightful temper. I believe that if she had been within the reach of a lethal weapon she would have killed him on the spot. She trembled violently from head to foot and her face, pink with temper a moment be-

212

fore, was now as white as her long, elegant gloves. At last she made an indeterminate sound that might have been a word, a cough, or an intake of breath. Then, before I could look at her again, she whipped around and walked jerkily through the open door and out of my life. It was years before I spoke to her again and when I did it was in vastly different circumstances.

I got up and drifted over to the smeared window, craning my neck around the intervening stack in order to see her climb into her car and shoot off up the incline in a flurry of blue exhaust. Uncle Reuben went back to his chair and slumped down in it, his Victorian eloquence spent and his heavy breathing betraying the fact that now the interview was over he was badly shaken by the turn it had taken. He sat for a moment pressing his hands on the desk and then muttered hoarsely, "Close the door, boy!"

I closed it and sat down near the window, exhausted, embarrassed and utterly wretched.

"I don't blame you doing what you did, John, and I certainly don't blame her daughter," he said, suddenly. "If she was my mother I wouldn't run away from her, I'd make her some toadstool soup, or push her under a bus when no one was looking!"

I said nothing; there seemed nothing adequate to say; and he mistook my silence and subjection for fear.

"You don't want to worry about any of her crazy threats, boy," he went on. "There isn't a thing she can do and her solicitor has already told her or she would have done it. I'll tell you something else, though. I think it would be a good idea all around if you cleared out of here for a bit. With her around and you going about your business, you never know what trouble she might go out of her way to begin! Go for a walk, boy, and let me think this out. Whatever we do ought to be done at once!"

I got up and stood beside him. "Thanks, Uncle Reuben," I said, and meant it, from the bottom of my heart.

I went out and through the town, turning my back on Sennacharib and taking the riverside road. For the first time since I had gone to Heronslea on the afternoon of my fifteenth birthday, Sennacharib was somewhere I did not want to be. At that particular moment it suggested scribblings on lavatory walls.

3.

It was mid-September when Diana and I surrendered. By the second week in October I had left Whinmouth and, apart from an occasional holiday, was to remain away for nearly three years. Uncle Reuben must have moved with uncharacteristic speed, for within a few days of Mrs. Gayelorde-Sutton's visit to the office, I was installed as glorified office boy on the staff of *The Illustrated Echo*, off Bouverie Street, E.C. 4. Here I remained for my period of exile, my home a bed-sitting room, within a twopenny Underground ride of the City.

It was sound judgment on Uncle Reuben's part to spirit me away from Whinmouth. The roar and bustle of London and the excitement of a new job in new surroundings enabled me to get my preoccupation with Diana into some sort of perspective and to isolate it from my everyday life of work, snack lunches and interminable journeys on the Underground. Soon I was able to enclose it in a kind of glass case, like a man living a shabby, hand-to-mouth existence who owns a single object of great beauty, something that is a source of comfort and inspiration to him.

Every night during those first autumn weeks, when my feet were aching from pounding asphalt pavements, and when I was shut off from the endless murmur of London and crouching over a minute gas fire in my second-floor back room, in Guilford Street, my mind would return to Sennacharib as an exile's seeking home, and I would follow again the wide curves of Teasel Brook, or climb up through the larch wood to the oak paddock and watch for buzzards.

I cannot honestly say that I was unhappy. Sometimes the very consciousness of exile brought with it a curious satisfaction, as though I were doing an enforced penance for some unrepented sin, and when I remembered Diana it was not with a lover's yearning. Part of my mind was occupied in preparing for the future, our future, and pondering the economics of our problem. With the other part I ranged the museum of the past, examining and analyzing each hour we had spent together and recalling every significant remark we had exchanged during our expeditions on the common, to the tower, or during our stay on Nun's Island.

I made no effort to get in touch with her, knowing that a botched attempt would jeopardize the future and very probably make things unpleasant for both of us. I had no idea where she had been sent, or what she was doing, and for a long time I made no attempt to satisfy my curiosity in this field.

Once, during a week's holiday in Devon, I nerved myself to creep through the Heronslea copse on the Shepherdshey road, but the house looked deserted and Nat told me that the family never seemed to come now, although they continued to maintain a large outdoor staff. After that I went back to my job and my uninspiring lodgings, waiting for her to find a means of getting in touch with me, and as the months passed it became easier to put aside all thought of her, often for days at a time, and catch up on a youth that seemed, in some ways, to have been petrified since the day Keeper Croker applied his half nelson and she rode out of the woods like a princess in a fairy tale.

I made a few friends among the junior staff. I even took one or two of the girl clerks and packers to the cinema. I learned to drink. I explored London and parts of Kent, improved my French at a night school, and even attended an Italian class one night a week. *The Illustrated Echo* was a pleasant office in which to work and the job suited my inclinations very well at that time. The *Echo* was a weekly magazine that made two quite separate approaches to its subscribers. The main part of the publication was devoted to what might be called social and historical flashbacks; the remaining pages were crammed with a wide variety of literary competitions, quizzes, and crossword puzzles, all rather more original than was customary in this type of periodical during the thirties. The editor,

215

Edwin Blackler, was a former *County Observer* reporter and an old friend of Uncle Reuben's. That was how the job had been secured for me, and I think I did my best during that first year or so to acknowledge this debt and convince Mr. Blackler that I was a very ambitious young man, anxious to advance in my profession and grateful for the opportunity to arrive in Fleet Street before I was twenty.

My work was at first limited to errand running and stamplicking, but after a few weeks, when I had impressed myself upon the chief subeditor by giving him an idea, I was promoted to a very junior position on the editorial staff and given a raise that brought my salary up to five pounds a week. Out of this I had to pay out more than two pounds for fares and lodgings, but even so it was a great advance on what I had been getting in Whinmouth, and by economizing on lunches I was able to accumulate money in a post-office savings account. The first year I was there I was tipped the winner of the Grand National and made an extra twenty pounds. This might have tempted me to speculate further on racing, but luckily for me Mr. Blackler heard about it and being of the same nonconformist cast of mind as his friend Reuben, he called me in and read me a terrifying lecture on the evils of gambling. This would not have deterred me from joining in the office pastime of spotting winners but I was anxious at that time to make a good impression on him and left the bookies alone.

A week or two after that I went to Blackler with a sheaf of ideas and he welcomed them, for it was difficult to find something new and sensational in the flashback field every week of the year. He at once set me to work collecting material and old photographs for a ten-page feature on Jack the Ripper, and afterwards on the South Sea Bubble and, later still, material for a pictorial inquiry into the assassination of the Archduke that had touched off the First World War.

It was exacting but absorbing work. Most of the day I trotted about London, keeping a careful tally of my bus fares and visiting record offices, embassies, museums, picture galleries, and the like. Sometimes I would have a slice of luck, as when I found someone whose aged father had been associated with the actor Booth who murdered President Lincoln, and I was able to hand in some unpublished photographs of the sixties and a wedge of secondhand theories about Booth's motives. Whatever its drawbacks, the job was never dull and left me free time in the evenings; I used this time to make myself thoroughly familiar with London and loiter in the Charing Cross Road bookshops.

This was not simply a means of passing the time. It was the result of some constructive thought about my future. I was determined, by now, to become a full-time writer, but the theatre interested me far less than it interested most young men and I greatly doubted my ability to write a novel. My strongest suit, I soon decided, was history, and I decided to put it to work in a way that was probably influenced by the *Echo*. It was an easy step from raking up material of a sensational aspect of the past to turning the same stories into full-length narratives.

My method of approach was naïve but nonetheless practical. I went through all the reference books relating to each subject that interested me and when satisfied that nothing had been published on it for the past half century, I noted it down and finally emerged with a curious list of characters who had never been presented to the reading public as anything other than two-dimensional people in the national biography.

My favorite among these was Margaret of Anjou, wife of Henry VII and leader of the Lancastrian cause throughout the Wars of the Roses. When I had amassed all the data I could find on her, I got a reader's ticket to the British Museum and from then on spent a good deal of my spare time under the famous dome. I bought a fat exercise book, a folding card table and a battered old typewriter, and with these tools joined the martyred army of literary geniuses living in the square mile around Euston Station. I think I was more in love with my role than I was with my material, but for all that the book began to grow under the title of *The Royal Tigress*.

It was cold and desperately lonely up there in a narrow bed-sitter, overlooking a car breaker's yard and acres of somber houses, but the room and the aspect were valuable stage properties, and as the story of the dynastic struggle took shape I congratulated myself on graduating from hack journalist to unrecognized genius. It was a kind of game I played and it helped to compensate me for the loss of the southwest wind off Whinmouth quay and the golden glare of the gorse thickets climbing Teasel Edge.

I suppose I had been working off *The Royal Tigress* for about three months when I came across an item in the gossip column of an evening paper. I had, as I said, made up my mind not to approach Diana, and because I saw no ready means of doing so I had been able to maintain this resolve. All the same, I kept half-hoping that she would contact me by writing to the *Observer,* in Whinmouth. When the months went by without her doing so, I began to wonder if Uncle Reuben, acting on the principle of doing something for someone else's good, might have received and held back a letter or letters. This doubt nagged at me so persistently that I was at length forced to write to him and ask if any letters had come for me. I knew I would get the truth. Uncle Reuben never committed a lie to paper.

He replied innocently that there had been no letters, and his reply bothered me. I began to lose some of my smugness about Diana's fidelity and, in the intervals between tracing the route the beaten Lancastrians had taken after Towton and in digging up photographs and material for the *Illustrated,* I wondered whether she had forgotten all about our pledges and had now regarded me as what she would have described as a "sixth-form pash." Every day I began to doubt her a little more, and every tug of doubt disturbed the comparative tranquillity of spirit I had painfully acquired since we had stood together beside the island bonfire awaiting the arrival of the pilot boat.

By midsummer I was in a ferment about her and my anxieties, added to a heat wave that made central London an insufferable place in which to work and sleep, combined to make me a very wretched and homesick young man.

I was in this self-pitying frame of mind when I got my first lead. It came at the cinema, during a brief newsreel dealing with Goodwood races. The winner of the cup that year was a Frenchman, and although I did not recognize the name when it was spoken by the commentator, I sat up when I saw Diana's French boy, Yves, mincing along beside his father as the winner was being led in after the race.

I searched the screen for Diana and would have been grateful to recognize Mrs. Gayelorde-Sutton among the spectators, but the item soon flashed by and although I sat through the desperately boring feature film twice in order to scan the newsreel again, I learned no more than the bare fact of Diana's friend's triumph.

That night, sleepless and half suffocating in my airless little room, I went over the social calendar of Mrs. Gayelorde-Sutton—Goodwood, Wimbledon, Hurlingham, Ascot, and so on—wondering if Diana was likely to return from wherever she was to accompany her mother to any of these functions, and if she did so, assessing my chances of seeing her at one or other of them and attracting her attention without risking a snub or worse from her parents.

I decided the chance was slim. Our paper did not cover social or sporting events, and the Gayelorde-Suttons always had the most expensive seats. Lacking a press card I was unlikely to get within hailing distance of them, even supposing they were present. Toward daybreak I thought up another half-baked plan, that of phoning the Gayelorde-Suttons's town house under an assumed name and accent, but this was a humiliating failure when I put it into operation the next day. A manservant at the other end of the phone at once asked my name and business and seemed entirely dissatisfied with my mumbled replies. Finally he rang off and I slunk away, telling myself that I was no good at this sort of thing and had no right to be within miles of Fleet Street. Any cub reporter, I knew, would have managed a good deal better than that.

I studied the glossies around Ascot time, hoping I might glean some information from the gossip column. Then I spent an evening or two picketing the house in Palmerston

Crescent but gave it up when an elderly constable, after eying me distastefully from the opposite side of the road, crossed over with the obvious intention of moving me on or charging me with loitering.

All this led nowhere and only served to increase my anxiety and frustration. Gone was the resolute attitude of my first months of separation. I had to get information of some kind. The next time I was in Whinmouth I made another cautious tour of the Heronslea copses, and even went so far as to get into casual conversation with an estate gardener in the public bar of The Rifleman. From him I learned that Mr. and Mrs. Gayelorde-Sutton were in America and "the maid was abroad somewhere but not along of 'em." It was the first definite knowledge I had had in almost a year that Diana was still alive, and although it comforted me somewhat (for I reasoned that this went some way toward explaining her failure to write) it did nothing toward re-establishing contact.

Nobody at home referred to Diana. Uncle Reuben had had a satisfactory report about me from his friend, the editor, and I could see that he had now completely forgotten the part Diana had played in removing me to London in the first place. Although, in some ways, I liked going back to Whinmouth, I was always glad when it was time to return to the privacy of my bed-sitter and the demands of *The Illustrated Echo*. In London I was able to keep Diana in her glass case some of the time. Down here she popped out of it every few moments, and the closer I went to Sennacharib, the more painful and depressing became my thoughts.

It was after my return on that occasion that I made my first real effort to put her out of mind altogether. I had written barely a page of *The Royal Tigress* since the night I saw Yves on the newsreel and now I forced myself to contemplate the empty prospects that faced me if I failed to get over Diana and discovered, after years of waiting perhaps, that I was nothing more to her than the partner in an adolescent prank. Sometimes I imagined I could hear her discussing me with a sophisticated friend, over a coffee on some exotic terrace by the sea. "Jan? Oh, we had a lot of fun when Mummy wasn't looking! He was frightfully stuck on me I believe, but the weeniest bit dreary, darling, taken all round."

I was certainly becoming a dull young dog, and one day Twining, the friendly, pimply subeditor, who was several years my senior, told me as much. Twining had married the previous year, after getting his girl into trouble, and now lived out at Twickenham in a semidetached. At the office he frequently bewailed his premature loss of freedom and inveighed against the economic miseries of marriage and parenthood.

"By God, young Leigh," he told me when he overheard me saying that I had no plans for the evening, "you single blokes don't know when you're well off, I'm damned if you do! Look, son, you're free, you've got dough in your pocket, you can go where you like and you can stop there until morning, with no one to chew the fat over you when you turn up with a hangover and a contented cow's look on your mug. What's eating a kid like you? Why the hell don't you see life while you've got the chance and before some calculating Judy puts tabs on you?"

Twining was no more than a chance acquaintance and never, during my stay in London, did he qualify as a friend, but by this time I felt a desperate need to confide in someone, so without reflecting much upon the matter I told him about Diana. I was surprised and slightly flattered by his interest. He asked me scores of questions about her and gave my answers a good deal of thought. Finally he blew out his cheeks and regarded me with amused contempt.

"Christ, kid," he said, "you've got it bad, haven't you? It's a good job you told me about this, though, because Uncle Twining is the very man to see you through it! I'll tell you what, let's knock off and go down to the pub for a jar. We can talk it over in comparative privacy down there."

I instantly regretted having told him. I was not much attracted to him and I was young enough and green enough to be shocked by his casual attitude to marriage. I had met his wife, a fluffy, talkative little blonde, and I pitied her.

Their marriage seemed a very shallow and tawdry partnership when measured against my dreams of marriage to Diana. However, there was no help for it now, so we adjourned to the local pub and carried our beer to an alcove, where he became jocularly confidential.

"Listen here, son, I'm years older than you and maybe it's none of my biz but damn it, I don't like to see a chap hooked the way I was and that's what you're heading into —you'll get married on the rebound to the first bit of skirt you meet the day the lady of the manor gives you the brush-off! Yes, yes, I know, that can't happen, you'll say, but it will, Buddy, it will and I'll tell you how and why."

He then launched into a colorful description of Diana's set, and he knew them well, for he had worked for a time on the gossip page of a daily.

"They're as hard as nails, son, and just as mercenary as their mothers, so don't get any ideas to the contrary. Oh, they're okay for slap and tickle when they're on the point of 'being launched,' and you really can't blame 'em, because the men they eventually do marry never have any lead in their pencils and somehow they know it, even at that age. That's why they run off with chaps like you and make hay while the sun shines, but when it comes to marrying, brother, they keep their eye smack on the ball! Nothing less than three to five thou' a year and a title if they can hook one. You can't blame 'em for that either. If you'd been brought up with someone to wait on you hand, foot and finger, and if you'd kipped in the Carlton at Cannes from the time you could remember, would you trade it to change shoes with an unpaid char and a fortnight at Margate with the kids every August?"

"But Diana isn't like that," I protested, angrily. "She hates the way she's been brought up and there's not an atom of snobbery about her."

He laughed unpleasantly, and although he was genuinely trying to help me I could have struck him across the mouth.

"I didn't expect you to believe me," he said. "You're a bloody little romantic and you've got it coming to you, but you'll believe me in the end, son. You'll look back on this

222

conversation and say to yourself, 'Old Twining was spot on! Old Twining knew his way around. Everything he said would happen *has* happened!' Damn it, man, forget the moonlight and roses for a minute and look on it from the practical viewpoint. How in God's name do you reckon you'll ever be able to keep a girl like that? Suppose you make the grade here? Suppose you land a good job with a national daily? Even then you won't take home more than thirty a week, and I daresay she spends that on clothes and make-up right now. Have another jar, on me this time —you look as if you need one!"

We had another drink and then two more. By the time I had seen Twining onto his train at Waterloo I was slightly drunk and very desperate. He leaned out of the compartment window and gave me a final piece of advice.

"What you need, Leigh, is a woman. Boy, oh boy, do you need a woman! *Any* woman! Take my advice, son, get yourself one tonight and start fresh."

I didn't take his advice at that time. I was far too timid to come to much harm in London and on the few occasions that a prostitute had accosted me I had always mumbled something unintelligible and hurried on my way, with my eyes at pavement level. I told myself, of course, that this was because of Diana but I don't think it was, not at that time. Uncle Reuben had forced himself to lecture me on this subject before he turned me loose in town, and when a closer familiarity with men like Twining encouraged me to take some of his dire warnings with a large pinch of salt, I was engrossed in my book and in grandiose dreams of the future. There was no room in my life for casual encounters.

The conversation, however, did have a sequel.

A week or two later Twining rang down from the subs' room and said that his wife had gone over to her sister's for the weekend and had taken the baby with her. He was on the loose for one Saturday afternoon and evening, and would I care to join him in a pub crawl? I said I had nothing better to do, and when we left the office about 2 P.M. he piloted me toward a battered Austin Twelve tourer, parked in our truck ramp.

"It's my brother-in-law's," he told me, gleefully. "He said I could have it until tomorrow and it's given me a swell idea. What do you say to a run out into the country, just to see what's growing down there?"

I much preferred this to the cinema and an aimless drift around the suburban pubs, but it was soon clear that Twining's curiosity about the country had nothing to do with wild flowers. We headed straight for Tonbridge, where he had once worked as an estate agent's clerk, and from an inn on the outskirts of the town he made a phone call and rejoined me in high feather.

"I've fixed a date with Peggy," he said. "She's a nifty little piece, an old girl friend of mine, and she's promised to find a friend. There's a hop over at Penshurst, you see, nothing much, but good for a lark, and listen—she says we can go back to her place after for coffee and sandwiches. We're in luck, son! Her old man kicked the bucket years ago and her old woman is deaf as a post and goes to bed at nine anyway."

I felt a certain amount of pleasurable excitement at the prospect of such an evening. Looking back, it seems incredible to me that I had arrived at my eighteenth birthday without ever having been interested in a girl other than Diana, but I know that this was so. I think I was more curious than eager to hold another girl in my arms and try someone else's kisses. Suddenly I began to feel almost grateful to Twining for including me in this philandering expedition.

We had tea and picked up the girls at Peggy's home, a largish, cottage-type house in a quiet, tree-lined cul-de-sac. Peggy was a slim, boyish-looking blonde—Twining was only interested in blondes—and she seemed delighted to welcome him back. I learned afterwards that they had been engaged for a time and it was obvious that she had no idea that he was now a married man.

The girl she brought for me was Madeleine. She seemed at first a vaguely disinterested young woman. Later I realized that this air was only assumed for my benefit, for when she forgot to pose she became friendly and talkative.

"I'm so glad you're tall," she told me, soon after we had

been introduced and had settled ourselves in the back of the car. "I can't stand little men at any price!"

"A little goes a long way," chuckled Twining, who was small himself.

He had already started to paw Peggy in the front of the car and settled down to enjoy himself with desperate resolution.

"Well, girls and boys, off we go! First stop The Bull, Hildenborough, second stop The Cock, Leigh—pronounced 'Li,' Mr. Leigh! Bull and cock! Highly appropriate, what?" and he laughed uproariously at his own feeble quip.

I glanced at Peggy to see how she would take this, for secretly almost everything Twining said was inclined to shock me a little, but she was obviously accustomed to his type of humor and only said, "Now George, behave!" as we roared out of town, Twining showing off madly with a series of rapid gear changes, and Madeleine looking out of the window with studied unconcern, as though already raising a line of defense against tepidity on my part.

I stole a cautious look at her as we went along. She was dark and pale to the point of being pasty. She had a full face and slightly pendulous cheeks, but her eyes were large and brown, with curling lashes that reminded me of Diana's. She had a ripe, sulky mouth and now that I was able to look at her more closely, I saw that she was a good deal older than Peggy, twenty-two at least, and apparently experienced with men. On the way out I rather wished we could swop girls, for Peggy's freshness and vitality appealed to me far more than Madeleine's sultry charm, but there could be no question of that, so I made up my mind that the sooner we had a drink or two, the better would be the prospect of a pleasant evening. I might lose my embarrassment at being paired off with a complete stranger, and she might loosen up a little and come halfway to meet me.

We stopped at the two pubs Twining had named. The girls had gins and lime and we drank beer. Peggy soon became very giggly, but I was right about Madeleine. After the second stop she made the running, nestling close to me, lifting my hand and putting it on her lap.

Soon I began to enjoy myself in a mild sort of way and the evening passed pleasantly enough. The dance was a jolly uninhibited affair, with plenty of loud laughter, bursting balloons, streamers, and squeals of delight from the patrons. We stayed until midnight and then made our way back to Tonbridge, Twining driving with one hand and mounting the curb as we swung into the quiet cul-de-sac where Peggy lived.

Peggy told us to be very quiet, and we all filed in through the back door. The coffee and sandwiches were there but they were mere pretexts. After a sip and a nibble Twining and Peggy retired to the front room, Twining winking at me as he left and pinching the little blonde's bottom with an air of a customer sampling goods.

There was an awkward silence after they had gone. Then Madeleine said, "You haven't been out with many girls, have you, John?"

I was prepared to bluff but she smiled and gave me a peck on the forehead. She looked much more attractive when she smiled and my shame at being spotted as an amateur was reduced by her good-natured approach.

"Never mind," she said, "I'd much sooner have you than that nasty piece of work in there! He's an absolute stinker and for the life of me I can't understand what Peggy sees in him."

I said that nobody could ever see what anyone else saw in anyone. I also admitted that her guess about my lack of experience was accurate. Her interest in this confession surprised me.

"Why?" she wanted to know. "Did you once go steady with someone?"

"Yes," I said, "for a long time—ever since I was a kid."

"But you're only a kid now," she laughed, and then, quite gently: "What happened? Come unstuck?"

"More or less."

"Want to talk about it?"

"No."

"I'm glad," she said. "Most of the chaps I get landed with do. I'm a universal aunt and it isn't very flattering."

She said this so solemnly that I felt sorry for her. I put

my arms around her and kissed her, lightly at first but more enthusiastically when she responded with a kind of desperate eagerness. She was a nice girl to kiss and I lost all my shyness after we had stood swaying for a moment or two.

"I like you, John, you're a decent boy, not at all the type I should expect George Twining to go around with," she said, rather breathlessly.

I told her that Twining wasn't a friend, just an office colleague, and she told me that she had recently been thrown over by a boy she expected to marry and that this was the second time, not counting friendships that hadn't amounted to much from the beginning.

"I can't understand that," I said. "You're jolly good company and I think you're pretty and exciting!"

I was alarmed by her reaction to this gallant speech on my part. I only said it with the intention of cheering her up but it had the effect of transforming her expression into something approaching radiancy. I had never had to say things like this to Diana. She didn't need to be flattered or courted, because it had been obvious to her from our first meeting that I regarded her as the most exciting person on earth. With Madeleine it was very different. She took my hands in hers and gazed at me with eyes as soft and wide as a heifer's.

"Do you think so? Do you *really* think so, John? Oh, I could hug Peggy for ringing me up tonight! Look—why are we standing like this? There's a sofa in the corner and we might as well make ourselves comfortable. Peggy and George will be necking in there until early morning."

My experience with girls might have been limited but it was wide enough to understand now why men had shied away from Madeleine. She wasn't content with rushing fences, she kicked her way through them. Before I knew what was happening, the lights were out, the back door key was turned and we were clinging to one another on the sofa. I don't remember taking an active part in these preliminaries.

It was an old and uncomfortable sofa and seemed to have been designed by someone who enjoyed making

227

things difficult for lovers. It had a hard, shiny surface and any sudden movement was apt to deposit one or both of us onto the floor. After two such humiliations we settled for this and made ourselves comfortable as possible with cushions. Here, after a great deal of kissing and clumsy caressing, my enthusiasm overtook hers, but her protests seemed to me very halfhearted and I persisted, so that at length she whispered, "Wait a minute, John—please!" and removed herself from me in the darkness. A moment later I realized that her protests had been lodged in defense of her dance frock and not, as I had imagined, on behalf of her honor, for when she came back to me she had removed her dress and we had soon pressed the encounter to its logical conclusion.

I don't remember feeling as guilty or apprehensive in my life and she sensed it at once.

"It was what you wanted, wasn't it, John?" she asked anxiously.

I made a tremendous effort to convey a gratitude that I did not feel and kissed her, misjudging the distance in the dark and kissing her neck instead of her face.

"Yes, of course, Madeleine," I said, and while the answer seemed to satisfy her it sounded to me like the words of a man confessing to a crime that would hustle him to the gallows.

I don't know how long we sat there, tired, cold and crumpled, but at last she got up, humming a snatch of a tune we had heard earlier in the evening. I can remember the tune. It was "Little White Lies," and whenever I hear it now, it conjures up a small wavelet of that vast tide of guilt and fear that poured over me as we slouched about Peggy's kitchen, making fresh coffee and waiting for Twining to emerge from the front room.

We said very little but it was clear that Madeleine did not share my crushing load of dismay. As she tidied her hair, pausing in her pattings and combings to give me swift, sidelong smiles, there was an air of smugness and complacency about her. At that particular time I hated her for it.

4.

My feelings of apprehension about this incident persisted for some time but my sense of guilt disappeared almost at once. In fact, as time went on and no dire consequences resulted, I began to feel mildly defiant about it, as though, by making love to a stranger, I had scored off Diana and punished her for demonstrating that she had outgrown our pledges and had no intention of renewing them.

All that winter this resentment against her mounted, and alongside it there grew in me a deliberate intention to vindicate myself as a man ill-used by a woman in whom he had reposed trust. It was a painful, gradual process. The plant that Diana had nourished in me over a period of three impressionable years had grown very deep roots, and it was not easy to extract them. When I first came to London the most innocent friendship with an office girl would have constituted a shameless betrayal of our Sennacharib vows. I am not claiming that this was a sensible attitude for a boy of my age and experience, but am simply stating that it was so. Even my confidences to a man like Twining had seemed an act of disloyalty and the passage with Madeleine was a bonfire of all my hopes and ideals at the time. Later the sense of personal betrayal left me and I began to rationalize my behavior, and this became much easier as the months passed and I made more friends among the staff, and one or two fellow lodgers. Twining was one of the first to notice the change in me and having surmised, quite accurately, what had happened between Madeleine and me while he was closeted in the front room, he lost no time in taking the credit for it.

"What did I tell you, young Leigh?" he chaffed, when he overheard me making a date with the switchboard operator at work. "You're a changed man since that night out we had in Tonbridge. You ought to hand it to that pal of Peggy's, she's made a man out of you! Have you seen her again? Has she come down on you for seven-and-six yet?"

He meant this as a joke and I accepted it as such, but if

he had known the hours of worry I had undergone regarding this very contingency he would have laughed his silly head off. As a matter of fact, I still had qualms about Madeleine and they were not wholly selfish. I could not forget her pathetic response to my lighthearted compliment and the eagerness she had shown to win my affection. If I had been as cynical as I am now, I should have wasted no sympathy on a girl who surrendered to a greenhorn like me after such a poor show of resistance, but in those days I was deeply ashamed of the fact that I had used her, not as a human being but as a means of defiance, a jeer at someone who had hurt me. It was because of these misgivings that I did not write to her, though she had pressed her address upon me when we parted. I don't suppose I should have seen her again, had she not passed a message to me via Twining, saying that she and Peggy were coming to town one Saturday and suggesting that we meet and go to a show. Twining, to his regret was unable to accept, but he advised me to meet her, and we had tea in Fuller's, and then went to a film. I had regarded the expedition as an act of penance, but Madeleine looked so attractive in a little blue and white pinafore frock and matching beret, and proved so agreeable a companion up to the moment of parting at Victoria Station, that I recklessly made plans to meet her the following Saturday and even found myself looking forward to the occasion throughout the week.

We made no reference during our conversation to what had taken place at Tonbridge. Confronted with her again and lacking all hope of privacy in London, I was too shy, while she, sensing as much, was apparently learning the value of tact. I was determined that on the next occasion we met we should have some privacy and although it was against house rules to bring girls into our rooms, I determined to risk it and laid in a simple supper, planning the evening so that we should have a couple of hours alone before her last train at eleven o'clock.

It was not a cold-blooded maneuver on my part. I was fond of Madeleine, and the prospect of making love to her again filled me with the kind of excitement I had once felt in keeping an early morning appointment with Diana at the tower. Even so, I am not pretending that it was more than the normal anticipation any youth feels for the company of a girl who he knows will accommodate him. During that week, whenever I thought of Madeleine coming all the way up from Tonbridge to spend a few hours in my company, I did so with a male arrogance that was new to me. I no longer regarded her as a weapon against Diana's indifference, and that in itself was significant, for it meant that the embers of the Sennacharib fires were now almost extinct. Chance, or another miracle, was to demonstrate how hopelessly wrong I was in this respect.

Madeleine's train was due into Victoria at three twenty, and I had a lunchtime call to make on behalf of the *Echo,* in Soho. After making the call and eating a quick lunch, I sauntered out into Piccadilly with an hour or so to spare, intending to walk slowly along toward the Ritz and cut across the park to the station.

I had reached Hatchard's and was idling beside the window absorbed in the new titles, when I heard a voice that made me spin around like a teetotum. There, paying off a taxi about five yards from where I was loitering, stood Mrs. Gayelorde-Sutton, and Diana waiting alongside her.

It was fortunate that they were not looking in my direction. I was so staggered by their appearance, and by the immense changes in Diana's appearance, that at least thirty seconds elapsed before I could collect myself sufficiently to turn my back on them and keep them in view in the plate-glass reflection. I stood there trembling as Mrs. Gayelorde-Sutton moved off past me toward the Circus and Diana crossed the pavement and disappeared into Fortnum and Mason's. Then, hardly able to believe my luck, I rushed in pursuit and watched her pass through the main part of the shop and turn into the dimly lit tobacco department. It was a convenient counter at which to observe her. I stood half-concealed behind a pillar and gazed and gazed at the elegant young woman who had replaced the tousled schoolgirl I had held in my arms under the tarpaulin on the night of the gale. I could never have believed that a person could change so much in so short a time.

She had developed a dress sense that rivaled her mother's. She wore a light, heather-blue coat with a wide fur collar and under the coat, which was open, a calf-length dress in a darker shade of blue, picked out with tiny white bows, like those on the dress of the celebrated Renoir girl. She had silk stockings, crocodile-skin shoes with three-inch heels, and a matching handbag as big as a satchel. Her hat was an outrageous piece of nonsense, a cross between a hussar's and a cossack's, flattened over the left eye and crowned with a blue tassel that matched her coat. Her thick chestnut hair had been severely disciplined, and although she was using plenty of make-up, the bloom and freshness of her complexion owed little to cosmetics but sprang from a radiantly healthy skin. Her cheeks had the soft glow of petals and her eyes, as huge and blue as I remembered, still held in their depths the laughter and mischief of Diana of Heronslea. It was all that was left, except perhaps the promise of her mouth.

Her figure had greatly improved. In her beautifully cut clothes she looked as trim as a model, her narrow waist emphasizing the firmness of her breasts and the long line of her shapely legs. My mind went back to the winter's day when she and her mother had come into Uncle Luke's quayside Mart to buy cottage furniture, and I recalled how gauche and insignificant I had felt when they inspected our seedy wares in the light of a single, naked bulb. Today the contrast was even more marked, for here she stood in one of the most exclusive shops in the world, once more giving the impression that she had paid the management a great compliment by entering it.

For a split second, as this memory crossed my mind, I was tempted to leave the place without speaking to her. Always unattainable, she now seemed to have removed herself to another planet, for how, I reasoned, could such an enchanting creature look at a down-at-heel wretch like me with anything but amused patronage? How could she be blamed for murmuring a few polite words and excusing herself gently but absolutely from a situation that could only bring us stuttering embarrassment? Then what remained of my pride came to my aid. It was an inadequate reinforcement but just enough to make me stand my ground. As she completed her purchase and moved away from the counter, I stepped out from behind the pillar and whipped off my ten-and-sixpenny trilby.

"Hello, Di!" I said, my voice not much above a whisper.

She stopped about a yard away, her lips parted, her eyes as serious as I had ever seen them. For several seconds we stood there facing one another, and then, with a rush of delight that made me want to shout at the top of my voice, I saw her cheeks flush with pleasure and she rushed forward to seize both my hands, hitching the shoulder bag to give free movement to her arms, and pulling me toward her so violently that the battered trilby I was holding slipped from my grasp and rolled on the carpet.

"Jan!" she exclaimed. "Oh, Jan, *Jan!*"

I was so moved by the warmth of her greeting that I was unable to say another word. As I stared at her, feeling the strong pressure of her gloved hands on my fingers, all the doubts and dismays of the past two years fell away from me like Christian's sins and went tumbling down into limbo. I was left with a lightness of heart that I could not hope to express in conventional greetings, for inside me, buried under a debris of loneliness and drabness, the spring and glory of Sennacharib stirred, bursting through the sour crust of London and soaring like the buzzards above the paddock oaks.

I must have said something when she proposed tea in the adjoining lounge, and I must have followed her to the little whitewood table in the alcove where we spent the next hour, but I remember nothing of this and not much of what we spoke about after the first breathless exchanges.

"Jan, it's been so long, so long!" she said, studying me from head to foot, her eyes dancing and flashing with excitement. "You've grown so! Stand up! Let me look at you! Let me take you in!" And when I stood somewhat shamefacedly (for she was the same uninhibited Diana and made no effort to keep her voice low): "Mmmmm! *Mmmmmm!* You're bigger and broader and more masculine than ever! I knew you would be, of course, but you've

233

filled out much more than I expected and you're still growing—you're over six foot now."

"Six-one-and-a-half," I said. "But now for heaven's sake let me sit down! I feel an absolute Charlie, standing up for inspection in Fortnum and Mason's tea lounge."

We both laughed aloud. That was what I found so remarkable about this meeting. Within minutes we were perfectly at ease with one another and the waiting months, which had wrought such changes in each of us, had been scattered like a drift of leaves. "Well?" she said, as soon as the waitress had set down the tray and turned her back on us. "How about me? Do you think I've changed at all?"

"You look absolutely wonderful, Diana," I told her. "Grown up—frighteningly so—and so marvelously pretty that they must be absolute idiots not to sign you up as a film star!"

She was pleased and did not mind showing it. "As a matter of fact they've tried to," she admitted. "Not here, though—I'm not the Elstree type—but in France, you know, where they only make films about precociously sexy little misses, who keep running away from convents. Now tell me more about yourself. What are you doing in London? What kind of job have you got up here? How does a husky like you keep all the flappers away? Tell me everything—*everything,* Jan!"

I told her almost everything: how and why Uncle Reuben had whisked me away from Whinmouth, all about *The Illustrated Echo* and about the book I was writing on Margaret of Anjou, and how I hoped it would be published before I was twenty; also something of how I had hoped and schemed to get in touch with her over the last year.

She nodded gravely when I came to this and said, "We'll discuss that later, Jan. In the meantime, I want to hear exactly what you aim to do in the future. Do you want to be a real London journalist, you know, Fleet Street pubs, a stained raincoat, frenzied dashes to trouble spots and all that? Or would you much prefer to be an author who crams a special subject and then unloads it on an unsuspecting public?"

234

It sounded as though she was disinclined to take my writing very seriously and I was slightly piqued. She noticed this at once and added, hurriedly, "Oh I'm not pooh-poohing the idea, Jan. I always knew you'd turn into *some* kind of writer but right at the back of my mind I always had a different kind of hunch about you. I had it from the first day we met."

"What sort of hunch?" I asked curiously.

"Oh, I don't know . . . nothing really specific, just something to do with land—farming, dairy cattle, poultry breeding, market gardening—that's in your blood, Jan, whether you know it or not."

"Is it?" I asked, lamely.

"Yes, Jan, it certainly is. I always recognized that because you can't feel about a countryside the way you feel about Sennacharib unless it's a part of your nerves and blood and bone."

"Do you mean that you'd be disappointed if I stayed a journalist all my life, Di?" I asked, puzzled by the sudden turn the conversation had taken.

"Yes, I think I would," she said slowly, "and so, in the end, would you, Jan!"

We had our tea and she told me a little about what had happened to her—how she had been abroad practically the whole time, either at a school in Tours or, during vacations, with the French horsy family near Périgueux. I did not give her my full attention. I wanted to think about what she had said. It was odd, I reflected, that none of the conversations we had had while riding and wandering in Sennacharib had led us to this subject—the prospect of my returning to the occupation of all my West Country forebears, up to the time that Grandpa Leigh took to swilling rum and rode to his death on Nun's Bay rocks, but it was difficult to think objectively in her presence, I was far too elated and excited. All I wanted to talk about was us—how we could start again, where we could meet, how much personal freedom she had, how often she went to Heronslea, and dozens of other questions directed at a single target—how soon we could be as important to each other as we had been during those days of isolation on the island.

Before I could explore this vital subject she glanced at her watch and said that she had arranged to meet her mother at four o'clock, at Brown's Hotel, where they were staying while the decorators worked on their town house, in Palmerston Crescent.

"It's being renovated from top to bottom," she said, "and the party is being held there on the eleventh of next month."

She told me then that this was to be the first of her coming-out parties and that there were to be a whole series of them throughout her season. Later on, in mid-June, she thought, there was to be a country party at Heronslea and about the same time she was being presented, just the way it had been planned, years and years ago.

"Don't look so tragic, Jan!" she laughed, reaching across the table and patting my crestfallen face with her glove. "I expect I shall survive it. Everyone else seems to."

I knew very little more about young girls' seasons or presentations at court than I had known when she had first described the ritual, but what did depress me as she outlined her program was the conviction that I had no place in any part of it. The whole silly business would remove her from me more effectively than she had been removed during the past two years. What made it even worse was that she now seemed to be reconciled to all the fuss and glitter that attended a season. There was none of the pouting disparagement that she had shown in our Sennacharib days. Coming out, I brooded, would mean constant chaperonage and behind that the shadow of serious competitors.

I said nothing about all this, for she gave me no opening. Although, from the very outset of our meeting, her attitude toward me was very frank and friendly, she made no reference to our former relationship. When she looked at her watch again I called the waitress and asked for the bill, but I dared not let her go without some kind of reassurance.

"When can I see you again, Diana?" I demanded. "We can't just . . . just meet and part again like this!"

She began pulling on her gloves and frowned at her hands. For a second, as she did this, I saw a wraith of the old Diana, muttering terrible incantations against the thieves of her freedom. Then the frown disappeared and she gave me a brittle little smile.

"You must leave that to me, Jan dear! The fact is, we *can't* see one another just yet and for the moment it really is 'hail and farewell,' but if you'll be patient, very, *very* patient, Jan, then something will turn up, something exciting maybe, the way it always used to, remember?"

And with that I was obliged to be satisfied, for she walked briskly out of the restaurant, leaving me to pay the bill at the desk.

When I had collected my change I hurried down the steps to the floor level of the shop and saw her standing just inside the main door, looking in my direction. As our eyes met she put her hand to her lips and waved. It was a clear hint that she did not want me to follow her into the street, and because I was uncertain and bewildered I hesitated long enough for her to slip through the doors and enter a curbside taxi.

Then I thought of Madeleine, hanging about Victoria Station, and conscience drove me to hail another taxi and drive to the terminus, where I arrived an hour after the scheduled arrival of Madeleine's train. I made a halfhearted search of the buffet and along the bookstalls and platform exits, but there was no sign of her. An inspector told me that a train for Tonbridge had just left and I supposed she had boarded it and was already making the cheerless journey home.

I never saw Madeleine again and I can never pass Victoria Station without a sense of shame.

5.

The chance meeting with Diana did not solve very much, for I was now bedeviled by fresh uncertainties. I went over her cordial but indeterminate attitude toward me but I found it impossible to decide how she looked upon our former relationship and whether, now or at any time ahead, she would ever regard our association as a prelude to marriage. To me, throughout all the time we had been separated, there had been but two possible solutions—either she would defy her parents on the day she attained the age of twenty-one, or she had already dismissed me as a presumptuous hobbledehoy with whom she had passed part of her girlhood. I had never demanded an "understanding" as to our plans when she was of age but I now felt that she owed it to me to clarify the situation. I had expected more from our reunion. I had hoped for a passionate reavowal, but in the absence of it a frank and unsentimental "old-pals" approach would have told me all I wanted to know. As things were, I could form no strong impression of her attitude; regarding essentials she had remained mysteriously neutral. All the next day I studied my impressions. There was the hint that I ought to turn my back on journalism and learn farming; there was her refusal to commit herself about future meetings; there was her abrupt departure, without even a handshake or a good-by, and looking at it from these angles it appeared that she was putting me in my place almost as ruthlessly as her mother might have done. Looking at it another way, however, I believed that I had grounds for supposing that she had one or more of her aces in reserve, and was, in fact, on the point of bringing off a characteristic coup . . . "If you'll be patient, Jan, something will turn up, something exciting maybe, the way it used to, remember?" If she had persuaded herself that our love had been no more than a phase of adolescence, then why had she been so explicit about the future? Precisely *what* was likely to turn up? Another chance meeting? A day in Sennacharib together? Or a wedding, with a fairy-tale ending?

On the whole I inclined toward the more hopeful alternatives. Diana had always been highly unpredictable, and I finally resolved to muster what patience I could command and settle down to await a summons. Fortunately for my employers it was not long in coming. All day my thoughts were full of Diana and there was no room left for research into the financial panic that followed the Young Pretender's march to Derby, or the Chartist agitation of 1832. In fact, I was becoming bored with the past and impatient with the present.

Less than a week after our meeting in Fortnum's, a Carter Paterson's man appeared in the office with a small crate, addressed to me personally. Inside was a magnificent Remington portable and a note from Diana on the label. All the note said was: *A little something to help poor Margaret over her labor pains! Love, Diana.*

I sat goggling at the wonderful gift for fully fifteen minutes, oblivious of everything save the astounding fact that she had made such a spectacular acknowledgment of my literary ambitions. Was it possible to read into her generosity a desperately serious intention to secure independence for both of us? All in all, I was elated with the turn of events and carried the typewriter home in triumph, taking up my manuscript and hammering away until the lodger underneath me knocked on his ceiling with a broom handle, something he had not had to do for months. I became so absorbed in the work, and found it so effortless after the maddening ribbon jams and type cloggings of the ancient machine, that I progressed at a very respectable rate and had the first draft finished by the last week in May. During those feverish weeks I stopped wondering about Diana. Perhaps her generous means of encouragement had reconciled me to leaving the initiative to her.

Then, halfway through June, I received a telegram. It read:

SEE LAST WEEK'S GLOSSY STOP HALFWAY HOME STOP PARTY HERONSLEA FRIDAY STOP GET WEEK OFF STOP TOWER EVERY MORNING 7 A.M. LOVE DIANA

I was not wildly elated by this communication, for journalism had been doing its best to convert me into a cynic and I began to suspect that Diana was now playing some kind of elaborate game. If she could send a telegram, I told myself, she could just as easily have written a coherent letter, and if she had to rely on a telegram, then why compose it like an agony column quote in a magazine serial?

I searched through the glossies in our morgue, thankful indeed that I did not have to go out and buy them all, and soon came across the feature to which she referred, a ten-page spread devoted to recent presentations, Diana's among them. There was the usual display of flashbulb photographs of debs at stately homes and night clubs, all the girls looking impossibly arch, and all the young men looking as though they would have preferred to be back in the Sixth, at Eton.

Diana's picture was no better or worse than the others. I found it impossible to identify the doll-like creature that blinked at the photographer over the hunched shoulder of an anonymous dancing partner, with the sveldt and elegant young woman who had greeted me in Fortnum's a month ago. The pictures and their captions made me even more impatient with the idiotic saraband that her mother was compelling her to dance, and I threw aside the papers and sat down to make what I could of the message.

The "halfway home" was easy. I supposed it to mean that the presentation part of the ritual was done with, and that the town parties, or the more important of them, had already been held. The date of the Heronslea party was plain enough but I might easily have read into the "get week off" a bold invitation to attend it, and clearly this was out of the question. I deduced, however, that she wanted me to be in the vicinity on the great occasion, and her last sentence, about a tower rendezvous, implied that no firm date could be arranged and that my best plan was to go there each morning in the hope that she could ride out on one or more occasions.

This was all very well and extremely promising in its way, but her theatrical secrecy and the obvious pleasure that she was deriving from it was instrumental in stoking up the resentment I had once felt while crouching like a thief in the Heronslea copse, waiting to escort her to the regatta dance.

Two years in London had done something to enable me to get Mrs. Gayelorde-Sutton into perspective. Although her spectacular snobbery and, more particularly, her tireless game of squiress-among-the-chawbacons had earned my disgust as a boy, it had nonetheless gone some way toward persuading me that she was a strong personality. Now I realized that there was nothing very special about her after all and that almost every district in Britain had a Mrs. Gayelorde-Sutton, most of them the product of rapidly acquired wealth in the period 1914-1918. I had discovered a little about the family, and how they came to acquire their money. Unlike his wife, Gayelorde-Sutton originated from a fairly prosperous industrial family, but they had never been reckoned as wealthy until Eric, the second son, secured large interests in a nitrate firm. His money now stemmed partly from this and partly from the timber business which had boomed so dramatically during the period of trench warfare in Flanders. Gayelorde-Sutton himself was reputed to have a first-class business brain and according to a city editor's clerk—the source of my information—would soon be knighted even as Diana had once predicted.

I was on the point of trying to change my holiday week when something happened to make an office reshuffle unnecessary. Poor old Uncle Reuben was knocked down by a racing cyclist while acting as a judge at the annual grass-track meeting of the Whinmouth Wheelers, and his injuries included a broken thigh, something to be reckoned with at his time of life.

Somebody phoned my editor and I was given time off to go down and see him, my leave being extended indefinitely after Uncle Reuben had written and asked if he could borrow me to keep the *Observer* going until he was fit enough to return to the office.

He never did return and I never returned to London.

When I visited him at the Cottage Hospital I was shocked by his appearance. I had never thought of him as anything but an elderly man, although he was still a year short of sixty when I joined the *Observer* staff. Now he looked as though he was dying. His eyes were tired and his memory, once so accurate about Whinmouth affairs, was hazed by pain and shock. He was delighted to see me and gripped my hand with an eagerness that I found very touching.

"Ah, John," he muttered, "sorry you've got to see me trussed up like a Christmas fowl, and sorry to bring you back here before you've had your fill of smoke! The fact is, I don't know how we'll manage if you can't take over for a spell. That's the trouble with newspapers, boy, even little unimportant ones like ours. You can't put 'em in cold storage when you run into trouble. I remember old Joe Arscott, who ran the *Clarion* over at Ferndale—he had to put a carnival edition to bed on the day his wife and kids were killed in a road smash. How do you feel about staying down here until autumn?"

I said I should be glad to remain in Whinmouth until he was up and about, but said nothing about Diana or the party. In my heart I was glad of the opportunity. Diana's return had awakened in me a wild longing for Sennacharib and an equally strong distaste for my stuffy little bed-sitter and the fumes and roar of London. I comforted him as best I could. He was more worried about the *Observer* than he was about his injuries. This was the first time he had ever been laid up and the first going-to-press Friday he had missed since he was a printer's devil, in the eighteen-eighties.

"Come up here as often as you can and tell me what's going on," he commanded, as though he was a wounded general addressing a flustered aide-de-campe in the midst of a battle.

I promised and went home to Aunt Thirza, who was equally delighted with my unexpected return.

"Why bless 'ee, John!" she exclaimed, throwing her fat, freckled arms around my neck. "Us'll soon 'ave the color back in they cheeks, and a bit more spread to your belly. Praper pasty you look, and I don't wonder, breathing nothing but they ole vogs an' vumes all this time."

I went up to my old room, which seemed even smaller than the one I had abandoned in Guilford Street, but the moment I threw open the window I found myself blessing the chance that had brought me back.

It was a still summer evening and the estuary looked

242

blood-red under the setting sun, its leisurely traffic of boats making hardly a ripple as they moved to and from the jetties. Far across the river, on a ketch moored beyond the tideway, a fisherman was hammering at something metallic and the sound of the blows reached me seconds after his arm was raised to strike. It made me think again of Huck Finn on the broad Mississippi, and I hoped that Diana was already at Heronslea and could see the bronze and heliotrope cloud formations over Nun's Head. Uncle Luke's favorite herring gulls, and lesser black-backed gulls, fished at their ease; Old Yelland, the pilot who had taken us off the island, stood on the quayside chatting to Ferris, the lobsterman, probably about football, for they were both vice-presidents of the Whinmouth Club. I stood there a long time, drinking the salt breeze and feeling older and more serene than I had ever felt in London.

I was up at the tower before seven. The Sennacharib bird chorus was deafening and the buzzards were there, looking as though they had been wheeling and mewing over the paddock oaks ever since I went away.

Foxhayes was aflame with gorse and heather and seemed to have put on its best clothes to welcome me home. From the tower summit I looked down on the long sloping larch wood and saw a wisp of smoke rise from the invisible chimneys of Heronslea, signifying perhaps that the family was in residence. Our room was much as we had left it but cobwebs had gathered and there was mold on the carpet strips, so I occupied the time tidying up and shaking the carpet from the window, keeping a sharp eye on the end of the ride from which Diana would emerge if she was coming.

She did not appear that morning or the next, but on the third day, the Monday of her birthday week, she came striding out of the wood and waved as soon as she had climbed the fence into the paddock. I was far too impatient to wait in the tower and ran down to meet her.

Even when we were hundreds of yards apart I saw that she was once more my Diana and not the girl I had met in London. She wore an old gray skirt and a sleeveless blouse, with a blue scarf tied countrywise over her hair.

243

We both broke into a run and when we met rushed into an embrace, laughing breathlessly as a pheasant kuck-kucked from the bracken at our feet and then running hand-in-hand for the privacy of Folly Wood.

We exchanged no greetings. The place we were in, and the careless, girlish clothes she was wearing exorcised the awe she had created in me when we last met. I felt no awe for her now, only the wildest tenderness and delight in her presence. It was as though we had been parted for a day, or were still alone on Nun's Island before the storm, and I could not wait until we had climbed the tower steps but kissed her mouth a dozen times as we clung to one another on the brier-choked path to the porch.

One thing was changed, and that the nature of the kisses we exchanged. They were no longer the kisses of infatuated adolescents, owing more to the wonder of discovery than to physical desire. We kissed breathlessly and greedily, and all the time our lips were touching she strained her body to me so ardently that I had to brace myself against the masonry. Her scarf came off and I plunged my hands into her hair, speaking her name as I had spoken it during our island adventure and hearing my voice sound strange under the stress of emotion.

At last we climbed the tower and she looked ruefully at the signs of decay.

"I've never been here since, Jan," she said. "I often started out to go but I never got beyond the paddock. It seemed so depressing alone . . . look, there are our buzzards!"

"They were here yesterday and the day before," I said.

"But they shouldn't have been! They're only supposed to show up when we're together."

"They knew you were in the offing, Di, and anyway, we're together now. I'm home for several weeks. How long will you be here?"

"Not long, Jan. After the party we're all going to Nice and this week it isn't going to be easy to see you, not even in the early mornings. So many people are staying, and Yves likes to ride before breakfast. I had to tell half a dozen whoppers to get here today. Oh dear, I wish I could invite you to the party but that's quite hopeless, even if you come as a pressman. Mother will be certain to recognize you after that frightful to-do at your office!"

Her mention of the brush between her mother and my uncle reminded me of its cause—her examination by a doctor after our escapade.

"What happened that time?" I asked her. "How did it seem from your end of the business?"

She did not mind talking about it. She described how, on the day after surrender, she developed a frightful cold and was locked in her room for more than a week.

"I didn't care anyway," she said. "I wanted to think and think about it all. I've never forgotten how sweet you were that time, Jan, and that's what made Mother's suspicions so beastly and ungenerous. She believed we had been lovers, of course, and it was only for your sake that I stopped letting her go on thinking so. It was when she started talking about police court proceedings, and got our solicitor in to talk jargon about it, that I had to let them know I was still a virgin." She looked at me without a trace of embarrassment. "I *still* am! Are you?"

I found it impossible to meet her gaze but she only laughed, reached out and pushed up my chin with the tips of her fingers.

"Oh don't look so dreadfully hangdog, Jan, it's different for men, isn't it? Was it with one girl or several?"

"One," I muttered, but she didn't seem to notice my distaste for the subject.

"What was she like, Jan? Was she pretty? Were you in love with her?"

"No," I admitted, relieved by her attitude but still miserably embarrassed, "I wasn't a bit in love with her. I'll never be in love with anyone but you, Di, and I think you're quite sure of that and always have been!"

"Yes, I think I am, Jan," she said lightly, "but I wouldn't have blamed you a bit if you'd found somebody else. After all, in most ways you've been a man for years. Sometimes I think you were born one."

"What are we going to do—about seeing one another?"

245

I demanded, not only anxious to change the subject but worried about the difficulties that continued to beset us.

"Well, we can't do a thing yet," she said calmly. "If Mother gets so much as an inkling that you're back in circulation, she'll let Heronslea and we'll never see one another at all."

The morning clouded a little and suddenly the tower room seemed dank and sunless.

"How long have we got to go on like this, Di?"

"I suppose until I'm twenty-one, Jan."

"And what then? If I'm back in Whinmouth for good, and running the paper, would you have enough guts to tell her and your father to go to hell and get engaged—properly, openly—without all this hole-in-the-corner routine?"

She smiled and for some reason I was sure that the smile was slightly forced.

"That's the second proposal you've made to me in this old tower," she said, "and it puts you one ahead; the one on the beach in Nun's Cove was really mine, wasn't it?"

I was determined not to joke about it this time and pressed her hard for a direct answer. The maddening frustration of the situation was more than I could bear. I had held her in my arms again and believed I had learned from her response that she felt about me the same way as I felt for her, but for all that I did not get my answer, not then, not for a long time to come. She turned away and stood beside the window, looking down over Sennacharib.

"Well?" I demanded, after nearly a minute had passed.

"You mustn't stampede me, Jan. Women are a lot wiser than men about this kind of thing. You're entitled to an answer and you'll get one, I promise you that, but don't panic me, don't drag an answer from me that is only part of one and has to do with biology rather than all kinds of other things."

"Such as economics?" I asked, grumpily.

Her head came up and she looked straight at me.

"Yes! Why not? That's the basis of our trouble, isn't it?"

I was alarmed at this and tried to talk my way out of it. Looking back I can see that my attempt was ingenuous but it seemed logical at the time. Eagerly I told her about the owner of the paper and printing works having willed his property to Uncle Reuben and how Reuben had promised that it would pass to me.

"It isn't the kind of money you've been used to and never would be," I argued, "but it provides a good living and later on, when I've got another income from books, we shouldn't be at all badly off. We'd have plenty to live the kind of life we want to live, and I daresay we could even manage to hunt if you wanted to."

She heard me out and I think my case impressed her. She smiled again, genuinely this time, and kissed me lightly on the cheek.

"Dear Jan," she said, and then, in the old familiar way, "dear, darling, sober, solid, dependable Jan Ridd! Will you wait until Friday? Everything's gone haywire at home and there's been so many things to see to. I want time to think everything over. We'll talk more about it then, I promise, Jan!"

"But Friday is the day of the party," I protested. "We can't even see each other then."

"Oh yes we can," she said, with a touch of her schoolgirl cockiness. "In a funny way you might even be *at* the party . . . if you want to be, that is!"

"But Di, talk sense! If I . . ."

"Listen," she said, drawing her brows together in a way I remembered her doing when she was planning mischief in the past, "all you have to do is to be handy at a certain time and wait for my signal. Then you walk straight in and I'll keep you in cold storage until all the others have gone to bed. It'll be wonderful that way, a simply glorious score off everyone, and a way of eating my cake and having it too!"

"Wouldn't it be far less risky to meet in Nun's Cove at any old time? We don't want another scene to spoil your birthday!"

The mischief went out of her eyes and she took my hands in hers and said, with immense seriousness:

"It's simply *because* it's my birthday—don't you see— that you're going to be at the party, Jan. Everyone I don't

247

care two straws about is there and I'm not going to dodge out and walk three miles to get a birthday kiss from the one person I really want to be kissed by! Does that sound unreasonable to you?"

I laughed, partly because she sounded so solemn but more, I think, because her words brought me great happiness.

"No, Di," I admitted very readily, "it sounds more reasonable than anything you've said so far."

"Well then," she continued, "you do just as I say. Now listen carefully—the party won't get going until the supper dance and . . ."

It was the usual hotchpotch of involved timing and theatrical nonsense. I was to come to Heronslea about ten P.M. and await her signal—the tune "Missouri City Waltz," played by the band, which would precede the buffet supper and provide my opportunity to enter by a little-used door that led through the flower room to the gun room. She undertook to meet me there and give me further instructions. We parted on this and I cycled back to Whinmouth with a sharp appetite and some misgivings, both outweighed in my mind by the memory of the eagerness with which she had run into my arms when I emerged from the tower to greet her.

It clouded over toward evening on Friday. I cycled as far as Shepherdshey Hill and left my bike in the gorse at the fringe of the big copse. There was no moon and I had a difficult time of it pushing through the wood to a spot where I could overlook the house. As I blundered along I wondered whether what remained of my boyhood was secretly enjoying this hocus-pocus, or whether I had consented to practice it because it was the only terms upon which Diana could or would continue our association. I never found a satisfactory answer to this query, the reason being, I suppose, that my reaction to the role of secret suitor was governed by the barometer of my faith in Diana. This went up and down almost hour by hour these days. Half the time I was convinced that she was only awaiting her moment of freedom in order to declare herself, at other times I was equally certain that she was using me as a kind of grappling iron to hang on to childhood. What she had said about my transmission from boyhood to manhood was true. The lack of a father throughout infancy, and the death of my mother before I was fifteen, had bridged the gap between boy and man in a matter of months and the process of growing up was further accelerated by Uncle Luke's helplessness when I went to help him at the Furniture Mart.

It had been so different for Diana. Consciously or unconsciously, her parents had done everything in their power to arrest her development, not only by working to rule and charting a conventional future for her, but also by surrounding her with hordes of servants, a circumstance that prevented her from learning to do the simplest thing for herself. She had revolted against this, of course, and her rebellion showed itself in her furtive association with me and her readiness at all times to flout authority. At the time of which I write, when she was physically mature but in most other respects two years behind the average working-class adolescent, this defiance of her mother's pattern of behavior was little more than the deliberate act of a spoiled child; it was not until later that it developed into a deep-rooted characteristic and fed upon its own appetite for acts of calculated irresponsibility.

When I reached the edge of the copse bordering the fenced paddock in front of the house, I saw at once that Heronslea was very much *en fête*. From where I stood it looked more like a roadhouse than a beautiful country home. Greenery and balloons festooned the façade and over the pillared porch, which was extravagantly floodlit, was a vulgar set piece in colored bulbs, representing a giant birthday cake. It crossed my mind then that Mrs. Gayelorde-Sutton was redoubling her efforts to supply her only child with gigantic helpings of the wrong pudding.

Nobody knew better than I that Diana, viewed objectively, was basically an uncomplicated and extremely affectionate child, without false pride and without ostentation. All she needed at that time was someone who could understand her natural high spirits and pull firmly on the reins when she frisked over the rails of common sense. She wanted a just, tolerant rule, tempered by strong, demonstrative affection. She needed someone to canalize her abundant energy into something mildly creative. All she was getting was unlimited dishes of caviar and ice cream, to be eaten in the glare of spotlights. She only had to raise a finger to command the material wants of a sophisticated woman twice her age, but now that poor Drip had been banished she might look in vain for a shoulder to weep upon. Looking at the glitter of Heronslea in the dark bowl below, I began to understand what had prompted the childish eagerness of her kisses at the foot of the tower a few days ago, and it struck me as remarkable that she was as fresh and unspoiled as she was, for her mother by design, and her father by acquiescence, had done everything humanly possible to convert her into an impossible little brat.

I could hear the band playing a waltz, and by avoiding the circle of light thrown by the decorations and porch lamps I was able to approach the house quite closely and look in upon the celebrations.

Although the afternoon had been overcast and rain now threatened, the temperature of the night was unusually high, even for mid-June. There was not a breath of air in the open and inside the overcrowded house it must have been insufferably close, for all the French windows opening onto the terrace had been flung wide, and every now and again little groups of guests drifted out onto the raised flags and sat at tables or on the low windbreak to sip their drinks. I recognized several of the guests. Lance Fayne, the M.P.'s son, was there and Gerald Brett-Hawkins, the landowner's son. As I watched, Diana herself came out with Yves, the French boy, and a knot of six or eight young people surrounded them, saying something that made Diana throw back her head and laugh. Then the music recalled most of them to the dance floor but one couple remained in shadow at my end of the terrace and as soon as the others had gone moved into a passionate embrace. It was all very smart, streamlined and jolly, but I turned away quickly when I thought that I might have to watch Diana being kissed by someone like Lance or Yves, and retired sulkily to the rhododendron clump to await "Missouri City Waltz."

It was a long time coming, and before I heard it heavy drops of rain began to fall and drip through the leaves where I was sitting. The moment the tune struck up I scrambled out and went around to the flower-room door, which was shut but unlocked. I went in, pushing through the litter of ferns and flower stems left by the gardeners and into the paneled gun room, where it was pitch dark.

I remembered this part of the house from my tour of inspection and after waiting a moment, to make certain that my entry had passed undetected, I opened the door a chink and listened to the music and laughter coming from the central hall. A manservant clumped past, whistling in tune with the band, and I remembered that the passage outside connected the wine cellar and the housekeeper's flat, with a back staircase halfway along it. Then, soundlessly save for a swift rustle of her ball dress, Diana was beside me, whispering

"Jan? Are you there, Jan?"

I found her hand in the dark and drew her to me. Her perfume banished the room's whiff of gun oil and resin and I kissed her bare shoulders.

"No, Jan, not now, there'll be plenty of time—I'll be missed, come quickly and don't say a word on the way!"

We stole out into the passage and crossed it to the stairs. The stairs led into the west corridor that branched off the central gallery, and a cacophony of music, laughter and plate rattling rose from the well of the big staircase. We turned our backs on it and slipped along the corridor to her side of the house.

"In here, *quickly!*"

She pushed me into her little suite and I saw that it was much changed from the last time I was there. It had been extended to include a little dressing room and a tiny bathroom, with a sunken bath. The simplicity of the room that had struck me as a boy was now buried under a vanload of hangings and antique furniture. It had the heavy, impersonal atmosphere of a modernized chateau. Although in good taste, the colors were too rich and the car-

251

pet was too thick. The rooms had Mrs. Gayelorde-Sutton's signature scrawled in every corner.

"I can't stay here, Di," I protested. "This is sheer madness!"

"No one comes in here and you can lock the door," she said, hurriedly. "Better still, *don't* lock it . . . leave it ajar, and if anyone comes along the corridor go into the bathroom and lock that. That's the last place anyone would expect to find a private boy friend!"

She giggled as she said this and I realized that she had been drinking. I think I might have resisted the idea of remaining hidden in her bedroom until the party finished in the small hours, but she gave me no opportunity. After drawing the heavy curtains she skipped out, blowing a kiss from the door.

It was about 10:30 by now and I knew that I could not expect her to return until after one A.M., at the earliest. Now that I was alone, however, I was exhilarated by the prospect of spending several hours isolated among her things. It brought a touch of intimacy to what had looked like being a damp and dismal evening, with my nose pressed against the pieshop window of Heronslea watching others enjoy themselves. There was triumph too, triumph over my dinner-jacketed competitors downstairs. Each was licensed to paw Diana in public, sharing her with a hundred others, but up here, cut off from the roar and clatter of the party, I was alone with the real Diana and secreted in a place where her dreams had flowered since she was a pony-mad schoolgirl.

I began to savor the privilege, stealing around and touching the things she handled every day, silver-backed hairbrushes, pots of make-up, the perfume spray, and even the pillow that held the scent of her hair.

I prowled across to the book alcove and found my own gift, the inscribed copy of *Lorna Doone*. Under the inscription was something written very indistinctly, in pencil, in Diana's handwriting. I took it over to the pink bedside light and deciphered it—*The tower, New Year's Day* and then a cross, signifying, I hoped, that this pencil mark was a record of our first kiss.

I examined her other books: Alan Seager's poems and several other books of verse, ancient and modern, Drip's classics that did not seem to have been read very much, and a row of Ethel M. Dell, Angela Brazil, Ruby M. Ayres that showed signs of constant use. I went back to *Lorna Doone* and sat down on a seat that looked like a pink, tilted plate resting on wicker legs. Outside heavy rain was drumming against the tall window and I read quietly until I heard someone cough in the corridor. Alarmed, I scrambled up and ran into the bathroom, locking the door and listening intently when I heard the bedroom door squeak, a faint clinking sound and then silence.

After listening for another five minutes I opened the door an inch and peeped out. No one was there but on the bedside table was a plate covered by a spotless napkin, and beside it an opened bottle of champagne. Diana had evidently remembered that I might want supper.

I was in fact extremely hungry and the sandwiches were very good. I had wolfed them all before I noticed two words scrawled in lipstick inside the fold of the napkin. She had written *Use toothbrushglass*. The message made me chuckle, for somehow it showed that the spiriting of someone like myself into a place of honor at her party was providing the hostess with more genuine pleasure than anything going on downstairs. I drank half the champagne and it gave me confidence and elation. I listened at the door to the sounds of revelry below—odd shrieks, bumps, *oohs, ahhs* and the contant undertone of saxophones. I tried to identify the tunes but failed, except in the case of "The Gay Gordons" which, judged by the uproar, seemed to be no end of a romp. My sense of private triumph mounted. I took off my shoes, tie and windbreaker and stretched myself on her bed, hazy with champagne, drunk with bliss. Suddenly I was quite sure that everything would work out perfectly, and lulled by reassurance I dropped off to sleep.

The prolonged rustle of her dress awakened me. I had turned off the bedside lamp and now only a chink of light entered the room from the corridor. I started up in alarm, cursing myself for being such a fool as to sleep with the door ajar. My mouth was dry from champagne and nervousness but Diana did not seem at all nervous. I heard her shut and lock the door. Then she called, softly, "Switch on the light, Jan, the small one."

I switched on and saw her smiling down at me. She was slightly tousled and her cheeks were flushed. There was the slightest suggestion of unsteadiness and this she exaggerated by clasping her hands behind her back. Her mascara had run a little and her lipstick was slightly smeared.

"I believe you're a bit tight, Di," I said, chuckling.

"Yes, I believe I am," she admitted deliberately. "Just the weeniest bit, that is, but not nearly so tight as most of them."

"Have they all gone?"

"All that *are* going. A baker's dozen are staying the night."

"I didn't hear any of the cars. I must have been sound asleep."

"Poor Jan! Have you been frightfully bored?"

"No, not a bit bored. I loved being up here, it was like being near you all the time."

She smiled vaguely, picked up the open copy of *Lorna Doone* and clicked her tongue in mock disapproval.

"Tch, tch! Jan Ridd wouldn't have gone to sleep uninvited in a maiden lady's bed!"

"Jan didn't get the chance," I told her.

She considered this, then dismissed it. There was something studiedly casual about her manner and I decided that it wasn't just the champagne.

"Do you want any more to drink?" she asked, suddenly.

"No," I said, "only water. My mouth is like a sandstone cave."

"I'll have a sip," she said, and poured a little into the toothbrushglass.

"Have you thought up how to get me out of here?" I asked.

"We'll think about that later. What time will it be light?"

"About five, I should say. What's the time now?"

"Two-thirty," she said, finishing her drink and glancing

254

at her diamond-encrusted watch. "If we allow half an hour to get you clear that gives us two hours. Right!" She suddenly became brisk and businesslike. "Turn out the light!"

She said it as a command and when the room was in darkness she slipped around the bed, drew back the curtains and threw open the window. The current of air was like a kiss. Away in the wood a nightjar screeched but the only other sound was the faint plop of raindrops falling from the rhododendrons under the window.

She remained by the window long enough to make me impatient. Then I heard her dress rustle and realized that she was stepping out of it.

"I won't be a minute, Jan," she said, and there was a strong tremor in her voice. She went into the bathroom and I heard water running. I knew then that she meant to give herself to me, not only because she wanted to but because to do so, here at this moment, was part of a planned ritual. This was the ultimate defiance, a surrender that mocked everything in her past and present, and it was to be here, on this special occasion, in the tabernacle of the enemy's temple! She had planned it this way, down to the last detail. All the time her parents had been sending out their gilded invitations, all the time the staff had been furbishing and decorating Heronslea, all the hours that she had been drinking, chattering and dancing with people her parents had chosen as companions, her mind was racing toward a different kind of milestone, one that marked the very end of her childhood.

For a moment, a few seconds only, I resisted the invitation. I told myself, breathlessly, that she was not quite sober, that no good could come of a gesture as wild and reckless as this, and at the back of my mind there was another scruple, a miniscule of doubt that I was not being used as Jan Leigh, a human being whom she desired and who was hopelessly in love with her, but once again as the banner of the undefeated, advancing against the ramparts of convention. It all added up to the feeblest resistance on my part and was swept away by the first touch of her lips. For a moment, as she threw her arms around me, I was choked with a tenderness and gratitude so vast and intense

255

that I played no immediate part in the embrace. Then I forgot to be grateful and all the tenderness I had for her was drowned under a sea of delight. I became rough and impatient to master what was so freely offered.

We lay without speaking for what seemed a long time. At first, so regular was her breathing that I thought she was asleep but she was not, for presently her hand moved gently across my face and began ruffling my hair, softly and rhythmically, as a mother strokes a sick child. Then I was bitterly ashamed of my roughness and almost wept to think of it. It was not the guilty feeling I had after my experience with Madeleine. As regards the act itself I felt only pride, but it seemed to me that my violence had given her cause to believe that she had been used impersonally and for that I wanted most desperately to apologize, only the words would not come. Like Madeleine she sensed my distress, using almost the same words.

"You're not sorry, Jan? You won't go away and hate yourself for it? You mustn't, you know, because it was how I meant it to happen and I'm glad it has! There's nothing furtive about us any more, you see, and nothing beastly either, as there would have been if it had been with anyone else. It's right that you should be the one and I'll never be sorry about it, *never*, do you understand?"

"I hurt you, Di!" I muttered. "And that's something I'll never be able to forget!"

"Oh nonsense!" she said, moving her arm and drawing my head onto her shoulder. "That wasn't your fault, stupid! It was inevitable. Anyway, don't remember that, just remember I'll always belong to you now, no matter what happens, or where I go, or what I do! Nothing can change that and it's what I always planned and wanted, right from the time I kissed you in the train that time, remember?"

Lying there, my head on her breast, I remembered so much, all of it sweet and uplifting. I remembered my first glimpse of her, riding out of the wood like a child-empress and banishing Keeper Croker with an arrogant glance; I remembered our short journey in the suburban train and her exultant claim as we pulled into the station. I remembered riding beside her into the wind on Foxhayes Common, under winter skies and in hot summer sunshine. I remembered even more vividly still our quiet days on Nun's Island, and her tremulous earnestness as we stood beside the signal fire awaiting the pilot boat. I remembered it all, every minute detail of it, and the memories filled me with a pride in my manhood that banished the shame of using her so fiercely and possessively. Her voice, and the nearness of her, healed the hurt and filled me with a sense of infinite peace.

I slept until she gently awakened me and I saw that the curtains were redrawn and the light was on. She was dressed in jodhpurs and yellow sweater and was beckoning, her hand on her lips.

"I've been on reconnaissance," she said, unsmilingly, "and it's all clear. We'll go out the same way as you came in, but don't say a word, not a single word, understand?"

We crept downstairs, through the gun room and out through the flower-room door. The sky was gray over Shepherdshey, but still dark toward the copse.

"When will I see you again, Di? It has to be soon!"

She put her mouth to my ear, kissed it and whispered:

"I'll write the moment I find out what's happening, Jan. Go now, dearest! And thank you for loving me, Jan!" There was no opportunity to argue, and no real need. I knew now that she would make it possible and that these things were always best left to her.

"I haven't wished you many happy returns," I said.

"Wish me now, then."

"Many happy returns, Di, many, many of them, and all as wonderful as this!"

She nodded impatiently and gave me a little push. I slipped across the paddock into the last of the shadows. When I reached the edge of the copse I looked back and could make out the long, gray shape of the house, but the garden door was shut and she was gone.

I experienced the same small spurt of disappointment as on the occasion of my first visit to Heronslea, when I was whisked down the drive in her mother's big car and looked at a closed door.

Part Two

Chapter Eight

IN SOME ways that period was the last of the old way of
life, not only for me—I was hibernating and barely conscious of the events that led, step by step, to the Second
World War—but for people like Uncle Reuben, Aunt
Thirza, the journeymen in the works outside our office, for
everyone who had seen the twenties and early thirties trying, and sometimes half-succeeding, to swim back into the
easy water of the Edwardian decade.

Some people would have it that the old-world isolation
of districts like Whinmouth disappeared in the slump of
'31, but this was not really true of our part of the world.
The slump never blighted Whinmouth. Down there wages
were always low and, as I have said, most of us lived by
taking in one another's washing. There are more people
unemployed in Whinmouth today, after nearly two dec-
ades of the Welfare State, than there were in 1931, and
Hitler was not even a concert-party joke with us until he
massacred half his supporters in the summer of '34. It was
only then, when the Nazis began to hit the world headlines, that we became aware that something shrill and hysterical was being shouted at us, something that made our
annual British Legion rally and League of Nations Union
meetings look genuinely parochial. Up to that time our interest in global politics was halfhearted, like our championship of Oxford or Cambridge in the Boat Race, or
reaction to Amy Johnson flying to Australia. We heard

258

about these things on the radio, and some of us read of them in the daily papers, but they were not as important to us as, say, the Chapel Hill tar-barrel race on Guy Fawkes night, and even when a General Election came along only about 60 per cent of the local electorate turned out to vote. We were far more vocal over Councilor Rawlinson's proposal to remove the Boer War obelisk from Fish Square, and the only national event in which we took a genuine interest was the two-minute silence around the war memorial, and the sale of Flanders poppies.

We had slipped from the nineteen-twenties into the nineteen-thirties almost without noticing, and we were almost halfway through the new decade before Hitler's name began to crop up in the public bars of hostelries like The Rifleman at Shepherdshey. After that, however, the tide of events carried us along at a pretty round pace. Almost everyone had a radio set by then and when Germany invaded the Ruhr, Mussolini pounced on Abyssinia, Hitler grabbed Austria, and the papers began to headline the Spanish Civil War and the Sudetenland problem, we began to realize that a bad train and bus service was not an absolute guarantee against invasion by the outside world.

Even in Sennacharib one was made aware of this, for on the plain outside the market town they had built a small airfield and the mew of the two buzzards became even more plaintive when silver-glinting aircraft zoomed in from the sea and skimmed across Foxhayes to land.

As a newspaperman, even a small-town newspaperman, I should have been far more aware of all that was taking place than in fact I was, but my grasp of global events was not much better than Aunt Thirza's. During the first part of this Gadarene stampede I was content to get through my routine work and dream about Diana, and when Diana wasn't there to dream about, the soundproof wall of self-pity I built around me excluded objective contemplation of the antics of grotesques like Goebbels and Ciano, and even, to some extent, of Mr. Chamberlain and his umbrella. Coming from a professional reporter this is a very lame confession, but it is true for all that; I date this period of personal detachment from the night that Diana and I became lovers, and I pedaled dreamily into Whinmouth just as the sun came up over Nun's Head and the gulls went about their early morning shopping on the sandbanks.

I was blissfully content for about a fortnight. I did not expect to hear from her until the family had settled in Nice, where they were expected to remain for two months. Uncle Luke's obstinate fracture kept him from taking any part in the weekly production of the *Observer,* and as it was now high summer I had plenty to keep me occupied.

Then I had a postcard from her, just a wish-you-were-here gesture but enough to keep me happy for another month or so. Then Uncle Reuben was told by his surgeon that he would never walk again and my concern for him was strong enough to put even Diana out of mind for a time.

The business was reorganized. I was made official editor a week or so before my twentieth birthday and later presented with a thousand shares in the firm, now operating under the title of R. & J. Leigh & Co. (Observer Press) Ltd.

When things settled down a little, and we had moved Uncle Reuben into a new bungalow on Dune Terrace, overlooking the estuary, I longed to tell Diana everything that was happening, partly from reasons of pride in my new status but mostly, I think, because I believed that these changes would have a practical bearing on our future. I even sat down and wrote her a long letter, but I did not post it. I was unwilling to take any action that might prejudice our meeting when she returned to England, and I knew her mother well enough to realize that promotion from junior reporter to editor of the *Whinmouth & District Observer* was not enough to qualify for the role of son-in-law. I had an uncomfortable suspicion, moreover, that even my winning the Irish Sweepstakes, or my sudden elevation to the post of Foreign Secretary, would not induce Mrs. Gayelorde-Sutton to forgive my part in the island escapade. There was no other course open but to await Diana's twenty-first birthday and because, deep in my heart, I was now quite sure of her, I could await that date —June 18, 1937—with dignity if not with patience.

I was happy enough in my work and I was saving money at what seemed to me a prodigious rate. I took to ranging those scattered parts of Sennacharib where odd and isolated houses had been built, hoping to find one with a sale notice exhibited, or learn of someone living there who was old and infirm and not likely to need it much longer. Up to now it had been a vain quest. There were not more than a dozen homes in the area and two-thirds of them were large, detached houses, quite outside the range of my pocket.

Then, in November of that year, the bubble burst.

I came home from a Saturday afternoon tramp across Nun's Head and Foxhayes to find a fat letter lying on Aunt Thirza's hall stand. It was postmarked New York and the unmistakable handwriting set my heart racing like a dynamo. I tore off my dripping mackintosh and carried the letter up to my room, shouting to Aunt Thirza that I would have my tea upstairs and work there until bedtime.

Aunt Thirza came up with a tray and it was not until I had heard her descend, and had locked the door, that I slit the envelope and drew out four folded sheets and a wad of tissue paper about two or three inches square. I unfolded the tissue first. Inside was a small lock of Diana's hair

It was softer and darker than I would have imagined but the sharp, neat twist reminded me of the broad lock that used to sweep down to her chin when I knew her first. Later on, when she began to attend West End hairdressers and the fashions changed year by year, this mutinous swath gave up its attempt to reach the corner of her mouth and fell in line with the long roll that touched her shoulders. I looked at the token a long time, almost forgetting the letter. Then I refolded the tissue, put it away in my wallet and settled down to read.

I have her letter still; this is what it said

> Hotel Plaza,
> New York.
> October 21st.

MY OWN JAN,
   This letter has been a long time coming, four months by my reckoning, and I suppose I could plead travel as an excuse.

Since leaving the Riviera, in July, we have been two-thirds of the way around the world, and I could easily say that the reason I didn't write was because I was at sea, or packing, or sightseeing, or anything else ordinary people say when they want to put themselves in the right. We aren't "ordinary people," Jan. We never have been and never will be. You've never pretended to me about anything, so I'm going to tell you the truth because I owe you that at least. The real reason I haven't written is that I hated telling you lies, and I was all this time finding the courage to say what I've got to say now, that we can't ever belong to one another as we thought we could all this time.

You've got to understand one thing straightaway. This isn't because of Mother—she doesn't even know we saw one another in London, or on my birthday, and I imagine she thinks I've completely forgotten you; maybe she has too, she's never mentioned you since that awful time she went to your office after the island business.

This is something I've thought about myself, day after day, since we became really each other's, and I knew it then, when I said good-by and perhaps it would have been more honest to call you back and say so, rather than sitting down and writing it cold-bloodedly, but I didn't and since then things have happened so quickly. We went away and have been on the move ever since. I've had to think about it at odd times when I was alone, which wasn't as often as I should have liked.

The thing is, Jan dear, I've learned so very much about myself in the last few months. I know now that it would be wrong to pretend I could be a good wife to you, and live in the country, even country as heavenly as our Sennacharib, because you would never have more than half of me. The other half would always be fretting for the kind of life you wouldn't even like, no matter how well-off you were, the sort of life your half of me has always sneered at when we've talked about it.

I said you had never pretended to me but I think I must have to you, although I do ask you to believe that I didn't do it consciously. The half of me that you've never met is the selfish half, that likes pretty clothes, smart hairdo's, racing cars, meeting people, going places as I've been doing lately, and all the things that come naturally to people who don't actually earn money but just *have* it. Said like that, this seems dreadfully crude, even snobbish, but I've tried to write it other ways and it always comes out the same. If this is the truth then let it be the truth. I'm a thoroughly spoiled girl and I've got used to

262

being spoiled. I can't cook, or sew, or make-do, and I don't think I'd ever learn. I could easily say that I would, for the man I loved, and I've heard heaps of girls say just that at school and even among the debs, but they don't mean it, not really, and all of them would rather be old maids than have to do it, or if they did they'd be hopeless at it and drive the man they married up the wall in the end.

I wouldn't do that to you, Jan, because you aren't just a schoolgirl pash but something much, much more. I've always known that and I'll always believe it, even if we never see one another again. The point is, going on and on like this isn't the least bit fair to you. It keeps you hoping and hoping when there isn't any reason to hope, but what is even worse, it stops you getting a proper kind of girl who would be a good wife, and that's the whole root of the matter—I'm living under false pretenses, and I've known that since about a year after we were separated and you went to work in London. It was very wrong of me to pretend when we met that time and even more wrong—something for which I'll never really forgive myself—to make you make love to me after the party. Any man, especially a man like you, would have a right to expect something different from this awful letter after that, and I can only plead that it happened because I do really love you in a terribly *private* kind of way, and when you put your arms around me and kiss me I just want you completely in a way I've never wanted anyone else who has kissed me or tried to make love to me. I suppose I wanted to *prove* this to myself! I had some sort of idea that if it happened the way I thought it might, then the "plushy" part of me that I've described to you would sort of wither away and leave just an ordinary woman in love with a man—the man being you, but you see, Jan, it didn't! Everything that's happened since—all the luxury cruising and travel and parties and what not—have only bolstered up this stranger to you and convinced her how impossible it would be to turn her back on it for good.

There is one way the half of me that you know will always survive and that's the physical way. Whenever I think of men *as men*, whenever I think of being made love to in the purely physical sense, I think of you and I suppose that will always be so and is just something that the person I marry (if I ever do) will have to put up with if he wants me. I can't alter this but I can be honest with you and say that this isn't nearly important enough to risk your happiness. People are quite right when they say sex is only part of marriage. If I've learned anything

263

from the silly way I've been brought up, it's that. It would be a heavenly part of a marriage to you, Jan, but not enough to make me into the sort of wife you deserve and should have. When I was cut off from all the things I've been used to and (for all the jokes I've made about them) really *like* having, we should have dreadful rows. I'd get snappy and you'd get sullen, and in the end we wouldn't have anything left but bed, and all the wonderful memories we had of Sennacharib, and places like the island, would get blurred. I wouldn't want that to happen and I don't think you would either. For me you have always been a marvelous adventure and it's far better to keep it that way, something to think about when we're old, a kind of reason for having lived at all, if you understand.

I feel very wretched about all this and I've been weeping buckets all the time I've been writing, but all the same I'm glad I had the guts to write it and I hope I have some left to post it!

Good-by now, Jan darling, and thank you, thank you, thank you for everything, for getting into so much trouble for me, for being so faithful, for being so patient, for wanting me so much, but most of all for being just you—my Jan Ridd.

DIANA

I skimmed the letter at first, my hands shaking and a sound like crashing waves in my ears. Then I went through it line by line half a dozen times, pausing and thinking about every sentence and every thought behind the phrases of every sentence. In the end I knew it by heart, every word and every punctuation mark. I had forgotten to light the gas fire and the room was as cold as a tomb. I was shivering, not from cold but from sheer, physical shock, as though I had just avoided being knocked down by a runaway truck and was picking myself up in the gutter, not quite certain if I was still alive.

There was a finality about the letter that stunned me. It was like death, not simply my death but universal death, a sudden cessation of the processes of life, a kind of change in being that blotted out sun and moon, that stopped tides flowing and things growing.

I had had doubts before, serious ones some of them, but never a blow like this, never a denial of the most important thing in my life that came, not from external agencies, like her mother and background, but from Diana herself.

It was over; finished! No more secret meetings, no irregular correspondence, no kisses, no Sennacharib, no future! Over, and decreed so by her, in carefully reasoned terms that made argument futile.

All this time I had been waiting and planning to snatch her away from the places and people prescribed for her, and all this time she had never wanted to escape from them for more than a few moments, as someone might stick his head out of the window to take a few breaths of air, or a fish might surface for a second before returning to the underwater world where it belonged.

That was what really hurt, the hideous, shattering sham of it all! For clearly it had been a sham, right from the night that she took me back to Heronslea on the pony, and we ate muffins and listened to Drip's musical boxes. Remembering this I recalled Drip's warning, and from this point it was fatally easy to gather together the clues that Diana had strewn along our path—her long silences between letters and meetings, her mysterious abstraction that time in Fortnum's, even the steady, almost calculating way that she had looked at me sometimes. It explained the odd remark she had made when we parted after the party night —"Thank you for loving me, Jan!" had not meant what I thought it had meant at all. In my male arrogance I had imagined it to refer to the act of physical possession, whereas it was now clear that she had begun composing this letter, or something like it, within an hour of our lying in one another's arms.

Blind rage ousted misery for a moment and I would have ripped the letter into shreds, had not Aunt Thirza called from the stairs at that moment.

"Supper, Jan! It's put out, so come and eat 'un while 'er's hot."

It is curious how compelling are the ordinary routines of life. I folded the letter, replaced it in its envelope, and went down into the kitchen, where Thirza mistook my glumness for overwork.

"Why bless 'ee, I dorn reckon you'd stop that there tap-tapping long enough to eat if I didn't drive 'ee to it," she

265

grumbled, ladling out liver and onions and pushing a huge plateful in my direction.

I ate her supper in silence. It was like munching my way through a dish of sand.

2.

For a week or more I hugged my misery to myself but at last, whether I would or not, I was driven by sheer wretchedness to share it with someone. I had to find a confidant. I had scores of acquaintances in Whinmouth but no real friends apart from Aunt Thirza and Uncle Reuben, and I inclined toward the latter. After all, Reuben had already been introduced to the problem, and Reuben had met Mrs. Gayelorde-Sutton. Outwardly he was a narrow-minded old bachelor, but what drove me to confide in him was the certainty I had of his deep affection for me, and a belief that a man of his age and experience might be able to give me worth-while advice. I was not disappointed; to the day he died I never stopped discovering Uncle Reuben.

I went to his bungalow and found him sitting like a stricken Cromwell in the big armchair, facing the superb river view. He had always been a very active man and he hated his inability to get out and about, and his dependence on the visits of cronies to bring him all the local news that did not appear in the *Observer*. He was always pleased to see me, however, and his face brightened up the moment I passed in front of his window. We exchanged a few banalities and then I went straight to the point, showing him Diana's letter.

He read it carefully, his hedgebank eyebrows drawing together in a puzzled frown. When he had digested it he said, very quietly:

"All right, boy, you'd better tell me the whole of it now, right from the beginning."

I told him everything. I described how we had met and how I had once lied to him about going to London to put flowers on my mother's grave. I told him how he and others had been hoaxed by our cover story of the journalistic

266

tour of Heronslea, and how for years Diana and I had used the local social and sporting events in order to meet without her parents knowing anything about me. I told him the full story of the island adventure, the dance that preceded it, and of our chance meeting in London. I finished with a truthful but shamefaced admission of what happened at the party, the previous June.

He didn't interrupt once but punctuated my story with a series of explosive little grunts. When I had finished he turned his big, gray eyes on me and I saw with relief that there was genuine concern in them, as well as pained bewilderment.

"Is that everything, boy?" he growled. "She wouldn't be in any sort of real trouble, would she?"

"That's everything I can remember, Uncle Reuben," I said, "and if she was in trouble you can be pretty sure we should have heard about it by now from the usual quarter."

"Ah," he muttered, "I daresay you're right at that."

He folded her letter and returned it to me. Like most printers he had been a snuff addict from boyhood and now he fortified himself with two enormous pinches and a volley of shattering sneezes. "Well now, tell me first what *you* make of it. Do you regard that letter as final?"

"There's not much doubt about that," I said.

He looked at me searchingly. "Isn't there? Then why did you come to me about it?"

Why had I come to him? Was it because I had been nursing this secret for years and had now allowed it to grow into an obsession, or was it because I wanted someone to blow on the ashes in the wild hope that a small spark had survived the cold douche of her decision? Had I come to him for sympathy or reassurance? To have my hand patted or to learn how to regroup my scattered wits for a counterattack?

He answered me himself, and the nature of his answer proved what I had long suspected—that underneath the harsh, radical shell of the Puritan there was an unrepentant romantic.

"See here, boy," he said, groping for his pipe and heaving his big frame half out of the groaning chair, "I'm a crabby bachelor, and have never had but one love affair in my life. It didn't amount to anything, not even as much as yours, you reckless young idiot, but it did teach me something about women. It taught me there's a right and wrong way to go about wenching."

I think I was more shocked by his admission than he had been by mine. Not only was it a great surprise to learn that he had once been in love, but his use of the word "wenching" was so uncharacteristic that it was almost as though he had started to tell me a dirty story.

"Who was she?" I asked wonderingly.

"She was the doctor's daughter, and in my young days a doctor was somebody in a place like this. Grace, she was called, Grace Dainton, tall and dark as a gypsy and as handsome a woman as you'd see anywhere, especially when she was up on her father's gig, driving a big gray up and down the town. We used to meet in the spinney, at the back of her father's place up on the Foxhayes road, and although I wasn't out of my apprenticeship at the time, and didn't have two pennies to rub together, she was mad to marry me and wanted us to run off when her father set about marrying her off to one of those Earnshaws, who owned the big brewery over at Whinford. Wealthy family and good-looking young chap, but she wouldn't have any part of him. You can't arrange these things, never could and never will! Here was me, several years younger than her and, as I say, without a penny in the bank, and there was this Earnshaw fellow, with all the money in the world and the first motorcar ever about here outside her door every night of the week. For all that, she'd get shot of him and come running down the spinney to me as soon as it was dark. Came in her nightdress once, aye, and bare feet at that!"

As he said this one of his rare smiles crossed his face. I was so astonished by his story that for a moment I forgot all about Diana.

"What happened, Uncle Reuben? Why didn't you marry her?"

He looked quite fierce for a moment and then, drawing on his pipe, relaxed and grinned again.

"Why? Well, for the same reason as you're disposed to take that drivel at face value," he said. "Mind you, this class nonsense was even worse in my young days! You were either born a gentleman or you were born to mind your p's and q's—none of this Jack's-as-good-as-his-master business you get nowadays. With Grace and me it wasn't only a question of money but a matter of birth and education. Now these Suttons aren't real quality, that's what makes the woman so insufferable! You're as good as they are and I daresay, if you went far enough back, you're the better bred of the two. When Grace Dainton begged me to run off with her I should have done it but I didn't, and not because I wasn't head over heels in love with her, because I was, but because I thought I'd be doing her an injury."

"You're sorry you didn't?"

He thought for a moment. "Yes, I am. I'm sorry for my sake but more for hers. I was doing her the injury by letting her go, because in the end she didn't marry anyone and by the time she was thirty-five she was a leathery old maid, grumbling over a sick father and putting flowers on the altar of St. Luke's Church. She died before she was fifty and all the money that had kept me from running off with her went to the Whinmouth Animals' Dispensary. They built that red brick place at the top of Fish Street with it and I never pass the monstrosity without wanting to spit at it."

"But this is different, Uncle Reuben!" I protested, impressed by his story but far from appreciating the parallel. "This time the boot's on the other foot. It's *her* who has had second thoughts about it, not me."

"Ah boy," he said kindly, "don't you believe it! She's written the letter, but what brought her to the point of sitting down to write it? She's a girl of spirit, just like my Grace was before I turned her into a sour old maid by shuffling about and apologizing for being who I was and what I was. Now you're doing the same thing, standing aside and letting her make all the decisions. Don't do it, boy, make some yourself, and right or wrong she'll come to respect you for it. If there's one thing a woman can't abide it's a man who lets her call the tune. Before you know where you are, it's unholy discord!"

I had expected censure and possibly kindly meant grow-up-sonny-advice, but certainly not an advocacy of aggression.

"I'll never have her kind of money, Uncle," I began, but he gave a loud snort of impatience and slapped his huge palm with the bowl of his pipe, the way I remembered him doing during the violent discussion with Diana's mother two years ago.

"Money! Class! Keep your station! Keep in line! What the devil has a generation of radical progress done for you, boy? There was some excuse for me when I was your age. You daren't let it be known you voted anything but Tory if you worked for a Tory or paid rent to a Tory landlord. But today—damn it, I don't often swear but you drive me to it—today there's more real equality than I ever dreamed possible. It's now, not 1884! You don't have to kowtow to people like the Suttons, just because they made a fortune out of nitrates and pit props in the war. If you want this girl as much as you say you do, then in God's name go in and get her! If she's been laughing at you behind your back all this time, then at least you'll soon know where you stand and be well shot of her! If she hasn't, if she's written you that mealymouthed letter because she thinks you've always accepted the situation and are therefore likely to go on doing so, then show her different. Thumb your nose at her background, tan her backside if you have to, and she'll want you the more for it! Maybe that isn't the kind of advice you thought you'd get from a dry old stick like me, but it's the kind I'm inclined to give you, seeing that you're no longer the moonstruck boy you were when you played truant on the island, but a man old enough to make love to a woman and then slink off with your tail between your legs, sniveling excuses about class and income!"

I was very much taken aback by this outburst but it did me a power of good, for it challenged my entire conception of the situation. He was entirely accurate in his assumption that I had never made more than a token attempt to kick over the barrier that separated us. I had accepted the limitations it imposed with a kind of masochistic fatalism, and although I had repeatedly told myself that I could do very little until she was legally of age, I now realized that this was only a cowardly way of evading the issue. The truth was, I had always stood in awe of Diana's background. Keeper Croker's agonizing half nelson still kept me in check. I raged at the necessity of coming and going to Heronslea by stealth, but I had never contemplated taking a stand in the middle of the big paddock and bawling defiance at the Gayelorde-Suttons. Uncle Reuben's comments, the first I had ever had on the subject apart from Twining's disparagement at the office and Old Drip's gentle dissuasion years ago, set me wondering whether Diana's behavior throughout our association had been conditioned by mine. I remembered now her curious, half-symbolic act in taking me over the Castle Ferry in order to show me her rough-tongued old grandfather; it seemed to me, looking back, that many times she had presented me with a tentative opening to challenge the opposition but had resorted to secrecy when she realized that I accepted stealth as a condition to our partnership.

All at once I began to feel a great deal more sure of myself. Uncle Reuben had greatly oversimplified the situation, but at least he was on the right lines, while I had been hopelessly off them for years. From confidant to whom I had been driven by unbearable loneliness he now emerged as a powerful and active ally.

"Look here, Uncle Reuben," I said, "Diana isn't twenty-one for more than two years yet. We couldn't marry without her parents' consent and, although I've got better prospects than most fellows my age, I haven't got enough to marry on. Just what is the best way of going about it?"

"Let me look at that letter again," he said, and when I gave it to him he sat hunched up for the better part of ten minutes, rubbing his nose with his forefinger and drawing his brows together so closely that they looked like a quick-set hedge dividing his face neatly in two. Finally he looked up.

"I'd let her sow her wild oats for a spell, and then catch her on a rebound," he said.

"But she's been sowing wild oats ever since I've known her," I complained.

"Down here . . . rural oats! . . . Wait until she's sown a bag or two in Mayfair! I know her sort all right . . . they provide all the copy for the 'silly' seasons and they either end up with a loveless marriage, or an overdose of drugs. Point is, you'll have to watch your timing but that won't hurt, you're young enough in all conscience, and you can use the interval collecting ammunition—money in your instance. If you want the real key to all this it's *here*," he went on rapping his pipe bowl on page four of the letter. "She won't get what she wants from those anemic guardsmen and younger sons, and the moment she realizes how badly she wants it, pounce, and good luck to you, boy! Now tell me what you've been up to this week and what you've laid by for the inside pages. I've had enough kiss-in-the-ring for one afternoon."

We talked on general matters, more easily and naturally than we had ever conversed in the past. When I left him there was a twinkle in his eye and he called as I reached the door:

"Feel any better for the heart-to-hearter, boy?"

"Better than I've felt for months," I admitted, gratefully, and hurried back to the office to give the Thursday proofs a good deal more attention than they had been getting since they became my responsibility.

3.

Uncle Reuben had lived his entire life in a rural backwater but his knowledge of the world was far wider than one might imagine it to be. His forecast in respect of Diana proved astonishingly accurate.

Over a year passed. It was December when I went to him for advice. The following spring, Diana was back in England and within two months of her return she was hard at work providing Fleet Street with silly-season material. She was doing it, moreover, in the company Uncle Reuben had predicted, that of guardees and younger sons, collectively known as Debs' Delights. Together with high-spirited companions of previous seasons they were recognized as the Bright Young Things. They were the very last legatees of the gay twenties.

Diana's recruitment into this set had its advantages. It made her movements easy to follow, even from as far away as Whinmouth. Regularly each month Diana and her boon companions made a bow to the newspaper-reading public, at first as participators in widely publicized charity efforts—balls, bazaars and dramatic entertainments—then as habitués of some of the more popular night clubs, later still as the organizers of bow-tie sprees and bizarre practical jokes, such as the digging up of a section of the Strand dressed as L.C.C. workmen, or the tarring and feathering of statues. It was all very gay and sophisticated, and I can imagine Mrs. Gayelorde-Sutton outwardly wagging a reproving finger but secretly being immensely proud of her daughter's antics, for they surely signified an acceptance of a way of life toward which the mother had been pushing her daughter since childhood.

Some of the left-wing newspapers were very scornful about these pranks and howled for less tolerance on the part of the police and a far tighter rein on the part of the parents, but the public as a whole gloried in the fun and I suppose most young people living quiet dull lives in quiet dull towns like Whinmouth, secretly envied Diana and her set their uninhibited exploitation of youth.

Certainly the newspapers played up to them, often devoting more space to a Mayfair treasure hunt than they would allocate Mussolini's latest bluster over Abyssinia. It was on one of these crazy treasure hunts, then the peak of West End fashion, that Diana's escort, a young man known as the Hon. Newton Symes, overstepped the wide limits of public tolerance and gave the Socialist press a chance to compare the antics of these young British socialites with those of French aristocrats, immediately prior to the revolution of 1789. The comparison was somewhat strained. Diana and the young Honorable had not killed a peasant's child by driving a coach over it, they had merely driven head on into a coster's barrow and when the man's truculent attitude annoyed them, had refused to pay compensation without recourse to law.

The incident left a bad taste in the public mouth and from then on even the sensational dailies began to lead their columns against the Bright Young Things, and publish a steady spate of letters from Tunbridge Wells, and Budleigh Salterton, deploring their wild behavior in and around London.

I did not see Diana all this time, neither did I write or attempt to get in touch with her. I watched her pranks from a safe distance, and I kept an eye on the calendar. Then, one day after she had been in trouble over a motoring offense at Maidenhead, and had been threatened with suspension of her driving license, I decided that it was time for a reconnaissance and took a few days' holiday in London. Before setting out I wrote briefly to her town home, saying that I would be delighted to say hello and take her out to lunch. It was the letter of an old friend, resigned to his dismissal as a lover.

When I got to my hotel a phoned message awaited me. Diana suggested that we meet in the sherry bar of Martinez's in Swallow Street, so I went there, booked a table for lunch and sat down to await her in the bar facing the dim foyer, placing myself so as to see her before she saw me. I went about it coolly, without any of the bubbling excitement I had experienced immediately before our earlier meetings, but I was too smug by a mile. It was I, not Diana, who was caught off balance.

She appeared some ten minutes late and I almost failed to recognize her. There was a jerky brittleness about her walk and bearing, as if she was playing at being a marionette. She was exquisitely dressed and groomed, but somehow the general effect was unpleasing. When I had met her by chance, in Fortnum's, her smartness was a part of her, personality merging with clothes and accessories, but now it was as though a convention of talented couturiers and hair stylists had gathered together and drawn up a

274

schedule decreeing "This is what the fashionable young woman of this season will look like; all else is drabness!" There was a cold uniformity about her appearance that banished the Diana of Sennacharib, replacing her with the kind of girl one saw leaning nonchalantly against an impossibly expensive coupé in magazine advertisements, and the transformation extended to her expression and features, from which the personality had been drained or neutralized. Her eyes had lost their glow, her mouth its mobility. Her chestnut hair still caught the light where it fell on the starched collar of her blouse, but it was no longer the kind of hair one wanted to stroke. It had a touch-me-not-it-cost-a-lot-to-arrange look about it, and this aura of prohibition invested her like an icy mist. It was as though the Diana I remembered and worshiped had died, giving birth to the Emerald that her training had conceived, so that for the first time since she had told me her name it suited her. She had a hard, greenish, gemlike quality that was fascinating at a distance, but repellent at close quarters.

She greeted me very cordially and I ordered two sherries. We chatted about one thing and another, much as two slightly acquainted cousins might have discussed members of their family. Then she ordered two more sherries and insisted on paying for them. It was during this second drink that I noticed that Diana was not yet dead but shut away in solitary confinement and trying, very feebly, to make her presence known. Twice Diana called to be let out, once in the bar, and again when we were lunching upstairs. The first time was when Emerald faltered for a moment and Diana reached out across the table, touching my shoulders with the tips of her fingers, saying, "They're so wide! I have to be sure they aren't padded, Jan!" The second occasion was when, halfway through the hors-d'oeuvres, she suddenly asked if I had been across Sennacharib lately. This time, however, Emerald was on guard and the word became *Senneckarib*, much as Mrs. Gayelorde-Sutton would have pronounced it.

It took me at least half an hour to absorb the transition and adjust myself to its almost macabre manifestations.

When I had succeeded in doing so, our passages became a sort of game, each maneuvering to catch the other at a disadvantage, like a judge and a competitor in a statue dance, where all movement must cease with the accompaniment. I think that on the whole I had the best of the exchanges, for behind her façade of guarded frigidity I thought I could detect a tiny flicker of guilt. She was rather like a woman who had sat down opposite me to settle a claim for damages, determined to yield no more than she was obliged to, but held in check by a conviction that, if the matter went to court, the decision would surely go against her

When we were sipping coffee the waiter came over to us with a bottle of cognac and Diana said she would like some. He poured a little into her glass but she laid her hand on his arm and kept it there, so that it became a treble. We had had a bottle of Beaune between us, as well as the sherry, and the effect of the alcohol now began to mellow her. She leaned back and smiled, no longer like a distant cousin, or a claim fighter, but like a rich aunt regaling a schoolboy nephew on a speechday outing.

"Are you doing anything particular this afternoon, Jan?" she asked, and although the question was an idle one I knew that it was important to her that we should extend the reunion.

"Have you anything in mind?" I said.

"As a matter of fact I hev!" she replied.

There it was again; "hev" not "have," a formidable echo of her mother.

"Well, Diana?"

"I'd like you to take me to the Tower," she said.

"The Tower? The Tower of London?" It would have been an astonishing request from Diana; it was an absolutely outrageous one from Emerald.

"I've never been," she admitted, "and I don't know anyone else who would take me. I heard a broadcast about the ceremony of the keys the other evening and said to myself, I expect Jan knows all about that place. *Do you?*"

"I've been there several times," I told her, "mostly when I was writing the Margaret of Anjou book. We'll go

276

if you really want to, we can get the Underground to the Minories."

She winced at the word "Underground" and I only just stopped myself laughing.

"I've got my flivver outside," she said, "providing you don't mind being driven by a woman!"

"No," I said, beginning to enjoy myself, "I'm sure you're a very good driver. Di."

She was too, as far as the mechanical processes were concerned, changing down soundlessly, judging distances with cool accuracy, and generally showing the same command over a car as she showed riding Sioux. I noticed, however, that she was impatient with less skillful drivers, and snarled at a man who slipped his clutch while trying to beat her over the traffic lights. In what seemed to me about five minutes we were on Tower Hill, where we parked and bought tickets at the gate. I showed her around. She did not seem specially interested in the block, the armory and the green, or even the crown jewels, which I thought might attract her, but she surprised me by dawdling beside the prisoners' inscriptions in the Beauchamp Tower, and asked me to tell her something about the people who had been imprisoned there. I was telling her about Lady Jane Grey, and how she had watched the headless body of her husband carried by shortly before her own execution, when I noticed that she was not listening. She had pretended to curiosity in order to allow time for other sightseers to descend the spiral staircase, leaving us alone in the half-light of the winter's afternoon. As soon as their steps died away she said:

'Well, Jan, don't you want to kiss me?'

The odd thing was that I didn't, not in the least, but it would have sounded so unfriendly to say so that I replied:

"If you want me to, Di."

"I do," she said, flatly, and tilted up her face.

As our lips touched I wondered if contact would free the real Diana and reduce this unpleasant parody of Mrs. Gayelorde-Sutton to a wraith as insubstantial as Lady Jane Grey, but it did nothing of the sort. Her kissing habits had changed like everything else about her This too

277

had conformed, and now the conference of hair stylists and couturiers had bowed themselves out, to make way for Continental love experts, who had reduced the art of kissing to a graded scale of intimacy—so much pressure, so much time, a place for each hand, a specified angle for the body. She kissed me near the top of this scale, her lips parted and her eyes closed. There was sensuality in the kiss but no hint of bestowal. Its effect upon me was to harden my obstinacy.

I wondered, even while kissing her, whether her town escorts would regard this kind of embrace as something practiced by the lower orders in cinemas and parks. She must have sensed my detachment for she suddenly stepped back and stared at the floor. Doing this she looked so childish and pitiful that I felt a sudden and inexplicable sympathy for her, and at once tried to make amends. I kissed her again, softly and very respectably, but this time she did not attempt to respond, but tore herself free.

"For God's sake let's stop playing 'if-only,'" she snapped, and walked past me and down the stairs.

As we emerged on the green a Yeoman of the Guard began shepherding the last visitors toward the main gate. I drew level with Diana and looked at her sideways, expecting to find her flushed and irritated, but she wasn't; the hard, poised look was back again and as we walked past the Traitors' Gate she said:

"Those beefeaters—do they stay here or do they come out sometimes?"

"They come up for air every so often," I said. "There's usually two or three of them hanging about the ticket office."

She did not reply to this, and the significance of the question did not occur to me until, months later, I read that one of the trophies of a Mayfair treasure hunt had been a beefeater's hat.

Perhaps this was why she had wanted me to take her to the Tower. At the moment she was obviously anxious to be gone and asked me, with the air of addressing a hitch-hiker, where I would care to be dropped.

"Nowhere," I said bleakly. "I've got to see a publisher and his office is near, I can walk."

It was a lie, but like her I had no wish to prolong the dismal occasion. She climbed into the car, started the engine, and revved up with unnecessary vigor.

"Well, so long, Jan! Thank you for taking me and thank you for a nice lunch."

We shook hands—that was the monstrously unreal part of it—we shook hands, and the gesture slammed the shutter on our adolescence. As she drove off, her engine making a series of sharp reports, a wave of sadness swept over me and the ache nagged at me all the way home to Whinmouth. Yet it was impersonal sadness. I was not mourning Diana so much as all things in life that promise so much and yield so little. I was sad for the sunny day clouded by rain, for the kitten that grows up to catch thrushes, for the juggler with the fixed smile who opens a glittering program and drops his clubs halfway through the first act, for anybody and everybody who grows up believing that the world is an oyster but never discovers the means of opening the shell. Behind this sadness, however, was a vague sense of relief. It was all over now! It was something that could be tied up like love letters and left to fade under a pile of holiday snapshots and old phonograph records.

I was free, really free, for the first time since that autumn afternoon in the larch wood a century ago, and I believe I faced this fact with the same kind of resignation as a man faces the prospect of learning to walk with an artificial leg. It could have been far better, but it might have been much worse.

4.

I said nothing to Uncle Reuben about the visit to London, but I imagine that he noticed my application to work throughout that spring and summer and probably related it to Diana in some way. In July I read that, following another motoring offense, her driving license had been suspended for twelve months.

Week followed week, with its usual round of petty sessional courts, council meetings, funerals, weddings, sales-of-work and the odd mild sensation, a fire or a sea rescue. I slipped into a swift rhythm, sometimes covering as many as a dozen jobs a day, and spending what spare time I had in boating and bathing. I went to a few dances and made two or three tepid friendships with Whinmouth girls. I had a ten-day holiday in Brittany, partly with the object of improving my French, which I had kept up by reading First Empire memoirs in the original, and occasional evening classes at the University. I went over to Uncle Mark's riding establishment now and again, and when the hunting season opened I even had a day or two out on one of his cobs.

It was a pleasant enough life. The riding and hunting, and sometimes an occasional shooting expedition at the invitation of local farmers, kept me in touch with Sennacharib. I remember crossing it under a gray, lifeless sky soon after my twenty-first birthday and bagging a couple of rabbits on Foxhayes Common, but I no longer thought of its gorse and plantations as in any way associated with Diana. I absorbed its color patterns and contours subconsciously, much as Uncle Luke might have watched the flight of a heron over the estuary, but it was now a background, not an Eden.

Then the fun began again with the Bright Young Things. They got into trouble with the Customs and Excise, at Dover, and one of them, whose name had been linked with Diana in the past, received a short jail sentence for smuggling. Later, around about Christmas time, Diana herself figured in a more spectacular scandal. She was a passenger in a glider that crashed on a row of suburban houses in Kent. The pilot was injured, but she escaped with bruises and was photographed for the newspapers standing beside the wreckage. In common with most people I became rather bored with all this nonsense and sympathized with the comment of a vitriolic columnist in a "progressive" weekly, beginning: *If Hitler seeks proof that our expensively educated young people are decadent he should follow the careers of certain ornaments of Mayfair these days. . . .*

Ordinarily these pranks would have aroused little attention but they were given prominence because of the sharp contrast they provided with the main news of those times —endless death and destruction in places like Addis Ababa and Guernica, a constant overturn of threats from the dictators, and irritated gloom among everyone with enough intelligence to wonder what was due to happen next. What irritated people like the gossip writer I have quoted was the impression that people like Diana had turned their backs on the rest of us, and despised us for wondering about the future. They certainly did give that impression, as though they were not only determined to live for the day but intended making as much song and dance about it as possible. The majority, who had to work hard for a living, envied them their freedom and probably found compensation in regarding their childishly high spirits as evidence of degeneracy.

Then something happened that could not be written off as a Mayfair rag. Diana and a young man called Irving, who was the son of a wealthy cement king, were involved in a fatal accident on a country road south of London. Their car collided with a motorcycle combination, containing a young husband and his wife—an expectant mother. The woman was killed outright. Irving and the motorcyclist were critically injured. Diana escaped with two cracked ribs.

At first it looked like just another road accident, but at the initial inquest (later adjourned in the absence of the injured parties) it emerged that Irving had been far gone in drink and would face a criminal charge if he survived. He did not recover, dying a week or so after the accident.

The next day the injured motorcyclist died and the hunt was up. Relatives of the victims howled protests through the press, and feature writers jumped in with whoops of triumph. Diana, as the sole survivor of the crash, came in for some very sharp interrogation at the resumed inquest. As a mere passenger in Irving's car, however, there was no painful sequel for her, and the papers rounded off the story by publishing pictures of her leaving the court, one

281

arm in a sling and the other shading her face from the cameramen.

Two days after these pictures had appeared, I came into the office to find a letter from Diana in my tray. It was a wild cry for help:

> MY JAN,
>
> I don't deserve the slightest sympathy, least of all from you, but I've been in hell since the business, and no one else is the slightest use! If you could meet me, wherever you like, I'd never stop being grateful! If you won't, tear this up and forget it. I should understand. It wouldn't make me stop remembering you as the nicest person I've ever had the luck to meet!
>
> With love,
> DIANA

I have said that I only remembered Diana impersonally, that when she disappeared in her cloud of blue exhaust on Tower Hill I had succeeded, at last, in turning my back on her. Since then I had adjusted myself to a routine in which she played no part at all. In essence this was true; I seldom thought about her these days, and when I did it was without bitterness. Her appeal showed me how grossly I had been fooling myself. The moment I read her cry for help I knew I must answer it, and I knew also that this would not be a matter of running to the aid of an old friend in trouble but the joyful stampede of a man hopelessly in love. Fortunately, I recognized this at once. It shocked me but I had the sense to go straight to Uncle Reuben and confide in him.

He was far more doubtful about her than he had been when I had sought his advice about her letter of dismissal.

"I don't know, Jan," he said, rubbing his chin, "she's gone from bad to worse, boy. Surely you can see that? There's a kind of devil in her, fed and watered by the kind of life she's been leading since you last saw her. I know that sort. Catch 'em young and you can do something with 'em, but now . . . how old do you say she is?"

I could answer that question with accuracy.

"She'll be twenty-one on the eighteenth of June," I told him.

"You want to go to her?"

"I've got to, Uncle!"

He looked at me sadly and nodded his big head. Inactivity had aged him. He looked more than his seventy years and tired to breaking point of pain and half-life.

"I daresay you're right, boy. It never pays to defy instincts. Go and see how the land lies at all events, but don't commit yourself to any tomfool promises one way or the other."

I wrote saying that I would come to London that night, and meet her at the Swan and Edgar's corner at eleven A.M. Then I changed into my best suit and drove to the junction for the night train. It was like a parody of my first journey to meet her, the time she had played truant from school. The London pattern was similar, too; a hunched walk through the drizzle of the January small hours, a breakfast in the Covent Garden area, a whiling away of time beside the Embankment, and finally a bus ride to Piccadilly.

It was all there but somehow the parallel was not a pleasant one. It was as though I was the victim of a malign compulsion forced to re-enact a lost youth in order to prove to myself that the original journey had been a dream and that here, years later, was the reality. When I jumped off the bus and crossed over to the rendezvous, the first person I saw was Diana, anxiously scanning the faces of pedestrians as they hurried to and from Eros. It was the first time she had ever been the first to keep an appointment.

I approached her from behind and touched her shoulder. She swung around with a sharp exclamation and I saw at once that she was in a state of extreme nervous tension. When she saw who had touched her she almost cried out with relief.

"Jan! I was terrified you'd cry off! I got it into my head that your idea of arranging to meet me here again was . . . well, a sort of pay-you-out trick. Can we go somewhere and talk? Where shall it be? Martinez? Fortnum's?"

She spoke with extreme rapidity. Each statement was a question.

"It was Lyons the last time we met here, Di, but we've moved up a bit since then," I said, trying a joke in the hope of calming her nerves.

The joke fell flat. "Was it? I don't remember . . . everything's muddled . . . maybe it's the shock, or the bump I got on the windshield . . . you decide—somewhere quiet, somewhere *inside!*"

I took hold of her arm and noticed that she was trembling. She looked so pale, and seemed so helpless and distraught, that I wondered at her doctor allowing her out. Her state of mind was reflected in the clothes she wore. She, who had always been so trim and fashionable, now looked as if she had grabbed any garment that came to hand and had not even troubled to arrange her hair or tidy herself before leaving the house.

She was hatless and gloveless and her lovely hands showed traces of London grime. The varnish on her nails was chipped and her make-up was sketchy, too much lipstick having been applied to one side of her mouth and not enough to the other, so that the cupid's bow looked almost clownish.

I was so shocked by her manner and general appearance that I was obliged to take command of her in a way that would never have been possible in the past.

"We won't go anywhere where you'll have to make an effort, Di," I told her. "What about a snack bar I know, for coffee and a sandwich in strict seclusion?"

"Anywhere," she said, gratefully, "anywhere at all! It was marvelous of you to come so quickly, Jan."

She grabbed my arm and hugged it tightly, as though she had no confidence in her ability to negotiate the traffic. We crossed into Lower Regent Street and made our way to a tiny taximan's pull-up that I knew in a side street behind the Plaza. There were no other customers at this time of the morning and the proprietor, a sallow young man with heavy sideburns, was out of earshot behind his zinc counter. I bought two coffees and two cheese sandwiches, carrying them across to an alcove at the far end of the shop. In the few moments it had taken me to get them she had made a brave effort to pull herself together and was now feverishly making up with the aid of a little hand mirror.

"I must look a terrible mess!" she said, sounding more like herself. "You've never seen me looking like this, have you, Jan?"

"Never mind that," I said, "just try to relax. We've got all day today and tomorrow as well, if you like. It's a lucky job your letter came on a Friday. I've put the paper to bed and I'm clear until the Petty Sessions, on Monday."

She sipped her coffee. It was very good coffee and she nodded, appreciatively.

"How much was this, Jan?" she asked, irrelevantly.

"Threepence a cup," I said, grinning. "I can run to that, Di!"

She smiled and it was exciting to see a trace of color return to her cheeks. She propped the hand mirror against the cup and, bending low, touched up her lips and tugged at her hair. Presently she replaced the things in her bag and straightened up, finishing the coffee in a series of quick gulps.

"I know places where they'd charge half a crown and it wouldn't be nearly as good coffee as this," she mused. "It was clever of you to know about a place like this but then, you lived and worked in London, didn't you? I keep forgetting that."

"On about thirty bob a week," I told her, "and it makes for careful housekeeping!"

I had been right to bring her somewhere like this. The traffic roar was very much subdued and there were no distractions, as there would have been in any of her usual haunts about the West End. She began to nibble the sandwich, gingerly at first but enthusiastically after the first bite or two.

"This is the first food I've had in forty-eight hours," she admitted. "I haven't swallowed a thing except pills since that awful inquest."

"What sort of pills?" I demanded.

"Oh, the usual . . . pheno and something else added," she said lightly, "but don't let's talk about pills, Jan. It's

285

lovely being here with you; it's making me come alive again. I feel a lot better already, my Jan."

It was callous of me but I wasn't big enough to resist it.

"So I'm your Jan again, am I?"

For a moment she looked exactly as she had looked when we were skylarking up on the common.

"Yes," she said, "whether you like it or not!"

"Do you want to talk about the accident? I've read all the papers had to say about it. We do get London papers in Whinmouth," I added, noting her look of surprise.

"Yes," she said, firmly, "let's get it over and done with. I've got to have somebody's opinion about what to do or I'll end up in the bin! It's odd, Jan, you go on getting further and further away from life and then, suddenly, a single jolt pulls you up and you see where you've been heading and at what a fantastic speed. Do you see what I mean?"

"You'd better start from the beginning," I said, "but don't tell me anything you might regret telling me later on."

"All right, Jan," she said, meekly, "but order some more coffee and sandwiches first. Get ham and plaster it with mustard. I've suddenly realized that I'm famished!"

I went over and bought more coffee and ham sandwiches. Out of the corner of my eye, as I stood waiting at the counter, I saw her take out a cigarette, stick it between her lips, pluck it out again and return it to the case.

"The papers only got half the story," she began, when we were seated again. "We'd been down to a country-club dance, near Maidstone, and Irving was so tight that I made him let me drive, even though my ban doesn't expire until midsummer."

This really frightened me. "*You* were driving? You mean, when it happened?"

She nodded and did not take her eyes off me.

"But how . . . I mean, does anyone know?"

"No one but you, Jan!"

I began to understand the reason for her semihysterical condition. All the time she was giving evidence at the inquest she must have been stricken with guilt, as well as terrified of what might happen to her if the truth emerged.

"How the devil did you manage to persuade the police that Irving was driving?" I asked.

"That was easy . . ." She said it with a touch of the old Diana, planning mischief in Sennacharib. "There was no one about, not until later, and I was the only one conscious. I did it all instinctively—defense mechanism I suppose you'd call it. As soon as I sorted myself out, a minute or so after the impact, I climbed out and pushed Irving into the driving seat. After all, if he hadn't died he'd have still been for it, for letting me drive! I was with him when I was disqualified, so he couldn't have said he didn't know about the ban."

"But how about the others, the couple in the motorcycle combination?"

"I didn't even see them until the ambulance men arrived. I didn't even know what we'd hit! It was all such a frightful shambles. We were piled up under a bank and my side hurt so much that I must have passed out myself after somebody had stopped and carried me into a house for first aid."

It didn't need a vivid imagination to picture the scene—four badly injured people, three of them half dead, in the wreckage of vehicles on a dark, lonely road; a bewildered motorist concentrating on the one victim of the crash who was the least helpless; a sleeping householder dragged from bed by thunderous knocks on the front door; phone calls, ambulance men, solemn police poking about among the mess, taking measurements. As a reporter I was familiar enough with the scene.

"What happened afterwards? After you'd all been taken to hospital?"

"The police came in the afternoon and took a statement. They had already been ferreting around the club where we'd been, and when they hinted that Irving was tight when he left there, I saw at once it was no good lying about details. Then Daddy sent his solicitor in and I made a statement to him. I didn't say any more than I could help, I just said I was dozing and never even saw the motorbike and sidecar."

"*Did* you see it?"

"Just about . . . it's all a bit vague."

Suddenly she lost her grip again and her eyes filled with tears. "It was when they told me the woman was expecting a baby that I felt like a murderer," she said, her fingers drumming on the table. "Sometimes I don't think I'll ever sleep again . . . all three of them, and the baby inside her killed, just like that! I wish to God I'd been killed too! I've been wishing it ever since!"

There was no point in offering her the conventional consolations, telling her she'd feel better later on, that time was a healer, that what was done was done and couldn't be altered. She was in too deep to be helped by platitudes and shoulder pats. She was racked with a misery that stemmed directly from a deep sense of guilt, and would probably suffer even more when the physical and mental shock of the accident had been absorbed. I was not sure that I could help her but I was certain that no one else could, least of all her parents or any of her society friends. Yet the responsibility of helping her, of calming her down and trying to rationalize the circumstances, pressed down on me like a slab of concrete. Only one approach suggested itself. It seemed to me that the most promising line I could pursue was to steer her back to the high-water mark of our association, to the moment when we had parted outside the flower-room door on the morning after her party.

"If I hadn't answered your letter what did you intend doing, Di?" I asked her.

She blew her nose and avoided my glance.

"I think I would have gone to the police and told the whole truth," she said. "Come to that, I still might. I would if you said I should."

"How would that help?"

"It would help *me*," she said, biting her lip. "I'd go to prison, I suppose, and that would help to wipe it out somehow!"

"*Were* you tight, as tight as Irving?"

"No, I wasn't. I'd had a few, spread over the evening, but I've been much worse than that other times and got the car home without a scratch."

"Yet you can't remember anything about the moment before the collision?"

"No, just a glare of lights and then an awful crash!"

"Were you blinding along, just before that?"

"How could I have been? The crash was at the end of a steep hill and I'd only just changed from third to top."

I began to see a gleam of light. Her threat of a confession had scared me and my brain was now working at top speed. I wasn't looking for facts, not real, solid facts, such as they drag from witnesses in court. What I needed were a few threads that I could weave into something that she could hold on to during the next few weeks. With relief I remembered that I had kept two or three newspaper reports of the inquest and had put them in my wallet to reread in the train. I took them out now and ran my eye down a column of print, stopping at the paragraph dealing with the evidence of the motorcyclist's brother, who had told how the dead man and his wife had left his home shortly before the crash. He admitted that the motorcyclist had "had a couple of beers." As one well versed in motoring cases I interpreted this to mean he had probably had five or six. Witnesses are generous to the dead, especially when big insurance claims are involved.

"Now listen, Di," I said, "and don't interrupt! First of all, forget that screwy idea of going to the police and confessing. It can't do anyone a ha'porth of good now and it will almost certainly land you in jail. Whatever claims there are will be fought out by insurance companies. I've seen a lot of this sort of thing and it's their job, and an absolutely impersonal one. If there were dependent kids it might be different, but there aren't and any admission on your part wouldn't amount to more than a bleat, and God knows how much it would complicate matters! That's point one—forget the confession angle, and don't even admit it to your solicitors, it would embarrass them no end. Point two is the accident itself. It's natural enough that you should feel to blame, but how do you know that you are? You only took a chance on driving because Irving was stinko, and if you'd let him drive you might have killed half a dozen people instead of two! As to the chap and his wife who were killed, they'd been drinking too—that's been admitted, and anyone who takes his pregnant wife out in a sidecar at night after sinking a few beers is sitting up and begging for it these days. It might even have been his fault, or at any rate, six of one and half a dozen of the other, so stop torturing yourself and write it all off as craziness on everyone's part. Look at it this way: if you had all four been injured and had come into court to give evidence on a motoring charge, what would have happened? I'll tell you. All four of you would have sworn on oath that you were doing about twenty miles an hour on your correct side of the white line, that you sounded your horn all the way up the road, that you dipped your lights like good little drivers and that you might have had one for the road but certainly no more before you set off! I've sat through dozens of these cases and they're all the same. No one is to blame. It's always the other fellow, and all it amounts to in the end is who is the better liar, or which of you has brought the slickest mouthpiece into court."

It was probably the longest speech I'd ever made and she heard it through, without taking her eyes off me. When I had said all I had to say she sat quite still, her head slightly to one side, her eyelids puckered at the corners, in a way that I remembered had heralded her short sudden laughs. The hunted look had disappeared. She had a natural color and her lovely hands, no longer fluttering, were clasped and pressed hard against her breast.

"You're marvelous, Jan!" she said at length. "You're an absolute tonic! You ought to have a room in Harley Street and get fifty guineas a time for sorting people out."

I wasn't at all sure whether she was trying to pay me a genuine compliment or half-laughing at me, the way she had often teased me when we had argued over something and I had seemed to her to champion stuffiness and caution.

"It's the way I see it, at any rate," I said, "and if you really want advice and not just a bit of 'there-there-now-now' I'll tell you something else while we're about it."

"Well?" She was smiling openly now, her teeth holding her lower lip, as though she was afraid a smile might offend.

"Cut loose from the Set and get to hell out of here, once and for all! Come back to Heronslea if you like but take it easy, at least for a spell. Stop chasing whatever your lot are chasing and grow up! We've all got to sooner or later."

She considered this a long moment, then she said, "When are you going back, Jan? Today?"

"I could," I told her, "but I shall have to travel down on Sunday night in any case."

"Would you take me with you—*now?*"

I had done my inadequate best to comfort her because it had distressed me very much to see her in such a pitiful state of depression. It had seemed important to me because, buried under the years of stress and disappointment that she represented, was the image of the person around whom my entire life had revolved, the girl who, somehow or other, had represented all the sweetness and joy of life. In the weeks that had followed our last meeting, on the afternoon we went to the Tower, I had persuaded myself that the Diana I had adored no longer had substance, that she had, in effect, been permanently superseded by the brittle, stilted upstart of Emerald, someone who, against all probability, had modeled herself upon Mrs. Gayelorde-Sutton and starved Diana of Sennacharib to death. Even the nervous creature that I had met an hour ago, outside Swan and Edgar's, was not really Diana but simply Emerald reduced to size, Emerald scared and threatened into something almost pitiful by worry and tragedy. Now, however, when this disheveled creature had sunned itself a little in my clumsy attempts at reassurance, it seemed to take on the flesh and spirit of a girl who had once galloped shouting through the larches into Big Oak paddock, and in as short a space of time I was back again at starting point, having my arm twisted by Keeper Croker, running to meet her from Folly Wood, holding her close as the raindrops

291

splashed down on the laurels through a short summer night.

"You mean come home for good, Di?"

"I'll be twenty-one in June. I can go where I like, do what I like. For that matter, there's no real problem now. Daddy is up to his neck in mysterious deals—I hardly ever see him—and after the inquest Mummy buzzed off to the Riviera and left here in a towering rage because I flatly refused to go. I'm glad now that I had that much guts."

"Then who looks after you at home?" I asked, wondering again at the strange callousness of parents who could smother a child with material benefits and yet be so niggardly in accepting responsibilities one associates with parenthood. "You can't mean that they stood aside during this business and let you battle it out on your own?"

"More or less—they got the best lawyers, of course, and Daddy paid the barman at the country club to say I had been wallowing in tomato juice," she said lightly. It was clear that she did not resent this incredible disinterestedness on their part and was so accustomed to it that it did not even strike her as unusual.

"It's something I just can't understand," I said, remembering anxious and carefully dressed parents in Whinmouth Court who invariably put in appearances when their sons or daughters were in trouble with the law.

"That's reasonable," she said, "for you've never really understood anything about our sort. You see, Jan, once you get caught up in big business, and the kind of life that goes with having a lot of money, you step right outside life as most people live it and sooner or later it warps you altogether. You don't have the same set of values about anything at all. I noticed that with Mother. That motorcyclist was a bricklayer, and once she knew this, Mother's sole reaction to the smashup was irritation arising out of unsavory publicity! Apart from that she didn't turn a hair. Daddy was a bit more concerned but, as I said, he's been terribly preoccupied with business lately and what happened to me was a sideline."

"But it's absolutely bloody inhuman!" I protested.

She lifted her shoulders, another gesture I had forgotten but now recalled.

"It's just *us*," she said calmly, and left it at that.

We went out of the cafe, down Lower Regent Street and across the Mall to St. James's Park. She walked freely now, swinging her arm and moving with long, even strides. There was no tension about her as we crossed the road, threading our way through slowly moving traffic, and her recovery left me free to think about the implications of her return.

Did her remark mean that she wished to cut loose from her parents forever and implement the pledge made on Nun's Island all that time ago? Was she agreeing to marry me after all, to turn her back on Heronslea and become a small-town wife who kept house and went shopping in Whinmouth? I suppose I should have asked her this at once, establishing our new position from the very beginning, but it did not seem to me a sensible thing to do at that time, it was too much like taking advantage of my temporary ascendancy and her highly emotional state. I knew that when I did get an answer to this vital question I wanted it to be an absolutely honest one. I was tired of finding her and losing her, and was sick to death of this interminable game of hide-and-seek. In addition, at this moment, Uncle Reuben's parting warning occurred to me— "Don't make any tomfool promises one way or the other."

I knew also, however, that I wanted her back. Diana had again banished the ludicrous Emerald and the only thing that really mattered was that Emerald should stay dead and buried, with Irving and the other victims of the crash.

"How about your things?" I demanded, suddenly. "There's a train at three P.M. from Waterloo. Could you make it?"

"If I don't then I never will!" she said.

I looked at my watch. It was ten minutes to one. We hurried out into Horse Guards Parade and hailed a taxi.

"It's platform ten," I said. "I'll get there early, buy your ticket, bag seats, and wait for you at the barrier."

She embraced me impulsively, and at the touch of her

cheek I knew I was once more fully committed, in spite of Uncle Reuben's warning and in spite of my own secret misgivings. We were beginning again, right from the start, and I could have shouted as much from the top of Nelson's column.

I made my way over to Waterloo, claimed my hand luggage and had a wash and brush-up. Then I felt I needed a drink and I had two double brandies with barely a splash. At half-past two I bought her single, first-class fare, and ten minutes later I was back at the barrier, having tipped a porter to save us two corner seats in a smoker.

At four minutes to three there was a small swirl among the crowds beyond the bookstall and Diana emerged, driving two porters before her like mules. Each man carried two heavy suitcases and each had smaller luggage wedged under his arms. Diana was carrying, of all things, an unwrapped saddle to which long, trailing girths were attached.

The little procession swept past, gathering me in its stride. There was absolutely nothing about the laughing, breathless girl who seized my hand that one could associate in any way with the hesitant bundle of nerves I had greeted exactly four hours ago. I had no time to wonder whether this was a good or bad sign, whether it indicated that I alone was responsible for the transformation or whether it implied that her mind was so shallow that shame, misery and guilt could find no lodging there.

We bundled into our compartment and she gave the porters ten shillings each. Then the whistle blew and the train began to move.

"Made it!" she said, triumphantly. "Sennacharib! Here I come!"

It was as though someone had been juggling with time, whirling the clock back through the years to the summer evening when we set out for the regatta dance on the borrowed motorbike. It was as though everything that had happened since was the slow unfolding of a long, muddled dream, in which joy jostled misery and triumph defeat, a dimly remembered seesaw of delight, laughter and heartache. I looked from her to her mountain of luggage and back again. Suddenly the sheer idiotic improbability of it all set me laughing until my eyes filled with tears, and Diana bounced down beside me and curled up like a kitten, tucked her long, elegant legs beneath her and throwing her weight against me in a way that sent her hair tumbling across my face. Then, still chuckling, I listened to the rhythm of the wheels.

Five minutes after Clapham she was sound asleep.

Chapter Nine

THAT WAS the best time of all, early spring homecoming.

I must have misjudged Diana when she bustled up to the barrier at Waterloo with her hundredweight of luggage. She hadn't wriggled from under the accident as easily as all that and during the first weeks in the West Country there were times when I sometimes wondered if her apparent recovery had been the last flicker of the flame that had burned in her so strongly throughout her adolescence. Her ribs still pained her and she was not sleeping well. She would meet me on Foxhayes, or on the wooden bridge over the Teasel inland from Shepherdshey and for an hour or so would talk and laugh in the old, familiar way. Then her expression would cloud over and she would move out of reach and at these times her hands were the clue to her thoughts. They were never still but constantly moved up to her hair, or plucked halfheartedly at whatever she happened to be holding, a riding crop, a twig, or, if we were riding, Sioux's mane.

It was the springtime of Sennacharib that started her real convalescence. Toward the end of the cold snap, when the long slope from the larch wood across Big Oak paddock was silent under February snow, her moods became less erratic and she was less disposed to soar from gloom to the brittle elation that I associated with Emerald and then, perhaps, drop back again, setting me the job of finding something to level off her mercury. We spent a great deal of time together, walking and riding on the afternoons when I was free and sometimes taking a Sunday picnic farther afield. When I was unable to be with her she spent much of her time with old McCarthy, the Scots gardener, who had always been a pet of hers. They worked together at potting in the big greenhouses and I did what I could to encourage this activity, for McCarthy, a gruff, unsentimental old body, always treated her as though she were an irresponsible child of eight, growling at her when she handed him the wrong tool and even slapping her hand when she did something that outraged his surly professionalism. He was fond of her for all that and championed her aggressively when I mentioned the accident and asked if he thought she was on the mend.

"There's nae wrong with yon lass," he muttered, "as couldn't have been put right by a lick with a razor strop years since. It's her folk that want it now, for raising the bairn the way they did! She'll do, if she bides down here in the open."

This brief conspiracy began an unspoken conspiracy between us. McCarthy held Mr. and Mrs. Gayelorde-Sutton in contempt, and would have been sacked long ago had he not been the means of Mrs. Gayelorde-Sutton's winning prizes at fruit and flower shows for miles around. I like to think that, in his view, I compared very favorably with most of the young men who had been Diana's guests at Heronslea. He knew everything that went on and Diana had probably confided in him from time to time, so that in the absence of the Gayelorde-Suttons I was able to come and go quite freely about the estate. The supercilious chauffeur, who seemed never to have recovered from the indignity of having to take me home in the Bentley that first night, continued to regard me as a tradesman delivering goods at the back door, whereas the butler, on the few occasions I encountered him, always looked fixedly over my left shoulder, as though determined to pretend that I was an optical illusion. The remainder of the staff, all Shepherdshey folk, were friendly.

My easy access to Heronslea had a curious effect upon

my new relationship with Diana. The very complications we had encountered in earlier stages of our courtship had, almost in self-defense, encouraged me to think of the future in terms of marriage. Now, with the clandestine element gone, the urgency of establishing right of access to Diana had disappeared. In those first weeks I concentrated solely on getting her well and later on, in the continued absence of her parents, there seemed to be no urgency in planning ahead.

I suppose, away at the back of my mind, I still thought of marriage as the ultimate outcome of it all, but I was not inclined to explore improbable ways and means of achieving it, as I had done so often and so fruitlessly in the past. It was enough, for the time being, to know that I was necessary to her and to watch her salvage more and more of the real Diana. It was enough for the time being, to hear her laughter ring through Sennacharib and watch her hair stream into the wind as she urged Sioux up the slope of the paddock. In some ways it was like reliving my happy boyhood but without the anxiety that had always attended our meetings here. There was Sennacharib, Diana and I, and with each day that passed, Sennacharib stirred more vigorously under its winter vest of sodden leaves and snowdrifts, and the southwest wind passed whispering through the marching woods as patters of rain coaxed dog violets, wild daffodils and crocuses from the banks of Teasel Brook.

One day in early March Uncle Reuben died, and much as I loved him I could feel no real sorrow at his death. He was tired of lying propped in a chair, watching the tides rise and fall over the estuary, and more than once had hinted that he was impatient to be gone.

We buried him beside his father and mother in the steeply sloping churchyard on the Foxhayes road, and went home to Aunt Thirza's to eat an immense funeral tea and hear what old Hawthorne, the Whinmouth Press executor, had to say about the future of the business.

The will was a very simple document. There was a modest cash legacy to Uncle Luke, another to the chapel, and a third to the Whinmouth Liberal Association. Reuben's

297

shares in the paper and printing works were equally divided between the sister and nephew of the original proprietor, and myself. These shares, together with those already given me, made me a full partner in the concern, with a guaranteed salary of four hundred a year, so long as I continued to work on the paper.

Diana questioned me at what I considered unnecessary length about my future as editor of Whinmouth's little newspaper. She had never been able to take the *Observer* very seriously, even less so after I had invited her into the printing office one Friday night to watch the old flatbed trundling out the weekly edition.

"It's all so terribly 'Caxtony,' Jan," she protested, laughing. "You really ought to sell out to someone much older and then use your little bit of capital to do something important. How much do you suppose it's all worth—your part of it, I mean?"

I discussed this with Hawthorne, the solicitor, who estimated that my share in the Whinmouth Press would now fetch some two thousand pounds on the open market. It might have been double this amount but Uncle Reuben had laid no claim to the freehold of the premises.

Two thousand pounds seemed a far larger sum to me than it did to Diana.

"It's not a fortune," she said, "but I daresay you could make a start with it. Daddy started with very little more but somehow I don't think you're cut out for his kind of hanky-panky. I suppose you wouldn't know what to do with stocks and shares if you had any, would you, Jan?"

"No, I wouldn't," I told her, rather crossly, for although I had by no means resigned myself to spending my life as a smalltown newspaperman, it still seemed to me infinitely preferable to the complicated occuaption pursued so profitably by Mr. Gayelorde-Sutton. I was a bit of a snob about high finance and I suppose this distrust had been nurtured by my fear and hatred of Diana's mother.

"Since we're discussing the subject, what *am* I cut out for?" I demanded. "I'm a good enough journalist for Whinmouth, but what I saw of Fleet Street while working in town didn't whet my appetite for anything more ambitious in that particular line."

Diana screwed up her eyes and her voice grew persuasive.

"I always see you as a farmer of one sort or another, Jan," she said. "After all, it's in your blood and you're never really yourself unless you've got mud on your boots. What I mean is, you always look like a fish out of water in town, whereas down here you're sort of . . . well . . . sort of *real* and *belonging,* if you see what I mean?"

I understood well enough what she meant. The older I grew the more I regretted that I had not spent my youth acquiring some up-to-date agricultural knowledge. Some of my happiest days had been at the county shows, plowing matches and other competitions organized by the Young Farmers Clubs in the area. I was keenly interested in forestry and land conservation and by this time I was on friendly terms with most of the farmers in the district, even those as far afield as Castle Ferry. In fact, farming and its tributary occupations had always seemed to me so much more vital than industry or shopkeeping, and Diana's vague encouragement started a smolder of thought that blazed up like a heath fire when an opportunity came my way to change course a week or so after Uncle Reuben's funeral. Before that, however, Diana piloted me on what was to prove a sentimental journey.

We had been cantering west from the head of Teasel Brook, intending to drop down the steepest part of the common toward the Folly Wood and then ride home via Big Oak paddock. At the junction of heath tracks, a mile from the main road, Diana pulled Sioux's head to the right and before I could catch her we had dipped down into Foxhayes Hollow, the farm once occupied by my grandfather.

It was years since I had been that way and I was surprised to find the old farmhouse shuttered and unoccupied. We hallooed, thinking that there might be someone living in the cottage beyond the farm buildings, but nobody answered, so we made a circuit of the yard and soon realized that the farm was derelict. Docks grew in the sties, a heavy barn door swung loose in the wind, and closer inspection of the buildings showed that the place was well on the way to becoming a ruin. Winter gales and the weight of February snow had shifted pantiles from the roof and beyond the begrimed windows of the kitchen we could see pools on the stone floor. The barn door creaked dolorously and there was such an air of decay about the premises that I called to Diana to mount and race me back to the common. She stood, legs apart, looking up at me.

"What's the matter, Jan? Don't you like the old place any more?"

"Not the way it is," I said. "It gives me the creeps!"

"There's nothing here that couldn't be made shipshape by a jobbing builder in a matter of weeks," she said. "Did you know old Yeomans, the tenant, had left?"

I remembered then that Yeomans had died more than a year ago, and that Uncle Reuben had told me he understood Yeomans' son was selling a holding in East Anglia and coming home to take his father's place. I told Diana about this as we cantered back along the rutted track to the open common but all the way home she remained preoccupied, and it wasn't until we were on the point of parting that she called, "Wait, Jan, I'm coming into town with you!" and climbed into my fifth-hand Morris Cowley and asked me to drop her off at the Gilroy Estate office, in Chapel Street.

"I've just remembered," she said, carelessly, "I've got to see the agent about some timber. Daddy wrote about it yesterday and anyway, I've shopping to do."

It was Thursday and I had all the proofs to read, so we arranged to meet on Saturday morning when the paper was out.

The next day, however, I had a visit from Hawthorne, the solicitor. It seemed that the nephew of the original proprietor of the paper was showing an unexpected interest in the property and had offered to buy me out, while retaining my services as acting editor at the same salary. He offered me eighteen hundred for my shares and a ten-year contract, breakable on either side at five years.

Hawthorne advised me to decline, pointing out that if I wished to continue as editor it was obviously better that I should retain some part of the control, but recent discussions with Diana on this topic had unsettled me and when I met her on Saturday afternoon I suggested we should leave the horses at home and tramp over the moor to the source of the Teasel. It was never easy to talk to Diana when she was astride a horse. Each conversation was spaced by a mad gallop or a breathless scramble over banks and ditches.

"You look terribly solemn today," she chaffed, as we crossed the covert and made our way upstream.

"And you look as if you were hatching up one of your hare-brained ideas," I countered.

She did indeed. There was a familiar "if-you-did-but-know" sparkle in her eyes, but I viewed it with tolerance, for it was clear evidence that she was now almost herself again. All the sun and wind we had shared during the last few weeks showed in her clear skin and lively bearing. I had never seen her look healthier or prettier. Emerald was banished and it was plainly Diana who skipped along in country brogues and a faded yellow sweater, moving like an eager girl discovering the country after a long spell in a city. Her thick chestnut curls looked as if they had never been within miles of a Bond Street stylist, and when the April sunlight fell on them they caught and held all the life and sparkle of the valley. The serenity of the countryside was reflected in her calm, untroubled gaze but its springing vitality was there also, as she bounded down the bank and hopped across the steppingstones at Teasel Curve and up again to the narrow footpath under the northern edge of Teasel Wood.

When we were a mile or so on our way, I told her of Hawthorne's visit and she showed the liveliest interest.

"Why, Jan, you must do it! It's the very thing! It couldn't have come at a better time, surely?"

I was by no means clear what the time factor had to do with it and said so, but she headed me off, strengthening my impression that she was deliberating some plan of her own that directly or indirectly involved me and perhaps both of us.

"It all adds up to what we were saying the other day,

301

Jan," she chattered. "The local rag is all right in its way, but it's . . . well, it's stuffy and parochial. It can never give you the chance to develop the real *you*, if you see what I mean? Do you remember that talk we had years ago, up in the tower, when I told you the kind of man I admired?"

I remembered it far better than she imagined; I remembered every last word.

"I know you still prefer the Scotts of the Antarctics," I grumbled, reflecting that, in spite of all the bold resolutions I had made on that winter's afternoon, I had done little enough in the intervening period to model myself upon the heroic lines she demanded. True, I had learned to ride, learned to speak French and risen from furniture delivery boy to acting editor of a weekly paper with a circulation of about five thousand, but I was sure that all this fell far short of her exacting standards.

"I gather you're in favor of selling the shares," I said, "but how about the job itself? I shall have to make up my mind soon and it seems to me that one thing is dependent on the other."

"Not necessarily," she argued. "Sell out, keep the money in a deposit account and say you'll stay on and run the paper just as long as you've a mind to, with a month's notice on your side only!"

"They won't wear that," I protested. "It's far too one-sided."

She stopped and caught hold of my hand, laughing and holding her head on one side.

"Oh Jan, Jan," she chuckled, "you're the world's worst when it comes to business! Can't you see this nephew is just drooling to get full control of that potty little outfit and that he'll agree to anything, so long as you part with your holding?"

"Suppose that's true," I said, "doesn't it indicate that he'll get rid of me the moment he gets his hands on them?"

"Well it might, but I doubt it. You're a jolly good reporter and it wouldn't be at all easy to find anyone to do all you do for the pittance you get. And even if it does, what matters? What can you lose, apart from the few pounds a week they pay you? You might have started

302

something else by then anyway, so do it—*do* it, Jan—sell out but don't be stupid enough to sign any contract about staying on as an employee, d'you hear me?"

She said this so aggressively that I was quite convinced that she was holding something sensational up her sleeve, something that had a direct bearing on the subject we were discussing. I knew her sufficiently well, however, to realize that no amount of probing on my part would persuade her to divulge until the suitably dramatic moment arrived.

"I know you're up to something, Di," I told her, "and I don't pretend to know what, but since we've gone this far we might as well go the whole damn way. I love you and I'm going to marry you—how or when I don't know, but somehow, someday, and not all the obstacles your people will put in the way are going to make a jot of difference in the end! I haven't harped on this subject before because I didn't think you were settled enough to talk about it, but you're more yourself again this afternoon than I ever hoped you'd be when I fetched you back here. Fine! I'll do what you suggest. I'll even explore the possibilities of getting a farming course at the Munhayes Agricultural College, over the river, but if I do, then I think you owe me two things, one following on the other."

"Well?" she said, looking a good deal surprised but not, I thought, in any way put out by plain speaking.

"First I've got to know if you really want to marry me, soon or a long way ahead, I don't give a damn which. Secondly, if the answer is what I hope it is, I'm jolly well going to speak to your father and tell him the truth about how things stand between us!"

Laughter still lurked about the corners of her mouth.

"Jan," she said, her eyes dancing, "that must be about the fourth or fifth proposal I've had from you. I'm beginning to lose count!"

"I'm not joking, Di," I told her, stubbornly. "I want to know exactly how you feel about it, for since you've grown up I've never honestly known whether you're serious, half-serious, or playing a long-winded game of bluff for both of us. Sometimes I thought I knew—that time after the dance, and again on the island, and again on your birthday, but every time something crazy happens. Now that I've got to make a decision about the paper I want something a bit more solid to decide me one way or the other."

She stopped walking then and stood looking at me, one leg crooked, with the sole of her shoe pressed against the last Scots fir in Teasel Wood.

We had now reached the point where the little river curved sharply westward, biting deep into the fringe of Foxhayes Common and forming a gully screened by young poplars, dwarf elms and flowering hawthorn. The water here was very shallow and the little shingle beach that sloped from the river bed to the sandstone overhang was as colorful as a fairy-tale bower. Primroses, periwinkles, windflowers, celandines and huge glowing dandelions grew there, against the whitish-green pattern of hedge buds. It was a favorite place for the blackbirds of which there were vast numbers in this part of Sennacharib. Their pipings rose shrilly above the steady wash of the stream and the whisper of Teasel firs. The inevitable buzzards were about: I had already seen them twice that afternoon. and now they were showing off over the distant larch wood, two wheeling, drifting specks, trying to pretend they were indifferent to admiration of their aerobatics.

After a long moment Diana took my hand and led the way down the cattle ford to the grassiest part of the beach under the hedge. There had been little or no rain for a month and the grass, facing sunwards, was as dry as straw.

"I've been a pig to you, Jan," she said, seriously, sitting and hugging her knees, "and you shall have something more solid, as you say, even though it does sound a little like another helping of treacle pudding. Sit down, take that Jan Riddish scowl off your face, and listen!"

She waited while I sat down beside her. "Nothing the Doones could do would stop me loving you more than I've ever loved anyone, so hang on to that for a minute and give me time to sort out my thoughts. First of all, I'm going to town again . . . no"—as I opened my mouth to protest—"not for good and not even for a week, but there's something I must do up there, something that has a bearing on us. It's not the slightest use pestering me to tell you what it is because it's still in the air and you'll have to trust me just once more, for three or four days, do you understand? As regards the sale of shares, don't do a thing until I get back, but keep it simmering. Tell them you want a day or so to think it over. If my idea amounts to anything, and I'm almost certain it will, then that little business will solve itself and we can settle the rest in five minutes."

"Is that all?" I demanded, as suddenly she shot out her legs and lay back, clasping her hands behind her head and looking as if she was done with talking and intended to luxuriate in the warmth of the sun.

"No, Jan, but it's all I'm going to say about business matters. I've got a lot more to add about loving you and needing you. I've been several kinds of a bitch to you over the last few years, and although I'm sorry for that, because you've been so wonderful to me particularly, when I was cracking up, I'm not promising that I'll ever be any different, because I know jolly well I won't be, not until I get the middle-aged spread, and by that time you won't care, because you'll be too busy reminding yourself that I wasn't always lined and stringy, or bulging and shapeless. There's something else—I wouldn't admit it to anyone but you—I'm like I am, not because of Mother and the way she's tried to push me since I was so-high, but simply because wildness and unpredictability are part of me. I've only got to be told that I must do something when a little imp pops up inside me and says 'I'll be damned if you do!' and that goes for settling down, and saying good-by to being young."

All this had the effect of relaxing me, and I chuckled.

"Don't talk as if you were getting in line for the Old Age Pension," I joked, but she was not disposed to share my mood and continued, very solemnly:

"I'm serious, Jan! I'm not the same as most people our age, not at all the same. Every person our age is frightened of growing old, I imagine, but with me it's not just the fear of growing old but the fear of growing *up*, and it's not simply worry either, it's a kind of blind panic that gives me nightmares. Sometimes, when I'm away from you, it gives me such a dreadful feeling of depression that I could run out and jump over Nun's Head!"

She said this so earnestly that it was impossible to tease her. In a way, indeed, I recognized it as the truth, a limited truth, for the fear she spoke of was all mixed up with the freedom of wealth as well as freedom to remain irresponsible, to go where she liked, say what she liked, and, if necessary, ride roughshod over all standards of behavior in her own world as well as mine.

"I daresay I'll grow out of this silliness sometime, and maybe it's as much a stage as every other stage a woman goes through from the pony craze onwards," she went on, "but in the meantime, and *because* I love you so much, Jan, I want to . . . well . . . to kind of insure against it in my own special way. What I've got in mind *is* a kind of insurance, as I hope you'll see after I've been up to London and back."

I chewed a grass stem, waiting for her to continue, but she fell silent and when I looked at her again I saw that her eyes were troubled and that her hands, freed from the clasp that had given her so relaxed a pose, were now nervously plucking at the leaves of some periwinkle stalks that clustered beside her. Suddenly, with a movement that was a kind of reflex, she twisted on her side and threw her arms around me.

"Jan, dear Jan! Don't ever leave me, not altogether! Not for good! Always come back, always *be* there! And love me now, Jan, love me in this heavenly place! Let it be a sort of marriage, our marriage, in Sennacharib! That would mean so much more to me than all the fiddle-faddle ordinary people have to go through . . . just love me, and make it certain, no matter what happens!"

I was to recall and ponder on that final qualification a great deal in the future, but I hardly heard it at that moment. My love for her and for the place we were in now mingled like two great streams, converging after independent courses down the steep hill. I gathered her up and covered her face with kisses, straining her to me as though we would merge ourselves with the very soil and fibers of the bank. It was much more than desire on my part, it was a consummation of all the years of longing and hoping and scheming to possess her. It was as she had demanded, a marriage before the altar of Sennacharib, a ceremony in which the setting assumed a personality, for as we clung together the hills and woods and valleys of Sennacharib seemed to reach out green and golden arms to enfold us in a vast, sensual embrace.

So vivid was this impression that to me the physical act was almost insignificant. It was immeasurably transcended by a spiritual accomplishment that gave me a sense of possessing her far more completely than anything stored in my memories.

We lay there in one another's arms until the sun passed beyond the big larch wood and its warmth left us for the estuary on the far side of the hill.

Then at last, we climbed back to the footpath and went along under the steep edge of Teasel Wood to the steppingstones, saying nothing and, for my part, conscious of nothing but a surfeit of tenderness and gratitude.

Chapter Ten

AFTER THAT events followed one another with the speed and improbability of a dream; indeed, in some ways the period that followed was more dreamlike than real in that I lost all sense of time. Even now days and weeks are jumbled together and events group themselves in what I know to be a perverse and inaccurate sequence.

Diana went to London on Monday, promising to return by the weekend at the latest but probably before. On Wednesday morning the phone rang in the office and when I answered it a soft, slightly sibilant voice asked to speak to Mr. John Leigh. When I told the caller that I was the person he sought there was a long pause; then the voice apologized rather gravely, and went on:

"This is Gayelorde-Sutton here, speaking from Heronslea."

I was so surprised that it took me a moment or so to recover but the caller had evidently anticipated this, for he allowed a period of grace. I could imagine him sitting there, erect in the study chair, his big head balanced on the long, thin neck, his mild eyes blinking at nothing.

"Are you sure I'm the person you want?" I asked at length, and when the voice assured me that this was so, I had to fight down a brief spasm of panic. It was no more than a spasm, for almost at once fear was succeeded by irritation and finally by a spurt of defiance. I felt that I had had more than enough of the Gayelorde-Suttons and their feudalistic notions. I was sure of Diana and that was all that mattered. If her father wanted a showdown then he could have one, and her mother too if she was standing behind her husband's chair, making the bullets that he was told to fire.

"Well?" I demanded, bluntly. "And what can I do for you, Mr. Sutton?"

His response disarmed me. If anything the voice was milder and more amiable than before.

"Ah, Mr. Leigh—I—er I—wonder if you would be good enough to call at Heronslea at your own convenience, and perhaps have a drink with me?"

"Well . . . yes," I managed to stutter, "I should like to, Mr. Sutton. I could come now if that suited you."

There was a flicker of enthusiasm or possibly relief.

"You could? Splendid! I'll expect you in half an hour, shall I?"

"Yes," I said and only just prevented myself adding "sir."

I backed out the old Morris and drove to Shepherdshey at about twenty miles an hour. I wanted time to think. I had known this family now for a number of years but this was the first occasion I had exchanged a word with Diana's father. I had no real quarrel with him, for as far as I was aware he had taken no active part in his wife's callous treatment of Diana after the island episode. From what I could piece together from Diana's conversations

308

about her parents, he was the purely passive force in the ordering of her life. She had often spoken of him contemptuously, as a man hopelessly under his wife's thumb, and I remembered now how helpless and pathetic he had looked when they hoisted him up on that big horse at the Heronslea meet. Quite apart from the summons, I was surprised to learn that he was in the West Country, having taken it for granted that Diana had gone to see him in London, and I could not imagine why he should suddenly take it into his head to invite me into his house for a drink, as though I were one of his daughter's friends whom Mrs. Gayelorde-Sutton approved and accepted. It occurred to me that this might be the result of Diana's "something concerning us," and that perhaps she had said something that caused him and his wife to hurry down to Devon in order to interview me, but I dismissed this at once; his manner on the phone had certainly not been that of an irate father, driven by a nagging wife to take the offensive.

I drove up the main approach and parked the car beside Gayelorde-Sutton's Bentley. Limousine and two-seater looked like a vehicular parody of the picture "Dignity and Impudence." I was hoping to demonstrate my determination by a fierce tug on the bell chain, but I was cheated of this by the sudden appearance of Mr. Gayelorde-Sutton on the doorstep. He had evidently been awaiting me and had come out as soon as he heard the car. We shook hands, casually on my part, limply on his, and crossed the hall to the study adjoining the pretty room that I remembered as being Mrs. Gayelorde-Sutton's morning room.

What struck me as unusual was that there seemed to be no servants about the place. Inside the study it was very quiet, so quiet indeed that I could hear a farm tractor bub-bubbing on the arable slope south of Teasel Wood almost a mile away. Mr. Gayelorde-Sutton's manner was so subdued that I thought at first that he was giving me the silence treatment and hoping thus to put me at a disadvantage. When I looked at him more closely, however, I soon realized that he was by far the more nervous. His hand shook as he poured a brandy from a Waterford decanter and his aim with the soda-water siphon was grossly inaccurate.

"You'll have brandy, Mr. Leigh?" he said, suddenly.

"Thank you," I said, sitting on a ribbon-backed chair near the tall window. I felt I could do with a brandy, and his was a very generous one.

He took his glass over to the desk, set it down and stood stiffly beside one of the bookcases. It was several years since I had seen him and the very first occasion that I had had an opportunity to study him at close quarters.

At this range the size of his head and thinness of his neck did not appear so ludicrously unlikely, but the over-all impression he gave was one of timid, secretive flabbiness. Face to face with him it was impossible to be awed by his presence, and I remember thinking how strange it was that a man with such a nervous disposition and possessing such an undistinguished physique had made his way so successfully in the city jungle. Yet when you thought about this perhaps it wasn't so strange. It was easy to imagine him sitting in board rooms listening to loquacious chairmen and accountants, saying nothing, blinking, drumming his long fingers, and then going away and sorting through the information he had acquired, filing it, weighing it up, discarding all irrelevancies before making a few telephone calls and going home the richer by several thousand pounds. He was the kind of man who would neither encourage nor discourage people but would let them talk and talk and writhe under his stolidity. Then he would use them, laughing drily at their weaknesses, so less apparent than his own but infinitely more vulnerable.

Perhaps I have been unfair to him. These were my first impressions and they were to be modified greatly as the interview proceeded. The moment my stubbornness emerged he became more human, and I think I helped to thaw him by taking the offensive.

"I suppose you're wondering what this is all about?" he said, after we had both taken a sip or two.

"Not really," I said, shortly. "I imagine that you want to talk about Diana."

He smiled, a very fleeting smile, the kind of grimace

that fond mothers sometimes claim as a smile when their babies burp.

"I know that you and Emerald have been close friends for a long time," he said.

"Since my fifteenth birthday," I told him, "and now I'm getting on for twenty-two."

"That's a long time to court a girl and an early age to begin!" he said, without taking his eyes off me, and without ceasing his rhythmic blink.

I was mildly surprised by his use of the word "court." It implied a certain regularity about an association that had always been clandestine, but before I could reply he suddenly stepped outside his board-room manner and became, if not affable, then at least heavily sincere in his approach. It was as though he had decided upon one approach but, after the preliminary exchanges, switched to another, suddenly making up his mind to project himself as a parent and not as a company director.

"Look here, Leigh," he said, lowering himself into his desk chair and placing his palms downwards on the red leather, so that his forearms formed a neat rectangle, "I don't think I'm being quite fair to you. The onus of this discussion is on me, since I invited you here, and the fact is, I know a great deal more about you than you imagine. I knew a little about you a long time ago and when I heard you had whisked Emerald down here after that unpleasant business in town, I made it my business to find out a great deal more. Now I daresay that appears somewhat presumptuous to you, but my daughter ha—*has* money coming to her, and certain inquiries on my part were obligatory. Do you follow?"

One thing puzzled me more than anything he had said. He was going to say "had money" and changed it, at the very last moment, to "has money." It was the kind of slip that a man like him ought not to have made and because my wits were razor-sharp that morning it told me more than it need have done.

"I've always known your daughter as Diana," I said, with the air of a man clearing the ground, "so can't we call her that for today? I can never think of her as Emerald."

311

"Very well," he said, gravely, "let it be Diana if you wish. I had a talk with her the night she came up to town and your name came into that talk. You won't mind my being frank?"

"Not in the least," I told him, folding my arms and looking, I hope, a good deal more self-assured than I felt.

"Right!" he said. "I take it you are genuinely attached to my daughter?"

That was something I could bite upon and I did, without the slightest hesitation.

"I'm a good more than that, Mr. Sutton. I'm in love with her and it's only fair to tell you that I'm going to do my damnedest to marry her. I don't know how or when, but nothing you or her mother can do or say will make any difference to my trying!"

It was a deliberately provocative statement on my part and I made it in the hope that it would galvanize him into terminating the interview. The situation was beginning to irritate me, partly because his board-room cat-and-mouse act was an affront to my pride but more, I think, because it somehow cheapened my estimate of Diana. All the years I had known her we had never found it necessary to spar as this flabby, blinking man and I were sparring now. If we had anything to say we had said it and if we hadn't, then we respected one another's privacy in a way that this man could never begin to understand.

My words, however, had an extraordinary effect upon him. He neither recoiled, nor flushed, nor displayed any reaction at all but sat perfectly still, blinking at an accelerated rate, so that I soon began to feel like a man who has pressed the trigger of a large blunderbuss and produced nothing noisier than a half-audible pop. Then, as I floundered about in this anti-climax, I was slowly conscious of his curious change of manner and expression. Quietly and smoothly his whole body relaxed, as though the frame of ice that had kept him so rigid had suddenly melted, leaving him free to stretch himself, uncurl his long fingers and flex his knees; but the strangest thing about this almost physical thaw was that it somehow reduced his stature and made him look as helpless and as pitiful as when he was

312

astride the big gray at the Boxing Day hunt. His face crumpled and his pursy little mouth twitched, as though he was on the point of tears. He realized this and it shamed him. He got up and turned first one way and then another, like a man suddenly awakened in a railway compartment and told he has slept past his station. Then he saw the glass of brandy on his desk and he snatched it up and drained it, slamming it down with such violence that I was surprised the vessel survived the shock. The brandy helped him to collect himself but he said nothing during the moment that it took him to come out from behind the desk and cross to the tall window, where he remained standing with his back to me.

"I'm glad you told me that," he said, quietly, "it helps a great deal. You see, my boy"—he suddenly swung around and faced me—"I'm going away . . . quite soon . . . a long way off, I'm afraid, and I shall be gone some time, some considerable time, do you understand? I asked you here because . . . well, because I wished to satisfy myself on certain things regarding my daughter."

He broke off but continued to look down at me. I sat twiddling the stem of my empty glass.

"Here—have another drink!"

I handed him the glass and he almost filled it. This time his aim with the siphon was totally inaccurate and I suddenly realized that he was a dreadful bundle of nerves. The board-room techniques that had sustained him throughout our opening gambits had now disappeared and he was quite lost without them, so much so that I began to feel slightly sorry for him. For the first time he looked as though he might be Diana's father, but the kinship was limited. He was as remote as ever from the Diana of Sennacharib but within hailing distance of the frightened girl I had watched scanning the crowds outside Swan and Edgar's a few months ago.

"I believe your name is John, isn't it?" he asked, after another brief silence, but before I could reply added: "Do you mind if I call you John . . . or Jan, is it?"

"John!" I said, hating the idea of his using Diana's pet

313

name, and longing for him to return to his board-room seat and drop his clumsy skittishness.

"Well, John," he said, "as I told you, I made certain inquiries, and I discovered two things—two things that led up to this talk we're having. One was the fact that you actually work for a living and the other is that you must think a great deal of Diana, or you would have sold out long ago."

"Just where does that get us, Mr. Sutton?" I asked him, but he had a much thicker skin than I supposed and clung desperately to his embarrassing affability.

"I'll tell you my boy, I'll tell you!" he squeaked. "You came up here on the defensive, didn't you? You imagined that I was going to make the same kind of scene about your association with my daughter as my wife once made in your newspaper office some years ago? Well, I'm not. Not at all! . . . As a matter of fact, I . . . I'm in favor of it. I've no objections at all and as far as I'm concerned you can marry my Emerald tomorrow, if she's agreeable. Now what do you say to that, eh?"

I had nothing at all to say to it. Once I would have been immensely flattered by this astonishing declaration but in those days I was far less certain of Diana and was also young enough to be taken in by an animated adding machine like Gayelorde-Sutton. Today, as a man full-grown, I was so incredulous and suspicious that I sat grasping his enormous brandy and glowered at him. There was something grotesque about his eagerness to put himself on the right side of me, and I found it impossible to accept anything he said at face value. His tongue seemed to be working independently of his brain, as though his head and mouth were master and apprentice, with the latter having been sent out by the former to try his luck at bamboozling the public. All the time he babbled on I could see the instructor squatting like Fagin behind the furiously blinking eyes and watching his bungling little Oliver make a fool of himself. Taken all around, it was a very unsavory experience, rather like a prolonged interview with an excited idiot.

"I was very glad when you persuaded her to come down

314

here for a spell," he went on. "Those people up there are no good to her, you know, and she's such a madcap that she'll probably get into worse trouble if she goes back among them. Now a nice, steady, pleasant young fellow like you . . . I daresay that's what she really needs, *all* she needs maybe, and if I was in your shoes, do you know what I'd do?"

"What?" I said, flatly.

"Why, I'd marry her and *keep* her down here! I'd give her some work to do, a family to look after . . . nothing really wrong with her that a decent home and roots wouldn't cure. . . ."

He said a great deal more in the same vein, but I recall very little of it, because I was no longer listening. What appalled me, I think, was not so much his arch line of patter—that might well have been borrowed from a second-feature film on the father-daughter relationship—but his complete and utter ignorance of Diana as a human being. He was as dismally miscast in this role of encouraging parent as it was possible to be, but with every word he uttered he convinced me that if indeed he and Diana had discussed our prospects, then neither of them had said anything worth saying. In other words, he was lying outrageously, but why? Uncle Reuben had discovered more about Diana after a glance at the single letter I had shown him than this man had discovered during a period of more than twenty years under the same roof. Where had he been all the time she had been growing up? What did he know about her that he could not have learned from reading newspaper reports on the antics of the Set, or a glance at one of her school reports?

Then, as I climbed slowly out of my disgust, and tried to peer at his hidden purpose objectively, I saw that there was something quite terrifying behind his blather, something so strange and unnatural that it almost stank. What this something was, and what made it so frighteningly evident to me, I had not the least idea, but it was there all right and it made me shiver, not only for myself but for Diana and everything surrounding her. I felt I wanted to take him by the shoulders and shake it out of him, like

315

money from his trouser pockets. I wanted to thrust my face within an inch of his and shout: *"Stop it, you old fool! Stop it, for Christ's sake! What's happened to you? Why are you suddenly handing me Diana as though you couldn't wait to get rid of her?"*

Then he was handing me a blank sheet of notepaper, with an embossed heading printed on it.

"I said I was going away," he ended at last, "and that's the address of my solicitors . . . good firm . . . sound people . . . go to them if you want to, but not until Emerald is of age, understand? We don't want her mother making more difficulties, do we, eh?"

"Where is her mother now?" I managed to ask, folding the paper mechanically, and stowing it away in my pocket.

"France," he said, offhandedly, "South of France. Spends most of her time there nowadays."

"You said you had a talk with Diana the night before last," I asked him, in a final attempt to extract a grain of realism from this senseless interview. "Did she give you to understand that we were eng—"

I never finished the question, for at that moment his desk phone rang and he snatched up the receiver like a greedy child grabbing a lollipop.

"Yes?" he snapped, and instantly his features took on the board-room mask of impassivity that they had worn when he ushered me into the room. All the eagerness and excitement ebbed from him, like air from a balloon. He even began to hold himself stiffly again, nodding and blinking an accompaniment to the insistent rasp of his caller's voice.

"Right!" he said at last, and then, still into the phone, "Excuse me a moment, I have someone here."

He put down the receiver and turned to me.

"I'm afraid that's all for the present," he said, distantly. "This is one of those timed, transatlantic calls and it happens to be rather important. Thank you for coming. I'll see you to your car."

I think this bland dismissal surprised me more than anything else that had taken place, but I was so grateful for the interruption that I made no protest and let him lead me into the hall and out onto the porch.

"Are you down for any length of time, Mr. Sutton?" I asked, for even then I found it impossible to believe that he could leave matters between us to remain as they were and would be obliged to ask me to call again after I had discussed this extraordinary interview with Diana.

"I can't really say," he said, vaguely, "but you'll be seeing my daughter again very shortly, I imagine."

"Before the weekend," I told him, "but . . ."

"Please excuse me now," he said, "that call . . . I've so much to do, so much to see to!" and he was gone, leaving the door ajar and myself standing openmouthed on the top step.

I did not return to the office but drove up over Foxhayes, to the highest part of the moor. Here I parked and tried to empty my mind of everything but four distinct puzzles that presented themselves as a direct result of the interview. There was a great deal I failed to understand, but to explore the subject as a whole would, I knew, result in lunatic confusion, so I deliberately separated the particular from the mass, and examined the most obvious puzzles one by one.

First, what had prompted Diana's father to send for me at all? Second, having sent for me, why had his initial reception been so formal and distant? Third, why had my frankness regarding the relationship between Diana and myself produced such a startling change in his manner? Finally, after having almost begged me to elope with his daughter, why did his interest evaporate at the sound of a telephone bell?

I looked at it carefully, point by point. He had sent for me, no doubt, in obedience to a demand on the part of Diana expressed during their talk the night she arrived in town, and this talk had a strong bearing on puzzle number three—his almost indecent eagerness to accept me as a son-in-law. It now seemed fairly clear that Diana had not only nagged him but threatened him, with what I could not even guess, for I knew absolutely nothing of the relationship of father and daughter. His stiffness on my arrival

317

at Heronslea might have a simple explanation. He was obviously a very shy man, constitutionally ill-equipped to make headway with any conversation outside the realm of business, but his abrupt switch from embarrassing amiability to downright rudeness was not so easy to explain. It was possible, of course, that the call represented the gaining or losing of thousands of pounds, and that the caller had jolted him back to the principal interest of his life, but this hardly explained the way in which he had rushed me out of the house and skipped back to the study without even pausing to shut the door. If the call had been of an excessively private nature he would surely have made certain that I was clear of the premises before he returned to the phone.

I teased myself with these speculations until late afternoon and I gave some thought to other aspects of the conversation, notably his slip of the tongue when he mentioned Diana's monetary prospects. This, in some ways, was the biggest mystery of all, for while I found it difficult to doubt the sincerity of his wishes regarding our marriage, it seemed odd that he had already made up his mind to disinherit Diana if she did what he appeared to want her to do. Had man and wife disagreed on this matter? Was the phone call an unexpected call from Mrs. Gayelorde-Sutton, thus presenting him with the opportunity to win her over or justify his sponsorship? Did Mrs. Gayelorde-Sutton know anything at all of what was going on? Was the slip about the money not a slip at all but an assumed one, intended to let me know that if I married Diana after her twenty-first birthday we could expect nothing in the way of a settlement? Did he still think of me as a person on the lookout for a substantial dowry? Was he such a poor judge of character that he failed to understand that I hated the very idea of marrying Diana without separating her, once and for all, from her family background? God knows, I had endeavored to make this much clear to him, but had he lived and worked among moneyed folk for so long that he could imagine no other spur toward marriage?

Finally I gave it all up and drove slowly back to town.

There was plenty of work to be done, an inquest and two weddings to be written up, proofs to be read, the layout to be sketched in, and I was hard at it, trying to make up for lost time, when the phone rang and I was relieved to hear Diana's voice on the line.

She was calling from London to warn me that it was unlikely that she could return until Monday. In the meantime, she wanted me to do something on her behalf, something rather urgent. I was so eager to tell her about the interview that I interrupted her before she had said more than a few words. The telephone was not the best medium for such an involved story, but I was so certain that she would want to hear every word that I began to gabble into the receiver at top speed. I was halfway through before I sensed that she was not nearly as surprised or as interested as I had anticipated. I broke off and said:

"Are you listening? Don't you want to hear all about it?"

"Of course I do, and of course I'm listening. Go on."

I was by no means reassured. She still sounded bored and impatient, but I finished the story and breathlessly awaited her comments.

All she said was: "I see! Poor Jan! It must have been dreadful for you!" Then, completely dismissing her father, she began: "Now listen carefully to what I want you to do . . ."

I was so dismayed by her lack of response that I did listen, but with growing bewilderment.

"First thing tomorrow I want you to drive up to Foxhayes Hollow, and give a verbal message to Harrington," she said, as if she had been a schoolmistress issuing orders for homework. "I want you to tell him to go down to the Gilroy Estate office, ask for the agent and get the papers from the Heronslea file. Tell him it's all satisfactory this end but Harrington is to take the papers home and read them, and have them ready for me when I come. Did you get that?"

"I'm a journalist," I said, grimly. "I'm accustomed to taking phone messages."

She chuckled at that. "Dear Jan, I can't wait to be hugged!" she said.

"If this is a Heronslea chore," I grumbled, "why the blazes don't you ring Harrington direct? He's your foreman, not mine!"

"Don't be so churlish, darling! Harrington is hardly ever at Heronslea and he's a frightfully difficult man to lay by the heels. Don't worry about Daddy, he'll be gone long before I get back and the weather up here is hot enough for swimming, how is it down there?"

"I'm damned if I'm going to talk weather with you, Di," I said, "and I'm getting bored with all these mysteries. Come on home and let's go riding."

"Monday," she said. " 'Bye now, darling."

She had only been away a few days but the sound of her voice made me ache for her. I sat on in the stuffy little office, copy and proofs forgotten, pondering her message and the strange, schoolmarmy manner in which it had been delivered, wondering at her lack of interest in what seemed to me a momentous development in our lives. Then, suddenly, I was tired of mysteries and complications. All the years I had loved her we seemed to have been enmeshed in an intricate web of conditions, provisos and prohibitions. I wanted to cut every strand, throw her over my shoulder and walk out into the open to a place where we could behave like a normal man and woman in love, like a normal couple who planned their own destiny and led normal, unrestricted lives. I pitched the proofs and the reports into the copy tray and locked up, slamming the door on the musty little office that had enclosed so many dreams since my wild need of her had driven me to seek my living there. Illogically my sense of frustration extended to the *Observer* and to the silent array of machinery that nursed it. The whole premises became mean, squalid and inadequate. Maybe she was right, maybe a man could never develop in a field as small and restricted as this business and this town.

I went home to have supper with Aunt Thirza and she found me very grumpy company.

Early the next morning I drove up to the main road and down the cart track to Foxhayes Hollow. Long before I reached the dip in which the ramshackle farm was situated I noticed that something was astir in the area. When we were last here the track had been grass-grown and straggling bushes almost met at several points; now deep tractor ruts showed in the lane and the undergrowth had been cut back to allow the passage of carts or trucks. One or two new bricks and traces of cement lay about and I wondered whether a new tenant had been found, perhaps some fancy friend of Diana's, who had enlisted her considerable influence with the Gilroy Estate.

Notwithstanding this, I was quite unprepared for the sight that greeted me when I bumped into the clearing. The farm and buildings had been transformed. A new slate roof had been laid in place of the weather-beaten pantiles, the ground had been cleared of rubbish, the barn door had been rehung and the greater part of the premises repainted in white and horizon blue. The farm now had a raffish, gaudy look, as though the person responsible for this work had borrowed some chintzy ideas from a magazine article on amateur farming. Builders' materials lay everywhere, and two early risers were already at work on the sties, operating a cement mixer. I recognized one of them as Davey, a member of the Heronslea permanent maintenance staff.

"What the devil is going on here?" I demanded, when he greeted me.

"Us is doin' the ole plaace up!" he said, phlegmatically. "Do 'ee know who's taaken the ruin?"

"Not a clue," I told him. "I'm looking for Harrington, the foreman. Is he around anywhere?"

"Aye, he'll be yer any minute, maister," said Davey. "Praper slave driver he be! Us be workin' overtime on this yer job, dawn till dusk. Praper bliddy hurry they be in!"

"Who?" I wanted to know.

"New tenants, pals o' the family I yeard, London townees, zo they say. Bought into the big house lease, 'er is," he added, nodding toward the farmhouse. "Always a freehold plaace in Ole Maister's time, but 'er's bought in now, zo they say."

I knew by Old Maister he meant my grandfather, for Davey was a Shepherdshey man and was just old enough to remember him. I don't think he recognized me as a Leigh or he would have remarked upon it. At that moment Harrington the foreman drove up in his old Ford and came over to us. He was a stocky, efficient man, who seldom wasted a word on anybody. He gave me a curt nod and told the concrete mixers to "put a jerk in it." Harrington knew that I was friendly with Diana. He had seen me riding with her and standing about in the stables. I gave him her somewhat cryptic message and he nodded, briefly.

"I'll see to it during lunch break," he said, and then scratched his chin and gave me a shrewd glance.

"You're a Leigh, aren't you?" he asked, suddenly. "Your people farmed here back along, didn't they?"

I told him that this was so and mentioned Uncle Mark, at the riding school, and Uncle Reuben, both of whom he had known as young men.

"That's funny," he said, "that's funny and no mistake!"

He shot another sidelong look at me. "You behind all this?" he asked, flatly.

"Me? This renovation lark? No, I'm not, and what on earth makes you think I am?"

"I dunno, maybe the fact that your name is Leigh," he said. "It all adds up."

"What adds up?" I demanded.

He told me then that his instructions regarding the extensive renovations on the farm had originated from Diana, who had told him that she was acting on behalf of her father because he was exceptionally busy. "He was down here yesterday, I heard, but he had left when I rang up this morning," he went on. "I've committed them for a real packet on this place. I didn't realize it was so far gone. It needed reroofing and pointing and some of the outbuildings will have to be pulled down and rebuilt. I suppose it's all right, but I would have liked an okay from

322

Mr. Gayelorde-Sutton before I went ahead with it. No sense in doing half a job. If they've had the place included in the Heronslea lease, they might as well make it habitable and workable but they'll be a damned long time getting their money back, if I'm any judge! The work that needs doing here will stand them in about three thousand."

"Do you mean to say that you haven't had direct instructions from Mr. Gayelorde-Sutton about the job?" I asked him, my stomach contracting.

"Not a word of 'em," he said, and his voice now sounded slightly anxious. "It all came through Miss Emerald. We rode out here together and saw what needed to be done."

I thought furiously for a moment, then I said:

"Look, Mr. Harrington, it's none of my business, but if you'll take a tip from me, go straight down to the Estate office, get those papers she talked about, see the agent and find out who talked to him about including this place in the Heronslea lease. Then, no matter what the Gilroy agent says, get on the wire to Mr. Gayelorde-Sutton as soon as ever you can."

He looked pained and indecisive. "It must be authorized," he argued. "Miss Emerald wouldn't do a crazy thing like that without consulting her father."

"Wouldn't she?" I said. "You don't know Diana Gayelorde-Sutton as I do! Take my advice and check up right away."

I left him standing there, hands deep in his breeches pockets, a puzzled frown on his brown countryman's face. Suddenly my brain fog had cleared. I was no closer to a solution of Gayelorde-Sutton's strange behavior, but I had rumbled Diana's plot. The penny had dropped when Harrington referred to my family link with the farm, and it had gone home the moment he told me that she had been acting independently in this matter. It was so simple that I was amazed I had not seen through her clumsy scheme long before, and I raced along the main road and down Foxhayes Hill to Whinmouth at a speed the old Morris had not traveled since she was new, in the early nineteen-twenties.

This was her idea of a bumper surprise! This was her plan to force me out of a profession that she despised into one that she considered far more befitting a gentleman-husband. This—a tarted-up Foxhayes Farm—was my advance wedding present likely to cost her father three thousand pounds, plus whatever advance rent had been promised for the inclusion of the farm into the Heronslea lease. Whether I liked it or not, I was to become a yeoman, operating a newly renovated 250-acre farm, as a Heronslea tenant, and all this before I had had so much as a day's training for the job.

I wasted no time wondering how this plan of hers tied in with Gayelorde-Sutton's sales talk of the previous day. Obviously he knew something about the farm, and was probably under the impression that I had far more capital than was the case. I could almost hear Diana lying to him: "He's only a journalist now, Daddy, but he's come into money and wants to farm!" I began to sweat at the thought of all the blarney she must have talked about me in order to bring a busy man like her father hotfoot to Devon, to have a look at his yeoman son-in-law.

The fact that here was proof that Diana really did intend to marry me, that she had abundant faith in my ability to become a farmer, and that she was willing to commit her father to heavy expenditure on my behalf made no impression at all upon me. The fantastic recklessness of her gesture made me shudder, and so did her estimate of my pride. All this time I had been her slave. Nothing she had proposed was too risky or improbable for me to condone it and act upon it. Twice she had claimed me as a lover and over and over again she had assured me that no other man meant two straws to her, yet she was still able to go calmly about the business of buying me with her father's money and enlisting me as tenant dependent upon her family's grace and favor as landlord and patron.

Before I clattered down Fish Street into Whinmouth I had a plan of my own. Gayelorde-Sutton had schemed, Diana had schemed, but neither had showed the least willingness to take me into their confidence. It was high time, I felt, that I started scheming, and I marched straight into

Lawyer Hawthorne's office and ordered him to sell my *Observer* shares for whatever he could get, providing the sale went through in twenty-four hours. He was startled and counseled delay, but I would not even listen to him. I had other things to do and shot off out of town again to my Uncle Mark's stables, behind Teasel Wood.

Mark had aged in the last few years and I knew that he was finding his muddled little business irksome and unprofitable. He was giving some promise of settling down at last and marrying one of his old flames, a hearty little widow who kept a boardinghouse in Jetty Road. He had been a frequent visitor there during her husband's lifetime and the last time I had seen him he had joked about her wanting to look after him. "Though 'er's a bit past it now, John," he added, with one of his lewd grins.

I found him standing in the little yard bullying Ned, his dull-witted stableman. When I said I had a proposition to put to him he led the way into his tumble-down cottage, which stood about a stone's throw from the loose boxes in the shadow of the beech copse. It could have been a very attractive little dwelling if Uncle Mark had kept it clean, but now its big living room was cluttered with harness and dirty cooking utensils and the great open fireplace was blocked with a rusty old stove and litter of every description.

"Do 'ee want that there cob after all?" he asked, for we had previously discussed the purchase of a neighbor's skewbald.

"No," I told him, "I want the whole shooting match if you're disposed to sell it!"

He gaped at me. "You mean it?" he gasped, unable to believe his good fortune. "You really want to take over yer? Horses and all?"

"Stables, horses, cottage, grazing, the lot!" I said. "What's it worth, Uncle?"

His eyes narrowed and he began to mumble something about me being Miriam's boy and therefore entitled to a special price, but I knew him very well and cut him short.

"It's no good asking a silly price," I said, "for I haven't got much and I shall have to spend several hundred doing the place up. What about twelve-fifty, lock, stock and barrel?"

"Damme, the horseflesh is worth five hundred," he growled.

"Don't be silly," I told him, "you couldn't get three hundred for all six of them at the horse bazaar. I'm not daft, Uncle Mark, but I am in a hurry, and I've finished with newspaper work!"

"Well that's a relief, at all events," he grunted, for his contempt for Uncle Reuben, and all Reuben's works, had not been buried in his brother's grave. "I'll practically give 'ee the place, John—fifteen hundred."

"Thirteen-fifty," I said. "It's all I can afford!"

He was far more eager to sell than I had anticipated. "Youm a bliddy old Jew!" he shouted, but we shook hands and I hustled him back to old Hawthorne to draw up a provisional agreement. In my absence Hawthorne had closed for nineteen hundred, so that I had a surplus of five hundred and fifty, less legal fees. As I intended to do the repairs by direct labor and to assist in the work myself, I considered this was more than sufficient. I had no clear idea what I would do with the place, but I knew that there was a good living in the livery stable, providing it was conducted on up-to-date lines, and I was sure that I could earn something more with the land, which comprised nearly fifty acres.

By five o'clock that day the two deals were complete. I agreed to remain at the newspaper office until a substitute could be found and later on I drove out to Shepherdshey to enlist Nat Baker's help in getting cottage and stables in order.

The old sexton agreed to work by the hour and we went up there before dark. I made a list of the furnishings I thought we should need and Nat explored the structure, pronouncing it to be sound, despite its great age.

Now that I had a place of my own, and a plan of campaign, however incomplete, I was as happy as a boy on holiday. It was Thursday when I bought the stables and by Sunday night Nat and I had transformed it. We made a vast bonfire of Uncle Mark's rubbish and persuaded Ned, the stableman, to scrub the loose boxes and give the horses their first real grooming in months. Aunt Thirza and Uncle Luke rolled up with a truckload of their best secondhand pieces and Thirza stayed on to help with the springcleaning, leaving the cottage reeking of strong carbolic soap that mingled with the stink of creosote Nat was plastering on the fence rails.

When they had all gone I toured the premises with a feeling of pride and achievement. I had a home, a small but promising home, and I had a means of livelihood, and both were inside the borders of Sennacharib!

I decided to move in the following day, and after giving instructions to Ned, whom I decided to retain, I left the car in the yard and walked home across Teasel Wood, down the escarpment and along the elm bank of Heronslea to Shepherdshey. For the first time in my life I looked at the big house with a feeling of equality. I awaited Diana's return with confidence.

3.

There was a letter on Monday morning, asking me to meet the eleven o'clock from Waterloo, due in Whinford about three-thirty. During the morning I had another idea. I went along to Awkright's Garage and traded in my old Morris for fifty pounds. He had some good secondhand cars in his shed, so I looked them over. There was a resprayed Alvis sports that had been involved in a crash. Awkright wanted two-fifty for it, but I beat him down to two-twenty-five. It had a long, wicked-looking bonnet fastened down by straps, and a deep-throated exhaust that sounded like an airplane warming up. I took it out on a trial run, paid him his hundred and seventy-five and drove home to the quay to change into my best suit. On the way to Whinford I stopped at Kennard's Nurseries and bought a huge armful of daffodils, narcissi, and purple iris. Then, feeling very artful and extremely pleased with myself, I drove to Whinford and awaited her train.

She came down the platform followed by the inevitable porter and luggage. I never knew Diana to travel light.

Wherever she went, be it only for the weekend, she took about a hundredweight of baggage. She looked extraordinarily chic and carefree, in her neat little two-piece and a close-fitting, Juliet-style straw hat that compressed her curls just so far, then split them over her shoulders. The moment she saw me she waved, broke into a run and kissed me half a dozen times. I told the porter to bring the luggage to the Alvis.

"Why Jan!" she exclaimed. "What on earth have you got there?"

"One of several things," I said smugly and stowed the luggage in the capacious trunk.

"Flowers too! Why, Jan, you're becoming almost gallant! Oh, I do love you so!" she added, ignoring the fact that the porter was still bustling around hoping to earn a bigger tip.

He almost groveled when I gave him half a crown but it wasn't the money, it was the Alvis and Diana. She climbed in and snuggled down in the red leather, shooting out her long legs and giving one of her luxurious, catlike stretches.

"Mmmmm-*mmmmm!*" she cooed. "Whatever's happened? Have you cashed in on your newspaper money?"

"You'll see," I told her. "We'll be making a call en route for Heronslea."

"You did give my message to Harrington, didn't you?"

"Yes," I said, "but forget Foxhayes Hollow for the moment, we'll go into all that later on!"

She looked at me half-smiling as I let in the clutch and we roared off up the Station Hill.

"Something sensational has happened to you while I've been away, Jan," she said. "You've grown about two inches!" Then, probing me: "What did you think about the renovations at Foxhayes Hollow? Don't you think Harrington is making a good job of it?"

"Fine," I said, "if someone has the idea of converting it into a roadhouse!"

She did not know what to make of that, and it struck me then that we were beginning to learn the art of sparring after the manner of her father, a method of conversation we had never found it necessary to use before, not even

328

when she was Emerald being conducted around the Tower of London.

"There's something funny about you this afternoon," she complained. "Is it the car that's making you sound so now-now-little-womanish?"

I made no reply to this so after a moment she said:

"What's wrong with what we're doing to Foxhayes Hollow?"

"It's chi-chi," I said, offhandedly, "the sort of place a man would build if his idea of a farmer was of a chunky man in tweeds, buckskin leggings and a pork-pie hat."

"A farm doesn't have to be a stinking midden, does it?" she said, rather snappishly.

"No," I said, "but it doesn't have to be quaint and hey-down-derryish either!"

We weren't getting along so well and I'm afraid it was mostly my fault. The car, the sudden break from the tyranny of a weekly paper, the business I had bought, and my still-smoldering resentment of her plan to convert me into a yeoman tenant without first consulting me combined to make me sound arrogant and patronizing. I stole a glance at her as we whipped along the road and noticed that she now looked unhappy. All the gaiety she had shown as soon as she stepped off the train was gone and she seemed to be groping for words that would resolve the curiously tense atmosphere of the cramped space under the hood. I wanted very much to stop, kiss her and tell her that everything was going to be all right, providing she granted me my little triumph, but pride, or more cockiness, still held me on a tight rein.

"What is it, Jan dear?" she said at last. "What's the matter?"

"You'll see in a moment, Di," I said, relenting a little. "Just have a little patience, five minutes' patience."

She fell silent after that and made no comment when I took the left-hand fork toward Teasel Wood instead of dropping down to Shepherdshey. I was beginning to be a little anxious now and my heart was thumping. I sensed her surprise as we turned off the road and dropped into low gear to negotiate the unsurfaced lane leading down to

Uncle Mark's place. Then we were there and I was handing her out of the car and into the cottage. She looked around with a mixture of surprise and dismay.

"Why have we come here?" she said.

The expression of distaste on her face frightened me.

"It's mine—*ours*, Di," I said. "That Foxhayes Hollow idea of yours is crazy. I don't want your family to stake me and I don't even fancy the idea of being their tenant. You ought to have discussed it with me before you did a slaphappy thing like that, and anyway, it can't even be legal until your father approves of it!"

Her face fell and for a moment she looked as if she were going to burst into tears; then her mouth hardened and her eyes blazed.

"Have you sold out and spent your money on this dump?" she demanded. "Have you been idiot enough to buy those old screws from your crooked uncle and set up as a riding instructor?"

"I've bought the stables, the stock and the cottage," I said, "and even if it doesn't look much now it will when it's had a bit spent on it. There's fifty acres and I won't need more than half of it for the horses. There's free grazing around here and I'm going to use the rest of the land for chickens. The cottage can be made very pretty and there's a good living here, Di."

"A living!" she almost screamed. "An existence, you mean! Five pounds a week profit on horses and two more on eggs, *if* you're lucky. You must be out of your head, Jan! Why, once Foxhayes Hollow is back in production—"

"I don't want Foxhayes as a bloody dowry!" I shouted, for suddenly I was hysterical with rage and disappointment. "Can't you get it into your thick skull that I don't want anything from your family but *you*?"

She calmed down somewhat but the superior expression that replaced her angry look was not an improvement.

"Do you really expect me to live here, like . . . like a Devon version of a poor white in the Deep South?" she said, calmly.

"Yes, I did and I do!" I roared. "If what's happened between us all these years means anything to you at all, you'd be happy to do it and help make a go of it. Damn it, you've always loved horses, and together we could build this place up until it was known all over the county. We could get more fields and better horses. We could do something together for once, free of all interference, and we should be doing what I always imagined you wanted to do—living together, in Sennacharib."

The look of disdain left her and she now stared at me with solemn, troubled eyes.

"Jan," she said, quietly, "this is real life. . . . Sennacharib was only a game!"

It was the most savage thrust that I had ever received from her and it hurt like hell, far more than any of the old wounds that her abrupt changes of mood, her eternal unpredictability, her erratic comings and goings in my life had inflicted. For a moment I was incoherent with rage and grabbed her wrist, pulling her toward me.

"You listen to me!" I thundered. "It might have been a game to you but it was never one as far as I was concerned! You say living here wouldn't be practical and you make it all sound childish and stupid, but I'm not going to let you walk out on me just like that, not after all I've been through on account of you! You can turn me and this place down with your mother's brand of arrogance but you won't forget me that easily. You'll remember me for at least a month every time you sit down, damn you!"

I had her fast with my left hand and with my right I reached out and snatched up a short switch from the windowseat. It was a light, improvised crop that had been overlooked in the general turnout. I pushed her away and flourished the crop like a dancing dervish, cutting the air with it and cursing her at the top of my voice. I was beside myself with rage and, for a brief moment, there was real fear in her eyes.

"Jan!" she said, and her voice seemed to come from the far side of Teasel Wood. "Jan, don't, *don't!*"

I struck her then, a single blow across her shoulders, and she shivered, pressing her hands flat against the wall and staring at me, her eyes wide with incredulity. The action did more to sober me than anything she could have said or done. I threw down the switch and for several seconds we stared at one another without moving. Then the fear left her eyes and her mouth began to pucker. She put up one hand and slowly rubbed her shoulder, without taking her eyes off me.

"You hit me!" she whispered, so quietly that I lip-read rather than heard what she said. "*You hit me, Jan* . . . nobody, ever . . . nobody . . ."

Her voice trailed away to nothing but her lips continued to move and her hand went on massaging the smart. Then, still without taking her eyes from me, her expression changed again, passing from utter bewilderment to a kind of savage intensity that I had never seen in the face of anyone, man or woman. The tears that had brimmed the moment before remained static in her eyes, giving them a kind of glaze and somehow magnifying them, as if I were looking at her through a powerful glass. Her mouth, which had crumpled like a child's, twitched into a firm line and two bright spots of color glowed on her cheeks, pulsing through the make-up. Her breast was heaving and she stood so tensely that, for a moment, I thought she was going to project herself forward and fly at me, clawing and biting, but suddenly her body relaxed and her head went back, her chin shooting up like the chin of a person suddenly and immoderately amused.

All my rage was spent. I ran to her and threw my arms around her, kissing her cheek and neck, burying my hands in her hair.

"Oh, God, why did you make me . . . *why*, Diana. . . ? What's happened to us? What *is* it?"

"Don't talk, don't say anything, Jan!" she said, and her voice sounded harsh, almost guttural. "Don't worry—fuss —we belong—always, so take me, for God's sake take me!"

She began kissing me then, not as she had in the dell beside the Teasel, and not even as she had kissed me when she was Emerald in the tower, but like a predatory savage, starved and desperate. Her straw hat slipped off and was trampled underfoot and we clung together in a frenzy for how long I do not know, perhaps for a few minutes, perhaps an hour.

At last I lifted her and set her down in the deep window seat, lowering my head to kiss her hands and wrists, fearful of breaking contact and conscious, as my lips touched her fingers, of their steady pressure on my face. Then I laid my head on her lap and she stroked my hair, gently and regularly, each sweep beginning at my temples and ending on the nape of my neck.

"I was mad, Di," I said, at length. "I felt like killing you and it scared me more than it scared you. I've never felt like that about anyone before."

"Forget it, Jan, I asked for it and I've always asked for it from you, right from the very beginning."

I looked up at her and saw that she was crying now. She looked about fourteen, no more, and I felt closer to her than at any time since we had stood together beside the island bonfire awaiting the arrival of the pilot boat.

"I'd really set my heart on the farm," she said, presently. "I'd got it all worked out and I felt terribly Machiavellian. It was because of that I was so beastly about this place, but I suppose my disappointment wasn't nearly as keen as yours." She looked around the half-furnished room. "It was a wonderful thing for you to do, quite wonderful, but then, why should I be surprised? You've always done things like this and I've always repaid you by being me."

She spoke very quietly and presently extricated one of her hands, opening the bag beside her and dabbing her eyes. While she applied lipstick I sat down beside her. Inside the cottage it was very quiet but outside the thrushes in Teasel Wood were singing their early evening chorus. I noticed Uncle Mark's switch on the floor and turned my eyes away.

"Did it hurt very much, Di?"

"Just enough, Jan!"

She smiled and then looked quickly away and I saw that she was blushing. "It's funny," she said, as though in explanation, "I've always heard that it's true, though I can't honestly say I really believed it when I read about it.

Women like brutes but just in short, sharp bursts, I imagine. I've never wanted you so much in my life. If you'd run out of the cottage, as I thought for one awful moment you were going to, I should have run after you, shouting that you'd forgotten your stick! I wonder just how much of our trouble in the past has been due to that? I wonder if the primitive part of me is terrified of your inclination to over-play your strong suit, Jan, and it's that that makes me want to run away every now and again?"

"What exactly is my strong suit, Di?"

She laughed and ran a hand down my cheek. "I told you years ago! Male gentleness—'Jan Ridd' gentle-ness—and only the really hefty men have it."

She got up and retrieved her hat, studying it ruefully.

"This is a write-off, like the farm idea. Wait here a minute."

She went out into the kitchen and a moment later appeared beside the car. Through the window I saw her gather up the armful of flowers that I had bought and carry them into the kitchen. Then she brought a large bowlful into the living room and put them down on the table. The gesture blew on the small spark of hope that remained in my heart.

"Why did you do that, Di?"

She gave one of her sly, mischievous grins and began combing her hair, glancing into her handbag mirror propped against the flower bowl. As she stood there, tugging at the knots, I was reminded very vividly of how she had looked during our island adventure, when she had combed out her hair in front of a handbag mirror propped on stones.

"I hate seeing flowers out of water," she said, "and any-way, this place needs color."

"Does that mean you'll give it a go?" I asked, trying to keep the tremor from my voice.

She went on combing. "This is how I see it, Jan," she said. "The thing I said that made you so angry—about Sennacharib being a game—well, that's a fact, you know, whether you like it or not. But there are other facts, and now seems to be the time to face them. What have you and I got in common, apart from our physical appetites and kind of spiritual hunger for the few square miles in which we grew up?"

"I believe we're in love with each other, Di," I told her. "That isn't a game, or is it?"

"You're in love with me, Jan, I'm sure of that, and whenever we're together in this place I'm very much in love with you. When I'm away from you I'm not, but for all that, I lust after you, the way I did just now. What qualifications have I got to marry a decent person like you? I can't cook, I haven't the faintest interest in housekeeping, I'd make a hopeless mother to children, and there's nothing I can do with my hands apart from spend money like water, the kind of money you'll never have! Mind you, I think it's damned sporting of you to want to take me on, and you do, don't you? You do, in spite of everything?"

"More than anything in the world," I said, "but not at the price of being financed by your family."

"Then your personal independence is more important than just marrying me?"

I considered this. I wanted to give her an absolutely honest answer. There was no point, at this stage, in bluffing her or myself.

"Independence wins by a short head, Di."

"You wouldn't have our maintenance staff up here to renovate the place and you wouldn't let me borrow from Daddy to restock the stable and lay out the rest of the place as a poultry farm?"

"No," I said, more definitely, "I wouldn't! I'd sooner risk waiting another five years and then make another pounce, by which time, I think, you might have found out what's worth having and what isn't."

"But you'd still be willing to risk it now? You'd still risk starting us off on the wrong foot and maybe making a terrible hash of it?"

"Yes, I would, Di! Taken all around, I believe that to be the lesser risk."

She was silent for a moment. Finally she tossed back her hair and carefully replaced the comb in her handbag.

"All right, Jan dear, we'll do it! All I'm promising is

that I'll try, I'll try damned hard, but you'd better keep this handy. You may need it oftener than you think!"

She picked up the crop and laid it on the table, regarding it seriously before turning and smiling down at me.

"Failing that there's always bed," she added.

I had imagined, over the years during which I had dreamed of this moment, that it would have the glow and excitement of an elopement, but now I discovered that it was far more like taking the first step of a journey into a remote corner of the world. Nothing was certain about it save that Diana was coming with me and nothing was certain about her beyond the fact that she only had to enter a room or pass within yards of me, to paint my world with the rainbow colors of joy and adventure. I did not ponder with these uncertainties but let go, happy to drift and careless of the quicksands and rapids that almost surely lay ahead. I got up and kissed her on the tip of the nose.

"Come on, Di," I said, "let's go down to Shepherdshey and put up banns before you change your mind!"

4.

We saw the vicar, an eager, gnomish little Welshman, and put up banns for a wedding in Shepherdshey Church on the Saturday following her twenty-first birthday. She did not regard the date as being of much importance, commenting on the certainty of her mother's continued absence in France, but I was taking no chances. If the vicar was taken aback by our frank discussion in front of him he had the good manners not to show it. He was a comparatively new man in the parish and his knowledge of the Gayelorde-Suttons was based almost exclusively on hearsay. We should have had a great deal more difficulty with the old vicar, who had been a regular diner at Heronslea.

We had high tea at a farm over on Nun's Head and when I took Diana back to Heronslea at dusk she suggested that we should wet the banns with a bottle of champagne.

"Hardly anyone's there," she said. "Most of the staff have been given a holiday, or shuttled up to the town house for some do or other. Anyway, I bought a record for you in London, and I'd like to play it. It's part of what you might call the Sennacharib overture, so I'm quite sure you'll approve."

The big house was oddly quiet. There seemed to be no one about but two or three living-in maids. The butler and chauffeur were missing, and for this I was grateful, but it seemed to me that, tonight of all nights, our healths should have been drunk by dear old Drip. When I asked Diana what had happened to her, she told me that soon after the island business Miss Rodgers had been pensioned off and now shared a bungalow with her sister in a remote part of North Wales.

"I write to her sometimes," she said, "but not as often as I ought. Before I found you, Jan, she was the only real friend I had. I tell you what. We'll honeymoon up that way and look her up. I've been everywhere on the Continent and never even seen Wales, or the Lake District. How about that?"

I said I should like that very much. Just to hear her use the word "honeymoon" was bliss.

She found some champagne, of the same year as that brought up to the bedroom the night of her party, and we opened it with a good deal of difficulty and laughter. Then she put the record on and sat watching me as music dripped from their impressive-looking radio phonograph. It was a more modern recording of the record we had burned on the island to start the signal fire, and I loved her for remembering. The nostalgic effect of the harmonies was so powerful that I could have wept, and seeing that her little surprise had succeeded, she came and sat on the arm of my chair, so that her nearness, her perfume, and the wildly improbable end to a very difficult day made me almost drunk with delight.

"I always thought those Student Corps' bellowings were a funny kind of theme song for two crazy kids marooned on an island," she said, "but I could never hear them afterwards without picturing you on your hands and knees in that leaky old cabin, puffing away at damp driftwood and trying to boil the kettle. Why, Jan, about a year after I was sent abroad, Yves' family, the French people I stayed with, took me to Heidelberg and I disgraced myself at a concert by bursting into tears and refusing to explain why."

As the record began to run down the phone rang and she got up to answer it. I was so deep in my trance of delight that I missed the first part of her conversation and only began to pay attention when I heard her say, "Is he in the hospital, then?" in a crisp, anxious voice.

"Who is it, Di?" I asked and, as though I had known that this phone call was going to shatter my dream as casually as a gale strips the petals from a rose, I scrambled up and hurried across to her. She made an impatient gesture, devoting her full attention to the phone.

"All right, Masters," she said, sharply, "I'll come at once. I can be there by soon after five. I'll catch the night train from the junction. Have the chauffeur meet me and we'll drive straight there, do you understand?"

She put down the phone and looked at me without seeing me.

"Daddy's had an accident, he's in the hospital, seriously hurt!"

"What kind of accident?"

"I don't know, Masters was very evasive, so I've got a strong suspicion Daddy's already dead and he was trying to break it gently. I shall have to go up right away, Jan!"

"Of course," I told her, slipping my arm around her shoulder, "but why catch the train? I'll run you up in the Alvis. We could be there about the same time." And I made to hurry into the hall for my raincoat.

"No, Jan!"

She stood quite still in the center of the big room, one finger plucking the corner of her mouth. "It's your press day tomorrow and you've got so many things to see to down here. You can't leave the paper just like that, the people you're selling out to might think you're letting them down and cry off the deal. If they did that I'd never forgive myself and it might spoil everything. You said you were under contract to keep it going until they got a substitute, and besides, I think I'd much sooner go by train.

338

I'm tired and I can try to sleep. I shall have plenty to do tomorrow, God knows. Masters says everyone is in a terrible flap!"

"How about your mother?" I asked.

"He says she's flying home but she won't get into Croydon until midday and anyway, she's not much good in a crisis."

"I'd gladly run you up, Di," I told her, "but in the circumstances maybe you're right about going by train. I'll stay here providing you'll promise to ring me breakfast time tomorrow and fetch me if I can be of the slightest use to anyone. Will you promise that?"

"Yes, of course," she said, and tried to smile. "Poor Jan! This was your big night and now . . ." Her smile faded, "Do you suppose there's some sort of curse on us?"

"If there is, it's not going to make a ha'porth of difference, you can rely on that!" I said grimly. Not even the thought that her father might be dying at this moment tempered my rage against him for snatching Diana away when we seemed at last to have emerged from the tunnel. "I'll run you to the junction. You'd better get some things, just a few things!"

"I'm not unpacked," she said. "I'll change and be down in ten minutes."

I occupied the time by phoning the junction and checking on the train. I had no real need to do this, for the train was the one that I had caught on my various dashes to town, after the *Observer* had been put to bed on Thursday nights, but I wanted to stop myself wondering how this thunderbolt would affect our plans and whether it would in some way postpone our wedding. There was a kind of desperation about my feeling for that coming-of-age date. For years now it had stood in the distant future, like a mountain peak that was clearly visible but unattainable. Only an hour ago it had seemed, at last, to be within walking distance, but now it had receded again and I was wretchedly uncertain of my ability to keep it in view. I told myself that this accident was a mere coincidence, that Diana had no real affection for her father and that we had agreed on the way down to the vicar's that neither he nor

339

Mrs. Gayelorde-Sutton had any place in our immediate future, but these arguments did very little to reassure me and we drove to the junction in silence.

The train was in and I found her an empty compartment and bought two cups of thick railway tea. We sat sipping them and trying to make conversation until the guard walked along and slammed the door. I jumped out and caught her hands through the window.

"Di," I said, piteously, for I was now in a turmoil of doubt and depression, "you'll come back! You'll come back the moment you can!"

She pulled me to her as the whistle blew and kissed me very softly on the mouth.

"Dear Jan," she said, "don't look so tragic. I love you and I'll always love you. And even if I couldn't come back, I'd need you and holler for you, the way I did last time!"

I was a little comforted by this and stood back as the train began to move. She remained rigid, framed in the window, not waving but just regarding me with the fixed gravity of a portrait staring down from a gallery wall.

Then a cloud of steam hissed up and she was gone, the last of the carriages snick-snacking past and beating out a metallic dirge. It thumped in my head all the way home and throughout the greater part of the night.

Chapter Eleven

THE NEXT morning every London paper carried the story in headlines. There had been no accident but there had been a resounding stock-market crash, involving a group of large trusts and a string of other firms, some of which had names that were household words. It was a Hatry scandal on a smaller scale, but a scale big enough to prompt Gayelorde-Sutton, as one of the most prominent figures in the group, to attempt suicide. He had swallowed two dozen sleeping tablets and had been found unconscious by his secretary. Two of the papers carried a stop-press announcement that he had died soon after midnight.

I bought all the London papers and went into the office, locking the door and telling the foreman printer that I was not to be disturbed. The old fellow looked at me anxiously.

"You feeling all right, John?" he asked and his eye took in the bundle of papers I was clutching. One flaring head-line was visible—CITY FINANCIER'S DEATH FOLLOWS MARKET CRASH—and the name Gayelorde-Sutton in the subsidiary headline. It was common knowledge in the printing shop that I had been mooning after Gayelorde-Sutton's daughter for years. You could never keep a secret of that kind in a town like Whinmouth.

"Yes, I'm all right, Fred," I told him, "but I've had a bit of a shock over this and I've got some important phoning to do. Keep everyone away for a bit!"

" 'Ee b'ain't caught you for aught, 'as 'ee?" demanded Fred, whose knowledge of stocks and shares were as vague as mine.

"Good God, no!" I snorted, and slammed the door on him.

I read the reports but they did not make very much sense to me. As far as I could understand, Gayelorde-Sutton's firm, or the one in which he figured most promi-nently, had gone bankrupt for over half a million pounds, and their ruin involved other groups in which he and his partners were concerned. One of the partners had fled to the Argentine and it was on his account that the Fraud Squad had been called in. The story was written in the consciously dramatic style that Fleet Street bestows upon this kind of news. There were pictures of Gayelorde-Sutton and his wife at Ascot the previous year, and another at Heronslea, labeled: *A financier's place in the country*. The caption implied a sneer and it was obvious that the jour-nalists knew a good deal more about the scandal than they could safely print at this stage.

When I had read all I could find on the subject, I asked

341

for directory inquiries and tried to get through to Diana's town house but, as I suspected, the line was blocked and no calls could be put through, although I tried several times.

Afternoon came but no call from Diana. I raced through the most urgent of my work and then rang Hawthorne and told him that I had no alternative but to abandon the *Observer* to the printing staff and hurry to London. I just told him it was on account of an urgent personal matter, involving a relative's sudden death, and I left instructions with Fred the foreman to answer Diana if she did ring and tell her that I was on my way. There was no through train until four P.M., so I filled up with petrol and drove across country to pick up the main London road, west of Yeovil. I kept my foot down and traffic wasn't heavy. I was nosing my way into Hammersmith about eight o'clock in the evening and I made straight for Palmerston Crescent.

I had no need to look for the house. There were parked cars all around the entrance and a little knot of reporters and photographers picketing the short flight of steps to the front door.

"I'm a relative, not a pressman," I told a photographer who warned me that no one would answer the door.

"You could be King-Kong, chum, but you won't make it!" he said, flippantly, and then, calling a thickset young man, told him that I was a relation and might have a new line on the story. Other reporters drifted over and I soon had cause to regret my feeble bluff.

"Where's his wife?" they wanted to know. "Is she down in the country?"

"I've just come from there," I said, "and the place is unoccupied. Mrs. Gayelorde-Sutton was supposed to be flying in from France today."

"She didn't turn up," said one of the reporters. "We've checked every airport."

I tried the bell again but the door remained shut. Bewildered and uncertain, I left the group and drove to the office of the *Illustrated*. I had a vague idea that the editor might be disposed to help me, for now I was beginning to regret my precipitate dash to town. I had no means of finding out where Diana was likely to be and, as always, I could only hang about waiting for her to get in touch with me. The editor of the *Illustrated* was sympathetic and made half a dozen phone calls, without the slightest result. Nobody knew where the Gayelorde-Suttons, mother and daughter, were hiding, but Fleet Street was anxious to find out before the story went cold.

It was a long time cooling off. There was even more about it in the papers on the following day, so I rang Fred at the *Observer* office and satisfied myself that Diana had not tried to get in touch with me. Then, in growing desperation, I made an exhaustive tour of her haunts—Fortnum's, Martinez's, various hotels, and even the homes of some of the Set with whom she had associated during her wild period.

It was all useless. Both Diana and her mother had vanished, and I came to the dismal conclusion that if the professions in Fleet Street could not trace them my own chances were negligible.

On the third day I trailed back to the West, where I took old Hawthorne into my confidence, but he wasn't much help. All he could suggest was that I should ask the telephone people to put through all the evening calls to the cottage where I was now sleeping. I did this as a precaution, and then hung about, racking my brains for a lead, any sort of a lead that would offer the slightest hope of tracing Diana.

Suddenly I found one, a folded slip of paper that had been in my pocket all the time, overlooked in my mad rush to and from London and forgotten under the merciless cudgeling I had given my brains during the last few days. It was the letterhead that Gayelorde-Sutton had handed to me during our interview and it gave the phone number of his solicitors. As I read it I heard his voice saying "Good firm . . . sound people . . go to them if you want to."

I could hardly wait to get in touch with them and put

343

through a call one minute after nine the following morning.

A dry, impersonal voice answered, saying that he was the managing clerk. I tried to speak quietly and reasonably, telling the clerk that I was an agent of the family, resident in Devon. Certain complications had arisen, I said, in respect of a farm Gayelorde-Sutton was purchasing, and as I was reluctant to worry the family at a time like this I had thought it best to contact the London solicitors. I gave the impression that I was in almost direct contact with mother and daughter.

The clerk went away and was gone for a few minutes. Then he told me that he was putting me through to Mr. Fellowes, one of the partners, and I repeated my story to him.

"I see," said a fruity voice. "Well then, I think perhaps you had better come to town and discuss the matter with us. None of our client's property can be sold or disposed of in any way, you understand, Mr. Leigh?"

I said that I realized this and made an appointment for the following day. Then I went up to the cottage and had the first real sleep I had had in more than a week.

2.

Mr. Fellowes, the owner of the fruity voice, was a heavily built man, about forty-five. He was so courteous, and made such a pleasant impression on me, that I decided to take him into my confidence. After presenting the letterhead as a kind of *bona fides* I told him how things stood between Diana and myself. I had to exaggerate the cordiality shown me by Gayelorde-Sutton, and I hinted that the family had intended to set up Diana and me in a farm newly acquired by the estate. I would have told any story to get to Diana and this was only half a lie.

Fellowes seemed keenly interested and when I had finished, and admitted frankly that Diana had vanished after I had put her on the night train at Whinford, his attitude became genuinely sympathetic.

"Why do you suppose she hasn't got in touch with

you?" he asked. "Could it be she's ashamed of what's happened?"

This had not occurred to me and privately I thought it very unlikely.

"Young women are very unpredictable about that kind of thing," he went on, "and her father has come out of this business rather badly. I'm afraid a lot of people have lost a great deal of money. I've lost a few hundreds myself, come to that! How about you?"

I said that I had never owned a stock or a share in my life and he smiled.

"Wise young man," he said lightly, but I could see he was summing me up and was by no means certain what to make of me.

"Excuse me for a couple of moments," he said, at length, and rang through to the outer office for Gayelorde-Sutton's file. A typist brought it in and he sorted through it, drumming his fingers and humming tunelessly. Presently he plucked out a large, sealed envelope.

"I thought the name rang a bell," he said. "This is addressed to you. It came in ten days ago, actually on the morning of the crash. Perhaps you'd like to open it in my presence?"

I was dumfounded. Not only did my name appear on the envelope, but Aunt Thirza's address was there and beneath it, in brackets, the alternative address of the *Observer*. Then I recalled Gayelorde-Sutton's admission—"I know a great deal more about you than you imagine." Well, here was proof of it. Inside the envelope was a single sheet of notepaper and another sealed envelope, with bulky enclosures. On the notepaper, in Gayelorde-Sutton's spidery handwriting, was a brief note:

DEAR LEIGH:

I was impressed by our talk. When you get this I shall be in no position either to oppose or assist your somewhat prolonged courtship. In the event of your taking my advice, however, I am making you a personal bequest of one thousand pounds.

You will find Emerald a handful and I wish you joy. I believe you are interested in horseback riding and my advice,

for what it is worth, is to keep her on a far tighter rein than
I did!

Sincerely,
ERIC GAYELORDE-SUTTON

Inside the second envelope were ten hundred-pound
notes.

I was so astonished that I sat staring at the letter until
Fellowes reminded me of his presence by a discreet legal
cough. I passed the letter to him and he read it, his eyebrows shooting up.

"Did you have any inkling about this?" he asked.

"Not the faintest notion," I told him.

"Then stuff that damned envelope in your pocket," he
said, gruffly. "I've mislaid my damned glasses again—can
you see them anywhere?"

I pocketed the money and handed him his horned-
rimmed glasses that lay on the desk before him. He blew
out his cheeks, like a motorist who has just avoided running over a dog.

"Will everything Gayelorde-Sutton owned have to be
sold up?" I asked.

"Even his clothes," said Fellowes. "The creditors might
get five shillings in the pound and then again they might
not! He didn't own Heronslea but there's a fortune in antiques down there and he did own the London house and a
place in Nice."

"What about Mrs. Gayelorde-Sutton?" I asked. "Surely
she had money of her own?"

"She had until a few months ago," he told me, "but
when things got sticky she transferred all of it to one of the
companies. I heard from her yesterday. She's penniless!"

I digested this for a moment, then I said:

"Look here, Mr. Fellowes, I don't need this money and
I . . ."

"What money?" he demanded, looking straight at me.

I thought for a moment. "Right, have it your way! Put
me in touch with her and I think I might be able to help
her," I said.

He looked hard at the ceiling. "I'm not authorized to

346

give her address to anyone," he said, slowly. "If the press got on to it the story would take another week or so to die a natural death! You've been a journalist, I don't have to tell you about that, do I?"

"No," I said, "but it seems to me that if I find her I might trace Diana, and I'm going to trace her if it costs me a thousand pounds! Talking of figures, is that very much, measured against the sums involved in these deficiencies?"

He smiled, then swiftly composed his features. "Like giving a donkey one oat," he said.

As we talked I noticed that he was fidgeting with the open file in front of him. A small sheet of notepaper, similar to the one I had given him as a *bona fides,* was now detached from the main pile. It edged across the desk, until it was about halfway between us. It was the top sheet of a letter written in a strong, feminine hand. At the top of the page was an address:

21 Drayford Gardens, Holland Park, W.9. Having noted the address I stood up.

"Well, I don't seem to have got much further, do I?"

"No," he said, blandly, "but I'm sure I wish you luck, Mr. Leigh! Don't forget this, will you?" And he returned Gayelorde-Sutton's note.

We shook hands and he showed me as far as the outer office, where we parted. He was the most human solicitor I have ever met.

I took an 88 bus along the Bayswater Road and on the way I thought about Gayelorde-Sutton's gift in relation to our interview of a fortnight ago. Some of the things that had puzzled me so much were now becoming clear——his talk of going away, which I recognized as a conventional smoke screen for suicide; his anxiety to get Diana settled and cushioned, to some extent, against the disaster that was then only forty-eight hours away; his frantic desire to be rid of me in order to concentrate on the phone call probably the final nail in his coffin. For all that, his last-minute efforts on behalf of Diana failed to impress me. Looking back on his grotesque heartiness, and knowing what was in his mind at the time, his clumsy bluff was like

347

the action of a drunk urging a slightly less tipsy companion to do something calculated to make him look foolish in the eyes of the sober. His letter was not the kind of letter a man should have written a few hours before taking his life. There was a sneer behind every word and the sneers suggested that, to some extent, he blamed his wife and daughter for the position in which he found himself at that moment. Pondering this I realized that nothing would induce me to use his money, that I had to get rid of it as soon as possible. If it was able to buy information regarding Diana's whereabouts then I was prepared to use it for that purpose, but in any case I had to get rid of it, soon!

I left the bus at the stop beyond Notting Hill Station and made inquiries in a shop. Then I found Drayford Gardens, a long and depressing row of four-story Victorian houses, stucco-fronted, Ionic-pillared and as grim as a city cemetery. Number twenty-one was divided into flats and on the plate beside the bell push there was no card bearing the name of Mrs. Gayelorde-Sutton. I took potluck and pressed the bell of Apartment Number Three.

A middle-aged woman with peroxided hair opened the door and I told her that I was a clerk with an urgent message from a firm of solicitors for a lady living in one of the flats but that I had unfortunately forgotten which number.

"What's she like?" the woman asked, affably enough.

I described Mrs. Gayelorde-Sutton as accurately as I could.

"Oh, that'll be the smart one who doesn't go out," she said. "Top floor, and a bloody long climb!"

I thanked the woman and followed her up six flights of stairs. On the third landing she pointed and I climbed two more flights, arriving on the floor that had been occupied by the maids when the house was occupied by prosperous Victorians. The landing was uncarpeted and there were two doors, divided by a strip of peeling plaster. I chose the door that had an empty milk bottle outside. Beyond it I could hear a faint whirring sound, like the pleasant drone of a sewing machine. The sound ceased the moment I knocked.

"Who is it?" called a voice, after a lengthy pause.

"A clerk, with a message from Messrs. Lammett & Fellowes, the solicitors, ma'am," I called back.

"Wait a minute!"

I waited, my heart pounding like a steam hammer, not only from the exertion of climbing all those stairs but from the prospect of seeing Diana again.

The door opened and there stood Mrs. Gayelorde-Sutton, as trim and elegant as she had been when I had last seen her in the West End. Apart from that, however, she had changed a good deal. Her drawn expression reminded me of somebody listening from the dock to evidence on the second day of a tedious trial.

For a long moment we stared at one another. Then, as I detected a movement to slam the door shut, I said:

"I really have got something for you from the solicitors, Mrs. Gayelorde-Sutton! I've just come from them, how else would I have the address?"

She considered this, her greenish eyes regarding me curiously but with none of their customary arrogance.

"You had better come in," she said, quietly, and stood aside.

The apartment was small, dark and low-ceilinged. What furniture there was reminded me of the pieces she had once bought at Uncle Luke's Mart. A one-bar electric fire was burning and under a single-shaded bulb stood a Singer sewing machine; around it were crumpled folds of material. It seemed almost obscene to discover Mrs. Gayelorde-Sutton in a setting like this, and I had a curious feeling that I was dreaming and had interrupted a game of Heronslea charades. It was as though at any moment all the lights would come on, and people would laugh, clap and call out the word that she was acting out on her sewing machine. Then, against all probability, I felt a rush of warmth for her, such as I had not experienced for her husband when he had patted my shoulder and used my Christian name. There was something about her in this shoddy setting that suggested enormous dignity, a dignity that had always escaped her when she was high-heeling across the parquet floors of Heronslea, or climbing in and out of her vast, black Bentley during shopping expeditions in Whinmouth. Behind the dignity there was something else, humility, and a kind of dogged courage in the way she moved around the room, clearing materials from the one easy chair and lifting her hand toward it indicating that I should be seated. The simple gesture humbled me as I had never been humbled by her in her lady-of-the-manor days.

"You're looking for Emerald, I imagine?"

Something else struck me as hopelessly irrational. The monstrous affectation had gone from her voice. She spoke like a normal person, tired perhaps but politely patient. There was no hint of tightly corseted vowels and tortured consonants. It was "Emerald," not *"Air-m'-lde"*; it was plain, simple "I," not *"Aies."*

"Yes," I said, struggling madly to adjust myself to this complete stranger, "I got your address by a trick but please don't let that worry you. I'll give you my word of honor now that I'll forget it the moment I walk out of here!"

She pushed materials from the sewing-machine chair and sat down, resting her hands on her lap. I noticed that the fingers were long and tapering like Diana's and also that they were ringless. Even her wedding ring was missing.

"She isn't here, I'm afraid. Did you think she would be?"

"I hoped that she would be. Do you know where she is?"

She thought a moment and her eyes avoided mine. "How long is it since you saw her?"

I spoke briefly of what had taken place between us on the day before the crash and how we had put up banns to marry a few days after Diana's coming-of-age. I mentioned the circumstances in which we had heard of the disaster, and of our parting at Whinford Station. She listened carefully to every word I uttered.

"Emerald's abroad now," she said, when I had finished.

"In Nice?"

"No, not in Nice."

"Then where? Or do you still think I've no right to know?"

"Yes," she said, quietly, "of course you have that right, Mr. Leigh, and I intend to tell you if you'll tell me something first. Exactly what did the solicitor say about Emerald?"

"He didn't say anything about her," I said, with a good deal of surprise, for her approach was so unlike all I recalled of Mrs. Gayelorde-Sutton that I had to keep reminding myself that I was addressing the right person. "I told you, I got this address by a trick, a quick bit of snooping over the desk."

More in the hope of convincing her that I was on her side than with any ulterior motive, I handed her Gayelorde-Sutton's letter. "I was given this by Mr. Fellowes," I said and waited while she read the note.

Her expression did not change but I noticed that her hands trembled slightly.

"What did Mr. Fellowes say about this?" she asked, in the same gentle voice.

"He pretended he had lost his glasses," I told her, and her lips twitched. It was not a smile but it was the nearest approach to one she had ever given in my presence.

"Well, that's very nice for you, Mr. Leigh," she said, returning the note, "but you don't have to marry her in order to keep the money, do you?"

"I haven't the slightest intention of keeping it!" I said, gruffly. "Diana tried to bully me into taking over a Heronslea farm but I turned that down, and this money either belongs to you or the creditors, it certainly doesn't belong to me!"

"That's rather silly," she said. "I should hang on to it now that you have been clever enough to get it out of the lawyers' clutches."

"Well, I'm not keeping it," I said, slightly nettled. "I'm leaving it here, and if you don't want it, put it back in the kitty and ensure that the creditors get 5/1d in the pound. Now are you going to tell me where Diana is?"

"Diana—Emerald is married," she said. "She was married last Monday, to Yves de Royden, a French boy she had known for a very long time."

"*Married*—you said?"

351

What meager light there was in that cheerless little flat seemed to fade, so that the erect figure of Mrs. Gayelorde-Sutton, seen sideways at the sewing machine, became blurred. The shock was very great. It was as though some-one had stolen up unseen and struck me a savage blow across the chest, and the illusion was so vivid that I put out my hands to avoid a second attack. The indistinct shadow in front of me rose from her chair and as she passed in front of me my vision cleared and there was Mrs. Gayelorde-Sutton, standing close beside me, her hand on my shoulder.

"Just sit still a moment," she said, "I'm making some coffee."

Even in the extreme stress of the moment I noticed that her voice was excessively gentle. It had never occurred to me that she might have a pleasing voice, for her natural speech had always been smothered under that stupid ac-cent. Now the recollection of her accent was like remem-bering the voice of a silver-toned contralto whose talent is being rendered grotesque by a botched accompaniment. I fixed my mind on this curious inconsistency while she bus-tled about in the adjoining room, turning on the gas and rattling cups and saucers.

In what seemed to be a moment she returned carrying a tray on which were cups, a coffeepot and a plate of choco-late biscuits. She cleared the table, swinging the heavy sewing machine to the ground as though it had weighed a couple of pounds instead of at least thirty.

Gradually the shock of her information about Diana be-came absorbed in a kind of competition that was engaging part of my brain, a crazy game of trying to relate the two Mrs. Gayelorde-Suttons, the one I remembered and had loathed and the one now moving about in front of me, doing things that I associated with Aunt Thirza and the housewives in the steep streets behind Whinmouth quay. It was like trying to place ball bearings in little holes under the glass of one of those tiresome tricks found in Christ-mas crackers. Every time I resolved the two personalities into a unit they slipped away, dodging one another and shooting off at a tangent. Presently I could bear it no longer.

"Why are you here? What are you doing in a place like this?" I asked her. "How is it that you aren't with Diana and what in God's name made her go off like that?"

"Which question would you like answered first?" she said—and this time she really did smile. Her smile reminded me of Diana's when she was making a special effort to appear patient.

"How do you come to be in this kind of house and living by yourself?"

"It was the best I could find at short notice," she said. "I shall be moving on very shortly, at least I will if I'm any good!"

"Any good at what, Mrs. Gayelorde-Sutton?"

"Dressmaking and dress designing," she said. "I'm even enjoying it in a way. Wasn't there once an emperor who became tired of ruling and retired to a monastery to make clocks?"

She had no more power to surprise me now and the weight of misery began to press down again. Diana married! Diana gone forever! Diana the wife of that narrow-faced youth who had once greeted us in a cinema foyer at Marble Arch, and afterwards whisked us to Victoria Station in his glittering sports car! She had hardly ever mentioned Yves since that far-off day. She had seemed absolutely resolved to share the cottage under Teasel Wood and ride out beside me over Foxhayes on eternal summer mornings.

Suddenly Mrs. Gayelorde-Sutton spoke again:

"How well did you know Emerald, Mr. Leigh?"

"I thought I knew her better than anyone on earth," I muttered.

She nodded. "I wouldn't go as far as that but I thought *I* knew her reasonably well. I knew that she was wild, willful, reckless, utterly unreliable, selfish, greedy, disloyal . . . I knew all that! What I didn't know was that she was such a pitiful little coward, even a worse coward than her father!"

"Are you trying to say that she married because she was afraid to stay in England after what happened?"

"No, that had nothing whatever to do with it. She was afraid of being poor, of having no money for all the things she's had lavished on her since she was a child, and it's hard for me to understand that. You see, I enjoyed having money, nobody more so, but I'm not in the least frightened of being without it. It was a challenge to be well off but is an even more exciting challenge to sell clothes and jewelry in order to provide a float to keep one's head above water while making a fresh start. You've always had to struggle, so perhaps you can understand, Mr. Leigh?"

I understood it well enough, but what I failed to understand was why the sale of her personal effects had not brought in sufficient money to give her a far more promising start than the one she appeared to be making. Her jewelry alone must have realized thousands of pounds. I was so curious that I mentioned this.

"No money or shares," she said, almost gaily, "but I only kept two hundred pounds from my sale of furs and jewelry. The main sum went in last-minute efforts to stave off the crash—I had several weeks' warning of it, you see —and what didn't was handed over. I've been all kinds of a fool in my time, Mr. Leigh, but I'm not a thief. These wretched people are entitled to every penny they can get, surely you see that?"

What do we know about anyone? I had always thought of Diana as a strong, inflexible person, someone who would ride out any storm and shout defiance into the wind. I had always thought of Mrs. Gayelorde-Sutton as a vapid, futile creature, with no more honesty in her soul than there was in her accent. The sheer impact of her character now helped me to hold Diana at bay for a few moments and I said, "You say you'll be moving on. What kind of plans have you got, and where do you hope this dressmaking will lead?"

"To a nice little one-woman business, I hope," she said, brightly. "I've an idea that I might open eventually in the Market Square, in Whinford. They need a place down there, and I daresay I should attract the curious and afterwards keep them as satisfied customers."

"Tell me," I went on, "did Diana know about the crash in advance?"

"I think she had her suspicions after her father turned down an increase in allowance and said no to a settlement."

"What settlement was that?"

"She wrote asking for a lump sum settlement in event of her marrying. My husband was hard pressed at the time and told her he could promise nothing definite at the moment."

Other certainties were creeping out of the mental fog of the last few weeks. I realized now what had been in Diana's mind when she had tried so hard to bulldoze me into taking the farm. Obviously she had banked on cadging a sizable lump sum from her father and using it to stock the place, at the same time getting all the renovations done free by the Heronslea maintenance staff. An unpleasant picture of our marriage, as she had seen it, began to emerge—Diana continuing to lead the life of a county belle, with myself as man-about-the-place and a proven bedfellow. She had never intended that I should become a real farmer, just a stallion, partly for use and partly for local window dressing. It was not a very flattering picture and it made me grind my teeth with rage and humiliation.

"Does she love this French boy?" I burst out, slamming down my half-empty coffee cup so hard that the liquid splashed the table.

"Love him? God bless my soul, does she have to? His family owns a tire factory! They're three times as wealthy as we were in our palmiest days."

She stood up, took a duster from the mantel shelf and carefully wiped away the coffee splash. Suddenly she stopped wiping and stood leaning on her hands, her back to me.

"One other thing, John"—she used my Christian name far less self-consciously than her husband had used

355

it—"and you don't have to tell me this if you'd rather not —were you and Emerald lovers?"

"Yes," I admitted, "on three improbable occasions and each a long time after the occasion you believed us to be, Mrs. Sutton!"

She straightened up and turned to me. "That makes it worse," she said, "because now that we've met you don't have to tell me that the initiative came from her. Frankly I always suspected her of being a sensual little baggage!"

My own thoughts about Diana were bitter enough but I did not want to listen to her mother's observations on the subject. I stood up to leave.

"Thank you for being so frank, Mrs. Sutton," I said, and held out my hand. "If you do open a shop in our part of the world, then I hope you'll let me know. I've got friends down there and I daresay I could pull a few strings with the local press. That usually helps with a new business."

"Yes," she said, pleasantly, "I might even take you up on that, John. I should like to see you again anyway, so perhaps you'll leave your address?"

I scribbled the name and phone number of the cottage on the back of one of her husband's envelopes and passed it to her.

"Teasel Wood Cottage. It's a pretty name," she mused.

"It's a pig in a poke," I said and started down the first of the eight flights of stairs.

3.

I suppose I should have learned something important from that interview, something of lasting value and not simply the bare fact of Diana's betrayal and a few of the reasons behind her scheming of the last few weeks. I could have learned, for instance, the right way to take a beating and to face life, bleak as it was, with dignity and courage, but Mrs. Gayelorde-Sutton had more guts in her great toe than I had in my hulking body and I was soon launched on a spring tide of self-pity and alcohol, much as Grandfather Leigh had launched himself two generations ago. It was no fault of mine that I did not end like Grandfather, dead and drunk over Nun's Head.

I suppose it was putting an unnecessary strain on myself to go back to Sennacharib and live a Crusoe life in the cottage all that summer. My sole companion during the days was Old Fred, Uncle Mark's lugubrious stableman, and apart from him I had few human contacts. Uncle Luke and Aunt Thirza came up there at first but I behaved very churlishly toward them and soon they stopped coming, as did the odd visitor from Whinmouth and Shepherdshey.

I hired out horses to people who wanted a ride but I never accompanied customers on their hacks, or gave lessons to beginners. I disliked my own company but I hated everyone else's. I spent most of the days exercising the horses alone, or digging in the extensive vegetable patch behind the loose boxes. The nights I passed in drinking, sometimes in the private bar of the Rifleman but more often alone in the cottage. Gin and French was my tipple and I accounted for a prodigious amount of it during that summer and autumn. The weather was generally depressing, with whole weeks of rain, leaden skies and brief, gusty intervals when the sun tried to warm the sodden woods and waterlogged meadows.

Sometimes I made a halfhearted attempt to put Diana out of my mind and tire myself with heavy spells of work about the tumbled-down premises, but these bouts seldom lasted more than a day or so. Soon I was back to brooding over the bottle or, what was worse, brooding along the vales and gorse plateaux of Sennacharib where every bush, every pattern of copse and hedgerow reminded me of Diana, of something she had once said or the ring of her laughter as I had heard it when we had cantered over this ground during the past few years.

I recall very little of that period, only an odd day or two here and there when I was so defeated and depressed that I set Margot, the best mare in the stable, at hedges and ditches that were beyond her power to jump. I won't say that I behaved suicidally but I was certainly indifferent as to whether or not we parted company at a hazard, and

357

sometimes I came home bruised and battered by heavy falls.

I deliberately cut myself from all contact with the town and village. My stores, such as they were, were brought up by Fred, and I seldom saw a newspaper. Had I possessed a radio, and kept in touch with the news, I might have derived savage satisfaction from the steady deterioration of affairs in Europe during those months. It was the period when Spain was bleeding to death, Mussolini was blasting and gassing his way into Abyssinia, and Hitler was screeching threats into loudspeakers at Nuremburg, Munich and elsewhere. As it was I had no interest in the victims of Guernica and slaughtered Abyssinians. I had plenty of troubles of my own and I was almost insanely jealous of them.

Sometimes, I think, I was a little mad, as on my twenty-second birthday, the cheerless anniversary of the day that I met Diana in the larch wood behind Heronslea. On that day, hell-bent on turning the knife in my wounds, I went out with the gun, eager to vent my spleen on any rabbit or pheasant that presented itself. I walked up to Teasel Bend, crossed the steppingstones and went along the edge of the wood as far as the Big Oak paddock. Here, just as I was climbing the rail, I spotted the two buzzards circling above their favorite hunting ground.

The sight of them convulsed me with rage. I jumped off the rail and ran shouting across the turf until I was about twenty yards short of the oak. It was at this very spot where I had first watched them, an hour or so before Keeper Croker pounced on me in the wood. I put the gun to my shoulder and fired both barrels.

They were too high to hit but on the report they mewed defiance and dropped swiftly down the slope to the trees. Then I felt a little ashamed of myself and abandoned the idea of shooting, humping myself back to the river and following it down as far as the track under the wood.

One of the few impressions I recall of that dismal interlude was the curious effect that one's mood has upon the aspect of a familiar landscape. Sennacharib had always held for me a holy significance. It was my private Arcady,

358

my Isle of Avalon, my Never-Never Land, and my greatest joy had been to watch the seasons change on the two-mile slope between the common and the first cottages of Shepherdshey. I had looked across the woods for the cloud formations driven by the south wind and my greatest compensation for the passing of summer had been the slow march of copper and rust red across the tops of the Heronslea beeches. It was always exciting to find a late foxglove on Teasel Bank, or early wild daffodils in the marshy part of the larch wood. I had always felt better for a walk or a ride up here, but now Sennacharib's power to heal must have crossed the Channel with Diana. The autumn colors seemed jaded and nondescript, it seemed always to be drizzling and the wind was forever in the southwest, driving sleet and shredded cloud across the estuary. Even when the sun shone, the undergrowth had the poisonous brightness of Stevenson's *Treasure Island,* and where the water had failed to drain away, acres of alien swamp had spread to the riverbanks. I suppose much of this was my fancy but it was how I saw it that year. Where there once had been magic there was dullness that pressed on me like a rain-soaked cap.

Autumn passed, then winter, with no snow but still more rain. I rode, walked, dug, chopped wood, groomed the horses, and withdrew more and more into myself until I was little better than a morose recluse, inhabiting an isolated pigsty. It was ten months now since I had said good-by to Diana on the station platform and I had almost stopped thinking of her as a person. She now merged into the general tedium of my life, at one with the driving wind, the gray, empty sky and the eternal drizzle. Then, one February afternoon, my life changed course again, but this time Diana's contribution to the switch was remote and indirect.

I had been over to Castle Ferry to find a sweep and try and get him to do something with the smoking chimney of the cottage. It was dusk when I returned and as I trudged up the muddy track I noticed to my surprise that the oil lamp was glowing in the window. I quickened my step, irritated at the prospect of an uninvited guest and determined to send him packing as quickly as possible. When I threw open the door I was amazed to see Drip, the friendly ex-governess, tending the fire.

She seemed to be very much at home. The room had been subjected to an intensive spring cleaning. Freshly washed curtains were drying on a line over the fireplace, a week's accumulation of dirty crockery had been cleared, the table laid for supper, the slated floor had been scrubbed, and all the rugs brushed and beaten. It astonished me that one person could have achieved so much during my brief absence.

Miss Rodgers did not look a day older than when I had last seen her, now getting on for five years ago. She was one of those plump, breathless little women who display far more energy than the lean, stringy ones, and her round, good-natured face was shining with health and the heat of the huge fire. In the soft glow of the lamp the room looked cozier and far more inviting than it had ever looked in my brief tenancy, or during the lengthy occupation of Uncle Mark.

"Come in and take your filthy boots off, Jan!" she said, as though we had been sharing the cottage for months. "I couldn't find slippers, so I warmed a pair of outdoor shoes. The fish is nearly ready and the kettle's boiling. You make the tea, while I cut bread and butter."

"Where on earth have you sprung from, Miss Rodgers," I asked, "and how the devil did you get in? I locked up when I went out at midday."

"You don't hide the key in a very original place," she said, smiling. "After I'd drawn blank under the bricks outside the door, I tried underneath the water butt. This place was a disgrace to a Christian! It positively stank when I came in and until the wind changed I was half suffocated by smoke. You'll have to get that chimney seen to at once."

Not knowing how to reply to this I said nothing, changing my boots and warming myself at the fire, where some fillets of hake were hissing in the long-handled pan beneath the spit. I noticed that the pan had been scoured. The smell of cooking put a sharp edge to my appetite.

360

"I came down from Wales last night," she said, "and called at your uncle's on the quay. As a matter of fact I stayed the night there, and your aunt is very worried about you. She has need to be, in all conscience. What kind of a man are you to turn your back on everybody like this, apart from living like a savage, and a very dirty savage at that?"

"It suits me well enough," I grumbled, but my mouth was watering for those fillets and hunger coaxed the sourness from my voice.

"It doesn't suit you at all," she snapped, "because you're really a very sociable person. You ought to be ashamed of yourself, a great hulking lout like you, mooning over a bit of a girl all these months! Haven't you got any pride? I'd be a charwoman before I let a man do that to me! Not that one ever has," she added, and winked so saucily that I laughed for the first time in months.

"And don't call me 'Miss Rodgers' any more," she pattered. "I've always known that you and Emerald referred to me as 'Drip' and I don't mind a bit because, as things have turned out, I'm not nearly such a drip as either one of you has turned out to be! Here"—she lifted the pan from the fire and tipped the fillets into a dish—"get that into you and when you've finished you and I are going to have a very frank discussion, young man!"

We ate a silent but enjoyable supper, finishing the new loaf Drip had brought and making inroads into a pound of the best Cheddar that came up in the same basket. Afterwards I helped her to wash up, and when all the crockery was back on the dresser we built up the fire and I sat opposite her, smoking. It was by far the most peaceful hour I had ever passed in that room.

"Well," she said, breaking the long, satisfying silence, "where do we begin, Jan?"

I asked her to tell me about herself and she said that her sister had died, and that she had suddenly been homesick for the West Country and had come down with the intention of buying a small property and ending her days in the district where she had spent the happiest part of her life.

"I *was* very happy at Heronslea," she said, "although you

361

may not have thought so. It almost broke my heart to leave and I kept in touch with the family right up to the time of the crash. I had a pension, of course, and it didn't stop when poor Mr. Gayelorde-Sutton killed himself. It wasn't very much but my sister and I ran a candy store and we managed very comfortably. Now I've got sufficient to last me out, providing I'm careful of course—but that's enough about me. Tell me everything about you and Diana—*everything,* mind you, no skipping the important pieces! Start from the time you two silly children were fetched home from that dreadful island."

I told her everything, how I had fared in London, how I had run into Diana outside Fortnum's, and all that happened afterwards, up to the day that I called on Mrs. Gayelorde-Sutton in Holland Park and began my nonstop sulk.

She listened carefully and made no comment. Then, without looking up, she said, "I had a letter from Diana last week. She's got a little girl called Yvonne and she's living outside a town called Saumur. Do you know it?"

"Not that part of France," I said, "but I've heard of it. It's somewhere on the Loire, isn't it?"

"That's right, but I'm surprised you've never been to Anjou. You speak French very well, don't you?"

"Yes," I said, glumly. "I learned to please Diana!"

She flushed a little at that and her head came up, her eyes regarding me seriously over the rims of steel-framed spectacles.

"Is that *all* you did on that account?" she demanded, crisply.

"No," I said, "not by a long chalk!"

"What else, Jan?" The voice was much kinder now.

"I gave up secondhand furnishings for small-town journalism and then small-town journalism for this. I left home for London and then left London for home. I nearly broke my neck learning to ride horses in order to be with her. I learned how to ride a motorcycle in order to take her to a single dance. I was always in and out of hot water on her account, but I'm not grousing at that, for I judged it was worth it and I got my payoff at the time. What I do begrudge her is *time,* Drip—the whole of my blasteu youth!"

She nodded as though she understood and sympathized and I fell into her trap. "All those years I never made a single friend," I said. "Do you know anyone else rising twenty-three who had grown up in a town like Whinmouth and not made a single real friend, male or female?"

"There was never another girl, Jan?"

"One, before Diana came back, but I only saw her twice. I dropped her like a hot coal after one fresh look at Diana."

Drip carefully removed her glasses and set them down. She did this as though she was playing for time before answering.

"Jan," she said, at length, "have you ever wondered what you might have done with your life if you hadn't met Diana?"

In all my moonings about Sennacharib during the past ten months I had never considered this. It was the sort of question that did not present itself, like a man wondering what it might have been like to have been born a woman.

"No," I answered, "I don't think I have, Drip. Can you tell me?"

"I can tell you precisely," she said. "If you hadn't met Diana that day in the woods you would still have been humping furniture around Whinmouth on your Uncle Luke's barrow!"

I considered this and accepted it as true but it did not seem to prove very much.

"I was happy enough pushing that barrow, Drip."

She made a gesture of impatience, a violent one for her.

"Don't you *see,* Jan? Everything you are as a person you owe to Diana! Diana performed a kind of miracle on you and in spite of what's happened I don't think you have any right to quarrel with it."

"Is it much of a miracle? I was Uncle Luke's errand boy at fifteen and at twenty-two I'm a bad-tempered hermit, living just as you said, like a grubby savage in a kraal."

"That isn't Diana's fault, it's yours! There isn't the slightest reason for indulging in this spectacular sulk, apart from the fact that I believe, deep down, you're enjoying it in a gloomy, perverse kind of way. Because of Diana you got yourself a better job! Because of Diana you learned to ride and manage horses! Because of Diana you learned a foreign language! Diana taught you to dance, taught you to look for adventure, taught you how to buy clothes, cured your accent, taught you your table manners if the truth's known, and goodness knows how many other things that you've forgotten or are in the process of forgetting, or have even come to believe you acquired by your own will power. *You make me sick, Jan Leigh!* Look at yourself in the mirror! Think about yourself!. Talk to yourself if you like, but if there's a spark of honesty left in you, you'll end up admitting that Diana enlarged your life and gave it a shape and purpose that it could never have had if you'd married one of those bovine girls I used to see pushing their prams up and down Whinmouth quay on Sunday afternoons. Now you can get that car out and run me back to your uncle's, but don't imagine I'm going to leave you alone! I'm moving in here; for the time being I've found my little place in the country. You don't have to pay me but you do have to pull yourself together, and you won't see the last of me until you have, so there!"

It was a long and vehement speech for Drip and it left her rather breathless, so much so that I laughed outright and she laughed to hear me laugh. I drove her back to Uncle Luke's and we all had a pot of tea in the kitchen before I returned home. The next day she kept her word, moving in bag and baggage, and we lived there, like aunt and nephew, until our world went mad.

It was a happy time, those last two and a half years under Teasel Wood. The stable prospered. I started a poultry farm, and Drip kept the premises as bright and cozy as a tea cozy in an illustrated fairy-tale book. She stayed on when I took a middle-aged Whinmouth gardener-groom into partnership and joined the army, in the autumn of 1939, and on that birthday, my twenty-fifth, she sent a cake to the battery in which I was serving outside Lille.

She took a big chance on that cake. It was made in the

cottage bread oven and she had piped it with a large, pink heart. In the center of the heart was my name, transfixed by an arrow, and the point of the arrow passed through her own initials, piped near the rim.

I was cutting into it during an air-raid alarm that had sent us to ground when Ginger Beavis, the bombardier, exclaimed, "Those marzipan dots around the edge! In this half-light they look just like emeralds!"

Chapter Twelve

THE FACT that I had learned French all those years ago, and had been sufficiently interested to improve it during my London period and subsequently, stood me in good stead when the war came. Or did it? I was soon winkled out of the friendly antiaircraft battery and attached to Intelligence H.Q. in Paris. When the big breakthrough began, in May 1940, I was hustled down to Bordeaux to make arrangements for the evacuation of civilian personnel.

The great exodus had hardly begun, so that the journey southwest was tolerable, but by the time I arrived in Bordeaux it was a city of bewilderment and seething rumor, with nobody from politician to refugee knowing what was happening, or likely to happen, hour by hour.

When the panzers smashed through the Allied line and the British army began its retreat upon Dunkirk, I had urgent instructions to get my people aboard. My immediate superior, a major, was badly wounded in an air raid on the harbor, and from then on I had to use my initiative, sorting out the claims of the various groups, civilian and military, French, British, Dutch, Polish and even Spanish, who besieged me for a passage to Britain.

It was a thankless, harassing job. For a period of four days I went without sleep and on the fifth, when I had dispatched two crowded coal boats and had seen another sink under a Stuka attack, I was too dazed and dispirited to take much interest in the war. Then a Dutch skipper came to me and put his thousand-ton tramp at my disposal. I sent my sergeant to collect any stray units in the area and get them aboard as soon as possible, for the Dutchman was as impatient to be gone as everyone else in that fear-crazed city and told me that, empty or laden, he intended to clear the Gironde on the early morning tide.

The weather was insufferably hot. At that stage of the evacuation I was operating from a slipway and ferryboat landing at Blaye, just across the river from Bordeaux, and I had commandeered the ferryboat office, a squat, one-story building near the water's edge. The would-be immigrants formed a long, untidy queue down to the waterside and a line of battered trucks, military vans, and hideously overloaded Citroëns and Renaults stretched from the ferryboat office to the main road, more than two miles inland.

I have never witnessed such a scene of chaos. The French, ordinarily a brave, philosophical people, had completely succumbed to the virus of panic and defeatism. They fought one another for places in the vehicle queue that led down to the berth of my Dutch steamer. Some of them wanted to go to Britain and picketed my office, shouting and gesticulating, each urging his or her claim to be saved from the Boche. Others were not interested in being evacuated but were trying to reach Bordeaux and join up with relatives from whom they had been separated on the trek west. It was useless to try to organize the fugitives and their vehicles. Car and truck drivers persisted in edging out of line and creating vast jams, and every now and again a fight started with other drivers and gendarmes who tried to stop them. Pedestrians clambered over the line of interlocked transport in the hope of bypassing my office and reaching the ship's gangplanks. The scene reminded me of Ségur's description of the passage of the Beresina during the retreat from Moscow.

Toward sundown, I locked myself in and did business through the window and I was here, praying for darkness to descend on the lunatic confusion, when my sergeant found me, fighting his way through the crowd and approaching near enough to shout a message to me.

"There's a Judy back up the road who says she knows you," he bawled. "She's stuck there, with a tribe of kids, about a dozen of them. She sent a note . . . catch! Did you ever see such a bloody shambles?" Then, having thrown his note, he disappeared, clawed down by two men who held him and screamed into his ears.

The message, a crumpled ball of paper, sailed through the window and fell beside my desk. I retrieved it without much interest, smoothing it out among the litter of papers. Then I nearly hit the ceiling. The note, scribbled in pencil, was in Diana's handwriting.

It said:

> Heard you were here, Jan—come and get me again! Be gallant, like Mr. Ridd!
>
> Love,
> DIANA

Just that; just as if we had lost one another in a Cup Final crowd!

I sat on, facing the hideous turmoil immediately under the window, indifferent to the grinding crashes of colliding vehicles and the shrill fury and despair of their drivers.

So much had happened during the last few weeks that no thought of Diana had entered my head. I had not even remembered that she was resident in France and had a French husband, for at last, at long last, the affairs of Europe had lapped over Sennacharib and were submerging it like a drowned civilization. Now Diana's note acted like an underwater beam, probing through the deluge and revealing a well-remembered contour. Looking down at her scrawl, as the last rays of the sun slanted across the road, I saw another stream, the tiny Teasel, chattering over its stones to Shepherdshey Bridge and its outfall at Nun's Bay. I saw the looming shape of Teasel Wood high above the left bank and the two vain buzzards, soaring and drifting above the larches of the plantation. It was all as vivid as a film flashed on a cinema screen. I had not set eyes on Diana or her handwriting for four years, yet a few words, scrawled on a crumpled piece of paper, had that much power to move me.

The moment it was dark I escaped from the ferry office via a rear window and crossed the fields, joining the stationary queue about half a mile inland. I went slowly down the line, shining my flashlight into the interiors of trucks and cars. Forlorn voices called to me but I ignored them. I was interested in only one refugee and at last I found her, on the grass verge beside a road junction where the road ran between high, sloping vineyards.

She greeted me gaily. We might have met after parting at the foot of Shepherdshey Hill the previous evening. Her car, a large Renault, seemed to be packed with sleeping children and there was a mountain of baggage tied to the roof with fencing wire. She saw me just before I spotted her and called out, so that I flashed my powerful flashlight in her face. She was much thinner than I remembered, and a long, gray dust cloak gave her unexpected height. Her hair was clamped under a colored handkerchief, tied tightly beneath her chin. Her voice had an unfamiliar timbre, acquired through speaking so little English during the past few years.

"Well, Jan!" she laughed. "Lady-in-distress, as usual! You really ought to have ridden up on a big gray and then we might have done an Uncle Tom Cobleigh into Blaye. The numbers would have been right—I've got five more in there for Widdicombe Fair!"

Her gay courage impressed me so much that I forgot to be amazed by the wild improbability of our encounter. In any case, she answered my question before I could frame it:

"It isn't exactly coincidence, Jan," she said. "I put a call through to British H.Q. and then the Bordeaux consul. The Bordeaux Johnny said a certain Lieutenant Leigh was the Big Cheese at the quayside, so I said 'J. Leigh?' and he said 'Yes' and I said 'A husky great chap, with shoulders so wide?' and he said 'How did you know?' and I said 'We're buddies!' and that was that!"

She had me laughing again, just as if there had never been a market crash, a suicide, an atrocious personal betrayal and, to end it all, a bloody great war. She was irrepressible, unique, the final, final word in cool cheek and inspired selfishness! No one but Emerald Diana Gaylorde-Sutton would push blithely through the swirl of foundering nations in order to put through the two long-distance telephone calls about shipping space for herself and five children, and no one but Emerald Diana Gaylorde-Sutton would have received anything but a howl of indignation from the other end of the wire! Even my own presence in that place and at that time did not strike her as incredibly providential but merely a kind of jolly surprise, like the acquisition of an unclaimed seat at a popular first night.

"Diana," I said, at length, "you're not only priceless, you're also the slightest bit tiddly!"

"Yes I am," she admitted, "but I wasn't greedy, I saved a noggin for you—and you look as if you could do with one, poor dear!"

She rummaged in the glove compartment of the car and handed me a half-empty bottle of cognac. I took a long, grateful swig. It was excellent brandy and helped me to match her mood.

"How did you really trace me? There must have been more to it than a couple of phone calls."

I sat down on the broad running board of the car and she seated herself beside me.

"Yes, there was," she said. "I saw this coming months ago so I wrote to Drip to make . . . well . . . certain arrangements. She gave me your Paris address and I called there, soon after you'd gone. The conversation I had with the Bordeaux consul was true. I gave you a build-up there!"

"In the meantime what the devil has happened to your husband?" I asked. "Is he boxed up in the Maginot Line, or somewhere?"

"Yves?" She laughed, unpleasantly I thought. "No, dear, he and his papa have gone over to the Opposition."

"Joined Jerry? *The Nazis?*"

It was the first I had heard of active French collaborators and I was shocked.

"Great possessions, Jan!" she said, shrugging. "They usually incline you to the winning side. After all, I ought to know, shouldn't I?"

It was neither the time nor the place to hold an inquest on her madcap marriage, so I ignored the opening and said, "Do they really think Jerry is going to win?"

"Don't you?" she said, quietly.

Did I? It seemed to me that I had never had a chance to study the possibility. Up until April it had not been a real war at all and ever since I had been acting as a kind of whipper-in to a traveling lunatic asylum.

"He won't beat us, not in the long run!" I growled, and she laughed, more pleasantly this time, and squeezed my arm.

"That's the stuff!" she said. "Death to the Doones!"

"By the way," I went on, "why five children? You haven't been that enterprising, have you?"

"Only the youngest, Yvonne, is mine," she said. "All the others belong to our Spanish gardener. His wife was killed in an air raid and as a militant anti-Fascist he's already on the run. Shall I wake up the kids now?"

"Yes, and you'll have to ditch car and baggage," I said. "We can make it over the fields, but for God's sake keep them quiet or we shall have half the French nation behind us! Give the kids the old Whinmouth Carnival treatment."

She laughed again. "You remember that, Jan?"

"I remember everything! Every damn thing that happened to you and me!" I said grimly.

She opened a rear door and prodded the children. They emerged yawning onto the road. Her own girl, Yvonne, was a pretty little thing, with jet-black hair cut in a straight fringe and huge brown eyes that stared up at me with solemn intensity.

"This is my Jan, Yvonne," said Diana briskly. "You've heard all about Jan, haven't you?"

"*Oui!*" said the child, stifling a yawn and then, after subjecting me to another solemn stare: "*Il est très gros, Mamma!*"

Diana chuckled. "Yes, I told you he was," she said, lightly. Then, "Come on, you others—Philip, Manuel, girls—this English soldier is going to put you on a big boat and take you all across the sea!"

The Spanish children formed a ragged line, Yvonne standing a little to one side, like a tiny N.C.O. on parade. Diana said something in Spanish to a child a year or so older than Yvonne and when the girl asked a question she replied rapidly in the same language.

"She wants to know if she's being taken to her father," said Diana, "but I told her that her father has to stay and beat Franco first."

"Good God!" I exclaimed, for nothing would have surprised me overmuch that night. "Is he coming in against us?"

"It's the same war to her," said Diana, simply.

"Poor little devils," I said, and the sight of the children, standing in pathetic, quasi-military formation as they knuckled the sleep from their eyes, reminded me sharply of all the misery and bewilderment I had witnessed during the last few days. Rage against the Germans rose in my throat like bile. I stooped and lifted the smallest of the Spaniards to my shoulder and Diana lifted Yvonne.

"You others hold hands and Manuel is to keep hold of the back of the soldier's coat," she said. "Don't chatter, any of you, and from now on do exactly as you're told!"

Reflecting that I would sooner have Diana than anyone else in the world to share this sort of adventure, I led the way off the road and over the shoulder of the vineyard. I walked slowly and carefully, keeping my torch to the ground. The little procession straggled along behind, Diana and Yvonne bringing up the rear, and in this way, without exchanging a word we reached the rear of the ferry headquarters.

I left them all outside and climbed through the rear window, to find Sergeant Bowles sound asleep on the floor. He had shuttered the window that opened onto the slipway and everyone outside seemed to be asleep.

"Christ! I was pretty sick when I got back and you weren't here," Bowles said, when I awakened him. "That bloody Dutchman is casting off first light and had the gangplanks removed. Orders came through on the phone an hour ago—we've got to go with them. He's flying the Yank flag, so we stand an even chance against Stukas, but it looks as though we'll ride home on the anchor chains!"

"There are six more outside," I told him, "and we have to get them aboard right now."

"It's dicey," he said. "They're already five deep on deck and the crew have got rifles and orders to shoot last-minute gate-crashers."

"We've got to try," I said. "They'll have to come aboard with us."

"Wait a minute," he said, "I've got an idea!"

He was a useful sergeant, a thirty-year-old Terrier who had been a chemist's assistant in Hereford less than a year ago. "We'd better use the dinghy and pretend we're only crossing over. I put two of the gendarmes to guard it—it's moored under the jetty."

"Okay—take four of the kids and then come back for me," I said. "I've got stuff to burn and I'll need half an hour or so."

We rejoined Diana and I explained what was going to happen. She passed on the instructions in Spanish and the children remained passive. They were adults in everything but size. Without a whimper they followed Sergeant Bowles down the slipway and I climbed back into the office.

"Hand Yvonne through to me and then come in yourself," I told Diana.

She passed the child through and I noted that Yvonne was sound asleep. I laid her down very gently on an old leather sofa and covered her with my greatcoat. Then I helped Diana to climb through, shuttered the window and switched on the flashlight.

"If we show much light we'll have everybody clamoring at the window," I explained. "Did you bring that brandy along?"

She passed the bottle and I swallowed half the amount that remained.

"Keep it," she said. "I can get plenty more, Jan."

"You won't find every mod. con. on that Dutch tramp steamer," I said, gruffly. "They're standing on one another now!"

"I'm not taking passage on your smelly old steamer," she said.

Overwork, lack of sleep and probably the emotional shock of meeting Diana again had combined to make me extremely irritable.

"Now look here, Di!" I shouted. "Let's not have any bloody heroics! This is everybody's last chance and if you don't believe me, take a peep outside."

"I never intended going, Jan," she said, "so please don't try to hector me! All I wanted from you was a chance to get the children away. I know what I'm going to do and my being here is part of the plan."

"You and your slaphappy plans!" I began, but she checked me by raising her hand.

"Listen, Jan, it's as I said, I've known this was coming all winter and that's more than Winston Churchill can say. The minute you've sailed I start back to the Loire to meet Ramond."

"Who the blazes is Ramond?"

"The father of those children, our gardener at Saumur."

"And what do you and Ramond intend doing? Fighting a civil war as a Lewis-gun team?"

"Not yet," she said, seriously, "but we probably shall as soon as the nights draw in, as they used to say back in Devon." She leaned back in the chair and clasped her hands behind her head, regarding me with that judicious mixture of amusement and affection that I had once found beguiling but now made me feel like a frustrated father coping with a willful child.

"Dear Jan," she said, "you haven't changed the tiniest bit! Still glum, truculent, explosive, but still utterly dependable! Just think," she went on, "in less than a week you and Yvonne will be in Heronslea. Will you promise something? Will you sit her up on old Nellie, and take her on the leading rein up the main ride and across Big Oak paddock to Folly Wood? I should like to think of her doing that for the very first time, with you."

I suddenly felt desperate about her. No trace of rancor remained and the hard shell of indifference that I had grown, scale by scale, since the damp afternoon that Drip had forced her way into my life and talked some sense into me, now cracked and fell away, leaving all the scars she had caused, sensitive to her glance, her touch, and the sound of her voice.

"Diana, you just aren't equipped to play cloak-and-dagger games with those bastards, and you've got to come!" I pleaded. "There'll be checkups, rationing, identity cards, God knows what kind of restrictions . . ."

She cut in, quietly but very decisively. "Don't be so insular, Jan. I'm French and I've lived over here a long time now. I know what's going to happen far better than you British amateurs. It's going to be tough but we've had plenty of time to arrange all this. We started getting an organization together months ago. That was why I took a duration lease on Heronslea."

She planned to surprise me and she certainly succeeded.

"You what?" I shouted.

"I did it through our old solicitors and it's all organized and paid for, with my funds transferred to London last January. Drip will explain everything when you see her. She's going to be in charge, you see."

"In charge of what? Damn it, when I was on leave last December they were making Heronslea into a Polish hospital!"

"That's all canceled," she said blandly. "It's going to be a refugee children's home and those Spanish kids and Yvonne will be among the first batch. As time goes on, I expect there'll be lots of others, all kinds of kids, who'll begin to turn up the minute they start bombing London."

"Are you operating through a government department?"

"Oh no," she said, "this is my own idea. It's a kind of dream I had when the war started, but now it isn't a dream any longer because meeting you has given it a kind of shape and solidity. You see, you've got a real stake in it now, because Yvonne is your child, Jan!"

She took advantage of my stupefaction to lift the flash-

374

light and direct the beam on the sofa, where Yvonne was still asleep under my greatcoat.

"That child . . . you mean . . . ?"

She put down the flashlight and reached across the table for my hand. She was smiling but her expression was as gentle and serene as I ever recalled.

"Didn't it ever creep into that great wooden head of yours? Didn't it ever occur to you as a remote possibility? No, of course it didn't! I can see that now. Well, it's true, for all that, and if you take a good look at her you'll see it is. She's got your jawline, your hair, your coloring, and a quite unmistakably Leigh gait. She'll have your obstinacy too, so watch out, or you'll have a problem on your hands!"

"Are you sure—absolutely sure?"

"Good Heavens, of course I am! I can count, can't I?"

"Does . . . does Yves know?" I managed to ask, after a long pause.

She looked just as she used to look when she was on the point of revolting against one of her mother's edicts. "He didn't but he does now," she said, grimly. "I wanted him to have something to think about when his Nazi friends began lecturing him on racial purity, selective breeding and all that claptrap!"

We were silent for a moment while she gave me time to absorb the information.

"When was it, Di?" I asked. "Was it that last time, that time when we quarreled and I hit you in the cottage?"

"No. Jan, before that. It was the day we walked up the Teasel and suddenly got tired of arguing about what we were going to do with your newspaper shares, remember?"

"Are you sure about that?"

"Absolutely, but does it matter that much?"

Somehow it mattered tremendously. It seemed to be of enormous significance that the attractive child asleep under my greatcoat was a living manifestation of Diana, of me, and of Sennacharib. Sitting there, in that shabby, airless little room, with the human wreckage of Armageddon lapping up to the very door, it mattered more than anything that our love, and our need for one another, had

375

combined with the sun and the wind and springtime of Sennacharib to create something tangible, something capable of inheriting the yearning we shared for those few square miles between the estuary of the Whin and the firs of Teasel Wood. For the cottage, where we had healed our quarrel by an act of love, was not Sennacharib. It lay beyond the wood and had never, in my mind's eye, been included in the domain, but the hollow under Teasel Bank, the quiet place where we had lain in each other's arms that sunny April afternoon, that was the very heart of Sennacharib! The conception of a child—our child—in such a place, gave a kind of symmetry to all that had happened between us since she had come riding down the larch wood to vanquish Keeper Croker with a glance. It made sense of so much that had seemed to me, in the years since she had gone, so empty, wasted and sterile.

"Was taking over Heronslea to do with us?" I asked her. "Is that what you meant when you said that running into me like this gave shape to that dream?"

"That's exactly it," she said, joyously, "and I don't even have to explain it, do I? It's as if everything that happened to you and me in Sennacharib was . . . well . . . a kind of prelude, but a prelude so complete in itself that what's happened since doesn't amount to a row of pins! This idea of mine means that the prelude hasn't been wasted, that maybe we were meant to live it not for ourselves but for a whole tribe of children, a representative bunch, a kind of juvenile League of Nations if you like. You and I managed to squeeze every drop of delight out of growing up in Sennacharib and this way we're passing it on as a sort of answer to all the horror that's piling up everywhere right now. Ordinarily it might be years before kids get a chance to romp and ride and laugh in places like Folly Wood, and on heathery places like Foxhayes, but this idea of mine makes it possible for at least a few kids to have that chance before they grow up and things get out of control, the way they finally did with us."

She paused, breathlessly, and I waited. "I suppose this all sounds a bit precious and fanciful, Jan, and I'll agree that it's madly uncharacteristic of me, but I'm not fooling about this! It's the only really imaginative thing I've ever done and I *want* it to happen, I want terribly for it to happen!"

I was going to beg her to abandon her crazy notion of staying behind. I understood, suddenly, why she was making this additional gesture. All her life she had resisted regimentation, and to Diana the very word "Fascism" must have been like a whiff from a sewer. She had been devastated by her husband's cynical espousal of the creed and in her own unpredictable way she was trying to atone for his degradation. In the years ahead many French people were to react in an identical way to their country's collapse, and I could see now that Diana had absorbed a great deal that was Gallic in essence. I don't say that I fully understood all this at the time, but I understand it now as clearly as though she had written it down and asked me to learn it by heart.

She looked at me anxiously. "You're not going to try to force me to go, Jan?"

"No," I said, gloomily, "nobody ever succeeded in forcing you to do anything that you didn't care to do, Di!"

"Then we can say good-by in here," she said.

I crossed to the rear window, where Sergeant Bowles' round, anxious face peered up from the yard.

"They're aboard," he whispered, "and I've seen the mate—high tide is at two and the skipper has given us fifteen minutes dead! Can you make it?"

"Yes," I told him, "I can make it! Take this other child down to the dinghy."

Diana had already lifted Yvonne, still wrapped in my greatcoat, and was now standing at my elbow. I passed the child down to Bowles and told him to give me five minutes to burn papers.

"For God's sake don't hang about," he said. "Never mind all that bloody office bumph, let Jerry have fun with it!"

He disappeared and I closed the shutter.

"Turn on the light, Jan, just for a moment, I must see you properly," she whispered.

I switched on a low-powered bulb and Diana stood

377

quite still, facing me, her eyes roving from dusty flying boots to the crown of my head.

"Darling Jan," she said, softly, and then, with a smile and a swift toss of her head: "You see, there were plenty of Doones left over after all! The whole of Europe is crawling with them."

It would have pleased me to have matched her panache but that would have been like playing horse holder to D'Artagnan. I could only take a long, long look at her, noting the strange and independent life of her chestnut curls under the kerchief, the luster of her skin and the wide, generous curves of her mouth. I held her in my gaze like that for about a minute. I memorized—as if I had need to memorize—everything about her, the strong grace of her neck, the swell of her breasts, the line of her thighs and the eternal promise of her eyes. Then I kissed her, not as a lover, but as a boy might kiss a mature woman who has been teasing him.

"Go now, Jan," she whispered, pushing me from her.

I remember de Maupassant saying somewhere that a deep and lasting love strikes the heart like a thunderbolt and leaves it a source of aching ruin, but my love for Diana was never like that. It was a slow-burning fuse that spluttered on and on throughout every phase of my life, sometimes sparking and sometimes smoldering but always inextinguishable.

I turned quickly and climbed through that wretched little window for the third time that night, and as I went I made an Orpheus-like resolution not to tempt fate by looking back. I broke that resolution and my final glimpse of her was standing framed in the window, her back to the light. It was a somber, theatrical picture, something to carry away, like the glowing memory of a Goya portrait.

I went down the slipway to the waiting dinghy. The broad Gironde, silent under the stars, looked uncannily like the Whin tideway from the summit of Foxhayes.

"Where's that damned woman?" demanded Bowles. "We can't wait . . . we . . ."

"She's not coming," I told him, "so for God's sake push off, *push off!*"

378

He gave me a quick, anxious glance. How was he to know that my life had been enriched by two loves, Sennacharib and Diana, or that one was the complement of the other?

I kept my promise and took Yvonne on the leading rein through the larch wood and across Big Oak paddock to Folly Wood. It was exciting to watch her big, solemn eyes study the parched countryside, comparing it, no doubt, to the green, flat country in which she had grown up. Later that same day, about an hour before sunset, I returned to the tower on foot and climbed the crumbling staircase to our room. Diana had once called it a "thought rendezvous" and I wondered now if its spell would work. It did, but not in the way I had hoped and expected. Standing against the window through which I had seen Diana come trotting out of the wood and across the paddock on Sioux, with Nellie on the leading rein as my first mount, I thought not so much of Diana but of the meaning of the struggle we were engaged upon. By this time even Shepherdshey had joined in, and at this very moment Nat the Sexton was leading his patrol of L.D.V.'s over Nun's Head. They were armed with rook rifles and two small-bore shotguns with which they were ready, if necessary, to do battle with tanks. I had only been on leave forty-eight hours but it was long enough to discover that Whinmouth and Shepherdshey were enjoying the war. No one could blame them for that. This was the first time anything like this had happened around here since Napoleon lay encamped at Boulogne, a hundred and thirty-five years ago. There were blackouts, London evacuees, bustling A.R.P. wardens and all the outward trappings of total war, but to any who had been involved in the rout of France it was all rather like a group of children playing cowboys and Indians. Up there in the tower I wondered how long this mood would last, how long Hitler would suffer it to last, and then I remembered my boast to Diana as we sat side by side on the running board of her crowded Renault outside Bordeaux.

Was it really possible that one day arrogant young Teutons would come jackbooting through the ferns and gorse of Sennacharib? Would high-explosives crash down on huddles of cottages like Shepherdshey? Would the road to Castle Ferry ever boil with panic-stricken women pushing handcarts piled with bedding? Somehow I couldn't imagine such things, and as I rejected the prospect I was able, at least, to think objectively of Diana, lurking about the woods and fields of Anjou in the company of homeless desperadoes like her Spanish gardener, risking her life—for what? Because she believed in democracy so passionately that she was ready to die for it? Or because she would find in this kind of adventure yet another excuse for hanging on to her youth and fending off the maturity that she hated to contemplate? I asked myself the question and told myself the answer. Diana never had and never would care two straws for democracy, but here was the best chance anyone had ever had of thumbing one's nose at strident autocracy. How long would the war last? How long would Diana last? How long would any of us last when Goering's air fleets had finished pounding the ports and airfields and switched to the cities?

It was very still up there in the tower. The Foxhayes blackbirds had gone to bed and the light was fading over Nun's Bay. There was no evening twinkle of lights from Shepherdshey or Whinmouth. People had had a long winter to perfect their blackouts.

Then the silence was broken by a pleasant sound that rose up from the central aisle of the larch plantation and carried right across Big Oak paddock to the edge of Folly Wood. It was the sound of the Spanish children laughing as they romped down the broad ride toward Heronslea, laughing perhaps at having evaded Drip's curfew, for it was past nine o'clock and they should have been in bed.

I listened carefully but the sound was not repeated. That did not seem to matter, for it had been unmistakable. Children were laughing in Sennacharib, so maybe there was something in Diana's crazy dream after all.

I went down the staircase to the wood. It was quite dark among the trees but I walked without stumbling. I did not need a light to find my way across Sennacharib.

The
Unjust Skies

"... Ah, when the ghost begins to quicken
Confusion of the death-bed over, is it sent
Out naked on the roads, as the books say, and stricken
By the injustice of the skies for punishment?"

W. B. Yeats

Reverie

THE ROOM was about ten feet by twelve, with height clearance at the end nearest the door and a single window set deeply into the gable recess. It was remote and airless, looking out over acres of rooftops, the kind of room that poets and artists starve in and threadbare young lawyers might have rented in the decade that saw the storming of the Bastille. I can't swear to the nature of bygone tenants but the room was certainly there in the eighteenth century, for just along the street was the hotel at which Charlotte Corday stayed when she came to Paris to kill Marat and Danton's home was barely five minutes' walk away.

Not that I did any walking myself, if one excludes the steady crunch from the door to the point where I had to crouch almost double, but I did do a great deal of thinking. There was absolutely nothing else to do. One might have said that I was "in retreat," like a visitor at a Trappist Monastery, and I took the opportunity to travel vast distances over devious routes, using years as mileposts. I was my own guide. I knew these routes better than anyone alive, including Diana.

It was difficult to pause every now and again during these random wanderings and reflect that Diana herself was not more than a couple of miles away at this very moment, that she was sleeping, eating and changing her clothes in one of the most luxuriously-appointed houses in the Bois de Boulogne district, in the company of her pale, enigmatic husband, Yves De Royden, the youth whom I had once met wearing pepper-and-salt knickerbockers at the entrance of the Marble Arch cinema, and who was now one of France's wealthiest industrialists and a prop of the Vichy government. I had to keep reminding myself that the tail-end of my reflections was not the final sequence of a dream but was, in fact, as actual as my fifteen-

383

year emotional see-saw with Emerald Diana Gayelorde-Sutton, now Diana de Royden, the spoiled only child of the man who had thought of himself as Squire of Heronslea, in Devon, and had grown bigger and bigger and bigger on a diet of Trusts and Corporations until, like the frog in the fable, he blew up and killed himself. It was even more difficult to remember that I was here in Paris, poised to kidnap Yves de Royden, and that only a few days ago Diana and I had collaborated in the murder of the man whose identity I now used, whose papers were in my wallet and whose actual clothes I wore.

Perhaps this reluctance to explore the very recent past was defensive. Perhaps my mind shied away from the squalid little incident on the Riviera, not because I regretted my part in it but because I had been a shocked witness to Diana's degradation at the hands of the man whose shattered body had been carted away in a trunk. Lying on my bed, waiting and waiting for the summons that would bring us together again, I preferred to bask in older sunlight, the warmer for being bottled like the memories of summers in our youth.

The sun seemed to shine more often then. It had been shining that October day, the afternoon of my fifteenth birthday, when I had first entered the lonely, purple-wooded estate that Diana and I (but no one else) came to know as "Sennacharib" because the blaze of gorse against the purple heather had recalled Byron's poem beginning:

"The Assyrian came down like a wolf on the fold
And his cohorts were gleaming with purple and gold . . ."

It was that same afternoon that I met Diana as she rode out of the woods to rescue me from the grip of one of her father's keepers and afterwards we had gone back to Heronslea to tea and Drip, her timid governess who became my friend and champion, played "The Lass of Richmond Hill" and "Allan Water" on her musical box.

After that there had been nothing and no one in my life but Sennacharib and Diana. It became essential that I should possess both and to do so I set to work with a single-

384

mindedness very rare in a fifteen-year-old odd-job boy, who earned five shillings a week in his uncle's broken-down second-hand furniture mart.

The really astonishing thing is I almost succeeded, would have succeeded had it not been for Diana herself. All the years of our adolescence we played hide-and-seek with her parents and evaded the course they had mapped for her, fashionable schools, trips abroad, presentation at Court, the social round, a suitable marriage. Once we ran away to Nun's Island in the bay and lived castaways' life for three days and when we were caught she was sent away to France and we did not meet again until a few days before her eighteenth birthday. I was a guest at that spectacular coming-of-age party, or rather a stowaway, smuggled into the house and later into her bed when all "the suitable young men" were driving off in their Austins and Lagondas. After that I was naïve enough to think of myself as her master but it was not so; she had only used me, as always, as the rope-ladder down the battlements, or the key to experience, or the banner of the undefeated. Her virginity had been reckoned in the casualty list.

The discoloration of the distemper on the walls of my hideout made curious patterns. Forests, moors, ruined castles and winding streams and here and there a grotesque caricature of a rustic face, like the face of my Uncle Reuben, editor of the weekly newspaper that I later came to own.

For a few moments I dismissed Diana and thought of Whinmouth, its steep, cobbled streets and untidy quay, its half-urbanised countryfolk and the stippled sky patterns over the estuary. It was here, as editor of *The Whinmouth & District Times*, that I had waited for Diana's return. Waited and waited, for more than two years. When she came I had had to fetch her and she was only the nervous ghost of the girl who had ridden with me into the wind across Foxhayes Common, or swum alongside me in Nun's Cove, for she had become caught up with the Crazy Set in London and had killed a motor-cyclist and his pregnant wife in a car crash. To this day nobody but me knew that she had been the driver of the killer car. Everyone else blamed the dead drunk they had fished out from under her.

It had taken me a long time to vanquish the guilt that tormented her but in the end my obstinacy won another round and there was a brief interval when she was the real Diana again. It was during that time that Yvonne, our child, was conceived in Sennacharib but I seldom had any luck, not with Diana, not with anyone or anything that mattered. Within a few weeks her father's fortune crashed and she and her mother were penniless. This should have strengthened my suit but the reverse was true. Diana slipped away again, and I began my long sulk in the cottage on Teasel Edge, to be rescued at last by Drip, her governess, and steered back to the broader current of life. Diana had opted for comfort and married Yves de Royden, the son of the French tyre magnate, and it was not until the exodus from France in 1940 that she sought me out once more and told me about Yvonne.

In the long summer evenings, when everyday noises in the street had been reduced to a murmur. I could hear the Nazi military traffic passing down the street. The drivers pushed their vehicles along with Teutonic arrogance, slamming the gears and snarling the horns. The cacophony reminded me of the wild panic at the Bordeaux ferry, where Diana caught up with me again and gave me our child and four other strays to convey to England on one of the last boats out of the Gironde.

It was something more than an evacuation on her part. She had got it into her head that somebody should make a gesture on behalf of the future and made me promise to use Heronslea, which she had somehow re-acquired with her husband's money, as a kind of haven for children, a place where they might hope to collect the dividends of our own youth, of hers and mine, earned in the days when Hitler was a joke.

And the odd thing was that this extravagant action of hers became a reality for now Heronslea was indeed a home for children uprooted by the war and it was here

386

that I had returned often during the last three years and watched Yvonne and the homeless Spanish children, and a rag-tag and bobtail of Dutch and French and Cockney kids romp in the coverts under the mild eye of Drip, the matron. It was here I had returned not so long ago with yet another secret and from here that I had set out on the curious journey that had led me, at last, to reunion with Diana, to cold-blooded murder in a Riviera villa and to this intolerably stuffy little room where the setting sun made memory patterns on the flaking distemper.

It had been a long, hard haul and homecoming seemed as far away as ever.

Chapter One

I NEVER pretended that I was in love with Alison, not even to myself. The strongest feeling I ever had for her was that half-jocular, half-affectionate need that a man sometimes has for a pretty spaniel bitch who follows him about and gets under his feet, waiting to be patted and teased at odd moments when the pressure lifts. She was aware of this and I don't think she resented it much. Our marriage had been a by-product of the blitz, a kind of short-cut blasted from old habits and necessities by the bombs. It had its advantages and one or two moments of enchantment but that was about all. If we brought one another no ecstasies we achieved something not often achieved by man and wife. We exchanged the sixpences of daily currency, a few jokes shared, an unexacting companionship and often a mutual if limited physical satisfaction. The world was in ruins anyway. It was not a time to go digging under the rainbow.

The poverty of our relationship did not lessen my sense of desolation when I looked down at her in death, lying still and small among the other victims of the hit-and-run raid. If I ever loved her at all, it was then. The fussy tidiness of her surroundings was an affront to decency and one had the sensation of something close to obscenity as nurses and white-jacketed porters moved to and fro beside this pitiful sacrifice, wondering, perhaps, when their spell of duty would end and whether they could get changed in time for the matinée at the Odéon.

I stood there looking down at the calm face and wondering at the prettiness of her dark hair until one of the porters touched me on the arm and said it was time to go. I went down the long, bustling corridors and out into the winter sunshine and the Flight-Sergeant was waiting with the jeep. I got in and he avoided my eye, concentrating on traffic problems made worse by a labyrinth of hosepipe and stationary fire-engines but as we entered the undamaged section of the town he pulled into the curb and said:

"There was a message for you from Group. Will you be going back to camp right away or staying here for . . . the time being?"

He had been going to say "funeral" but stopped himself in time.

I forced myself out of a reverie that was leading me down the months and years to the time when I had first met Alison, then lost track of her, then found her again in a NAAFI queue soon after Dunkirk. I was glad he checked my thoughts because I knew they would lead to another dead-end where I would stop and begin bullying myself for the injustice I had done her by marrying her.

"What was the message about?"

"Couldn't say but the Winco sounded edgy. Would it be about your remustering air-crew?"

"No," I told him, "I failed the medical two days ago."

"You ought to be cock-a-hoop over that!" he said.

"I'm not, especially now. Would you be? If you'd just seen your wife killed by the bastards?"

He considered this. "I'm not married," he said, at length, "but if I was, or if it had been my kid-brother or my best pal or someone like that, I don't think I'd let it panic me into bloody heroics! I've had all that, it's a racket from beginning to end. One in ten are coping with Hitler and the other nine are on the mike or making dough.

Sit tight and begin again when it's over. That's my advice, but then, I'm a regular, I only came in out of the cold!"

I was only half-listening to him. My mind had switched to the summons from Group. It would serve as an anchor before I was washed back into a sea of bitterness. It was not simply the death of Alison but the entire, stupid pointlessness of life, the everlasting menace of black-outs and syrens and pincer-movements and postings and rationing and untidiness that were being heaped on the plates of youth; it was a world that had promised so much and turned out to be a stinking refuse-yard in a corner of a dirty city, a place where all nervous energy was drained away searching for something worth having among a shifting mountain of sodden newspapers, rusty tins and stained, stopperless bottles.

I caught the Flight-Sergeant looking at me sideways. He was only an amateur cynic and his kindness popped through the conventional crust of the regular.

"You need a drink," he said, "you need one damn bad, son!"

We had several drinks and it helped. When I went in to see the Winco I was sufficiently clear-headed to remember that he had lost his only son at Narvik and also that nobody had any time for a bore walking around with a chip on the shoulder. People are not interested in your griefs and disappointments although the majority pretend to be, at least for an hour or so. After that they make excuses and slip away, to the bar around the corner or to the lavatory if their brush-off technique is rusty. I remembered this just in time and sidestepped his condolences.

"Sorry about the air-crew," he said, "but something will turn up. Maybe it already has——take a look!"

He handed me the signal from Group. The message quoted my name, rank and number and ordered me to report to H.Q. immediately for an interview. It didn't say what the interview was about so I looked at the Winco for a clue.

"Soon as I heard about your wife and the hit-and-run I phoned Groupy Stevens," he said. "You don't have to go over now, I expect you've plenty to see to!"

No, I told him, I should like to go now and see what they had in mind. Underneath the weight of wretchedness concerning Alison I could still feel the smart of my failure to pass the air-crew test because of a defect in one eye. It seemed such a damned silly reason for failing and made nonsense, of all the trouble to which I had gone to transfer to the R.A.F. from the Gunners after returning from France, in June, 1940. Now I could see no prospect of getting into the real war and was already beginning to regret the transfer. My old battery was in North Africa and if I hadn't been childishly impatient I should have been with them and thousands of miles from all this dreariness. I said:

"Haven't you got a clue why they want me, sir?"

"My guess is some kind of Intelligence job," he said. "Groupy Stevens is mixed up in that, or was. It's probably interpreting. You speak fluent French don't you? By the way, you never lived in France did you? How come you speak it so well? I never got beyond 'Ou est la plume de ma tante?' Could never get my tongue round those bloody 'rrrrs!"

I guessed from this speech that he had information he was holding back and also that he had been looking into my service documents. I let it pass, however, for he was a cagey old bird.

"I learned French to show off to a girl," I told him. His eyebrows went up and he grinned. "I always heard you could learn it better in bed," he said. "Was it a French girl?"

"No, about as English as they come!"

"Was she impressed? Was it worth the effort?"

"Not really, it was all part of an act, a hell of a long act in a play that was a terrible flop!"

I could see that his curiosity was aroused but I cut the interview short by asking for my railway warrant. He said I could borrow the jeep I had used to go down to the hospital so I went up to the mess, tried and failed to eat a spam sandwich and drove off across the Downs to Group H.Q.

There was a good deal of phoning at the Guard Room.

I might have been an escaped Luftwaffe officer trying to hijack a Spitfire but at last they signed me in and told me to report to Group-Captain Stevens. The Winco was right, Stevens was acting as Intelligence Officer and was enjoying it enormously. There was an air of small-town Thespian rehearsal about him and his office, as though at any moment a man wearing a deerstalker would sidle in, address him as "X-54" and write in code on the blackboard. I was so struck by this that I hardly noticed an officer wearing Free French flashes on his battledress who was sitting over by the window and trying to look as if he was there by chance.

"This officer is from General De Gaulle's H.Q. He's er . . . closely involved," said the Group-Captain, looking more apologetic than any Group-Captain should look in the presence of an Acting-Pilot Officer.

The French officer made a sharp sitting bow and then stared out of the window. I had time to get a good look at him. He was about thirty, slim and good-looking, with regular features, darkish hair and cheek bones that were a shade too prominent. He had shapely hands and long, thin legs that he held pressed closely together, as though he was finding it difficult to maintain his passive role.

"Sit down, make yourself comfortable," said Stevens affably and I had the impression that he too was unsure of himself. I was glad then that I had presented myself for interview. The extreme novelty of the situation took my mind off Alison.

The Group-Captain glanced at some papers and I recognised my service record and medical history folder.

"I understand you speak fluent French, Leigh," he began. "Have you ever lived in France?"

"No sir," I told him, "I studied it for a hobby when I was a boy and then spent several holidays there."

"You were over again with the B.E.F. and came out via Bordeaux?"

I told him this was so and again got the impression that he would have preferred to have interviewed me privately but the French officer sat on, hands on knees, perfectly still and somehow critical.

"Just before you left Bordeaux, in June, 1940, an Englishwoman put some children in your care and you brought them to England with you?"

It was my turn to feel uneasy and I wondered if this was the beginning of a come-back. A man in uniform always thinks of a come-back first. It never occurs to him that an investigation involving his private life can mean anything but trouble. I decided to counter-attack. I wasn't in the mood to be cross-examined, not even by a Group-Captain.

"That is so, sir, and one of the children was mine. The woman who brought her to me was her mother!"

I expected both the Group-Captain and the French officer to react to this but neither did and I realised then that my screening had been a thorough one. They knew about Yvonne and they knew about Diana and me and that was why I was here.

We stopped fencing and the air of restraint left the Group-Captain but it remained with the Frenchman. Stevens looked at the papers again.

"This woman was British, the wife of a Frenchman," he said, almost as though he was confiding in me.

"Her married name is de Royden," I told him, "and her husband is, or was, mixed up with Laval and the French Fascists. Before Madame de Royden married she was called Gayelorde-Sutton, Emerald Diana Gayelorde-Sutton. Her father was the well-known financier who committed suicide a year or so before the war!"

Suddenly the Frenchman chipped in, addressing me in French, not the carefully articulated French that a polite Frenchman uses when he addresses an Englishman but French that whipped across the room like short bursts of a machine gun.

"You were Madame de Royden's lover before her marriage!"

It was not exactly an accusation but it was couched like one and because of this it annoyed me. I couldn't see that it was any of his business.

"We were to be married shortly before her father died and she eloped to France!" I said, controlling my temper. Then, to Stevens: "With respect sir, I think I ought to

392

know what kind of assignment this is before I go into my civilian history. There's no reason why I should want to hold anything back and it's all in the statement I made the day I disembarked at Plymouth in July, '40. I was given to understand that I was volunteering for a straightforward Intelligence posting."

"That's true," said Stevens, easily, "but I hadn't even seen your application before Captain de Royden showed up and when I rang your Wing-Commander he told me about your losing your wife in the hit-and-run." He smiled and looked like an amiable uncle for a moment. "Listen, Leigh, suppose we stop here and start up again when you've had time to cope with your private affairs? You've just had a bloody awful shock."

Before the Frenchman could protest I told him the Wing-Commander had made this offer before I came over to Group H.Q. but I preferred to go through with the interview now that it had begun.

"Very well," said Stevens, "maybe you'd better take it from here, de Royden!"

I must have been numb with shock or the name would have registered the first time he used it. As it was, and notwithstanding the line of questioning, it was not until then that I connected the Frenchman with Diana. I turned my head and took a good look at him, searching my memory for details of Yves de Royden's features and then remembering that I had absolutely no recollection of what Diana's husband looked like. It was fifteen years since I had met him, for a few moments only, in the foyer of a cinema and he could not have been more than seventeen at the time. The Frenchman met my surprised stare with fortitude and the mutual scrutiny ended in a draw.

"We speak in French please," he said, crisply. "First it is necessary that I know how fluent you are. I came here to recruit for the De Gaullist group in the Paris sector. It is fair that you should know at once that I am a cousin of Madame de Royden by marriage. de Royden himself is now working for the Germans, not merely the Vichy French. I also feel it fair to tell you that I have all the necessary information regarding your association with Diana

393

de Royden before and since the war, and that I obtained most of it from Madame herself!"

"You saw her recently?"

"But of course. She is working for us. She returned to her husband shortly after the Occupation!"

I was unable to conceal my surprise but he was a very well-bred man and lowered his glance to give me a moment to recover. I needed that moment badly. It was almost two years since I had parted from Diana at the Bordeaux ferry during the chaotic collapse of France, and ever since I had carried a mental picture of a hunted, harried creature, moving about Occupied Territory by stealth in the company of fugitives, carrying out desperate little acts of sabotage and living, if indeed she was still alive, just outside the range of a firing-squad. It was the kind of picture that fitted all I knew of the wild, unpredictable creature with whom I had romped and ridden in Devon woods during the halcyon period when we were growing up together at Heronslea. It was the kind of life that would satisfy her insatiable appetite for excitement and adventure. The first present I had ever given Diana had been a copy of *Lorna Doone* and one of the last things she had said to me, after telling me that Yvonne was our child, had been: "There were plenty of Doones left after all, Jan! The whole of Europe is crawling with them!"

Now that picture was seen to be as false and as fatuous as so many other pictures of Diana that had enslaved my imagination since the day of my fifteenth birthday, when she had ridden out of the woods to rescue me from one of her father's keepers.

"She is reconciled to her husband?" I asked at length, and Stevens cocked an eye as though the interview was now beginning to interest him in an unofficial capacity.

The Frenchman lifted one shoulder. "How else could she be of any use to us? Before she was playing games. At that time, Paris was full of amateurs!"

The way he said this, his voice grating with contempt, deepened the impression of steely, cold-blooded efficiency he had already conveyed. I saw that I had a lot to learn about resistance fighters.

394

I said: "The reconciliation must have been difficult M'sieur. Diana told me that when her husband joined the Quislings she told him that Yvonne was not his child. He must be a very tolerant man to overlook a thing like that."

de Royden lifted the other shoulder, as though shrugging off another trifle.

"She did not tell him the child was yours," he said. "My cousin does not know of your existence. That much I have been able to check. Otherwise I should not have bothered to trace you!"

Stevens cleared his throat, as though he was desperately anxious to be excused but the Frenchman ignored him. It was rather comforting to see a Group-Captain treated with so little respect.

"Madame de Royden has been reconciled to her husband for more than a year," he went on. "It has been useful having her there living with him but now we have run into difficulties." He paused a moment, wondering how to phrase the next sentence. Finally he continued, "It is because of those difficulties that I came to England to find you, Pilot-Officer Leigh!"

He flushed slightly as he said this and I sensed that his presence here was in some way an affront to his dignity and professionalism.

"Diana sent you to me?"

"We will come to that. We *may* come to it!" He corrected and here Stevens chipped in again, rather to the Frenchman's annoyance.

"The fact is, Leigh, you failed your medical for air-crew and then volunteered for Intelligence. Are you at all interested in Special Operations? This wouldn't be our own S.O.E., it would be General De Gaulle's outfit!" He had been on the point of saying "mob", but the eyes of the Frenchman stopped him.

"I hadn't thought about it," I said truthfully, "but now that I do, I don't think I'm ideal material for that kind of job. I can't see myself as a cloak and dagger man, sir!"

The Group-Captain turned to de Royden.

"How is his French?" he demanded, and when the

Frenchman replied: "Good; unexpectedly so!" he grunted, as though disappointed by the reply.

I was curious about the De Gaullist's rancour. Now that I had spotted it, his disapproval of my proposed enrolment was apparent in every word he uttered.

"How do *you* feel about it, Captain?" I asked him.

He seemed to look at me for the first time. His keen, ice-blue eyes travelled from the top of my head to my shoes and back again. Then, pursing his lips slightly, he said:

"Not ideal, as you say. You are too tall for one thing, but you could pass as a French Canadian, from Montreal possibly, and you might resist torture for the requisite four hours providing your convictions were at stake. You would find it hard, however, to shake a man's hand, bring your knee into his groin and then stick a knife in him. I doubt if training could achieve it!"

"I doubt it as much as you, Captain!" I said, but against the rising tide of my dislike of the man I could not help being struck by his obvious efficiency. The Englishwoman from whom I had learned French was the wife of a professor from Montreal.

"This 'ironing out of difficulties' you mentioned, would it entail cold-blooded murder?"

"It might. Who knows?"

"Of Yves de Royden?"

The De Gaullist raised both shoulders and composed his features into an expression of boredom.

Group-Captain Stevens had had enough. He was not playing M.I.5, any more, he was miles out of his depth. I could see that he not only shared my dislike of the Captain but extended it to all Continentals, exclusive of "good" Germans.

"Why can't I give the man the letter and be done with it?" he said, grumpily.

The Frenchman lifted his hands. It was a gesture of renunciation. Stevens flushed and poked around his wire tray until he found a single sheet of foolscap folded in three. He opened it and glanced at it like a tired schoolmaster marking a fourth-form essay. Then, with a faint sigh, he passed it across the desk to me. I recognised Diana's handwriting.

How much control do we have over our loyalties? A single glance at the sailing, fishing-line loop in the "J" of "Jan Dear" blotted out the present, effaced Stevens and the Frenchman and all but banished the ache of Alison's death. It not only conjured up my own youth but the youth of the entire world, when life was as full of promise as an unwrapped Easter Egg and I used to lie in wait for the postman as he pottered along Whinmouth Quay and stood fumbling outside the door of my Uncle Luke's second-hand furniture mart with letters from Diana. They always arrived in longish blue envelopes, edged with a thin line of gilt and they were scented, not with perfume but the curiously musty smell of school that always seemed to me to combine the smells of chalk-dust, blotting paper and fine summer dust. The first glimpse of the greeting choked me, and as I struggled to master my emotion I heard the voice of the unpredictable French officer addressing me across the years:

"Perhaps, m'sieur, you would prefer to read it in private. Important decisions should be made in private, preferably in the open!"

I was immensely grateful to him and got up and left them, turning my head away as I passed into the narrow corridor and down the wooden steps on to the tarmac. Far across the field a Wellington was warming up and an airman, driving his petrol-wagon like a chariot, was whistling "Pass the Ammunition". I went out of the wind and sat down on a concrete armadillo, the single sheet of paper fluttering in my hand.

"Jan Dear," it ran, "Raoul will be giving you this. Don't be put off by Raoul. He's our sort but something happened to him when Yves and the rest of the family went over to the Doones. He's terrifyingly professional and one can't really expect him to understand why I need you and must have you if I'm to do what they want me to do. So I told him about 'us' and Sennacharib, I had to if I was to begin to convince him and in a way I think I did. Anyway he gave in and I don't think you'll disappoint him. You always came before and I know you'll come again. I don't deserve this loyalty but Sennacharib does and, after all, that's what the war is about, isn't it, Jan? Isn't it, Jan, dear? My love to you, Jan, as always, the same love that has such long roots. Diana."

That was all, and through it ran a note that was as familiar to me as the English landscape and the air I breathed. Yet there was present an unfamiliar strain, a kind of hysteria that had no place in Diana. I had not expected anything specific from her. In all her life she had never paused long enough to set down a logical sequence of thoughts, the way a woman might when making a shopping-list. There was no mention of our child and no hint presupposing I might, at long last, have formed a new attachment. The sheer, animal wildness in the woman had always rushed down on me like this and swept me along like an old leaf in a gale. Always the force of her personality had been violent enough to sweep me along until it spent itself and it disappeared over the hill, leaving me breathless, bewildered and alone once more. I knew as I read this deliberate mixture of nostalgic appeal and demented demand that the same thing would happen again, that if I allowed myself to be caught up in this whirlwind I would be blown half across a continent at war and then rolled into some desolate corner and forgotten, perhaps for weeks or months, but more probably for years. Yet this time there was a difference. The appeal, direct as it was, was not aimed at the heart directly but fired from behind a smokescreen of patriotism and I sensed that it was false patriotism because Diana had never cared two straws about democracy, or any kind of freedom but the freedoms she demanded for herself. "That's what the war is about, isn't it, Jan?" was hypocrisy. It was not an appeal to a fellow-champion of individual liberty but Diana's way of asking me to extricate her from a new kind of emotional maze into which she had wandered. Sennacharib, the symbol of our freedom, was her bait.

I read the letter again and again, looking and hoping for a more honest plea, for an interpretation that might have helped to convince me that two years in Occupied Europe had matured or disciplined her but there was no evidence of this. It was not the letter of a woman faced with a tragic crisis calling on her mate but the demand of a venturesome spirit who has dared just too much and squeals for a lifeline. If the first reading amazed me, the second reading amused me, for the light it shed upon Captain de Royden's frigidity. I could imagine Diana pouring out her tale to this competent, hardbitten man. I could almost hear her saying: "But, Raoul, dear, I'll be perfectly reliable if you get Jan! Jan and I always did everything together! Jan's wonderful! Get Jan and we'll work as a team!" and I could visualise de Royden's incredulity that a woman caught up in his kind of business could remain so naïve and still persuade herself that her fight against the Nazi war was a game of hide-and-seek in Heronslea woods on a summer's afternoon. Then, as I thought this, I realised that to Diana this was exactly what it was and that he, de Royden, knew this but accepted it, like all the other risks he faced. In the old days Diana's delight had been to tilt at authority, any sort of authority, a day-by-day campaign to out-wit schoolmistresses, governesses, parents, bye-laws and Acts of Parliament, and it was from this challenge that she drew her vitality. She must have welcomed the war as the greatest challenge of the century. As I thought about this, I understood de Royden's shrugging dismissal of her activities . . . "Paris was full of amateurs at that time," and it seemed to me that what had probably happened was this; by early 1941, France had absorbed the shock of its defeat and real resistance fighters like Raoul de Royden had begun to emerge, discarding amateurs and forming a hard core of partisans dedicated to the task of salvaging French honour. Diana was useful and had easy access to the enemy's citadel, so Raoul and his colleagues had enrolled her and flattered themselves, poor fools, that they would make something of her, that she could be taught to submerge her individualism in the movement, the cause, the crusade. Then, as always with Diana's mentors, they had broken their teeth on her but rather than give up they had listened when she cried out for me. They had humoured her, fancying perhaps that they knew all there was to know about a spoiled, wayward girl who had been given her own way in every single respect since she was a rich man's child at Heronslea. Yet how much did they really know of her? How much compared with me, who had served so brutal an apprenticeship?

I folded the note and went back into headquarters. When I re-entered the office Raoul de Royden was standing by the window, his slender hands clasped behind his back. The Group-Captain, for want of something better to do, was fiddling about with a station timetable spread out on his desk. They both looked at me expectantly when I handed de Royden the letter. It was the only letter I had ever received from Diana that I had let out of my possession.

"No dice!" I said and was not much surprised by de Royden's look of relief.

Group-Captain Stevens relaxed, becoming his old bumbling self in an instant. It was clear that he had regarded the entire episode as blush-making nonsense, dredged from the pages of a second-rate thriller. This was not the British way of making war. In mind and temperament he was only one 'page on from the charge of lancers at Omdurman and the thin red line at the Alma and Waterloo.

"I can't say I blame you, Leigh," he said, heartily. "Dammit, if you happen to have the stomach for that kind of thing we've got our own circus, haven't we? I daresay Buckmaster might employ you!"

He shook hands and acknowledged the Frenchman's half-salute with a nod. Clearly he wanted to be rid of us both.

"I'll keep my eyes open, Leigh," he said by way of dismissal. "Command ought to find some use for you. Never heard a fellow rattle off French like you do!" He said it as though the ability to converse in a foreign language was something slightly shameful, like a talent for seducing married women.

de Royden and I went out on to the tarmac and across to his jeep parked outside the mess. When we were on the point of parting he said, stiffly: "Any message?"

I pondered, wondering if I was under an obligation to explain the reasons why I had rejected his invitation. There were a number of contributory reasons of which the subtle influence of Alison, now beginning to make itself felt, was one, but the basic reason had nothing to do with Alison or with the process of growing up after years of emotional stalemate. It had instead to do with a sense of justice involving her husband, Yves de Royden, for I realised that in a sense Diana had tried to serve him as she had served me, ruthlessly and with a callousness that was almost obscene. Well knowing what acceptance might involve she had not hesitated to invite me on to a stage where I would be ordered to kill him, and kill him treacherously. I had too much sympathy for him to want to kill him, too much indeed to bear him any malice, or regard him as an enemy. For a moment I considered trying to explain this to de Royden, then I realised that he must know it without my telling him.

"No, Captain," I said, saluting him, "no message. Just 'no dice'!"

He started the jeep and roared away towards the main gate and I went looking for the padre. I had to make arrangements for Alison's funeral.

Chapter Two

THE COASTAL town near the camp might have possessed a limited charm in Dickens' time but it had very little now. It was a marriage between a bungalow town of the "twenties" and a mid-Victorian Spa. Painted shanties and red-brick villas grew like a pink and green rash along the battered esplanade and most of their pre-war occupants had gone elsewhere. Those who remained flitted about the rusting coastal defences and in and around the bomb sites as though the war had no more to do with them than the scare that had prompted the building of the half-ruined

401

Martello tower on the foreland. It was not the kind of town one would wish to remember and when I saw its cemetery, the tidiest area for miles around, I changed my mind about using it. I thought of taking Alison back to Whinmouth and burying her on the western edge of Sennacharib but I soon dismissed the idea. She had never visited Devon and the shadow of Diana and Sennacharib had come between her and fulfilment. I settled for a tiny churchyard behind the Downs, where the chalk road crossed the valley, climbed the next fold and lost itself in birchwoods.

My experiences as a small-town reporter had prejudiced me against public funerals. Alison had served in the A.T.S. and the local Commandant rang my camp and suggested a quasi-military funeral. She seemed to think I ought to welcome the idea and was hurt when I turned her down. In the end I went out there alone and the service at the graveside was conducted by the local rector, attended by his sexton.

It was a mild, windless day and up here the countryside looked battered but friendly. The sky was clear over the chalk hills and the woods were blue black on the horizon. Around us was a kind of patient emptiness that suited the occasion.

When it was over the rector and the sexton went home and I entered the little church to sit for a while. It was a fourteenth-century building, not much restored, and I passed down the central aisle and sat in a front pew, trying to think about Alison a little. I found I was unable to do this. My eye kept roving to the scroll-work on the reredos screen and comparing it with the reredos carved by Drake's seamen in the Shepherdshey parish church at home. I found myself wondering what kind of men would sail round the world and come home reinforced in their belief in Providence and if any such men existed today. I thought then of Raoul de Royden with his aura of vicious despair and wondered if his religious beliefs had survived the two years of reprisal and counter-reprisal in the Underground Movement, or if he had any religious beliefs to begin with. I thought I ought to feel sad and desperately lonely but I didn't, just depressed and indecisive. While I was musing, I heard, almost without hearing, a single foot-fall on the stone slabs at the far end of the church and then the faint protest of a pew bench as somebody sat on it. The interruption braced me and enabled me to focus my mind on Alison again and I went searching back over our brief period together, looking and looking for a memory that could hold its own with my first love. There was none but I decided that this was neither my fault nor Alison's. How the hell could two people build a relationship when each was chivvied about from camp to camp, their minds occupied by scores of minor irritations, food shortages, cigarette shortages, black-out precautions, button-cleaning, syrens and overdue trains? Since September, '39, the whole vista of private life seemed to have acquired a grey, prison-like aspect. Colours had faded and such laughter as remained had taken refuge in the clichés of the parade ground.

I sat on, watching my peace of mind drift over the horizon and I began to wonder whether I was developing into the kind of man who makes a kind of hoard of his troubles and disappointments. Self-pity is like alcohol, creating its own appetite and the loss of Alison, following the cul-de-sac traipse of my courtship of Diana, began to seem inevitable, a thread of personal destiny that was never meant to lead anywhere but into a desert. A discreet cough remind ed me that I was not alone. I got up and walked down the aisle towards the porch. When I was within a few steps of the door I saw a woman in a coloured headscarf rise from the rearmost pew and step forward to intercept me. The woman was Diana.

I don't know why I wasn't astounded. I should have been, for nothing whatever in the conversation I had had with de Royden had led me to suppose that Diana had ac-companied him to England. He had spoken of her as if she was still living with her husband in Paris, or on one of their country places in the south-west. I knew enough of the Underground Movements in Europe to be aware of the coming and going of prominent agents, but if I had thought about it at all I should have dismissed her journey here as an impossibility. In wartime all civilians, even civilians linked with partisans, do not come and go between enemy countries like tourists. They stay put, whether they like it or not, and even women as egocentric as Diana are subject to restrictions imposed upon all conquered peoples. Yet, as I say, I was not very surprised and perhaps this was because, for some time now, I had been living in a bad dream where the improbable is the norm. She advanced, smiling a little tremulously and tilted her chin. The gesture had in it a faintest suggestion of defiance and it was this rather than anything else about her that accomplished recognition.

'Hallo, Jan," she said, very quietly.

Outwardly she was changed far more than I could have imagined. I knew her age to the day. She was four months short of twenty-nine and when I had last seen her, close on two years ago, she had looked as taut and fit as when she rode across Heronslea paddocks on her spirited gelding, Sioux. Now there was a curious heaviness about her that slowed her down and hinted at the approach of middle-age. Maturity, a curiously accelerated maturity, showed clearly in her face. Her blue eyes, once so bold and impudent, were veiled and uncertain, as though they had forgotten how to chase the laughter that had always lurked at the corners of her wide mouth. There was no laughter there now although the mouth had not grown up with the rest of her features but retained its girlishness, childishness almost, yet seemed pathetically anxious to adapt itself to the rest of the features. Her hair was unchanged too, the same thick, heavy curls that always seemed to possess an individual life of their own and to wage cheerful guerilla war against any covering Diana clamped on her head. Now they were pushing against the folds of the scarf and spilling down behind the ears and a shaft of sunlight crossing the church porch lingered for a moment about her shoulders so that I saw the lustre that had impressed me the first moment I set eyes on her in Heronslea larchwood.

I looked at her for a long moment without speaking and the peace I had tried so hard to find settled on her like a butterfly, just out of reach. The hate and frustration and boredom and desolation ebbed from me and I knew at once that nothing had changed and that nothing essential ever would change.

She said, touching my hand: "Did you come alone, Jan? Is nobody here but you?"

"Just the parson," I said and the huskiness of my voice surprised me.

"He's gone," she said, "he drove off as I came in," then: "Do you want to stay here or is there somewhere else we could go?"

"How did you get out here?"

"By bus. There's another back at five."

"I've got a jeep," I said. "We can go through the wood and up to the Old Ring. Do you know this area?"

"No," she said, "I've never been here before."

That was all we said at that time. It was like a pair of studiously polite strangers meeting in a park. Nobody overhearing us would have imagined that we had grown up together, lain in one another's arms, conceived a child now nearly eight years old, or been separated by a world at war. And nobody would have imagined that I had just buried my wife.

We went out into the churchyard and down to my jeep at the lychgate. A blackbird piped in the yew clump and across the valley an engine fussed over its trucks. Apart from these two distinct and isolated sounds the landscape was silent and empty of life.

A doubt seemed to strike her as she opened the door of the jeep and began to climb in.

"You don't mind, Jan? You wouldn't rather be by yourself? If you would, I . . ."

"Damn it, get in!" I snapped, and then, relenting. "I'm glad you're here, Di," and meant it from the bottom of my heart.

We drove out across the valley and climbed the hill through the woods to a plateau, fringed with firs. It was, I imagine, a favourite summer picnic spot in peacetime, but there was nobody here at this time of year. We could see

405

the camp and the sprawling town spewed along the coastal strip and beyond it the blue-grey line of the Channel. I knew somehow that she was comparing it with the view from Foxhayes over Nun's Head and also that she was homesick and desperately unsure of herself. I think she had relied upon surprise to win a headstart and when she found me shockproof she was at a loss how to begin.

"How the hell did you get over here?" I asked her presently.

"What does it matter?"

"It does matter. We've got to begin somewhere so let's begin there!"

"It wasn't all that difficult," she said, deliberately. "I refused to put anything on paper and they badly needed a progress report on Yves' activities at the factory and I was the only one who could supply it so I blackmailed Raoul and he had to arrange it. It would have been impossible last year but we've got secret landing grounds now. I came over in a Lysander and I'm going back in one!"

She had found and used her sally-port.

"You're going *back* in one!" It hadn't occurred to me that she was here temporarily, that she would run the frightful risks of a return journey to accomplish her crazy plan of enlisting me in the Resistance.

She looked at me with genuine surprise. "Well, of course I'm going back! I've got to go back, whether you come or not!" Then, a little pompously: "After all, this isn't a private war, Jan!"

"You're trying damned hard to make it one!" I retorted and she looked at me very steadily, almost pityingly, I thought. Under her scrutiny I lost my advantage.

"I don't think I am, Jan," she said, "but you are! Even Raoul understood that much!"

"Look here, Di," I protested. "Raoul absolutely disapproves of the whole thing! You went to work on him the way you used to work on me when you'd made up your mind about a certain course of action. Raoul may act tough but I daresay he's as gullible as the rest of us!"

"Raoul was right about something else," she said. "You

hate me so much that you can't imagine I may have grown a little or learned anything."

"I don't hate you, Di, but I don't believe you're any different, or ever could be."

She sighed and looked away, out over the crest of the hanging wood to the sea. "All right then, let's talk about something else, Jan. I haven't very long, I've got to be back in town this evening. Tell me about your wife if you like, tell me if you made a better job of marriage on the bounce than I did! You should have, because you didn't really marry on impulse. What was she like? Anything like me at all? They say men always fall for the same kind of woman."

"Alison wasn't in the least like you," I said, "not in the smallest particular! Here . . ." and I dragged out my wallet and gave her a snapshot taken during our three-day honeymoon in Anglesey the previous September.

As Diana reached out to take the photograph I noticed that her hands were shaking. Not simply trembling, as from nervousness or embarrassment but shaking so badly that she had difficulty in closing her finger and thumb on the creased print. She saw that I had noticed this and bent her head. Her cheeks were flushed and there was nothing pretty about the blush that coloured them. It was a hard, brickish blush and made her skin look coarse. She looked closely at the snapshot.

"She was pretty, Jan, and very dutiful-little-wifey! Just like I imagined, in fact, just right!" and suddenly she returned the photograph and turned her head away but not quickly enough to conceal the tears that brimmed over and ran down her cheeks. I had never seen her weep before and her tears embarrassed me. I put the snapshot away and gave her a moment or two to recover. She made a great effort to do so but it was not wholly successful.

I cleared my throat and said: "Look, Di, why the hell don't we have done with this nonsense? You've got out of France by a miracle, so why not call it a day and go back to Drip and Yvonne in Heronslea. I don't know, maybe after the war we could start from scratch again. I can't think how but we might, or *you* might! All I know is, right now you're in a far worse state than when I took you home after that accident before the war. You aren't fit to go stealing milk bottles, never mind pitting your wits against those bastards!"

By the time I had finished she got herself in hand and blew her nose on a handkerchief about two inches square.

"Raoul didn't even begin to make you understand, did he?"

"He didn't try," I said.

"It was a mistake expecting him to break the ice," she went on, "I didn't realise how thick it was!"

She put her hand on the door-catch and turned, facing me squarely. "Oh God, how you must have hated to let it fester like this! It's odd but when we met that time during the fall of France I didn't notice it. You were on your dignity and the same old stiff-necked Jan, but there was no rancour gnawing your heart out! Why *was* that? Why didn't I notice? Was it because you were touched by finding out Yvonne was your child or has it built up in you because you found somebody else? Did Alison teach you to hate me? Could anyone be so bloody jealous of the past?"

"Alison wasn't jealous of anything or anybody. That was about the one thing you and she had in common!" I said.

"Then perhaps my timing was bad. Is that it, Jan? Is it seeing me so soon after losing her?"

Was it? I didn't know. I was beginning to wonder if I knew anything worth knowing about Diana or Alison, or even how to jog along living for the day, as most people seem to be able to do without much trouble. I didn't know whether I wanted to spend the rest of my life mooning over this woman or to turn my back on her and forget she ever existed. Millions and millions of words have been written about first love but no one has ever explained why the roots it sends down tug this way and that, tearing the heart out of you, uplifting you, plunging you down a vertical drop into a pit of seething, scalding emotions. First love ought to be a steady and sobering something that enables men and women to measure distances and calculate

408

risks. It ought to be a simple melody that is easy to remember, not an overture played by a brass band.

"We've only got about an hour, Di, providing you really are going back with your cousin," I said.

"I'm going back," she said and lifted her hand from the catch. For the first time since we began talking, there was hope in her eyes.

"Right," I said, "then don't let's waste the hour starting innumerable hares. Let's go over it all sanely and logically as I imagine your tough-guy relative has already done. First, tell me just what you hope to achieve by staying married to a toad like Yves de Royden? Tell me, what have you achieved so far and what have you got lined up for the future? He's working for Hitler or Raoul said, but Raoul dribbled out information like a Security Officer lecturing a recruit. Is it Raoul's intention to blow up his factories or cut his throat or hold him to ransom, or what? And anyway, where do you fit and where, in the name of sanity, would I if I was crazy enough to sign on for the job?"

My tirade had given her a chance to compose herself. When she answered she was within hailing distance of Diana planning a swoop on one of her mother's Conservative fêtes.

"Well, Jan, which question do you want answered first?"

"Any of them! Give me the griff! Don't keep hinting at a sensational *coup d'état* without telling me who's to be made king."

She was silent for a moment, considering, then she said:

"Do the words *'Vergeltungswaffe Eins'* mean anything to you?"

"Not a thing. The only German I know is *'Kamerad,'* *'Mein Gott!'* and *'Gott mit uns!'* It is German, I suppose?"

"It means 'Reprisal Weapon No. 1' and Yves and his father are helping to make it at this moment."

"One of those dreary Secret Weapons? We've had a string of them starting with the magnetic mine. Is this one so special?"

"We don't know what it is, we haven't a clue so far.

We've been exploring blind alleys ever since Rance arrived and took over."

"And who is Rance? A Jerry scientist?"

"No, he's French, or pretends to be. He was in charge of one of the de Royden experimental labs in the south-east but six months ago Yves' father installed him as Director of the Paris factory."

"I thought Yves was the boss."

"So he is, in a way, but he and Rance are very close, at least they work closely together. It's a poisonous relation-ship."

"How do you mean, 'poisonous'? Is Yves a queer?"

"Not in the accepted sense," she said casually, "at least, I don't think so. At first I thought Rance was his boy-friend, but . . ." She faltered for a moment and then went on, "Rance definitely isn't a queer, he's just . . . just one hundred per cent evil!"

"How does this relationship affect you? You have noth-ing to do with the factory, do you?"

"Nothing whatever, but socially I'm expected to pull my weight."

"You mean, entertain and that sort of thing?"

"Especially 'that sort of thing'!"

I digested this. It sounded like the plot of a Continental film but not really any more improbable than many things that had happened to Diana. Once again I made the effort it needed to remember Yves from the one occasion I had met him and from the pictures I had seen of him in the days when I was a lovesick reporter keeping track of Diana through the glossy magazines and gossip columns in the papers. All I had was a memory of a slim, un-distinguished-looking young man, always faultlessly dressed, always hovering in the shadow of his race-going father, always suggesting but never quite establishing the outward mannerisms of a pansy.

"Never mind about Rance," I said, "tell me about Yves. What kind of man is he and what kind of marriage did you have before Jerry took over?"

"It wasn't a marriage at all, Jan," she said, but without bitterness, "it was an arrangement. Yves is extremely in-

410

telligent and very ambitious and his main interest was always the firm and its future. Most of the de Roydens are playboys—Raoul was until the Nazis turned him into something more positive—and the old man, Yves' father, is a kind of rumbustious patriarch presiding over them and their social legend." She saw this confused me and tried to enlarge it.

"It must be difficult for you to understand. We've got an entirely different kind of upper crust over here, a good deal healthier, I'd say, and anyway less vicious. I learned my way around easily enough because I spent a good deal of time in France, you remember, after mother found out about us and determined to keep us apart. I lived with the de Roydens then and went everywhere with them. In a cussed sort of way, Yves' father is very fond of me, even now."

"Did you ever live with Yves as man and wife?"

"Oh yes, for a year or so and then he backed out and began to devote more and more time to his factories and I went about with his set, mostly his relatives. His father was good to me. They have a curious sense of snobbery, they don't mind lovers as long as one stays inside the family circle. It's a very wide circle."

I think she thought that she was going to shock me with this information. There was an element of masochism in the admission but I wasn't shocked, just puzzled that a woman of her positive energy and courage had been prepared to pay this kind of price for wealth and security, yet even this shouldn't really have surprised me. All through my youth and early manhood I had been fighting her background and I only won the odd skirmish. Every major engagement had resulted in a humiliating defeat, all the way to Waterloo.

"You see, Yves had a dream," she went on, presently, "the kind of dream a certain class of northerner had over here halfway through the nineteenth century. He believes machines are superior in every way to human beings, more efficient, more useful and a whole heap more predictable. That's why he was able to adapt himself to the Occupation and pay lip service to the Nazis' political philosophy. He

411

sees the world as a kind of vast factory, controlled by a select few who understand why the wheels go round. Nothing else touches him at all and all the battle-cries and patriotic claptrap on both sides are just the cries of children playing in the street. In his Shangri-la everything is controlled by buttons and switches and the Nazi programme, with a master-race using experts like him to control serfs, would suit his book far better than a democracy hamstrung by demands for welfare, week-ending and individual privacy. He's not unique, of course, I daresay you could find a handful like him in every country in the world, particularly Russia and America but they don't take over because no other industrial nation has Germany's tradition of obedience."

Listening to her I began to understand a little of France's collapse. You couldn't learn this kind of thing from political hand-outs or radio news-bulletins. I also understood something of the dismay of men like Raoul de Royden, who were intelligent enough to have guilty consciences over their contribution to what happened in the West in the summer of 1940. Away and beyond this, however, I was impressed by Diana's grasp of the situation and by the evidence of a certain maturing of mind and spirit that was quite new about her, at least as far as I was concerned. In the old days she had never cared a fig for politics, national or local, and was bored by newspapers and popular talking-points. It was clear that she had been doing some thinking lately and had discussed these things with somebody reasonably well-informed on the Collapse. I wondered if it was Raoul, although he had not struck me as a man who would discuss politics with a woman.

"How close are you to that cold-fish cloak-and-dagger merchant?" I asked her and she smiled, touching my knee and tilting her head in another gesture I remembered.

"Not with Raoul," she said, "not even in the old days. I'm not his type and since he joined the Resistance he's been celibate. We take our pleasures as sadly as the British these days, Jan."

I thought for a moment, realising that even now I had not learned very much about her or the situation.

412

"How is it you won't be missed? The round trip is bound to occupy several days."

"I've got two alibis," she said, "men and antiques. Both are permissible within reasonable limits and, anyway, Yves and Rance are both on an inspection tour in Germany."

"This Secret Weapon, have you really got on to something, or is it too Top Secret to talk about?"

"We've got very little but the name as yet. I happened to see a file with the words *'Vergeltungswaffe Eins'* on the outside. The rest is pure conjecture so far."

"That's pretty vague, isn't it?"

She laughed for the first time since we had met that day. I had forgotten what a joyous sound Diana's laughter could be.

"Oh Jan, you haven't changed a bit! Do you expect the Nazis to drop leaflets about it during one of their Baedeker raids? Of course it's vague, and there's only a hundred to one chance we shall ever get any direct information on a thing as big as that but we've found one bit of jig-saw and all over Europe people who hate their guts are staking their lives looking for other pieces! When we get five or six we can start guessing. The point is, I've got the best view, the *only* view, as far as the de Royden contribution is concerned. I know where Yves goes and who he sees. Whatever I pass on is sifted and sorted and pieced together by people who are experts in their own particular field."

"I can appreciate all that," I said, "but what I don't get is what makes you think I could do anything but make a bloody great fool of myself in this business. I can imagine some clot of a C.O., or amateur Security Officer, suggesting I volunteer, but not you, unless you've completely forgotten the kind of person I am. I could never keep you in the dark about a birthday present."

"There's such a thing as double-bluff," she said, "and it so happens, by a series of coincidences, that you're qualified to play it. You're about as far removed from the run-of-the-mill Undercover Strong-Arm type as it's possible to be, and that's not a bad disguise to start with, but you've got several bonus qualifications you don't even know about. You speak French with a Canadian accent, and not at all as most Englishmen speak it. You've had a certain amount of technical training with the artillery and you've worked in the antique trade. If necessary, we could pass you off as a Montreal-educated picture expert. Not a soul knows you over there and you might even get into the house if you have to. We've been over all this with your Special Operations Executive and if you don't trust me you might trust them. They've done a pretty good job so far."

She made a convincing story of it and for a moment or so she almost fooled me. Then the months and years I had wasted thinking about her paid off, and I knew she was only weaving in and out of an elaborate smokescreen. There was no point in letting her do it indefinitely, so I called her bluff.

"It's personal, isn't it, Di? One hundred per cent personal!"

She looked at me like a child caught in the act of spending her Sunday collection penny. For a moment I was quite sure that she was going to laugh, as she always had laughed when I walked away from one of her firework displays. But she didn't laugh. She looked straight at me for a few seconds, her expression so deflated and hopeless that she seemed almost plain and middle-aged. Her eyes were bleak and dull and the curious brickish colour returned to her cheeks. Then, without a word, she slipped the catch of the door and heaved herself out of the jeep. Turning her back on me she began to walk swiftly across the waste patch towards the road.

I was after her in a second. I couldn't bear her to go like this, without a word about our child or Sennacharib, without the remotest prospect of ever seeing one another again, to slouch off like a tired, defeated saleswoman who had had a door slammed in her face. I knew that I was throwing in the sponge again. Nothing she had said had shaken my belief that she was on a hopeless tack and that I had, or could ever have, any place in her work outside

414

her imagination. Nevertheless I ran after her, calling. The past was too strong and its road too brutal.

I caught her up on the lip of the plateau where the silver birches began and the path met the road.

"Does it mean as much as that, Di? *Does* it?"

She stopped and faced me. If she had ever been honest with me for a single moment of time over the years I believe it was then.

She said: "It was my only chance, Jan. My very last chance, but you were right, it is purely personal."

She began walking again and it was not another bluff, she had made her decision, but I caught her arm.

"Listen, Di, why can't you pack it in and go back to Heronslea? Old Drip would look after you and damn it, there's Yvonne, you owe her something! You'd be happy there, I know you would and anything that needs healing would get healed. The bloody war can't go on for ever. There must be an end to it sometime and maybe we could begin again down there. It isn't impossible, is it?"

She continued walking, shaking herself free. "It was impossible for you, wasn't it? And I know it would be for me! There's a rule about these things, Jan. 'Take what you want and pay for it.' I took what I wanted when I panicked and ran off that time, and it still has to be paid for somehow, sometime. I'm tired of living in debt! I want to pay up or finish!"

She had lifted the curtain slightly, not much perhaps, but enough to afford me a glimpse of the crowding forces that had compelled her to make this journey and do her utmost to involve me in her atonement. She wanted very badly to fight her way out but she needed me on hand when she did it. If we were together there was a chance, a very slim chance, and I think this flash of understanding gave me the final push.

"Okay, Di," I said, breathlessly, "okay, I'll do it! I'm not much good on my own either!"

She stopped and faced me, regarding me intently as though trying to make up her mind how much my decision was due to weakness and how much to conviction. Then she nodded and walked slightly ahead of me back to the jeep. For the first time I got a really good look at her. She was breathing hard and I was almost sure that she was pregnant.

Chapter Three

DIANA AND her associates were hustlers. I don't know who was backing them at De Gaulle's headquarters, but whoever it was.he must have had direct access to people who counted. It was early February when I surrendered to her. By the sixteenth of the month I was cleared at Free French H.Q. and three days later I began my course.

It was a very strenuous course and the demands were far more than physical but I was grateful for it. I went to bed exhausted in mind and body and there was little opportunity to brood on past or future. By mid-April I had passed out, having learned all they had time to teach me about the use of explosives, how to use a portable radio transmitter and how to hit somebody with a revolver. I had also learned how to kill a man with my hands without making more than the minimum amount of noise, and how to make some kind of show at parrying awkward questions about my papers and identity. It was all imparted with laconic objectivity, as though my instructors shared my own doubts regarding my ultimate usefulness. There were times when I almost made up my mind to call their bluff and drop the pretence that I was likely to be of service to them. Then the memory of Diana's face as she jumped out of the jeep would return and I would call a truce with myself and let things take their course. I had a curious feeling of helplessness about events, as though I was standing off and watching an old friend make a fool of himself and was unable to decide if and at what point I should intervene. It was as though I engaged in some kind of game played at a distance with Diana, not the Diana who had come to me in the little church within half an hour of Alison's funeral but the Diana of Sennacharib and Heronslea far back in the past. It was loyalty to those days that kept me at work going through the motions of training as a cloak-and-dagger man. It was a very odd sensation, this fourth dimensional feeling, but it was also a spiritual sedative. I wondered if it would disappear when they asked me to plunge head-first into the desperate business or whether it would be replaced by terror, the nightmarish terror of facing responsibilities I was incapable of shouldering. In the meantime, however, I cannot say that I experienced physical fear, only this curious, half-dreamy sense of detachment at finding myself plucked from the current of the old, boring war and groomed for entry into a very different kind of conflict.

After an initial briefing I was given a week's leave and went down to Heronslea, in Devon. I had been home several times in the days since Dunkirk but this time it was different because I knew I might be seeing it for the last time and my reunion with Diana had reinvested it all with something of its former enchantment, a quality that it had lost the day she abdicated from Sennacharib.

It was the best time of year to return. After I had dropped in to see my Uncle Luke and Aunt Thirza at the Quayside Furniture Mart, and watched the same fishermen lounging on the same bollards alongside a harbour cluttered with beach obstacles dating from the invasion scare of 1940, I went up the hill and along the chalk road that skirts the edge of Foxhayes and took the high-banked lane to Folly Wood and Big Oak Paddock above Heronslea. Diana was with me all the way. I saw her among the primroses that hung in great clusters along the banks, and in Folly Wood, and beside the early bluebells round the foot of the old tower that had been our rendezvous. I scrambled up the steps and entered the crumbling, mould-smelling room at the summit, the place where I had given her a copy of *Lorna Doone* for a fifteenth birthday gift and received her first, impulsive kiss. I came down and crossed Big Oak Paddock to the wood, looking about for the two buzzards who were symbols of our association but they were not to be seen, they seldom were unless we were together. Then, at length, I dropped down the central ride towards the big house, passing the glade where she had ridden out from the young trees to rescue me from Keeper Croker's half-nelson. This was the beating heart of Sennacharib, this was the spot where it had begun all those years ago. It was what happened here, in this clearing, that had set my feet upon the least rewarding of all quests, the pursuit of lost youth, and this struck me so forcibly that I paused, as though half-decided to turn my back on it all, to grow up, to try a new side of the hill. It was no use, the pull of Sennacharib was too strong and I went on down the ride and came at last to Heronslea.

"Drip", Diana's old governess, greeted me with tears in her poppy blue eyes and was obliged to wipe her gold-rimmed spectacles before she could embrace me whole-heartedly. She was the only person on earth who knew the real story of Diana and myself for she had been present at the very beginning of it, the afternoon of the October miracles. I wished heartily that I could confide in her and seek, if not her advice then at least her solace, but that was not possible. I was a very amateur secret agent but I was not so amateur as to realise that the word "security" was rather more than an excuse for bullshine to men like Raoul de Royden. I listened to Drip's prattle about the hopelessly rapid growth of the evacuee home at Heronslea and all the problems attendant upon tending two score children of mixed nationalities in a remote corner of the country and when she had talked herself out I told her that I was posted overseas. I said nothing at all about my meeting with Diana.

"Do you know where you'll be going or shouldn't I ask?" she said tremulously, for she loved me more than anyone on earth.

"You shouldn't ask," I told her, smiling, "but it's probably just Canada, for air-crew training!"

"Oh," she said, brightening at once, "that isn't so bad, is it?" then, tentatively: "I . . . I don't suppose you've had any word from Diana?"

"No," I lied, "have you?" There was a remote possibility that Diana had communicated with her in some way.

418

There had been one letter, early in the war, through the Swiss Red Cross organisation.

"No," said Drip, sniffing, "nothing more, but I wonder and wonder, sometimes half the night long. I suppose you do, don't you, Jan?"

"Not so much as I did," I said, "I never knew anyone more able to take care of herself than Diana."

"That's true," she said, cheering up again. Drip was probably the most gullible soul ever to attain the age of eighty. Suddenly she got up and pointed: "Look, there's Yvonne! Doesn't she remind you of Diana on a horse?"

I looked through the tall morning-room windows to the small paddock. A dark, intent-looking child was walking a barrel-bellied pony alongside the palings and she was deep in conversation with a rangy boy of about ten. The boy had a curiously sturdy walk and carried himself like a proud peasant.

"Who is that boy?" I asked Drip, and she reminded me that he was Manuel, the son of Diana's Spanish gardener and eldest of the five children I had brought home from Bordeaux in 1940. "He's very devoted to Yvonne," Drip said, "she's a kind of queen here and he's her Prime Minister!"

"Poor little devil," I said, remembering so much.

I realised that I must do something about Yvonne and do it without awakening Drip's suspicions. She knew that Yvonne was our child, of course, but Yvonne—if she thought about it at all—must still think of herself as the daughter of Diana and Yves de Royden. It seemed to me quite wrong to go away without telling her the truth, so I said: "How much does she remember about France and Diana?"

"Not very much, she isn't an introspective child. I can't recall her ever having referred to her supposed father, or to her early childhood in France, but she still thinks Diana is fighting Germans, like the Spanish boy's father."

"She ought to know about Diana and me," I said. "Suppose the pair of us bought it?"

" 'Bought it'?" said Drip, looking very puzzled. The poor old soul wasn't at all familiar with wartime slang.

419

"Look, Miss Rodgers," I went on, "nobody knows what might happen to me or to Diana. I'm not out looking for medals but hundreds of chaps get killed training and Diana might die a natural death before the war's over. Suppose we both died? The kid's financial future is okay, I imagine, Diana's funds in London will take care of that but I'm damned if I'd want her to go on thinking she had a Quisling for a father. I think I'll talk to her tonight."

It was obvious that the prospect shocked Drip. She belonged to an age of uniformed governesses and afternoon calls, of tea under the chestnuts and family prayers in the breakfast room.

"Surely she isn't old enough to understand . . . ?" she protested.

"I'll have to do the best I can," I said, "I know I'm right about this and I know that Diana would agree with me."

"Very well, Jan," she said, meekly, "you do what you think is right and when you go you'll write, won't you, you'll write whenever you can?"

"Whenever I can," I compromised, "but sometimes it isn't easy from overseas, sometimes mail is forbidden. What time does Yvonne go to bed?"

"When it's getting dark," she said, "I can never get her in until then. She's even more self-willed than Diana was and sometimes we have quite a scene over it. I do wish she'd set a better example to the others."

"You and I were always wishing people would set examples," I said, "and it never got either of us anywhere, did it?"

I went into Yvonne's room at dusk. She had a room to herself in the east wing, where Drip's old quarters had been when she was resident governess at Heronslea. The old mansion was impossibly large but even so it was getting overcrowded. The staff and children numbered over thirty and I used a camp-bed in one of the lumber rooms. Drip had told Yvonne I was calling on her and she was sitting up in bed awaiting me. So far our relationship had been easy without being intimate. I think she regarded me as a kind of uniformed Uncle, who popped up from time

420

to time with packets of Naafi chocolate in his haversack. I don't think I was very important to her at that time and I know she didn't think much about me when I was away.

I sat down on the end of her bed and studied her. Temperamentally she favoured Diana but physically she was four-fifths Leigh, with my countryman's build, dark hair and gipsyish complexion. She was a very assured child but there was laughter behind her eyes and a kind of quiet ruthlessness that was another of her mother's legacies.

I came straight to the point, she was the sort of child likely to appreciate this.

"What do you remember about living in France, Yvonne?"

She looked surprised and then composed herself conventionally, clasping her hands behind her dark head and looking up at the arched ceiling.

"Funny things that don't go together!" she said. "A lake near a castle, a castle like this!" She sprang up suddenly and flicked through a book of nursery rhymes until she came to a page illustrating a conical-towered chateau, the kind of tower the Lady of Shalott lived in on the island in the river.

"Yes? What else? What about the lake?"

"Mummy used to take me there to see irises. Huge irises they were, much bigger than ours here and a different colour. Yellow, I think! She used to sit there and tell me about England and Heronslea. She must have told me a lot because when I came here I knew it, you know . . . I could sort of find my way about! Sometimes it seems I dreamed everywhere else. Mummy liked living here didn't she?"

"Yes, she did, very much," I said, "we had a wonderful time about here when we were young."

I groped for something to focus her attention and remembered the pony she had been riding earlier in the evening. "She taught me to ride on a pony like yours. The first time I fell off and cut myself. Drip had to bandage me up."

"Did you live here too, Jan?" she asked, and I could see that she was now genuinely interested.

"No," I said, "I lived in Whinmouth and I wasn't really allowed up here, but we didn't take much notice of that! Mummy and I spent all our holidays here and even when she was away at school I used to come here a lot. Drip was the governess and she was always on my side. You see, Yvonne, Mummy was very rich and I was very poor."

"Are you still poor, Jan?"

"About the same, but it doesn't matter so much now as there's a war on and money doesn't count all that much. Winning the war is all that matters, beating Hitler!"

This held her interest but it did not seem to be getting me much farther so I plunged.

"Mummy and I were very much in love with one another, right from the first time we met! We were going to get married."

"What stopped you? The war?" Her logic disconcerted me. She had exceptional reasoning powers for a child of eight but although her remark offered me a way out I was reluctant to use it.

"Not exactly," I said, "Mummy went off to France and married somebody else and I didn't see her for a long time, not until that time she brought you and the gardener's children to me and I took you back to England on the boat."

"What on earth made her go to France and marry somebody else?" she demanded, almost indignantly, I thought, and somehow her indignation brought her closer.

I didn't know the complete answer to this and doubted if I would ever know it, so I said:

"People in love don't always know their own minds, Yvonne, they do silly things on the spur of the moment. This was one of them I suppose. But the point is, people who love one another sometimes have children. You know about that, I suppose?"

She looked at me sharply and I saw that her mouth was quivering with laughter.

"You needn't fuss, Jan," she said, "I know how babies come, we've got cows and pigs and all sorts here and Old Mac' let us see one of the cows calve. Then Drip told us but said we mustn't talk about it, and was jolly angry with Mac' but we do—talk about it, I mean!"

I was grateful for the cows and for Old Mac's indifference but still I had not arrived.

"People aren't exactly like cows, Yvonne," I said, "but they sometimes have babies without being married. Your Mummy and I aren't married, not yet that is, but we had you and you belong to me and her."

I expected almost any reaction but the one I got. She nodded slowly, not surprised, or pleased, or even puzzled but somehow sympathetic.

"Like Alice," she said, resignedly.

"Who the hell is Alice?" I exclaimed. I felt like a drill instructor who had just watched a first-day recruit strip a Bren gun in record time.

"She was a maid here," said Yvonne, calmly, "and she got fat and had a baby. She wasn't married either but Rachel, the other maid, said she ought to have been. To a sailor," she added as a kind of postscript and while I still gaped; "Drip was awfully mad about *her*, too. She won't let her come back now that the baby's being minded!"

I gave it up, feeling that any further comment would have been fatuous. Instead I put my arms round her and kissed her dark curls. They were tighter, more disciplined curls than Diana's, as blue and black as storm clouds over Nun's Head.

"I'm going away, Yvonne," I told her, "but I'll come back, I promise."

It was then she said what seemed to me a remarkable thing: "Are you going to look for Mummy and bring her back here?" she asked, simply and without emotion.

"I might even do that, Yvonne," I said and turned out the bedroom light.

She called as I reached the door.

"Jan!"

"Well?"

"Will you be flying now that you're an airman?"

"I might. Why?"

"Fly over here and do a victory roll. Do it on my birthday. It's next Thursday."

"I'm sorry, I'll be away by then, but I'll ask one of the others to do it, if not Thursday, then one day soon after!" Uncle Luke had told me that Polish pilots operating from the base at Shepperton sometimes shot down a hit-and-run raider along the coast. I hoped to God they would do so in the next few days.

I went out into the paddock and down the beach avenue for a pint at "The Green Rifleman". I felt happier and less confused than I had felt in years.

When I was a boy growing up in Whinmouth I was very interested in war. I never missed an opportunity of coaxing the men who attended British Legion rallies to relate anecdotes of Ypres, the Somme or naval engagements, like Jutland. It seemed to me at that time that to fight in a war would be a glamorous, adventurous occupation and I remember that I was always disappointed and disgusted when characters like old Tom Pigeon, the Dockmaster who had served from Mons to the Armistice, dismissed those four years as a journey across a wasteland. I remember one particular thing Tom said when I was interviewing him for a November 11th edition of the *Whinmouth Gazette.* Hardly bothering to look up from his revolving of the dock swing bridge, he grunted: "You'm asking me about war, Sonny? Giddon with'ee, there baint nowt one can say about it! Most o' they years I was idle, and all of 'em I was wet'n cold, or parched an' sweaty. T'other odd minute or zo I was zo bliddy scared 'twas all I could do to stop maakin' a mess o' meself!"

It was a reasonable estimate, taken all round. I was in France throughout the winter they called "The Great Bore War" and until the Nazis broke through and we ran for the coast I had been both bored and half-frozen. Then, after the panic of the invasion summer, I was bored and sweaty, like almost everyone else in Britain and now, nearly two years later, I had exchanged boredom and a sense of futility for the semi-permanent bellyache of fear.

I was scared all right, from the top of my scalp to the tips of my toes. I woke up in the night sweating with fear. I toyed with plates of spam and powdered egg unable to

424

swallow more than a few mouthfuls and when I remembered what I had let myself in for, and what was likely to happen to me, I thought of myself as a man needing a brain specialist. A soldier serving in an ordinary unit isn't scared until he sees the enemy coast or hears the scream of a bomb or shell but I kept reminding myself that I wasn't attached to a unit of any kind but was sweating it out by myself, without a soul to confide in, and with absolutely no idea of what was expected of me. There was only one useful by-product of those days I spent waiting for my final briefing. I was completely cured of my endless pursuit of Diana and wished heartily that I had never set eyes on the woman, or had had the strength of will to tell her and her cousin Raoul to fight their private war any way they wished and leave me to fight mine in company of my own choosing.

And then, as always in war, came the anti-climax. The briefing was simple and straightforward and my despatch to the Continent nothing like what I had anticipated in terms of risk, excitement or even route. My ideas about the passage of agents to and from occupied territory were as hazy as any ex-civilian's. Up to that time I had been a gunner, a temporary interpreter, a transport officer and a trainee in the R.A.F. I had never been asked to do anything more heroic than fire a few rounds at a distant target, to ditch lorries or collect evacuees for shipment to Britain. I had imagined, up to that time, that secret agents behaved more or less on lines laid down by the authors of spy-fiction churned out by the ton during the 'twenties and 'thirties. I should have read Maugham's "Ashenden", he was much nearer the mark. There was no disguise (apart from a short, pointed beard I was ordered to grow) and there were no secret codes and poison pills. There was no fearsome parachute drop or complicated cross-country journey involving moments of indecision at checkpoints and station barriers. Instead, I was given a perfect set of papers in the name of a certain Hervé van Orthes, a fine arts expert and insurance assessor of French-Canadian extraction, and after an uneventful journey in the belly of a Free French submarine I was set ashore a few miles west of Villefranche, on the Riviera, and told to make my way to a villa on the eastern rim of the resort to await identification by a contact named "Olive." I arrived in France knowing very little more than when I had parted from Diana's cousin in the Group-Captain's office.

The curious thing was I felt cheated. Cheated but also vaguely relieved. They had given me what seemed to me a vast amount of paper money and this, with my personal documents, hand luggage and an automatic revolver with which I had fired a dozen or so practice rounds, was my entire equipment as a spy, agent or saboteur. It all seemed to me absurdly amateur, as amateur as the notion that Emerald Diana de Royden, née Gayelorde-Sutton, of Heronslea, Devon and Palmerston Crescent, S.W.1, was also dedicated to the fumbling, fictitious business. For all that, I lost my bellyache and almost, I say almost, began to take on full awareness again and look about me with faint stirrings of excitement.

I had never previously visited the Riviera. Throughout my service and during pre-war holidays I had lived in the north, in Paris and the south-west, all of which I knew reasonably well. Yet for many years now I had associated the Riviera with Diana. In pre-war days it had been one of her seasonal playgrounds and her mother, who made a fetish of appearing fashionable, had once owned a villa here, not in Villefranche, but further along the coast, behind Nice. Living out my uneventful life as official chronicler of the fêtes and funerals of Whinmouth, I had thought of the Riviera as somewhere I would never visit, like the Royal Enclosure at Ascot or the Centre Court at Wimbledon. Before the war, Diana and her family made an annual pilgrimage to all these places and I had followed them via the pages of the glossy magazines. That was the extent of the gulf between us, she the daughter of the financial wizard and me the small-town reporter on a Devon country newspaper. It had always seemed to me an unbridgeable gulf and I still thought of it as one. That was why I had eventually come to terms with it and married Alison but now I had to remind myself that Alison was dead and that Diana had whirled round again and I was re-entering her world,

426

not as a lover or husband, but as a callow opponent of the most ruthless tyranny in the history of the world. It all seemed so improbable that I found difficulty in believing it real.

I located the villa easily enough, a newish, rather baroque dwelling, built into a rocky shelf above a coastal road that wound behind the town and towards the Riviera proper. It was built of whitened stone and in the bright Mediterranean sunshine it hurt your eyes to look at it. It had a pretty garden surrounding it and the enclosure was gay with rock plants and flowering shrubs. There were scores of other villas within view but this one looked as if its owner had more money than his neighbours. It had a squat, squarish tower, with glass on three sides and a finely gravelled drive leading up to the entrance and branching off to a large double garage roofed with green tiles. Its garden and approaches were meticulously weeded and along its frontal veranda was an awning of red and white canvas. Viewed as a whole it was conventional but impressive.

There was nobody in the garden so I went up the drive and looked in the garage which was empty of cars but housed some brand-new servicing kit. The green sun-blinds were down at the front and I was unable to peep through the windows, so I went up some steps and round to the back where the triangle of lawn and rock-garden drove into the cliff face at an angle of about thirty degrees. I put down my bag and tried the back door. It was open so I went in, closing the door behind me.

The kitchen was as luxuriously appointed as everything else in that villa. The sinks and cupboards were new and highly polished, the gadgets devious and very modern. There was a water-softening apparatus and a glass-fronted liquor cabinet containing scores of interesting-looking bottles. There was a wealth of coloured glass, not all of it for practical use and a double row of gleaming utensils clamped to the walls. The general impression I got was one of orderliness and scrupulous cleanliness. I went on through a glass-panelled door and called out but nobody answered and after a long pause I slipped the safety-catch of my automatic and held it in my pocket, moving across the cool hall into a large, low-ceilinged lounge, dusky in filtered sunlight. Everything was new and everything was expensive-looking. Whoever owned the villa seemed to have made himself very comfortable.

The main room giving on to the terrace overlooking the sea was furnished in the taste of a person who is trying, self-consciously perhaps, to break away from the traditional without seeming eccentric. There was a great deal of Swedish glass and wrought-iron, one or two tortured looking lamps and a bookshelf full of French classical novels, bound in red Morocco. The carpet, a blue and silver Chinese, was a work of art and there was a grand piano shrouded in a dust sheet. I prowled about wondering what kind of person would live in a place like this, and why he or she was prepared to let it be used as a rendezvous for strays like me and the enigmatic "Olive". I inspected the shower-room and then noticed one of those retracting ladders leading to a room in the gable. I pulled the cord and the ladder descended noiselessly. It was obviously very well-oiled. I went up and pushed open the trap. The place had been used as a box-room and there was only one tiny window which was draped so that for a moment or so I was puzzled to discover the source of light. Then I saw that three tiny glazed apertures had been let into the floor immediately above the light fittings of the living-room, kitchen and hall downstairs. It seemed to me an odd device and when I looked more closely I noticed the rawness of the cuts in the joists and a trickle of new sawdust. The peep-holes had obviously been an afterthought and when I checked downstairs I realised that they were invisible from below. I poked around among some cartons and looked behind the boarded partition, where some trunks were stored but the boxes were empty and presently I went down again carefully closing the trap and retracting the ladder.

It was now close on midday and the pep pills I had taken the night before were beginning to lose their effect. I stifled a series of yammering yawns and had a wash at the kitchen sink in an effort to stave off sleep. It was very cool and peaceful inside the house and the occasional swish of a passing car ascending the hill did not disturb the sense of security I felt in there. The pantry shelves contained plenty of food but I was not in the least hungry and presently I went into the big room and found myself a book. Then I remembered that I had neglected to check the bedrooms, which were situated on the western side of the entrance hall, one at the back and one at the front. The back room was completely bare. The other was magnificently fitted up with mahogany furniture in Second Empire style and had a double bed, canopied in grey silk and hung around with tassels of gold wire. Suspended from the canopy frame was a gilt cherub, fat and leering. The accessories on the glass-topped dressing-table were exclusively feminine and the perfume I found there was as expensive as everything else in the villa.

There was a very comfortable armchair in this bedroom and I sat in it, musing, and presently kicked off my shoes and put a cushion behind my head. It was a ridiculous thing to do but, as I say, the serenity of the setting and the comfort of the surroundings were tempting after the stresses of the journey and the uncertainty with which I had set foot in France that morning. At all events in a few seconds I was sound asleep and the thud of the book falling on to the thick carpet failed to recall me. Sprawling there, snoring and oblivious, I was a sitting target for anyone who appeared and if the villa had been blown, as were so many of our refuges in areas patrolled by the Vichy police, I should have ended my career as an agent within twelve hours of beginning it.

I awoke to the sound of running water. Someone was in the shower-room either taking a bath or hoping to convince me that they were taking one. I leaped to my feet, sick with fright and my hand shot into my jacket pocket for the automatic. It was still there and I grabbed my shoes and glanced at my watch, horrified to discover that it was now seven o'clock. I had been asleep for almost seven hours.

It took me a few minutes to pull myself together and rub the drowsiness from my eyes. I saw that the sun was low over the bay and the roofs between the villa and the waterfront were bathed in soft, pinkish light. I craned my neck round the angle of the terrace and could just see the tail fins of a car parked at the entrance of the garage. Then, listening intently, I heard the sound of running water cease and someone open the shower-room door and shut it again. I was at a loss to know how to announce myself or if, indeed, I should do so at all. I had expected the contact "Olive", or someone deputed by her, to meet me when I arrived at the villa and after satisfying myself that it was unoccupied, I had relied upon seeing a visitor before I was myself seen. Now more than eight hours had passed and we were both in the house but neither, presumably, knew the other was here. My mind was still juggling with the situation when I had another shock, an even bigger one, for the door snicked open without the slightest warning and standing there, wrapped in a mauve bathrobe, was Diana.

I was dumbfounded. I don't know why but it had never occurred to me that "Olive" might be Diana, or that Diana would be anywhere but with her husband, or with Raoul and his confederates in Paris.

I had been told so little and was so new to the game, that I had never speculated upon the identity of my contact. The word "Olive" did not suggest a person to me but a kind of password into the network of the Resistance.

Then another thing struck me. The woman standing on the threshold was vastly different in appearance from the stocky, rather ravaged-looking creature who had sat beside me in the jeep immediately after Alison's funeral. She was a reincarnation of the Diana I remembered in the period just before her marriage, a woman with a clear skin and a trim, attractive figure and long, pretty legs that revealed their shape through the folds of the robe. In contrast to me she seemed perfectly relaxed. Her eyes sparkled, reflecting the periwinkle blue that I had marked the moment I saw her ride out of the woods at Heronslea. She looked splendidly healthy and the contrast with her appearance on the last occasion we had met was more striking than her presence.

She stood in the doorway looking at me with an expression of tolerant amusement and as her mouth puckered into a smile, a great rush of yearning and warmth and joy gushed over me and through me, so that I was unable to utter a single word but simply stood there gaping at her, one hand hanging at my side, the other clutching the butt of the automatic in my pocket.

"Sleep well?" she said, cocking her head on one side in a way I remembered when she was teasing, then, when I continued to gape:

"You never told me you snored, Jan! It was awful, like floodwater running through the grating under Teasel Bridge! What a good thing I didn't marry you after all!"

I found my voice at last and withdrew my hand from my pocket. I said: "How the hell . . . ?" but she had noticed the movement of my right hand and suddenly became serious.

"Have you got a gun in there?"

"Yes, here," and I took it out and handed it to her. She looked at it critically and then expertly snapped out the magazine and flicked the safety catch on and off.

"You shouldn't keep it loose in your jacket. Safety catches get clogged with bits of fluff. Either it won't come off when you need it or it shoots when it feels like it. You should have a shoulder holster or at least a piece of chamois—look!"

She took an almost identical weapon from the pocket of her bathrobe. It was protected by a little holster made of wash-leather.

"Do you pack a gun even when you take a bath?" I asked, but her eyes did not smile. "It isn't part of a dressing-up act," she said, and I felt deflated. She noticed this at once and smiled again, throwing up her head and pulling off her turban so that her lovely mass of hair tumbled. Her hair had always been her loveliest feature. It was dark chestnut and there was so much of it. It had always seemed to me to have an independent life of its own and play games with her. Sometimes it almost talked, hissing like the larches in Heronslea woods. If you were riding behind her at a gallop it seemed to shout into the wind.

She returned the gun and I replaced it in my pocket, wrapping a handkerchief round the barrel.

"Are you 'Olive'?" I asked, partly because I felt vaguely uncomfortable under her critical scrutiny.

"Yes," she said, "it's a dreadful name! I always hated it. It conjures up a vision of a pudding-faced girl with adenoids who works in a chemist's shop!"

"I once knew a librarian called Olive," I said, "and she wasn't a bit puddingy. As a matter of fact she was ash blonde and very pneumatic."

"Where was that? Not in Whinmouth, I'm sure!" she said, but with genuine interest.

"No," I admitted, "it was when I was working on the illustrated weekly in Fleet Street. She married a compositor." Then: "This is a bloody silly conversation, let's pack it in, Di!"

"All right," she said, "I expect you're hungry."

I was, ravenously hungry and my mouth was parched with the back-kick of the pep pills. "I could eat anything, preferably hot," I said, "but first, how did you know I was here? I'm damned sure I should have jumped up if anyone had opened the bedroom door."

"You left your grip in the kitchen," she said lightly but managing to convey reproof. "Anyway, I was expecting you and I went outside and looked through the window. I could hear those snores through the glass. That's a good reason why people should sleep together before they make up their minds to marry. You can get a divorce on those grounds in the States. Come into the kitchen unless you want a shower first."

"I'll take a shower later," I said and we crossed the hall into the spotless kitchen. I could smell coffee and it made my mouth water.

What impressed me most I think was the ease with which we found the guidelines of our old relationship. There was no fumbling, no casting about for handholds and useful crevices. We arrived at the summit at once, as if there had never been that tense meeting after Alison's funeral, as if we had come together again after a separation of about a fortnight and were attuned to one another like a man and woman approaching their silver wedding. It was a kind of miracle this fusing of our personalities, this renunciation of past and future. In the old days we had often been separated for long periods but when we met again it was never quite like this, not even during our happiest spells. Always there had been mutual shyness, a brief but painful waiting-for-the-train-to-start atmosphere and usually it was never dispelled until we had embraced. I sat at the little metal table and watched her pottering to and from the electric cooker in her feathery mules, trailing a yard or so of towelling and throwing the damp curls out of her eyes and it made me ache with joy to see her so engaged. I felt like a newly-wed husband who had returned home unexpectedly and demanded a scratch meal and I had to keep reminding myself that we were here on desperate business, a couple of amateurs pitting their wits against thousands of professionals. She poured the coffee and then came up with a vast plate of ham and eggs. It was the most heaped-up looking plate I had seen for nearly three years and I complimented her after the first few mouthfuls.

"This is wonderful! I've never seen you cook anything before, Di." She was pleased but made a show of concealing her pleasure.

"Everyone cooks over here," she said, "men, women and children. It's only in Britain that women are the exclusive drudges."

While I was drinking my third cup of coffee she ran the bath. When she came back she had discarded the robe and wore an inadequate black brassiere, black lace panties and one stocking. She stood by the stove, tugging at her hair with a fancy-looking comb. I remembered then that Diana never seemed to want privacy for dressing or undressing. It was not that she was deliberately provocative, or liked to display herself, but she liked to dismiss modesty as a tiresome, old-fashioned notion. I looked at her objectively for a few moments and then my curiosity got the upper hand.

"You were pregnant in February, Di. What happened?"

She stopped combing and looked at me steadily for a moment.

"We'll talk about that later," she said.

"All right, Di," I said, cheerfully, "but hadn't we better talk about the job? No agent ever touched down with a sketchier brief than me and sooner or later somebody will have to tell me something. Or will they?"

She thought hard for a moment, contracting her brows and making a slow circular movement on her chin with her index finger.

"Raoul will be down presently and he'll brief you before Rance arrives. But that shouldn't be for at least forty-eight hours. I thought we might take a sort of holiday. We might never get another chance." Then she looked at me less certainly. "It's up to you of course. About the holiday, I mean."

"Is Rance the Svengali type you told me about? The one who works for the de Royden outfit?"

Her expression changed. For a moment or so she looked hunted.

"That's him and that's really why you're here. It's also why they told you to grow that ridiculous Van Dyke beard!"

"I don't get it," I protested.

"No," she said, deliberately, "you won't yet, but you will when Raoul and the others show up. The point I'm making is this, we'll be up to our eyes in it within a day or two and maybe, if we're lucky, it will be all over this next week. We can't do a damned thing one way or the other until Raoul gets here, so why can't we let it ride and enjoy ourselves? We can even go out in the car if we want to. The whole idea of your being here is that you should be seen. I've got all the props, clothes, papers, the lot."

"*My* props?"

"That's it. Well?"

"I'm presumably under your orders or Raoul's orders but it's like I said, I don't even know why or what in hell I'm supposed to do. If you know you might as well tell me. Do you know?"

434

"Only the bare bones," she said, reluctantly, "not the details."

"All right, then give me the bare bones and then we'll talk about the holiday. First, however, for God's sake, get something on! I'm human and I can't be expected to concentrate with you standing there looking like a pin-up in 'Men Only'!"

She brightened at this, as if she had begun to suspect that I was unimpressed. She threw me a swift smile and drifted out into the hall, returning a moment later in a jazzy-looking kimono. It was a startling and voluminous garment but she left it flapping and sat down on the edge of the table, crossing her legs and lighting a cigarette. I wanted to laugh again. She was acting the conventional French tart in a second feature film and doing it rather well.

"We've found out what Yves and his father are up to, more or less," she said. "It's the propelling unit of a missile, some kind of bomb that is supposed to home under its own steam. It's one of the famous secret weapons but not quite so secret as it was when Raoul and I came over. Rance is their key man, that's why he left the factory in the south and came to Paris. They've been working on it for more than a year."

I was not much impressed by this. Like most British servicemen, I had never taken Hitler's secret weapons very seriously. We had heard so much about them ever since the first month of the war. There had been the magnetic mine, which was countered in a matter of days, and since then the Press were always running stories of new and devastating devices. The very fact that the newspapers could print such stories drew the sting from the menace, for nothing worth reading had appeared in the British press since September, 1939. Over there, security was a cult, like the blackout and digging for victory. Some of my scepticism must have revealed itself to Diana.

"It's more serious this time," she said. "Raoul's people have given it top priority. Nobody knows how far they've progressed with it and Yves' unit is only concerned with our part of it, possibly the direction-finder, or more probably the propulsion, we don't know yet. We've got a three-fold job and I only know the first leg. That's straightforward enough, the impersonation of Pierre Rance!"

I noticed two things about the way she said this. One was that Rance's Christian name was a slip of the tongue, and that she had not meant to use it, the other that the slip had embarrassed her. She recovered herself almost at once but not quickly enough to prevent her gaffe from registering. She made what was for her a singularly inept attempt to mask her confusion by slipping off the table and crossing over to the stove. Once there, she kept her back towards me and pretended to be busy with the coffee pot. I gave her a moment or two and then said:

"You still haven't told me where I come in, Di. You don't have to and maybe you'd better stop there."

She thought about this for a moment and then turned, pressing her hands against the stove and looking at me very steadily.

"I can tell you that, Jan," she said, quietly, "there's no point in your not knowing now. Your job is to double for Rance. That's where the beard comes in. You're very like him, extraordinarily like him! Not exactly a double but close to it, close enough to take a chance, at least, so I've always thought. It was my idea originally and in the end Raoul backed me up. You're almost exactly his height and build and you've got his colouring and even . . . sometimes that is . . . his way of holding himself!"

I began to glimpse one or two outlines in the fog that had surrounded my part in this business from the beginning and in some ways I found them humiliating. Until then I had had no alternative but to assume that my presence here, and the fact that Raoul de Royden had taken the trouble to seek me out, had been based wholly upon a whim of Diana's. If I hadn't known her so well the premise would have been ridiculous. People like Raoul, and the men who screened volunteers at the Free French Headquarters in London, did not engage recruits at the behest of a woman but Diana was not simply a woman, or even a tested ally. She was the wife of a very prominent collaborator and the mere fact that she was not in an internment camp argued that Yves must stand very high with Vichy and the Nazis. I had assumed that she had struck some kind of bargain with them and that I was involved in that bargain. I knew, none better, how ruthless she could be at getting her own way and if there was a person capable of going to any lengths to exploit her usefulness that person was Diana. Yet it seemed to me that Raoul had engaged upon the business of enlisting me half-heartedly, that he did not believe me capable of serving his cause effectively. If I really was this man's double then he must have considered the project seriously and must, moreover, have convinced a number of shrewd and suspicious men that such a possibility did in fact exist outside the realms of Diana's imagination. This led me directly to Diana's slip when she had used Rance's Christian name, Pierre, so that I was not at all surprised by her next remark.

"I was Pierre Rance's mistress, Jan. I suppose I still am, or he imagines that I am. It was his child I was having."

The lost, pitiful look that I remembered seeing when we had talked in the jeep returned and it had the strangest effect upon her because, although the fear remained in her eyes, it somehow communicated itself to the corners of the mouth and caused the skin on her cheeks to flush that curiously mottled colour I had noticed on the previous occasion. For a moment or so she looked almost raddled. Then, with a conscious effort, she regained control and health seemed to flood back into her face. She straightened up and the fear and uncertainty in her eyes was extinguished by a flicker of challenge, half defiant, half appealing. That was the wonderful thing about Diana. She never went under for long, she never ceased to fight back.

"We don't have to go on with this, Jan," she said.

"We do," I said stupidly, "we're committed, aren't we?"

She made a gesture of impatience.

"I don't mean the job! . . . I mean us! All sorts of things will become clear if we don't force it, if we don't hold one of your famous inquests. I think that was half the trouble with us. You always wanted an inquest, you would never do what I did for so long, let everything go down with the sun and start fresh in the early morning. Will you do that now, Jan? Will you? Until Raoul gets here?"

It was not an appeal but a supplication. I saw her mouth quivering and suddenly all the realities of the situation slid away like a cliff erosion. Suddenly there was no betrayal, no lost years, no Yves, no Rance and no war. The only thing that had the least significance was her little girl's mouth, her anxious eyes and the mass of tumbling hair that seemed to rally to her appeal. I pushed back the chair and crossed to her, throwing up her chin and grasping a handful of her hair and twisting it until it spilled out between my fingers. I knew then how fatuously I had lied to myself about her, how many futile years I had spent creating an image of her that was totally false. There was really nothing spiritual about my yearning for her, not since the day we first met and I was a boy just entering his sixteenth year. I cared nothing at all for her faults or qualities as a person, for her gallantry, her crude selfishness and her hopeless and baffling unpredictability. All I wanted from her was what any man wants from a woman whose entry into a room in which he is standing causes his pulse to quicken and his mouth to dry. I wanted her naked on a bed, her mouth to mine and her breast under my hand. I wanted to give and receive, over and over again. Everything else was deception.

I think she must have realised this simultaneously for in that first, frenzied embrace it seemed to me that our youth reflowered. We might have sat in conclave for a month, solemnly retracing old routes, scratching among the errors and omissions of the years without learning a fraction of what was revealed to us in that moment. She was right, of course, right about the inquests. They had always been too many and too searching and what sterile verdicts had they produced? Bitterness and resentment turned sour in the heart and futility. It was like digging holes to house the rubbish taken from other holes.

I lifted her and was surprised to find how little she weighed. I looked down at her for a moment, choked with tenderness, and her heavy chestnut curls, worn even longer than when she was a girl, swung down below my knees. I walked with her into the bedroom and kicked the door open and shut. She opened her eyes as it banged and there was triumph in them, relief also, a world of gratitude and relief. I knew then that I had found a way out of the cul-de-sac and that the Odyssey I had thought over and done with years ago was scarcely half completed. I knew also that whatever happened here, and however closely and dangerously we became involved with people like Yves and Raoul and Rance, we would achieve something and achieve in partnership.

It was still dark when I awoke. Through the gap where the curtains should have met I could see one or two stars and a few lights down near the harbour. After a moment or so I knew that Diana was awake too and touched her cheek. I smiled when I thought of us lying here in Rance's four-poster, and how we had not even paused to lock the outside door, or pull the curtains properly, or take out the guns and place them within reach. It was a droll way of fighting a war, far removed my conception of marching under the Resistance banner but the reflection made no difference and sounded no alarms. My brain still had a cramped corner for the war but my body, relaxed and drowsy, had renounced it altogether. Presently it occurred to me that at least I should lift her arm from my chest and get up and lock the back door but when the thought caused me to stir slightly, her hair fell across my cheek and again I lay perfectly still. She said:

"I can talk now, Jan. Here, while it's still dark. I used to hate waking in the dark, but not any more. Do you want to go to sleep again?"

"No," I said, "I'm too happy to sleep, Di, so talk if you want to."

"First about Pierre Rance," she said.

"No," I said, "not about him. Damn the past. We've done with it at last!"

"No, Jan, not now we've got this chance to start out again."

"Who was it put the ban on inquests?"

"This isn't an inquest, Jan, it's a map. We need a map or we might get lost again."

"All right," I said, for gratification had drowned me in tolerance, "tell me about this Rance!"

"I never lost the physical image of you, Jan, and it's important that you should believe that. Never for an hour, not after all that time. I did everything I could think of to lose it, drink, casual affairs and later on, living dangerously and trying to lose myself in the cause, you know, like a frustrated woman taking the veil! But it was pretty pointless, all of it, and sometimes at night I ached so that I'd get up and go looking for a man, any man! Whoring without a fee!"

"Don't, Di, let's take it as read!"

"No," she said levelly, rising and turning on her elbow, "because it doesn't hurt any more and I want you to understand. I want that more than anything! Then Raoul found me and took me on, so that for the first time in my life I felt vaguely useful to someone other than you and the ache ceased, not much but enough to make me hope. Up to then, I had been using the Resistance like the bottle but under Raoul it did take on some kind of meaning and purpose. I thought I was getting somewhere but that spell only lasted about three months."

"Well?"

"Then, out of the blue, Pierre appeared and because he seemed to me a kind of distorted double of you he pushed me under again. Right under! I went down deeper than ever and the wonder is that I didn't kill myself. I can't understand now why I didn't because I had nothing to live for and if someone had told me this miracle could happen I wouldn't have believed them."

"No two men are that alike, Di," I said, "and you never have been that much of a fool. I don't resent Rance, not in the way one might imagine I would, you obviously needed him, or someone like him and to feel jealous of him would be as stupid as you resenting Alison."

"He doesn't seem much like you now, Jan, and I'm certain he won't seem at all like you when he comes again but when Yves first introduced us I almost cried out. It was uncanny. I kept on wanting to call him 'Jan' and when he saw what was happening he jumped to the wrong conclusion and lost no time in following up. He's a one hundred per cent bastard but he's very bright, not just scientifically and where money-making is concerned but really bright and in some ways utterly original. I think he was rather flattered at first but later on, when he realised I wasn't in love with him and was only substituting him for someone else, the sadist in him had a field day! I believe he knew I was flirting with the Resistance and he used this to improve his hold on me. It was about then that I conceived his child and the only trick I ever won against him was keeping it from him!"

"How the hell did you manage that?" I asked, disturbed in spite of myself. Di wasn't easily frightened and the fact that she was obviously terrified of this man made him that much more important.

"I was lucky," she said. "Before it became obvious he and Yves went off on the inspection tour of Germany and by the time he returned I had got rid of it. That wasn't very difficult, Raoul arranged it all. As soon as he heard you had agreed to come he said this was essential but I should have done it anyway unless you had turned me down."

I wondered at this for in some way it made me responsible for the course she had taken.

"You mean you would have had the child if I had backed down on the invitation to come here?"

She was silent for a moment. Then she said: "Yes, I would, because I'd made up my mind to let go. I hadn't nearly as much guts as I thought I had and I certainly hadn't enough to do myself in. I suppose one is born with a certain amount, Jan, and uses it up, bit by bit. I don't think courage breeds. You begin with so much and the older you get the more carefully you have to husband it. You can fire it away in quick bursts or in single shots but there comes a time when the magazine is empty. Do you believe that?"

"It's arguable," I said. "Courage is a very difficult thing to analyse but never mind all that, what had you decided to do when I almost backed out, that time in the jeep? If it wasn't suicide, what do you mean by 'let go'?"

"Just—'let go', let things take their course. It would have meant betraying Raoul and the others but I was so damned tired, I didn't shrink from that. I didn't care very much what set of idiots were in power and come to that, I don't now, not madly so!"

It was an astonishing confession from a woman in her situation but I believed her. It wasn't really as cynical as it sounded but that was something I had to find out. I was as green as the next man when I arrived in France but I learned the true state of affairs very quickly. One did under the various pressures. The white and black inevitably merged into grey and all that has happened since the overthrow of Hitler has justified Diana's pessimism.

"Why didn't you stay in Britain when you had the chance?" I asked her.

She threw out her right hand and switched on the bedside light. It seemed that she didn't need the dark any more.

"That isn't obvious to you? Not even now?"

"No, Di, no it isn't! It was an escape and you were sure of me and Yvonne. We could have made our fresh start on home ground. What difference would it have made?"

"Why, all the difference in the world," she cried. "I've lived all my life without achieving anything at all and to have come back and used you in that way would have been more despicable than anything else I've done! In some ways it would have been as futile as tying up with Pierre for the rest of my life!"

She rolled over and clasped her hands behind her head, drawing up her knees and addressing the ceiling.

"You and I were destined for something splendid, Jan, something we could do together, because of one another and for one another! I like to think this is it, this is our final try! In the old days, loving and needing each other was enough. There was always the opposition—my background and people, your rather snobbish pride in being poor and what's happened since then is an altogether bigger challenge, it's the march of the faceless little men, with their hideous machines and squalid little minds cluttered

442

up with rules and regulations and prohibitions and tidy conceptions of an orderly, graded society!"

"But damn it, Di, you said you don't believe in Democracy!"

"Democracy is a word! So is 'Fascism' and the swastika is only the trademark! Half the people opposing Hitler at this very moment are moving in his direction without even knowing it, and when they've dealt with him, because he's thrown their machines out of gear by being so damned impatient, they'll set to and finish what he started. People like you and me will always find themselves in opposition or gaol! I shouldn't be surprised if the war doesn't speed up efforts to convert Sennacharib into a nice, tidy park, with 'By Order' notice boards and concrete ponds and circular flower beds and God knows what other sanitary improvements! Both sides have already deified science and they're out to convert every one of us into a bigot or a cog! Well, we're going to take a crack at the toughest bunch and if we survive we'll go on fighting for the rest of our lives, even if we're the last champions above ground!"

"Well," I said, catching her mood at last, "you've made it plain what we're fighting against but what the hell are we champions of? That's something I've never really understood!"

She thought for a moment.

"I suppose of everything that grows and thrives in Sennacharib, the wind in the larch wood and the free flight of our special buzzards, the right to walk and love and breathe how we like, where we like and if we like! Of our absorption into the rhythm people call God and a lot of other silly names—oh, I don't know, you can't put a thing as fragile as that into words but you don't need to, Jan, at least, you *used* not to, you feel it, sense it, belong to it! Trying to define it is pointless, don't you see?"

I saw well enough and reflected that she hadn't changed much after all. She was still Emerald Diana Gaylorde-Sutton, riding into the wind with the banner of the undefeated on her stirrup.

I said, kissing her shoulder: "That's enough, Di! We've

got at least forty-eight hours you said, so let's take that holiday!"

She laughed and threw her arms around me, rocking me slightly as a child rocks a doll. Over her shoulder I saw the first, wispish glimmer of dawn and more lights winking on the hillside.

Chapter Four

WHEN I was a schoolboy I thought of France as a strange country where women in frilly underwear danced the can-can in the streets and naughty old men patronised brothels advertised by red lamps. When I was a year or so older I thought of France as a place dotted with turreted chateaux and peopled by grave peasants, who paused in their toil to acknowledge the Angelus. Then, in early manhood, I travelled in France and found it broad and flat, almost treeless and half-populated, its friendly, shabby people inhabiting crumbling little towns with unpainted shutters and streets hard on the feet.

In the spring of 1942 I discovered a new France, a country where the misery and shame of occupation and betrayal showed in people's faces, where the bulk of the population hunted the necessities of life in a vicious black market and a minority risked their lives hitting back at the conquerors, but, in so doing, lost the tolerance that had distinguished Frenchmen in the past. I think the most astonishing thing about France at this time was its political confusion. Under the hammer of the Gestapo and the Vichy *milice* Resisters had split into scores of unco-ordinated little groups, and it seemed that no power on earth could organise them to work for their liberation as a team.

Some owed allegiance to the extreme Left and some to the official Free French organisation in London. A few co-operated intelligently with the British movement, directed

444

from Baker Street, but the majority clung to their independence to the very end.

I suppose that Raoul de Royden's group was as official as any. It had the backing of De Gaullists in London, but I had the impression, then and later, that this support dated from the time de Royden and his associates told London of their active interest in reprisal weapon number one, the sinister-sounding *Vergeltungswaffe Eins*. The fact that Raoul de Royden was a member of the family concerned in the manufacture of the weapon must have given the London screening officers a headache, but at last he was cleared and trusted, and official backing advanced his personal prestige in France. He must have been extremely adroit at double bluff, because when I arrived in Villefranche he was not on the run but operated quite openly and was still on the payroll of the Vichy army.

At that time, of course, not even Raoul knew the true nature of the weapon or what parts of it were being tested in factories owned and operated by Diana's husband. All he did know was that some kind of missile was being developed in Germany and that either its direction-finder or propulsion unit was being built in one of the de Royden workshops. For a long time he and his intimates worked on the assumption that Rance, the principal boffin of the firm, was engaged in designing a new master gyro (Rance, it seems, was a recognised expert in this field) and it was this that led them to shadow Diana's lover and get a line on his real activities. Then, soon after Diana's visit to Britain, they had a stroke of luck. A foreman at the de Royden Vincennes plant went over to the Resistance and told Raoul's group everything he knew. It tied in with information the Allies already possessed and plans were set on foot at once to strike a counter-blow.

The original plan was to get the British to bomb the factory and destroy the plant, but this was soon discarded, partly because the work was widely dispersed and no one could be sure where vital damage could be effected but also in deference to French workers engaged on round-the-clock shifts and therefore vulnerable to air-attack. Apart from the danger of killing civilians, there was another factor that deterred the R.A.F. Total dislocation of a factory always meant that thousands of French workers were thrown out of work, and whilst the Allies were not over-sentimental in this respect, a raid that closed a large factory prejudiced employees in ·favour of Laval's pro-German government.

Ultimately, a different approach was found. It was decided to promote a three-fold offense. Rance, as a key-man in the enterprise, was marked down for assassination by the Resistance and Yves de Royden, whom the Allies thought they could coerce and use, for kidnapping. At the same time it was hoped that these two strikes would lead to the acquisition of blueprints and perhaps a prototype of the weapon or such parts of it as were in an advanced state of production. I had nothing whatever to do with this back-room planning. All that Diana was told was that on a certain day Rance was to be eliminated and that afterwards I was to impersonate him in the attempted kidnapping of Yves and the search for blueprints and prototypes.

Diana and I were alone at the villa for two days. We moved about openly for it was thought the villa might be under routine surveillance and my presence, as Rance, would allay suspicion. On the third day we received a telephone message that Raoul de Royden was on his way down to us and he arrived that same afternoon, so quietly and unobtrusively that we never discovered whether he came by car or on foot, or whether he entered the house by the back door or front.

Diana and I were listening to Mozart records in the big room when suddenly he was there standing just inside the door. I don't know how she reacted but I know that I felt extremely foolish at being discovered lying full-length on a divan, with Diana squatting on the floor, her head against my legs. It was almost as bad as being surprised in bed with one another and if Raoul had arrived an hour or so later that might have been the case.

I leaped up and he smiled, superciliously I thought. I remembered then that Diana had told him the full story of our idyll and the recollection of this increased my embarrassment. He was faultlessly dressed in the uniform of a tank regiment and he looked like a staff officer who has surprised an airman and a Waaf behind a haystack. He said, with as much irony as we deserved, "You seem to have made yourself very comfortable here, M'sieur!"

Diana was not impressed by his manner. "Don't sound so damned stuffy, Raoul!" she said, scrambling up and switching off the radiogram. "What did you expect us to do? Play a hand of écarté?" He smiled and relaxed. I could see that he was fond of her and that she could manage him far better than I could hope to do.

"I'll make some coffee," she said, then, hovering: "When do you expect Pierre?"

"Tonight!" he said briefly and I noticed that she winced. She left us without another word and remained in the kitchen for the next twenty minutes. When the door was shut I said: "She's all right about everything else but she's terrified of him! She thinks he knows that she's involved with your people!"

"That's very probable," he said, "but it won't matter after tomorrow. If he does suspect her he hasn't communicated his suspicions to Yves or anyone else."

"How can you be sure of that?" I demanded.

"I am sure of it," he said, irritably, "and there is no necessity to go into tedious explanations, my friend! What kind of pistol did they give you?"

I showed him my small automatic and he sneered.

"That is quite useless! I will lend you something more reliable."

Suddenly I was tired of being pushed around, it had gone on for too long and seemed to be the prerogative of too many people. I said:

"Look de Royden, my life is important to me. I've gone a long way with all of you in the sacred name of security but I'm damned if I'll go another step until someone tells me what's expected of me!"

He smiled, unexpectedly, and for a moment looked almost genial.

"I'll wager Diana has told you more than she ought, Jan Leigh!"

"Whatever Diana told me was unofficial. I want to hear it from you. As far as I can see I'm doubling for this character Pierre Rance. His name makes her sick with fright and I'm not asking why; I think I know why. What really bothers me is this. If I'm standing in for him how comes it he's still alive and is coming here? Diana says he's due to be bumped off. The point is, when?"

He smiled again but this time it was a tight-lipped smile.

"I can tell you that; tonight!"

"Tonight? You mean on his way here?"

"No, after he arrives, after you've had an opportunity to study him at close quarters. Killing him is easy enough. Doubling for a stranger is not nearly so easy. Watch the way he stands, walks, talks, look for the odd gesture. Then, when you're satisfied, kill him!"

"*I* kill him?"

"Why certainly. Who else?"

I stared at him with dismay. The sopnists declare that there is no difference between killing an enemy who happens to get in your way during a wartime operation and killing a man in cold blood but there is a difference, a very great difference if *you* have to do it. People who tell you that kind of thing usually take care to use theories for live ammunition. I opened my mouth to say something like this but thought better of it and remained silent. I knew any protest from me would invite his contempt and irritation. He looked at me intently for a moment.

"Well, my friend?"

"Does Diana know I am to kill him?"

"If she hasn't taken that much for granted she has even less imagination than you! However . . ." he shrugged and seemed suddenly to tire of the discussion and turn his attention to my prospects of understudying Rance satisfactorily. "There is a certain likeness and we might employ it successfully, that is, unless we are unfortunate enough to run into someone who knows Rance well. I think perhaps that you should bide your time when he gets here. Watch him closely for a few hours and then dispose of him early in the morning!" He turned aside. "Why is

448

she so long with the coffee? I should like a drink. You have not even offered me a drink, Jan Leigh!"

He said this as a feeble effort at jocularity and as he said it he reminded me of a headmaster patronising a schoolboy in out-of-school hours.

I crossed to the cocktail cabinet and poured him a brandy. He drank it off and returned the glass for more. "Be a little more generous with our friend's liquor," he said, still trying to sound affable.

Diana came in with coffee on a tray and set it down without a word. She had got herself in hand during her absence in the kitchen and was now trying even harder than Raoul to appear casual but she didn't fool me for a second. I noticed that her hands shook when she placed the tray on the marble-topped table.

"How do you recommend me to go about it?" I asked, presently, since Raoul continued deep in thought.

"I have given it a great deal of thought," he said, now sounding less like a headmaster but like an employer about to reject an employee's claim for a rise in salary. "I should imagine that even a raw hand like you could achieve it with reasonable efficiency, that is, unless Emerald has changed her mind on the matter!"

They exchanged looks, hostile looks, I thought, and then Diana turned away. I noticed that whenever he wanted to sound ironic he always called her "Emerald". It was a name she hated and told me so the first day we met.

"I can't do it and I've told you why, Raoul!" she said, flatly. Then, as though anxious to be gone, "I'll tidy the other rooms, we don't want him alerted by something trivial. You don't want me any more, do you?"

"No," said Raoul, more kindly this time, "our friend will find it easier if you are not in a position to anticipate."

I was glad he dismissed her. I was having a hard battle with myself and her presence would have made it a good deal worse. She went out and I heard her opening and shutting drawers in the bedroom.

"You will do it with this, from up there!" he said, shortly, and bent to unzip a kind of cricket-bag he had brought with him. At the same time, straightening himself, he

449

jerked his hand towards the ceiling and at once I remembered the little glazed apertures in the attic floor.

"Was it with something like this in mind that you loopholed the loft?" I asked.

"Yes, indeed!" he said, approvingly, obviously relieved that I had shown a limited amount of promise by noticing them. He reached into his bag and took out a short, murderous-looking carbine. It had begun life as some kind of sporting gun but had been adapted for close-range, single shot firing. He handled it lovingly.

"You could hardly miss at that range," he said, "providing you choose the right moment, of course. Don't move about at all unless it is absolutely necessary and if you do move, move on your belly. We cut three holes just in case, but I recommend the bedroom."

"How about the body?" I asked, feeling as if I was speaking a banal line in a theatrical production of the Whinmouth Thespians.

"I will call for it tomorrow," he said, "and afterwards we will move on to the next stage!"

Suddenly he dropped his patronising manner and became almost likeable.

"Have a drink, Jan Leigh," he said, "have one now and then leave it alone. And do not imagine that I fail to understand your misgivings! After all, we are supposed to be civilised and have been several centuries learning to respect the sanctity of human life. One cannot jettison all that in five minutes. It took me several months and some complicated balancing of accounts!"

"Personal accounts?"

"No," he said, pouring me a large brandy, "not especially so. I think it was the transportation of the French Jews that put me in credit. You probably heard about it yourself?"

"No," I said, "only the mass extermination they are doing in Europe as a whole."

"French ghetto-clearing was rather special," he said. "A few months ago orders came to root out all the registered Jews and separate the children, even the children of two and three years of age. They and the parents were transported to Germany in separate convoys, packed like beans in a box. Most of them were probably dead when they arrived and it is certain that all are dead at this moment. There were four thousand children in that convoy!"

I swallowed my brandy but it did not seem to do me much good.

"I've read a good deal of history," I said, at length, "but one doesn't find this kind of thing anywhere, not wholesale extermination of children, if one discounts Herod. What I find so hard to understand is the attitude of the rank and file. Why the hell don't the fathers among the extermination squads prefer death to that kind of job? What stops them losing all control and turning their guns on their officers? British troops would, so would French and Turks and even Japs, I imagine!"

"It has gone on too long," he said. "There have been isolated instances of it and there will be again but mass mutiny, that kind of mutiny among the S.S.? It is asking a little too much, my friend! It is a matter of conditioning. If you had been present at their pre-war youth rallies you would understand a little better, I think!" He stopped musing and became businesslike again. "Would it help if you were conditioned yourself? We have . . ." he glanced at his wrist watch, ". . . an hour or so. I could describe to you what happened in a village near my birthplace last December!"

"No, Captain de Royden," I said, "I can manage, it's just a question of getting used to the idea. We had better employ the time on the gun and by having a look round upstairs."

He nodded and gave me a quick and useful lesson on the weapon, disengaging the magazine which held five shots and showing me how to steady my aim by employing the sling as a shoulder strap. Then we went into the hall and lowered the staircase. There were plank catwalks between the rafters and he sent me down again to listen while he belly-crawled about upstairs. I heard no sound but doubted whether I could have moved as noiselessly as he did. Then he called me up again and drew my attention

451

to the hideout behind the cistern and said that I would have ample warning to retreat there when I heard the stair cord pulled but that it was unlikely Rance would have occasion to come up before I had a chance to kill him.

"He will be thinking of other things," he said. "She still exerts a considerable influence over him. We have already established that, otherwise we should have found some easier method of disposing of him. We chose this way because it promises to be tidy."

I pondered this remark as we went downstairs and Raoul summoned Diana and told us a little of his future plans. Once Rance was dead and I had stepped into his shoes, we were to set out for the small factory where we might hope to find blueprints in the safe. In the meantime I was to show myself in the area in case Rance was being shadowed by a personal bodyguard employed by the Germans. It was a possibility we could not overlook for a hue and cry over Rance would be sure to complicate the capture of documents and might well alert Yves.

I don't know whether it was Raoul's act in taking me into his confidence or my recognition of Diana's fear of Rance that gave me the confidence I needed, but soon I began to feel less reluctant to murder him.

Towards sunset Raoul assumed his brisk, military personality again and wished us a formal farewell. When he had gone Diana said I had better go over the villa thoroughly and make doubly sure there was no trace of my presence. I did this and then it was dusk and time for me to take up my position. I had to force myself to ask her what kind of programme Rance would have in mind when he arrived. Would he be likely to collect her and take her down to the town for a meal or a drink or would he want to go straight to bed?

"It depends where he has been and what he has been doing," she said uncomfortably. "I'm not the only woman he sleeps with. He has a mistress in Nice and another in Paris."

"Raoul told me that they were confident that you still had considerable influence over him," I said.

"They're probably out of date," she replied, dully.

452

Her apathy worried me on two counts. Unless she perked up when he arrived he might easily deduce something from her manner but quite apart from this I was beginning to be seriously concerned for her.

"Look here, Di," I said, recklessly. "Why don't we have done with all this bloody nonsense? Why don't I crown him the minute he comes in and have done with it?"

"We have to do it the way Raoul planned," she said. "He has a good reason for everything and I swore to him that I wouldn't question his orders if he agreed to getting you here!" She straightened her shoulders and made a big effort. "This is damned silly," she said, "and I'm not helping much, am I? Just think of those Jewish children. I heard Raoul tell you about it, I was listening outside the door!"

Somehow the admission comforted me, perhaps because it reminded me of the old Diana, a shameless eavesdropper if she thought eavesdropping paid. I pulled the cord of the stair and rested the carbine against the rail. Then I kissed her gently and reminded her of one of the things we had discussed before Raoul arrived.

"This is a sort of beginning again, Di," I said, "so don't let's forget where we hope it might lead us. I'm not scared any more and you mustn't be, not with me within call. I won't botch it and all you have to do is to keep him happy and relaxed. If you can't do that you've lost your touch. Remember how long it took your mother to rumble what was going on between us all those years. I don't think they'd know now if we hadn't panicked and eloped to Nun's Island!"

She smiled and held me closely for a moment. Then I took the carbine, climbed the stairs and closed the trap. She pulled the cord and I was isolated in the roof. There was no way of lowering the stairs from above.

The little window was set high up in the wall facing the sea but it was almost dark when I settled in and the only real light came from the peepholes, three thin pencils above the kitchen, living-room and main bedroom. I slung the carbine and moved about in the gloom, checking the field of fire from each hole. Then I knelt over each, sighting the carbine. Dependent upon where Rance stood, I thought I could get a line on him anywhere but the bedroom loophole was the most promising, for elsewhere there were portions of the room I couldn't cover, no matter on which side of the apertures I stood. As I said, the peepholes had been glazed and the loft was almost soundproof, far more so than its counterpart in a British-built bungalow of this type. Up here it was like looking down into a fish-tank and one felt far removed from anyone below. When Diana, drifting restlessly between terrace and main room, bent over the radiogram and switched it on I had to strain my ears to catch a murmur of the music and even when she turned it up and glanced towards the ceiling, as though asking me whether or not I could hear, I could not recognise the record. She turned it low again and helped herself to a brandy, a very generous one it looked from where I crouched, and she was sipping it when I saw car lights reflected on the little window and a yellow beam swept across the rafters. It might have been any passing car but somehow both of us knew at once that it was Rance's. She jumped up so quickly that she almost spilled her drink and I padded over to the window and saw a car reversing into the short drive. Someone got out, said something to the driver and then stood aside as the car started up again and drove off down the hill. The passenger walked up towards the front door.

I was tempted to shoot him then and get it over. The range was short and he was silhouetted against the final glimmer of daylight but I remembered just in time that I was scheduled to impersonate this man and had therefore better get a much closer look at him. He stood under the window a moment as if fumbling for a key and then Diana opened the door and I crept back to the peephole over the living-room. The music was still playing, I could just hear it, but for several minutes the room remained empty. Then he came in alone carrying a fat briefcase. He had left his coat, hat and bag in the hall.

I suppose we prefer to think of ourselves as unique individuals and perhaps a prejudice in this respect helped to

454

reassure me as regards the likeness between us, or rather the lack of it. He was certainly my build and colouring, and the short Van Dyke beard and moustaches we wore did something for the match but we were only doubles in the sense that a pair of Guardsmen look very similar when they are pacing the same sentry beat in identical uniforms. He did not move like me, or hold himself like a man who had lived most of his life in the country. He had a town look and a slight stoop, as though he had spent long hours over a desk and I noticed that he found the light in the big room too strong for him and squinted before turning off the centre-light and then one of the table lights. I was worried about this for I needed light and now the room was half-full of shadows.

He stood for a moment directly under my spy-hole and I saw that his hair was thinning on top and that his hands were not at all like mine but long and rather elegant, the hands of a man who has never worked at a bench. He had the air of a student, resolved and purposeful, a man whose moments of indecision would be confined to trivial things, when to eat or drink, what paper to buy, what train to catch. I can't say why I got this impression but it was there all right. He looked a difficult, obstinate individual, big and strongly-made yet petulant and wilful and looking down on him I believe that I began to understand Diana's physical fear of the man. No one could have mistaken him for anything but a Latin and I wondered again at Diana's curious substitution of him for me. Taken all round it was not very flattering on her part. Again I could have killed him with a single shot and no margin for error but I did not, I just knelt there looking down on him and wondering. Presently he called something over his shoulder and Diana came in. I realised at once that there was something odd about her, a change in her manner and expression, in the way she moved and looked, and also that these changes were not part of an act to lull any suspicions he might have. It was a physical change and for a moment I was puzzled. I had never seen her looking quite like that, perky yet somehow stilted, jaunty in a rather fatuous way as though she had taken too much to drink and was defiant on this account. Then she went close to him and my bewilderment increased, for she looked up at him in a way a woman looks at a man when she has made up her mind to rouse him. Yet there was a good deal more than desire in her approach and it seemed to me that either she was overacting, or that she had told me less than the truth about their relationship. There was almost adoration in her approach, as though she was in the presence of the one man in the world who mattered to her, whose touch and affection were vital to her immediate happiness. He did not show any noticeable reaction to this but stood off, looking at her with what seemed to me amused contempt.

They pottered about down there, Diana making all the running and they exchanged a few remarks. I caught a word here and there but not enough to follow the drift of their conversation and I cursed Raoul for failing to convert the loft into a listening-post. I felt quite futile looking down and being able to see their lips move without hearing what they said. Now it was like looking out from a fish bowl. At length he sat down and she brought him a drink which he sipped and put down on a coffee table beside him. Then, having swallowed all her liquor, she suddenly slammed down the glass and reached over his shoulders, clasping her hands across his chest and laying her cheek alongside his in a sensuous but amateurish fashion. It was like watching someone who was half-drunk trying to parody a scene from a film, and it made me feel like a Peeping Tom squinting through a suburban window. I was struck by the expression of abandon in her face. Her lips were moist and slack and her eyes dilated in a curiously unpleasant way.

Then another curious thing happened. Suddenly, as though irritated by her, he shrugged her away, stood up and stretched himself, yawning and tapping his mouth. She looked at him uncertainly for a moment and when he turned and said something she hung her head, looking almost abject. I could not be certain but it looked as though there were tears in her eyes.

I was so absorbed in what was going on that I quite forgot what I was doing up here and pushed my carbine on to the narrow catwalk between the rafters. I saw him pick up and finish his drink and take his briefcase over to the table where he peeled off his jacket and opened the case, spreading his papers on the desk and seeming to forget her altogether. She said something more but he made no reply and after looking at him intently for a moment, she turned on her heel and drifted out, closing the door.

I was now able to devote my full attention to Rance and did so with a certain relief. Casually he consulted a notebook and jotted down one or two figures in a small ledger. Then, after pondering a moment, he began to sort through a bulky file holding what appeared to be drawings and sketches and I wondered if we were going to have the luck to find what we sought in his possession without the risk of raiding the factories. He sifted through the drawings without much interest until he found what he was looking for, a folder measuring about eight inches by six. This, I decided, must be something important so I craned my neck until I could look beyond his hunched shoulders. He flicked open the folder and drew out the contents, a bunch of cards that he spread fanwise in front of him. They were not plans or lists of figures, just pornographic postcards half as large again as ordinary postcards and printed in lurid colours. I could see them so clearly that I could recognise them as a series featuring two sleek, fuzzy-haired young men and a plump olive-skinned girl, all South Sea Islanders or natives of that hemisphere. They had been photographed in some extraordinary positions, sometimes as a pair and sometimes as an acrobatic threesome.

Suddenly I wanted to laugh and the chuckle stuck in my throat causing me a few seconds of acute discomfort. The momentary discomfort restored my sense of reality and I decided that I might now get on with what I had been instructed to do, that is, to shoot him tidily and efficiently whilst Diana was safely out of the room. I slid the carbine towards me and lifted it, adjusting the shoulder strap and aiming at the hairline on the forehead. Surprisingly so, I now felt no repugnance at what I was going to do and my aim was as steady as if I was sighting a target card. I realised what it was that had steadied me, the pictures and his way of studying them. In a matter of seconds his stature had been reduced to that of a bored little man grubbing about in search of erotic stimulation. Until then he had been grave and dignified, and his attitude to Diana's pawings aloof and remote, but now killing him was like swatting a fly on the window-pane. I was within a split second of squeezing the trigger when the door opened and Diana returned.

She was wearing a garment that I had not seen before, a pseudo-Oriental kimono in a shade of deep purple, with so much gold thread about it that its folds were semi-rigid. It looked an uncomfortable and vulgar gown and seeing her draped in it annoyed me. She had loosened her hair and taken off her shoes and stockings. I was quite certain that underneath this ridiculous robe she was naked.

Perhaps it was this kimono that emphasised her second change in personality, a far greater one than that which had taken place when Rance had entered the room an hour or so earlier. This time everything that I knew as Diana was absent. She was not only a parody of the woman I had known in my youth but a complete stranger to the Diana I had held in my arms during the last few days. The impression that she was drunk or drugged was much stronger now. Her movements were listless and the colour had gone from her cheeks, her complexion reminding me of how she had looked on the day of Alison's funeral. I knew with absolute certainty that she had forgotten I was waiting within a few yards of her to kill this man and that she had surrendered unconditionally to whatever spell he exercised over her. She was completely submissive but there was also a kind of pitiful eagerness in her approach to him. The transition was not merely astounding, it was terrifying.

Then, as he looked up and saw her, things began to happen in a way that suggested at once a kind of ritual, something that was fully understood between them, something that had happened before. He paced about the room, addressing her in what was clearly a hectoring tone and all the time she listened very attentively, like a chastened pupil receiving teacher's lecture. I thought again that she

458

must be acting but then I realised no actress alive could give a performance of that standard.

At last he stopped barking and went back to the table, sitting and taking up the pictures one by one and handing them on to her in a patronising manner that suggested he was doing her a great favour. She looked at each of them and clearly they excited her, for she began to anticipate them like a greedy child being fed with sweets. He humoured her for a while and then barked another order and she went over to the radiogram and selected a record. Having put it on she poured two drinks, a large and a small, and carried them across to the desk. He was busy for a moment shuffling his precious postcards and when they were bunched he picked up his drink and she reached for hers. She did this so tentatively that I was not very much surprised by what happened next. He slapped the back of her hand with such force that I heard it strike the edge of the desk. She leapt back a pace and her bruised hand shot to her mouth but she did not take her eyes off him and her expression was still reverent to the point of worship. He poured the contents of her glass into his and began to sip, giving her another order as a kind of afterthought.

I was trembling now and my hands were so sweaty and unsteady that I doubt if I could have used the gun. As it was I was far too fascinated by what was going on below and when I looked again she was standing over by the radiogram, very still and straight; I could hear the faint purr of the record and follow its beat by the steady tap of Rance's foot. Then he seemed to mellow and said something that made her smile. In a single movement she threw off the gown and began to walk across the room, not towards him but past him as his foot stopped tapping and he leaned forward, studying her intently and keeping up the rhythm by gently clapping his hands. She crossed in front of him again and reached the radiogram and then turned again and repeated the walk in exactly the same way, to and fro, along the entire length of the room and all the time he did nothing but watch her and clap his hands. It was not simply a case of a timid tart gratifying the demands of an eccentric customer, it was much more like a marionette moving back and forth on the end of a string and was the most degrading performance I have ever witnessed.

She had passed under the peep-hole about a dozen times when Rance seemed to warm up and take a more positive part in the ritual. Leaning forward as she moved a step beyond him he delivered a heavy smack on her buttock and another to match it as she passed on the way back. She took no notice whatever of the assault but it seemed to destroy his gravity for he threw back his head and howled with laughter.

The two blows broke the spell that the repellent spectacle had cast over me. I managed to choke back the shout of rage and grab the carbine, bringing it into position and waiting until Diana was at the blind end of the room, then pulling the trigger with about three times as much pressure as is consistent with accurate aim.

The roar of the gun filled the loft and set my ears ringing. There was a tinkle of falling glass and I saw that I had missed him by a yard.

He did not throw himself down or reach for a weapon, or do anything that a man at whom someone is shooting might be expected to do. He just sat back in his chair and looked inquisitively at the ceiling and his inertness gave me a moment or so to pull myself together and work the bolt.

I was quick but not nearly quick enough. Almost before the glass had fallen into the room Diana leaped into vision and hurled herself at Rance and in the very act of leaping, God knows how, she had seized a paper-knife that lay in the ink tray. It was a ridiculous weapon and could hardly have done more than break the skin of a man wearing clothing but as the two of them crashed over she lunged at him again and again.

I saw all this during the second or so that it took me to level the carbine and at the same time I saw that to shoot into the melée behind the desk might be fatal to the wrong person. For the time being the carbine was useless and I knew that I was obliged to break out of the loft at once.

There was only one means of doing this, to burst through the ceiling and I grabbed at the cross-beam connecting two rafters, swung myself up and projected myself down with every ounce of strength in my body.

The space between the joists yielded readily enough but the lath and plaster did not break as completely as I had hoped. For a few seconds I was held by my waist, my legs swinging free in the vast cloud of dust that the puncture had released into the room. Then, as I threw my arms above my head, my weight carried me down and I fell within a few feet of them, striking the desk top and rolling against the curtained window.

I suppose the whole incident only occupied about seven or eight seconds but it seemed much longer and a good deal had happened while I was on my way down. Diana's leap had carried her over and beyond Rance, so that she had landed face downward beyond him and overset a tall standard lamp, the main source of light after Rance had dimmed the others. What light remained came through the clouded glass panels of the hall door and it was by no means adequate for in-fighting among broken and over-turned furniture. Rance must have been an extremely active man. In spite of Diana's spring, which had knocked him over the back of the chair and full-length on the parquet floor, he was up in a flash and had pinned her down before she could rise on hands and knees. He had her in a vicious neck-lock, his forearm under her chin and in a matter of seconds he would have broken her neck.

In what must have been a reflex action I found my automatic and whipped it out, struggling violently to free myself from the curtain which had ripped away from its rings and brought down pelmet and pelmet board. I rolled about helplessly for a moment, wrestling with the heavy folds and cursing at the top of my voice. Then I managed to free myself, dive across the surface of the desk to grab Rance by the hair, groping for a place to jam the muzzle of my gun. In that moment we must have looked like the characters in his postcards. Diana was stark naked and Rance almost so, his shirt and singlet having been torn the length of his back. Then I found his temple and pressed the trigger.

I heard no explosion so I pressed it twice more and he shuddered so violently that I lost my grip and was left with a handful of his hair.

Diana was screaming and I screamed back at her, shouting for light and ultimately scrambling to the door and switching them on. Rance lay on his back among the folds of the curtain with half his head blown off. Diana was leaning against the tilted cocktail cabinet and there was blood on her shoulder and down her left leg. Some of the bottles had tipped over and the room reeked of spirits. The desk chair was splintered, the curtains lay in a heap and dust from the ruined ceiling was spreading into every corner of the room. And all the time the radiogram continued to wail its off-beat, tuneless rhythm.

"Are you hurt? Are you okay?" I shouted, grasping her shoulder. It did not occur to me that the blood might be Rance's.

She made a hopeless gesture and I realised that she was still fighting for breath. I picked up the purple gown but she shook her head so I dropped it, picked her up and carried her into the bathroom where I pushed her under the shower and sluiced her with warm water. She neither assisted or hindered me. Only when I began to dry her did she rouse herself and take the towel, so I left her there, returned to the big room and helped myself to a drink. I needed one badly but I didn't take one into Diana. What she needed more was time to pull herself together and a pint of black coffee.

A few minutes later I heard her go into the bedroom and I switched off the lights, partly because the scene sickened me, but also because the large window was now without a curtain. Raoul had stressed the fact that he wanted Rance eliminated tidily and I began to wonder what he would say when he called for the body in the morning. After another drink, however, I felt a good deal better and, working by pocket torch, I started collecting Rance's papers and stuffing them back into his briefcase. I wasted no time examining them, there was far too much to do.

I went through Rance's pockets and emptied them of everything, wallet, identity papers, letters, fountain pen and loose change. I also took his wrist watch and cuff links and would have peeled off the remains of his clothing but it was blood-soaked and no use to anyone. I did, however, take his shoes which fitted me tolerably well. Then I rolled him in the remains of the curtains and tried to tidy the room. There was nothing I could do about the gaping hole in the ceiling but I lowered the stairs and retrieved the carbine. I mopped the floor and rolled up the bloodstained rug and the remains of the chair, stuffing them into a cupboard pending final disposal. By this time it was getting on for dawn and I heard Diana stir, so I went into the kitchen and brewed coffee. I would have preferred to have disposed of Rance's body at once but I did not know where to put it. In the end I pushed it behind a divan and locked the living-room door. Then I banged on the bedroom door and told Diana to hurry. I was already ashamed of the botch I had made of things and I did not want to annoy Raoul further by keeping him waiting.

When Diana joined me in the kitchen she was subdued and very composed. She wore a high-necked sweater which only partly concealed the bruising left by Rance's grip and her voice, when she tried to talk, was not much above a whisper. For a time we sipped our coffee in silence but I could see that she was groping round for some explanation of the miscarriage of our plan. She kept looking at me with a half-smile, then flushing and looking away again. At last she said:

"Don't blame yourself, Jan, it wasn't your fault. It wasn't mine either but you'd better pretend it was, otherwise Raoul might call the whole thing off!"

"You mean he'll have no confidence in me after this balls-up?"

"The idea was to make Pierre disappear. The police would not have known where to begin. Now they'll get a headstart right on his doorstep."

"Then Raoul should have got one of his bloody hatchet men to do the job in a back alley," I grumbled, "I warned him I wasn't his man!" After another long pause, I cleared my throat and went straight to the point. I had to know two things, how much she remembered of what had happened after she had returned to the room in that idiotic Chinese gown, and whether it was possible to hope that Rance was now out of her system for good.

"Were you doped, Di? Did you slip anything into that first drink you had, after I went up to the hideout?"

She looked at me slyly, still half smiling.

"Don't you know? You were watching, weren't you?"

"Yes, but you could have taken dope just before or just after he got here! My guess is that you pepped yourself up for the occasion!"

"You're getting to be quite a sleuth, Jan," she said, and reaching into the pocket of her slacks she produced a small phial containing a yellowish powder and threw it on the table.

"What is it, for God's sake?"

"Does it have to have a name?"

I took the phial, extracted the cork and sniffed the contents. It had no smell but I sensed a sharp pricking sensation in my nostrils and my eyes watered violently. When my vision cleared I had an extraordinarily heightened sense of color. Everything in the room seemed to be made up of dazzling blues and pinks and yellows.

"It's got a long South American name," she said, watching me. "I never could pronounce it and I can't even spell it! I only know that its effect is just what he said it would be, a reversal of values. That was its original purpose in Central America when the Aztecs used it. Everyone inhaled it before a religious festival."

"Why?"

"Because it converted the leery old priests into minor Gods fit to minister to the Almighty Gods! You can see how useful it was if you had to do business with someone like Rance!"

"Is this all you have?"

"It's all *I* have, there may be more in his baggage."

I got up and fetched Rance's grip from the hall. I had already been through it but I gave it a thorough going-over, feeling the lining of his spare suit, examining toilet accessories and probing the lining of the case. Finally I was satisfied that there was nothing among his effects that matched the powder in the phial.

"He didn't take much himself, he preferred giving his women the pushover," she said when I returned to the kitchen.

"How the hell . . . ?" I began angrily but she cut in, placing both hands on the table and looking straight into my eyes.

"Don't look so 'holier than thou', Jan! If you want to hear I'll try and tell you!"

"You could have done that days ago," I said, bitterly.

"I couldn't," she said quietly, "because I thought I was over it! I was really. That was the last shot."

"That's what they all say!"

She sighed and got up.

"It's no use, Jan, maybe you'd better tell Raoul when he gets here!"

"Doesn't he already know?"

She looked at me with surprise.

"Good God, of course he doesn't! Do you think he'd have a junkie in his outfit?"

I thought about this for a moment and decided that she was probably right; I said:

"Look, Di, I honestly believed we were on the level this time, really on the level! No lies, no half-truths, no reservations! A one hundred per cent fresh start."

"So we were," she said.

"We weren't, Di! You told me about the drink and the boy-friends, you didn't add that you were a dope addict!"

She was silent for a moment and I noticed that all traces of the drug had disappeared. She was calm and rational and her natural colour was returning. I was prepared to believe she had only taken a minute dose, enough perhaps to enable her to face Rance.

"I'm not an addict," she said, at length, "I took one shot about an hour before he got here. You saw what he was like. Maybe even you will concede that he rated that much in the circumstances!"

"I can understand you taking the stuff, Di," I said, "but

465

what I don't suppose I shall ever understand is how a person with your kind of guts ever got tangled with him in the first place! Do you have enough words to make me understand that?"

"One word—'penance' maybe!"

"Penance! Great Scot! On *my* account?"

She was involving me again, even in her drug-taking, even in her subjugation by a rat like Rance, and as she said this I remembered how mercilessly I had been involved in everything she had ever done or thought or experienced in her triumphs, frustrations and dreams, her emotions and madcap adventures, in every damned thing she had ever attempted, right back to the days when she had used me as an excuse to play truant from school.

"Well, Di, say what you have to say but for pity's sake let it be the truth! Don't leave the usual rabbit in the hat for the next crisis."

"There won't be another crisis, Jan, not our type of crisis. We're back together, really together now that that swine is dead. And we'll get back to Sennacharib again, you can depend on that!"

I couldn't but it did me good to hear her say we might. I poured fresh coffee and we sat in the airless little kitchen facing one another. It occurred to me that it was a distorted reflection of the night after our first quarrel, when she sought me out in the middle of the night and came into my aunt's kitchen dripping wet to make her peace.

"There's a great deal you do understand about me, Jan," she said, "but a lot more you don't! My obsession with Pierre Rance is something I might be able to make you understand over the years, but I couldn't do it now, not in a single sitting, I could only rough it out, maybe."

"All right, then rough it out before Raoul shows up."

"The Doctor Jekyll and Mr. Hyde theme isn't a literary cliché, pointing the good and evil in people," she said, "it's real enough, particularly in a person like me, whose early life has been cushioned. You know how I was brought up, cut off from every normal emotional experience, fenced round with nannies, chauffeurs and banker's drafts!"

466

"They didn't worry you all that much, Di, you found plenty of holes in the wire!"

"They had their effect, nevertheless. Why do you suppose so many of my set kicked over the traces in the Thirties?"

"You got over that, Di. I ought to know, I nursed you through it, or thought I had, God help me!"

"That's where you really came in, Jan! I daresay that surprises you but it's true for all that. Until then and throughout all the time we were kids you were just one more hole in the fence! Did you ever realise that?"

I had not realised it because my pride had never let me. All the same, it made sense, it explained her fiendish unpredictability and the way she would disappear for months at a time only to return every time she needed a shoulder to cry upon.

"What about your eighteenth birthday?" I reminded her. "You're not going to tell me you weren't a virgin after all!"

"No," she said, evenly, "I was a virgin and you were certainly my first lover but what took place then was prompted by curiosity more than anything else. You demanded the whole truth, Jan. It's not my fault if you find it indigestible."

I did find it so; it stuck in my throat like a sponge soaked in vinegar.

"And after that? The time Yvonne was conceived, and again when we agreed to get married at the cottage?"

"Good God!" she exclaimed, "why be so morbid about it? Why the hell do men have to put such a premium on an act of physical gratification? I'm not talking about isolated acts of sexual communion, Jan, I'm talking about spiritual desolation, the kind I experienced when I renounced every chance I ever had of living a decent, normal, healthy, happy life! That's what I mean when I say you didn't really mean anything until I turned my back on you, finally and irrevocably and found myself married to a queer! That's when I began fighting back and went into training for a man like Pierre Rance. Can't you begin to understand?"

"Not really, Di," I said, "at least not to that extent! If it had been a matter of finding a normal man or half-a-dozen normal men, yes; but a pervert like him, someone who could only see a woman through a twisted mirror and get warmed up on pornographic pictures, a man who could want a woman to parade up and down while he walloped her behind! Not that, Di! Not a person with your pride and vitality! It isn't simply obscene, it's a contradiction of every law in the universe!"

"That's just what it isn't, Jan," she said, "and I should know because I'm the person who experienced it! I couldn't get the good so I reverted to the evil and being the kind of person I am I dredged as deeply as I could! I'll tell you something else! There were times when I actually enjoyed Pierre Rance, enjoyed his warped inventiveness and his twisted approach, enjoyed being beaten and humiliated by him, because somehow or other he was the ultimate evil, just as sharing Sennacharib with you was the ultimate delight! When I was parading for him last night I had completely forgotten you were in the house. I only remembered you when I heard the shot and saw him glance upward. Then I came to and I wanted to stamp him out of existence! Well, that's about the middle and both ends of it and I'm done with him at last but if you still think I'm too big a security risk then maybe you'd better tell Raoul and carry on alone, if he'll have you after the mess we made of everything!"

I was silent for a moment but there was no real decision to make. All the time she had been talking my mind had been finding excuses for her that stood up, and making allowances for all she had been through since she had turned her back on Sennacharib. I knew that I wasn't going to mention the drugs to Raoul, that I was going to invent an attempt on Rance's part to kill her which had necessitated my leap through the ceiling. I knew also that this confession of hers was indeed the whole truth and that we might still break through into Sennacharib again and find the sun.

She said: "One thing more, Jan. Between now and then, will you promise me something?"

468

"Well?"

"Take the lead, Jan! Start telling me what to do and meaning it!"

"How about Raoul?"

"Stand up to him, too! He isn't always right. Damn it Jan, Britain's still fighting and we ought to have some real say in what happens!"

I thought about this for a moment, particularly her emphasis on my leadership and reflected how much grief might have been avoided if she had given me this advice years ago. But perhaps it wasn't her fault at all, perhaps it was mine.

Chapter Five

RAOUL DE Royden appeared about eleven o'clock. Two of his hatchet men were with him, as chilling a pair as I had ever hoped to meet, one shortish, barrel-chested and sallow-skinned, the other tall, drooping and badly scarred about the face. They looked like a sinister comedy team and neither of them spoke a single word while they were with us, although the fat one coughed so persistently that conversation between Raoul, Diana and myself was interrupted from time to time.

Raoul looked aghast at the mess in the front room. After unwrapping the curtains and satisfying himself as regards Rance, he addressed me unsmilingly: "How did you kill him? With a bomb?"

Diana spoke up. "Your plan wasn't so bright after all, Raoul! If Jan hadn't come down that way your ghouls would have had two bodies to dispose of, one of them mine!"

He looked interested. "So? What happened?"

I told him as much as I wanted him to know and I didn't care a damn whether he believed it or not. All I wanted now was for Diana and me to be out of the house and into the fresh air. To me the whole place stank of blood and filth. I could look at Rance's shattered head unmoved but I could not forget what he had represented in Diana's life. This was going to take time, a lot of time.

I gave Raoul all the personal effects I had taken from Rance, together with the briefcase. He raised his eyebrows when he came to the postcards and passed them without comment to his henchmen, who sat against the wall like a pair of bored patients in a doctor's waiting-room and studied them with quiet detachment. When they had seen them all the fat one shuffled them and then dealt them out like a hand of cards. They retained about half-a-dozen apiece.

"There's nothing here that will help us much except the keys," said Raoul, at length, closing the briefcase.

"You wouldn't expect him to carry the kind of documents you want on his person," said Diana, and it struck me that she was beginning to tire of her cousin's patronage.

Raoul got up and walked about the room, tapping his teeth with his fingernails. "Maybe I was wrong," he admitted, presently, "maybe I should have let Pepe cut his throat in a back alley, but I abominate disorder!"

"Rance didn't strike me as a man who would be caught in a back alley," I said and realised that I too was beginning to question the infallibility of this man. "My advice, for what it's worth, is to get him out of here as quickly as possible and then concentrate on the factories or Yves!"

He made a sign to his two acolytes and they went out, returning a moment later with an old-fashioned black trunk, the kind of trunk suburban murderers leave in left luggage offices. It was all so theatrical that I winked at Diana.

The thin man threw open the trunk and I noticed that it had been lined with oiled paper, to avoid leakage, I imagine; they dumped the body inside with about as much ceremony as a pair of butchers handling a carcass after closing time. They stuffed the bloodstained curtains on top and then slammed the lid, locking it and lacing it with rope. I had the impression that they had earned their living doing this sort of thing since they were little boys. Then they marched out carrying the trunk and I saw, on glancing through the window, that they had arrived at the villa in a removal van. They did not return to the house but sat on the tailboard, munching slabs of bread. Raoul noticed my morbid interest in these characters.

"They are good boys," he said, "they do what they are told without comment!"

Diana and I made no reply to this but sat watching him uneasily as he sifted through the many keys on Rance's key-ring.

"The question is, which is which?" he said, finally, and made the remark sound as if it was a profound summing-up of the situation.

Diana made an impatient gesture. "It doesn't matter a damn which is which," she said. "Why don't you leave the rest of it to Jan and me? You can tidy up here one way or another, strip the place and dump it all somewhere, or set it on fire and cover our tracks for a few days. The point is, whatever you do, for God's sake take us into your confidence, Raoul! We've eliminated Rance but that isn't what Jan came over for, any one of you could have done that sooner or later. We want Yves and we want a blueprint. Well, let's get to hell out of here and try for both! I don't know about Jan, but I'm bored with all this wait-until-you're-a-little-older routine!"

The speech expressed my sentiments so exactly that I gave a grunt of approval and was relieved to notice that Raoul seemed to take her advice in good part. He had been shocked by the disorder in the house and perhaps Diana's frankness helped him to marshal his thoughts.

"Let's all have a drink," he suggested and rummaged about in what was left of the cocktail cabinet, pouring three brandies and motioning us to join him at the table.

"There have been some new developments," he said, when we were seated. "First of all there is no prototype in existence, of that we are now certain. Secondly, the major part of the work has been concentrated at the Lyons factory, and has an S.S. guard right round the clock! Diana's father-in-law spends most of his time down there so it is useless to go there and try these keys on the offices and safes of the premises unless we can be sure he is absent. The thing to do would be to entice him away while our friend here impersonated Rance and made a discreet search. It is just possible that one or more of the guard detail know Rance well, but that is a chance we might have to take. If we drew blank there, we could go on and try the keys in the Paris offices. There are five all told but the most likely is at Vincennes. It would mean hit and miss but sooner or later we should stumble on what we were looking for!"

"Stumble is about right!" said Diana, brutally. "What is Yves supposed to be doing all this time? You don't imagine he would be taken in by Jan? We couldn't call at a single one of those factories without the chance of coming face to face with Yves. The whole plan is suicidal, but quite apart from that, it's woolly! I thought you people had things lined up a lot better than this!"

Raoul shrugged: "Have you an alternative plan?" he asked.

"Yes, I have," said Diana. "I suggest we go straight for Yves and make him lead us to the right safe at gunpoint! That's the only way you can make real use of me, isn't it? Otherwise I'm a mere hanger-on and now that Jan's involved it won't do, Raoul! I mean to have a say in this, do you understand? I can smuggle Jan into the house and if any of the servants see him they'll accept him as Pierre. Not one of them knows him well and we can choose our time and maybe get in without any of them seeing him at all. Then I'll manoeuvre Yves on the spot for Jan and we'll go the rounds of the factories in the Mercedes. Two of us can take care of Yves and you can follow at a distance. Once we've found what we're looking for, you can take over and we'll rely on you to get us home with the loot!"

It delighted me to hear her in this kind of form. It was like listening to the old Diana planning mischief in and about her father's estate. Her eye was bright and she radiated confidence. It was almost impossible to imagine that a few hours ago this woman had been dominated by a man like Pierre Rance and I noticed that Raoul was impressed in spite of himself. He was a proud man but he was very far from being a stupid one, liable to adopt a mulishly obstinate attitude to a plan because it was somebody else's. He sipped his brandy slowly, exploring the various situations that might develop from the direct approach she suggested, weighing up chances and balancing them against risks. His passion for neatness and orderliness was an integral part of him. Confusion ruffled his natural civility so that he could seem petulant and intractable but I now decided that I was correct in my earlier surmise, Diana could handle him if she was given half a chance.

He said, "I must sleep on this. I must admit it has possibilities. You and Jan will drive back to Paris at once. I will meet you there at my apartment. Tomorrow night."

"How will you get there? By train?"

He smiled. "I am still nominally in command!" he said. "Leave me the crumbs of authority!"

"Do I notify Yves, or bounce in on him?" Diana asked.

"You must telephone Yves en route," he said, "from Avignon or Orange. You will say Rance is otherwise engaged down here and has ordered you to return."

He stood up abruptly, and held out his hand to me.

"Next time, try and make less mess, my friend!" He looked up at the hole in the ceiling and clicked his tongue rapidly, reminding me of Aunt Thirza when she came upon her husband littering the kitchen with wildflowers and birds' eggs. "What else can we do with this place but burn it?"

I watched him descend the drive and motion to his thugs on the tailboard. It must have distressed him to note that they were eating their bread without first having washed their hands.

Diana spoke over my shoulder. "He is rather a sweetie, isn't he Jan?" She might have been drawing my attention to one of Heronslea's elderly rustics, pottering into the public-bar of the "Rifleman" in Shepherdshey Village.

That was the very beginning of the best time of all between us, the long, leisurely journey across France, from the Mediterranean to Paris, with Rance's elimination behind us and the unpredictable ahead. Now we were far closer than we had ever been, even in the best of the good days. There was a reflowering of the old relationship speeded by the stimulus of achieving something together, even though there seemed every likelihood of sacrificing our lives. The nagging fear of death, capture and torture left us for good. I was excited but it was almost a pleasurable excitement. Looking back on that time I know that even the most alarming moments were far preferable to the empty years we had passed in isolation.

We travelled leisurely. There was no need to hurry for little could be done until Raoul had had time to prepare the ground in Paris. He had to check on Yves' movements, consult the technical men of his group and get our minimum terms of reference as it were; after that, he had to set up some kind of escape route on our behalf. As regards what we hoped to find on de Royden premises my original briefing was already out-of-date and Raoul was not a technician himself, relying upon information supplied him by undercover men such as de Royden's ex-foreman. None of these could take part in the actual raid for every one of them was suspect, as indeed Raoul would have been had he actually presented himself at one of the factories. The security checks on all these establishments were stringent. That was why the group had gone to such extravagant lengths to obtain a passable double for Rance. His identity had a double advantage, his person was familiar at the checkpoints and would hardly be questioned if he tried to pass them in company of Yves but his papers, which we now possessed, were more important still, for security guards would be certain to pay more attention to written permits and to the changing rota of stamps, passmarks and signatures, than to a physical recognition of the man. Under German occupation, Diana warned me, possession of the correct documents was more vital than any actual resemblance I might or might not possess to the faceless thing now lying in Raoul's black trunk.

We set out in Diana's sports car, the white Cadillac convertible that I had seen in the garage of the villa and

474

Diana drove all the way. She was an excellent driver and we could have covered the distance in half the time, but the Provençal sunshine was inviting and as I had never been through this part of France, I welcomed an opportunity to look about me and listen to her lively commentary on the area and her comparisons with our own southwestern region.

I had never realised until then how Continental-minded she was, or how insular most British provincials, myself included, had become in the turbulent pre-war decade. She had spent a good deal of her girlhood down here and her perfect French, plus the fact that she had been here since the first day of the Occupation, enabled her to take a detached view of the effect of total defeat upon the French nation. She was very fond of the French peasant and small business man but she had nothing but contempt for the rich industrialists and politicians who had sold the country to the Germans. She knew both these classes very well, having lived and moved among them since her marriage, but since the war she had taken pains to study the outlook of the ordinary folk in the departments. When I remarked that signs of enemy occupation were not obvious in the small towns we passed through, Diana laughed.

"What did you expect, Jan? Squads of Gestapo men ransacking houses? Firing parties in the market places? Why, ninety-nine out of a hundred of these poor devils are far too occupied getting two square meals a day to bother with war! Many of them still don't know what really happened in the summer of 1940. Ever since the 'twenties', France has been run by a shady company based on Paris and Jacques and his wife had to grow cynical or go mad! Resistance only concerns the odd romantic like Raoul, or the person who has a very practical reason for hating the Nazis, like the families of the prisoners-of-war they still hold. But it's much deeper than that really, this distrust of politicians and power groups and fat businessmen and stiff-necked soldiers. Particularly soldiers! For hundreds of years now these people have seen armies come and go, pillaging and exacting, bullying and cadging. We British made hay down here, didn't we? During the Hundred

Years' War and since? Then there were the religious wars, the Wars of the Fronde, the Seven Years' War, the Napoleonic Wars, the Franco-Prussian War and God knows how many others, all excuses for free billets, impressments, confiscations, conscriptions and every other harassment. Our people in Devon haven't faced this kind of thing since the Monmouth Rebellion and that was only a ripple lasting a few weeks. I can prove my point as a matter of fact. I was taking some horses down south a year or so ago and I had to stop for forage at a farm near Blois. It was an isolated place and just as I was coming away a French military convoy drove up. It was quite obvious that they were French but judging by the panic you might easily have imagined they were Tartars bent on rape and loot! The family ran in all directions, shouting warnings and concealing everything they valued. It was an interesting object lesson, I can tell you!"

This was how Diana looked at things. She had never been a scholar, an amateur politician or even a wide reader but she had a remarkable facility for standing outside everyday life, looking in on it and learning something of interest from every personal encounter. She had watched garage hands repair her cars and could now strip a car like a professional. She could fly an aeroplane and distinguish at a glance between the genuine and the spurious in a room full of antiques. She knew the background history of every country she had visited. She was a first-class judge of horse-flesh, an expert rider and a passable linguist and if you were alone with her for any length of time you were continually surprised by her casual skills and the extent of her general information on all manner of unexpected subjects.

Beyond Orange, where she put through a personal call to Yves, we bought some food and a bottle of wine and drove off the road to picnic in a wood of flowering chestnuts. It was very still and pleasant in there under the arched branches, with greenish light filtering through the leaves and sunlight teasing the long grass and bracken fronds. The peace of the wood discouraged chatter and for a long time we sat watching the lightest of breezes ripple

476

through the grass stems, bending and chivvying them the way the south-west wind behaved in Big Oak Paddock above Heronslea larchwood. I knew that she was comparing this place to Sennacharib and balancing our chances of ever getting home to Heronslea together. I watched her closely as she sat with her back braced against a chestnut bole, her eyes fixed on the mock-panic of the grass army under the gentle onslaught of the breeze. Then, my love for her and my joy in its rebirth, spilled over me like a giant summer wave and I rolled over and laid my head in her lap, revelling in the softness of her thighs and the caress of her fingers in my hair. For several minutes she continued to stroke, absently and vaguely and then awareness returned to her and she looked down, smiling, and I thought I had never seen anything so pretty and engaging as her slightly parted lips and the sun-gleam on her teeth.

"Do you want me, Jan? Here? Like in Sennacharib?"

"No, Di, not here, not yet!" And the strange thing was that I did not, for any expression of the yearning I felt for her would have seemed futile and trivial, an exercise in the humdrum physical domination of the female by the male. I sought no such domination, only the fusing of two human beings and blessed relief from the torment of eternal loneliness.

It was when we had crossed the former Vichy demarcation line that I began to be aware of the shadow over France. Every soldier who had been involved in the 1940 debacle had returned to Britain with an understanding of Nazis that one could never distill from propaganda and radio news bulletins, or from the bellicose thunderings of Churchill. I had witnessed the panic out of Paris that summer but even these memories were not so chilling as the sight of a young German officer lounging against a big, black car parked outside a town hall displaying a notice board printed in German. To me, imaginary or not, there was a kind of twilight about the towns we passed through and the only time it lifted was at a checkpoint outside Paris, where French police inspected our papers and the gendarme who returned them winked in blameless recognition of the fact that a German sentry occupying the sentry-box immediately behind him was staring at us with unwinking hostility, based no doubt upon his resentment at having to stand in full kit under the warm sun whilst his comrades were swilling beer in the guard-post. I mentioned this to Diana, as we drove through St. Cloud and she laughed.

"I sometimes feel sorry for the poor devils," she said, unexpectedly. "Most of them are fed up and far from home, and I can't help suspecting that even the dimmest of them are beginning to doubt the final issue. I used to watch them mooching about in the early days, trying to take an interest in Napoleon's tomb and the Arc de Triomphe but so obviously hoping the pretty girls would unbend!"

"Haven't any, by now?"

"Precious few, although I think some would like to; some of them are rather handsome brutes, aren't they? Here is where you drop off, Jan!"

She stopped at a roundabout within sight of the Arc and opened her capacious handbag, glancing in the mirror and adding a few touches to her make-up. She was trying to appear casual but was not succeeding very well. She had difficulty in gauging the amount of lipstick to apply and as for me, my mouth was dry and the old, familiar beast began to claw at my belly. I had an address to go to, a rooming house in the Avenue de Medecin, on the left Bank, not far from the Pantheon but it depended wholly upon Raoul when we met again. I had strict orders to stay indoors until I was visited or summoned.

I got out, collected my hand luggage and stood hovering by the car. She grinned and said:

"It's like those days you used to see me off on the Waterloo train, Jan! It never started soon enough, did it, and when it did, it always stopped again a few yards down the platform! Then we had to begin—'Well . . . ?' all over again."

I admired her panache but I could not match it, much less improve upon it. I remembered too vividly the last time I had seen her off from Whinford Junction, the time

478

she had never returned, and I wondered, dismally, if the same thing could happen again.

"How long do you think it will be, Di?"

"Not long, Jan, I won't let it be. A day or so, perhaps. Certainly not more than a week."

We had not parked in the best of places and an impatient truck driver hooted behind us.

"Kiss me, Jan!"

I reached over the empty passenger seat and kissed the tip of her nose. Her eyes were clouded and she whipped her hand from the wheel and squeezed my arm.

"Dear Jan! My Jan!" she said, and let in the clutch. I watched her shoot into the flow of traffic and stood shakily alongside the kerb, savouring a valediction that was a password by now. The first time she had ever used those words in parting had been sixteen years ago in a suburban train when she was a precocious schoolgirl of fifteen. As I picked up my grip and walked slowly along the tree-lined pavement towards the *Etoile,* it seemed to me only the day before yesterday.

Chapter Six

RAOUL CAME on the thirteenth day. It was the first time I had seen him in civilian clothes and they reduced him both in stature and dignity, so much so that I felt justified in complaining about my interminable isolation. He had shed his military brusqueness with his tunic and polished leggings, and when I told him I had been so bored that I had been on the point of committing the deadliest sin of an undercover man, that of putting my thoughts on paper, he only smiled wearily and said: "That would have been harmless, my friend, providing you lit the fire with your deathless prose each morning!"

I asked eagerly after Diana, how she was making out with Yves, and whether he had shown any curiosity about her parting with Rance. This time his smile warmed a little.

"I keep telling myself I was mad to allow myself to become involved in this adventure," he said, "for how can a wife teach her husband to drive? Sometimes I think both you and she are using the Resistance as marriage brokers. Come now, you may be as tender and solicitous as you choose when you have accomplished what you were sent here to do!"

Then he relented. "She is managing very well! Yves was curious about Rance but the story stood up. He is supposed to be in Italy with another woman and that pleases Yves. He probably derives a certain amount of pleasure from Diana's presumed jealousy. It is a very curious marriage!"

"You people make a cult of understatement," I growled. "It's a bloody outrageous marriage and all I care about is terminating it! When do I start?"

"Tonight!" he said and twinkled at the effect he produced.

"Tonight? But good God, man, what about my briefing? I don't even know what I'm supposed to get from him before I knock him off!"

He opened the door and glanced out on to the stairhead. I caught a fleeting glimpse of one of his henchmen, the tall, drooping one, lounging against the cast-iron bannister with a slung Sten gun on his shoulder. He shut the door again, locked it and took a long, fattish envelope from his inside pocket.

"You will have until dusk to study this, Jan," he said. "It is a list of possibles and the maximum we can expect. All you need to do is to persuade Yves that you understand it, so that you are not fobbed off by trivial or irrelevant papers. He will attempt that if you fail to impress him sufficiently. You might have to threaten him with death on the spot. You might even have to beat him, but be sparing, we want him in one piece and it might be very difficult to get his co-operation if he is injured. Later on, if things go as we plan, we might try and get him across the Channel. It has worked with one of the biggest Quislings in Holland

480

who was worth all the trouble, they tell me. One can never be sure with that kind of man. On the other hand he might have unexpected reserves of courage. Many of us have. Perhaps you have yourself, Jan?" and he looked at me with one of his quizzical half-smiles.

"I'm not frightened of Yves de Royden," I said, "and given the advantage of surprise I haven't much doubt that I can cope with anyone in the house who tries to help him. That's not what bothers me, it's getting Diana clear after we've done our part of the business."

"That won't be so difficult," he said, "not if you operate without damaging the ceilings! You'll go out by Lysander and we have that arranged for tomorrow night!"

I was elated by this information. I had pictured a much longer delay, a period of lying up in some dismal room like the one I occupied now and then a ticklish journey out of Paris to some God-forsaken coastal rendezvous with a submarine. If Raoul meant to smuggle us out by aircraft, we ought with luck to be back in England within forty-eight hours and imagination took flight with the Lysander. A few days making out reports and then leave and a rail warrant to Sennacharib! My spirits soared. It was a wonderful tonic after thirteen days in that airless attic under the tiles.

"You had better give me the drill, Raoul," I said. "I assume Diana already has hers."

He took a small tracing from his side pocket and crossed over to the window, beckoning to me to follow. The tracing was a detailed plan of de Royden's Paris house, one section devoted to the ground floor and one to the first floor where Yves had his study-office.

"As to getting in, that should be perfectly simple," he said. "Diana will unlatch this garden door and you might even get up to the study without meeting any of the servants. She will try and arrange that for you!"

I smiled at this and he asked the reason. I was tempted to tell him this side-door routine was familiar to us, that she had performed an almost exactly similar introduction on my behalf the night she was eighteen when I had entered Heronslea by the garden door and listened to the invited guests romping their way through the Gay Gordons downstairs, but he was not in the mood to relish confidences of that sort. I noticed that he was taut and having a struggle to conceal the fact in case he infected me.

"Very well," I said, "I'm inside and upstairs. What then?"

"If you do meet any of the servants do not forget that you are Rance," he said. "Only the butler, Harvé, knows Rance well. The others may have seen him half-a-dozen times when he called at the house but it is very unlikely they will challenge you. It is essential that you get upstairs without disturbing the household. You need at least half-an-hour closeted with Yves in the study or, if you are unlucky enough to encounter him elsewhere, you will have to take him into the study for that is where the safe is, and that is the only place you are unlikely to be disturbed. We have briefed Diana very thoroughly on this point. She is going to do everything in her power to get him there and keep him there but one can never tell. After all, he is in his own home and can move wherever he likes!"

"Does he work in his study in the evenings?"

"Usually after dinner, but not always. You cannot count on it."

"Are there likely to be documents you need in that study?"

"No, almost certainly not, but there is an index book, or so Diana believes, a book that contains the names of hundreds of sub-contractors and the products they supply. That would be extremely valuable to us. It could be the basis of a major sabotage campaign prior to the Allied invasion, or even before that. Diana says she would recognise the book. It is red and indexed in ivory. Bring that whatever happens."

"We then leave by the same door?"

"Mon Dieu, no! By the front door, openly! To go out the way you came in would be to set everybody wondering. Yves never uses that door and you would have to circle the house to get to the car."

"Where is the car?"

He referred to the map:

"In the courtyard, here. It is his own car, a black Mercedes. Diana will drive you to the factories. You will sit in the back, with Yves on your left. The side he sits is important. He will be furthest from the concierge huts when you stop at the entrances to show your papers."

"Won't his car be admitted without those formalities?"

"Certainly not! Yves discharged a man only last week for failing to examine his identity card at the Vincennes gate. The fact that it is his car will probably keep the gate-keepers on their toes!"

"We call at the Vincennes workshop first?"

"That is the most likely. After that, Orly, and then the other three, but don't worry about the routes, Diana has worked these out."

"Where will you be?"

"Following, but not too closely. Don't worry if you don't see us. Pepe, my man outside, is a clever driver and can tail a car like an American speed cop. You probably won't know we are around. When you have finished your round, Diana will bring you to my apartment. It is in a street near the Avenue des Capucins, not far from the Madeleine. Any questions?"

"Several," I said, although the assignment sounded far more straightforward than I had anticipated. "If I have to kill him, do I stay to make my own search of the safes, or run for it?"

He thought hard for a moment. I could see that he had worried about this and had not fully made up his mind. Finally he said: "You run for it, my friend, but I shall despair of you if you are obliged to botch it as badly as you did the last job! We need Yves de Royden alive. If he is killed, it will complicate things very much, perhaps fatally for a good many of us! Anything else?"

"Yes," I said, "about this list you've given me. My study-ing it won't help, I'm no technician and I know very little about what he makes inside those factories. Suppose I show it to him and demand his co-operation there and then? Would that be an idea?"

He sucked in his cheeks and then blew them out again, smiling but ruefully. "You have a genius for confusing

483

things, my friend. Let me put it this way. We are after the contents of those safes. You are bound to bring us papers of no importance at all, but we have someone who can do all the piecing together that is necessary, providing Yves doesn't hoodwink you and leave top secret material behind. The index book is recognisable. For the rest, use your own judgment when the time comes, but we want him delivered to us alive! With him *and* his papers we may show a handsome profit on this plan of yours!"

I had forgotten that it was my plan, or rather, Diana's, and that Raoul had been a convert to it. One thing about it still worried me, however. How far, if at all, did Yves trust his wife at this moment? Was it possible that a man could condone his wife's association with a man like Rance yet still accept her as an ally? Had he lived with Diana for years without discovering anything at all about her? Was it possible that he was playing a waiting game and hoping to pounce at a moment when he could strengthen his position with the Germans by handing over not only his wife, but a whole group of people like Raoul and myself?

"Have you actually seen Diana in Yves' presence since we killed Rance?" I asked.

"Yes," he said, "I have seen her once," but volunteered no further comment.

"Did it strike you then that he still had no suspicion she was working for us?"

"My friend," he said, "you will not be able to satisfy yourself as to that until you meet him. Ah yes, I remember, you have met him, but that was long ago, before he sold himself."

"To money?"

"No, my friend, to machines. Today he thinks only in terms of machines. This makes him an excellent technician but a bad judge of the human heart."

I had to be content with this for he passed on to details of route, clothing, equipment, telling me what I should carry in my pockets and what I should not carry, that I must walk from the hideout to the Bois de Boulogne and set out before dusk, so as to reach there in time to make

484

myself familiar with the approaches to the house. Diana's zero hour was fixed at ten fifteen, that was the time she would make her final check on Yves and the garden door. He showed me how to get into the shrubbery bordering the house on the south side and finally insisted on taking another look at my automatic.

"It is a child's toy," he said disparagingly, "but I am bound to admit it, it was more than enough for Rance."

"What did you do with Rance's body?" I asked.

"You are not gathering material for a detective novel," he said, smiling.

We had a drink from a flask he carried and presently he left. It was five o'clock and traffic was heavy in the street below. I sat down on the bed to make what I could of the schedule he had given me.

The area where the de Roydens had their town house was a section that seemed to me to have an affinity with the rest of the capital. It stood aloof, like a shy, elegant woman caught in the eddies of an autumn sale. There are parts of London that try hard to shake sister suburbs out of their clothes but residential Paris has an aloofness all its own, and on this particular night, with not a leaf stirring and the dry heat of the day pulsing in the stones underfoot, it seemed the loneliest place on earth.

It was about nine-thirty when I reached the gates and gave them a gentle push. They were not locked and I was thankful that an orchard-robber's entrance was unnecessary. Diana had also been successful in dealing with the parking-area light, for that side of the house lay in deep shadow. I kept close to the laurels and worked my way towards the little court, guided by a glimmer of moonlight reflected by the polished wing of a car. It was the Mercedes Benz, a huge, sleek monster, trumpeting wealth and privilege, a car that would have warmed the heart of Diana's mother when the family cruised around Whinmouth in a Rolls with a chauffeur at the wheel and the rear seats crowded with expensive-looking dogs.

There was a subdued light in the entrance hall and its glow lit part of what appeared to be the dining room adjoining. I took a quick peep over a box hedge to see if anyone was moving about. No one was and the room was empty as far as I could see. It was furnished with heavy, period pieces and I studied it for a moment savouring the irony of the situation. All through my adolescence I had stood outside Diana's private world looking in, a ragamuffin at a barrier, a boy with his nose pressed against a pie-shop, not wanting the pies but the girl to whom they were being served on a silver platter. Always I had to remain under cover, an eye cocked for keepers and dogs and my body braced for ignominious flight; now, incredibly, here I was again, subject to the same restrictions and tensions.

I moved into the deep shadows where the shrubbery ran down close to the house and found the door marked on Raoul's plan. Its glass panels were reflected by what I imagined to be the lights from the kitchen on my left and it could be reached by two steps approached by a path beside a small glasshouse. I looked at the luminous dial of my watch and saw that it was ten minutes to ten, twenty-five minutes to zero hour. I backed into the shrubbery and found a place where I could keep the garden door under observation. Then I settled down to wait.

I think those twenty-five minutes were the longest I have ever lived through. Apart from the faint glow of the kitchen lights, the house on this side was in darkness and in the shrubbery this darkness pressed down on me like a weight. I could smell freshly-clipped privet and it reminded me of a terraced street in the Brixton suburb where I had lived as a child before my parents died and I was sent down to Devon. The fragrance made me think of my mother for a moment, of the strained, anxious look she always had and of the rustle of her clothes when she came in to tuck me up at night.

Down near the *Etoile* I could hear the faint purr of traffic and overhead an occasional rumble of thunder. I wondered if there would be a storm before morning and if so what effect it would have upon our plans. Then my thoughts were swung back on the door as I heard the scrape of a shoe and saw a shadow reflected behind the panels. I knew the shadow must be Diana's and that she was making a final check on the door. It was the first glimpse I had

486

had of her for almost a fortnight and it steadied me even though it was only there for a matter of seconds. Then it disappeared and a light went off and on nearer the front of the house. I guessed that this was a signal intended for me and when I looked at my watch again I saw that it was now exactly fifteen minutes past ten.

I panicked for a moment, groping for my pistol and wiping my sweating hands on the lining of the jacket pockets. Then I relaxed and moved forward to the garden door.

It opened quietly and I was in a stone passage laid with uncarpeted flags. Recollecting Raoul's briefing, I moved along it until I came to a broader door, faced with baize. I gave this a gentle push and it opened, letting in a flood of light from the hall where ornate lamps burned on each side of the stairs. I stood for a moment listening, one hand on my pistol butt. Behind me, in the kitchen regions, someone was singing and clattering pans and plates but the noises came from a safe distance. I was on the point of slipping into the hall when I heard steps on the stairs and opened the door a crack to see an elderly manservant descending with a tray and glasses. He looked tired and dragged his feet a little. I was getting ready to brace myself behind the angle of the door in case he came my way, when he turned and walked away in the opposite direction, disappearing on the left of the vestibule beyond the staircase.

The moment he had gone I moved into the hall and made for the stairs. I had put my foot on the first of them when I heard her voice.

"Jan!"

She was standing on the first landing, looking down. She was wearing a beautifully-cut evening gown the colour of old gold and the lamplight from the landing above her fell directly on to her head and set her hair sparkling and glowed on her bare shoulders. She looked very lovely, lovelier than I ever remembered as she stood with one hand on the newel post and the other hanging loosely by her side. Then I noticed that this hand held an automatic pistol. The ugly little weapon seemed so incongruous that it

487

was almost laughable, as if she was a beautiful hostess playing charades with a houseful of jovial youngsters.

I went softly up the stairs and reached her side. She was utterly composed, so much so that her expression and pose might have indicated abstraction. As I breathed her perfume, I found it very difficult indeed to focus my mind on the reason why we were standing here, each holding a pistol and on the brink of a desperate enterprise. All I could think of in those seconds was her loveliness, the tumbling vitality of her hair and the deep blueness of her eyes. I wanted to let my hands slide over her bare shoulders and down over the roundness of her breasts to her waist, I wanted to bury my lips in her hair and draw warmth from her cheeks and mouth. I realised that I was trembling, but it was not from fear. She said, quietly:

"Did you see Hervé go down?"

"Yes, a moment ago."

"Where did he go?"

"Behind the stairs, to the left of the front door."

She nodded. "The dining room, he fusses about in there every night at this time, but don't mind him, keep close to me."

"Is Yves in the study?"

"Yes, and we haven't much time, he intends to go visiting and he's already told the chauffeur. Come, don't waste a second."

She glided on ahead, up the second short flight and into a broad corridor that branched from the first-floor landing. As I followed, I noticed one or two pictures on the staircase. They were Corots and Fragonards, small but very valuable, each skilfully lit from below. There was a deep yellow carpet on the floor and where the corridor branched, a huge Louis Quinze commode, heavy with ormolu. It crossed my mind then that every time Diana introduced me into a house its atmosphere was one of outrageous wealth.

Halfway along the corridor she stopped and laid her hand on my shoulder. Beyond was a closed door, and we were now in a cul-de-sac, with unrelieved walls on each side.

"Follow me straight in," she said, "and don't bother to lock the door behind you. First we must cancel that chauffeur and get him out of the way!"

For the first time she spoke with urgency. I took my automatic from my pocket and followed at her heels as she threw open the door and marched in, closing the door with a side kick. We were alone with Yves de Royden, each pointing a gun at his head as he sat in a pool of lamplight at a huge, flat-topped desk placed at right angles to the fireplace. Before he could look up a buzzer sounded at his elbow.

"Answer it!" she rapped out. "Tell Martin you won't be needing him after all!"

I have never seen a man more astounded. He sat slumped down in his comfortable chair, with one plump hand stretched towards the house telephone and the other resting on a sheaf of papers spread across the desk. In that few seconds I got a good look at him and my first impression, dominating all others, was how pitilessly the years had used him. I fixed his age at thirty-four, three years older than Diana and only two years older than me, but he looked at least forty-five, with the lamplight shining on his bald patch and glinting on his prim pince-nez spectacles. Somehow I had never expected him to look like this. When I had met him all those years ago he had been slim and narrow-faced and now he was plump and round-headed, the kind of man who might have passed for a rapidly ageing executive in a bank or an insurance company, with a son at university and a daughter keen on tennis and sports cars. He didn't look French at all but rather middle-class British, a family man who takes a first-class every morning from Esher or Sevenoaks and spends the day in a centrally-heated office, surrounded by juniors hoping to please him and ask for a rise. He had pursey little lips and an exceptionally pale skin that looked as if it might be moist and soft to touch. He did not look as if he ever needed to shave.

Diana had issued her command in a quiet voice but when he continued to sit staring up at her, she repeated it, her voice rising half an octave.

489

"Answer it, Yves! Tell Martin you won't need him!"

He swallowed twice and then moved his left hand nearer the switch. Simultaneously the buzzer sounded again and she forestalled him, jerking her head towards me as an instruction to keep him covered and snatching up the little receiver.

"Martin? Madame here! You won't be needed, I shall be driving M'sieur's car myself! Yes! Go to bed!"

She replaced the receiver and the strain left her face.

"That's done!" she said, lightly. "It worried me when I heard him ask Martin to stand by!" She addressed Yves directly: "You won't be going over to see Labortine to-night," she said, "instead you'll be taking a trip with us!"

He spoke at last, in a whisper.

"Who *is* this? What is he doing here?" Then, clearing his throat, "Why are you waving that gun at me? Are you out of your senses?" He sounded like a petulant junior master who has surprised boys skylarking in the dormitory.

There was no great urgency now that the chauffeur had been headed off so I thought it might help things along if I introduced myself and made it quite clear that we meant business.

"I'm a British agent," I said, "and I want certain papers from your safe. Afterwards we shall be making some calls on your factories. We have other men outside and they will follow us everywhere we go, so don't try anything silly!"

He paid very little attention to me which I thought odd in view of the fact that I was supposed to be doubling for his friend Rance. Instead, he directed his astonished gaze at Diana, now rummaging in the safe behind him.

"You must be out of your mind!" he said, slowly. "I suppose you realise I shan't be able to protect you if this piece of foolishness becomes known!"

It struck me then how fatally wealth can warp a man's judgement. Here he was, two guns pointing at him and his safe being ransacked by his own wife, yet he still found it impossible to believe that we were in earnest or had serious intentions of thwarting him, or were in fact doing anything more than to interrupt his work. The safe was

490

open and his keys swung from the lock, in all, about a dozen clamped on a stout ring. At my request, Diana tossed over the ring and I noted that it contained six small keys of intricate but almost identical pattern. I thought it very likely that the safes at all five factories were to a standard design and pocketed the ring, moving round beside him and taking care to keep the barrel of my gun within a foot of his round head.

"The book is here," said Diana, over her shoulder and she pulled out a wedge of papers and threw them on the desk. Prominent among them was a red-covered book about the size of a small ledger. It was indexed and was obviously the one we sought. I flicked over the pages and found each covered with small, precise handwriting.

"Is that his handwriting, Di?"

She glanced at a page and nodded. I slipped the book in my hip pocket.

He followed each movement with the same expression of irritated concern. Now he reminded me less of a schoolmaster than of a testy husband, engulfed in a spring-clean and having to sit by and see all his papers disturbed.

"That book can be of no possible use to you!" he blurted out. "Put it back at once! At once! Do you hear me?"

Diana laughed and slammed the safe door.

"That's the lot, Jan!" she said. "Show him the list and I'll see if I can talk some sense into him!"

I thought he had shown slight reaction to my use of the word "Di," but now I was sure that he had picked up her "Jan." He swung round towards me and let both his hands rest on the little gilt lions decorating the armrests of his swivel chair.

"British!" he said, "*British,* you say! What the devil can the British want with my business records?"

"What do you suppose?" said Diana, sitting on the corner of the desk and throwing one long leg over the other. She looked very much at ease sitting there in her lovely yellow gown and looking down on him with a smile.

"Do you imagine they don't know about you in London? Do you think that you and those bastards you work for are the only people concerned with *Vergeltungswaffe Eins?*"

The mention of the weapon shook him. For the first time, I think, he took us seriously and his prim little mouth contracted as though he had tasted something sour. He began to get up, but Diana motioned him down and he obeyed her, very promptly, I thought.

"First of all, let me get you up to date," said Diana. "Pierre Rance is dead and buried! Jan and I killed him. We needed his papers!"

He received this news stolidly. The only sign that it might have shocked him, if indeed he believed it, was a faint flush that came to his cheeks. Diana went on: "We are going downstairs and out through the front door, Yves. We shall drive first to Vincennes, then to Orly, then to Juvisy and so on. Don't make trouble on the way, or at the gates. I shall be driving and Jan will be sitting right beside you! He's deadly. He put three bullets in Rance's head in the dark!"

"There is nothing the slightest use to you in any of these safes," he said, addressing me rather than Diana.

"We'll decide that," I told him, "in the meantime this is a list of the documents we're looking for."

He took the envelope and glanced at the contents. Again I thought of a pedantic schoolmaster, now engaged in correcting botched examination papers.

"You can take your choice," I added. "Give us the relevant stuff or we'll take everything and burn what we don't need. We might even spare ourselves the trouble and lay on a first-class blitz."

He had got himself well in hand now. It was like looking down on a skull with the power to see through the flesh and bone and watch the processes of thought squirming underneath. Finally he said: "Why should I do this? Why should I help you in any way? If you really have killed Rance then you mean to kill me, so why shouldn't I make a run for it the moment I arrive at my establishment? I might get shot but I should have the satisfaction of knowing the pair of you would be caught. The difference would be that you would undergo several unpleasant experiences before the end. I daresay the Gestapo would enjoy coaxing information from you!"

It was a cool speech for a man in his situation and I admired his logic and his guts. Diana looked to me for a lead, clearly she was surprised at the way he pulled himself together. I said: "Listen, de Royden, I've got to turn you over to the Resistance as soon as we've made a tour but don't deceive yourself that they are going to dispose of you! They have something quite different in mind. They are going to ship you over to Britain and give you a chance to turn King's Evidence! You can save your neck that way, either now or after the war, when the De Gaullists begin weeding out you people and standing you up against walls! You're not stupid and you know very well Germany can't win the war now. They had their chance in 1940 and threw it away!"

He was silent for a moment. Then, when he spoke, he shocked us both.

"I assume you are my wife's lover," he said, not accusingly or even testily but as a simple statement of fact, almost the way Stanley might have said "Doctor Livingstone, I presume?"

"If you had as good a memory for human beings as you have for facts and figures, you might even remember him," said Diana, still perched on the edge of the desk. "You once gave him a lift in your first sports car, but it was a long time ago!"

He closed his eyes and I could see he was trying but failing to recall me. Then he looked straight at me and said: "My wife already has access to certain funds in London and elsewhere. I could treble them if you wished and pay out through Madrid, or a Swiss bank. Suppose you take what you need and leave me to get on with my work? It would be quite safe to do so, I could hardly inform on you without involving her in a one-way journey to Dachau or Sachenhausen. You may find it difficult to believe but I should be unwilling to accomplish that, providing that is, she undertook to get out of my life altogether! You would have everything you need for the rest of your lives! You might find me more rewarding than the Armed Services."

493

It had never occurred to me that he would attempt to bribe us, but I believe his offer was a genuine one and that he would infinitely have preferred to be rid of her in this way rather than expose her and see her thrown into Fresnes gaol and turned over to the Gestapo. Perhaps it was pride and nothing else that prompted this proposition or perhaps he felt that his stock with Vichy and the Germans would be worthless once it became known that his wife had introduced a British agent into his home and factories and attempted to hand him over to the De Gaullists. Diana looked hard at him for a moment, wrinkling her brows. Then, without comment, she slipped off the desk, picked up his briefcase and began cramming the papers into it.

"We'd better make a start, Jan," she said and I motioned to him to get up and walk before us to the door.

"You are both making a fatal mistake," he said, as I switched off the desk light and prodded him in the small of the back.

Diana went ahead and stopped to peer over the stairhead.

"Bring him down slowly," she said, "I'm going to check on Hervé! He had better know we're going out!"

She ran lightly down the stairs, holding her dress with her right hand and concealing the gun in the folds of the material. I followed with Yves immediately in front and as we reached the hall I heard her talking to the butler in the dining-room. A few seconds later she reappeared with a coat thrown over her shoulders. She paused for a moment, putting her automatic into a small evening bag and stuffing the bag into the pocket of her coat. Then she opened the door and we passed out into the mild night and walked towards the car. Just as we reached it thunder rumbled overhead. The storm seemed to have come much nearer whilst I was in the house. The time was now five minutes past eleven.

I opened the door of the car and pushed de Royden inside, taking care to seat him on my left. Diana had a car key of her own and started the engine at once. A moment

494

later we were sliding away and turning into the avenue. In less than a hundred metres she had built the speed to around fifty and all this time Yves de Royden said nothing at all.

I looked behind to see if we were being followed but there was no sign of Raoul's car or of any other vehicle. The streets were almost deserted and the gloom of the semi-blackout hid the houses on each side of the tree-lined thoroughfares. In about twenty minutes we slowed down alongside a high brick wall and stopped at a pair of wooden gates, over which a single light was burning. In its feeble gleam I saw the name *"de Royden Fils"* painted on a notice board nailed to the gates. The place seemed deserted.

Diana tooted the horn and almost at once a panel in the gate slid back. Diana got out and spoke to someone inside who flashed a powerful torch in our faces. de Royden stirred as the beam fell on us and I gave him a prod in the ribs. Then the torch was turned away, the gate creaked open and Diana got back into the car, driving it into the yard and stopping again. An elderly Reservist shuffled over and I lowered the window to present Rance's identity card. The janitor glanced at it, then at me, and finally at de Royden.

"M'sieu!" he said, stepping back, and waved us through.

Diana drove further into the yard, reversed and pointed the car toward the gates. As I got out, I noticed that the watchman was closing them again.

"Take over for a moment," I told Diana and went over to him.

"This is a spot security check," I told him. "Don't alert the night shift. We are inspecting on behalf of the Todt Organisation."

The man looked startled and uncertain. I turned away and over my shoulder added: "Leave one gate open, we shall only be here a short time!"

I went back to the car and Diana said: "Over there, up the short flight of steps!"

She went ahead and Yves followed her, hunched and silent. We passed up the steps and on the platform at the top I gave Yves his key ring.

"Open up," I said, "and don't waste time about it!"

He selected a key and opened the door. We passed in and Diana closed it behind us, switching on a light. We were in a large building set out with rows of desks like a school. On each desk was a hooded typewriter. At the far end was a wooden barrier and an inner office marked "Private". We walked down the aisle and tried the office door, finding it open. We went in and turned on the light. I looked all round it but there was no safe.

"It's behind the filing cabinet," she said and I wondered how she had acquired this kind of information without arousing suspicion.

"I should like a drink," said de Royden, suddenly. "There is cognac in the second drawer."

I thought I could do with a nip myself so I opened the drawer he indicated to its fullest extent. Inside were various odds and ends. ink, pens, receipted bills and a few metal castings of bolts with two inch screw nuts attached to them. There was also a half-size bottle of Courvoisier which I took out and uncorked. There was a carafe and glasses on the table and I poured a measure, helping myself first and then pouring another.

"Not for me," said Diana, when I glanced at her. She was tinkering about the bottom drawer of the filing cabinet and as she spoke I heard a sharp click and the cabinet swung round to an angle of forty-five degrees to the wall. It was just as she said, behind it was a small wall safe.

Yves had his drink and it seemed to lift him out of his lethargy. "I should like to have another look at that envelope!" he said. very civilly.

"Watch him while I tackle the safe," I told Diana and she came over to the desk, taking out her automatic and sitting down immediately opposite her husband who slumped into the desk chair.

I tried the small keys and the third one sprang the lock. There was no combination. For a man engaged in highly secret work, de Royden was very miserly when it came to buying security. There was not a great deal on the shelves,

496

a bundle of what appeared to be deeds, a large cash box containing a considerable sum of money in new notes, and a small pile of ledgers.

"Most of this is nonsense," he said, lifting my list, "it has little or nothing to do with German contracts. The only thing that can possibly interest you are the drawings of the cylinder and the jet with which it is fitted!"

For some reason I was certain that he was not bluffing. I was so sure that I left the contents of the safe undisturbed and came back to him.

"Where are they? Here, or in one of the other offices?"

He seemed to ponder for a moment.

"You promise me British protection from the De Gaullists? I get prisoner-of-war status?"

This was a teaser, but I had to take a chance on it.

"I can only guarantee you your life, I have no authority to bargain about your status. My rank is only that of Captain."

He opened the centre drawer of the desk and took out a large blotter, a commonplace thing bearing the advertisement of a garage in the Auteil district. He lifted a corner of the blotting paper and extracted from beneath it a sheaf of drawings on linen-fold paper.

Very few people and certainly not me, knew anything at all about jet propulsion in those days and I was now looking at the drawings of a Heath Robinson outfit in terms of today. In the drawings, numbered Two and Three, a cylinder had been broken down into various component parts, air intake, flap valve grid, combustion chamber and so on and although I had received a very limited technical briefing, my common-sense, together with Yves de Royden's manner, told me that I now had something under my hand that was likely to prove extremely valuable to the Allies. So strong was this impression, that I decided not to bother with the other documents in the safe. We already had de Royden's briefcase and the index book that Raoul wanted, and these, together with the drawings, seemed to me a worthwhile haul. I still meant to visit the other factories according to plan and make certain there was nothing else worth taking but I made up my mind not to prolong our stay at the Vincennes office. Time was getting along, we had less than five hours of darkness left and I meant to be off the streets before dawn. I told Diana to lock the safe and bring the keys, and I motioned to de Royden to get up and move on ahead of us.

Diana turned off the lights and we went through the typists' room and down the concrete steps to the yard. Taken all round, I felt very satisfied with our progress and now that Yves had voluntarily handed over the drawings I suppose I must have relaxed my vigilance somewhat. I quickened my step to walk beside him as we made for the car.

The janitor had followed my instructions and one gate, just wide enough to enable us to pass out, was hooked against the wall. The janitor himself was standing beside his hut over which there was a single shaded lamp that lit up the gate area, but its light did not penetrate to where the car was standing. Diana was not more than a yard or so behind us and we passed out of the circle of light thrown by the lamp at the head of the steps and into a patch of shadow marking the limit of the gate lamp's glow. It was here, some ten steps from the car, that de Royden made his bid.

At the time, of course, I had no clear idea what had happened. All I recall is a sudden flash, like a firework exploding in my face. Then I was down on one knee with de Royden standing over me brandishing something. I was by no means fully conscious, but I was not much more than stunned. I could see but without fully comprehending what was happening and although I felt no pain, my other senses must have been functioning, for I heard the crack of a pistol and saw Yves drop what he was holding and dash for the open gate. I even realised what it was he had dropped after using it to strike me a vicious but glancing blow on the right side of my head, it was one of the heavy bolts that had lain in the drawer from which I had taken the cognac. The drawer had been left open, and he must have snatched one in the odd second or two that I spent glancing at the drawings after he had taken them from beneath the blotter. Considering that both of us were watch-

498

ing him it was a notable sleight of hand, for not only had he snatched it from the drawer but had somehow managed to slip it into his pocket and keep his hand on it ready for an opportunity to strike.

Immediately he had dropped the bolt, he dashed for the open gate and this was the worst thing he could have done, for he ran straight into the pool of light. If he had doubled back into the shadow we should have lost him in the maze of outbuildings with which he was familiar and if we had wasted a moment or so pursuing him, the janitor could have slammed the gate and raised the alarm. I suppose he lost his head, or he might have been winged by Diana's single shot.

He ran like a hare and was more than halfway across the wide yard before I realised that he was not going to strike me again. Then, with a roar, the Mercedes leapt forward, so suddenly that it seemed to spring into the air. It shot across the yard and overtook the running figure at a point exactly between the two gate pillars, where a wide patch of road was lit by a suspended lamp above the weighbridge. It swung hard left and the wing struck the fleeing figure in the small of the back, pitching him forward and upwards like a ball. Then, as he fell back, the wing caught him again and flung him against the stone pillar of the gate. At the same moment, the car braked and skidded on the gravel, slewing round and striking the pillar with a grinding crash. The watchman ran out into the road and stared at the car and then at Yves, who was lying under the wall. In these few seconds, Diana reversed the car a yard or so and there was a squeal of tortured metal as the wing dragged away from the stone. A second later, she was beside me, supporting me under the arms.

"The car, Jan! Get to the car! Hurry, Jan! Hurry!"

My vision steadied but the blood from a deep gash on the side of my head was pouring down my cheek. I found that I could walk but I had to lean heavily on her as I staggered across to the car and slumped face foremost across to the driving seat. She pushed at my legs and slammed the door and the next moment she was beside me

499

and we were roaring past the watchman, now crouched over Yves under the wall.

Diana headed the car back into the city but even in my confused state of mind I realised that there was something seriously wrong. The beat of the engine was harsh and irregular and we tore along to the accompaniment of a hideously loud clanking. I remember being puzzled by this noise and it was not until we stopped in a narrow street between rows of what seemed to be warehouses that I realised the clanking was caused by a trailing, offside wing.

I had managed to check the flow of blood somewhat with a duster that I found in the glove pocket but I was still too dazed to be able to marshal my thoughts and Diana's urgent voice came to me through an orchestra of buzzings and hummings.

"Let me see it! Lean over this way, never mind the blood!" and she shone a torch on the wound. Then the torch went out and I saw her fumble in the glove box. A flask was pushed against my teeth and I gulped down a few mouthfuls of spirit. "There!" she said, "you'll have to make an effort, Jan! We'll have to leave the car and go on foot! Can you walk? Can you walk if you lean on me?"

The cognac had restored me a little and I was able to make a clumsy pad of the blood-soaked duster, stuffing it under my hat and cramming the hat low on my forehead. The wound throbbed and smarted like the very devil.

"Why can't we make a dash for Raoul's in the car?" I asked her.

"Because it will attract attention wherever we go! Everyone will remember us passing and if we weren't stopped by the police, they'd trace our route. We stand a far better chance on foot! Come on, Jan darling, make an effort. Wait! Give me your gun!"

I fumbled for the automatic and passed it to her and she slipped it into her handbag, leaning over and opening my door. I got out and stood swaying but in a moment she was beside me, her arm tight around my waist.

"Now! Lean on me all you want to, but keep going, Jan, *keep moving!*"

We lurched along the street and emerged on to a road

500

running north from Vincennes. I recognised the spot as being fairly close to the Place de Grève. One or two cars sped by, but there were no pedestrians about and we began walking slowly along the inside of the pavement, using the shadow of the shops that lined the route. Once or twice we stumbled over projecting hoardings and awning poles but we finally reached the Place, where Diana hesitated a moment before plunging into a narrow street on the left.

Awareness came and went, like gleams of sunshine on a winter's day. Sometimes I knew approximately where we were and what we were doing, then a blanket would descend and I could only cling to her supporting arm with both hands and drag my feet like a hopeless drunk. Several times I fell but always she dragged me up again and we pushed on, staggering from side to side and sometimes actually striking the walls on my side of the road.

"How about Raoul's car?" I demanded, during a flash of comparative clarity, "he was supposed to be following wasn't he?"

"He'll have lost us," she said, "I had to zig-zag after I left the factory. I can find my way from here but we'll have to cross two main roads. Wait here a minute and have another swig!"

She half pushed me down against a wall between two buttresses and thrust the bottle into my hand.

"Where are you going?"

"To see if we can cross. They patrol the main roads at night, and the checkpoints down here are close together."

She was gone for about five minutes and I had another drink, fixing the rough bandage more firmly under my cap. The duster had stuck to the wound and the bleeding seemed to have stopped. I made a tremendous effort to collect myself, splashing my face with water from a puddle in which I was sitting. Diana came back and whispered:

"It's all right, there's a post about a hundred metres down the road but they won't see us if we're quick. Come on!"

She sounded almost as if she was enjoying the excitement. I got up and put most of my weight on her and together we emerged from the side street and slipped across the main road into a shadow on the far side. We turned right and moved back in the direction of the south side of the Place but before reaching it, ducked into a maze of side-streets, some of them not much more than alleys, until we came to a passage that ran between two high walls plastered with advertisements. At the far end of the alley was another main road and when we reached it, Diana stopped and left me again, returning almost immediately.

"How do you feel now, Jan? We're almost there!"

"How the hell do you know where we are?" I asked her, helplessly. "We might be in the middle of China, for all I know!"

"You could lose me in China, but not in Paris! I've had over a month to study street-plans. Now listen carefully. There's a street opposite and the far end of it comes out about two minutes' walk from Raoul's place but there's a check-point at the entrance of the street and a gendarme outside it, smoking. You can see his cigarette end from here, over there near the sentry-box."

I looked out and saw the vague outline of a man. He was leaning against the side of his box and as I watched, he stood upright, flipped his cigarette butt into the road and strolled to the edge of the pavement.

"Can't we double back and get across somewhere else?" I suggested, but humbly because the decisions were now hers.

"No," she said, "it would take us too long. It will be daylight soon and we must get to Raoul's while it's dark! Then we can lie low for a day or two and get your head attended to. Now listen—I'm going across to the gendarme to turn on the charm! He looks bored to death and obviously hasn't been alerted yet, or he'd be keeping a much sharper look-out. I hope to God that watchman at Vincennes takes his time reporting and it looks to me as if he has, or perhaps Raoul has attended to him. Keep me in view and dive across the moment you get the chance, do you understand?"

"Yes," I said, "but how will you get away when I'm across?"

"Great God!" she said sharply, "he's on duty, isn't he? It won't take very long!"

The remark meant nothing to me at the time. If I thought about it at all, which is doubtful, I probably gathered from it that she meant to distract the gendarme's attention while I tottered across the road and into the shadows on the far side but I do recall that I made another great effort, finishing the brandy, standing upright and edging along the wall to a spot where I could watch them without showing myself.

I saw her emerge into the street, walk straight up to the sentry and say something to him. At the same time he moved nearer his box and the sentry post light fell on them. They remained talking for a moment and presently she threw back her head and laughed. The sound came to me quite clearly across the twenty yards or so that separated us. Then he reached into his tunic pocket and took out a packet of cigarettes and she held out her palm and he counted several cigarettes into it. It seemed a very odd thing to do and puzzled me somewhat until I remembered that cigarettes were currency in Paris, particularly among low-grade prostitutes. Then I would have cried out and crossed the road if my legs had not buckled under me so that I cannoned off the wall and fell flat on my face. I suppose I lay there several moments, weeping with pain and weakness and perhaps something else, the thought of Diana being pawed and sweated over by a gendarme in a shop doorway. Then my head cleared again and I forced myself to reflect what would almost certainly happen to us if her ruse failed and we were marched along to the nearest police depot. Within an hour or so teleprinters all over the city would be broadcasting the news of Yves' murder. All exits to Paris would be sealed and Gestapo cars would cruise over every yard we had covered since midnight. The Mercedes would be found and reported as soon as it was light and our trail would be picked up within minutes. By the time Parisians were brewing their acorn coffee, we should be under lock and key, probably at the Gestapo headquarters in the Avenue Foch. After that, I should never see Diana again and a firing squad would be the best we could hope for.

Savagely I pushed myself up and lumbered across the road into the shadow at the mouth of the side street. I found a nook behind a refuse bin and crouched down waiting, my heart hammering and one side of my scalp feeling as though it was being stripped from the skull by pincers. The thunder that had been threatening all night now began to rumble overhead like the passage of a train and heavy drops of rain began to fall, beating out a slow tattoo that synchronised with the throb of my wound. I sat there for perhaps ten minutes before Diana rejoined me, reaching into the darkness and touching me on the shoulder.

"Quickly, Jan, straight ahead! Don't let go of me and walk on your toes!"

I noticed that she was breathless and as we passed under a lamp at the far end of the short street I saw that her headscarf had been thrown back and her hair disordered. Then I saw that her beautiful dress was disarranged and rage rose in my throat and I caught her by the hand and stopped her dead.

"Damned swine!" I shouted, but she shook her head, lifting my blood-caked hands and kissing them, as a mother might comfort an hysterical child.

"We haven't *time*, Jan! Not now! Later we'll talk about it, but not now, dear, not now! Keep moving, Jan! Keep hold of me, we're almost there!"

We set off again and blundered forward, turning right towards the corner of the street where the awning of a cafe projected over the wide pavement. Just as we reached it, the storm burst, half-stunning us with its hiss and confusion. Lightning forked across the sky, making the street as bright as noon-day and the darkness that followed bible black.

It might have been the stunning contrast between the glare and the darkness that extinguished the final flicker of consciousness, or perhaps I had reached and passed the extreme limit of my endurance and used up the final dregs of my will-power. Whatever it was, I remember nothing

504

more of that nightmare journey and still less of what occurred during the next few days. The last thing I recall
after the first lightning flash was rain bouncing from the
awning at eye-level and the neat stack of chairs and tables
pushed against the wall under the cafe window. I know
now that we were actually in the Avenue des Capucins
and not more than a hundred yards or so from Raoul's
apartment but I had no notion of this at the time. I
clutched at the nearest awning pole and missed, falling
against the stacked chairs. Then thunder crashed again
and I was whirled away on the storm.

Chapter Seven

THE NEXT thing I remember was an uneasy swaying motion, as if I was lying in a bunk at sea and the illusion was
increased by the bitter taste of bile in my throat as though
I had just finished retching and was lying back exhausted
by the effort. Then, to my right, I saw a low-powered bulb
that winked like a baleful eye and when I raised my hand
to ward off its beam I discovered that my head was covered with bandages passing over my cheeks and under my
chin and piled so thickly that my head felt twice its normal
size.

The movement must have been noticed by someone
because a cool hand closed over mine and guided it away
from the bandages and then rested for a moment on my
forehead bringing a sense of reassurance and comfort.

Later, at intervals, came a series of impressions, of
being lifted, of the murmur of voices, of wind in my face
and a curious throbbing sound near at hand. This beat
seemed to continue indefinitely and finally it settled down
into a steady rhythm. Under its compulsion I lost touch
with the debris of reality and slipped into a dream world
that had Sennacharib as its background.

It was a very pleasant, soothing dream in which I rediscovered every corner of our personal Shangri-la, from the rutted, high-banked lanes that led down to Shepherdshey, to the pine-dotted uplands beyond the larch wood and Big Oak Paddock. I even saw buzzards wheeling and fox-gloves growing on the outskirts of the coppices and heard a chorus of blackbirds in Teazel Wood and under the eaves of the old, ruined tower, but the strangest thing about it was that I knew all the time I was dreaming and that the dream had a time-limit; I knew that soon someone would ring a bell or blast a hooter, and I would be whisked away from the fields and woods and dumped down in more mundane surroundings, an army hut, or the airless attic under the tiles in the Avenue de Medecin. And presently this happened, precisely as I had suspected. A bell tinkled and I opened my eyes and found myself in a freshly painted room with a wide window through which the sunlight streamed and a plump young woman in a nurse's uniform was in the act of drawing the curtains on an ambulance passing by. It was the ambulance bell that had summoned me.

When the nurse saw that my eyes were open she looked startled and then, but with too much effort, she smiled and said: "Hullo there? Would you like some tea?" in the kind of voice one uses to cajole an idiot or a scared child.

I said that I would like some tea and that I was hungry and she seemed madly delighted by this information and scampered out of the room with a swish of starched skirts, leaving me to grope around for some explanation of where I was and what I was doing in a strange room and a strange bed.

It was a feeling of gross constriction round my neck and chin that gave me my first clue. The bandages were still there, about a hundred yards of bandage, it seemed, and they reminded me of the fact that I had been struck on the head, a very long time ago it seemed, but the memory of the pain introduced other memories of storm and flood. Then, as I fumbled about in my mind, I was able to recall just how I had received the blow, and even the iron bolt that had inflicted it and from here it was a logical step to that crazy totter across half Paris and the picture of Yves de Royden lying huddled under the factory wall, then Diana advancing across the street to the gendarme's post and finally her voice in my ear reiterating—"Keep moving, Jan! Keep going!"

The recollection was like a landslide, first a trickle, then a stream and finally an avalanche that must have sent my temperature soaring for as the sequences became clearer, I struggled up and shouted at the top of my voice. The nurse came running and threw her arm under me, easing me back into a prone position and making little soothing noises that even then I thought sounded ridiculous.

"Where the hell am I? What's happened?" I demanded.

She looked at me doubtfully, as though debating with herself whether or not to enlighten me but as I made another move to sit up, she came down on my side.

"In Cheriton Bishop Cottage Hospital," she said, as though Cheriton Bishop was a capital city and required no amplification. "It's quite near the airfield, but we don't have many Service boys in, you're only the second since the war started! They've got their own sick quarters, you know!"

She was a V.A.D. and took her duties very seriously and I realised that I should have to humour her a little.

"Cheriton Bishop? What airfield?"

"Why, Pockington Manor!" she said, a trifle shocked, "you were admitted two days ago! Early in the morning. You had a very nasty bump on the head and you oughtn't to talk. I'll fetch the tea now!" and she popped out again, rustling like a dowager at a ball.

I considered this information slowly and carefully, like a man who has discovered a curious object on a market stall. Two days ago. Early in the morning. And Pockington Manor was a satellite about twenty miles from my parent station, in Sussex. I wondered how the hell I could have arrived here, more or less intact, when the last thing I remembered was passing out under an awning in the middle of an early morning thunderstorm in the Avenue des Capucins. It struck me as being about as improbable as crashlanding in a moon crater.

I felt the side of my head under the wad of bandages

and found it very tender. When I moved my jaws my skull throbbed and a curious icy sensation swam across my forehead. The V.A.D. came back with a loaded tray containing a mug of tea and some wafer-thin slices of bread and butter. She placed it on my knees and helped me to settle myself. The tea was gloriously hot, sweet and satisfying.

"You can have as much as you can drink," she said, "you've had concussion!"

I thought of covering local V.A.D. displays for the *Whinmouth Observer* in my youth—"In cases of shock, no alcohol but plenty of hot, sweet tea" and nibbled at the bread and butter. Somehow my appetite had evaporated.

"Did I come here alone?" I asked, and it seemed to me that if she answered in the affirmative I should have flung the tray at her.

"Why no," she said, "there was a lady, one of those French Resistance people. I must say I admire them! They must be terribly brave!"

I framed my next question very carefully, like a man asking a specialist to tell him the truth about a suspected disease.

"The lady, was she all right?"

"Certainly she was all right! Worried about you, of course, but not knocked on the head, if that's what you mean!"

I sat back contentedly. The tea tasted like nectar and suddenly I was desperate for a cigarette.

"Can I smoke?" I demanded.

"Well, just one," she said, "I'll take a chance on it as nobody said anything about smoking. Here . . ." and she pulled a packet of Players from her apron pocket, stuck a cigarette in my mouth and lit it, standing back to watch the effect. It must have pleased her. I exhaled a vast cloud of content. So we had made it, Diana and I. After all the excursions and alarums. After all the tensions and risks. We were home again, together, and Sennacharib was only four hours' train journey away.

The plump girl watched me, not professionally but with an awe that I found flattering.

"How did you get that crack on the head?" she asked, presently, the sensationalist evading the trainee.

"With a bolt," I said, "a damned great iron bolt and there was a nasty square nut on the end. Like a mediaeval mace!" I added, with a touch of pride.

"You were very lucky," she said.

"Lucky?"

"Lucky it didn't fracture your skull! Mr. Digby-Warren says so. I heard him say it!"

"Who is Mr. Digby-Warren?"

Again she looked a little shocked. "Our specialist," she said, as though discussing Pasteur or Simpson, "he comes Tuesdays and Fridays and he was here on a case when they brought you in."

"Why didn't I go into R.A.F. Sick Quarters?" I asked.

"They were rather full, but I think the lady had something to do with it. She got you here, too, a private ward! They were going to put you in the Men's!"

I grinned a little at this. I had a swift vision of Diana throwing her weight and money about among a batch of duty officers and hospital porters.

"Where is she right now?"

"In London," said the girl, "and that reminds me, I gave her my word of honour I'd phone the moment you came round! I've got the number here!"

She scrabbled in her pocket and it was clear that Diana had made a great impression on her. She was an impressionable girl and clearly the Digby-Warrens of this world took shameless advantage of it.

"You do that," I said, "tell her I'm sitting up and taking nourishment. How long do you think I'll be here?"

"Oh, I wouldn't know that," she said, "I'm only a V.A.D." and she swished out to make the call.

I lay back and finished the cigarette. Then, almost in the act of crushing the stub, I fell asleep again, this time dreamlessly, and when I opened my eyes again Diana was sitting in a wicker chair with her back to me. It was full day again and the morning sun played games in her hair. I watched her for a few moments, drifting along on a tide of thankfulness. Then I called over:

"What's cooking, Di?"

She leapt up as though she had been jabbed with a hat-pin. Standing against the light she looked wan and tense but then, quite suddenly the strained expression left her and she smiled, threw back her curls and rushed across the room.

"Oh Jan! Jan, darling!" and she flung herself down beside the bed, seizing my hand and showering it with kisses. In all the time I had known her she had never done anything like that. Even when we had lain in one another's arms, it had always been bestowal on her part and gratified acceptance on mine. The hand-kissing was a kind of abdication in itself and perhaps because I was weak it brought tears to my eyes. I withdrew my hand and stroked her hair.

"How long is it since we made that trip, Di? It can't really be weeks or months."

"It's just days. How far back do you remember, Jan?"

"Blacking out under the awning during the storm."

She looked mildly surprised. "I didn't think you'd remember that far," she said, "I thought you would stop remembering about the time we left the car!"

When she said this, it struck me that she had hoped this was the case for it would mean I should have no recollection of the incident with the gendarme. Then she became brisk. "What do you want to know first? Or shall I get some breakfast in? I've got this place organised. No visiting hours and that sort of nonsense. I've given them a new X-ray outfit!"

I laughed, but inwardly so. What Diana couldn't charm out of people, she purchased outright.

"It was a good idea, don't you think?"

"Wonderful," I said, then, "Never mind about breakfast, that'll bring Florence Nightingale in. Just tell me how the devil you managed it all!"

"It wasn't really me," she said, "it was Raoul mostly and that hatchet-man of his, the moronic, gangling one he calls 'Pepe'! They stole an ambulance and I put on fancy-dress. Then we drove all the way to the pick-up ground near Le Mans and Jerry waved us through half-a-

510

dozen checkpoints! We got quite careless towards the end."

"But before that, Di, before you found Raoul?"

"Well, there wasn't a great deal to that either. When you passed out, I dragged you behind those stacked chairs at the cafe. You're a frightful weight, aren't you? I piled them all over you and then I went on to Raoul's. We were nearly there fortunately." She gave a little chirrup of laughter, as though she almost enjoyed the memory of the experience. "That dress of mine wasn't very suitable for the job in hand was it? I ripped it right across the seat getting you under cover and I went all the way down the Avenue des Capucins with my bottom showing! Raoul was there, luckily, half crazy with worry, poor lamb! He sent his man for you and you were in Raoul's place within ten minutes. He even got a tame gendarme to help get you there!"

Lying there listening to her recital was like rediscovering her all over again. There was absolutely no trace of the fitful, raddled woman who had accosted me after Alison's funeral, or the cowed, pathetic creature who had helped me to kill Rance, or even of the self-possessed woman who had partnered my pounce on Yves. She was young again, young and gloriously vital and one felt that at any moment she would suggest changing into jodhpurs and taking her mare Sioux for a gallop over Foxhayes. There was a bubble of laughter and devil-may-care under her droll bedside manner and I wanted very much indeed to kiss her hair.

"Well, you've got me as far as Raoul's. What then?"

"I thought we ought to lie up for a month or two, until the hue and cry died down and you were better but Raoul said this was crazy and we ought to get started right away, particularly as he had an air-lift laid on and it would have been very complicated to cancel it and lay on another. He went out and got hold of an ambulance just like that and we made a run for it that same afternoon. In the meantime he got hold of a Resistance doctor who patched you up and gave you a terrific amount of dope to keep you quiet. I don't suppose you knew a thing about that though, how could you?"

I noticed that she made no reference at all to Yves and it did not seem to me that the omission was due to reticence.

"What about those drawings and the other stuff we managed to get?"

Her face fell and she smiled, wryly.

"They were useful confirmation, but they told me in London that they already had that much information on Reprisal Weapon No. I."

"Do you mean it wasn't worth the risks we took to get them?" I said, deflated somewhat.

"Oh, I wouldn't say that," she said, "maybe they don't like their agents to get big-headed! In any case, old Raoul was pleased with the sub-contractor's book and his people are going to work through the list, workshop by workshop. I expect they've already started on them by now."

Her information regarding the plans should have brought a feeling of anticlimax. It seemed ridiculous to have taken all that trouble and all those risks for "useful confirmation", and a list of targets for Paris saboteurs, but lying in that clean bed, with Diana smiling down on me, I was able to get the war into a better perspective. We had done our best, a pretty good best, I thought, and we were still alive and together and almost home. Suddenly the junketings of armies and secret services and the whole ebb and flow of the global struggle seemed far away and trivial, something that did not concern us very much. I knew that Diana shared this outlook for she dismissed the plans and reverted to the personal. "How do you suppose Yves got hold of that iron bar? We slipped up badly there, didn't we?"

She talked as though we had just lost a game of tennis, or had been placed third in a jumping contest at a local gymkhana. Listening to her, it was impossible to imagine that she, personally, had driven a Mercedes full-tilt into her husband and flung him against his own factory wall like a pheasant slow off the ground. I knew then that if we were really beginning again I was the one who would have to bring the subject of Yves into the open and uncover the real reason for her murderously quick reaction to the crisis in the yard. Had she acted instinctively to save our lives? Did she regard him much as a soldier regards an enemy occupying a position that had to be taken? Or was there something altogether more complex and subconscious behind the killing? Had it been opportunism on her part, a chance to be done with all the muddled and futile years which Yves de Royden represented in her life? This was something I had to know now, so I said:

"Do you feel anything at all about Yves, Di? Or might you begin to feel when the excitement has died down?"

She looked me squarely in the eyes. "Not a thing, Jan," she said, "and the fact that I don't has absolutely nothing to do with the certainty that he would have turned us in if he had made his getaway!"

"What has it to do with, then?"

"With what Yves represented. It's like I said, I never have seen this war in black and white like you, and the others opposing Hitler. Yves was right out in front of the arrogant idiots who took a wrong turning about a century and a half ago and won't be happy until the whole damned lot of us are robots! I'm glad I wiped him out! It's one less and an important one and the fact that I was his wife had nothing whatever to do with it. He just had it coming to him, like Rance. If they don't make a clean sweep of them after the war they'll bob up again so the more we kill now the better our chances in the 'fifties and 'sixties. There isn't much of a chance, anyway. The few people who want it our way aren't nearly ruthless enough." She looked at me doubtfully. "Sometimes I don't think you are!"

She was right about that and I envied her her cold-bloodedness. I had no regrets at all about killing a man like Rance, but Yves was different. He had his dream like the rest of us, and in some ways that dream was objective and selfless. I granted her its menace. All the things that were meat, drink, sun and air to romantics like us were so much sentimental trash to the planners, the watch-the-wheels-go-round brigade to whom Yves had dedicated himself. All the same he was still a human being and a rather pathetic one, a man who had given her his name and let her go her own way so long as she didn't get in his. It was difficult to share her simplification of the issue and the effort of trying made my wound throb. Diana read as much in my grimace.

"We've got the rest of our lives to go into all that, Jan," she said, gently. "Let's shelve it and concentrate on getting you out of here. I've put in a longish report in town but they'll need another from you of course. I told them you'll come to town the moment you get out of here. The specialist is coming again this afternoon and he'll give you some idea when that will be!"

"Where will you be in the meantime?"

She looked evasive. It was strange that she should still use these routine subterfuges when she wanted to deceive me about something. She never would realize that I could read her expression like the morning headlines.

"I'm going down to Heronslea to see Drip and Yvonne," she said. "Then there are certain things I've got to do about converting funds, and feeding them into the place. I can't get my hands on a penny of Yves' money in France, of course, but there's enough to go on with over here, providing it's approached intelligently."

"Can you actually use his money?" I said, less surprised than shocked.

"Oh yes," she said gaily, "there's no such thing as war in International Finance! In time I daresay I can get hold of all the money in Madrid and Geneva. Then I've got to buy a car. I've already got my eye on one and when the time comes I'll pick you up in it and run you to town. Then, when you get your survivor's and sick leave, we'll go home together. Will that suit you?"

"It's all I want, Di," I said, earnestly, "I can't think of another thing I care a damn about!"

"Good," she said, bending forward and kissing me lightly and having done so she laid her cheek alongside my bandages and slipped her cool hand into the open front of my pyjamas jacket, and let her fingers slide across my breast and under my ribs. At this precise moment the plump V.A.D. marched in with breakfast but Diana made

514

no attempt to withdraw and the wretched girl almost dropped the tray trying to avert her glance.

"Did you bring any for me?" asked Diana, cozily.

"Why, of course, Madam," said the girl, as though it was quite usual for hospitals to serve early morning visitors with breakfast.

"Then I've got a present for you for being so nice to my Jan," said Diana, disengaging herself and opening an enormous white handbag that she had somehow acquired in the interval after our escape.

The girl looked startled. "You needn't do anything like that, Madam! It's wonderful to feel caught up in the real war at last! Ohhhh no, no, I couldn't . . .!" and she backed away as Diana produced a brooch set with small emeralds. It probably cost her something between fifty and a hundred pounds. "No, really, I should get into trouble, I . . .!"

"Oh rubbish!" said Diana, impatiently, "I bought it for you! If it sets the matron and sister by the ears don't show it to them, or just say your boy-friend bought it for your birthday!"

I wondered if the V.A.D. had a boy-friend and if she had, whether he would ever be able to afford a gift like that. Coming from most people the present would have seemed vulgar, but not from Diana. She could bestow expensive gifts in such a casual way that they were always acceptable. The girl stared at the brooch, absolutely overwhelmed, so I said:

"Let's eat! I'm ravenous!" and the girl gulped, pocketed the brooch and took refuge in her professional duties.

Chapter Eight

I WAS detained in Cheriton Bishop Cottage Hospital for the better part of three weeks. de Royden's blow had come very close to cracking my skull. The sharp edges of the screw-on nut had done the damage, stripping the scalp and causing lacerations that made probing difficult and very painful. Digby-Warren, the V.A.D.'s heart-throb, was not so competent as he liked to pretend and in the end they had to call in an R.A.F. specialist who was satisfied that there were no bone splinters in the wound. He warned me, however, that I might have severe headaches for a month or so, but insisted that there was no permanent injury. The headache warning was timely and I used it to get two months' sick leave on discharge from hospital.

My old fuddy-duddy Group-Captain came to see me before I left and was very pleasant in a guarded kind of way, about my efforts in France. He said that when I was fit I could join Group H.Q. staff as an Intelligence Officer and I told him I would be glad to take the job. There was no immediate prospect of being posted abroad and the action I had seen in the last few weeks was more than enough to satisfy me for the remainder of the war. I was frank about this and the old chap chuckled.

"Oh I daresay you might get a jolt when the Second Front opens," he said, "but that won't be for a year or more. These clots who attend rallies in Trafalgar Square and chalk slogans on walls haven't a clue what is involved. They want to see you over at Free French H.Q., by the way, but you'll have heard about that?"

As soon as I felt fit I went up to town without waiting for Diana, who had done one of her disappearing acts again although she phoned every night. I didn't worry about her now that she was home and dry. I thought it might be a good idea to let her get re-acclimatised in private. She sounded happy enough and Drip wrote me saying how popular she was with the children and how fit and cheerful she seemed.

The visit to the Air Ministry and Free French H.Q. did a good deal to restore my sense of proportion. Up to that time I had never been more than half reconciled to Diana's view of the war, her "six-of-one-half-a-dozen-of-the-other" outlook, with a modest bias in favour of the allies. Diana saw the struggle as a war within a war and I had always felt her unorthodoxy had its roots in her antipathy towards any kind of discipline or collective effort. A

516

few hours at the centre of the Allied web enabled me to get a glimpse of things from her viewpoint. de Royden's money and position must have opened windows on the breeding ground of war that had been denied people like myself, and there were, as I saw, plenty of excuses for the cynicism. All her life Diana had moved in an atmosphere of deals, mergers and on the higher levels of what the Americans now call "payola." It was she who had told me of the encouragement given to Fascism by groups of French and British politicians. All this is generally known now, but it wasn't then, not to the rank and file fighting the war. Had it not been for her, I doubt very much if I would have recognized the childish place-seeking and pettiness that fidgeted under the mantle of patriotism in the offices where plans were hatched and invitations were sent out to the little folk to die gloriously on behalf of this cause or that. I saw and was questioned by half-a-dozen minor notables, French and British, during my stay in town and not one of them impressed me as much as, say, Raoul de Royden, or a Grenadier Guards sergeant whom I happened to see during the Dunkirk debâcle polishing his boots at a road block while he awaited the appearance of German tanks north of Lille. I was very glad to turn my back on it all for a couple of months and when I pocketed my leave pass and crossed London to keep my appointment with Diana, I felt like a schoolboy going on holiday after a gruelling first term at school. One side of my head was shaved to the skin and the headaches the specialist had promised were prowling around on the edges of the scar but these were minor worries. I knew now what it felt like to enjoy what the trench veterans of an earlier war called a "Blighty" and I meant to squeeze every drop of satisfaction from our incredible luck.

Diana had phoned to say she had got her car and would pick me up at any point I named as soon as I was through. This was too good a chance to miss so I told her, chuckling, that I would meet her outside Swan & Edgar's at eleven o'clock on the first morning of my leave. The sharp angle of Piccadilly and Regent Street had been our adolescent rendezvous. Here she had come whenever she had played truant and I was able to travel up from Devon on a football excursion, and here she had appeared after her harrowing experience at the inquest on the victims of her car accident. Our association was like that from the beginning. Localities played an important part in it, for the dream we shared encouraged us to respect the backgrounds in which it had begun. It was foolish, I suppose, and even childish, but for us at least it had significance.

I wondered what kind of car she had been able to find and when she coasted round from Regent Street and pulled up alongside the kerb I laughed aloud. It was clear that she too was a victim of nostalgia, for she appeared driving an outrageously flamboyant sports model of the 'twenties, with wire wheels and a bonnet as long as a horse. It was a 1927 model with an engine-throb like a badly-serviced fighter plane and thick leather straps to hold the bonnet casing in place. Its exhaust growled and spluttered when she slipped into neutral and its last owner had painted it silver and blue. To sit in that car was to be transported back to a world of "Old Boys" and "Chin-Chins", to a time when people danced the Charleston and used words like "topping", to days when girls wore skirts inches above their knees and young men strummed "Ain't She Sweet" on five-shilling ukuleles.

Diana was delighted at the impression the car made on me. She crouched low in the bucket seat, her curls imprisoned under a headscarf and we zoomed down Piccadilly and through Knightsbridge and Hammersmith to the Great West Road, playing hard at being kids again and enjoying every moment of it. I forgot the war and Rance and Yves and the tenderness of my skull. I was young again and more in love than I had ever been.

Notwithstanding its age the car had plenty of power and Diana pushed it along at a spanking pace. Soon Staines and Salisbury were behind us and after sandwiches and a drink in a pub I took the wheel and we turned on to a second-class road and crossed the border into the wooded country of east Somerset.

There had been a long, dry spell and the cow-parsley in

518

the hedges was bowed with dust. Women in aprons stood at cottage doors and watched us pass and old men in corduroys lumbered in the fields, looking like figures in a Moreland landscape. There was a kind of timelessness down here that banished not only World War II but all that had happened since August, 1914. It was like driving backward into the 19th century.

As we crossed the Devon-Somerset border and neared the coast I could sense her mounting excitement. She sat more upright and turned her head from side to side, sniffing the air like a pointer and when we came out on to the winding white road that led to Castle Ferry she suddenly laid her hand on my arm. It was about three o'clock and the mid-afternoon sun beat down on the castle ruin that crowned the hamlet and the shallow river that divided it.

"Let's have tea here, Jan! Let's see if Old Gramp's still about and whether he's pushed up his ha'penny ferry charge to wartime prices!"

I stopped the car outside the Castle Inn and we looked across to the ferry landing. I recalled so vividly the summer afternoon we first came here when she had introduced me to the foul-mouthed old boatman who plied to and fro for a halfpenny, a dirty, unsavoury old man, who stank of sweat and beer. I had been horrified when Diana had confessed that he was the skeleton in the Gayelorde-Sutton cupboard and her grandfather paid so much a month to keep his identity secret so that his daughter, Mrs. Gayelorde-Sutton, could reign as the Lady of Heronslea, only a dozen miles away. I remembered too, Diana's purpose in telling me this closely-guarded secret; "a tonic" she called it, administered in order to encourage me to believe that I was as good and better than a Gayelorde-Sutton and combat the inferiority complex that had been fostered in me by her mother's airs and the family's riches. I had loved her for this and I still did.

We couldn't locate Gramp and his ferry service seemed to be suspended, so we ordered tea in the Castle Inn.

"Doesn't he know even now that you're his grandchild?" I asked her, while she was pouring out.

"No," she said, "but I'll confront him sooner or later. I

sent him money through Drip before the war and I believe she still keeps an eye on him. You know Jan, I simply loved having that old pirate for a grandfather! I kept half-hoping he would stagger into the drawing-room at one of mother's 'At Homes' and breathe stout and blasphemies over the local Conservatives! I wonder what happened to mother in the end?"

"Good God!" I exclaimed "Do you mean to say you don't know?"

She looked mildly astonished. "Well, naturally I don't. How should I? I haven't set eyes on her since the crash. She never wrote and you haven't mentioned her again!"

This was true, but it was something that surprised me a great deal. Why hadn't I told her about her mother? Why hadn't I described how I had tracked her down weeks after Diana's flight and told how Mrs. Gayelorde-Sutton had met the challenge of sudden penury? Was it because I was still afraid of the past whenever it involved the opposition? I said:

"Look, Di, we'd better settle something right here and now before we go another yard into Sennacharib. It's absolutely vital to both of us! We've got to really start afresh, before we get tangled up in loose ends, before we get drunk on nostalgia!"

"Well, Jan?"

She said this patiently, almost dutifully, and again the certainty crossed my mind that she was hiding something, holding something back, making one of her fireworks that would presently be lobbed at me and explode in my face. I can't say why I felt uneasy, but I did. There was something deliberately vague about her smile, as though I was a child who had asked a question that couldn't be answered until I was grown up.

"Look here, Di," I burst out, "there's something behind all this and I'm damned if I want today spoiled by mysteries. I hate mysteries, yours especially. They always end in muddle and heartbreak!"

She ceased to smile and ceased to look superior. She put down her cup and looked steadily across the table.

520

"Jan," she said, levelly, "are you quite sure you still want to marry me?"

I spluttered for a moment but she didn't smile at my confusion as I expected she would; she just waited, her expression mild and relaxed.

"Great Heaven, of course I want to marry!" I said at last. "I should have thought I'd made that much clear by now! Don't tell me you're awaiting a formal proposal!"

She dropped her glance a little and began to trace patterns on the table-cloth with a cake knife.

"What I mean is, you don't have to marry me, Jan! I'd never want to be parted from you again and I've made up my mind I won't, ever, no matter what happens! But that still doesn't mean you have to marry me. You might like to think about it, you know—just drift, until after the war."

"I've been drifting for years," I said, "and I'm coming ashore! Besides, there's Yvonne to think of! Have you talked about us to Yvonne?"

"Yes, I have," she said, in the same quiet voice, "but I wouldn't dream of marrying you for that reason alone. Leave Yvonne out of it for the time being!"

"What exactly are you getting at?" I demanded, and for the life of me I didn't know. She said, slowly:

"It isn't as if there had only been Yves. It would have been easy enough to wipe out one mistake, one impulsive, selfish act, one betrayal even! But there was also Rance and I suppose I'm glad now that you saw what you did see at the villa. I don't think I could have made you understand if you hadn't!"

I began to get a glimmering of what she was trying to say. Perhaps the memory of her emerging into the street towards the gendarme, and rejoining me a few minutes later with her dress disordered, did as much to enlighten me as the act of abasement I had witnessed in the villa. What she was trying to convey, I think, was her natural drift towards haphazard promiscuity, the twopenny valuation she put upon sexual encounters and their triviality when measured against the kind of relationship that had grown up between us over the years.

"I want you and I'll never be satisfied with anyone else, Di," I said urgently, "but there's a qualification and it's this—don't let's take the easy way out and live in the past, let's try and build a different kind of relationship that lives in the present and admits to a future! We can't undo one jot of what's happened but for God's sake, let's both try and learn from it and use our experience to find tranquillity and mutual trust! Does that make sense, Di? *Does it?*"

"Yes," she said, in the same mild tone, "it makes all the sense I'm looking for so now I'll jump the gun! Pay the bill, Jan, and let's go on, but not directly to Heronslea. We've a call to make en route!"

"Call on whom?"

"You've waited this long, Jan, you can wait another fifteen minutes. I thought we'd be weeks getting around to this, but it seems you're in too much of a hurry, so I'll go along with you!" She faced me squarely as she rose. "From now on I'll always go along with you. You're the boss, Jan! Don't forget that, don't ever forget it, for your own sake and mine. Not even if you have to wallop me into remembering every so often!"

I hadn't a notion of what she was talking about or on whom we were supposed to call but her forthrightness intrigued me and I paid the bill and we went out to the car. The discussion had given my headache a foothold and my wound was nagging, so she drove and we took the road that skirts Foxhayes Common and winds away from the coast and along the edge of the plateau, then down the Teasel Valley with the larch plantations of Heronslea to the west and the pines of Teasel Wood to the east.

It was early August and the country was drowsy with evening sunshine. Always at this time of year Sennacharib's banks were lush with waist-high bracken and behind the bracken foxgloves grew in majestic ranks, a guard of honour all the way to Teasel Bridge. The magic of Sennacharib silenced us, soothing the ache in my temples and wrapping us in an embrace of sounds and patterns and scents that was balm to the spirit. It was very still up here and when we stopped at the approach to the bridge I could hear the blackbirds rustling in the thickets and the long sighs of Teasel beeches, always an undertone to the whispering larches and spruces higher up the slopes. This was the very heart of our country and as we lingered there Diana turned her face to the sky and pointed.

"There! Over there, a hundred yards below Big Oak!"

It was true. There were our buzzards, the pair she always declared could never be seen unless we were in company, and a sense of fulfilment stole over me as I saw the two specks wheeling and gliding in their search for wind currents over the coverts.

"That clinches it," said Diana. "Until now I wasn't absolutely sure, I still thought we ought to have waited but not now, it's a come-on sign! We'll take the cart track up under the wood to your cottage! Don't argue, don't waste another second!"

I began to share her excitement although I couldn't imagine who would be expecting us at the end of the winding track. I knew of no one who would be likely to occupy the cottage to which I had retired after Diana ran away. It was here that Drip, her governess, had found me shortly before the war and soon after, when I joined up, Drip moved into Heronslea to look after the children. As far as I knew the place was a ruin by now, I had not visited it since the Autumn of '39.

But it was not a ruin. We rounded the final bend and she brought the car to a halt in the little clearing beside the stables. This was a courtesy title for a ramshackle array of sheds but there was nothing ramshackle or seedy about the property now. The whole place had undergone a very determined attempt at renovation. The garden beds had been weeded, the grass cut short, the cottage and sheds were newly painted in farm-wagon blue, the fences shored up with freshly-cut timber and there was even a wisp of smoke drifting from the squat chimney above the red pantiles of the roof. It looked, in fact, just like a cottage in a child's book of fairy-tales, the kind of place that Red Riding Hood's granny occupied.

Still far too overcome to comment I got out of the car and went up the short brick path to the front door. It opened easily on freshly-oiled hinges and inside the big living-room a bright fire burned and each piece of furniture gleamed in the reflection of the flames. There was a delicious air of cosiness about the room, the judicious mixture of oak, brass and copper combining with new wine-red curtains and a profusion of rugs to produce an atmosphere of repose and warmth and permanence. In the kitchen beyond somebody had been hard at work for hours, scouring and red-bricking the floor.

I went back into the big room and across the little passage to the main bedroom. In here a great number of changes had taken place. My old iron bedstead had gone and in its place stood an eighteenth century four-poster lacking its canopy. I recognised it as the bed that had once stood in Diana's suite in the west wing of Heronslea, at the time of her coming-of-age. The low-ceilinged bedroom had always been rather dark and airless, and I had always been intending to enlarge the window looking over the Teasel Valley. Now somebody else had carried out the improvement and the window had not only been widened but fitted with diamond lattice panes. The stonework at the edges of the frame was old but the mortar was barely dry. There was a lovely Chinese carpet on the floor and two pictures, a small Fragonard, that I also recognised as former Heronslea property, and a larger picture of an autumn hunting scene that I did not recognise but seemed to me an impressive piece of work of the Stubbs school. There was a Sheraton side table set at an angle in the window, with an elegant little dressing-table mirror on it and a long row of pots, bottles and Coalport trays. In the furthest corner beyond the bed was a lovely walnut jardinière holding a sheaf of crimson and lemon-coloured gladioli. I stood at the end of the bed and took in every detail of taste and care that had gone into the making of the room.

Diana's step on the uneven bricks of the passages roused me. She had followed me into the house and taken off her coat and hat. She had carried in our luggage and put it on a heavy oak chest just inside the door and she was standing watching me with an intentness that suggested anxiety.

"Well, Jan?" she said, so softly that I sensed rather than heard her question.

I stepped out of the bedroom and took her in my arms, holding her very close. We stood thus for a moment and then I shut the door and led her into the living-room. We sat down on the couch under the window, where Drip had once sat sewing through the long winter evenings when she was coaxing me out of my sulk.

"You haven't said anything, Jan. You like it, don't you? It's how you wanted it and *where* you wanted it?"

"It's quite wonderful, Di," I told her, "not simply the place itself but the idea. It's the most wonderful thing anybody ever did for me, or thought of doing for me!"

She looked so relieved that I laughed. "Did it ever occur to you that I wouldn't appreciate it?"

"It's rather a long story, Jan," she said, breathlessly. "Are you sure you want to hear it now? Maybe we ought to let Drip know we've arrived and we can't phone, I didn't put a phone in."

"Drip can wait," I said, "she obviously expected you to bring me here, or she wouldn't have lit the fire. We'll stay here now. You won't get me to budge!"

"Come now, Mr. Leigh, how can we do that before we're churched? You haven't even carried me over the threshold!"

"I can do that right now!" I said and gathered her up, kissing her hair and eyes and mouth and then planting her down on the low settle where she clung to me, laughing like a child whose mischief has delighted an audience of adults.

"Oh, it's all worked out so differently from how I planned," she said breathlessly. "I meant us to come here the day we were married but the moment I crossed the border of Sennacharib with you, Jan, it all washed over me like a wave and I couldn't wait, not another minute! The first evening I returned here I was disappointed in a way. It was wonderful to be back, of course, but it wasn't the same, with you lying in hospital and me not knowing how soon you'd be out. I got so restless that I had to do something, so in the end I took Drip and Yvonne into my confidence and soon everybody knew and everybody wanted to lend a hand! We only just finished in time. I was terrified you'd leave that ward and pop up when we were halfway through!"

"What gave you the idea, Di? What began it?"

"Oh, it goes back years," she said, "back to the day you bought this place from your Uncle Mark, and got it ready for me while I was in London, remember? I was an absolute bitch on that occasion, so much so that you took a stick to me when I poured cold water on your idea of love-in-a-cottage, remember?"

I remembered. It seemed centuries ago.

"You deserved it," I reminded her, "but you made up for it immediately afterwards!"

"It was a lesson well learned," she mused, "though it did take rather a long time to sink in! I thought about the way I behaved a great deal afterwards and I could never really forgive myself for being so blind and brutal! Even if I make allowances for being immature, it doesn't absolve me altogether, I might at least have pretended to be impressed and then cooled off gradually!"

"Never mind all that," I urged, "tell me how you went about this transformation. Was everyone in the secret but me?"

"Almost everyone. Drip and Yvonne were the principals but your Aunt Thirza was very useful and so were the girls from the village. You really are accepted as the Squire of Heronslea now you know. I don't quite know how it happened, but it has! You see . . ." she wriggled herself into a more comfortable position, tucking her legs beneath her, tilting her head so that some of her heaviest curls tumbled over the headrest of the couch, "I remembered something that you once said to me when I tried to bulldoze you into taking over the tarted-up Foxhayes Farm, and becoming one of Daddy's tenants! I remember you saying 'I don't want anything from Heronslea but you!' and it seemed to me that now you finally had me then it was up to me to show you I appreciated the fact! Do you follow?"

"Not altogether," I admitted, "but go on."

526

"Well, everything here, the land, buildings, furnishings —everything is *yours!* All it needed was a good spring-clean and one or two little improvements, all of which you paid for without even knowing it!"

"Would you mind telling me how?"

She laughed again. "You've been giving Drip an allowance and she's been hoarding it. She paid for the repairs and the cleaning up, and we got in local labour so it didn't stand you in at very much. About a hundred and fifty pounds all told."

"Come now, Di," I protested, "I'm not that stupid! I've been in the antique business and that four-poster, or just one of those pictures in the bedroom, cost a damned sight more than a hundred and fifty!"

"Oh, the bedroom!" she said, "that's different! That's my contribution! Hang it all, Jan, you don't begrudge me the right to give you a wedding present of some sort, do you? Besides, I always liked that bed, it was always a very special bed! Do I have to remind you why?"

"No," I said, chuckling, "but what about the rest of the bedroom furniture? The Fragonard that used to hang in Heronslea hall, the side table, the carpet and all the other things? And how the devil did you come by the bed and the picture anyway? They were sold when your father went bust. I know that because your mother had to sell everything to pay creditors."

"That's quite true," she said, "but I made a few enquiries from the Whinmouth auctioneer who put them under the hammer and I was able to trace the bed and the Fragonard. I would have traced several other pieces if only they'd kept you in hospital another few days!"

I got up and wandered round the cottage, sniffing the smell that is peculiar to all country cottages, a pleasant combination of yellow soap, heath, peat and old timber. I felt swept along on a tide of exhilaration but beneath this was a current of security that washed away every trace of bitterness and uncertainty. Diana had done this! Without prompting! Without long-term planning! She had looked into me and diagnosed my hurts, not only those for which she had been responsible but all the self-inflicted wounds as well. It was a remarkable accomplishment and I loved her for it.

"We'll make up for everything, Di," I promised her, "and we'll do it here and now! We'll obliterate every damned thing that tried to destroy us, money, pride, Rance, Yves, the war, the lot!"

"Oh, I wouldn't be so sweeping as all that," she said, smiling, "nostalgia is all right in moderation. This for instance!" and she opened her handbag and took out a small package tied with tinsel string, the kind they use for Christmas presents. "Open it!" she said, smiling and watching me fumble with the fastening.

I peeled off the paper and opened the carton. Inside was a musical box about the size of a large cigarette pack and I recognised it at once. It was Drip's musical box, the pride of her collection, the one that played "Allan Water" and had been set going in Heronslea kitchen the evening we met.

"Where the blazes did you get it?" I asked, amazed and more moved than I had been by the cottage transformation.

"I begged it from her," she said, "it seemed important somehow. Play it! Just once! Then we shall have to go on to Heronslea and let them know we're here."

I pressed the spring and started the music. The clear, tinkling notes had the sweetness of a remembered perfume. We sat quite still listening and it seemed to me that everything in Sennacharib was listening too. It was one of those intervals that etch themselves into the memory so indelibly that every single detail of scene and sound and smell remain in the mind for ever. I marked the shaft of afternoon sunlight striking a wisp of chestnut hair under Diana's ear, and heard the solemn, measured tick of the grandfather clock in the corner but it was the scents of the old room that made the deepest impression, burning oak, wax polish, the whiff of the open sea through the window, and Diana's nearness. The scent of her hair was the essence of all I had ever sought in a woman and Sennacharib.

"Oh God, Di," I told her, "I've never been as happy as I am now!" and I fell on my knees beside her and buried my face in her lap.

"It was rather like following a trail, Jan," she said,

quietly, "you know, one that wandered through all sorts of country, parched and pleasant, up hill and down, but led somewhere worth the effort! It wouldn't have been the same if it had gone smoothly from the beginning. Sooner or later, Jan, the magic would have gone from it but now it never will, I promise you, *never,* you understand?"

The musical box played itself out and over Heronslea larch woods the shadows lengthened. Gulls sailed in from the bay, wailing news of rough weather and their cries echoed across the valley.

I took her by the hand and we went out to the car. Neither of us spoke again until we had coasted down into Shepherdshey village and turned in at the beech avenue that led up to the big, white house.

Chapter Nine

HUSTLE NOTWITHSTANDING we were unable to marry that week or the next. There were various formalities concerning Yves' death and estate and arrangements involving the re-organisation of Heronslea. Form-filling and business chores never bothered Diana. She sailed through them like a cheerful apprentice putting up the shutters before going on holiday. She seemed to have made herself very popular with the children and was always in demand, giving riding and swimming lessons, telling improbable stories and organising games. I marvelled at her vitality and the ease with which she had sloughed off the experiences she had undergone in France. Sennacharib had not only rejuvenated her physically, it had restored to her all her zest for living and originality so that now the entire establishment seemed to revolve around her and take on some of her glitter.

The only person whom she did not seem able to dominate was Yvonne. Yvonne still preferred my company but perhaps this was because Diana had usurped her as Queen of Heronslea. Yvonne did not resent this but slipped out of the limelight almost gratefully and spent a good deal of her time with me, sometimes watching her mother's high jinks with a curiosity that was grave but amusing.

"I *know* what she's like," she said to me suddenly, when we were standing by the paddock rails witnessing Diana's spectacular clearance of some bush jumps she had built for the children. "She's like the gale, you know, Jan, the one that comes in from over the river, bending all the trees and making a fearful to-do and then, when you're least expecting it, goes whooping over Teasel Wood and leaves you out of breath!"

It was a very accurate description of Diana in her present mood and when the gale had blown itself out I remembered and thought about Yvonne's remark.

They were rewarding days. The sun seemed to shine from first light until early evening when Diana and I crossed the small paddock and went up through the larch wood to Big Oak, Foxhayes or Tower Wood. Nothing had changed up here, not a bush, not a 'old in the ground. The oak where the buzzards lived had seen a dozen wars come and go and the steep lanes intersecting the coverts and heathland were gay with campion, stitchwort, viper's bugloss and the periwinkles that matched Diana's eyes. Together we made many sentimental journeys. Sometimes we turned our backs on the open country and went to swim in Nun's Cove and one hot afternoon we rowed over to Nun's Island and found Crusoe Jack's ruined cabin, where we had lived throughout our three-day elopement. We even found the cross that Diana had made to mark the grave of the two unknown seamen, lost in the wreck that gave the island its name and we laughed at our earnestness in having conducted the burial service half-a-century after the bones had been laid there.

It was during our visit to the island that I thought I had hit upon the hidden cause for the curious physical shyness that had entered into our relationship. During the brief interval at the villa, whilst we were awaiting Rance, we had sought and found relief in one another from the desperate tension of the vigil, but now, when there was no tension and we had all the privacy lovers could desire, we kissed like a pair of shy sixteen-year-olds playing hide-and-seek with each other in the maze of inexperience. I attributed this to the magic of Sennacharib and to the sheer wonder of being alive to receive its benediction. When we had been alone on the island as adolescents we had not made love and the shameful examination to which Diana had been subjected on her return home had proved unnecessary, a fact which astonished her parents. Now, after all these years, the same invisible chaperon accompanied us through the glades and across the beaches we knew so well and there was no need to possess her for now she was already possessed in the deepest and most satisfactory sense. I could look at her for minutes at a stretch, marvelling at the firm maturity of her breasts and the long sweep of her thighs, loving the tumult of her hair and the full curves of her mouth and yet do so without desire, without needing to touch or undress her, and enjoy her nearness and warmth and enthusiasm for love. That afternoon, as we sat watching the sun play on the tide-race over towards Whinmouth, I mentioned this lull and she laughed and shook her head.

"Oh no, Jan, it isn't that, not really, and it isn't a virginal phoenix arising from the ashes of our spiritual marriage in this setting. It's something more mature I imagine, or perhaps more primitive! You know the old superstition about the groom seeing the bride the morning of the wedding? Well, we're getting a bigger kick out of the hopeful journey than we shall from the arrival and I say 'we' because I understand exactly what you mean. I've never felt like this in my whole life, not about any man and not about you, never so utterly and comfortably sure! To make love now might invite a depressive reaction!"

"How long is this reticence likely to last?" I said, and I must have sounded slightly anxious, for she shouted with laughter. "Oh, until about ten minutes after we've left the Register Office in Whinford, I should say!" and she kissed me so boisterously that the invisible chaperon ran halfway down the beach and then stopped and came back, but slowly and hesitantly.

It was when we were on our way back to the mainland that I suggested we should call on her mother and bury the pre-war hatchet by inviting her to be one of our witnesses. I did not look for enthusiasm on Diana's part. She and Mrs. Gayelorde-Sutton had detested one another since Diana was a child but their antipathy had very little to do with me, it was there long before I appeared on the scene. To my surprise, however, she raised no objection.

"Why not ask Old Gramp, the pirate, to stand in for me?" she said. "It might be fun. Mummy would have to acknowledge him publicly!"

"Let's not go hunting trouble," I told her, "It usually finds us easily enough. No, I'm serious, Di. It's damned childish to maintain the feud and I've got nothing against your mother, in spite of the fact that she was a bitch to me in the past. As a matter of fact I rather admire her for starting up again the way she did. She showed more spunk than any of us when it came to the touch!"

"Okay!" Diana agreed, "we'll pay a social call on the exiled Squireen of Heronslea and you needn't worry, Jan, I'll behave! As a matter of fact I'm curious to discover whether she still puts all her vowels on the rack! She's running a dress shop, you say?"

"It's rather more than a dress shop. It's called 'Marcelle' and I've never been there but I've heard it's sensational. Bond Street in a Devon market town! We'll go over tomorrow morning, I'll ring her tonight."

"No, don't!" said Diana, her voice bubbling with laughter, "it'll be so much more fun to catch her on the hop. She must have heard we're back in the district but the last thing she'll expect is a social call from me. I'm glad you suggested it, Jan, I'm looking forward to this!"

She might have welcomed the prospect of a reunion when I mooted the idea, but her high spirits began to ebb the moment we arrived outside "Marcelle's" establishment about eleven A.M. the following morning. I could see she was overawed by the outward aspect of the shop and this put her at a disadvantage. I wondered briefly how a mother and daughter could have arrived at such an impasse. I knew how deeply Diana had resented her mother's efforts

532

to keep her in a social straitjacket all those years, and I was equally aware of how disappointing Diana had proved to a woman whose entire nervous energy was expended in establishing herself as a county hostess, but there must have been far more to it than this; the antipathy must have reached back into Diana's nursery days when the first attempts were made to halter a spirit as wild and reckless as Emerald Gayelorde-Sutton. Perhaps Diana's joke had substance; perhaps Old Gramp, the ferryman, really did number a pirate among his ancestors.

Diana gave the shop front a long, steady glance, then she pulled herself together and marched forward as though advancing up a strongly-defended glacis.

It was just the kind of shop that a person like Mrs. Gayelorde-Sutton would create, having once persuaded herself that there was nothing shameful in earning an honest living. I had always conceded her good taste, even while detesting her pretensions. Now I had to admit that she had shown a great deal of imagination in opening this kind of a salon in the shadow of Whinford Cathedral.

Her premises were hemmed in by antique shops, bookshops and pseudo-sophisticated cafes, and were approached by a gate opening on a conservatory that was decorated *á l'Espagnole,* with a wrought-iron well-head and a group of Picasso-style pictures. On the far side of this court a short flight of stairs led to the salon proper, a long, low-ceilinged room, lit by skylights and softly-shaded lamps, and fitted with gilded Empire mirrors and a row of cubicles, each screened by peach-coloured curtains. There was a peach-coloured carpet and one or two Récamier couches dotted about. There was also a First Empire commode that must have cost her two hundred pounds and beside it an exquisitely carved stool that would have fetched half as much again in a London sale-room. The general atmosphere was one of cosy luxury and was probably designed to prepare customers for the prices they would be asked when they stepped inside.

I entered on tiptoe—it was that kind of place—and Diana, after inspecting the furnishings and fittings, gave a low whistle of approval.

"She was flat broke, wasn't she?" she queried. "Where the blazes did she get this kind of money again? Was it a bank advance, or a sugar-daddy?"

I said I had no idea, that the last time I had seen Mrs. Gayelorde-Sutton she had been sitting at a sewing machine in a dreary flatlet at the top of a Holland Park boarding house. I was prepared to swear that she had told me the whole truth when she had confessed to having no money at all, but it was plain that she had found money somewhere and had used it to great advantage. The place oozed prosperity and bankers' blessings.

We were directed to a padded seat by one of the high priestesses of the establishment, a small-waisted young woman with a crown of carefully coiffeured curls and an accent that reminded me of Mrs. Gayelord-Sutton in her palmiest days.

"Modom? Ai'll see! Taike a seat, will yew?" and she hesitated a moment, as though assessing the depth of my pocket. "Who shall Ai say?" she added bleakly.

Diana giggled and to cover her giggle I gave my name, adding "Captain" in the hope that the rank would give her confidence. It didn't, I should have promoted myself to Brigadier. The girl gave a toss of her head and disappeared through a door marked "Private", reappearing in a moment but ignoring us in favour of a mountainous, blue-haired customer, whose thighs rubbed together as she walked.

"Well it was your idea, Jan," crowed Diana, "she's going to give us the velvet brush-off because we don't look prosperous enough!"

The chuckle died in her throat, killed by a gasp as the door marked "Private" opened and an old man emerged. He walked slowly, head bent, his eyes on a long, fat envelope he carried.

"Great God!" she exclaimed, "it's Gramp, collecting his remittance!"

It was indeed and a sadly spruced-up Gramp in a suit of excellent broadcloth and sporting a fringe of well-washed whiskers. The only recognisable item about him were the toes of his rubber sea-boots peeping from under the turn-

534

ups of his carefully-pressed trousers. He was so intent on his envelope that he did not notice us, although he passed close enough for us to inhale the odour of mothballs that had replaced the more familiar whiff of beer, tar and sweat. In spite of his finery he looked ill-at-ease, like Shaw's Doolittle the day after he had inherited the fortune. Diana was still staring after him when a bell tinkled and the high priestess popped the fat woman into a cubicle, popped into the office, popped out again and ushered us into The Presence. The office was even more impressive than the salon. It was decorated in a severely utilitarian style, with streamlined filing cabinets and a cluster of anglepoise lamps. Mrs. Gayelorde-Sutton sat behind a huge flat-topped desk, lined with lacquered trays, quill pens, a silver inkstand and other useless but expensive-looking objects. The thing that astonished me most was her youthful appearance. It was sixteen years since she had highheeled it into my uncle's quayside store, buttonholing me with —"Boy! Boy! Ai want to see some furniture!" and I knew that she was now well over fifty. In the pink glow of her desk lamp she could have passed for thirty-five. Her dark hair was tinted and she was very carefully made-up but she still possessed the trim elegant figure that had once made all the leery old longshoremen in Whinmouth gape after her as she drifted up and down Fish Street on her shopping expeditions.

If she was surprised to see Diana she did not show it but remained seated and greeted her with a carefully articulated: "Well Air'm-alde! End *how* are you?" after which she looked calmly at me and said: "Keptin Leigh? Naice to see you again!"

Her outrageous accent, which had taken a brief holiday when I had called on her in Holland Park, had returned to roost but with a difference, as though during its vacation it had undergone an intensive commercial course. In the old days it made you shudder. Diana was quite right, the vowels were stretched as upon a rack, and half the consonants were leap-frogged. Now both vowels and consonants had a reasonably square deal and the timbre of her voice was deeper having lost most of its aggressiveness. It was a successful business woman's accent and no-one could quarrel with it, so long as it was used to dominate silly customers who came into the salon with preconceived ideas of what suited them. When Marcelle claimed that she "dressed" people, she meant it, she did everything but put the clothes on their backs.

Diana was almost routed by her mother's majestic seizure of the initiative but she made a valiant rally and bent over the little figure at the desk to bestow a swift kiss on the top of the head.

"You look wonderful, mother, absolutely wonderful! Doesn't she, Jan? And quite horribly successful in a world of dreary utility clothes and lets-all-pretend-we're-in-uniform collections!"

I thought we would come to the point. The interview had its amusing aspects but I was finding it embarrassing. I said, flatly: "Diana and I are getting married, Mrs. Gayelorde-Sutton, and we thought you ought to hear about it from us. We would like you to be there if you'd care to come. It will be at the Register Office here, on the third Saturday in August and we'd like you to be a witness!"

She blinked once or twice and then grimaced. A nervous twitch of her small mouth had always done duty for a smile and I noticed that it still did. She picked up a red leather diary and flicked through the pages with exquisitely manicured finger tips.

"August? The Fifteenth? Let me see! About what taime?"

She might have been making an appointment for a fitting and Diana, who had by this time recovered her poise, came so close to laughter that I had to catch her eye and frown. "At eleven o'clock, Mrs. Gayelorde-Sutton!"

"Yes . . . yes, Ai ken do that! Ai'll make a note! *There!*" and picking up a gold pencil she wrote "Diana's wedding" in the space reserved for the fifteenth of the month.

Her methodical briskness was beginning to unnerve me and Diana, noticing this, came to my rescue.

"Yves was killed in France," she said, "he was working

536

for the Germans!" Then, before Mrs. Gayelorde-Sutton could comment, added: "I saw my grandfather here just now, the old ferryman at Castle Ferry. I've always known that he was my grandfather!" and waited.

A flicker of emotion showed in Mrs. Gayelorde-Sutton's face but it was no more than a flush and a slight contraction of the jaw muscles. Then it was gone and she was calm and impersonal again.

"Thet's so, he was here. He comes to see me once a fortnight. He's a partner, of a kaind!"

"A partner?" Diana made no attempt to hide her amazement. "You mean you . . . actually acknowledge him, mother?"

Mrs. Gayelorde-Sutton toyed with her pencil. She had never possessed the smallest sense of humour but there was at least irony in the glance she gave me before looking back at Diana.

"Ai daresay Mr. Leigh told you about mai circumstances thet time you ran off and married," she said, quietly. "Ai had no money at all! *At all!* you understand? Ai had to get started somehow and when Ai opened down here before the war, Ai was sadly under kepitalised, you follow?"

"Well, where does Gramp come in?" demanded Diana. "He never had two pennies to rub together and if he did it went on beer! I sent him money through Drip . . . Miss Rodgers!"

"Thet's so and he told me about it," pursued Mrs. Gayelorde-Sutton and I could see that she was enjoying herself. "As a matter of fact, your grandfather advanced me money to secure this lease! He had an allowance from me when your father was alive, you know!"

"He had five pounds a week," said Diana, bluntly. "I know that because I once looked in your handbag and saw the cheque stubbs!"

Mrs. Gayelorde-Sutton winced slightly, as though the confession was a personal affront.

"At all events he was able to help me," she went on, "to the extent of two thousand pounds!"

"That was exactly the sum I sent him!" said Diana and

537

I began to cough, for I could see that this interview promised to develop into one of their familiar free-for-alls and felt that should be avoided at all costs. The cough worked, both Diana and her mother taking the hint. Diana simmered down and Mrs. Gayelorde-Sutton bit her lip, checking the sharp retort that she was on the point of making.

"It was kaind of you to think of him," she said, finally, "but as things turned out it was all for the best. Instead of wasting the money, he invested it. He left his kepital in the business and now he draws forty pounds a month. It suits us both very well, but of course, if you need thet money, if it was a loan and not a gift . . ."

"It was a gift!" said Diana hastily, "so forget all about it, mother!"

I could see that Mrs. Gayelorde-Sutton was relieved but she covered up very well and came as near to smiling as I remember her doing.

"Ai'm very glad you and Mr. Leigh are getting married," she said, and she meant it. Then, turning to me, "Ai'm sorry that Ai failed to make it my business to get to know you properly a long time ago, Mr. Leigh!"

For Mrs. Gayelorde-Sutton this was an abject apology, but Diana burst out in protest.

"Oh, for God's sake, Mother! Don't keep calling him 'Mr. Leigh'! We aren't living in Jane Austen's time and he isn't asking for my hand! He's got it! We've already had a child and she's aged eight! It's 1944 now and there's a hell of a war on, so why not relax and call him 'John'? Help her, Jan darling, she's obviously sold on you! Give her a kiss and then let's all three have a drink on it!"

It was remarkable to see how even Mrs. Gayelorde-Sutton was unable to resist one of Diana's attacks. For a moment or two she looked miserably embarrassed and her hands fluttered, just as Diana's did under stress, but in the end she was won over and tilted her face so that I could plant a kiss on her cheek. It was a clumsy effort on my part but it must have touched her for she made a gesture that caught me by surprise, slipping her hand over my wrist and giving it a quick, nervous squeeze. It was so swift and gentle a movement that it was like the flutter of a small bird's wing, yet it was reassurance of a kind and I was grateful for it.

She touched first one bell and then another and an acolyte suddenly appeared from behind some curtains at the rear of the filing cabinets.

"Modom?" sighed the young woman, arching a pair of mercilessly plucked brows.

"We should laike some sherry, Doreen! Bring the decanter and three glasses! Amontillado, Ai think. Yes, Amontillado!"

The young woman disappeared and Mrs. Gayelorde-Sutton eyed Diana, this time professionally.

"What will you be wearing?" she demanded.

"I hadn't thought about it," replied Diana, and her mother gave a little shudder.

"You used to be very interested in clothes," she said sadly, and Diana replied, "Oh, I still am! I had a book of twenty-six coupons issued to me when I got back but I haven't one left. Why don't I look at something while I'm here?"

"We'll have our sherry first!" said Mrs. Gayelorde-Sutton, taking command again as Doreen returned with glasses and decanter on a silver tray.

We sipped our sherry and I took little part in the subsequent conversation which was mostly about clothes, and the effect of the German occupation of Paris upon styles and materials. I was content to listen for it was interesting to note how quickly their mutual suspicions disappeared once they found a common ground. Sitting there, as they conversed in a kind of Pidgin English, I reflected that clothes had been the one subject that they had been able to discuss without acrimony and it crossed my mind that if Mrs. Gayelorde-Sutton had climbed off her county pedestal years ago, and opened a business with Diana as junior partner, they might even have grown to like one another.

Presently Mrs. Gayelorde-Sutton said: "Don't bother about coupons, Ai've something heah that mate interest you! Why not slip it on?" and they drifted into the salon while I helped myself to a second glass of her excellent

539

sherry, congratulating myself on the unexpected success of the expedition.

The woman called Doreen came in—her attitude changed now that Diana had been hooked, and she flashed a professionally welcoming smile in my direction.

"Do hev a cigarette while you are waiting!" she said and proferred a crystal box half-filled with gold-tipped Turkish. I thought then what a pitiful waste of talent Mrs. Gayelorde-Sutton's pre-war activities had been, just so much frantic pursuit of a will o' the wisp called Social Prestige, together with an almost hysterical compulsion to impress people who did not care to be impressed, people like Whinmouth fishermen and Shepherdshey labourers. It had taken her husband's suicide and a bankruptcy to launch her on a career for which she was superbly qualified, for here her natural fastidiousness and her outrageous accent were just part of her stock in trade, like the curtains, furniture and fitted carpet, and she was fulfilling herself in a way that she had never been able to do as Squireen of Heronslea.

Through the open door that led to the Salon I could hear mother and daughter chattering away like neighbours over a fence and when Mrs. Gayelorde-Sutton looked in again I saw that her carefully-arranged face was pink with pleasure.

"*Do* come and look Mr. Leigh . . . er . . . John, Ai think we've hit on something, Ai really do!" and she bobbed back as I followed her into the salon.

Diana was standing in front of a full-length mirror in a cubicle with the curtains drawn aside. She was wearing an extremely well-fitting suit of light wool in a rich turquoise blue and a hat I can only describe as a double handful of crushed petals, held in place by a broad band of ribbon that looped under her thick curls and fastened above the nape of the neck. She looked enchanting and Mrs. Gayelorde-Sutton was hopping about like a painter who has just put the finishing touches to a masterpiece. Diana turned slowly towards me and let her left eyelid droop.

"Like I said, it's supposed to be terribly unlucky to let you see me, Jan, but Mummy insisted! I think it's wizard

540

and I'll never let Paris give itself such airs again! What do *you* think?"

I said humbly that she looked adorable and bowed acknowledgement to the impresario.

"Of course, we wouldn't give it a second look under normal conditions," said Mrs. Gayelorde-Sutton, "but it stands out today because there's almost nothing available. Ai'll get one of the gels to run up a blouse from this," she went on, flourishing a length of material that she was holding like a dipped standard. "The hat really *is* a little pet! A positive little pet! Don't you think so, Mr. Leigh . . . er . . . John?"

"The most outrageous hats look sober on Diana!" I said and a procession of Diana's hats from her childhood onwards flashed before my memory like a reel of film, red Tam-o'-Shanters, grey Cossack caps, Bergère and Highland bonnets, crushed down and lopsided hussar shakoes, all manner of folkish and quasi-military creations.

"Well, Ai'll tell you both something," said Mrs. Gayelorde-Sutton, now sounding like a rich aunt about to bestow a blessing. "Ai'de laike to make Diana a wedding gift of thet suit and thet hat! It's so much more *precktical* then giving a gel toast racks and suchlaike, don't you think?"

I murmured my thanks and Diana beamed.

"Why yes, because it's *you,* mother!" she said and she could hardly have put it more strongly for her mother blushed and said: "Well, Ai'll . . . er . . . see Doreen about the blouse . . ." and she hurried away in a pathetic attempt to hide her embarrassment.

Diana shook with silent laughter.

"Oh Jan, you've got to hand it to her, haven't you? She's absolutely terrific against this backdrop and I'm so glad you talked me into coming!" She swept out of the cubicle, wound her arms round my neck and kissed me warmly on the mouth. We left feeling something substantial had been accomplished.

During this period I was sleeping at the Cottage and Diana had a room at Heronslea. This was less of a concession to Drip's sense of propriety than to an attempt on

Diana's part to win Yvonne's confidence. Yvonne's reserve when Diana was around was the only cloud in the sky at that time and it bothered me more than it bothered Diana. I had a suspicion that Yvonne resented sharing the Heronslea throne with her mother, but Diana was more discerning and declared that she was jealous of the attention I paid to mother. This was probably the truth. In my previous visits I had devoted myself almost exclusively to Yvonne. Diana was very understanding in this respect and did everything possible to counteract it but in the end she had to appeal to me for help so I took Yvonne up to Big Oak one afternoon and had a long talk with her, probing her feelings regarding our marriage and doing what I could to supplement the talk I had had with her shortly before I left for France.

I think I was inclined to be a little irritable with the child and I soon discovered that I had made insufficient allowance for the weakness of the hold Diana already had upon her when she passed into my charge in 1940.

"Look here, Yvonne," I said, after we had topped the large wood and were walking across the short turf of the paddock, "it wasn't your mother's fault that she had to part from you. She sent you over here because the Germans had came and then stayed on to fight them."

"I can't remember much about that," Yvonne replied, glumly, and then, with the frankness of her mother that I found astonishing in a child not yet nine: "What's eating you Jan? Why are you so stuffy this afternoon?"

I remembered just in time that I was talking to Diana's daughter and that no one was likely to be less impatient with a compromise.

"Mummy thinks you don't want things to change. She thinks you don't want us to get married and live together after the war!" I said, feeling like a gambler who is staking a month's salary on the turn of a card. Yvonne considered this, gravely. The statement caused her no shock or embarrassment. She accepted it for what it was worth and pondered for a moment.

"Well, it's true I don't want anything to change, Jan," she said coolly, "but I suppose they have to and I daresay

542

I'll get used to it! I never thought much about Mummy before she turned up here. I know you tried to make me remember her every time you came, but then you would, wouldn't you? I mean, you're bound to, because you're madly in love with her!"

"Yes, I am!" I said, feeling a pricking sensation behind the eyes, "and I always have been, Yvonne! That's something you'll understand much better in a year or so!"

"Oh, I understand it now," she said, screwing up her face and looking so like Diana that I almost choked, "but you see, Jan, you can't expect me to feel the same! At least, not all at once! It's like . . . like someone grown up coming to stay with us, don't you see? I mean, she's beautiful and a wonderful rider and everybody goes for her but she's still someone who—well—who has popped up from nowhere, if you see what I mean!"

I did see what she meant and I was touched by her honesty, touched and to some extent reassured. She had my colouring and build and gait but fundamentally she was all Diana. She couldn't pretend about anything, not for an hour, not for a second, and not even to someone she loved and admired. I don't know why but I felt relieved and grateful for this discovery and after that I didn't give her lack of enthusiasm for Diana another thought.

We went on across Foxhayes and round the fringe of Folly Wood and when we were returning down the dusty Shepherdshey road to Heronslea Yvonne slammed the door on the subject by saying, with a sly, sidelong glance:

"Don't fret, Jan! It'll all come out in the wash, like Doris said!"

"Who's Doris?" I asked, grinning and running my hand over her dark mop of curls.

She stopped and looked surprised. "Gosh, don't you remember? Doris was the girl who had the sailor's baby— the one I told you about!"

"Ah yes!" I said, conscious of a tumult in the pit of my stomach, "I remember now," and we turned in at the lodge and walked up the long avenue of beeches to the house.

I was awake about five-thirty on my wedding morning and lay still in the big four-poster thinking luxuriously of inconsequential things, of the grain of the polished mahogany of the canopy pillars, the sense of purpose in the face of the gallant chasing the serving-wench in the Fragonard picture, the pleasant sough of the early morning breeze fluttering the little muslin curtains that Diana had fitted over the enlarged window. Then I got up, knowing I should not sleep again and not wanting to miss the freshness of this particular day stealing over Sennacharib.

I looked sideways in the speckled glass of the dressing-table mirror and examined the slow growth of new hair over the side of my head that had been shaved clean by the surgeon who had first dressed my wound. It was coming along very leisurely I thought and reflected that this was a clear sign that I was past my prime, and moving up towards the brow of the hill. Then I grinned at myself, thinking of the snort of contempt Diana would give if I told her I was getting old. I sluiced myself with well-water, slipped a pair of flannels and a sweater over my bathing trunks and went out whistling, moving along the winding path that followed the ridge of Teasel escarpment and looking west across the valley to the blue-grey stillness of Heronslea Woods.

It was an almost windless morning, with a clear sky and the promise of warm sunshine later on. I climbed up through the pines and chestnuts, listening to the shrill chorus of the birds, starting a cock-pheasant from the bracken and sending him whirring across the valley squawking indignation. At the top of the rise, where the trees thinned, I could look back on the whole of Sennacharib to the winding Teasel, Shepherdshey church and cottages and beyond into the wooded triangle of Heronslea estate. then southward to the sea and Nun's Island still half-hidden in haze. I paused up here and breathed a kind of prayer over it all, or perhaps it wasn't really a prayer but an incantation to the wood spirits and hedgerow sprites who had shared this place with us since we were children. It all seemed so utterly remote from war and the Nazis that I might have been inhabiting another planet in an age before any Cleverdick turned his misguided energies to devising guns and submarines and barbed wire.

Then I hurried across the clifftop and down the landslip to Nun's Cove where nobody was astir and the sea looked cold and placid. I left my slacks, sweater and towel on the tiny quay and waded in, finding that the water wasn't as cold as it appeared and swimming with slow strokes to a moored boat about a hundred yards offshore.

I hung on to the buoy rope a moment getting my second wind, then pushed off and made for the tip of the long, curving breakwater that bounded the eastern edge of the bay. I swam slowly, enjoying the loneliness of the scene and the physical release that movement through placid water brings to a swimmer. When I reached the rock barrier I climbed out and picked my way up the boulders to a point overlooking the next cove, a tiny sanded bay no more than a hundred yards across and isolated from the village by the bulk of Nun's Head. Here I gasped, my eyes level with the summit. In the exact centre of the beach, wavelets breaking round her feet, was Diana.

She wore no costume and was standing quite motionless, perhaps thirty yards away, her eyes fixed on the southernmost point of Nun's Island across the bay, but it was not her presence or nudity that caused me to smother the hail that rose to my lips. Rather it was her pose which was one of complete rigidity and preoccupation, with her arms raised and extended seawards, as though absorbed in the performance of some archaic rite.

This impression was so strong that it would have been folly to distract her and I felt this most forcibly in the first instant of sighting her. It was obvious that at that moment she wanted to be alone and unobserved and to break the spell would have been unforgivable. It struck me then that she was engaged in a form of supplication that had nothing whatever to do with Christianity, or with any known cult, but with something that had its roots in far-off centuries when tribes acknowledged allegiance to the things about them, the moon, stars and winds, to the red sun now rising from behind the headland and laying its rays across the bay.

Diana looked beautiful but her beauty transcended the physical, pulsing upwards and outwards, like ripples of colour and sound and striking the eye and ear as something both seen and heard. I crouched close against the rock watching her, watching the waves swirl round her feet and the light breeze ruffle her curls, worshipping her with my eyes and my soul, and as the sunplay scattered diamonds across the bay the strong, pinkish light found her sturdy thighs and seemed to caress her breasts and belly with a sure, loving touch. What was even more wonderful to see was her reaction to this, for she smiled and swayed ecstatically, like a woman pleased with the power she exerts over a lover.

Perhaps a full minute I remained there motionless and then, but with infinite care, I backed away and slipped into the water, swimming with careful strokes to the quay where I had left my clothes. Absent-mindedly I dried myself and dressed, thinking over what I had seen and reflecting that this was perhaps the strangest and most compelling discovery I had ever made about Diana and wondering whether I should admit to having seen her at her devotions. It was a difficult decision to make. At first I thought the better way would be to let her nurse her secret for as long as she wished. Then I thought that this would be a betrayal of Sennacharib, for Sennacharib was something we shared and if our lives together unfolded, as they promised at this moment, then I had a right to understand the compulsion that lay behind her action. Perhaps it was necessary that I should understand it, for it seemed to me that the key to her entire complex character lay in the impulse that had driven her down to the beach at first light to perform this act of obeisance.

I had still not fully made up my mind when I took the path across the landslip to the Teasel plateau and here fate decided for me, for as I reached the junction where my path joined the track leading over the headland to the cove, we came face to face and both stopped in our stride.

I don't think she was surprised to see me or if she was she recovered more quickly than I did. For a few seconds she looked angry, as though I was a trespasser caught in a private garden, but then she smiled and gave me a moment or so to master my embarrassment, or perhaps to consolidate her grasp of the initiative.

She was wearing an old grey skirt and a heavy sweater and her hair was not damp, so that I guessed she had not actually entered the water. Then I recalled that she had gone into Whinford for a hairdo the previous afternoon and that she never used a bathing cap.

"Well, say something!" she remarked, after what seemed an almost intolerably long pause.

"I've been for a dip!" I said foolishly and she laughed, breaking through the barrier by stepping up to me and kissing me on the cheek.

"You've got trunks and towel in your hand," she reminded me and then, "All right, Jan, you never could keep me guessing could you? You saw me didn't you? I don't mind, not really, though it is rather a shame after all these years! If it had been anyone else mind you, I think I'd kill them to stop their silly tongues, but you . . . my Jan . . . well, maybe I'd have told you myself in the end!"

I said nothing. I was wondering how she could have kept a thing like this all to herself in the days when we were growing up here together. She went on, as though dismissing the subject altogether, "I could do with a coffee, couldn't you? Let's make one at the cottage on the way back. Then I'll leave you to get into ceremonial. You'll have to do it all on your own, won't you? You really ought to have found a best man from somewhere, but who?" She gave me one of her shrewd, sidelong glances, the parent of the glance her daughter had given me a day or so before, "You've never had a male friend, have you? At least, not one of your own generation!"

"No," I said, only half-jokingly, "I never had time to cultivate one, I was always too busy keeping track of you!"

We climbed to the edge of the wood and down through the grove to the path along the eastern bank of the Teasel.

"You were worshipping, weren't you, Di?"

"In a way," she said, "but I don't much like the word. It conjures up visions of morning service in Sunday best and a lot of pi-faced people singing 'For All the Saints' Why don't we settle for 'acknowledging'?"

"Acknowledging what?"

She gave me another tolerant glance.

"You're a bit exasperating sometimes, Jan! Imagine you, of all people, asking such a damned silly question? Acknowledging *this*"—and she swept her arm round in a half-circle that took in Heronslea Woods, the Teasel Valley and the gorse-covered crown of Nun's Head.

Someone who knew her less well than I might have been fobbed off with the answer, but I wasn't. I had had a good long look at her as she had stood by the tideline and I had been near enough to note the intense concentration and earnestness in her pose and expression. She had not been playing a game with herself, or expressing a purely physical exhilaration as someone might in an idle and relaxed moment, she had been taking herself very seriously indeed. I was piqued by her evasiveness. It was as though she had denied me access to her body or had set limits on the liberty of my hands and lips, but I had no wish to pursue the matter. I had an uneasy feeling that it would lead to a quarrel so I went into the kitchen, poured milk into a saucepan and set the cups.

When the coffee was made I carried a tray into the main room but she was not there. I called, getting no answer, and went into the bedroom. She wasn't in the cottage and she wasn't anywhere outside.

It was unreasonable I suppose but at once I succumbed to the wildest panic. I ran to and fro, shouting her name and I think I was more frightened then than at any time during our adventures in France. It was like a final echo of all her other disappearances and I raged about, sick with dismay. It was so true to the merciless rhythm of our association. One day she was there and the future glowed, the next she was gone and the future stretched before me like a desert that had somehow to be crossed before I could find her again. It had always been this way; holidays then term, elopement to Nun's Island and then two empty years to follow, the ecstasy of her surrender on the night of her eighteenth birthday then her letter rejecting the future; her

548

return, broken in nerve after her road accident and then her abrupt flight the night her father killed himself. Here and gone, kisses and protestations, then silence. Yet always, long after the silence the trumpets again, as at the Bordeaux Ferry during the panic of 1940 and the sound of her footsteps in the church after Alison's funeral.

I had no idea what I should do, how I should begin to set about looking for her and telling her she could keep as many secrets as she wished, I was too shocked to stop and reflect how childishly I was behaving. I suppose I was conditioned to disappointment where Diana was concerned and this time it reduced me to the helplessness of a small child lost in a fairground, running this way and that bleating its misery.

I went back into the cottage and foraged in the old bacon cupboard beside the fireplace, fishing out a bottle of cognac that she had put there two or three days before when we were laying in stocks. It was unopened and I was far too impatient to find a corkscrew. I struck the neck of the bottle on the edge of the fireplace and slopped a measure into a cup. As I raised it to my lips a voice said:

"He knocked off the neck as one well accustomed to the habit!"

Diana was standing inside the cottage door, leaning against the great oak doorpost and smiling across at me with an expression that was half amusement, half concern. I remember the quotation, it was from '*Treasure Island*' and I recalled too that Israel Hands, Flint's treacherous master gunner, was one of Diana's favourite characters in fiction. I swallowed a mouthful of the spirit and it rallied me, so that I was able to grin shame-facedly and quote back at her.

" 'By Thunder but I needed some o' that!' "

I offered her the bottle but she shook her head.

"It's all right for the groom to reek of brandy but it's asking too much of the bride!" she said, picking up the cup of luke-warm coffee.

I had imagined that I was familiar with most of her moods but this one baffled me. She was composed and deliberate yet still half-inclined to mock and tantalise. But behind the mockery was gentle laughter and behind that again a wisp of uncertainty.

"Did you really think I'd run out on you, Jan? Did you really believe that?"

"Yes, I did!"

The uncertainty mastered the laughter, driving it from the corners of her mouth and clouding her eyes. She swallowed once or twice and stopped fiddling with the cup handle.

"I suppose I deserve it!" she said, sighing.

"Deserve what, Di?"

"Distrust; to that extent!"

I forgot everything then under one of the shuddering waves of tenderness that had always drowned me at times like these. I ran to her and pulled her close to me, letting my hands slide over her shoulders to her waist.

"I can't explain it, Di! The fear was crazy but it was real! By God, it was real!"

"Yes, I know," she said, "that's why I stopped teasing and can e back!"

"I didn't want to pry and I'll never want to, Di, I promise!"

"There's nothing to pry into, Jan, nothing you wouldn't understand, *nothing*, you hear?"

We stood like this for a few moments and outside everything seemed still and timeless. I remembered other moments like this, just a few of them spread over a long period of time. Each was a tiny interval of unimagined nappiness, worth waiting for and hoping for, worth every penny of the toll they demanded. Diana said:

"I'll tell you, Jan. Tonight!"

Then she slipped away and was gone and I heard her swishing through the bracken as she took the short cut aown to the river and across the chestnut grove to Heronslea. I went to the window and waited to see her emerge from the trees at the stepping stones, a tiny, girlish figure in shapeless grey skirt and sweater. She didn't wave or look back and a moment later she had scrambled over the low wall into the estate and was lost among the big timber.

550

I washed the cups and cleared the broken glass from the fireplace. Then I went in to shave and change.

She kept her promise and told me that same night.

After an explosion of tenderness Diana always slept but I never did, or seldom so. A man is reluctant to close the lid of the coffer that contains proofs of his personal triumphs and nothing I ever achieved came within hailing distance of winning Diana, or having her asleep in my arms under Sennacharib stars. It was immature I suppose, this conscious gloating at my time of life, but I made no apologies to myself for it, then or later. Diana never ceased to be the Arthurian damsel snatched from the tower or the girl of all the cheap popular melodies of the 'twenties. We get older and greyer but we don't change that much, not in essentials.

She lay with her head on my shoulder, breathing deeply and quietly and her hair alongside my cheek stirred to the rhythm of her breathing, bestowing the lightest of kisses. I thought of the verse in Genesis that had puzzled me as a boy; ". . . and Adam knew his wife, and she conceived and bore Abel" and felt I understood it so well now, that old, Biblical verb "knew." I knew Diana as I had never learned to know her in previous encounters scattered thinly across the years and remembered with a tinge of guilt that sprang perhaps from Puritan ancestry, and all the sermons I had sat through in Uncle Reuben's Gothic tabernacle down on Whinmouth quay. After all, they had not been so frequent, these encounters and none so rewarding as now. Fear had gone from them and impatience, so had urgency and the goad of tomorrow. The war was still on and I was pledged to engage in it, but war was a global concern. My war was won and the spoils were under my hand.

I lay there with a shaft of moonlight cutting across the foot of the bed, half-listening to the night sounds of Sennacharib, noises that were so much a part of the place that they might have been scripted into the pages of a play or film, the south-west wind soughing through the trees, an owl hooting, the far-off murmur of the rising sea under Nun's Head. I thought of the first time we had lain thus after she had smuggled me into her room and all her coming-of-age guests had driven off, flushed with liquor and bawling their good-nights. It seemed so improbable and so long ago that it might have happened to two other lovers in another century. I thought of the next occasion when we had consummated what she had called "a marriage in Sennacharib" in the glen beside the Teasel and created our child, Yvonne, to inherit the woods and moors and sky that had been our inspiration. Then I remembered the third time, when Diana's contempt for the dream had enraged me and I had struck her and after that, the curious release she had sought in me from the fear of Rance at the villa. Not one of these experiences had been a genuine act of love for each had its source in emotions alien to the need we had one for the other. In all of them there had been abstract factors, curiosity, a search for reassurance, a conquest of fear or self-disgust but tonight all these things had been absent from our union and it seemed to me that, no matter what happened in the future, these particular spectres would never bother us again. It might not have been so had we married in some other place. As it was, we had arrived together and now there was a shape to it all, a shape and a sense of purpose. We had found the speck of light at the end of the cave and the shadows had achieved substance that could be touched, even as I could touch Diana now and listen to her steady breathing and feel the kiss of her hair on my cheek.

I passed my hand down over her head and across her bare shoulder to her ribs and she drew a long breath and stirred, catching my hand, lifting it to her breast and holding it there. She said, briskly considering she had been sound asleep a second before:

"I didn't tell you, Jan! About this morning. I promised, didn't I?"

"Forget it, who cares?"

"*I* care! It's important in a way. I hadn't forgotten, I was waiting for the right moment and this is it, Jan!"

"Very well, then what?"

"You were right, I *was* praying. 'Supplicating' I suppose

you'd call it. Not just for us though, for a son. Several sons!"

I was mildly amused at her gravity and by the issue she seemed to want to make of what I now regarded as a piece of exhibitionism, a little play each of us acts for ourselves, openly as children but secretly as adults.

"He's on the way," I said, feeling sleepy now but my reluctance to discuss the matter made her impatient and she gave me a little shake.

"Listen Jan! Don't go to sleep! You could have slept while I was asleep. Why didn't you?"

"I was thinking how adorable you are and how possessive!"

This mollified her somewhat and she chuckled. Nobody was ever more serious than was Diana about love-making when actually engaged upon it yet nobody found it more amusing in retrospect. It was a kind of reflex. She not only laughed at her lover's enthusiasm, but at her own.

"The first time I ever went down to the beach at that time of day was before I met you," she said. "It was the summer before I met you and I was nearly fourteen. I had religion. Quite badly!"

"You never had religion and you certainly never had it badly!" I said.

"Oh, but I did! How could you know? You hadn't set eyes on me! We had only just arrived at Heronslea but before that I'd been confirmed at St. John the Evangelist, in Palmerston Square and I was chock full of sin!"

"You still are," I said, but I was attentive now. I always enjoyed Diana's confessions. They had a kind of off-beat primness that perched on her like a saucy jackdaw on the shoulder of a bishop officiating who was at a royal wedding.

"At first it wasn't anything special," she went on. "All girls that age go through it and dream of taking the veil. I don't suppose boys do, they don't appear to at all events. Well, because Daddy had so much money and because Mummy used it so vulgarly this hit me quite hard. I suppose I found difficulty in fitting it in with the poor inheriting the Kingdom of God or the rich threading the eye of the needle!"

It made sense. Diana had always been ashamed of her mother's ostentation and I imagine that, at the age of fourteen, it must have been painful to live it down in a community as forthright as ours.

"I did all the usual things about it," she continued. "I prayed and prayed and asked God to make us poor and I even talked to the local rector about it—you remember—that dreadful little man who took snuff and toadied to Daddy when he moved in as Squire. He did his best to make me feel comfortable again, told me it was a trust and that I must learn to use it for the benefit of the less fortunate! Even at this distance that seems outrageous hypocrisy on his part. I can understand him better now, however, he was an absolute pig for port!"

"Never mind the rector, tell me about your conversion to paganism!"

"Well, it happened that very morning, the morning I was down there by myself. You've read *Pilgrim's Progress* and you remember when Christian got to the top of the Hill of Difficulty and his bundle of sins went rolling down, giving him wonderful freedom of movement? It was exactly like that! Bunyan knew his stuff. I went down there very early to the exact spot where you saw me yesterday and it just happened. I saw the sun come up over Nun's Island and spread across the bay, and it was all so big and wide and wonderful that the kind of religion I'd been practising up to that moment seemed a shrivelled little thing, like a . . . like an old peapod on top of a dustbin! I thought 'They've been having me on! It isn't like that at all, it hasn't anything whatever to do with Churches, or your Uncle Reuben's Chapel where they whine about the blood of the Lamb, and the Holy Spirit, and repentance and renunciation and fornication and God knows what else! This is it,' I thought, 'this is really it! The sun and the patterns on the sand, the smell of the wet weed and the swoop of gulls, the scent of the gorse and the song in the larches, the shepherd's crook curve on the top of the tallest foxglove

554

and the kind of curtsey that cow-parsley makes when its lace is weighted with summer dust!'

"I tore off all my clothes and said my new prayers there on the tideline and one of the things I prayed for was someone to share it with, someone who would listen and understand! I suppose I was so damned lonely, Jan, until you came and after that you were caught up in it, in a sense you *were* it, and as I matured the sensuality of Sennacherib seemed to centre on you, so that I shook at the knees every time you touched my hand, or said anything that I could construe into the discovery that you wanted me as a woman and a mate! You could have had all of me before I was fifteen but it took me a long time to realise that men don't develop at anything like the speed of women or that men like you idealise women and sometimes frustrate them to the point of eruption! I learned to control myself of course. You would have scared off if I hadn't but it wasn't until that time we were on the island alone that I learned how to come to terms with your male gentleness and even be grateful for it! Anyway, I've rather wandered from the point, what I really wanted to tell you was that this sense of being at one with the Seasons, and with everything that grows and dies and is born again in Sennacharib, stayed with me and is still with me. Looking back on everything that has happened, this is the only really consistent thing in my life and it's locked up in you and only you! That was why, on the day we were to be married it seemed essential that I should acknowledge it and put into words the primaeval need of every woman, to bear male children for the man who is the focal point of her existence. I was doing just that when you saw me! I was admitting that my happiness depended upon that and begging the life-force in Sennacharib to make me fruitful at once and often! Is it so fanciful, Jan? *Is* it?"

It wasn't in the least fanciful, not from her and certainly not expressed as she had expressed it. It made so many things clear that had never been more than half-clear in the past. It tied up so many loose ends and closed so many uncalculated columns, even underlining the answers and turning the page. It accounted for some of the things that had shocked and puzzled me, for her unpredictability, her eternal restlessness, her sudden, impulsive demands to be taken by force, to be used roughly and masterfully and then flattered and coaxed and spoiled! How could I have understood all this as a boy growing up in a small, remote community, with nothing but a few books and my instincts to guide me? How could I have been anything but troubled and frightened by the pressure of her child's body to mine when I parted from her after our stolen hours and secret meetings? And afterwards, when she was so wayward and elusive, when she had disappeared from Sennacharib for months and sometimes years on end? Did she do that because I failed to soar with her but had remained boorish and churlish, rejecting what she offered because the offer was premature, or because the time was inopportune, or because measured alongside her, I was poor of spirit?

I didn't know the answer to this and I made no attempt to seek it. I was too busy rejoicing that she had made it her business to tell me these things here and now, and that she had had the sensitivity to hold them back for the right time and place. I said: "It's not in the least fanciful, Di darling. It might sound so to others but it doesn't to me. I understand every word of it. I've been damned arrogant all the way, imagining even you could never feel as I did about this place. I realised that you could hear the theme but I thought you missed the grace notes. It's very obvious that you didn't and I'm sorry I was heavy-footed and smug. I'll make up for it, you can depend on that!"

She threw both arms around me and held me so closely that I could feel the beat of her heart.

"You were never heavy-footed, Jan, never! If it hadn't been for you that feeling I had down there on the beach that morning would have never taken root, it would have blown away on the first new excitement, a pony, a holiday abroad, a flirtation at a party!"

"Is having another child all that important to you, Di? We've got Yvonne!"

"Yvonne *is* me. I want to reproduce *you,* Jan! That's

more important than anything, apart from being a good wife to you!"

I could understand this, or partially so, but it wasn't all that important to me, not really, not if I was completely honest with myself. My imagination had never carried me beyond Diana to the contemplation of Diana's children. I loved Yvonne, but Yvonne was a by-blow and I remembered how incredulous I had been when Diana told me that she was our child and had laughed at my amazement. We might have more children or we might not, it was something I was happy to leave to chance.

"Why is it so important Di?"

"Two reasons and I don't know which comes first. I know which ought to but I'd have to think about it."

"What reasons Di?"

"I've got a good deal out of life, Jan, but so far I've put precious little into it. Up to now you've always been the giver and I want to change that, I'm determined to change, and it isn't just a first-night resolution, believe me. I've wanted to do it ever since I ran away and married Yves. Making you a good wife, and giving you children, seems to me about the sanest way of making up lost ground."

"But why does it have to be a boy?"

"That's the other reason—continuity! It's the pattern and the rhythm. I know why you always felt like you do about Sennacharib. It isn't just me, you know, it isn't just because we met and fell in love here or because all your happiest hours were spent here. It's deeper than that, deeper than you know! What have I to do with this place really? My family came here a few years ago to play at being Squires. We bought our standing-room for hard cash, but your people didn't, they earned it! There were Leighs working Foxhayes Farm centuries back and some of the dirt on their horny hands was passed on to you. You would have belonged here in spite of me, I only helped to glamorise it when you were an impressionable boy. I want to contribute to that continuity; to me Sennacherib is just you. It's a lot more than me to you, that's why it has to be a boy! It's the difference between owning a place and being a weekly tenant!"

I lay there listening to her and wondering if there was anything in what she said, whether in fact my love for the place was an ancestral memory, or whether it was a by-product of the woman who lay beside me; I wondered whether the sense of belonging that I had experienced walking my first mile up the Teasel Valley, would have taken root had it not been nurtured by the girl who rode out of the woods on a pony and gave vitality and purpose to a boy's dream. I didn't know and couldn't tell and musing on it I fell asleep.

When I awoke it was full day and the sun was streaming through the open window and making the dust motes dance. Outside in the thickets the blackbirds and finches were chattering like an impatient audience and inside, both hands tugging at her hair, was Diana. Not Emerald Diana Gayelorde-Sutton. No longer Madame de Royden. Plain Diana Leigh, wife of John Leigh, of Teasel Cottage, Shepherdshey, in Devon. I crunched this knowledge like candy, then I stretched and called:

"Di! Mrs. Leigh! Wife!"

She stopped combing and turned her head, looking over her shoulder so that her lovely hair slipped forward and swung into the sunlight, catching great greedy handfuls of its radiance and playing with it like a miser toying with gold. She put down the comb and crossed to me, kneeling beside the bed, placing her hands alongside my cheeks and bending her head so that her curls shut out the light. Then, very gently, she began to rock as though I was the child she wanted so much.

Chapter Ten

A MAN remembers exciting times, the good and the bad. He remembers most of the high tides of his life but only occasionally do they coincide with those of the community in which he lives. It was this way with me. Some of the stones that marked the miles for me did the same for the Allies in their struggle with Hitler but not many, and none at all in the months that followed our home-making on the slope overlooking Heronslea Woods.

They were placid months, despite the war and my trivial part in it. The calendar was marked not by the advances and retreats on the Heronslea war map maintained by Drip but by a succession of leaves and departures, by the march of the seasons across the bracken and gorse thickets and the slow change of the beeches from bright green to crimson and then to gold and finally to dulled bronze.

I managed to get down there pretty frequently in those days, for they were very tolerant with me at Command H.Q. They seemed to think that I had earned a break approximating to that given to bomber crews after a tour of operations. My duties at Command H.Q. were not exacting, for the most part I interrogated returning crews and helped with the business of sorting and interpreting photographs and general information relating to Western France. I was shameless in wangling forty-eight hour passes and two or three times, when there was work about, Diana travelled to the market town close by and put up at "The Mitre", the haunt of boisterous young bomber-crews living on wallop, nerves and borrowed time.

One of the most satisfactory developments at this period in my life was the steady improvement in the relationship between Diana and Yvonne. It was not spectacular but it was obvious, even if one made no special effort to look for it. They were never like mother and daughter but they soon found a mutually satisfactory compromise, that of a couple of sisters with a wide gap in their ages, one tolerant and inventive, the other, thrustful and dominant, the way a certain terrier behaves when it finds itself in the company of a bigger dog who is willing to engage in a rewarding frolic. It seemed to suit them very well and I encouraged it.

Meanwhile, the war rolled on, hopefully but with little indication as to when it was likely to end. Italy dropped out and Russia began its counter-attacks. Lancasters and Halifaxes pounded German cities to rubble and there was endless speculation about the date of the Second Front. More and more Americans began to appear and the daylight bombing offensive began. Losses were formidable and the "We can take it" mood of the earlier part of the war was replaced by a collective yawn on the part of the British public. People in trains spoke less of pincer-movements and more of petrol shortages or the unpleasantness of the local black-out warden. Then, in the first week of May, 1944, the chopper came down.

I was summoned by the Chief of Intelligence and asked if I was prepared to undertake a special operation involving an almost immediate return to France. I say "asked" because this was technically true. This kind of job was never thrust on anybody and people like me were given the doubtful privilege of volunteering for duties coming under the heading of "special operations". I had absolutely no appetite for glory. I hated Fascism and I believe I was prepared to do as much as the next man to win the war, but I wanted to do it in company, as a member of a Lancaster crew or a cog in a technical ground unit. I wanted most desperately to survive. For the first time in my life my thoughts were tidily arranged and my personal future was predictable. I wasn't looking for medals or kudos and there was nothing awaiting me in Nazi-occupied Europe but the loss of everything I had won back from life during my former gamble.

The Chief was very comfortably seated behind a large map of north-western France that took in all of Brittany and parts of Anjou, Maine and Lower Normandy. He was a comfortable-looking man, a pre-war turf celebrity with the kind of assurance that comes from inherited wealth and the civilian rank of County Lieutenant. I admired him without being able to like him. His confidence was derived not so much from his present Air Force rank and social status as from his attitude to the war as a whole, as though it was a foxhunt that had worked itself into a tedious muddle and needed to be sorted out by an expert.

We talked a little about my Service record and at his request we conversed in French. His French was very bad, far worse than he knew, but he spoke it with so much assurance that I was half-convinced that it was I who had learned it at a crammer's in the nineteen-twenties. It soon leaked out that he wanted me to contribute towards the temporary isolation of a section of French railway lines that would be used by Germans reinforcing the north-western sector of the Atlantic Wall. It was my first clue as to where invasion was likely to strike.

The next thing that emerged was the fact that my name had been put forward for this particular job by Raoul de Royden, who had left the Paris area after our flight and had been engaged in the backbreaking task of co-ordinating the various Resistance groups in the area under survey. The Chief told me something of what was intended in the way of aerial bombardment and said it would aim at cutting railways, blocking tunnels and isolating the combat areas. He didn't actually say that there was going to be an invasion here but he might just as well have admitted it.

"The idea is to isolate this area for at least seventy-two hours," he said. "I don't know why, it's not my concern, but I imagine there's some kind of feint or raid on, a largish one, I should say!" He pointed out the course of rivers and railways and told me where the heavy Lancaster raids would occur, mostly against bridges over rail cuttings and waterways. Then he came to the point without wasting time on ascertaining whether or not I was willing to volunteer for special duties a second time.

"This chap de Royden seems to be highly thought of at De Gaulle's H.Q." he said. "We had a signal yesterday with your name on it. It seems that this chap is in a spot and wants a British liaison officer that he can rely on. Before we go into details what kind of feller is he?"

He might have been asking my advice on the employment of a beater at a grouse shoot.

"He's the toughest egg they've got in the field," I said, "and one hundred per cent reliable! He was educated over here. At Marlborough!"

"Really?" He was obviously very relieved to hear this and promoted Raoul de Royden from porter at the Gare du Nord to reserve in the county cricket team. He then came as near to animation as was possible with a man of his antecedents. "Tell me about him! Tell me how he came to get caught up in this cloak-and-dagger circus!"

I told him what little I knew of Raoul de Royden and mentioned that he was a cousin of my wife's first husband. I could see he knew all about Diana and me. He was even worse at concealing what he knew than he was at expressing himself in French and it occurred to me that he was a classic example of British Service snobbery at its worst. He possessed certain qualifications for his job but he would have got it anyway and within days of joining the staff.

He said, in his best old-boy voice:

"I see! Well now, this chap de Royden has to pull out. Seems he has other things to do! A strike has been laid on that is supposed to synchronise with ours. There's a loco-motive repair depot here"—he pointed to a small town called Ghislaine St. Père, just south of the Loire—"and the Resistance people intend to wreck the breakdown train before it can get here," and he indicated a tunnel linking two main lines from the south. "Our fellers will soak that place on a certain date—you'll get the date later of course —but the whole damn thing will be useless unless the French blitz that repair train soon after it sets out. It'll start within minutes of the attack on the tunnel. This likely chap, de Royden, has sent a demand through that he must have a British officer to take his place at once and he spe-cifically asked for you. I imagine it saves him the trouble of getting to know a complete stranger."

He did not mean to sound unflattering, it was just his way of stating a hunch. I said, reluctantly:

"Suppose I went over, would I get my local briefing from de Royden personally?"

He had obviously not considered this and said he would find out from "someone on a rather higher level". Then, but archly, he reverted to Service slang.

"That's the griff, Leigh old man! You'll get all bumff later on but this is all I'm authorised to tell you now. Point is, I'm not ordering you to take it on, it's not exactly a piece of cake, is it?"

It wasn't a piece of cake. It was a sour lump of dough

562

and my stomach confirmed the fact. I could guess what had prompted Raoul to send the S.O.S. over the crowded wire. By now he had probably despaired of playing referee to about half-a-dozen rival partisan groups and had realised that, in his absence from the scene, the only possible solution would be the appointment of an official British agent under whom the enthusiastic locals might be persuaded to forget their countless personal jealousies and mutual mistrust. The job itself did not look too difficult but the chances of making a getaway after it was accomplished were vague.

"Do I have to make a decision now, sir, or do I get a chance to think it over?"

He looked at me as though he was the head prefect and I was a grubby third-former asking for permission to cut games.

"I'm afraid you have to say 'yes' or 'no' now," he said, bleakly. "Dammit man, we are rather heavily engaged, what with one thing and another!" Then, self-consciously, he softened a little and added: "After all, strictly speaking this isn't my show you know, its an S.O.E. pidgin! Maybe you'd care to take it up with them!"

"No sir, it's not the job I'm querying. If Raoul de Roydon set it up, then it has a good chance of succeeding. It's a personal matter. Could you give me fifteen minutes?"

He smiled and became almost human.

"Why naturally. Dammit, not all that panic, is there?" and we both stood up.

I went out into what had once been the walled garden of a great country house. The May sunshine wavered on the lichened blocks and there was that most evocative of early summer scents, the smell of wallflowers. I sat down on a piece of stone near the sundial and looked across the wilderness of neglected garden to the huddle of grey buildings that had been coachhouses and were now doing duty as a carrier-pigeon centre. Birds were strutting on the weedy lawn and I envied them their ignorance of the part they would be expected to play in the coming offensive. I told myself that I ought to have expected something like this, that I had been drugged since Diana and I had homed on Sennacharib, that there was no reason at all to suppose the British military machine would consider me immune from further risks simply because I had solved my personal problems. Evidently they had yet to solve theirs and I was being asked to assist. A good many men who were well satisfied with their lives right now would be asked to face death or mutilation before the summer was much advanced.

I could refuse of course but it was not solely the look in the Air Commodore's eye that I feared. That wouldn't last anyway. He would soon find some other mug and forget all about me, my name as well as the proposition he was putting to me. What nagged at me was my responsibility toward Raoul de Royden and the rag-tag-and-bobtail he led. Raoul was a dedicated man, dedicated in the way that I had been dedicated, and to a dream. It was a different dream perhaps—but was it? Diana said we were at war in defence of the right to walk freely at Sennacharib, whereas Raoul was fighting for the nation that had shamed him and sold his generation to a pack of thugs for an unspecified number of francs. It amounted to the same thing, the free determination of an individual to use or to waste his life as he chose, and I wondered what Diana's advice would be if she was able to look at the matter objectively. Could she do this? Could she help me if I ignored the look in the Air Commodore's eye and stalled for time to go home and discuss it with her?

I turned my back on the prospect. I had enough pride to want to work this one out alone. How much did I owe Raoul de Royden? How much did I owe the Allied cause? How much did Britain or the British owe me? If it had not been for de Royden, Diana and I would not have come together again, never at least in the sense that we were together at this moment. And if the Allies had not stood up to the Nazis in 1940 Sennacharib would have ceased to exist, for me or anyone else, of that I was certain. For me, Sennacharib *was* the nation. It was the part of Britain, named on the map, and the Britain that was not marked on any map. It was the cluster of thatched cottages and hedged fields and the rash of suburban estates on the edge

564

of the industrial cities. It was Cobden and Doctor Johnson and Cromwell and Chaucer; it was Wilberforce and Shaftesbury and the Tolpuddle Martyrs; it was Tennyson's *Idylls of a King* and it was the *Song of the Shirt* and Dickens' London; it was the Union Jack and the Mother of Parliaments. I owed it a damned sight more than it owed me or could ever owe me, notwithstanding loyalty to Diana's lovely body and the music of her laughter in the morning.

I took my hands out of my pockets, straightened my tie and went to knock on the Air Commodore's door.

They sent me on a forty-eight that same evening, with a promise that I should get my initial briefing and despatch date the following Monday afternoon. For this, they said, I would have to go over to S.O.E. Headquarters in Baker Street. There was an inter-service background to my particular job and S.O.E. were the boys with the latest "gen."

Diana guessed what had happened the moment I entered the room and when I told her the details she was silent for a long moment. Then she said:

"Don't let's discuss it here, Jan, let's go up to the paddock beyond the larch wood. I must have time to get used to this."

"There isn't any time," I said, "I'm already committed, Di!"

"I know but I've got to adapt myself to it, so let's get out of here and go up to Foxhayes."

We went out and down the slope to the river, then over the wooden footbridge and up the nearside of the Heronslea coverts to Big Oak Paddock. The primroses were gone and the foxgloves were budding. For wildflowers it was an in-between season. There was only campion in the hedges and on the edge of the wood a thin mist of bluebells. We walked a mile or more without exchanging a word and then, as we were crossing Big Oak, she said:

"I'm glad in a way, Jan, there had to be a readjustment We might as well get it over with right now!"

"What kind of readjustment? Damn it, we've been happier than I ever dreamed possible! You have, haven't you?"

"Yes, but there's a flaw, Jan. In one way I've succeeded better than I hoped but in another I'm still a bloody failure!"

I stopped and pulled her round so that she faced me.

"Don't say that! Don't ever say it! You've been wonderful in every way and I'm more in love with you now than I ever was!"

She looked at me steadily and there were tears in her eyes. Diana was sparing with tears and whenever I saw them I was frightened.

"What is it, Di?"

"I can't give you any more children, Jan. Never, you understand?"

I was shocked by the despair in her face and voice. I took her hand and led her to the broken stretch of fence opposite the buzzards' oak. She sat down, her hands in her lap.

"It's true, Jan, I've been everywhere, to everyone and its unanimous. They all say the same thing!"

"Who have you been seeing? When? And why the hell didn't you tell me?"

She lifted her shoulder. "Does it matter? I went to the best. The last was Foster-Hayne, in Welbeck Street. He's supposed to be the best in Europe. I've been up to town four times when you were away. I kept hoping that one of them would come up with something new and I could hope. If that had happened I should have told you at once. You believe that, I suppose?"

It was in character when I thought about it, this desperately secret search for reassurance. There had always been secretiveness in her way of doing things, a passion to solve the really big problems alone and come up with the answer when she was ready and not a moment before. I took a deep breath and came to terms with it at once. Perhaps I could never convince her that children were not important. They might have been once and they might have been still had it not been for Yvonne but now their importance was insignificant. All that mattered to me was that

566

we would continue as we were, the complement of one another physically, spiritually and emotionally. Nothing else mattered at all. She forestalled my attempt to explain this yet again.

"You'd better hear the whole truth now Jan. Then we'll talk about your going to France again!"

"Talk yourself out Di," I said, trying not to sound as exasperated as I felt, "then I'll have my say and you're going to listen to it and think about it!"

"It was the child I got rid of just before you came to the villa. I told you Raoul arranged it but he didn't, I lied to you then and I never thanked you for not bullying the facts out of me. Most men would have tried, you know!"

"What about Rance's child?"

"I took a chance, a big one as it turned out, and this is the pay-off. I suppose the sane thing would have been to have asked Raoul to find me somewhere reliable but I didn't. The only thing that seemed to matter then was to start afresh and how was that possible with his child in my womb? I wasn't even sure when you would arrive and there was no time to be choosey. I just went ahead and as I say, this is the pay-off!"

Things began to fall into place, little things that had passed half-noticed at the time. I remembered her elation last Christmas when she thought she was pregnant and what had seemed to me her unreasonably bitter disappointment when she had learned that she was not. I remembered too odd trunk calls and a couple of trips to town and one or two long silences between us when her manner had suggested that she was preoccupied with a part of her life still hidden from me. I had never probed and never wanted to know more than she wanted to tell me but this was not due to consideration on my part but a kind of fear that whatever emerged would cloud the present. I wasn't even curious, I felt that I knew the real Diana and I wasn't interested in the wild, pacemaking creature of the period between past and present. I said, in reply:

"I don't seem able to convince you about the unimportance of children so we'll accept that it's terribly important to you. What concerns me vitally is your health and your

567

peace of mind, so tell me all you have to tell me about both. I'm sure it isn't as serious as you make it out to be and anyway, it was wrong of you to keep it to yourself this long!"

"I don't know how much you know about these things," she said guardedly. "Men seem to spend a lot of time laughing at sex but most of them are incredibly ignorant about it. It's a miracle you never guessed anyway."

"Women who don't have children but want them as much as you usually go to specialists and have an operation. I know that much," I said, "I'm not seven or eight any longer!"

"Oh yes you are, Jan," she said gently, "in most ways you are and certainly in this field. Not that I'd want you different, except that it's difficult to make a child grasp the essentials of this issue! I underwent a clumsy abortion Jan! Not only the neck of the womb was torn but the womb itself. It's not uncommon in those kind of circumstances. Maybe I left it too late, I don't know. Anyway, it happened, about six weeks before you arrived in France."

I tried to remember how she had looked when she surprised me asleep in Rance's villa but I could only recollect that she was no longer pregnant and had seemed so much more alert and vital than when she had sat beside me in the jeep after Alison's funeral. There had been fear in her eyes certainly, but that, having regard to the tension and Rance coming, was not surprising.

"When did you first know about this?" I demanded. "Did you know when we were married?"

"No, not until after the miscarriage in January. If I had known before I hope to God I should have had the guts to tell you but I doubt it, knowing me."

"Stop being tragic and stick to the facts," I said. It was clear that she was very much upset but I could see no profit in guilt. We had shared enough guilt to last us both a lifetime.

"The facts are very simple Jan," she said. "Four specialists have had a good look at me and only one, Foster-Hayne, recommends a Trachelorrhaphy."

"What's that?"

568

"It's a repair to the womb. I could give you more details but they wouldn't mean very much to you."

"We can go into all that later," I said. "Is it a reasonably simple operation or is it dangerous and complicated?"

"It's very straightforward."

"Well why not have it, not now but after the war when I can be here all the time?"

She gave me a look that was tender and pitying, the look a harrassed mother gives a little boy who had suggested that the family money troubles can be solved by emptying his moneybox.

"That might be the answer if the problem was confined to the womb, Jan," she said. "You asked for the facts and you're entitled to them, so here they are. Any kind of operation would be a risk as far as I'm concerned. Foster-Hayne told me my heart wouldn't stand up to a major op."

This was a shock that I couldn't ride out, not then, not just like that, as if she had told me that the water-pipes had frozen, or that somebody down the road had had an accident and broken a leg. I stared at her but in her eyes I read only concern for me. There was no fear, just a deep and communicated sadness.

"Are you absolutely sure about this?" I managed to croak at last. "I always thought you were as strong as a horse! You've always behaved as if you were! You've never had an illness that I know about!"

"It surprised me, that part of it," she said, "but don't waste time quarrelling with Foster-Hayne's opinion. He knows his business, Jan. He's been consulted by members of the Royal Family in his day."

"But why? *How?*"

"Drip said I had rheumatic fever when I was three. I didn't even know about it until I asked her and that's probably the basis. The kind of life I was leading until I caught up with you again did the rest, I imagine. It's the other half of the bill, Jan."

It was obvious that she had contemplated telling me all this for a long time. She had had leisure to select words and phrases but the care she had used in choosing them, in trying to reduce the facts to a trickle was wasted effort on her part. I had first to fight the rush of panic, the feeling of slipping through a hole in the bottom of life and clawing at anything to check my descent. I tried very hard to do this and after a few moments of floundering I believe I succeeded for it seemed to me that everything depended upon my doing so, on my relating the various factors and marshalling them into some kind of order. Diana's womb had been violated by the use of clumsy instruments. Diana was unlikely to conceive another child. Diana could have a formidable sounding operation to put matters right, but Diana also had a weak heart and might die at any time and from any source of aggravation! Those were the links in the chain leading us into this impasse and how the hell could I ever find my way out again?

Diana's voice came to me as though from a distance.

"We mightn't have so long, Jan, and it seems stupid to waste even a part of that time. That's why you have to arrange for me to come with you or at least follow on the moment it can be arranged!"

This was worse than anything she had said before. This was a perfectly monstrous suggestion and I shied away from it like a horse throwing up its head at a flapping tarpaulin.

"*No!*" I shouted, "no, Di, not that! For God's sake let's nurse our capital, not squander it like a pair of lunatics!"

I expected her to react passionately to my denial, to storm and beg and plead and reason, but she did not, she sat musing, a grass stem between her lips, as though pondering something utterly unrelated to what we were discussing. At length she said, composedly:

"You don't think my plan is logical, Jan?"

"No, of course I don't!" I bellowed, wretchedness and confusion making me sound pitiless, "it's the silliest bloody suggestion you ever thought up and it isn't even possible! Do you imagine they would turn you loose over there again? You, whose face has been plastered over every newspaper in the country, a person known to half the Quislings in France with a detailed description in the files of every police officer in Occupied Europe? What

570

good would it do? If what you tell me is true how long would you last, even if you weren't recognised and slammed in gaol within hours of arriving? Can't you see there is only one thing we can do?"

"Well, Jan," she said, patiently, "and what's that?"

"Forget this fixation you've got about a family and nurse your health, at all events until after the war when we can set about finding the real answer together! We have to ride it out, quietly and sanely, to play it safe for your sake, my sake and Yvonne's sake! I should want to see all those specialists and talk to them one after the other, I'd want to explore the entire bloody background, every inch of it you understand, and then do the best thing that suggested it-self! I'm going to do that, d'you hear? I'm taking over here and you'll do what you're told, *everything* you're told and I'll double check that you do!"

The sadness left her eyes and she smiled.

"Very well Jan, you do that," she said meekly. "I don't remember promising to love, honour and obey but it was implied I imagine. It was just an idea, I get them from time to time but they don't always work. I've had some pretty feeble ones in my time as you can testify!" and she got up, shaking the grass from her skirt. "Now suppose we begin by going over to Heronslea and telling Drip as much as we think she ought to know?"

"We'll do that," I said, "and after that I'm going to write a long letter to that Foster-Hayne, whoever he is. We'll see him together and if I'm not a hundred per cent sat-isfied we'll go up Welbeck Street and Harley Street knock-ing on the doors like a couple of hawkers!"

I said this and meant it but I was not by any means as sure of myself as I sounded. For one thing I was discon-certed by her surrender. It was utterly unlike her to abdi-cate in this fashion but I had had more than enough for one day and was glad to tell myself that by talking to Drip we were beginning to nibble at the problem. Drip had known about the rheumatic fever and might come up with some more information. She would doubtless fuss and flutter but afterwards she would do anything she could to help and I trusted her as I had never trusted anyone Drip had been in on my problems from the very beginning.

As we recrossed Big Oak and entered the larch cover leading down to Heronslea, Diana took my hand.

"We'll make it sound as trivial as possible Jan, but afterwards, for the rest of the time we're together, will you promise something? Will you not refer to it again or not until the last possible moment? It's Saturday now and you'll be leaving first thing Monday. You can phone Foster-Hayne and try for an appointment early in the week. Wednesday is his private patients day and I could come up then. If there's time that is!"

"There'll be time," I said savagely, but there wasn't.

There never is for the really essential engagements.

Chapter Eleven

I SUPPOSE it would not be right to say that Diana and I never enjoyed luck. We had our breaks and throughout our long association we took full advantage of them, but sooner or later, usually sooner, the sheer, bloodyminded cussedness of life snapped at our heels, and then we were fugitives trapped in a sea of treacle. We always found a path that led out of the morass but soon we were back in again, calling directions to one another and blundering about until we managed to touch hands and make another attempt to find solid ground. It was this way throughout the next ten days.

We made the appointment with Foster-Hayne and because of the special circumstances he agreed to see us the following Tuesday. His receptionist made it sound as if she was personally reprieving a condemned prisoner and one felt she expected to hear a sob of gratitude over the phone.

To keep the appointment we arranged to travel up on the first train on Monday. On Sunday afternoon, however, a wire arrived instructing me to report back to unit "imme-

572

diately repeat immediately". Ordinarily I should have ignored this but the kind of job I was engaged upon always gave one an uncomfortable feeling that people's lives might depend upon sticking to the rules. In any case, it did not seem to matter all that much so I caught the night train and arranged to get in touch with Diana as soon as she arrived in London the following day. In the event this proved impossible. I was despatched on a special three-day demolition course within half-an-hour of arriving back in camp and was driven straight into a security belt where every serviceman and civilian was incommunicado. Outward mail was forbidden and there was a sentry on the only available telephone.

I cursed and raged but that was the limit of my protests. There was absolutely nothing else I could do about it and I pictured Diana hanging round the hotel waiting for my call, or trying to contact me at my base unit where everybody derived enormous pleasure from being unhelpful to civilians.

I took the course, a concentrated study of how to operate a new kind of explosive which was an improvement on the small plastic mine then coming into general use. It had been designed for saboteurs and from what I could see was likely to be very effective. In addition to being extremely destructive it was easily portable. A man could carry half-a-dozen in a knapsack.

On the Friday morning I raced back to town and called at the hotel en route. Diana had been there but had left, presumably to return home. She had probably got some inkling of what was happening and had given me up as a bad job. Foster-Hayne's receptionist told me our appointment had been cancelled early Tuesday morning. This time she addressed me as if I was a professional assassin.

Before reporting back to base I phoned Heronslea. Drip told me that Diana had left as arranged on Monday but was not yet back. I guessed then that she was on her way home and there was nothing to do but kick my heels until her train got into Whinford Junction and then allow another hour for her drive back to Heronslea. I made another tentative appointment with the specialist for the following Wednesday but I had no great hopes of being able to keep it. Then, murderously bad-tempered, I reported back to base where the Air Commodore informed me that I was to travel to France that night!

Diana's train should have got into Whinford Junction about seven and she could have been back at Heronslea by eight, providing she got a taxi or a lift. There was no branch line train to Whinmouth after seven-thirty.

My own deadline was eight-forty-five and at eight-thirty I phoned again. Diana had still not arrived. In desperation I went on to the airfield and climbed into the Lysander. By this time I was so depressed that I did not reflect upon my destination. The aircraft could have headed for the Arctic Circle, or crashed head-on into Windsor's Round Tower for all I cared and this mood did not lift until I saw the landing lights of the French reception committee. No man ever went into action with a bigger chip on his shoulder.

The first person I met as my feet touched the soil of France was Raoul de Royden who embraced me, French fashion, as the Lysander roared away and little figures darted past me in the darkness staggering under the can-nisters of arms and explosives that I had brought with me. In less than three minutes we were in an open truck and being driven through the woods and as we bumped and lurched along the track the urgency of my personal prob-lems slipped away like a bunch of lodgers unable to pay their account. It was as though I was suspended between two worlds, that of Diana and Sennacharib and this strange, active darkness that was alive and menacing and yet, in some ways, as reassuring as a stronghold. I turned my back on my worries with the heavy resignation of a man taking his last walk to the scaffold. I made up my mind that I would never see Diana again in the flesh and that I would die here within a few days but when we did meet again it would be in the spirit, over the larch tops of Heronslea coverts or on the swell of Nun's Bay and that here we would at last merge into the scents and soil and russet-clothed slopes of the few squares miles that had made us so dependent on one another. There would be no more stresses, no partings, but fulfilment in timelessness.

Perhaps the tablets I had taken en route had something to do with this fancy which might have continued indefinitely had I not, on leaving the lorry at what seemed to be a good-sized farmhouse, been attacked by a sickness that was so violent that Raoul was obliged to support me by the shoulders. After the retching my head cleared and the sense of being dead and disembodied gradually left me. Raoul helped me into the building and sat me down near an open window, waiting without comment while a woman brought me some coffee in a two-pint mug. I drank the coffee and it did me a great deal of good. When I had emptied the mug Raoul said:

"I am glad you came tonight, my friend. If it had been tomorrow you would have been thrown to the lions!"

He swept his hand in a wide circle and I noticed for the first time that we were surrounded at a respectful distance by a circle of about half-a-dozen men, every one of them clutching some kind of firearm and all looking down at me with expressions that ranged from mild astonishment to disgust. I had been so distressed by the nausea that I had failed to take note of them. They were a desperate-looking bunch. I noticed one fellow particularly, a broad-shouldered, bearded ruffian, with a sub-machine gun braced across his bandoliered chest. He looked exactly like an illustration of a Mexican bandit in a Boys' Magazine, complete with slouch hat and top boots. He was the one who looked scornful but I discovered later that this implied no special criticism of me, it was his habitual expression.

Raoul looked sharply from the men to me and decided to ignore my lapse.

"As it is, I can give you one hour. Then I must be gone and these others must disperse. It is stupid to congregate near a dropping zone. Ordinarily we would have parted company at once."

He said something in very rapid French to the circle of men and the only word I caught was "cannister." They reacted at once. The bandit sat down by the stove and lit a pipe and all the others vanished like a chorus of pantomime robbers. The woman who had given me the coffee went out after them and shut the door.

I glanced at Raoul and noted the startling change that had taken place in him during the ten months that had passed since he engineered our flight from Paris.

In the glow of the single oil lamp his hair looked almost white. He was much thinner than I remembered and his spareness accentuated his height and emphasised a slight stoop. The skin of his face was taut, so stretched that it gleamed like ivory when he crossed the lamplight and one could see the movement of the bones underneath. His expression, when I looked at him closely, reminded me of the blankness one sometimes sees on the face of a ventriloquist manipulating his dummy and feeding himself with gags. One way and another he looked as if he had been through a very bad time indeed.

"You can ignore Simon," he said, "he is inclined to deafness and he's a Walloon. He won't understand very much of your French."

He sat down on the bench beside me and took out a map and a brandy flask, spreading the map on the table and taking a long swig at the flask.

"You had a briefing about the repair train?" he asked, and when I nodded, "It is planned ten days ahead, a week on Monday, unless we get a cancellation. We usually do. London is very free with its cancellations. They sometimes cost lives over here. You will be in command and Simon is your deputy!" He went on to explain details of the locale and some of the more obvious hazards, the amount of explosive that would be needed, the various points along the line that should be reconnoitred before the ambush was arranged. He spoke sourly but rapidly, as if he was in a great hurry to be gone and when he came to discuss the men recruited for the job a note of bitterness entered his voice.

"It is essential to have someone fresh to direct the strike," he said, "most of these fools would let the train pass while they settled their own differences! Simon is the best of them but he's a Communist and one never knows what secret orders he has been given. You will have twenty to thirty men with you and they belong to at least four separate groups. Several will be Communists and perhaps

576

half-a-dozen De Gaullists The rest are locals, good enough at a pinch and necessary because they know the terrain, but if you run into trouble don't rely on them, they are amateurs!"

I had a look at the map and asked him questions that seemed to me relevant and necessary. He brushed most of them aside and told me that Simon would find a man to take me along the line as far as the depot and that it was useless to discuss further details until I had made the tour. It was also hopeless, he said, to attack the depot itself. The Germans had a guard company stationed there and the only possible chance of wrecking the train would be when it was actually en route to a break in the line.

"The sole object of this strike is to prevent the train getting to the tunnel after it has been blocked! Keep that in mind and don't let any of these clowns persuade you to do anything else. They will try but you must ignore them. Only the tunnel matters. If the train goes out to repair routine breaks in the line after an air attack, let it pass and return. No matter how great the devastation in this sector it always goes back to the depot at sunset, they never risk leaving it in the open."

"Why the hell doesn't the R A.F. hit the depot and be done with it?" I asked.

"You wouldn't ask that my friend, if you had seen where they keep it overnight," he said, and rose, extending his hand.

I was dismayed by his hostility and perhaps more so by his apparent lack of interest in anything but the job on hand. I might have been a stranger to him and Diana might not have existed. He had not referred by so much as a single word to the death of Rance or Yves or to our escape a year ago, or to anything at all except the waylaying of the railway breakdown train planned for the following week. He had not even commented on the war situation generally or the possibility of expelling the invader from France. What concerned me most, however, was his lack of interest in plans for a withdrawal.

"Assuming everything goes satisfactorily how and where do I lie up?" I demanded.

"The De Gaullists in Charmont St. Père have that in hand," he said, "or should have. It is their responsibility. Simon will be in touch with them and you will probably get your instructions next week. In the meantime this is your base."

I had to leave it at that. He was not the kind of man with whom one could argue about personal insurance. I said, half apologetically:

"Diana and I are married now. She has heart trouble and isn't too well, Raoul! Did you know?"

"I knew you were married," he said, and then, with what seemed to me an almost shameful effort to appear more friendly: "I hope you get through it in one piece, Jan! I don't expect to, I've already had more luck than any two men deserve!"

"It can't be so long now," I said. "When the invasion comes nothing can stop it and Jerry is already chin deep in trouble in the East. Isn't it a question of who gets to Berlin first?"

"Jerry!" he said, and again, bitterly, "*Jerry!* You British are incurable! Even now 'Jerry' is still the losing cricket side!" His eyes became vacant for a moment. "You see my friend, I have forgotten how to pretend to be British. I think I have forgotten everything except how to hate!"

Before I could reply he crossed over to the silent, pipe-smoking Simon and touched him on the shoulder.

"Look after my friend," he said, "he is a relative—of a sort!" and then, hitching his rifle, he was gone, leaving me to make what I could of his inadequate briefing and cryptic conversation. He left behind him an atmosphere of defeat and staleness, as though each of us were engaged in an enterprise that was not only lethal but futile.

Simon knocked out his pipe and pointed to the door with the stem.

"I learned Englisch on banana boats," he grunted, apropos of nothing. "I like to spik it, if you can!"

"By all means," I said, feeling deflated and hating the sharp taste of bile in my mouth. "Do I wait here until you bring someone to take us on reconnaissance up the line?"

"Roger!" he said, stroking the short barrel of his sub-

578

machine gun. "I bring him by daylight. It is safer to look in daylight when I bring the railwayman's clothes. You are not hungry after you empty the stomach?"

"No," I said, "I'm not hungry but I could use some sleep. Show me where I can sleep until you come back with Roger!"

He looked mortally offended. "Rachele will show you!" he sneered and stalked out, banging the door. Presently the woman returned and conducted me to a loft over an open shed where they kept their carts and farming machinery. I climbed the ladder and lay down in the hay, not expecting to sleep soundly or for long but I did and Simon had some difficulty in waking me when he came back shortly before noon the next day. He stood over me with the same contemptuous expression as I scrambled to my feet like a schoolboy late for call-over.

"We go take a look," he said, casually, "I have food for both of us!" He slapped a knapsack he wore and threw at my feet a shapeless bundle of clothes he was carrying.

"Leave the explosives here," he added and abruptly descended the ladder while I changed into the loose cotton blouse, corduroys and a greasy railwayman's cap he had brought along.

I knew that he was trying to dominate me and suddenly I felt almost hysterically angry, angry with myself for sticking my head into this noose, angry with Raoul and this boorish Walloon for the stink of hopelessness they had introduced into the enterprise, angry with the Air Commodore for closing the loophole through which I might have escaped, but angriest of all, I think, with Diana for weaving miles of Lilliputian bonds round my life and leaving me as helpless as Gulliver. Sullenly I thrust my personal equipment under the hay and dragged on the coarse, skin-chafing trousers and clumsy boots. I thought: "If I get out of this, *if* I get out of it, I'll begin watching out for Number One! I'll watch out for myself like nobody's business! I'll stop being a combination of Don Quixote and bloody Sir Galahad; I'll stop hanging bicycle tyres round my neck and getting sent off on everyone's business but my own! If I get free of this I'll stop rowing and drift for the rest of my life! I'll be myself at last and everyone else can go to hell!"

I went down the ladder in a dangerous mood to find Simon and an undersized little Breton sitting on the pump trough talking to the woman.

"Roger says we should go across country to the depot and not walk down the line until it is dark," Simon said.

"Roger will do as he's bloody well told and so will you!" I growled. "Take me to the nearest point of the line at once! We'll start from the tunnel end and work south to the depot and we'll do it in daylight! *Now!*"

The effect of this outburst surprised me. A warm and childlike smile stole across Simon's seamed face, displaying a row of broken, discoloured teeth. He took his right hand from his pocket and began to stroke his gun in long, sweeping motions, as though it had been a cat.

"Goot!" he said, and to Roger, who looked ill at ease, "what did I tell you? Capitaine de Royden is nobody's fool. He picked this man. The man gives the orders! Me? I am tired of playing soldiers in the dark!"

"That being so you won't need the artillery!" I said, snatching his beloved Tommy gun and tossing it to the woman. "Is Roger armed?" Simon glared at the guide. "Give the Britisch your pistol!" he roared and the man dragged a Luger from his blouse and handed it to the woman who remained impassive.

"Put the guns with my equipment in the loft," I told her briefly. "Now we march!"

"That's bloody goot!" said Simon happily. "Now we march!" and he transmitted the order by planting a well-directed kick in the Breton's behind.

The outburst, or possibly the immediate results of it, did a good deal to reconcile me to my situation during the next day or so. I still thought of my life as more or less over, and I had the strongest conviction that never again would I hold Diana in my arms, but the job itself lost its aura of hopelessness and futility and became a routine task to be carried out in a certain way and to a time-table.

Simon, the Mexican-looking bandit, seemed to take a liking to me and through him my control of the score or so men selected for the strike became a reality instead of something dreamed up by the liaison officers of the British Special Operations Executive and the London De Gaullists. I made a number of reconnaissance trips along the line and I visited the tunnel itself, also the small town of Ghislaine St. Père beyond and later, by night, the repair depot situated some twenty kilometers to the south. The Loire at this point ran in a great, wide bend and the main line railway bridge at Ghislaine St. Père was undamaged by bombs and permanently guarded against the attempts of local saboteurs. I could understand now why headquarters had chosen the tunnel as the point of attack. Its temporary destruction would neutralise two main lines instead of one, and was sure to cause enormous dislocation further south in the area where the enemy's reserves were stationed. In our area there were few German units and what there were were of poor quality. Apart from sporadic Resistance activity the Germans had had no trouble in this part of France. There was a company of Reservists in the citadel of Ghislaine St. Père and other units within call, but an agent was able to move about far more freely than in the industrial areas further north. I had a railway pass permitting me to be abroad after curfew and as some of the men working with us were railways employees (the best recruiting ground for the Resistance Movement throughout the war) I was able to take my time about choosing an ambush point and hatching out a feasible plan.

Raoul had disappeared into the blue and my only contact with the central organisation and London was via a courier working for the De Gaullists in the Tours area. He brought me a revised date fixing the attack for the night of Sunday, June 4-5th, and I laid my plans accordingly, setting up an ambush at a point about twelve kilometres south-east of the town and five kilometres from the train's point of departure. I soon realised why a more direct attack upon the depot itself had been ruled out. Not only was it heavily guarded but the train was housed in chalk cliff where a natural cave had been enlarged to accommodate it. It was proof against air attack and could come and

581

go to any section of the line where it was likely to be needed.

The point of ambush I selected was a deep cutting where the line ran between two sections of woodland giving excellent cover at this time of the year. On the Friday before the attack I had a conference with section-leaders and issued their instructions. They received them equably enough but it was obvious that there was considerable mutual antipathy between the various groups, particularly between the De Gaullists and the Communists. Had it not been for Simon's outspokenness I should have wasted a great deal of time pacifying them. One of the main causes of contention was the disparity in arms between the sections. The Communists possessed greater and more modern firepower, yet they refused to part with a single rifle or grenade. They had always been more enterprising in raids on small garrison posts and had armed themselves at a considerable cost. They now had a morbid fear that if they surrendered their arms the weapons would be used against them after the war. I gathered this and other useful information from Simon who, once you got accustomed to his banana-boat English, proved an observant and intelligent fellow. He was a great boaster and, in most ways, immature in his judgments, but I had a feeling that he would prove a good man in a crisis. The more I saw of him the more he seemed to belong to the world of boys' fiction. He was bandit-buccaneer and medieval freebooter in one but there was no doubt about his fanatical hatred of Fascism, or the pleasure he derived from killing Germans.

On Friday morning I had done all I could to prepare for the strike and turned my attention once more to my own plans for ensuring a personal withdrawal from the scene the moment the blow had been struck. I had no illusions about the thoroughness of a German comb-out after the raid and I wanted to put as great a distance as possible between Ghislaine St. Père and myself within an hour of the attack. Simon and the section leaders were not specially interested in my survival. I was there to co-ordinate the attack and after that I could go to the Devil as far as they were concerned. The heavy pessimism that had obsessed

582

me since my last parting with Diana reduced the urgency of an escape plan but presently the instinct of self-preservation asserted itself and I took myself over to the village where the courier lived in the hope that he had received some instructions from London by radio. He had, it appeared, and he was as keen to pass it on and be rid of it as a thief holding hot money. The previous day, he said, he had been given a message instructing me to report to a photographer's shop in Ghislaine St. Père but for what purpose he did not know. Radio location units had been very active in Tours and the operator had had to close down and decamp before the message could be completed.

I made the best of this information and returned to the farmhouse, leaving a message for Simon saying that I was going into the town to keep the appointment. In the event I did not arrive there until after midday because I had to make a detour in order to check arms and equipment at the dump in the woods. When this was done I borrowed a bicycle and cycled towards the river. I took my time. It never paid to hurry to a rendezvous in Occupied France and I wanted an opportunity to check on the contact before I presented myself.

It was a warm, sunny morning and the old town looked pleasant and welcoming, its mediaeval buildings flanking the great river, its broad streets astir with shabby provincials busy with their meagre shopping. Nobody paid any attention to me and I saw no Germans, at any rate, none in uniform.

I turned right along the waterfront and soon located the photographer's at the junction of a street leading up to the towering fourteenth-century castle dominating the town. It was a trim little shop, well cared-for and recently repainted. There was a single window displaying wedding pictures and advertisements and behind the shop a studio with windows that looked out on a yard. No one had seen me enter the alley leading to the yard so I stayed there, looking across at the studio window about twenty yards away.

Two people were sitting at a table, eating. One, a woman, had her back to me and the other, a small-featured, walrus-moustached man, presented his profile. He was talking a great deal and gesticulating with his fork. The woman seemed to be listening and throwing in a word every now and again. She had a great mop of peroxided hair under a wide, straw hat and wore a voluminous cloak, the kind of garment French women wear at fashionable race-meetings.

When she leaned sideways to reach for the coffee pot I saw that she was wearing dark sun-glasses.

I studied the pair for a few moments and satisfied myself that they looked harmless, although it struck me as rather odd that the blonde wore her cloak and sun-glasses indoors.

About two yards from where I stood, beyond the open yard-door, was a short flight of steps that led to the flat above. I thought I would make doubly sure by getting inside without their knowledge, so awaiting my chance I slipped across the alley and up the steps to the back door without anyone knowing that a visitor had arrived.

The stairhead door was open and I entered a large and sunny room, full of the hideous furniture with which the average French tradesman clutters his home. Then, thinking myself the cleverest man in the business, I slipped behind a curtain and composed myself to wait until someone arrived.

About twenty minutes passed before someone mounted the steps and entered the room. I could tell it was the woman by the click of heels and when she passed close to the curtain I could hear her breathing. She drifted about for a moment and then took a seat facing the window and lit a cigarette but she seemed unable to relax for almost at once she got up, crossed to the door, locked it and sat down again. A whiff of her perfume reached me where I stood behind the curtains and I heard her chair creak and rustle as she fidgetted.

Suddenly I began to feel foolish. It occurred to me that I had taken theatrical precautions but I reminded myself of the fate of other agents who had walked blithely into traps set by the Gestapo or French Quislings. Ordinarily we worked only with people we actually knew and entered the houses of those of whom we had first-hand knowledge

584

but it was the circumstances rather than the background of this appointment that worried me and perhaps also the fact that orders for the rendezvous had come directly from London and not through the local group. I reflected that Simon, for instance, had no clear idea of where I was and that if I failed to turn up at our next meeting our entire operation would be jeopardised.

I glanced at my watch and saw that it was now close on thirteen hundred hours and my failure to appear, no doubt, accounted for the woman's restlessness. Her obvious uneasiness, however, convinced me that she must be genuine so at length, with a preliminary cough, I stepped smartly from behind the curtains and covered my embarrassment with a bow.

"Madam!" I said and spoke my code name.

The effect was farcical. The blonde leaped to her feet with a cry of alarm and gave back so quickly that her high-heeled shoe caught in the edge of the rug and she fell on her side and rolled over on her face. Her straw hat and her sun-glasses fell off and her skirt shot up, revealing wide-legged panties and a generous expanse of bottom. She made a partial recovery and a swift movement with both hands rescued decency. Then, as she jerked herself upright, it was my turn to gasp. The blonde on the floor was Diana!

I don't think I have ever been so astonished in my life. Every other surprise I had had up to that time was a lift of the eyebrow compared to the amazement I felt staring down at Diana, her expression a comic mixture of dismay and alarm. Her posture was equally undignified. She had one leg exposed as far as her suspender-clip and her ridiculous blonde hair flopped over her shoulders like a vast, yellow mat.

I tried about half-a-dozen times to say something but all that emerged was a series of squeaks.

We must have stayed like that all of thirty seconds, Diana absorbing the shock of the fall and fright, myself gaping down at her, gibbering and fluttering my hands like a man confronting a spectre. Then, in a single swift movement, she scrambled up, jumped forward and grabbed my hands. Colour flooded her cheeks and she hopped up and down, one heel hanging by a shred of leather, her chewed-looking tresses bobbing up and down, the light of laughter and mischief rapidly ousting shock and surprise from her eyes.

"Oh Jan, Jan!" she bubbled, "I might have known you would have done something like that, you solemn, deliberate, cautious, play-it-safe old clot! It's *me*, Jan! Really me! Take hold of me—there!" and she flung her arms round my neck and kissed me half-a-dozen times without pause.

Very slowly I began to relate this laughing, bobbing ghost to someone real and tangible and gently disengaged myself from her enthusiastic embrace. All manner of sensations flooded in, driving out the dazed bewilderment that had paralysed me the moment her floppy hat and sunglasses had fallen off but in the van of my emotions came a horrid, gnawing fear, an absolute certainty of impending disaster that clawed at my belly and milked the strength from my limbs. My knees buckled and I flopped down on the window ledge behind me.

"How—*how* did you get here? *Why* are you here? *Why? How?* In God's name, Di, what's the meaning of this bloody tomfoolery?"

She pouted but the laughter remained in her eyes. Lifting her foot she ripped away the trailing heel and sat facing me, crossing her legs and folding her hands with deliberate primness, like a Victorian governess about to commence the day's lessons.

"Did you really think I'd let go that easily, Jan? Do you imagine I was impressed by all the mumbo-jumbo idiots' talk over in England nowadays? God bless my soul, I sized up the average British male years ago! All this secrecy and counter-signs! All those awful 'Hitler-is-listening' posters in trains and cafés! *How* did I manage it? It was easy! When you turned me down I waited until you were out of the way and offered my services to the De Gaulle outfit! I had luck, mind you, your sudden disappearance into a sealed-off Coastal area gave me the chance I was waiting for! The French were a pushover. A Frenchman realises that a woman's place in the world isn't confined to the bedroom and the kitchen! There's no 'not-quite-the-thing-y'know-for-the-ladies-to-poach-a-feller's- preserves,' about *them*! They accepted me at once and let me volunteer for this particular strike, they didn't even tell the S.O.E. until after I'd gone!"

"Did you come alone? Were they that stupid?"

"No," she said, gaily, "I came over with Claude Perry, one of their new agents. He's downstairs right now but don't tell him more than you can help because he isn't much good. He only volunteered because he simply couldn't stay away from his Lucille any longer. Lucille is his wife and they were parted after the Germans moved in. She's been running the shop since he got involved in the Resistance. She's rather sweet, very docile and pretty, absolutely your type, Jan!"

It was the same Diana down to the last smothered chuckle behind a barrage of impudence, gaiety and cheerful contempt for all male prejudices.

"It's the most outrageous piece of idiocy I've ever heard of!" I protested, but as I said it I was conscious of a glow of pride in her courage and enterprise, and a delight not far removed from smugness to have proof that her love for me was strong enough to take such a risk.

"Do you know what I'd like to do right now?" I added.

"Yes I do! Drag me off to the nearest despatching unit and throw me into a Lysander marked 'Returned Unopened'?"

"No," I said, "you're only half-right! I ought to turn you upside down and tan your behind as it should have been tanned years ago, regularly, at least once a week and with the broadest slipper available! I remember my Uncle Reuben gave your mother that advice years ago!"

She laughed, tossing her ruined hair over her shoulders.

"That's your privilege, Jan, now that we're respectably married but postpone it until after the real strike! You'll need to conserve the strength of your sword-arm and I don't suppose I could run as fast after you'd done with me!"

She got up slowly and looked ruefully at her shoe.

"Just look what you've done to my heel, popping out on me like that! God, I thought my number was up! How long were you playing hide-and-seek before I came in?"

"I got a glimpse of you from the alley beyond the yard," I told her. "You were sitting at a table with Porthos, or Cyrano de Bergerac, or whatever lunatic you talked into bringing you here!"

Her eyes opened wide. "You saw me and didn't recognise me?"

"I only had a back view squint at a range of twenty yards. Have I got Sam Weller's 'hextra-special-gas-lamps'?"

"But great heavens, you ought to have known by instinct! This is dreadfully humiliating and when we get home I'll pop a strange girl in bed with you one night and see if you can tell the difference in the dark!"

"*If* we get home!" I said, heavily for fear was returning to my heart.

"Oh pooh to that!" she said, becoming a boisterous schoolgirl again, "We'll make it all right! We've only used up about seven of our lives and once the invasion begins it should be a piece of cake! Jerry will be running around like a hen wired up with a fox! As a matter of fact, Perry and I have already worked out a plan. Some of his men are taking part in your raid, so when it's over come straight here and leave the getaway to me!" She suddenly became serious, or serious for her: "That bunch you're working with is a suicide squad, Jan! If you join up with them you'll be in the bag in twenty-four hours!"

"Now let's get this straight, Di," I said, fending her off as she came closer and tried to rub herself against me like a cat, "and let's get the business sorted out before you start your phoney Delilah tactics! You're not coming on this strike and to show you that I mean what I say I swear to you that I'll resign from it myself unless you stay under cover until I get back!"

"I'll settle for that," she said promptly, "I'm only interested in getting you clear!"

"That promise isn't good enough," I told her. "You said the same thing and in precisely the same tone of voice

588

when I thought I'd talked you out of coming here in the first place!"

"Jan," she said, sitting down beside me, shooting out her legs, turning in her toes and letting her hands rest limply on her lap in an attitude I remembered, "now that I'm with you again I don't want to take any active part in the business. I only want to be sure that you get off safely and that's the absolute truth! I tried to get that across to you at home but you shouted me down, so I decided to make a demonstration of loyalty-cum-independence and that's the reason I'm here! Life just wouldn't have any meaning without you and if anything did happen I'd want most desperately for it to happen to both of us, within call of one another or better still touching hands. I know you won't have any patience with this but it has to do with my not being able to give you a son! If I was carrying one for you now, or had any hope that I would be soon, then I should have accepted your decision and stayed on in Sennacharib, waiting and praying for you; as things are I can't afford to take the least chance of having something final happen to you all that distance away! Do you believe this, Jan? I wish you'd try anyway, I wish that more than anything, except perhaps that we win through in the end and have each other for the rest of our lives!"

How could I resist that kind of declaration? It was impossible not to believe her, not to worship her for her gallantry and deep, abiding loyalty to the past and future. I took her in my arms as gently as if we had been sitting before our log fire in our home above Teasel Valley. Perry and his wife, Lucille, left us alone until late afternoon and in the evening we went over our escape plans. At dusk I made my way back to the base where I told Simon of Perry's offer to bring eight well-armed men into the field. Simon's hatred of the Boche was strong enough to overcome his distrust for the De Gaullists and he sent a message through the grapevine accepting the offer and naming the rendezvous.

"Eight you say? Okay! Maybe we rub out eight more Boches!" he grunted. "We do not need their popguns but who am I to refuse more dung for French fields?"

I was only half listening to him, I was wondering how long it would take Diana's tarty-looking hair to grow out and whether it would ever regain its lustre.

Perry, the De Gaullist with whom Diana had returned to France, paid us a courtesy call the following morning and I was thankful that Diana had not taken it upon herself to accompany him. He and Simon took an instant dislike to one another. Perry was a gracious, spirited little man but he talked too much for Simon's taste and I think the rival groups would have quarrelled on the spot had not Perry's party brought along a plentiful supply of ammunition and distributed it without political discrimination.

We all three got down to business and picked a team of twenty men, twelve from Simon's party, including myself, and the remainder from Perry's group. It was agreed that the actual ambush should be left to Perry and that Simon's men should act as covering party on both sides of the track for the repair train would have an escort of some thirty riflemen and at least one machine-gun team. We set up pickets to advise us on the results of the R.A.F attack and others to warn us of the departure of the train from the depot. Perry passed me a personal message from Diana who was based on his shop in the town. He told me that Diana had made arrangements for me to link up with the De Gaullists after the strike and I was to make my way there the moment the attack was over. She promised to have reliable transport waiting to take us both due west to the coast and was arranging hideouts en route as far as Quiberon, where Perry's local group would do their utmost to get us taken off by submarine.

I checked once more with the telegraphist but no further orders had arrived from London. This did not surprise me, the lines were grossly overloaded and there was a general air of nervous expectancy among all the Resistance groups. Oddly enough this was not reflected among the Germans. During my previous stay in France, when the prospects of invasion were remote, the enemy had shown far greater tension. The few Germans that I saw in and about this area seemed to be taking things very calmly

590

but there was probably a good reason for this. Information coming in from the north and east pointed to the fact that they were preparing to make every effort to repulse any attempts on the part of the Allies to get ashore in France. I did not know then that the German High Command was convinced that the main attack would fall much further north, and had grouped its defences accordingly. Down here, in the Loire area, they had only second-rate troops and very little armour.

We took up our ambush position at twenty hundred hours. The day had been overcast, with rain threatening all afternoon, so that twilight did not linger and we were able to make our way to the point of attack in twos and threes, some by bicycle and others on foot, depending upon our several plans for withdrawal.

Simon was in excellent spirits. He had his men well in hand and although he carried a flask of spirits himself he sternly forbade drinking among the others. Perry, whom we met in the wood above the track, was rather jittery but the men who accompanied him seemed tough, truculent types, four of them dependable village tradesmen and a fifth a huge blacksmith who carried a long-handled sledge hammer, presumably to use upon those parts of the repair train missed by our bombs and explosives. We had already set up a field telephone connecting our posts and now there was nothing to do but wait for word to come from the picket keeping watch over the depot. We estimated that the repair train would start out an hour or so after the air strike and would therefore pass our ambush point shortly before daybreak.

Shortly after midnight we heard the wail of the town air-raid syren, soon relayed by the syrens in outlying districts. At a quarter to one we heard the distant drone of aero-engines and the bark of flak batteries. A goods train clattered through the cutting but we let it pass and when it had gone Perry's team went to work on the line with his own and my dwarf mines, while Simon posted his men along the lip of the embankment.

Presently the sky became quiet again and although the alert was still on in the town I decided that the flak battery

591

we had heard must have been firing at bombers passing on their way to a target further east. Then, at about ten minutes to two, the flak started up close at hand and this time the presence of bombers in the immediate area was unmistakable. The growl rose to a steady roar as the Lancasters and Halifaxes made their preliminary bombing runs and suddenly there was an almighty crump as a stick exploded some three or four miles north-west of our wood.

Tension broke along the line and the men began to exchange comments, to be cursed by Simon into an uneasy silence. Then the raid began in earnest and a dozen or more bombs exploded, culminating in a final one that sent prolonged echoes rumbling in the valley like peals of thunder. I decided that this must be the bomb we had been awaiting for it was clearly a block-buster and I told Simon to check with his patrols. He came back after a brief interval in high glee.

"The bloody tunnel kaput!" he bellowed, forgetting his own wrathful injunctions for strict silence, "I get the word from Maurice! The bloody bombs they bash the bugger right in, you hear?" and he executed a little jig of triumph that drew a harsh chuckle from the phlegmatic blacksmith standing nearby. I told him that we needed confirmation that news had reached the repair depot and he shot off to the nearest phone picket again. Half-an-hour passed and the sky began to lighten in the east. I waited impatiently, for the men had been promised a night attack that would give them some advantage over machine-gunners.

It was after three o'clock when one of Simon's men reported that the locomotive at the depot had steamed up and a few minutes later Simon, breathing confidence and brandy in equal proportions, hurried over to my bush and said that the train had started and was carrying as escort a platoon of infantrymen and two light machine-guns, one on the engine-tender and one on the rear truck.

"Then we must concentrate on both ends the minute she goes up," I told him and we split our covering party, Simon taking charge of the rearward squad and leaving me and my half-dozen to cope with the machine-gun on the tender.

It was almost daylight when I heard the train clanking up the incline. At that moment the all-clear wailed in the valley below and the men relaxed, relieved that the ordeal of waiting was over. When the train rounded the furthest bend I was surprised not only by its size but by its appearance of strength. An armoured box-car was coupled to the tender and behind this was a string of flat-topped wagons bearing the lifting gear, grabs and tackle, five trucks in all, each with its quartet of steel-helmeted soldiers aboard. At the tail of the train was another armoured box-car, with a searchlight on top of it and a squad of soldiers ringing the light, their rifles at the ready.

The De Gaullist team allowed the engine and the first two wagons to pass their point of ambush. Then the blacksmith pressed the plunger and we tensed ourselves, expecting to see the crane-bearing wagon rise in the air, dragging forepart and hindpart of the train from the tracks. Nothing like this happened. The charge exploded with the reluctance of a damp rocket, fizzing and coughing with just sufficient power to lift the central wagon from the tracks but not enough to topple it on its side.

The train did not buckle and disintegrate as we had hoped, it merely shuddered along the whole of its length and ploughed on for a few yards, grinding over the sleepers and coming to an uncertain halt. The entire operation was such an anti-climax that it was almost laughable.

The interval between the time the blacksmith pressed his charge and the wheels of the locomotive stopped revolving was about seven seconds, fortunately too brief for the escorting troops to understand what had occurred. At the end of that period I detonated the smaller, subsidiary charge, located towards the rear of the train between the last wagon and the searchlight car and this was far more effective than its predecessor. With a blinding flash the fifth wagon heaved itself up and partially disintegrated, hurling the load twenty feet in the air and upending the searchlight car so that it stood balanced on its forward coupling looking like a squat, smoking tower. The coupling links of the fourth and fifth cars snapped under the strain

593

but the two cars behind the crane did not even leave the rails. The shock, however, was sufficiently violent to spew most of the soldiers into the cutting where some of them, shaken but otherwise unhurt, scrambled up and ran in all directions.

For a minute or so we had it all our way. The machine-gun in the hindmost box-car was out of action and the twenty or so men flung from the wagon were too dazed and shaken to offer much resistance. Firing broke out on both sides of the line and half-a-dozen Germans dropped as they scurried round the wreckage or ran directly against the muzzles of the saboteurs. One man, helmetless and half-crazy with terror, ran up the embankment straight at me. I shot him twice with my Colt, the second man I had killed. I hit him first in the cheek and then in the stomach. He ran on to within three yards of me and then went down on his knees staring at me stupidly and making vague protests with his hands.

Then, and with deadly precision, the machine-gun in the forward section of the train opened fire on my side of the line. A stream of bullets whipped into the foliage and three of my party were hit, one of them the blacksmith, who pitched forward and rolled head over heels down the embankment. I heard Simon's whoop from lower down the train and in one more minute the battle was fully joined, the forward machine-gun pumping bullets into our part of the woods and effectively pinning us down with our faces pressed into the earth.

As I crouched there a bullet whipped the length of my back and broke the skin of my behind but I did not know this until later for I felt no pain and only realised that I had been hit when I made a dash to get into better cover. Then my half-severed belt snapped, dropping away and depriving me of my spare ammunition pouches. As I ran I had to leap over three bodies and fire from the rallied troops on the far side of the line was now whacking into the branches about my head.

By this time Simon had launched his attack, jumping down on to the line and roaring like a bull as he hurled hand-grenades at the knots of men who had scrambled up

594

the far bank. He seemed to have forgotten all about his precious sub-machine gun but was obviously enjoying himself. It was not until he was across the line, and preparing to rush the bank, that he unslung his gun and raked the bushes in which the fugitives had taken refuge. We had posted a small party on this side but either they had fled or been accounted for by riflemen taking cover under the derailed wagon. The party of Germans on the bank faced front and fought like demons, holding on to the escarpment to the last man but Simon's dash won the day. There was a wild outcry of yells and then all the escort troops at his end of the train were shot down.

While this little battle was being fought I rallied four or five men behind the upended searchlight car and was on the point of advancing against the forward machine gun when suddenly I realised that it had ceased firing and that its team, together with half-a-dozen stragglers, were now beating a retreat into open country up the line.

There was no time to pursue them. Our job was to wreck the train and after posting flank guards on both sides of the track we placed charges under each of the wagons. In ten minutes or so it was done and all four of the trucks went up, Simon himself attending to the locomotive and tender.

It was now broad daylight and the battlefield was a shambles. The reek of cordite set everyone coughing and the little cutting was blocked with splintered wagons and twisted machinery. The crane, buckled in the centre, lay like a footbridge between the embankments and down at the front of the train wounded men were screaming behind a thick pall of smoke. We could do nothing for them and did not even turn aside to discover whether they were German or French. Simon made a hasty count of the German dead within the immediate area and told me that we had killed fourteen, not counting the wounded, two of whom were still lying beside the track. Just then the flank guards came in with three prisoners, the eldest of them not more than twenty. They stood in a row with their hands raised and Simon shot them down almost absentmindedly. Of our party, eight were dead and we had three wounded.

Among the dead was Perry, the De Gaullist agent, shot between the eyes during the rush down the bank and now lying beside the upended truck, his automatic still in his hand.

"Now we vamoose, bloody quick!" grunted Simon, snatching up German rifles and hitching them to his shoulder. "You, Roger!" he bawled to a guide, who was trying to staunch the flow of blood from the thigh of a man on the track, "Don't you play bloody nursemaid to Baptiste! Collect all the guns lying around! Take them back to the hut and bury the bloody things! This is bloody war, ain't it'"

Neither Roger nor the wounded man could have understood a word of his jargon but his intention was clear and the man abandoned his first-aid attempts and jumped to obey the order.

"The Boche take one hour maybe to get reinforcements from the town and kom back!" he went on in his atrocious argot, nodding in the direction taken by the fugitives. "You kom with me? I got a motor cycle in the woods and we go for hiding!"

I told him that this was impossible, that I had arranged to contact another agent in the town and follow a line of flight already planned. He was not disposed to argue the point.

"Okay, okay! You do as you bloody please, Mister! From now on all is himself!" Briefly he surveyed the scene around him, obviously deriving great satisfaction from the chaos. "It was the goot strike!" he said. "They noddings get through here for the month! Then we chase the bastards to Uncle Jo, eh?"

I said briefly I hoped so and looked around for the De Gaullist who was supposed to have accompanied Perry and myself back to town. I found him sitting with his back against a tree, his feet at a wide angle and a German submachine gun between his knees. His face was drained of colour and a dark stain was spreading through a wad of improvised bandages wedged under his armpit. He was a Breton of about my own age, a big, sun-burned man, whom I had only met the previous evening. When he saw me looking at him he made a pathetic attempt to salute.

"Take my bicycle, m'sieur!" he said, speaking between clenched teeth, "I stay here and get one or two more when they come back!" Then, apologetically: "Is it possible you have cognac in that flask, Capitaine?"

I gave him my flask and he thanked me, politely. There was nothing more I could do for him and I doubt whether he was alive to press the trigger when the Germans returned to the scene.

I scrambled round the wreckage and climbed the northern bank, making my way to the cart track where the De Gaullists' bicycles had been stacked. I took the first one to hand and pedalled away towards the town, thankful to have found a means of getting there ahead of the survivors of the escort, who had headed away in the opposite direction and would have to make a wide circuit back to the river bank. As I rode I reflected grimly upon our chances of getting clear of the area before a general alarm was raised and the district was cordoned off by other garrison troops alerted by telephone.

Chapter Twelve

I ENTERED the town from the south-west and from the top of the steep street that led down to the bridge I could see signs of activity in the area of the tunnel mouth, near the railway station, although there was no evidence of the air raid damage from this side. It was still early but there seemed to me to be an unusual number of people astir and those I passed looked preoccupied and distraught. I abandoned the bicycle at the top of the street in which Perry's shop was situated and went on down towards the riverfront, walking slowly, as if I had come out to inspect the air-raid damage.

Just before I reached the shop I squinted along the tree-lined boulevard towards the bridge and saw a black Mercedes, preceded by an armoured car, turn left on to the waterfront and head directly towards me. Neither vehicle was travelling fast but a helmeted German stood on the turret of the armoured car and appeared to be scrutinising each house as he passed.

I was tempted to duck into the alley that I had used when I reconnoitred the house but I changed my mind and took refuge in the cabin of a parked refuse-van, whose driver was nowhere in sight. As I slammed the door I saw a troop carrier, crammed with troops, descend the hill from the opposite direction. It looked so much like a converging movement that I took alarm and ducked to the floorboards.

One of the most reassuring things about fighting Germans is that they are quite unable to go about their business without creating an uproar that gives their opponents warning of their immediate intentions. As the armoured car and the troop carrier approached one another there was a great deal of bellowing and banging and it was obvious that some kind of house-search was in progress lower down the water-front. I peeped out and saw Germans thumping on doors and milling up and down the boulevard nearer the bridge. Their behaviour made me sick with anxiety for it was clear that they had information about the approximate location of agents but were not certain which house sheltered them.

At that moment I smelled burning and on taking a peep saw a thick column of smoke issue from the upper window of the photographer's immediately opposite. I was on the point of leaping out of the van and dashing into the shop when Diana appeared at the window, waving a rag and shouting down at some Germans hammering on a door fifty yards down the street. She seemed to me to be deliberately attracting their attention. I was so confused that I sat immobile as half-a-dozen men came pounding along to the scene of the fire. At the same time Diana disappeared and the whole area became enveloped in smoke and there was a lot of shouting and the crash of breaking glass. Then, with a soft explosion, the whole upper storey blazed up, flames shooting from the window and licking under the eaves of the roof.

I hesitated no longer but jumped out of the cab, colliding heavily with a woman who had run screaming from the alley alongside the shop. The impact was so violent that she staggered and almost fell. I made a grab to steady her and saw that it was Madame Perry, still in her nightdress. Her face was convulsed with terror and I don't think she recognised me but before I could speak Diana herself tumbled through the smoke-screen, a bundle in one hand and a Luger pistol in the other. She saw me and shouted something I failed to catch, at the same time grabbing Madame Perry by the neck and bundling her into the cabin of the refuse-van.

"Start her up, Jan!" she shouted, running round the bonnet, leaping in the offside door and slamming it shut.

I obeyed automatically, pressing the starter button and ramming the stiff gear into bottom. We shot off through the smoke cloud, just missing the offside wing of the troop carrier that was descending the hill. The vehicles actually touched and I swerved, mounting the curb and bumping back on to the pavement.

Behind us all hell was loose. Beyond the billowing clouds of smoke that now filled the street we could hear the roar of flames and the shouts and yells of the troops. Someone loosed off a burst of automatic fire in our direction but I ignored this and concentrated on the road ahead, urging the van up the hill and across the square under the castle. For the moment my only concern was to get clear of the town and into the wooded country beyond. I said no word to Diana or to Madame Perry, who was wedged tightly between us severely hampering my steering.

On the far side of the square was a narrow archway through which I had entered the town that morning. Three German soldiers, one of them an officer, were in the act of erecting a roadblock on our side of the arch and two twenty-gallon oil-drums were already in position supporting a heavy baulk of timber. As we roared up the two privates were about to close the left side of the gap and were carrying a third drum between them. I rammed the accelerator to the boards and steered straight for the gap, which was just wide enough to permit the passage of the van.

The officer saw us first and shouted, leaping back against the castle wall and fumbling with the flap of his holster but before he could draw his pistol I had crashed head-on into the other men, knocking them and their oil-drum over the half-built barrier. From her side Diana leaned out and fired point-blank at the officer, her bullets ricochetting against the masonry. One of them passed over my head, shattering the offside window of the cabin. Then we were through and heading for the open country at top speed. I had just enough wits about me to take the road that forked away from the direction of the railway and head towards a belt of woodland a mile or so out of the town.

"Take the track to the right past the clearing!" Diana yelled at me across Madame Perry. I saw it just in time and slewed the van hard right, skidding round in a half-circle and shooting into the trees. Two hundred yards further on I stopped, flung open the door and jumped out and as I did so Madame Perry rolled sideways, her head and one arm projecting from the cabin. She was stone dead, her neck broken by the burst fired at us in the town.

Diana climbed out and came round to my side of the van. She seemed miraculously calm and looked down at the corpse without emotion.

"It was better than starving to death in one of their stinking camps!" she said quietly. "Where's her husband?"

"Dead, up at the railway cutting," I told her, "I never even had a chance to tell her, damn it!"

"It's just as well," said Diana. "How did your show go, Jan?"

"Pretty well!" I said bitterly, "we might even get a medal for it!"

"You smashed that repair train!"

"We blocked the line with the debris. Everybody was satisfied!"

She put her hand on my arm and looked hard at me. "What's the matter Jan? What is it?"

"I'm sick to death with all this bloody killing and running!" I shouted hysterically, "sick to bloody death of it, you understand? Back there we had to kill prisoners and leave men to bleed to death on the blasted railway track! Now there's just you and me, and where the hell do we go from here?"

She didn't attempt to reason with me, seeing my hysteria as a reflex to the excitement of the last few hours, and perhaps the tensions of the days that had preceded it. Under a dead weight of fright and revulsion the eternal spark of my love and admiration for her still glowed but for the moment I felt spineless, flabby and utterly used up. It was she who would have to take the initiative now and I think she realised this.

"First we have to get rid of Madeleine," she said, "help me carry her."

We lifted the dead woman from the cabin and carried her across to an evergreen growth on the edge of the wood, setting her down in a hollow and covering the body with twigs and leaves.

"It was strange that you should dive into this refuse-van without even knowing," she said, as we turned away. "I had it parked for our getaway and meant to use it as far as Le Mans. We can't now of course, we'll have to ditch it and steal something else!"

"What the hell was happening back there!" I demanded, "the men who got away from us couldn't possibly have got into town and raised the alarm yet!"

"Your ambush is a sideshow now," she said, "the R.A.F. knocked hell out of that tunnel last night. Direct hits, half-a-dozen of them! That line will be out of commission for weeks."

This was good news but I could not see that it helped us very much, except maybe to slow down pursuit. I asked Diana how the Germans had located the area where Perry lived and why a house-to-house search was being conducted along the river front when I arrived. She said she supposed that Perry had been recognised or that his wife had talked indiscreetly. She had been uneasy about them for days and would have arranged an alternative rendezvous had she been able to contact me in time. "I hate saying 'I told you so, Jan'," she added, "but you see now that it would have been far better if you hadn't been so bearish, and let me take part in the ambush. At least we should have had a clear start!"

"Well, you know this country better than I do, so you can take on from here," I said, grumpily. "Do we go west to the coast, south to where we were picked up last time, or dodge around trying to locate Simon's outfit and throw ourselves on his mercy?"

She stood thinking for a moment. It was quiet in the wood and the sun was strong over the clearing. Thrushes were singing in the bushes where we had laid Madame Perry and it was only with an effort that I reminded myself we were hemmed in by men who would give a month's pay to kick us to death, or string us up to the nearest tree.

"We leave the van here and walk due east until we find help or can cross the river and strike the Paris railway line," she said. "Our papers will pass a train check and it's always safer by rail. If we can get to Paris we can contact Raoul and he'll find us somewhere to hide until the Germans pull out. I'm like you, Jan, I'm about through with the war! From now on let the army and the air force take over, we've done our share, God knows! By the way, I suppose you heard that the invasion has started!"

I gaped at her, astonishment driving out fear.

"*Our* invasion? 'D' Day?"

She smiled, retrieved her bundle from the cabin and struck off through the close-set pine trees with me trotting alongside like a child.

"When did you hear about it?"

"Oh, at about two A.M.," she said, "a courier came round and told us that it was to be today. I wonder how they're getting on?"

"But *where*? Where is it? For God's sake, Di, don't sound so casual about it, it's the biggest thing that ever happened and if it's true it'll make all the difference to our chances!"

602

"Oh no it won't, Jan," she said, realistically, "it'll make things a lot worse. Every Hun in France will be trigger happy and every road crawling with troops. We might even get shot up by our own side if we show our noses in the open. The courier said they had landed in Normandy, somewhere near Caen, but it's no good nagging me because I don't know any more than that. The tunnel raid was a masterpiece. All troops in this area will have to use the roads now that we have air mastery, so shut up about the invasion and concentrate on us! Take a look at the map—I never was any good at geography—and tell me exactly where we are, then I'll rack my brains about this part of the country. Yves and I spent a lot of time hereabouts before the war but today I can only remember the topography of Sennacharib!"

We stopped in the thickest part of the wood and I had a close look at the map she produced from her bundle. I soon discovered where we were, about ten miles south of Ghislaine St. Père, in the heart of what the tourists know as 'the chateau country'. Unfortunately, we were a hundred miles from the area where we had been flown out by Lysander the year before and a district where we might have found a temporary refuge. Diana was right when she claimed that rail travel was safer than movement on the roads for now, when the British and American air forces dominated the skies over France, German transport made use of even third-class tracks, the kind favoured by fugitives like us. They also travelled a great deal by night and the only safe way to avoid their convoys and patrols was to move directly across country, the rougher country the better. Down here there were far more uncultivated patches than one could hope to find in the north but there did not seem to be many woods marked on the map and Diana thought we should hole up as soon as possible and seek help at one of the farms as soon as it was dark. There was something to be said for this but my instinct was to put as much distance between ourselves and our field of recent activity as was possible for a pair of foot travellers. After a brief discussion we pushed on to the edge of the wood, crossed some ploughed fields in which we felt very vulnerable, and plunged into another belt of woodland that was not as dense as it appeared from a distance. It was, however, invitingly extensive and we went through it until we came to a narrow glade, dotted with clumps of rhododendrons. Inside the largest clump we burrowed out a nest and after a meal of bread and goatsmilk cheese, washed down by a draught of local wine from Diana's bundle, we made ourselves as comfortable as possible and slept. As I dropped off I reflected that, all in all, we had been luckier than we deserved and that Diana's mad escapade in following me to France had already saved my life. Without the refuse-van she had borrowed, I should never have got clear of the district and although I did not know it until weeks later I was, in fact, the sole member of the ambush party to survive. Simon's men and all the surviving De Gaullists were caught and shot within two days of the attack.

It was almost dusk when I awoke to find Diana sitting cross-legged and smiling down at me, the map spread on her lap. She looked as serene as if we had been on a Foxhayes picnic and the only thing that recalled our present plight was the barmaid brassiness of her hair.

"Has anyone been near?" I asked, sitting up guiltily.

"Not a soul," she said, "and I've explored nearly half-a-mile down the path, almost to the edge of the wood!"

"Didn't you sleep? We've got to walk all night and you should have rested while you could."

"Nonsense," she said, "you've slept enough for both of us, and as it happens we don't have to walk all night, we've got transport and we've got a plan!"

"If you've been risking our necks breaking into places ... !" I began, half expecting her to tell me that she had a stolen car parked in the glade, but she told me to hold my tongue and listen.

"The trouble with you Jan is that you'll never surrender the 'Victoria-papa' standpoint! Now I admit that it's rather cosy to be cossetted and protected sometimes, but it's a luxury I can't afford at this moment. I told you I know this area and for every contact you've got in France I've got fifty! That's why I followed you over here. I was convinced that something like this would happen if you were on the run in Invasion Week. Now listen! When you were snoring I searched my memory for someone I know who is not only reliable but within comparatively easy reach and at last I hit on the right bod, André Lancier, who lives in Tours. We'll go to him straight away and he can hide us until we are overrun by the Allies or can establish contact with Raoul!"

"Is he one of the De Gaullist contacts? Did they give you his address?"

"Of course they didn't and I don't even know whether he's connected with the Resistance! I haven't set eyes on the man since the war but I'm a good enough judge of character to be sure he won't let us down . . . at least . . ." and she smiled secretly, "he won't let *me* down!"

I was in no doubt at all as to what she meant by this. Lancier, whoever he was, had been one of her lovers and a year ago my pride would have smarted at seeking help from him. Now I was more philosophical and found the situation not without irony.

"He was a vet," she went on, "and quite a famous one. I used to meet him at Longchamps and I once stayed at his villa, in Biarritz. He was handsome in a rakish kind of way and his wife fancied herself as a painter. Some of the avant garde boys kidded her that she really could paint and she was so grateful that she not only slept with them one after the other but paid handsomely for services rendered!"

"You upper-bracket French must have lived like a bunch of alley cats!" I growled. "No wonder you were a pushover when Jerry moved in!"

She laughed so loudly that I had to shush her.

"Oh Jan!" she exclaimed, "your most endearing characteristic is your seventeenth-century Puritanism! It runs in your veins like holy water and whenever you come face to face with the flesh you scowl like a Cromwellian troop-chaplain carrying bible and sword into the tents of the ungodly! Don't ever change, will you? Don't ever get tolerant and broadminded, I couldn't bear it, I should pine away for my Pilgrim Father!"

Gaiety seemed to bubble out of her, lending excitement and sparkle to everything within range of her laughter, and in spite of our desperate situation I wanted to take her in my arms and use her as roughly as she loved to be used; I wanted to demonstrate to her just how lusty a Puritan Father could be when he was tempted by an unrepentant pagan. I checked myself, however, and asked her how she intended to get us to Tours, reminding her that every cart-track would be crawling with Nazi transport.

"We don't use the roads, silly," she said, "we travel by boat!"

"Boat? On what?"

"On the river, the Cher. It's over there through the trees and there's a punt waiting for us!"

She showed me our approximate position and I saw that Tours was about forty miles downstream, where the tributary flowed into the Loire.

I weighed the risks and decided in favour of the punt. Night travel on a river was not without its dangers but it was far safer than stumbling over open country in the dark, and trying to cross rivers and main roads in search of the railway lines.

"This fellow Lancier, the vet," I asked, "how do you know he's still there? And even if he is how can you be sure he won't turn us away? There must be thousands of Nazis in a town the size of Tours!"

"At least I know him," she argued, "and what's the alternative? To knock on doors and trust to strangers? We might be lucky and then again, we might not. The current will carry us to within a few miles of Tours and we can lie up on one of the islets en route. Jerry will be guarding bridges and landing points but he won't have a garrison on every island in the river."

It made good sense. With any sort of luck we ought to be able to drift downstream in two or three nights, depending upon the strength of the current and I remembered that all the rivers in this part of France were studded with islets offering good cover during the hours of daylight.

"Okay," I said, "let's have a look at the punt!"

We wriggled out of the rhododendrons and stood silently in the glade, sniffing the air like a couple of hunted animals. It was almost dark now and the wood was alive with small, scuffling movements but they were not noises that worried a countryman. Diana took my hand and we moved off, pushing through the trees to the river bank. It was lighter here and we could just see the far bank, and, slightly downstream, a shadow on the water edge.

We went along the bank and down the shingle. Judging by the sound of the wash the current was strong and the area was clearly deserted. The punt was fastened to a staple driven into the corner pile of a ramshackle building and on feeling it I concluded that the wood was rotten all through. I gave the chain a sharp tug and the staple came out, the current catching the end of the punt and swinging it against the piles. There was an inch or so of water in the boat and the seats were wet with slime but it was seaworthy for it had been moored in two feet of water and still floated level. I groped under the thwarts and found the pole as Diana settled herself in the stern. In the darkness I heard her giggle.

" 'She loosed the chain and down she lay'," she quoted and then, with a ripple of laughter, "Cast off for many-towered Camelot, Sir Lancelot!"

Navigation was fiendishly difficult. The swirl of the current kept edging us towards the left bank where there were shingle bars and a seemingly endless tangle of willows trailing the water. When we fended off into midstream the current spun the boat in slow, ponderous circles, so that I was obliged to dodge from bow to stern and risk upsetting us in an effort to maintain headway. For all its difficulties, however, the cruise was relaxing, for Diana was in high spirits and kept up a flow of adolescent backchat as we bumped and butted our way downstream. Later, when the moon rose, our progress was a little easier and we passed under a long footbridge that was, as far as I could see, unguarded. No lights appeared on the banks and when the first glint of day showed in the sky above the woods I began to feel guardedly optimistic about our chances. The river at this point was not navigable for craft larger than row-boats and it now seemed to me that if we exercised reasonable care we stood a good chance of drifting down within reach of Tours and establishing contact with her friend Lancier.

About four-thirty A.M. we moved out to a broader stretch of water and right ahead I spotted a railway bridge resting on tall, stone piers. Feeling certain that a bridge of this size must be guarded I eased the punt into the left bank and peered around for a place where we could lie up during daylight hours. The woods here were thin, offering insufficient cover and there were one or two houses on the further bank. As it grew lighter I spotted an islet about a hundred yards downstream. It was very small but it was wooded and the chances of spending the day there undisturbed were better than if we remained close to the towpath. We made a quick dash for it, crossing over, driving the punt into the undergrowth and making fast to the roots of a willow. The branches of the same tree provided an excellent screen and I was sure that we could not be spotted from either bank. We scrambled out and circled the tiny haven, choosing a place where we could keep the right bank under observation. Here, beneath close-set birches, we made a camp and stretched ourselves out, Diana keeping watch while I slept for I was worn out by my efforts with the pole.

Diana woke me when it was broad day and put her hand on my mouth, jerking her head towards midstream. I sat up and peered through the leaves. A skiff containing two men, one of them wearing the field grey of a Wehrmacht Reservist Corps, was drifting within twenty yards of our hideout but the occupants did not appear to be searching for anybody. The soldier had a fishing rod and his companion, a squat peasant about fifty years of age, was sculling in a leisurely fashion, a short pipe gripped between his teeth. Once or twice the reservist looked curiously towards the island and then the current carried them down towards what looked like a large railway maintenance shed on the left bank. I watched the point where it had disappeared for a long time, my Sten gun at the ready but no one else appeared and the river remained empty. We made a meal of stale bread and the remains of the goatsmilk cheese. Diana also produced some malted milk tablets and with these, doled out at intervals, we kept our hunger in check.

"We're going to starve before we locate that vet!" I told her.

"Oh, we can do what Huck Finn did, put in somewhere and borrow a chicken!" she said, gaily. "I think it's all turning out rather well, Jan. It makes me feel young again to be living on an island again with you! If only we had my old Decca gramophone and those Gilbert and Sullivan selections!"

For all my anxieties, however, it was impossible to withstand her gaiety and the sense of schoolboy adventure that she managed to infuse into our desperately serious situation. In some ways I think that day was among the most serene that we ever spent together. There we were, hidden by a thin screen of bushes from men who would have beaten us to death, with practically nothing to eat and the prospect of a twenty mile cruise to dubious safety ahead of us, yet we lazed and talked as though we were back in Sennacharib with nothing worse to fear than a downpour of rain. We discussed all manner of things, our youth, our child Yvonne, what we should do with Heronslea after the war and how I should earn a living on my twelve acres of Teasel Wood, plus the little I had been able to save since my enlistment. Then, I recall, we moved on into wider fields and discussed the future of Europe and what the Allies would do to guard against a third bid by Germany for world domination. I told her what her kinsman Raoul had said about the certainty of an attempt on the part of statesmen to bring about a status quo, and leave the scars of the First World War unhealed, but she pooh-poohed this possibility and said that the 1918 War had been an affair of soldiers, whereas this one had involved whole populations. It was therefore more than likely that people would demand a bigger say in the reshuffle. Then, shrug-

609

ging our shoulders on the twentieth century, we went on to discuss religion and philosophy.

"We're all so damned smug about our combustion engines and modern surgery and washing-machines!" she said. "We equate these kind of things with progress, whereas they seem to me to have absolutely nothing to do with teaching people how to enjoy their little day. I used to be terribly impressed by fast cars and power stations and what-not but they're only toys really!"

Enthusiasm crackled from her. "Have you ever read anything about Ionian Bacchic cults Jan, those wonderful orgies the Greek women indulged in while their husbands had their heads down in elementary mathematics!"

I admitted wryly that my knowledge of Greek mythology was limited to Kingsley's "Heroes".

"Oh dear," she said, laughing, "I'll have to give you a short course when we get home! There were only two main cults practised and one, the worship of Dionysius, was a kind of feminine-inspired safety valve, you know—a reaction to Orphic gloom and pre-occupation with the future of the soul. The women got fed up with all the prohibitions just as I did at Heronslea and used to go up into the mountains and make whoopee! The more you read about the history of philosophy the more you realise that this tug-of-war between taking life as you find it, or preparing for after-life by soul-searching and self-denial, has been going on since the year dot. Now me, I'll take Pan to Jehovah every time! There's a personal element too— your Puritanism was always a kind of challenge to me and I used to get a terrific kick out of persuading you to peel off your dun-coloured doublet and hose and chase me across Arcady! It always gave me a sense of achievement to watch the satyr kick the Obadiah-bind-the-wicked-with-links-of-iron in the pants, and do battle with his conscience the minute the fun was over!"

It made me smile to relate this admission with well-remembered bursts of sensuality on her part but there was some truth in what she said. Perhaps after all, it was her pagan enthusiasm for life that had fascinated me all these years; old Dionysius crying out to be done with Puritanism and playing safe.

We dozed off when the noonday sun beat over the clearing and kingfishers flashed across our peephole. Then, but without a trace of her customary impatience, she roused me, leaning over me and letting her hair brush across my face. She had thrown off her windcheater and underslip and her breasts were bare. I kissed them without urgency for there was a timelessness about this place that banished the sense of danger. For an hour or more we lay in each others arms, like foolish lovers with the world before them and presently a friendly mist stole over the river giving us confidence to move about the islet and make preparations for our second night's voyage.

The sun went down and birds rustled in the thickets. The current warbled among the reeds and shingle bars and soon one or two lights showed on the furthermost bank near the bridge. Twice, while we were waiting for complete darkness, long goods trains went clattering over the river and thinking to avoid the risk of drifting into the glow cast by a third train I told Diana to hurry and scrambled into the punt to unhitch the mooring chain. I was standing with the chain looped round the stump and looking over my shoulder at Diana who had one foot on the stern thwart when the searchlight beam fell on us. Two seconds later the first burst of fire whipped into the branches above my head and showered leaves and twigs into the boat. There was no challenge, no warning sound of any kind, just the hard, white glare and then the harsh tattoo of bullets in the trees. Diana, poised midway between the shingle and the stern, was holding my Sten gun. Her Luger and my colt were in the boat with our bundle. There was no chance to do anything but duck and make a grab for the guns but I missed the bundle by a foot and landed face foremost in the inch of water at the bottom of the punt. I heard Diana shout and although I could see nothing and was half-stunned by the violence of the plunge, I knew that it was not a cry of pain she uttered but a warning. Then the peace of the tiny creek was shattered by a hideous outcry, shouts, splashes, the roar of an outboard motor, and behind all these noises a steady rattle of machine-gun fire and the whack of bullets cutting into waterlogged timbers of the punt.

Somehow I managed to struggle to my knees and saw Diana in the identical position she had occupied when the light went on, one foot on land and one on the edge of the punt, but as I cried out to her to jump she brought up the Sten gun and fired two short bursts, one to the left and one to the right, both clean over my head. At the same moment she braced herself against the stump to which the punt had been moored and pushed hard with her foot so that the shattered boat shot away from the beach and swung into the current, spinning in a wide circle well clear of the beam which played directly into the mouth of the creek, picking out every leaf and stem that grew there. I suppose I must have been about ten yards from the islet when I heard her shout again and her voice carried over the uproar as the current took a firmer hold on the wallowing punt, slanting it across the river towards the eastern bank above the bridge.

"Dive, Jan, *dive!*" she shouted. I lurched forward as the punt went under and the midstream current rolled me over like a barrel and the roar in my ears shut out the confused medley of sounds concentrating round the beam of light.

I did not know that I had been hit twice, once in the thigh and once in the calf and was losing blood rapidly. I felt no pain or no shock beyond that of immersion in cold water. All this had happened in less than fifteen seconds and for the next half-minute I forgot everything in an instinctive struggle to survive, and swim slantwise across the stream, dragging a numbed and useless leg. It was not until my chest bumped on the reedy fringe of the bank that I realised even approximately what had happened, that Diana was on the islet fighting it out alone and that I had no means whatever of getting to her or taking part in the battle. She had the only weapon and one magazine of bullets. Everything else was at the bottom of the Cher. I could still see the searchlight in the distance, and hear a far off jumble of sounds, but whatever was happening out there was as remote from me as a battle a hundred miles away. I tried to run along the bank but at the first stride I fell back into the river, sobbing with rage and helplessness as I dragged myself ashore and tried to crawl up the bank. The effort of that three-yard crawl was my last conscious act. The blood drained away from me and my senses left me as I gained the towpath. I remembered someone close at hand shouting something in my ear but the sound of the voices reached me as a pub babel penetrates the brain of a man stupefied with drink. The newcomer put an arm under my shoulder but I could make nothing of what he said or was trying to do. Then he slipped away altogether and the next thing I recall was the strong smell of resinous wood in my nostrils and a kind of pressure on all sides, as though I was lying in a cage made of strong smelling pine logs, with bars so close set that they shut out all but a chink or two of light.

For a long time I lay still, trying to relate factors that baffled me and intruded between me and the resinous smell, the curious sensation of stiffness as though I was pinned by the legs, and the dim awareness of the cagelike structure of my surroundings. Then, with a sickening rush, I remembered Diana and my final glimpse of her braced against the stump firing the Sten into the searchlight beam. With a cry I started up and a sharp spasm of pain ran from toe to groin, licking along the leg like a tongue of flame. My surroundings suddenly became significant. I could see that I was not in a cage but a kind of nest made of faggots, and that the strong, resinous smell came from bulkier pine billets half filling the shed or out-house where I was hidden. Where the logs were carelessly stacked I could see a triangle of light and beyond it the wall of a building. I put down my hand and discovered that my right leg was bandaged and splinted and that I was unable to move, however desperate my need. A shadow crossed the triangle of light and wooden sabots scraped on stones and I called "Diana!" and again, as loudly as I was able, "Diana!" not because I had the slightest hope that the shadow was hers but in defiance of the terrible conviction that she was dead. A man jumped into the shed and tugged at

613

the faggots, enlarging the chink and thrusting his head and shoulders into the aperture. He was a middle-aged peasant with a pale, narrow face and a tuft of wiry grey hair pushing under a beret too small for his head.

"Mother of God, be silent!" he hissed, "they are searching the wood now!"

Before I could reply he had disappeared and I heard him moving about in the yard between his cottage and the shed in which I lay. Presently he went away and it was quiet again. I could hear birds in the trees and now and again the far-off rumble of trains crossing the bridge.

I must have slept a fitful sleep of despair or perhaps my temperature rose and I was delirious for when I became fully conscious once more the sun patterns on the wall of the cottage told me that it was evening and the throb of my injured leg was less urgent than my raging thirst. I thought about water deliberately, torturing myself rather than let my thoughts range back to the skirmish on the islet and what had become of Diana. That way I could pretend to hope that she was secreted somewhere not far off and that the moment the hue and cry died away we would be reunited and hidden until my leg healed and we could continue our flight to Tours.

When it was almost dusk the peasant returned bringing some coarse bread and a bowl of vegetable soup which I swallowed without a word. I then asked for water and he called over his shoulder to someone in the yard. A moment later a shapeless woman with a pitifully anxious manner approached the gap in the faggots and passed him an earthenware pitcher and a tin cup. He watched me drink a pint and in a guttural accent that might have been Basque or Spanish, he said:

"They are gone, M'sieu! They are satisfied that you were either shot or drowned! They are now searching the river banks downstream below the bridge. Tonight we shall bring a doctor to dress your wounds. They are not serious wounds but you lost much blood on the way here!"

I digested this for a moment, scouting for courage to ask him the question that tormented me.

614

"Where am I? How far from the railway bridge?"

He shrugged. "Four or five kilometres, M'sieu. They would have searched the cottage more thoroughly but they do not suspect me. I have never worked for the Resistance, I have been employed on the maintenance of the bridge ever since the Boche came, you understand?"

His eyes searched out my reaction to this statement and I could see that it cost him a considerable effort to admit to having worked for the Germans for years. Perhaps because of my own misery I was sorry for him.

"I heard that the British and Americans had landed," I said. "Can you tell me how the invasion is going?"

"They say it is a big success and that the Boches are already on the run."

"Who says this?"

"The Resistance groups but the German railway police say otherwise. They say Churchill has been thrown into the sea in Normandy!"

"Which do you believe?"

"I believe the Resistance, M'sieu! The Boche is clearly very much frightened and cannot hide his fear!"

I lay quite still for a moment, licking my lips and mustering my entire mental and physical resources like a man preparing to jump from a high wall into darkness.

"Where is the woman agent I left on the island?" I said finally. "Did they kill her?"

He answered me casually, "No M'sieu, they took her alive! She was driven to the Mairie in Buzot Vernay and will probably be taken on to Tours, or perhaps to Orleans!"

I tried to sit up and he raised his hand, prohibitively.

"Where is Buzot Vernay? How far from here?"

"Ten kilometres, a small place. A Boche railway unit is based there, not more than a dozen men and some of them older than I am."

"Was she wounded in the fight?"

"I think not, Henri says not!"

"Who is Henri?"

Suddenly the woman spoke from immediately behind him. I had not noticed that she was still there.

"Henri is a fool who will get us all shot!" she snapped.

The man shrugged again, implying the futility of reasoning with a woman.

"My wife is against it! My good sense is against it also but I think it is now time we did something to protect ourselves! When the British get here we will be denounced, they will shoot all the people who have worked for the Boches!"

He said this not so much to me as to his wife and I had a conviction that they had discussed this subject often and with plenty of give and take.

The pain in my leg became active again and the spasm made me gasp. When it receded I said, slowly:

"What is it that your wife is against?"

She shouldered him aside and approached the aperture talking directly down at me.

"Henri wishes to organise an attack on the Mairie and rescue this woman!" she said, bitterly. "I say that is suicide for all of us! The Germans have guns and bombs and all we have are a few rabbit-guns and some bottles filled with paraffin. The men would be killed and afterwards the Germans would come and shoot all of us on our own hearthstones. In any case it would be useless, the woman will have been moved to Tours by now. She will not even be in Buzot Vernay!"

Somebody whistled from the yard and they left. I tried to ponder their information calmly and usefully. Diana had been taken alive, though how I could not begin to guess. She had then been driven to this place Buzot Vernay, the nearest market town perhaps, and there the Germans would interrogate her pending a report to the nearest military post. She had been captured with arms in her hands and the penalty for this was death, never less. She might be dead now, lying in a shallow grave near the wall under which she had been shot, or she might be hanging from a tree as a warning to other partisans. There were rules in this game we had been playing since she had climbed into the jeep beside me after Alison's funeral. If you broke one of the rules, like getting caught for instance, you lost your stake, every farthing of it. Sometimes, when the game was absorbing, you forgot this but sooner or later you were sharply reminded of it and now was such a time. This was total war and there were no qualifying verdicts for the losers. You struck and ran away, as on the occasion when we had killed Rance and Yves, or you struck and got caught and were eliminated from the contest. Diana had known this when she followed me back to France and I too had known it and had accepted it but remembering did not help now. It did nothing at all to sweeten the bitterness of defeat.

I thought back on the final rally in the creek where we had spent our last hours together. She could have made a bid for it and jumped into the punt as it swung out into midstream. We could have plunged into the river together and struggled for the bank but she had rejected this choice and done so deliberately. Instead she had braced herself against the mooring stump and pushed with her foot, giving the sinking punt enough impetus to carry it into the current so that when it did go down I had a chance of evading the searchlight beam. She had done much more than this. She had stood in the open firing at the searchlight, drawing both beam and bursts in order to increase whatever chance I had of getting clear. She had done all this, coolly but instinctively, because this was what she had returned to France to accomplish and all for what? Because she had a crazy notion that this was my due because, in her eyes, she was unable to fulfil herself as a wife.

The harder I sweated out a reconstruction of the final scene the more snugly all the pieces fitted together and the picture that resulted from the assembly was a hideous one, that of a bruised and battered woman hanging from a tree with open wounds fouling her body.

The peasant returned to the chink and pushed his head between the billets.

"Henri has come," he said briefly, "and the doctor will be here soon. My wife was right, the woman has been taken to Tours! She went there this afternoon by ambulance. You are very lucky, M'sieu, they have abandoned the search of the banks and are now sure you were drowned!"

That was all. Diana had gone to Tours by ambulance and they had stopped looking for me. I was very lucky.

Chapter Thirteen

WRITE IT down they said. That was the thing to do, take pen and paper and write it all down. Start at the beginning and don't stop until you've got it out of your system like tainted food. Then you'll start living again and only remember the good times.

But there are some times I can't remember at all, whole days and weeks when a kind of greyness wraps itself round the memory like summer evening mists over Nun's Head when the only thing that reminds you of the sea is the dolorous clang of the bell-buoy offshore.

It was this way after Diana's capture. I stayed in the shed until I was moved on to a more permanent hideout and then, when I could get about with a stick, to a series of hideouts in farms, tradesmen's houses and once a disused brewery. I met a great many people, most of them anxious to impress themselves on my memory, either because they were proud of the risks they were taking or because they regarded me as a form of insurance against a speedy Allied victory. But I do not recall the face or personality of a single one of them. They are like figures in the background of an impressionist painting, suggested by a few strokes of the brush.

I know by the calendar that this lost period lasted almost nine weeks, and that during the latter part of it I took an active part in the upsurge of partisan activity south-west of Paris. I must have proved a morose and rather frightening oddity for here and there, when the fog shreds for a few moments, I can remember hitting out at the enemy like a blinded savage and killing without thought, pity or pleasure. Up to then I had killed but two men, Rance and the young soldier in the railway cutting. Both killings had robbed me of human dignity and left scars on my spirit that are still capable of producing an ache but this is not true of the men I killed afterwards.

I was sure that Diana was dead or about to die. Every time I thought of her standing before a Gestapo examiner I had the urge to smash and destroy, and sometimes the means to find this release were at hand.

There was the time I had taken part in an attack on a mobile flak battery near Chartres where the guns were successfully halted and blown up with mines. One lorry driver survived, a boy of about nineteen, who pleaded that he was a pressed Hungarian. I shot him through the head whilst the leader of the local Resistance group was interrogating him. A few days later another group-leader came to me with a story that they had captured four S.S. men during a reprisal raid on a farm. The men were tied to trees in the forest of Maintenon and I went there by truck and emptied a magazine into them. I noticed then that my savagery shocked the partisans and that they ceased to contact me or seek my advice, but I could operate without them. There was a Vichy policeman in a village who my hostess said had been an active Fascist before the war, and had been responsible for selecting local hostages in 1942. I did not check her story. I waylaid him on his way home one night and clubbed him to death with a pick-handle.

As I say, these killings left no scars. I can only remember them as one might recall blood-curdling illustrations seen in a book during one's childhood. I daresay I was partly insane with rage and misery and shame, shame at having left Diana alone on the islet, humiliation at being free and alive when she was dead or under torture in Tours gaol.

Then Raoul found me and shocked me out of this coma. On the seventh of August, the day of the abortive German counter-attack at Mortain, he sought me out to tell me that Diana was not dead and that she was not in Tours but in the Gestapo prison at Le Mans and that the discovery of her identity had saved her life. He said that she was being held as a possible hostage against the surrender of the Nazis in France.

I suppose he expected me to show delight, but my spirit was far too bruised and battered for this. I could only gape at him as he told me all he knew, that the break-up of telegraphic communications during successive waves of air attacks had delayed recognition until her dyed hair grew out and someone inside the prison had recognised her as the woman who had driven a Mercedes into her husband and run away with her English lover. By that time the German hold upon France was tenuous and all prisoners with any claim to importance were being set apart as bargaining counters. They would not kill her, Raoul said, but would almost certainly convey her to Germany when they pulled out or perhaps before. Every day political prisoners were being taken away to places like Dachau and it was generally known that they were guarded by special squads of fanatically loyal S.S. who had orders to kill them en masse if and when orders came from Hitler's headquarters.

I suppose I should have been relieved to have news that Diana was still alive but in some ways her new status increased the hopelessness of reaching her. Raoul was not much help, not on that occasion, for he was all but breaking under the terrible strain of holding the enthusiasm of the partisans in check. He was now a grey ghost of the trim young man who had enlisted me eighteen months before. His hair was white and his eyes, red-rimmed and permanently narrowed, held in them the expression of a man driven to the edge of physical and mental exhaustion. Notwithstanding this he had compassion for me and said there was a possibility that he might get advance information of a mass transfer of prisoners to the east. If this took place and convoys bypassed Paris, using second-class roads, there was the prospect of a successful ambush. In the meantime, there was nothing either of us could do but wait and maintain contact with his source of information inside the gaol. He parted from me with a stern warning not to spread this news among the local partisans.

"The victory will be too late when it comes," he said,

gloomily, "far too many good men have died already and if the general uprising is premature most of the survivors will follow them. These people would do well to remember what happened in Warsaw recently!"

His visit did not do much to uplift my spirits, but it did help me to get a grip on myself and nurse the small spark of hope he left behind. I stayed inactive in the Chartres area for a few days and was there when the Germans began their retreat over the Seine. When that happened it would have been easy for me to have slipped through to the Allied lines but I did not even think of doing so. If I preserved my own life then I wanted it to be of some use to me, to have turned my back on Diana and left her survival to chance would have increased my self disgust to a point where I should probably put my revolver in my mouth and pull the trigger.

On the night of August the eleventh I got a message from Raoul asking me to meet him at a rendezvous not far from Rambouillet. I went there at once and found him installed in a disused quarry. Round about him, armed to the teeth, were some thirty or forty partisans and it was clear that a major strike was in preparation. He said that news had arrived that a large convoy of political prisoners was being moved from Le Mans to Germany and travelling through Belgium to Holland via road or rail. Little more was known except that the convoy was unlikely to cross Paris. The capital was now on the point of rising, communications were bad and the German garrison unreliable since the failure of the attempt to assassinate Hitler in July. The Germans in charge of the convoy, he was informed, would almost certainly be S.S. who could be relied upon to obey their instructions to the letter. If the convoy came by road arrangements had been made to waylay it not far from its point of departure. If it went by rail the job of attempting to stop it would be taken over by the Belgian partisans, who had already freed one trainload near Malines.

This was the best news I had had in a long time and I felt immensely grateful to Raoul. He smiled thinly at my enthusiasm.

"Ah my friend," he said, "for you this has become a personal war!"

"It always was," I told him and offered him some Pernod I had brought along. He shook his head.

"That's no use to me any more Jan," he said and slouched off to make contact with his telegraphist lower down the wood.

He returned an hour or so later and had got himself thoroughly in hand. He was no longer tired and dispirited but issued his orders crisply. His lieutenant, a fugitive Jerseyman, followed him about, reiterating his commands and enjoying reflected authority.

"We move at once," Raoul said, "they are coming by road." Then, to me, "I am putting you in the charge of Paul to prevent your enthusiasm running away with you! You are concerned only with one inmate of those trucks, my responsibility is spread somewhat wider, you understand?"

He indicated his squat little lieutenant who was encumbered with a home-made bazooka and the man stepped up to me as if I had been a prisoner.

We heard the convoy grinding up from the valley a few minutes before its masked headlights showed in the scrub country at the foot of the escarpment. From our ambush-point it looked like a segmented glow-worm, writhing up the long gradient, and beside it pin-points of light moved to and fro as though marshalling its progress. Word regarding the convoy's composition reached us by field telephone. There was an armoured car at each end of a string of six lorries, and the pin-points of light were motor cyclists acting as mobile flank guards. Raoul made his plans accordingly. We split up, some twenty men on each side of the road with a forlorn hope to deal with the motor cyclists and bring them to action before they could sweep the road with their light machine-guns.

Raoul took charge of the party on the bank whose orders were to concentrate on the forward armoured car. The Jerseyman and I were in the rearward party, lying on open ground in advance of the bazooka which we hoped

622

to bring into action when Raoul's group opened fire on the leading car.

We were aware that each lorry would have its complement of guards, armed with automatic weapons but we dared not fire on the lorries without endangering the lives of the prisoners. We could only hope that the detached guards would engage us the moment battle was joined and thus give us a wider field of fire.

We set up no road blocks. Any kind of obstruction would be spotted by the motor cyclists at a distance and give the gunner of the leading car time to sweep the hedges. There was practically no cover here and everything depended upon a swift, overwhelming stroke. That was the reason Raoul had chosen such an unlikely place for an ambush.

I felt almost elated now. Perhaps the nearness of Diana improved my nerve or perhaps the prospect of immediate action gave me a genuine physical release. I knew that some of us were certain to be killed in the returning fire and that as I was attacking from the more open side of the road it was more than likely that I would be among that number but the prospect of dying here on this bare stretch of upland did not depress me. If it happened it would be an atonement for a great deal more than my failure to rescue Diana on the Cher, it would be a kind of grand cancelling-out of all my failures in her respect, the failure to win her in the days long before anyone had ever heard of Nazis and extermination camps. If this was to be the end then it was a fitting climax to everything that had gone before and if she survived and I died then at least I could claim to have caught her up in the last stride and she, being Diana, would credit my account accordingly. This silly, vainglorious thought steadied me as I lay in the coarse grass listening to the steady whine of the approaching convoy and the stutter of the motor cycles. Around me was complete silence but behind each clump of grass men were waiting and sweating with the image of death in their eyes, each perhaps exploring some secret dream such as mine and wondering about the girl who had given it singularity.

The two scouts breasted the slope one behind the other, their exhaust fumes tainting the upland air. We let both of them pass and they chugged on down the short stretch of straight road towards Raoul's ambush. Thirty yards in their wake the first armoured car levelled out and changed gear, its silhouette passing before us like the snout of a primaeval monster heaving itself out of the murk. Close behind, at intervals of about fifteen yards, came the canvas-topped lorries, a guard with an automatic rifle sitting beside each driver and two more on each tailboard.

At first sight of the coal-scuttle helmets I heard the little Jerseyman hiss and I reached out my hand to steady him for we had received strict orders to hold our own fire until the convoy had been halted in front. So the six lorries trundled by, traveling at about fifteen miles per hour, for the climb had been steep and as each vehicle topped the rise it faltered for a moment as the driver groped for his gears. Then, at the tail of the procession, came the second armoured car and finally one more motor cyclist.

The rearguard was exactly level with us when the first grenade was flung at the leading car more than a hundred yards down the road. Within seconds of its detonation the Sten guns of Raoul's party went into action and flashes of orange lit up both sides of the road. Then, as I fired my own burst at the last motor-cyclist, the Jerseyman's Heath-Robinson bazooka boomed off at the car and the shock of a direct hit lifted its near-side wheels from the ground so that its bulk seemed to prance before crashing down on the road surface. Before the bazooka could fire again the Germans were pouring a murderous fire into the scrubland immediately behind us.

I saw my man crumple over his handlebars as his motorcycle bucketed round and roared across the road straight into the low bank, mounting it and throwing its rider backwards across the road to within a few feet of where I crouched. After that all was smoke, confusion and outcry, with grenades exploding on all sides and above their roar, the rattle of small-arms and machine-guns.

The bazooka charge had hit and damaged the nearside turret of the armoured car but it had not killed the crew.

Their machine-gun was now firing at point-blank range and as our men stood up to hurl grenades at the stationary vehicle they were cut down in a swathe. It was Paul the Jerseyman who silenced this gun, abandoning the bazooka and running straight in under the blister of the car to level his automatic rifle at the men on the turret. Perhaps the gunners were not killed by the Jerseyman's volley but died in the swirl of flame that suddenly shot upward and outward from the shattered vehicle. Only one man succeeded in scrambling down, landing in a heap at my feet and I shot him through the body before he could scramble upright.

Then, from immediately beyond the blaze, I heard something that made my flesh crawl, an agonised and continuous screaming from the prisoners in the lorry and forgetting everything I ran past the burning car towards the hindmost vehicle and rushed headlong into a German who was standing with his back to me pouring Tommy-gun bursts into the interior of the van.

It took me a moment or so to understand his intention. It seemed such a stupid and incongruous action, to stand still with his back exposed and shoot into the laced-up canvas of the hood. Then, as I understood what he was doing, I lost all reason, flinging down my gun and grasping him with both hands and at the same time hurling myself backwards so that we rolled together under the tailboard. The German landed on top of me but was helpless in the grip I had on his throat.

How long we wrestled there I cannot say but it could have only been a matter of seconds before our struggles carried us against the offside wheel and I was able to improve my grip by thrusting my fingers between his chin and helmet strap, forcing his face against the fishtail of the exhaust pipe. The pipe was red-hot and his violent heave as he touched the metal separated us for an instant. In that second I was able to draw my knife and stab him through the neck but before he was dead I was on my feet again, screaming for lights. It was just as Raoul had stated, I was engaged in a purely personal war and I forgot that the battle was still raging further down the line or that grenades were still exploding beyond and behind me as attackers converged on the vehicles.

From the moment of the first explosion to that when I had disposed of the man under the lorry and run the length of the convoy to the slewed-round armoured car at the head of the procession was probably no more than three minutes. In that space of time the battle was won although odd, sniping shots and the roar of an occasional grenade continued for five minutes more.

By then every German in the convoy had been accounted for and the last two, who eluded the Jerseyman's group and began to run back down the hill, were killed by a long burst from a sub-machine gun posted on the other side of the road.

Just then the moon sailed out behind a bank of cloud and the stretch of road could be viewed from end to end, a long, untidy string of vehicles, its tail-end lit by the glow of the blazing armoured car and at the summit of the car the doll-like figure of a man half in, half out of the turret. I heard Raoul shouting and turned back towards my end of the convoy, stumbling over bodies and calling Diana's name aloud. Men and women began to emerge from the lorries, some of them still screaming, others laughing and shouting as they rummaged among the dead for the keys of their handcuffs that linked them two by two. Somewhere in this ghoulish mob was Diana but for the moment I was too shocked and breathless to conduct a search. Away at the back of my mind, pinned there by fear too awful to be faced, was a certainty that she was lying in her blood behind the curtains of the last lorry, killed by the fire of the man I had stabbed to death under the tailboard. Raoul found me at last and seized me by the jacket, shaking me savagely and telling me to help restore some kind of order into the chaotic scene. He had to shout at the top of his voice for the din was now deafening and everyone seemed to be running in different directions and cursing those who got in their way.

Slowly, section by section, partial discipline was restored and we began a half-hearted search of the lorries hustling those who remained inside into the open. Head-

626

light masks were prised from lorries that had been backed across the road and the beams were directed on the centre of the road. The screaming and the shouting died away to be replaced by a continuous murmur as grotesque pairs shambled into the circle of light, joining the few prisoners who had already freed themselves. I shouldered my way into the groups, staring at every face but Diana was not among them.

Ignoring Raoul's shout I turned away and ran to the last lorry beside the burning armoured car. It was as light as day down here and the debris of the engagement lay all over the road. Here was the man I had killed, the two other men I had shot and just beyond them a group of five Frenchmen killed by the opening burst of the car's machine-gun.

I hardly glanced at the bodies. Tearing aside the remnants of the canvas hood I peered inside, calling and calling. Another dead German lay on his back on the tailboard and behind him was a huddle of figures piled one on top of another like carcasses in a slaughter-pen. One or two still moved, making feeble gestures with arms or legs and another, sitting with his back against the partition, called out to me in an agonised voice.

"Is there a doctor there? A doctor, for the love of God!"

Raoul had pursued me and now I wrenched his torch from his hand, tossing bodies this way and that and flashing the beam on each face. In the furthermost corner I found her, handcuffed to a tubby little corpse clad in the clownish pyjamas of a political prisoner and splashed from neck to waist with his blood and her own.

I remember being aware of the terrible stench of the lorry and then of plucking helplessly at the short length of chain that linked Diana's wrist to that of her companion. After that I must have fainted for the next thing I recall is sitting with my back against the low bank with Raoul forcing a flask against my teeth and repeating the same words over and over again, like an incantation.

"She is alive, my friend! You hear me? *Alive* I say! Emerald is *alive*, Jan, do you hear?"

627

Slowly, through a roaring tide of revved-up engines and the babble of voices, his words penetrated my brain and I grabbed the flask and gulped down mouthfuls of the raw spirit. Beyond us the partisans were already making ready to depart. Our own transport had been brought up and the German lorries were being driven off the road and ditched. The space beyond the glowing armoured car was being used as a clearing centre for our wounded, fourteen of them laid in a row and behind the bank on which I lay men were burying the dead, German and French, in two common graves. I could hear the chink of spades in the flinty soil and the burial parties passed and repassed, dragging bundles wrapped in tarpaulins taken from the trucks.

I looked across at the wounded, some of them sitting up, with fresh bandages showing white against the murk of the moor, a few lying still under German greatcoats. Farthest from me, at the very end of the line, the light of the burning car flickered on a great mop of chestnut hair.

With a great effort I pushed myself away from the bank and lurched over, Raoul following, the flask still in his hand.

"She will live, Jan!" he repeated. "They will give her every care at the convent and no one will come for her when we get her there. They are busy saving themselves from now, I promise you! I promise this, my friend!"

I hardly heard him. Kneeling there in the road I let my hand run through her hair, lifting it away from her waxen face. She was breathing in great, shuddering gasps, like a person plucked from a winter sea and the unit doctor walked down the line and glanced at her, balancing a hypodermic syringe in his hands. Raoul sighed and walked away. Couples came and lifted the men beside her, easing them gently over the tailboards of make-shift ambulances and covering them with the clothing of the dead.

"Will you go with her, Capitaine?" the doctor asked, presently. "She is not in pain, not now. You could sit in front and hold her in your arms perhaps?"

I gathered her up, wondering at the smallness of the effort required and the doctor reached out and steadied me as I swung myself over the tailboard and wedged myself

628

against the canopy. Beyond, along the entire stretch of road, the purposeful bustle continued, lights bobbing, men calling softly to one another, gears groaning and tyres crunching under the fitful moon but to me it all seemed to be taking place on the edge of a dream, or as though I was looking down on it from a great height. The weight of Diana on my knees was so trifling that I might have been carrying a small parcel wrapped in cloth.

As the ambulance turned and moved off down the hill I slipped my hand inside her blouse and felt the beat of her heart. She stirred very slightly and then settled back, her breath becoming shorter and less audible. I held her closer in a desperate effort to offset the bumps in the road.

Chapter Fourteen

ONCE I had worried about the prospect of her undergoing a single operation. Now I had to sanction a series and they were performed not to save her life but to prolong it, season by season, sometimes, it seemed to me, month by month. Yet her heart survived them all and she became "a case". They even wrote about her in "The Lancet".

After her fourth operation we took her back to Heronslea and settled her in the large bedroom of the west wing that had once been her mother's.

It was September again then, the first September of the Peace, and summer lingered in the curving row of beeches that marched down to the Shepherdshey road. There was, as yet, no hint of autumn in the coverts behind the house and the sky over Nun's Head remained blue for more than two months. Only in the west, beyond the wide estuary of the Whin, was there an occasional promise of November gales and the days of soft, seeping rain that would precede them. We pushed her bed against the tall, recessed window so that she could look south and west across miles of red ploughland to the sea.

She had changed a good deal during her last and longest spell in hospital. Before that, and during her periods of waiting, she had been restless, usually rational and reasonably patient but sometimes deeply depressed and fighting hard to conceal it. Now her fretfulness had been ironed away by drugs and she had won through to a kind of disciplined tranquillity. She smiled naturally once more and seemed to enjoy what she read during the periods I was occupied elsewhere.

When she was settled I returned to London and pulled strings to hurry my discharge, ultimately jumping the queue on the pretence of farming. I had no intention of farming, indeed, I had no plans at all beyond fighting for Diana. Everything else was of little consequence but even I found it impossible to extract a straight answer from the various doctors and specialists who visited her. Each seemed guardedly baffled. Some said one thing and some another. Some hinted that she might not only survive but walk again; others that although the spinal wound had healed the two bullets had caused so many complications that even a partial recovery was very doubtful. None gave her more than a few years and one said the best we could hope for was that she would recover sufficiently to use a wheeled-chair. After over a year of this I became gruffly impatient with the entire medical profession and took to relying on my own guesses, gloomy or less gloomy, according to my needs.

All this time Diana and I exchanged very few words about her health or future. When we were alone we talked about other things, Yvonne and the children, books and furniture, anything to mask what was always uppermost in our minds. It was like a game, each seeking to bluff the other and both knowing that every word we uttered was a deception. As I say, however, all this changed when she came home after the final operation, the one that was designed to remove bone splinters and give her a chance to build up her strength for a more extensive probe in the distant future.

The day I was demobilised I came back to Heronslea in a mood that was neither relief at being free to resume normal life, nor dejection that I had paid such an appalling price for victory. I had learned by this time to settle for monthly reprieves. Diana was still alive and I was thankful for that but I found no pleasure in the kind of things that amused those about me, the bonfires of blackouts, the promise of an end to rationing, the annihilation of the wretched perverts who had pushed Western civilisation over the edge. I could feel no relief in the end of it all, I could only continue to blow on the tiny flame deep in my heart and hope that some day, a year, ten years or twenty years ahead, a miracle would enable Diana to climb the long slope of Teasel Edge to our cottage or cross the larch coverts to Big Oak Paddock and Folly Tower. As long as the flame was there I could keep a sense of proportion.

I went into the big kitchen and found Drip supervising the preparation of the children's supper. The Peace had not done much to reduce the population of Heronslea. All the Spanish children were still there, with a dozen waifs Raoul had collected and sent over from France, the orphans of men killed in half-forgotten skirmishes on lonely roads, or the children of poor devils who had died in Dachau and Belsen. There were one or two British children who had come to us as evacuees but had no homes to which to return and there was a Danish couple, a boy and a girl, whose father had been one of our best agents before he was betrayed and shot at Tromso. It was a miniature League of Nations and in some ways a more hopeful one than its predecessor.

What was going to happen to these strays when our five-year lease ran out was problematical. Diana's critical condition had absorbed me completely and I hadn't given the matter a thought. If Drip was depressed by Diana's helplessness she did not show it but prattled on about how pleased Diana would be to see me and how I might surprise her with the seven o'clock supper tray.

I took the tray and trudged up the broad, curving staircase, my twelve-year-old daughter Yvonne skipping along at my side. She had Youth's contempt for illnesses and I could not help feeling how closely her attitude resembled that of her mother's at the same age. Diana could never stand invalids or sick rooms and excused her impatience by declaring that her vitality was an affront to the bedridden.

As we went along the corridor I stole a sidelong glance at the child beside me. She had the odd gait of the Leighs and my own big bones and dark complexion but basically she was her mother all over again, engaging, yet displaying a kind of savagery in her determination to swim clear of human woes.

Diana was sitting up in bed reading an anthology of British and American verse. I had noticed during my flying visits that she turned more and more to poetry. She said she found it difficult to concentrate on novels and she had always been bored by magazines and newspapers. When we entered the room she marked the page and put up her lips to be kissed. Her face was much thinner and she seemed terribly fragile but I was delighted to notice that her hair had at last regained its former lustre and displayed no trace of the barmaid rinse that had clung to its roots all the time she had been in and out of hospitals.

I noticed the inner change almost at once. There was a stillness about her that I had never seen before and it lay deep in her eyes, like a soft light shining at a distance. She held my hand while she joked with Yvonne about the Spanish boy Manuel, who continued to shadow our child like a big, sombre dog and was madly jealous of anyone else who showed her the slightest attention.

"Has he proposed again?" Diana asked, half-seriously.

"Yesterday! When we were fishing off the Whin sandbanks!" Yvonne told her, gaily.

"Ah, I never had a proposal in a boat," said Diana, winking at me. "Almost everywhere but never at sea. Isn't that so, Jan?"

I mumbled something about the night we had run away from home and taken refuge on Nun's Island.

"Nonsense!" said Diana firmly, "you were terribly glum that night! You were scared stiff that someone was going to arrest you for abduction and I never believed we'd get there! I don't think we should have if the tide hadn't been

632

ebbing and you couldn't possibly have sculled back to Whinmouth!"

She dismissed me for a moment and talked to Yvonne about Sioux, her aged hunter, now content to amble about the small paddock dreaming of the days when he could have cleared the white rails at a bound.

"Can he still be ridden?" she asked, "could Jan ride him if he kept to a walk?"

"Good Lord, yes!" Yvonne told her, "Manny and I took him up the main ride on Sunday and he kept wanting to trot!"

The information seemed to please her. "That's wonderful!" she said, "he's indestructible. Do you know how old he is, Jan?"

I calculated back to the Boxing Day meet in 1927, when Sioux had been presented to her by her father. He was a two-year-old then, just broken and would now be rising twenty-one.

"By God but he could skim along!" said Diana without wistfulness, "I was scared of riding him that day, do you remember Jan?"

"You didn't look it!" I said, wishing that Yvonne would either conceal her impatience or go away.

"I'll tell you what, Yvonne," Diana said suddenly. "Go and catch him, saddle him up and Jan can take him as far as Big Oak tonight. You'd like that, Jan wouldn't you? I've got a dressing between seven-thirty and eight!"

I raised no objections. For some reason that I didn't understand, she was anxious that I should ride Sioux again, so I told Yvonne to do what she asked and the child rushed away. I heard her shouting for Manuel as she ran down the stairs.

"She absolutely loathes these duty visits!" said Diana, calmly.

"I'll have a word with her," I suggested, but Diana shook her head vigorously.

"For God's sake, don't, Jan! It's right that she should feel this way about sick people! I don't want a little Flo Nightingale mooning about the place. Yvonne's attitude is healthy and normal, so don't make her feel that she's expected to waste hours practising small-talk at the bed-side!" She smiled and took my hand again. "I know you don't feel that way. Mind you, *I* should, if it was you lying here, but then, you've always been madly Holy-Graily haven't you? You probably get a hell of a kick out of sick-visiting!"

It was very encouraging to hear her talk this way again. We had not had a conversation like this since that final day on the islet. I noticed then that her cheeks had a bloom and that she had gone to a great deal of trouble with her make-up.

"You look very pretty tonight, Di," I said and to my delight she flushed and crushed my hand to her mouth. Her lips were warm and very soft. It was like being touched by a petal.

"Kiss me Jan," she said suddenly and then, raising her head, "kiss me properly!" and the moment I touched her lips her long, slender fingers slipped over my head and tugged playfully at the hair on the back of my neck. It was a favourite trick of hers and the gesture fanned the pitiful flame of hope into a glow.

"Jan," she said quietly, when I had settled myself against the bedhead and put her head on my breast, "how long have I got? Will you tell me your guess?"

She spoke in a level tone, as a person might ask a casual question. Her words descended like an extinguisher.

"Don't say that, Di! It isn't brave and noble, it's just bloody stupid!"

"Oh no it isn't, Jan," she replied, but just as quietly, "it isn't stupid whatever else it is! I don't know how much you know or suspect, I don't know how much of the real truth they've told you or to what lengths you're capable of deceiving yourself about me. You can think what you like but I'm the one who has the right to decide exactly how we face up to this thing and I'm damned if I want myself padded round with shock-absorbers. They may prevent bed-sores but I'm more interested in fresh air!"

"I've talked to half-a-dozen doctors and specialists and not one of them said the same thing," I told her, truthfully.

"You can't be better informed than any of them, so don't let's speculate until we have to!"

"That isn't strictly true anymore, Jan," she said, "I wormed the truth out of Parker-Strachey the day before yesterday." Parker-Strachey was the Scots surgeon who had performed her last operation, a taciturn, rather prickly celebrity with a European reputation and the kind of man impatient with everything outside his profession. I had not liked him much but that meant very little, I disliked them all.

"What makes his opinion so special?" I demanded.

"Oh I don't know," said Diana, glancing up with laughter in her eyes, "maybe it's his objectivity. He's more adult than the others so I took a chance on him."

"Well?"

"I insisted on seeing him alone before I was discharged. At length I managed to persuade him that I was a big girl now and didn't fall for the now-now-soon-be-better line of patter!"

"What exactly did he say?"

"He told me it wasn't simply a question of spinal damage, they'd more or less coped with that, and that as the heart had held out all this time it probably wouldn't kill me now. My real trouble is pernicious anaemia. He admitted that he was damned surprised I'd weathered the last op.! Would a man like Parker-Strachey tell a patient all that if it wasn't true?"

"He may think it's true, it's only his opinion!"

"Dear God!" said Diana smiling, "how pig-headed can a man be? Of course it's true and of course he's right! It's a matter of months or weeks, and that's why we've got to stop playing 'I-spy' Jan. I'll go along with all the others, with Drip and Yvonne and the nurses, but not with you! There's too much at stake and too little time, don't you see?"

So it was here. The tiny flame had finally gone out and it was Diana who had extinguished it. I said, in a whisper:

"If you're so sure why do you ask me 'how long' ?"

"I wanted to know if you knew as much as me and now I'm satisfied that you didn't! It was a loaded question, Jan, right in the 'Have you stopped beating your wife?' category!"

What astonished me was not her fearlessness—I would have expected that for she had always had three times as much guts as anyone else—it was the consistency of her character. Her approach to dying was a kind of bridge linking the laughing girl of twenty years ago to the mature woman whose objectivity could so easily be mistaken for bravado but was really something much more fundamental and admirable. I thought awhile, then I said:

"We've come through a good deal together, Di, and maybe we can get through this. I don't give a damn what Parker-Strachey says, he doesn't know you as I do. To him you're just another patient and these chaps are wrong as often as they're right. You can't expect me to sit here and accept that kind of verdict. If you want to act as though it was final then go ahead—make what dispositions you like and I'll listen and carry them out for you, but I'm incapable of resignation as far as you are concerned and all I promise to do is to humour you until you've talked yourself out! Is it the estate or money? Is that what you mean when you talk about time?"

"No," she said, "mostly I lie here and worry about you, Jan! You're my biggest headache! You always have been, you know!"

Although she smiled she wasn't joking and I knew exactly what she meant. To her, ours had always been a very lopsided relationship and even before she married Yves she never mastered her guilt-complex about me. It kept cropping up in letters and conversations. She had a conviction that somehow, by falling in love with her as a boy, I had missed my way and that she had wasted my life or destroyed its potential usefulness. In a very limited sense this was true. I had never succeeded in outgrowing my boyhood emotions and had directed every ounce of my nervous energy into winning her, but as she reminded me of this I remembered Drip's declaration, the one the old governess had made when she found me living as a recluse on Teasel Edge shortly before the war. Drip had said: 'All that you are you owe to Diana! . . . Diana taught you to live, to look for adventure, even such things as how to buy clothes and how to cure your accent! She taught you your table manners if the truth's known . . .' The memory of this was sufficiently clear for me to be able to quote aloud exactly what Drip had said on that occasion. Diana listened, gravely.

"Well, I suppose there's something in it," she admitted, "but for all that I always longed for a chance to justify myself, *really* justify myself! Now I won't have that chance and it's the one thing I can't bear! Even if I lived to a ripe old age I could never be a wife to you. We've had two years it's true but more than half of that had been something and nothing. That isn't much return on an eighteen year investment, is it?"

Was it? If, with foreknowledge, I could have put back the clock to October, 1927, to the exact moment before I had met Diana Gayelorde-Sutton as she rode out of the woods to rescue me from Keeper Croker, would I knowingly have chosen a path that lead away from Sennacharib and down the road to a come-day-go-day existence as a Whinmouth worthy? It wasn't an easy question to answer. It might have been, if we had come through unscathed but it wasn't now.

She knew very well what I was thinking and the fact that I hesitated must have caused her some distress for I saw her teeth bite into her lower lip and she seemed to be pondering deeply. Finally she said:

"Very well, Jan, we won't have a show-down, not yet! Go for your ride but come in before you go to bed and tell me how old Sioux stood up to your weight. Oh, one thing I forgot, Parker-Strachey will be here tomorrow and maybe you'll want a pow-wow. Will you see him alone or shall we make it a threesome?"

I couldn't take any more just then so I kissed her swiftly and left without answering. I went out into the yard to find Yvonne waiting with Sioux. She was right about the animal's agelessness. As I climbed into the saddle he tried to buck me off and Yvonne, watching, squealed with delight. I turned his head into the rear drive and crossed the small paddock to the larch coverts. The sun was setting over the estuary and the sky about Nun's Head was splashed with huge, formless dabs of crimson and indigo. There was so much savagery in the spectacle that it was with relief I turned my back on it and passed into the green funnel of the woods.

Parker-Strachey, the specialist, arrived the following afternoon and we saw him together. Although a dedicated man he seemed to me to be far less positive than any of his predecessors. It was clear that he had conceived a grudging admiration for his patient but whether the source of this lay in her war record, or in the fortitude she had displayed under his care I never discovered. Such conversation as I had with him was limited to her health.

It was from Parker-Strachey that I learned, for the first time, what was really the matter with her and what havoc those murderous bullets had caused. He told me unequivocally that he would not gamble on her survival until winter but he also succeeded in convincing me that Diana herself infinitely preferred death to the life of a helpless invalid milestoned with sustained periods of agony. Slowly, over the next few weeks, I came to terms with the situation, at least, I persuaded myself that I had done so and this was all that mattered when I was alone. When I was with her I continued to reject the monstrous idea altogether for she was so relaxed, spiritually and even physically relaxed, that it was difficult not to convince oneself that she was slowly regaining her strength.

We used to sit together for long periods, sometimes without saying much and when we did, discussing abstract subjects or things that had happened and people we had met.

She was now reading nothing but verse and her bedside table was stacked with collected poems and anthologies, English, American, French and even German. She seemed almost to feed on these and poetry coloured most of her thoughts.

She had her favourites, Yeats, Hardy, Sassoon, Blunt and Wilfred Owen but she re-read poets who had sparked off her enthusiasm as a girl, Tennyson, and our old friend

638

Alan Seager, the American boy who had died on the Somme and who had seemed to us at the time to crystallise adolescent love more effectively than any of the better-known writers. I think I was rather jealous of these old and new friends. They seemed to be able to bring her far more comfort and tranquillity than I was able to and once I admitted this, expecting her to laugh at the idea, but she didn't, she just said:

"Oh, they're useful as substitutes Jan, and some of them teach real values but they can't compete with you! I'm still interested in the flesh. Kiss me and see! Touch my breast —there, leave your hand there! It's warm and firm and real, so much more satisfying than reflected sunshine! Besides, your turn is coming."

I wasn't by any means sure what she meant by this hint and I didn't ask. I was grateful for morsels and swallowed them thankfully. It was a great joy to realise that she was still vital enough to want caresses and kisses, and to discover that, virtually helpless as she was, she was still able to stir me as effortlessly as when we were both young and hungry for one another. Her concern for me in this respect was one of the sweetest things about that time. She would contrive all manner of artful little tricks and subterfuges to rouse and satisfy me, and when I remember this now I can never understand how I had ever thought of her as a selfish woman. She took immense pains to overcome the natural reluctance I had to stimulate either her or myself in the physical sense, and she did it with such maternal gentleness that after a time each manifestation was a joy and a lover's triumph.

She took great pains with her appearance and I never saw her when she wasn't well-groomed and composed, with her hair carefully brushed and her skin glowing. It was only when I was away from her that Parker-Strachey's words made any sense and then I had to scratch about for tiny crumbs of comfort in the specialist's warning that, as time went on, she would become utterly helpless and that emergency arrangements would have to be made to feed her. No merciful coma would blot out periods of pain and all that would be left to her was a clear brain with which to measure her present helplessness against the memory of the woman she had been. Then, when I remembered her immense vitality, I could only wish that she would die in her sleep, taking the gulf between present and future in a single leap, but this prayer was never once completed. Always it fled under the softest pressure of her fingers, or the caress of her glance as I entered the room.

She was quick to notice the effect that this see-saw between fatuous hope and gloomy fatalism had upon my nerves and as usual, she had a prescription for it.

"You've got to get out more, Jan!" she urged. "You must ride and walk about Sennacharib all the time you aren't actually beside me! That's the only way you can live with it and if you won't do it for yourself, do it for me! I can only see two aspects of Sennacharib from here and I should like to know what's going on in the north and east."

I suppose she was half-jesting but I took her at her word and after that I went out on Sioux every day, returning to tell her where I had been and whom I had met. I thought I knew that area better than anyone alive but I was wrong. There wasn't a bush or a tree or a rabbit-run that she had forgotten and sometimes she caught me out on a short cut, or a point where an overgrown track crossed the upper reaches of the Teasel. It was as though she had taken hundreds of thousands of close-up photographs of the country that lay between the sea and the London road across Foxhayes, and it was her pleasure, whenever she was alone with her thoughts, to sift through them and interpret each picture yard by yard. Since her return here the entire heritage that had once been shared between us had passed to her and all I retained now was a few square miles of scrub and coverts, almost identical with any other rural backwater. God knows, I did not grudge her the inheritance, realising at last that my claim on Sennacharib had been physical whereas hers rested upon her kinship with forgotten and neglected gods and goddesses of whom she alone was aware.

She was at one with this pagan cult as never before and I think it contributed to her tranquillity. Up to then her worship had been a kind of game that she played with herself, as when she stood naked on the beach the day we were married, but pretence was behind her now and sometimes, when I saw her looking out across the ploughland to Nun's Head, she was as much in communion with her deities as a priest before an altar.

This was proved by what happened a day or two before my thirty-third birthday, in the second week of October.

The Scots surgeon had been down again that afternoon and this time she insisted on seeing him alone. I hung about on the stairhead while they were closeted together and once or twice I heard the murmur of voices raised in argument and once Diana's soft ripple of laughter. When he came out he was looking very puzzled. All traces of his professional arrogance disappeared when he took me by the arm and asked if I could find him a drink.

I led him into what had once been Mrs. Gayelorde-Sutton's morning room and gave him a stiff whiskey and soda.

"By God, yon's a fey lass!" he muttered, pushing forward the glass for a refill and then, watching me closely from under his sandy, tufted eyebrows: "Will ye no' tell me something aboot this 'Sennacharib' nonsense?"

I was astonished by his request. Sennacharib had always been a very jealous secret between us and I could not recall a previous occasion when she had discussed it with a stranger. Parker-Strachey was not the type of man who encouraged one to bare one's soul yet now he was curious to interpret something that she had confided in him. I told him, briefly, the circumstances surrounding our first meeting and a little of what had happened in and around Heronslea prior to her runaway marriage to Yves. Then, feeling it might help, I described Diana's behaviour in Nun's Cove on the morning we were married three years before.

He listened carefully. Finally he said:

"Ah, then there's no help for it! Has she spoken aboot takin' her up there?"

"Up where?" I asked, mystified.

"Ach, to the top o' the hill, mon!" he said, irritably. "I

641

dinna ken *where* exactly but I thought you would!" He puffed furiously at his pipe for a moment, staring hard at me. "Mind you," he added suddenly, "I'll have none o' the damned nonsense aboot a horse! If ye go then ye'll go up by car, and ye'll give her a bare five minutes, d'ye ken? Five minutes by the clock!"

I had no clear idea what he was talking about but he seemed reluctant to be more communicative and told me I had best continue the discussion with Diana. Then he left, glad to be gone. Perhaps he was ashamed of having lost his professional composure in front of a chawbacon.

I went up to Diana and found her flushed and excited and before I had crossed the threshold she called across to me.

"He said I could go, Jan! He told you about it, didn't he? He wasn't just humouring me because if he was . . ."

I was alarmed for her and hurried across to the bed, putting my arm round her and drawing her close.

"He said you wanted to get up, Di, and talked about taking you up to Foxhayes but you can't possibly ride there! You must know that, Di!"

The flush died on her cheeks and she became quiet and submissive.

"I do know that, Jan. I suppose that was asking too much but I thought, with you riding Sioux and holding me . . ."

Suddenly her mouth crumpled and her eyes filled with tears. She looked so much like a child that it was like watching a 'mix' on a film when the director is using the flashback technique. Then, with a big effort, she rallied, arresting the transformation and checking the tears. She was quite silent for a moment and I could almost feel her getting to grips with her emotion.

"What can it matter now, Jan? It isn't much to ask and I'll do it on my own if I'm cheated of it! At all events I'll try, I'll try damned hard if you let me down! You'll have to lock me in, I swear it!"

There was so much of the old, defiant Diana in the threat that I smiled and capitulated.

"All right Di, if he's prepared to accept responsibility

642

for it! Five minutes he said and it'll have to be in a hire-car. You'll have to wait for good weather too and you'll have to put yourself absolutely in my charge, do you understand? It'll be a military op. and I'm the C.O., is that clear?"

She looked artful and nodded twice and at once I began to regret having promised, wondering how the devil I was going to explain such an act of folly to Drip or to the nurses, and wishing that I had had the forethought to get Parker-Strachey's permission in writing. She knew me well enough to avoid the subject for the rest of the day and the day after that but now and again I caught her cocking an anxious eye at the sky over the Shepherdshey elm clump and when the weather improved, and the temperature rose above average for the season, I had a strong conviction that she would pick my birthday for the day of the excursion.

On that day I went down into the stable yard about seven o'clock to find the early morning sun climbing the eastern wall and the air as soft and mild as in early May. There was a mackerel sky over Teasel Edge and the lightest breeze stirring the leaves of the big copper beech beyond the arched gate. I stood there for a moment listening to Sennacharib shaking itself awake. Birds rustled in the rhododendron brake where the paddock sloped away to the brook and Shepherdshey Village. Beyond the rail old Sioux cocked an eye at me, awaiting the mangold I threw him whenever he was about to be brought in and saddled. The sight of him revived the mad notion I had been considering and rejecting ever since Parker-Strachey had spoken to me of Diana's plea. I stood irresolute for a moment longer and then the old magic of the place began to work, driving out reason and commonsense like a sheep-dog dispersing a flock-jam in a gateway.

I crossed the drive, vaulted the rail, caught Sioux and led him round to the loose-box. As I sorted among the harness in the tack-room I heard his strong teeth crunch into the mangold and he had almost finished it by the time I found what I was looking for, a great, broad, old-fashioned side-saddle that had lain there for years. It was a

Souter and its leathers were as strong as the day it had been made. I examined it carefully before throwing it across Sioux's back and I chose the best girth in the room, a new nylon cord of Yvonne's. When I was mounted, I reached across to the top shelf and grabbed a thick, plaid rug and a tether rope and threw them over my shoulder. Then I gave Sioux his head and we lumbered out of the yard and up the main ride towards Big Oak Paddock.

I passed the glade where I had been grabbed by Keeper Croker and bore right through the plantation until I emerged on the western edge of the Teasel Valley that looked directly across to Teasel Wood to the eastern border of Sennacharib. Here, where I could see right down the valley to Nun's Head and the bay, I could pick out every important landmark, the wooden footbridge marking the farthest limits of Shepherdshey cart-track, the high wood itself, the square mile of larch coverts behind and the wide sweep of purple and gold of heath and gorse that had given Sennacharib its name. This was the spot where, in Springtime, primroses hung in huge, trailing clusters and foxgloves marched through bluebells to the edge of the escarpment. There were no wild flowers now save an odd, obstinate campion, or one of those hardy periwinkles that seem indifferent to seasons and come out whenever they smell the sun.

Sitting there on Sioux I was absorbed in the scene that was familiar in every detail yet always had the excitement of a discovery. Then, shaking the reins, I went on down to the winding stream where I dismounted and ran out the line, tethering Sioux to the bridge rails but giving him enough rope to crop grass on both sides of the path. Leaving the plaid rug close by I walked back down the cart-track to Heronslea and breakfast.

I went up to Diana about nine-thirty meaning to tease her a little before telling her that today was the day, but I should have known better. She read my intentions before I was halfway across the room and sat back on her hands, her eyes shining with excitement.

"It's today, Jan! It is, isn't it? It's this morning? *Now?*"

644

"When the sun gets up a bit," I promised, "and I still haven't had the nerve to tell a soul!"

"Oh to hell with them all, you don't have to! They wouldn't understand, not one of them, not even Drip!"

"All the same they'll have to know," I said, "because the car will be calling at the front and I couldn't possibly get you out unobserved. Have you finished with your tray?"

"I couldn't eat anything, I was too keyed up," she said. "Ask Millie to take it away and help me to get dressed. No, wait! . . . Tell Drip and get her up here. We shall need help and I can handle Drip better than I can the day-nurse!"

"Are you absolutely resolved on this, Di?" I asked, nervously.

"Yes I am and if you let me down I'll never forgive you! I mean that Jan! It's more important than anything I've ever asked of you!"

I didn't care any more when she said that: I didn't give a rap for all the doctors, nurses and play-safers in Christendom. Diana wanted to drink wind in Sennacharib and that was the only thing left for her, and the whole world could pay forfeit so far as I was concerned. I owed no loyalty elsewhere. As long as she drew breath I was Diana's, body and soul.

I went out and told an incredulous Drip what we were going to do and while she followed me about croaking protests and fluttering her hands, I phoned Maddocks, the car-hire firm in Whinmouth and asked them to send their largest car up to Heronslea and leave it in my charge for an hour or so. As I replaced the receiver I was confronted by the day-nurse.

I had had very little to do with her but I knew her for a competent, humourless woman. She now addressed me like a sergeant-major tackling a truculent recruit.

"I can't have you doing this, Mr. Leigh! It's outrageously stupid and I'm quite sure you realise it is!"

I told her that I had the specialist's permission but she dismissed this with a chopping motion of her large, meaty hand. "Mr. Parker-Strachey hasn't seen her for several days and to take my patient out in a car, even for an hour or so, might be fatal for a woman in her condition!"

Suddenly I was impatient with them all, with every last one of them and with the whole process of prolonging life at all costs. I saw now that Diana was absolutely right and that she in her weakness had more vision than all of them lumped together and stuffed into trunks labelled "Fragile", "With Care" and "This Side Up".

"Damn it woman, what the hell can it matter now?" I yelled, glad of a chance to bully someone. "She's going to die, isn't she, so mind your own bloody business and stay out of this!"

The nurse faltered but only for a moment. Her mouth shut like a trap.

"I've got my responsibilities," she snapped, "and I can't let you do it, even though you are her husband, and in spite of what Mr. Parker-Strachey said or didn't say!"

The implication that I was lying about the specialist maddened me and I could have struck her in the face. As it was I walked round her, mounting the stairs and turning my back on her high-pitched protests that ended with a threat of instant resignation. I hesitated long enough at the head of the stairs to call down and tell her to pack her things and go, for the world was closing in on me now and I could see but two things clearly—Diana, her lips parted and her eyes shining, and outside Sennacharib, waiting and rustling under its autumn mantle. Nothing else was of the least importance, not Drip shuffling about the bed-room, her veined face swollen with tears, nor the shrill-voiced nurse threatening and abusing, nor the wondering children who appeared from nowhere and peeped from the corners and corridors like mice. None of these people had any significance at all. Neither had the spectre of death marching before me like a guide.

I made Drip help me lift Diana from the bed and we sat her half-upright on the divan, pulling on her underclothes and stockings and foraging in the wardrobe drawers for one of her thick, high-necked sweaters. I spoke no word to her until I heard the toot of the car as it turned into the main drive and crunched up the slope. Then I gathered

Diana in my arms, kicked open the door and marched down the broad staircase into the empty hall. On the steps stood Yvonne, staring at us in silent wonder, one finger pulling at her lower lip, one long, bare leg crooked behind the other as she leaned on the pillar of the portico.

"Are you taking Mummy away?" she asked simply, as the driver jumped out and ran round to the rear door.

"No, Yvonne, certainly not!" Diana told her, "I'm out for a whiff of fresh air and it's Doctor's orders! Run and tell Drip not to worry any more!"

The child nodded. Her innocent acceptance of the situation affected me so strongly that I could say nothing more and it was left to Diana to tell the driver that he could wait inside until we returned the car. He looked puzzled as he helped me to settle her in the back, propping her sideways on cushions, with her feet resting on the folding box-seat opposite. Then he stood aside as I got into the driving seat and re-started the engine. The big car slid down the drive almost soundlessly and I turned left into the village and left again into the track that led up to Teasel Footbridge. Diana's reflection seemed to fill the mirror and her face glowed with pleasure.

"Dear Jan, *my* Jan!" she said and her voice was strong and steady that for a moment I had an insane notion that we weren't in a car at all but galloping side by side over the heath, myself a short head in the lead. Then the car breasted the long slope and passed between the high-green banks dividing Heronslea elms and the Teasel slope, emerging on to more level ground where the track petered out and Sioux was cropping grass at the water's edge.

I heard Diana gasp as I applied the brakes.

"Jan!" she said, and then: "Oh no . . . *no* . . . ! You didn't, you couldn't have!"

I got out, opened the nearside door and freed her of rugs. She lay quite still staring at me while I untethered the horse, checked the girths and led Sioux across to a slab of granite marking the gateway of a field long since reclaimed by the Common. Then I went back to the car, lifted her out and carried her to the stone, steadying her against my shoulder while I bunched the plaid rug I had left there and wedged it between seat and pommel. Sioux stood perfectly still as I climbed carefully into the saddle, gathering the reins in my right hand and giving the old horse's flank a tap with my heel. He moved forward at a steady walk, stamping across the plank bridge and up the winding slope between the gorse patches to the spot under the larches where I had paused earlier in the day.

The sun hung over Teasel Wood like a great burnished cauldron and its rays searched out every drop of moisture on the slope and set them shimmering like ten million gimlet-points. The breeze came sighing across the dip and called down to us as a genial giant might hail a pair of pigmies. The scent of Diana's hair mingled with the scent of peat and hoof-crushed bracken as she stirred in my grasp, firmly but slightly adjusting her perch and causing me to tighten my hold under her thighs. Without exchanging a word we gained the top of the hill and I edged Sioux round in a half-circle so that we could look down the long valley to the sea.

"Is this the place, Di?"

"Yes, Jan, this is it and I didn't even have to tell you, did I? You can see more from the top of the Tower but never so clearly. This was the place where it all began, remember?"

I remembered. Oh God, God, how clearly I remembered! It might have been an hour ago, a gawky boy in a shoddy, ready-made suit all stuck about with burrs and shredded beech leaves and a laughing girl, less than a year younger, wearing expensively-cut riding clothes and sitting a well-groomed pony with her long legs swinging free of the stirrups and her mouth curved in a half-smile as she said: "You love it, don't you Jan? You feel about it just like I do! You *do*, don't you?" And the boy, looking across the bowl of guineas flung slantwise across a purple mantle, had replied: "It's Sennacharib!" and quoted opening lines of Byron's poem.

"The Assyrian came down like a wolf on the fold
And his cohorts were gleaming with purple and gold."

There it was, exactly the same, untouched by slumps, and booms and invasions and blitzes. And here we were, exactly eighteen years older, a healthy full-grown man and a woman at the gates of death. It was a full circle and had within its sweep the rhythm and shape of the seasons and of everything that grew and died and enriched the earth.

I don't know how long we remained there, five minutes perhaps, or ten, or much longer. Then she gave a slight shudder and lifted her hand, pointing up the valley towards the hogsback of the Common where the heath met the sky. I saw at once what she was pointing at, two dark specks dancing across the skyline and growing rapidly larger as they veered and twisted along the course of the stream below. It was the buzzards and their sudden appearance made me cry out. Swiftly they came, growing bigger each second, alternately beating and gliding as they tested the currents and displayed their matchless windcraft, soaring, dipping, recovering and sideslipping, and all the while uttering their long, mewing cries of triumph.

Silently we watched them pass at eye-level along the valley, make a sudden turn as they neared the village and bank away to the east behind the highest firs of Teasel Wood.

As they disappeared the warmth went out of the sun and over the whole valley there was silence and a sense of suspension. Diana, said sleepily:

"I knew they'd show up, Jan! We'd better go now and thank you; thank you again, Jan . . . *my* Jan!"

She said nothing more as we picked our way down the peaty track to the bridge. She was not asleep however, for every now and again her eyes opened and seemed to be fixed on some point over on the right, beyond the elm clump of Heronslea boundary wall. I lifted her down, settled her in the car under the rugs and retethered Sioux. Then I backed along the lane towards home.

The day-nurse had taken me at my word and resigned, so I phoned Parker-Strachey and told him what I had done. He made no comment, merely grunted and promised to come down again before the end of the week.

I looked in after lunch and Diana was deeply asleep, one of her favourite anthologies open on the coverlet. I picked up the book and saw that some of the poems were marked in pencil. There were two heavy strokes beside the final verse of an excerpt from one of Edgar Lee Masters' *Spoon River* pieces, called *Lucinda Matlock*. The lines she had marked were:

> *What is this I hear of sorrow and weariness,*
> *Anger, discontent and drooping hopes?*
> *Degenerate sons and daughters,*
> *Life is too strong for you—*
> *It takes life to love life.*

She did not seem to be any the worse for her adventure when I went up after breakfast the following morning. She was quiet and thoughtful but apart from the flurry of excitement she had shown over the expedition she had been subdued for some days now and submissive to those attending her. She said that she wanted to write some letters so I fetched her pen, notepaper and envelopes, promising to come again before I went over to Whinmouth with the weekly order and telling her that if the letters were ready I would take them to post. She seemed to ponder this a moment and then said that there was no hurry about them and Yvonne could take them in the afternoon.

I left Heronslea about midday and ate lunch with my Aunt Thirza and Uncle Luke in their kitchen behind the Quayside Furniture Mart, where I had lived as a boy. I told Uncle Luke about our ride to the top of the escarpment and because the old man was a passionate devotee of the countryside he sympathised and understood but Aunt Thirza, a practical body, clicked her teeth and said, in her richest brogue: "You'm praper daaft, the pair of 'ee! Alwus 'ave bin, ever since you was tackers and 'rinned off to live on that there rock in the bay an' catch your deaths-o'-cold! Bade is the place for her, 'till 'er starts to mend, so why dorn 'ee settle for it boy?"

I carried out Drip's shopping commissions and it was dusk when I drove down the hill to the Shepherdshey crossroads. Yellow lights were showing in the village as I climbed the long avenue between the carefully-spaced beeches of the drive and autumn seemed to have unpacked and settled in at last. Already the greens were fading and the trees looked as they always did at this time of year, like two neat rows of candles, glowing red and gold in equal proportions.

Then, as I turned into the gravelled half-moon under the porch, I saw that something was wrong. Drip was trotting up and down the terrace in her apron, and it needed an emergency to get Drip to show herself out of doors in an apron. The moment she saw me she jumped up and down and beckoned and as I ran up I noticed that tears were streaming down her face and she could hardly speak for sobs.

"I waited and waited . . . I tried to phone your aunt's . . . quickly Jan! Doctor Fosdyke's there now . . . !"

I ran through the hall and up the staircase. The local doctor was standing with his back to me looking out of the window and the night nurse was beside the bed, holding Diana's wrist. Fosdyke turned when I crashed into the room and nodded curtly to the nurse who went out without saying anything.

"I've put through a call to Mr. Parker-Strachey," Fosdyke said, "but he can't get down here until late tonight. Is there anyone nearer you'd like? Someone from Plymouth or Bristol?"

I shook my head and he turned back to the window. She was breathing very lightly and her hand, when I took it up, was warm and dry. Where the lamplight fell on her face it struck a sharp angle of the pillow, so that her mass of hair lay in a section of shadow that made it seem as dark as a gipsy's. Her eyes were closed but once her lips moved and I bent low to catch what she said. I only heard four or five words and recognised them at once. They were from the poem she had underscored and they showed that the testimony of Lucinda, of Spoon River, was in her mind at that final moment. She said: " . . . *too strong for you*" and then, after something I could not catch, *"love life"*. After that she lay very still for nearly an hour and at last

Fosdyke came and touched me on the shoulder. I put her hand under the sheet. It was not until I did that that I realised she was dead.

Chapter Fifteen

WHEN WE were children Diana and I promised one another that whoever survived would make sure that the other was cremated and their ashes scattered in Sennacharib. Young people make such pacts, for at that age, death is something that only happens to other people. We had long arguments as to the most suitable area for scattering. She could never make a choice between Folly Wood and Big Oak Paddock. I favoured the other side of the Teasel, where the broad, sandy path ran along the western edge of the wood.

The biggest effort I ever made in my life was that needed to honour this light-hearted pledge. I wanted nothing whatever to do with Diana's funeral. I had a horror of discussing the disposal of her body with an impersonal man like Kinglake, the local undertaker, and my instinct was to leave all such matters to Drip or whoever would undertake the task. I won this battle over my cowardice. The pull of loyalty was just strong enough to hold on and I got Doctor Fosdyke to call in his partner and arrange the cremation. I didn't go to the city Crematorium but left poor Drip to go there alone. I went instead to find old Nat Baker, the Shepherdshey Sexton, who had known Diana as a girl and asked him if he would perform the final act on my behalf. He was a big, good-natured fellow, genuinely fond of us both and agreed very readily without asking for reasons or directions. I let him choose his own spot, knowing that it would be somewhere inside Sennacharib and not wanting more exact knowledge.

The next day he waited for me at the lodge and told me, briefly, that it was done. He stood thinking for a moment, his big, grey head cocked on one side, as though listening for a distant sound.

"'Er was a rare maid for the open," he said presently and then touched his cap and shambled off. It was an epitaph that would have pleased Diana.

So it ended and yet it did not, not as one might have supposed and certainly not as I had expected. There was a great gap that I could not bridge. I was somehow rooted to the moment I had turned Sioux's head down the slope after the interval we spent watching the buzzards. I moved my body sluggishly about the place but my brain was hardly functioning at all. Most people kept out of my way and those who did not, like my well-intentioned Aunt Thirza, were rudely rebuffed and soon went their way.

I believe almost everyone agreed that the madcap outing had hastened Diana's death, but nobody reproached me about it and I had no regrets. I was very glad now that I had taken her up there and the bitterness of my loss would have been even greater if I had denied her this last service. Even so, from the moment of her death my senses atrophied. I did not feel grief so much as a kind of stunned confusion, which made it impossible to fix my mind on any one aspect of our private tragedy. After a day or so I went through the motions of living, talking to Drip and Yvonne, and eating what was put in front of me but I could not sleep. I lay for hours at a stretch with a bedside light switched on and one of Diana's anthologies on my knees.

I tried very hard to read the book and make something of the poems she had marked with pencil strokes but the words and phrases meant nothing at all. They buzzed about on the edge of my consciousness like a swarm of flies. Only a fragment of one poem got through to me and made me wince, some lines of Yeats' *Cold Heaven* that ran:

"*. . . Ah, when the ghost begins to quicken
Confusion of the death-bed over, is it sent
Out naked on the roads, as the books say, and stricken
By the injustice of the skies for punishment?*"

For the rest, a black, hopeless despondency settled on me, perhaps not alone the result of shock but a delayed reaction to the strain of the war that had been held in check by the sustained anxieties of Diana's illness. Now, when the focal point of my life had been removed, futility wrapped me like a wet fog and my mind was free to conjure with facets of horror and despair that must have stamped themselves on my memory during my service on the Continent. They were odd and often unrelated snapshots but each was dreadfully stark and clear. I remembered things like the foolishly lolling head of the young German I had shot in the cutting, and the toughness of the throat muscles of the S.S. man I had killed under the prison-van in the ambush and these memories merged into a general picture of hopelessness and paraded up and down before a background of ruined towns and country roads choked with the debris of a civilian exodus. The prospect of Sennacharib, in its autumn coat of red, gold and purple, was blotted out by a much larger canvas of a ruined continent and a civilisation slowly bleeding to death.

Presently it seemed to me that it was pointless to continue such a march when the means to end the journey were at hand. On the morning of the twelfth day after Diana's death I took my twelve-bore from the tack room, slipped a couple of cartridges in my pocket and went out across the small paddock to the larch covert.

I am not sure, even now, that I meant to take my life. I was too confused and desolate to make such a clear cut decision and perhaps what I did was simply a childish gesture, a shrill challenge to someone to prove to me that there was a future worth having, not only for me but for everyone.

I left no note and I went quite openly at eleven o'clock in the morning, when the larches were whispering under the steady pressure of a south-westerly breeze and the previous night's rain dripped from their leaves, covering the floors of the glades with a soft, russet mush. Under the spell of the same crazy compulsion, I located the actual tree under which I had offered Keeper Croker a farthing damages for my trespass, and here I slipped cartridges into the breech and stood the gun against the tree, listening in tently but not by any means sure what I would do next.

Then, out of the silence of the wood, I heard the overture of the third and final October miracle, a faint and far-off drumming and the crackle of broken twigs.

The sounds, distant as they were, did not at first register for what they were, the passage of a fast-moving horse up the long, central ride of the wood. Instead they struck me as a routine wood-noise, a solo played above the steady drip of the leaves and the whisper of the wind in the larches. Then, as the hoofbeats grew louder, a sense of guilt and shame stole over me and I thrust the gun behind the tree and walked forward into the glade. It was here that I heard Yvonne's voice calling my name.

"Jan! Jan! Where are you, Jan?"

I began to sweat and tremble then and looked over my shoulder to make sure that the gun was out of sight. Reassured, I stumbled forward to the southern end of the glade and at that moment, riding at a fast canter, Yvonne swept round the bend and up the slight incline.

She was mounted on her own pony, Peggy, a barrel-chested little mare with vicious stable manners, and as horse and rider appeared I gasped at the astonishing likeness between the child leaning forward over Peggy's short back and my memory of Diana moving down that same path on Nellie, in October, 1927. They had the same seat, the same rapturous identification with the pony's thrust, the same easy grace in drawing rein and half-rolling from the saddle in what looked like an effortless but was in fact a minutely-judged, movement and as she lifted her gloved hand and pushed back her hard little hat beads of perspiration showed on her forehead. She drew her glove across them laughing and talking through her laughter, the way Diana had done times without number.

"Drip said you'd gone up to Big Oak! She said you'd gone shooting but I told her she must have made a mistake because you haven't shot since the war, have you? Mummy told me why, she said that *you* said everything found it hard enough to keep alive without show-off sporting types popping off at them at fourpence a cartridge! Is

655

that true Jan, or was she pulling my leg? Won't you *ever* go out after pigeons and pheasants again? Or don't you count game we kill to eat?"

I took a deep breath like a man who, against all expectations, has risen to the surface after a desperate struggle under ten feet of water. I said, painfully:

"Diana wasn't teasing, Yvonne. It's true I don't get any fun out of shooting now. I never was much of a sportsman. I once gave the Heronslea huntsman a bum steer when Diana and he were right on top of a fox! I told him the fox had turned right-handed to the cliffs when it had gone up country to Foxhayes. Did she ever tell you about that?"

The confession interested her and her eyes opened wide.

"No, she didn't, and I can see why," she said. "She must have been ashamed of marrying someone who would do an awful thing like that!" Then, grinning: "I say, Jan, where did it happen?"

"Just over there!" I said, pointing through the trees to the blurr of Teasel Wood, "but it's true that I did bring the gun along today. I didn't shoot anything and got tired of lugging the damn thing around. But why aren't you over at Whinford with your grandmother?"

"Oh, I can't breathe in towns, even little towns!" she said, carelessly. "Besides, everyone was patting and 'poor-dearing' me!" She looked at me very steadily for a moment. "I don't feel that way about Mother, Jan, and I know she'd hate it if I did! I like to think of her as . . . as . . . well, as someone who was killed in the war, someone who was always taking chances for the hell of it! She *was* like that, wasn't she Jan?"

"Yes," I said, "very much like that and you're right about her not wanting us to mope and snivel! You go right on thinking like that about her, Yvonne! She'd want it so, I'm sure!"

Suddenly the conversation seemed to embarrass her and she turned aside, fondling Peggy's muzzle. She remained like that for a moment and then she looked at me with a swift, sly grin, one of the grins that had heralded Diana's

656

counter-attacks against grown-ups inclined to shush-shush and now-now.

"But *you're* moping, Jan. Drip says so and anyway, any fool can see you are!"

The manner in which she said this, or perhaps the look of concern that lurked behind the grin released in me a flood of affection such as I had never yet felt for her. Until that moment she had been a gay, mischievous and slightly dominating child but now, suddenly, she was so much Diana's daughter and such a part of Sennacharib that I cried out with pleasure. I threw my arms round her and hugged her. "I was, Yvonne, but not any longer, not any more!"

She submitted to the embrace with a comic dignity and then, extricating herself and dropping Peggy's rein, she fished into the pocket of her riding jacket and came up with a fat and very grubby-looking envelope.

"What's that?" I demanded, my heart thumping as I recognised the handwriting under the smears.

"It's a letter," she said, gravely, "*the* letter! You can have it now! I wasn't to give it to you until you were in the right mood. Mummy gave it to me the day before I went to Whinford." She looked down at it and grimaced. "I say, it is a bit messy, isn't it?"

I took the letter and she watched me expectantly as I slipped my thumb under the flap and pulled out several neatly folded sheets.

"Was this the letter she wrote before I went over to Whinmouth, the one I offered to take and she said you could post?"

"That's it," said Yvonne, "but there weren't any more, she was days writing that one, or so Drip said!"

I stood thinking for a moment. Suddenly it seemed unnaturally still in the wood. The breeze had dropped and the larches were silent. I could feel strength flowing back into my loins and moist, salty air filling my lungs. It was an extraordinary sensation, almost like coming round from an anaesthetic.

"Were you going anywhere special or were you just out looking for me?"

657

"Nowhere special," she said, evasively, I thought. "I meant to take Peggy up to Foxhayes and give her her head to Teasel Ford. She hasn't had any exercise since I've been away. All the others are scared of riding her!"

"All right Yvonne," I said, "you do that and I'll read the letter. If you aren't back soon I'll walk up to Big Oak and meet you in about half-an-hour. Then we can go down to lunch together!"

She nodded happily, obviously glad of an excuse to be off. Disdaining the stirrup she belly-rolled into the saddle and thumped her heels into Peggy's flanks. They were off in a second and in ten more were out of sight round the bend.

As the thud of hooves died away I went up the glade to a spot where a larch had been uprooted and had fallen to form a handy seat beside the path. I sat for a moment feeling the edges of the folded sheets. Then I smoothed them out and began to read, slowly, and with the kind of relish a man feels when he mulls a favourite passage in a much-read book. The letter was dated the day before her death. It began:

"My Jan; I don't know how long it will be before you get this; that depends on you. If I was writing to Yvonne she could have had it straight away, but then, Yvonne is even more of an extrovert than I was at her age, so it isn't necessary to write to her at all! My guess is that you won't be able to absorb the little I've got to say until the old spell of Sennacharib has stolen up on you again, relegating me to a role of first mate instead of captain. Sennacharib and I have always been jockeying for precedence and lately I've had the edge on her. Surely that was my due as the fading heroine on the couch!"

I let the pages rest on my knee for a moment while I absorbed this preamble. Foremost among my reactions was an astonished admiration that she was able to jest so determinedly in the face of death. Surely this was the kind of courage that I had needed so often and so desperately during the last few months yet had never glimpsed, much less won. She went on:

"I had to write this letter for two reasons, one big and

658

one insignificant. Let's get the little one out of the way first. It's money! While you were away getting demobbed I had two sessions with a London solicitor. You know the firm, they were nice to you that time I ran away and told you where to locate my mother, though what good that ever did you I never did discover! They told me then they had almost finalised Yves' affairs and when everything is settled I shall get (or rather you and Yvonne will get) about a fifth of the original estate. I haven't a clue how much this will amount to but they say it should be enough to endow Heronslea as a children's playground (I almost used that dreadful word 'home') for years ahead. I'd like you to go on with this, because I think it will be damned good for you, and give you a chance to develop the one characteristic of yours that I have adored since the day we met. You know what I mean—your great, woolly bearish male-gentleness which always spills over and drowns everything else about you, even your dreadful obstinacy! Don't have any qualms about using Yves' money for this purpose. After all, he and his kind broke up the background of the children and it's clearly just that they should help to reconstruct it! Keep Heronslea going with the money and never go very far away, or if you do, not for long because I'll always be here or hereabouts and I'll be as jealous as a burned witch if you ever turn your lumping great back on me for good!

"Now to the main reason for writing. What's to be done about you, Jan? I told you this has been my biggest headache since I was sure about what was going to happen and when. This is something about which it isn't at all easy to be objective because, you see, I've so loved having you all this time and sometimes I've been so proud of this one thing in my life that it made me sorry for every other woman in the world! I've loved being able to 'come inside out of the rain', I've loved all the things we've shared and all the fun we've had, but most of all I've enjoyed our joint suzerainty over Sennacharib for nearly twenty years. Most people have never had anything like this Jan, and I suppose this is why I don't feel resentful of dying at thirty-two."

There was a blot here and the writing became almost illegible but the blob was not the result of a tear. It was plain that the physical effort of penning this letter had taxed her strength beyond limits. She continued after a breathing space and the writing was firm and clear again.

"Where was I? I know . . . listing my dividends from you. Well, Jan, as I say, I've loved all the spiritual part of our partnership but I've also enjoyed the physical side, right from the very beginning, from the first kiss in the Folly, the day you gave me 'Lorna Doone', to our last day on the islet before we got bounced by Jerry and even beyond that, right up to recent days, when I coaxed you into kissing me as a woman ought often to be kissed, invalid or not! I always got the old-fashioned kind of thrill out of touching you and lying in your arms and even yesterday, when you were holding me on Sioux, it was just the same, like a cat being stroked and stroked in front of a warm fire!

"What bothers me, and what I'm really writing this for, is how much I've given back? Since we got married as much as I could and without any effort on my part I can assure you! But over the whole time not nearly as much as I would like to have given, and this leaves me with a feeling of inadequacy every time I think of it. I believe it would have balanced out if I could have hung on a few more years, or if I could have given you sons like I wanted to, but as it is my one big regret about the way things have turned out is that you really aren't equipped to make a fresh start on your own, not unless I can still bully you into beginning again! I could do this all right if I could employ the standard artillery! I'd have you seeing sense and eating out of my hand as soon as we had disentangled ourselves but wait, wait—what am I saying? I want you to stop eating out of my hand, don't I? Otherwise what point is there in all this feverish scribble?"

The writing had tailed off again and there had been another pause. I could imagine her battling and battling with her weakness and marshalling all that remained of her vitality for the final effort. She resumed:

"I'll have to risk short cuts Jan. What I want most desperately to say is this: teach yourself to accept everything that has happened between us as a phase and not the be all and end all of life! You're as strong as a bull and you'll live another fifty years. You'll see all sorts of changes and have all manner of new experiences *if you let yourself!* And *do* let yourself, Jan, please, please, so that my claim on you wasn't so bloody greedy after all, so that everything we brought to one another doesn't go stale inside you, and make you heavy and dull and unresponsive to everything else about you! And by 'everything' I mean life *outside* Sennacharib. Keep gambling and exploring, Jan! Get married again if you want to and have six more children. I don't care *what* you do, so long as it's something demanding, something that helps you develop into a bigger and kinder and more genuine person than even my Jan! Don't let the memory of our love stunt that growth the way it's tended to in the past. *Use* it, Jan, don't tie it up with blue ribbon and stick it away in a drawer, because if that happens our love will have been so feeble and useless that you might just as well have stayed in that Whinmouth junk shop where I found you and married someone who thought of you as the man who paid the rent and made love on Tuesdays and Saturdays, instead of someone who always thought of you as a force and a wonderful way of life!

"Goodbye now, Jan, and thank you for everything, absolutely everything! I hope to God this letter does what I meant it to do because then I won't have a conscience and at least there'll be one person left to thumb his nose at the Doones and stir himself to kick some of them in the pants! Because that's all *I* ever made of Democracy. Maybe it's all there is to be made of it—that, and the right we claimed so often, the right to walk in moonshine holding one another's hands!"

That was all, save for the scrawling signature and the usual cross contrived out of the final flourish of the last 'a' in Diana.

I read it over three times before I heard the thrumming of Peggy's hooves returning down the ride. Around me Sennacharib maintained its unnatural stillness so that I heard twigs break under the pony's shoes all the way down the slope from Big Oak. Before horse and rider came round the last bend I got up and there was a spring in my legs that had not been there when I sat down. I put the letter in my hip pocket and rubbed my hand across my eyes and then I was ready, or as ready as I ever would be. The letter had done what it set out to do. I could begin again. I had good enough directions.

Afterglow

THAT WAS the end of it all, or almost so; it wasn't quite the end because there was a Spring postscript to that letter, pages that might well have gone into the grubby envelope but somehow didn't because she was unable to write more, or perhaps because she was too modest, though "modest" is an odd word to use about Diana.

I kept the home going as she insisted and in a sense did find myself again or enough of myself to be useful about the place. When the ache was less urgent I went through her things and one evening, when I was packing up her books, I found a half-used writing pad on which was scrawled, in her handwriting, the cryptic words: *"This is awful—fourth draft—try again . . ."*

I thought for a moment that the self-criticism related to the earlier drafts of the last letter she had written. In moments of exasperation Diana had often addressed herself and she might have done so on paper, it was a characteristic that suited her exactly. But I soon discovered that the words did not refer to the letter for when I turned the page I found a draft poem that was clearly original.

I had always flattered myself that I knew everything about Diana. I knew her likes, dislikes, prejudices, her sources of enthusiasm, quirks, characteristics, moods, preferences, the lot! Yet here was something that I had not known! I had not known that she wanted to write verse. I had always imagined that the poetry inside her was satisfied to use her personality as its outlet.

The discovery excited me very much and very pleasurably. I went to the window, holding the notebook to the light. The verses had been written in pencil and were difficult to decipher. There were many crossings out and here and there odd words written in the margin but at last I made out the text and it was with a deep sense of discovery that I realised it was a faltering but terribly earnest attempt to express all she felt about Sennacharib. It was called "Senile Countryman" but some hidden reservation had caused her to set it down in the third instead of the first person. It ran:

> *He found his faith in the foxglove bell*
> *His creed in the clustered stars*
> *Of Ladies-lace, where dust-bent stems*
> *Played games with sunlight bars.*
>
> *In the moist, gold shine of the celandine*
> *He hunted Heaven's grace.*
> *Sermons he heard in every copse*
> *And many a gorse-grown place.*
>
> *He did not need the parson's plea*
> *To note a godly hand*
> *In the age of the oak or the bluebell smoke*
> *On an April-stirring land.*
>
> *His psalms were sung to the tissing larch*
> *His hymns to the purple heath*
> *To the iris clump on the marshy edge*
> *Of the shallow lake beneath.*
>
> *His prayers were said on a beech-leaf bed*
> *Where the drifts lay deep in the lane,*
> *And his saints rode out on a South-West squall*
> *To kiss his poll with rain.*

Thither he'll go when his time runs out
And his loins have lost their swing
No fear in his heart but sorrow perhaps
In not outliving Spring.

Senile? Perhaps, but less I think
Than those who work by night
Earning, yearning, tax-returning,
Under electric light.

I whipped through the leaves of the book hoping for more completed poems. There were odd lines and phrases, most of them scratched out with a fine impatience, and I was beginning to think that this must have been her sole essay in poetry when I found, on the very last page, another almost completed poem entitled "Codicil." I read the first line and then I stopped. It was as though Diana had stolen up behind me and whispered in my ear. I sensed then that the room in which she had died was not the place to read it but that I should take it to its source, the high ridge under the larch wood that overlooked the valley all the way down to Nun's Head, the place where Sennacharib had been christened the day we met and the one to which we had returned that last day.

I put the notebook in my pocket and went out, crossing the paddock to the elm clump and passing a gap in the hedge that led along the Teasel bank to the wooden bridge. It was an early evening in late March, the hour and season when the valley is lit with a curious light that is neither silver nor white but something in between, when the blackbirds are active in the thickets and the smell of peat is lifted and jockeyed by the breeze coming in from the sea, when the tall timber on Teasel Edge stands darkly against the sky and the half-mile rank of beeches guard Heronslea like a row of sentinels. Only the birds broke the intense stillness as they fidgeted in and out of the clumps. Primroses and campion splashed the hillside under the banks and there were violets hiding under the yellow clumps and here and there a few celandines. For the first time since Diana had gone I knew peace, real peace that warmed me through, so that blood began to flow in my veins and my senses stirred as from a long, troubled sleep. I could see and hear and smell Sennacharib again, and the sense of re-awakening so quickened my step that I almost ran up the long slope to the wooded spur.

Here I sat down on the stump with my face to the sea and read her poem. It was, I thought, a kind of blessing on me for having found the courage to honour our pledge for now I was certain that she was here, all about me, in the flesh, in the spirit, in person. Pandora's chest had been emptied and all the devils had gone, leaving Hope to hammer on the unlocked lid. I did not need to seek out old Nat, the Sexton, and get confirmation of the spot where he had laid her. I knew that it was here and could only be here, for she had written:

> *On Foxhayes edge go scatter my ashes*
> *Above the ground in sunlight splashes,*
> *Where all about my . . powdered bones*
> *The trefoil weaves between the stones,*
> *Where what I was feeds foxglove roots*
> *And robust April parsley shoots*
> *Five miles or more from churchyard drab*
> *Where, underneath a lettered slab,*
> *The body that has served me well*
> *Would bloat in clay, pathetic shell.*
> *At Foxhayes edge atop the grass*
> *I'll sense successive seasons pass*
> *I'll see the beeches overhead*
> *Turn tangerine and rusty red*
> *I'll hear the sky-seen of their leaves*
> *Wind-gossiping to younger trees.*
> *Then, with the fall of blue-smoke dusk*
> *I'll settle in the rustling husk*
> *Of brittle, sun-dried bracken stalk*
> *To hear the spruce and larches talk*
> *And see the lovers come and go;*
> *Or later, when the New Year's snow*
> *Builds up in drifts below the hedge*
> *Crisping the blades of dock and sedge*

I'll wait content, to stir in sleep
The hour the earliest violets peep.
For with them all the wood will rustle
Under the west wind's old-maid's bustle,
Lifting perhaps a speck of me
And bearing it, due south, to sea.

I sat very still for a long time while dusk stole over the wood and lights began to twinkle in Shepherdshey village. I was searching the sky and in the last few seconds of light I saw what I sought, two specks plummeting over Teasel Wood. I was not in the least surprised that they should be there at this hour. Diana had always promised that they would come wheeling in the moment we were reunited.